NICHOLSON

LONDON STREETFINDER

London Streetfinder
© Robert Nicholson Publications 1989

Based upon the Ordnance Survey Map with the sanction of the Controller of Her Majesty's Stationery Office. Crown Copyright reserved.

London Information
© Robert Nicholson Publications

London Underground map by kind permission of London Regional Transport

All other maps
© Robert Nicholson Publications

Designed by Robert Nicholson and Romek Marber.

Published by
Robert Nicholson Publications
16 Golden Square
London W1R 4BN

Great care has been taken throughout this book to be accurate but the publishers cannot accept responsibility for any errors which appear, or their consequences.

Printed in Great Britain by
Scotprint Ltd, Musselburgh

ISBN 0 948576 332 (Cased edition)
86/2/35
ISBN 0 948576 340 (Paperback edition)
86/2/325

Symbols

†	Church
⊕	Hospital
🚗	Car park
🏛	Historic buildings
	Small buildings
	Schools
	Sports stadium
⊖	London Underground station
	British Rail station
	Coach station
✈	Air terminal
	British Rail terminal
PO	Post office
Pol	Police station
→	One ways
⋯⋯	Footpath
50 ▶ ◀ 100	Figure indicating the direction of street numbering and the approximate position

Outer area

⟝─────────────⟞ ½ mile

⟝──────────⟞ ½ km

Large scale   Central area

⟝────────────────────⟞ ½ mile

⟝──────────⟞ ½ km

ROBERT NICHOLSON PUBLICATIONS

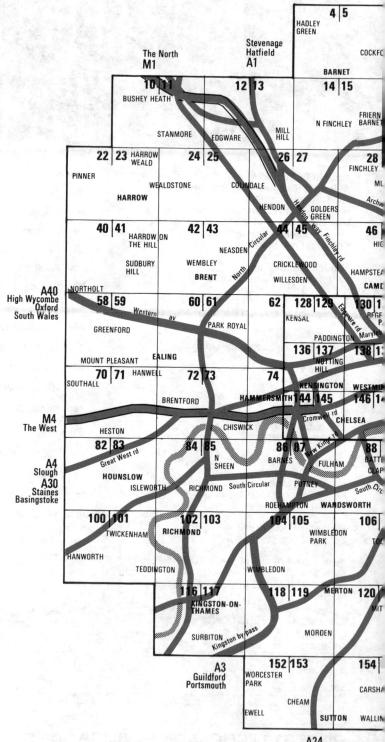

4 | 5
HADLEY
GREEN

COCKFC

The North
M1

Stevenage
Hatfield
A1

BARNET

10 | 11
BUSHEY HEATH

12 | 13

14 | 15

N FINCHLEY

FRIERN
BARNET

STANMORE

EDGWARE

MILL
HILL

22 | 23 HARROW
WEALD

24 | 25

26 | 27

28
FINCHLEY

PINNER

WEALDSTONE

COLINDALE

ML

HARROW

HENDON

GOLDERS
GREEN

Archw

40 | 41 HARROW ON
THE HILL

42 | 43

NEASDEN

44 | 45

46
HIG

SUDBURY
HILL

WEMBLEY

CRICKLEWOOD

HAMPSTEA

BRENT

WILLESDEN

CAMD

A40
High Wycombe
Oxford
South Wales

NORTHOLT

58 | 59

Western av

60 | 61

62

128 | 129

KENSAL

130 | 1
REGE
P

GREENFORD

PARK ROYAL

PADDINGTON Marylel

MOUNT PLEASANT

EALING

136 | 137
NOTTING
HILL

138 | 1

70 | 71 HANWELL
SOUTHALL

72 | 73

74

KENSINGTON

WESTMI

BRENTFORD

HAMMERSMITH **144 | 145**

146 | 1

M4
The West

HESTON

CHISWICK

Cromwell rd

CHELSEA

82 | 83
Great West rd

84 | 85
N
SHEEN

86 | 87
BARNES

New King's rd

FULHAM

88
BATT
CLAP

A4
Slough
A30
Staines
Basingstoke

HOUNSLOW

ISLEWORTH

RICHMOND

South Circular

PUTNEY

South Cir

ROEHAMPTON

WANDSWORTH

100 | 101
TWICKENHAM

102 | 103
RICHMOND

104 | 105
WIMBLEDON
PARK

106
TO

HANWORTH

TEDDINGTON

WIMBLEDON

116 | 117
KINGSTON-ON-
THAMES

118 | 119

MERTON **120**
MIT

SURBITON

Kingston by-pass

MORDEN

A3
Guildford
Portsmouth

152 | 153
WORCESTER
PARK

154
CARSHA

CHEAM

EWELL

SUTTON

WALLIN

A24
Dorking
Worthing

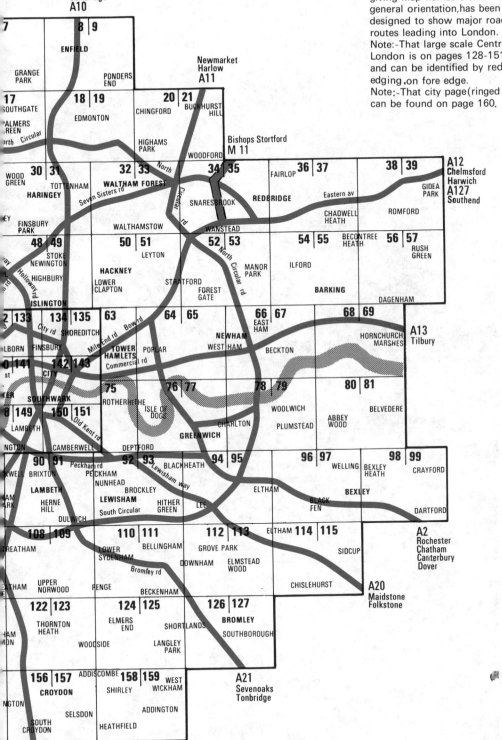

Key to map pages

This general map, apart from giving map numbers and general orientation, has been designed to show major road routes leading into London. Note:-That large scale Central London is on pages 128-151 and can be identified by red edging on fore edge. Note:-That city page(ringed on 142) can be found on page 160.

Cambridge
A10

7

8 | **9**

ENFIELD

GRANGE
PARK

PONDERS
END

17
SOUTHGATE

18 | **19**

EDMONTON

PALMERS
GREEN

North Circular

Newmarket
Harlow
A11

20 | **21**
CHINGFORD | BUCKHURST
HILL

HIGHAMS
PARK

WOODFORD

Bishops Stortford
M 11

30 | **31**
WOOD
GREEN | TOTTENHAM

HARINGEY

Seven Sisters rd

32 | **33**
WALTHAM FOREST

North Circular

rd

34 | **35**
SNARESBROOK

FAIRLOP

36 | **37**

REDBRIDGE

Eastern av

CHADWELL
HEATH

38 | **39**
GIDEA
PARK

ROMFORD

A12
Chelmsford
Harwich
A127
Southend

FINSBURY
PARK

WALTHAMSTOW

WANSTEAD

48 | **49**
STOKE
NEWINGTON

HIGHBURY

50 | **51**
LEYTON

HACKNEY

LOWER
CLAPTON

North Circular rd

52 | **53**

MANOR
PARK

STRATFORD

FOREST
GATE

54 | **55**

ILFORD

BECONTREE
HEATH

BARKING

56 | **57**
RUSH
GREEN

DAGENHAM

ISLINGTON

2 | **133**
City rd | SHOREDITCH

HOLBORN | FINSBURY

134 | **135**

Mile End rd | Bow rd

63
TOWER
HAMLETS
Commercial rd

64 | **65**

POPLAR

NEWHAM

WEST HAM

66 | **67**
EAST
HAM

BECKTON

68 | **69**
HORNCHURCH
MARSHES

A13
Tilbury

0 | **141**
st

CITY

142 | **143**

75
ROTHERHITHE

76 | **77**
ISLE OF
DOGS

78 | **79**
WOOLWICH

PLUMSTEAD

80 | **81**
ABBEY
WOOD

BELVEDERE

8 | **149**
LAMBETH

150 | **151**
Old Kent rd

CHARLTON

GREENWICH

DEPTFORD

CAMBERWELL

90 | **91**
BRIXTON | Peckham rd
BRIXTON

LAMBETH

HERNE
HILL

DULWICH

PECKHAM
NUNHEAD

92 | **93**
BROCKLEY

LEWISHAM

South Circular

Lewisham way

BLACKHEATH

HITHER
GREEN

LEE

94 | **95**

ELTHAM

96 | **97**
WELLING

BLACK
FEN

BEXLEY

98 | **99**
BEXLEY
HEATH

CRAYFORD

DARTFORD

108 | **109**
STREATHAM

LOWER
SYDENHAM

UPPER
NORWOOD

PENGE

110 | **111**
BELLINGHAM

Bromley rd

DOWNHAM

BECKENHAM

112 | **113**
GROVE PARK

ELMSTEAD
WOOD

CHISLEHURST

ELTHAM **114** | **115**

SIDCUP

A2
Rochester
Chatham
Canterbury
Dover

A20
Maidstone
Folkstone

122 | **123**
THORNTON
HEATH

WOODSIDE

124 | **125**
ELMERS
END

SHORTLANDS

LANGLEY
PARK

126 | **127**
BROMLEY

SOUTHBOROUGH

156 | **157**
CROYDON

SOUTH
CROYDON

SELSDON

ADDISCOMBE **158** | **159**
SHIRLEY | WEST
WICKHAM

ADDINGTON

HEATHFIELD

A21
Sevenoaks
Tonbridge

A23
Redhill
Crawley
Brighton

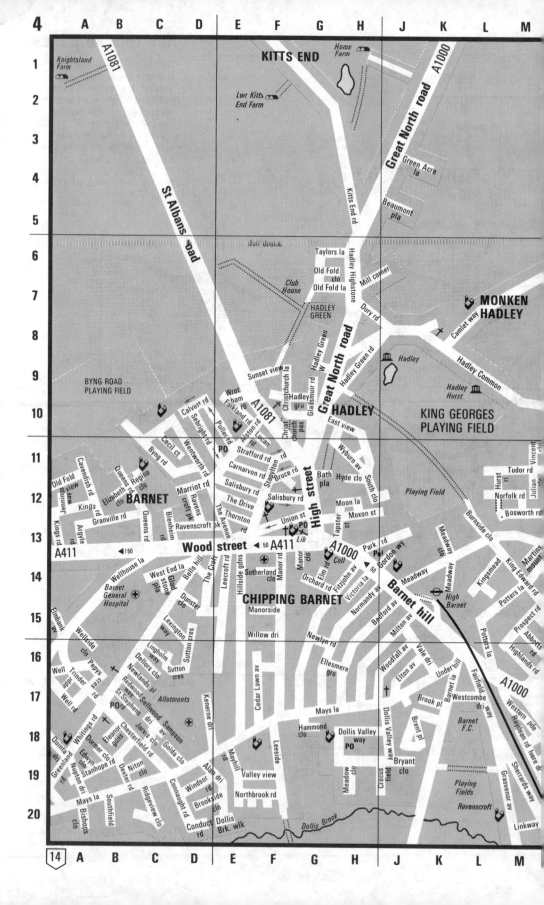

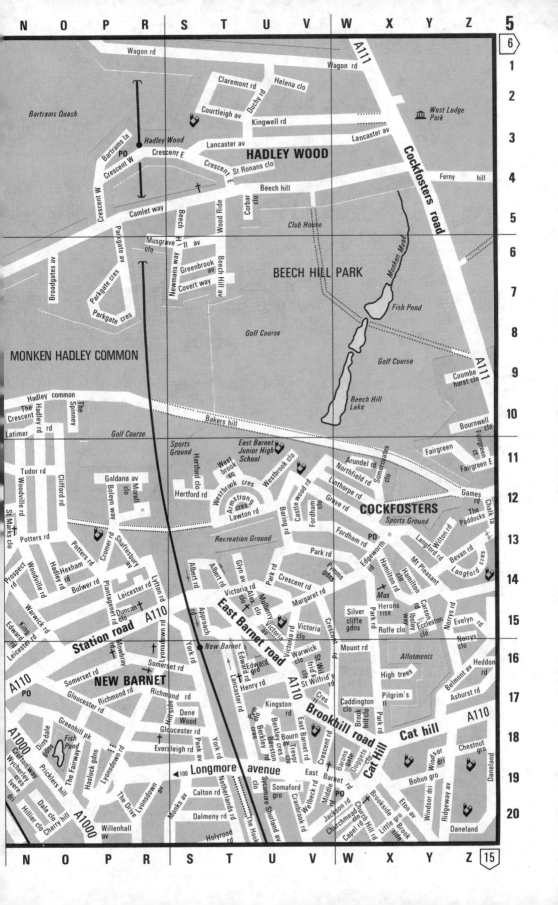

Wagon rd

A111

Wagon rd

Claremont rd

Helena clo

Courtleigh av

Duchy av

Kingwell rd

West Lodge Park

Bartrams Quash

Lancaster av

Lancaster av

Hadley Wood

Bartrams la

PO

Crescent E

HADLEY WOOD

St Ronans clo

Crescent W

Crescent W

Crescent E

Ferny hill

Beech hill

Cockfosters road

Camlet way

Corbar clo

Parkgate av

Beech la

Wood Ride

Musgrave clo

Club House

Hill av

Parkgate cres

Newmans way

Greenbrook av

Beech Hill av

Covert way

BEECH HILL PARK

Broadgates av

Monken Mead

Parkgate cres

Fish Pond

MONKEN HADLEY COMMON

Golf Course

Golf Course

A111

Coombe hurst clo

Hadley common

The Crescent

The Spinney

Hadley rd

Bakers hill

Beech Hill Lake

Bournwell clo

Latimer

Golf Course

Fairgreen clo

Sports Ground

East Barnet Junior High School

Fairgreen

Tudor rd

Galdana av

Hertford clo

West brook sq

Arundel rd

Northfield rd

Somersettes

Fairgreen E

Woodville rd

Clifford rd

Morell clo

Boleyn way

Hertford rd

Westbrook cres

Westbrook clo

Lynthorpe rd

Games rd

St Marks clo

Armstrong cres

Castle wood rd

Fordham clo

Grove rd

COCKFOSTERS

The Paddocks

Chalk la

Potters rd

Lawton rd

Baring rd

Sports Ground

Langford rd

Wilton clo

Recreation Ground

Fordham rd

PO

Bevan rd

Prospect rd

Potters rd

Cromer rd

Shaftesbury av

Albert rd

Glyn av

Park rd

Edgeworth rd

Mt Pleasant

Langford rd

Woodville rd

Hadley rd

Hexham

Albert rd

Crescent rd

Proms gdns

Hamilton clo

Hamilton rd

Bulwer rd

Leicester rd

Lytton rd

Victoria rd

Margaret rd

Mus

Herons rise

Carson rd

Ibsley

Eccleston clo

Evelyn rd

Warwick rd

King Edward rd

Leicester rd

Duncan clo

Plantagenet rd

Mowbray

Station road A110

Approach rd

Alex clo

Mulberry clo

Victoria rd

Victoria

Park rd

Silver cliffe gdns

Rolfe clo

Norrys rd

Norrys clo

A110

New Barnet

York rd

New Barnet

Edward gro

East Barnet road

Warwick clo

Mount clo

Allotments

Heddon rd

A110

PO

Somerset rd

Henry rd

St Wilfrid's clo

St Wilfrid's rd

High trees

Belmont av

Ashurst rd

Gloucester rd

Richmond rd

NEW BARNET

Richmond rd

Lancaster rd

Kingston rd

Brookhill road

Caddington clo

Brook hill clo

Pilgrim's ri

Park rd

Cat hill

A110

Greenhill pk

Dene Wood

Gloucester rd

Pym rd

Berkley rd

East Barnet rd

Cres

Windsor dri

Chestnut gro

Everleigh rd

York rd

Berkley cres

Beeston

Bourn rd

Trevor clo

Crescent rd

Daggers gate

Daneland

Fish Pond

Greenhill pk

Lyonsdown rd

Park av

Barons gate

Cat Hill

Bohun gro

A1000

Dinsdale gdns

Pricklers hill

The Fairway

Hasluck gdns

◄100 **Longmore avenue**

Calton rd

Netherlands rd

Somaford gro

Cranbrook rd

East Barnet rd

Sycamore clo

Shurland av

Welbeck rd

Middle clo

PO

Jackson rd

Churchmead clo

Church Hill rd

Brookside

Little gro

Brook side

Windsor dri

Ridgeway av

Crafton way

Wycherley cres

Ivere dri

Dale clo

Cherry hill

Hillier clo

A1000

The Drive

Lyonsdown av

Monks av

Dalmeny rd

The Hook

Capel rd

Eton av

Daneland

Willenhall av

Holyrood rd

1
2
3
4
5
6
7
8
9
10
11
12
13
14
15
16
17
18
19
20

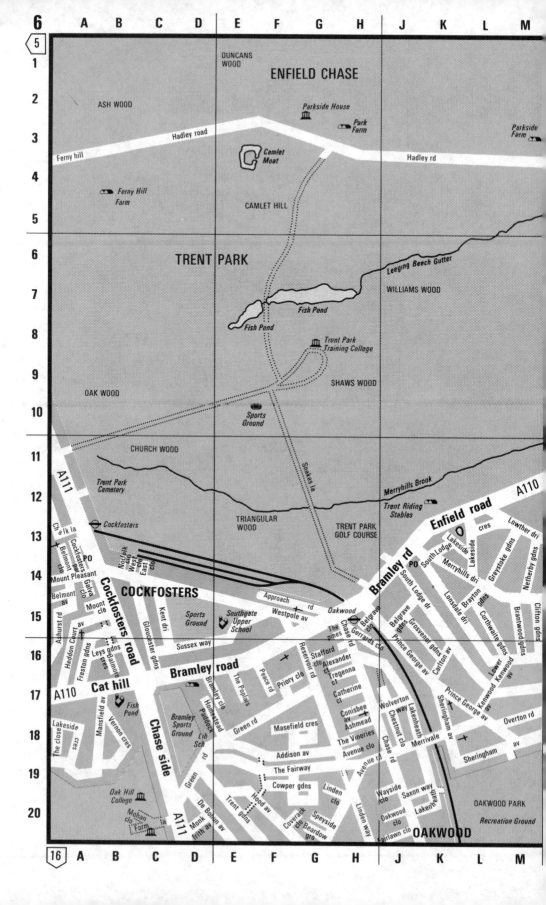

ENFIELD CHASE

DUNCANS WOOD

ASH WOOD

Hadley road

Ferny hill

Parkside House

Park Farm

Parkside Farm

Hadley rd

Camlet Moat

Ferny Hill Farm

CAMLET HILL

TRENT PARK

Leeging Beech Gutter

WILLIAMS WOOD

Fish Pond

Fish Pond

Fish Pond

Trent Park Training College

OAK WOOD

SHAWS WOOD

Sports Ground

CHURCH WOOD

Snakes la

Merryhills Brook

A111

Trent Park Cemetery

Trent Riding Stables

Enfield road

A110

Cockfosters

TRIANGULAR WOOD

TRENT PARK GOLF COURSE

Bramley rd

Lowther dri

cres

Lakeside

South Lodge

Greystoke gdns

Netherby gdns

Ch alk la

Cockfosters West

PO

Norfolk West clo East clo

Merryhills dri

Lakeside

Brayton

Clifton gdns

Belmont clo

PO

South Lodge dr

Lonsdale dri

Curthwaite gdns

Branwood gdns

Mount Pleasant

Galva av

Belgrave gdns

Grosvenor gdns

Carlton av

COCKFOSTERS

Belmont clo

Approach rd

Oakwood

Belgrave gdn

Prince George av

Lower Kenwood

Ashurst rd

Mount clo

Westpole av

The pines

Gerrards clo

Kent dri

Sports Ground

Southgate Upper School

Chase

Cockfosters road

Gloucester gdns

Wolverton way

Prince George av

Kenwood

Heddon Court

Leys gdns

Balmore

Sussex way

Stafford ct

Alexander ct

Lakenheath way

Chestnut clo

Sheringham av

Overton rd

Freston gdns

cres

Bramley road

Reservoir rd

Tregenna ct

Catherine ct

Merrivale

Cat hill

Mansfield av

Vernon cres

Bramley clo

The Poplars

Peace rd

Priory clo

Conisbee ct

Ashmead

Sheringham av

A110

Fish Pond

Chase side

Bramley Sports Ground

Homestead Paddock

Lib Sch

Green rd

Masefield cres

The Vineries

Avenue clo

Chase rd

The close

Lakeside cres

Green rd

Addison av

Avenue rd

Oak Hill College

De Bohun av

The Fairway

Cowper gdns

Linden clo

Wayside clo

Saxon way

OAKWOOD PARK

Recreation Ground

Mohan clo Farm

la

Monk frith av

Hood av

Trent gdns

Coverack clo Beardow gro

Speyside

Linden way

Oakwood clo

Lakenheath

A111

Fairlawn clo

OAKWOOD

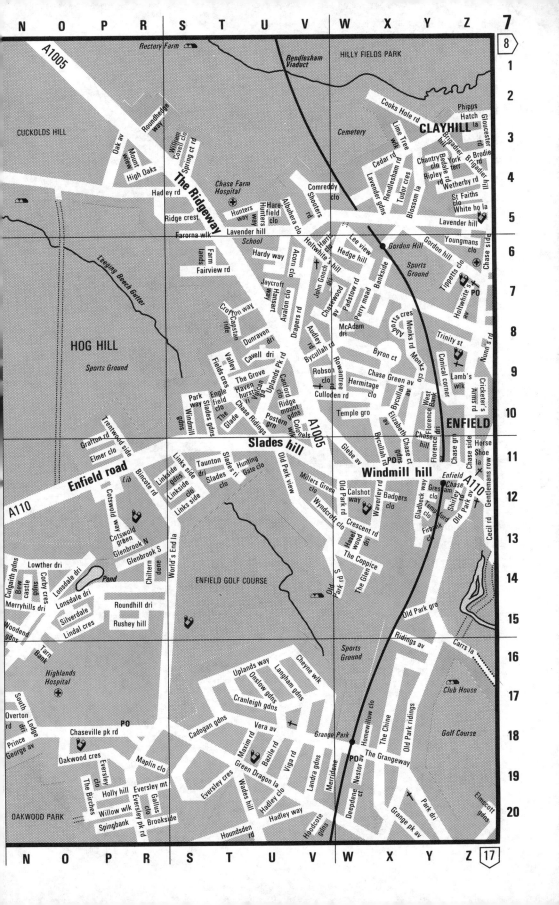

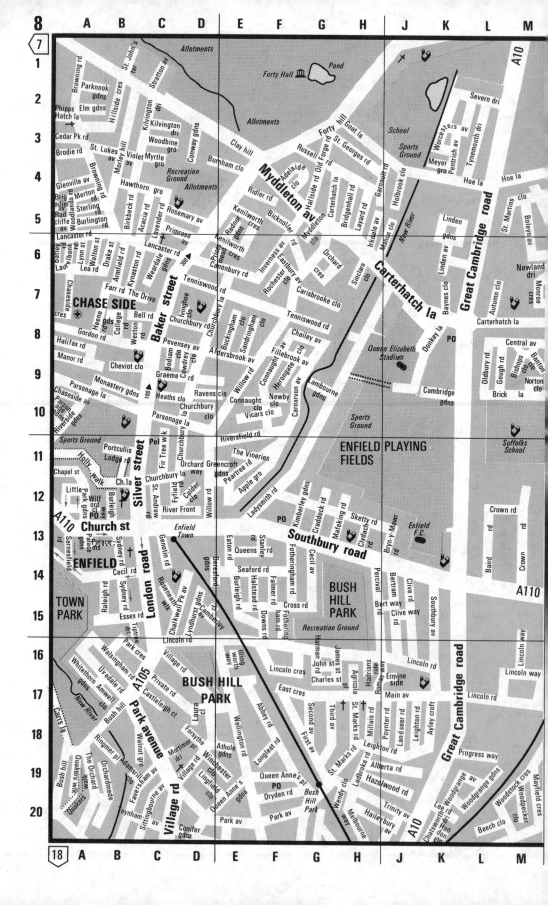

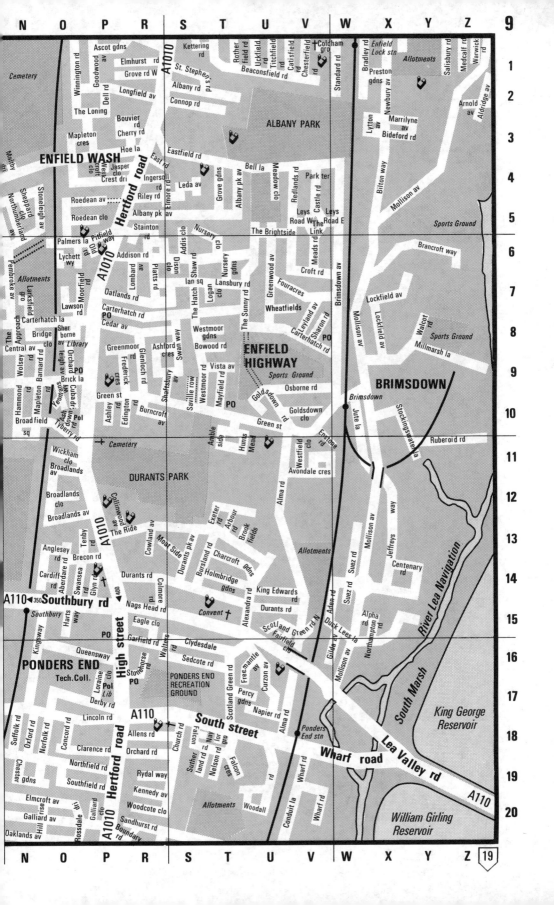

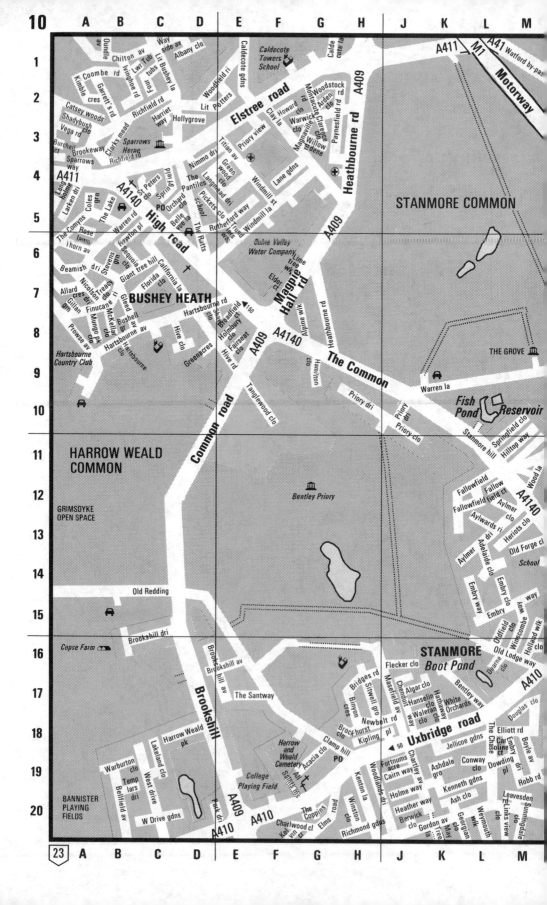

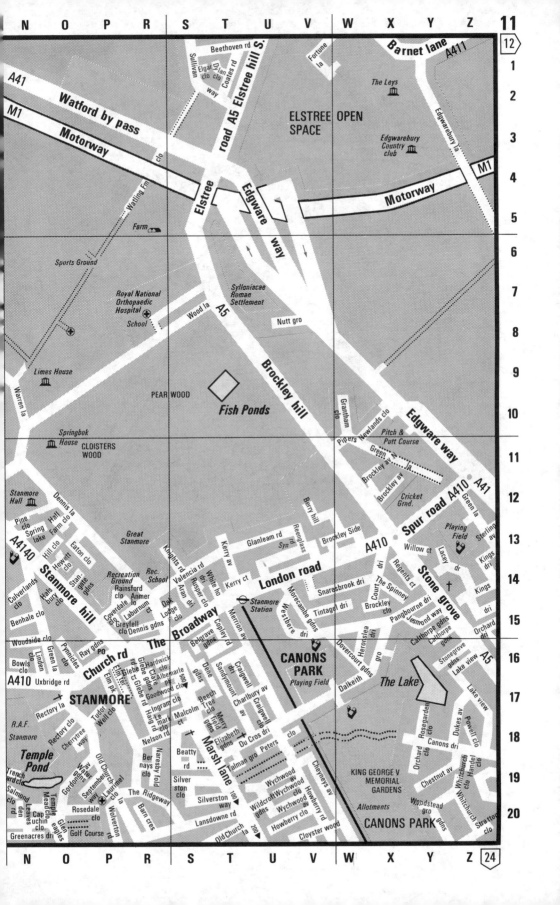

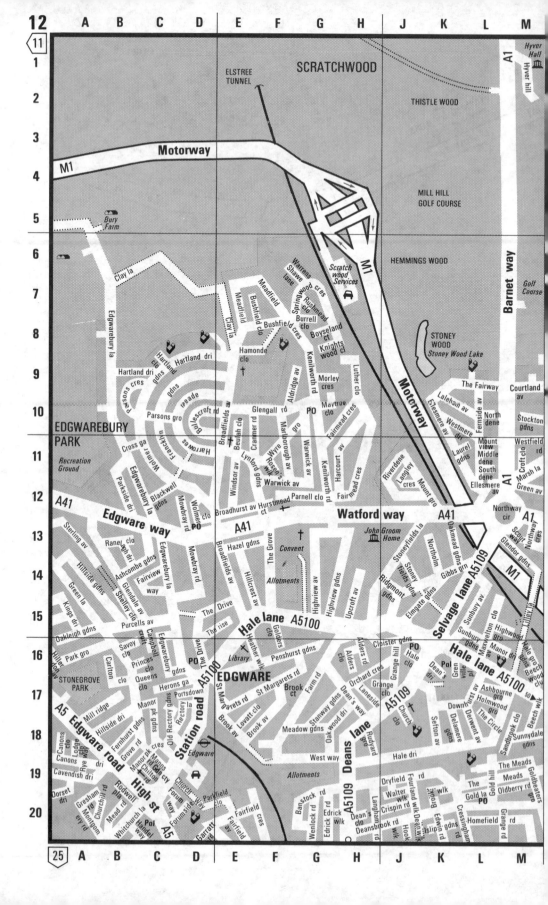

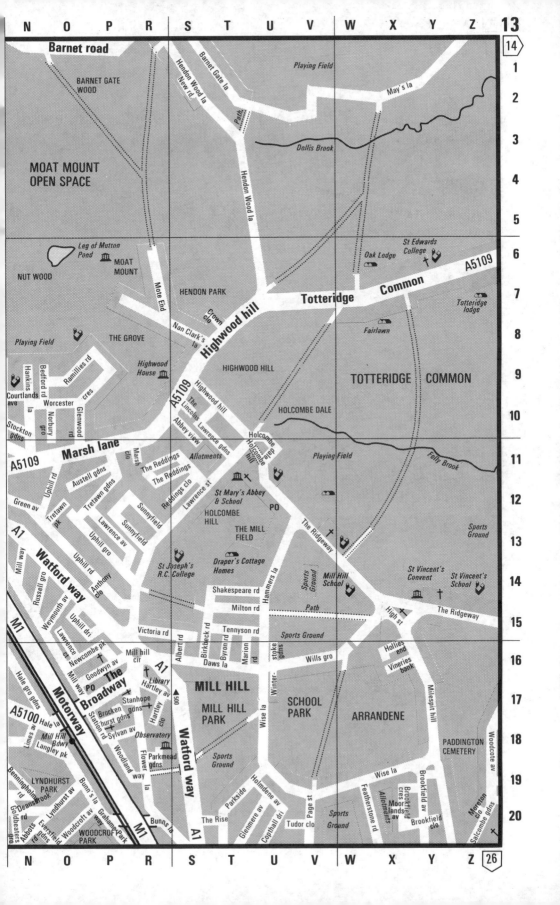

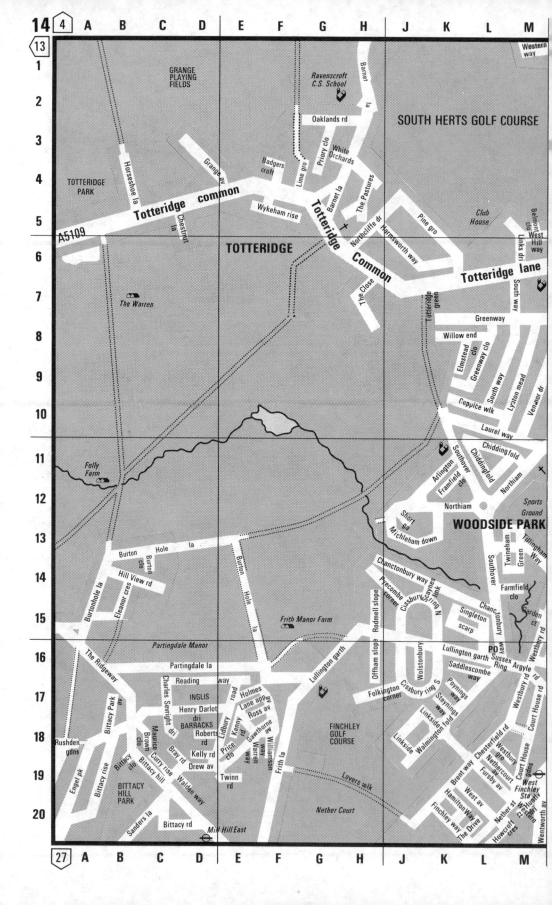

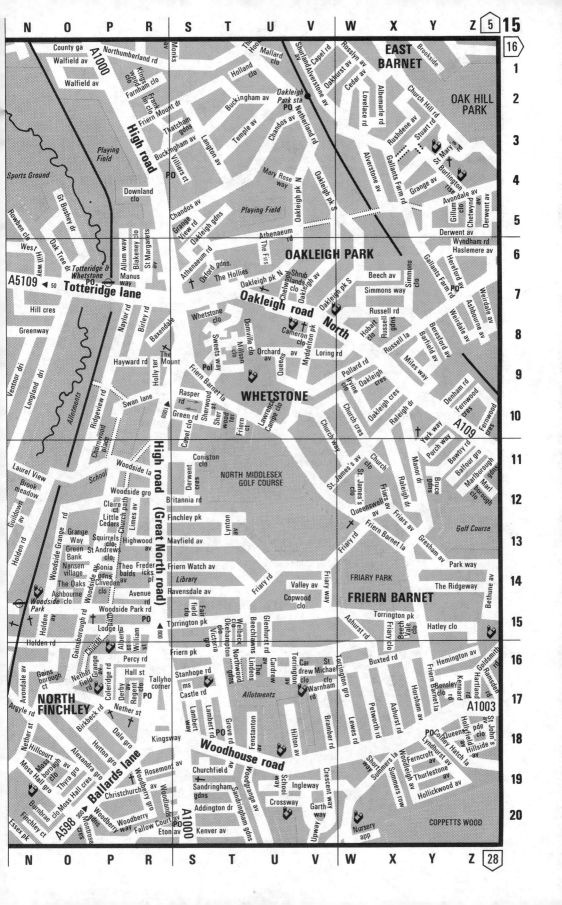

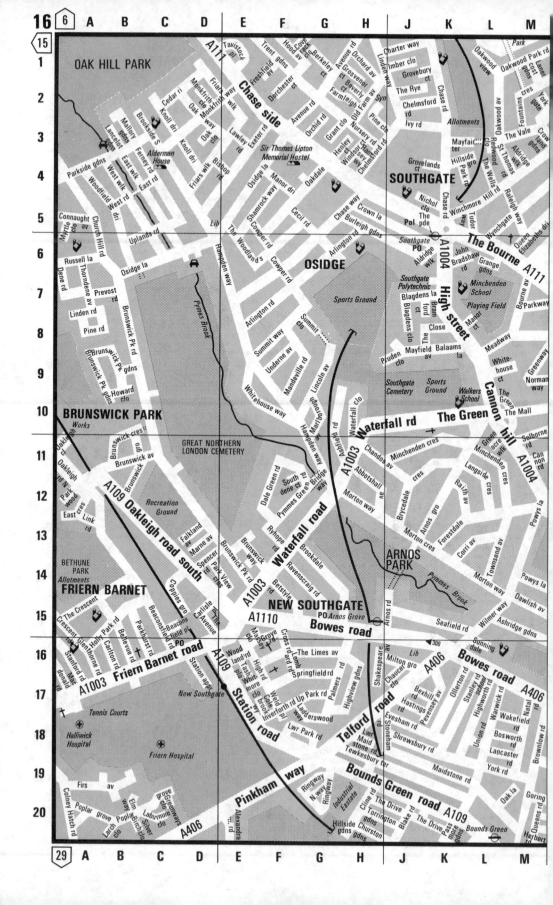

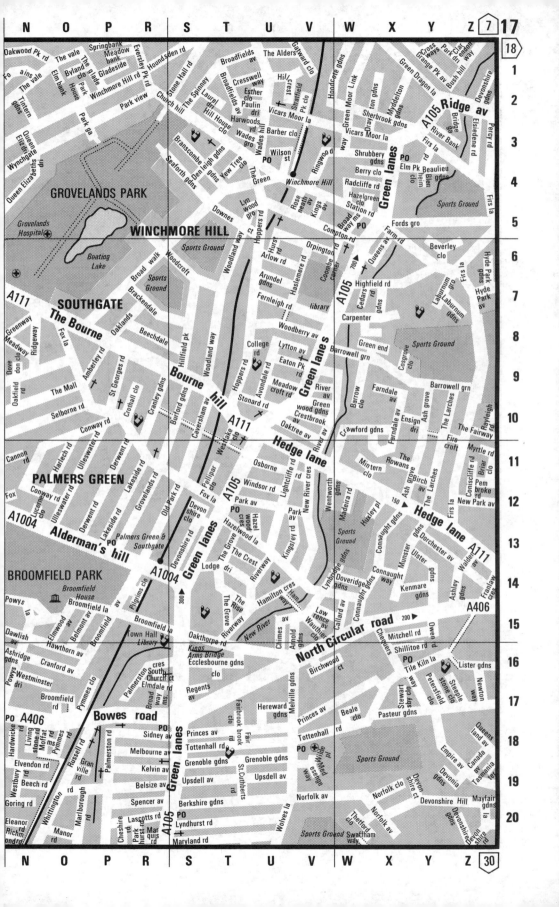

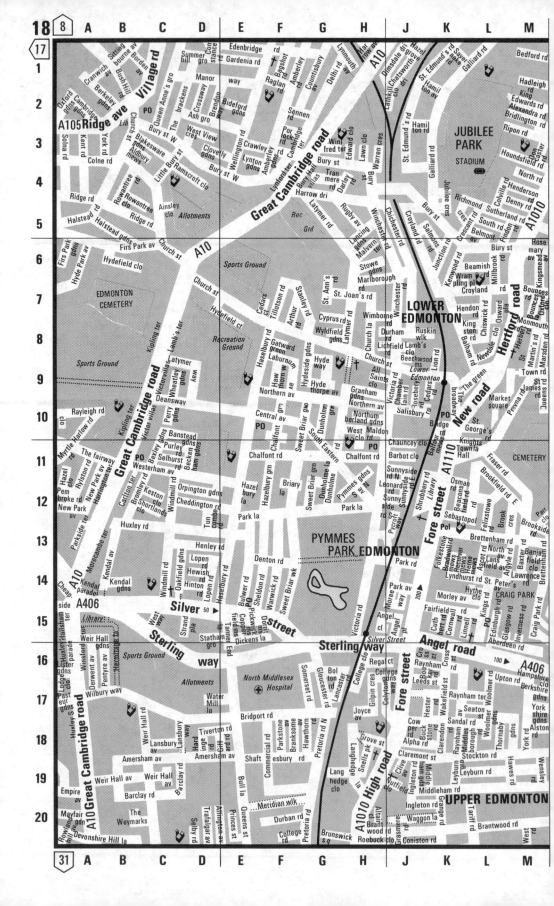

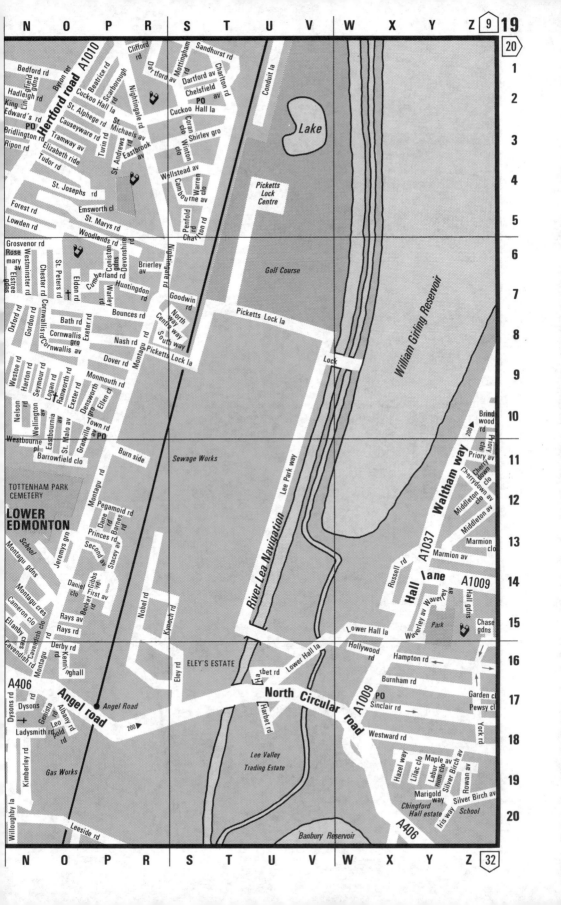

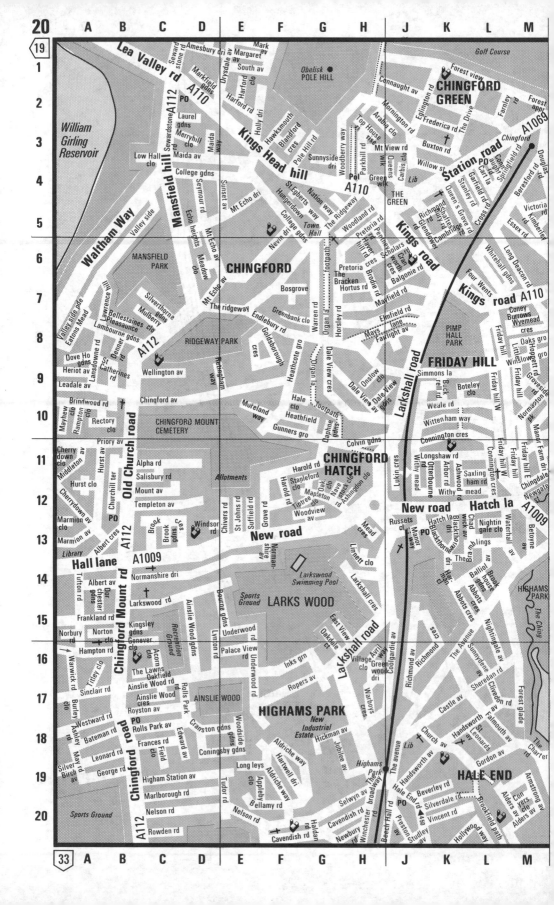

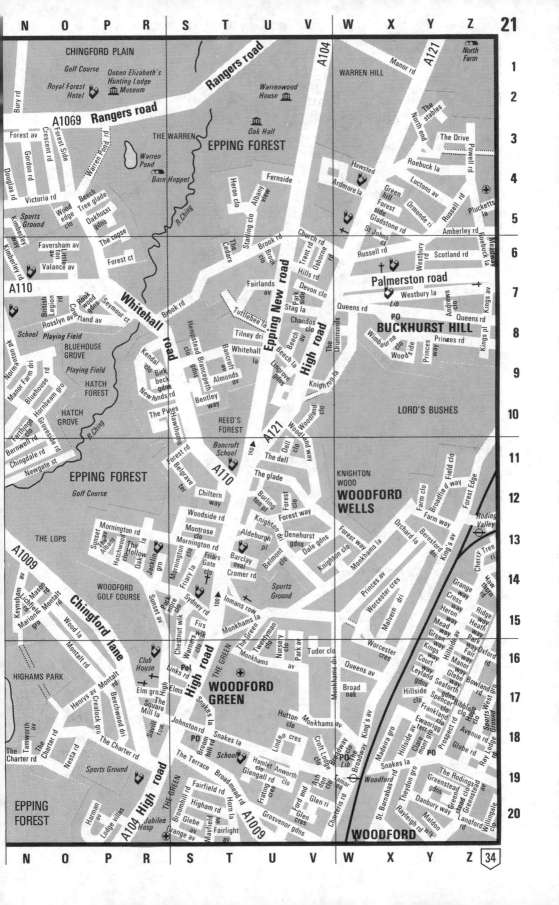

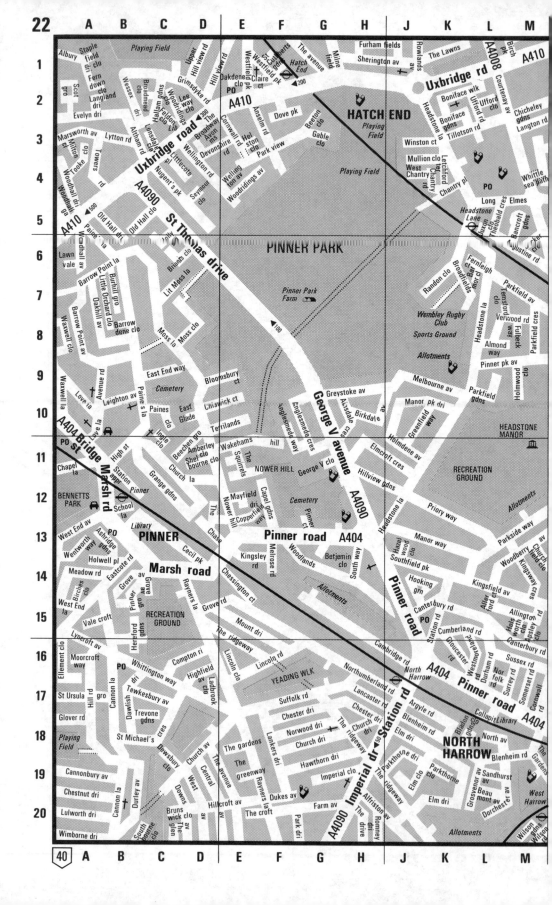

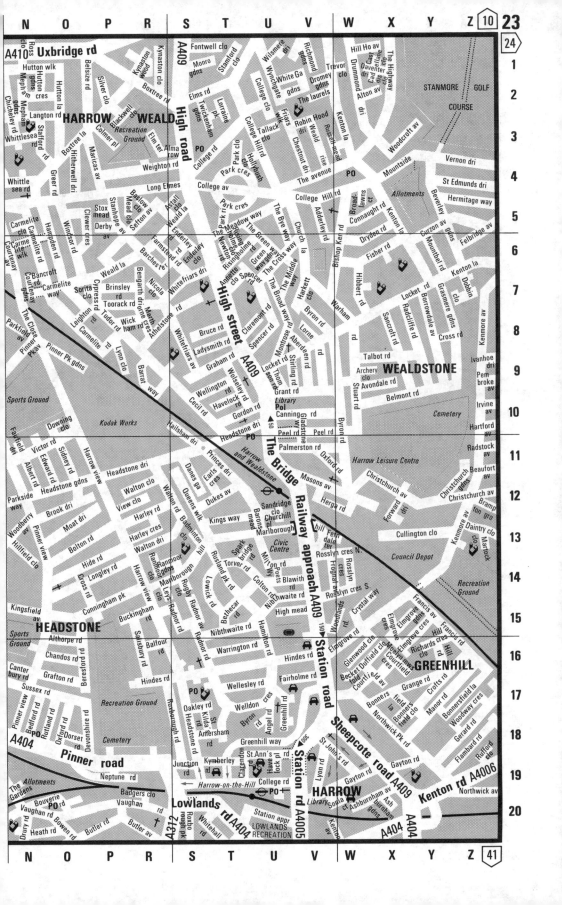

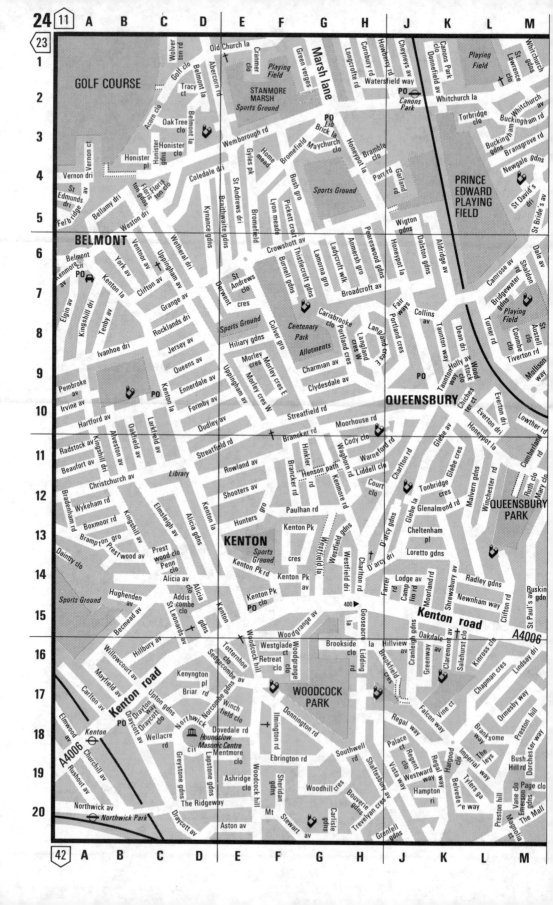

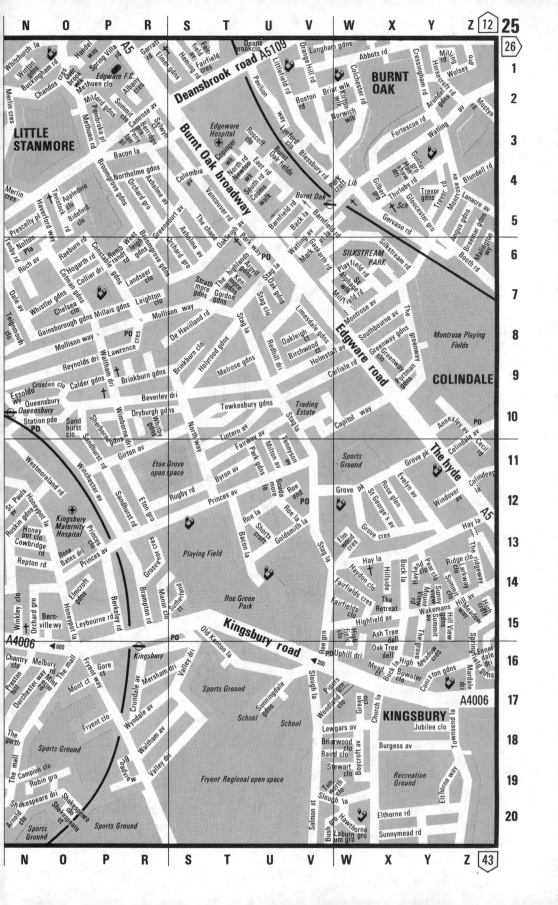

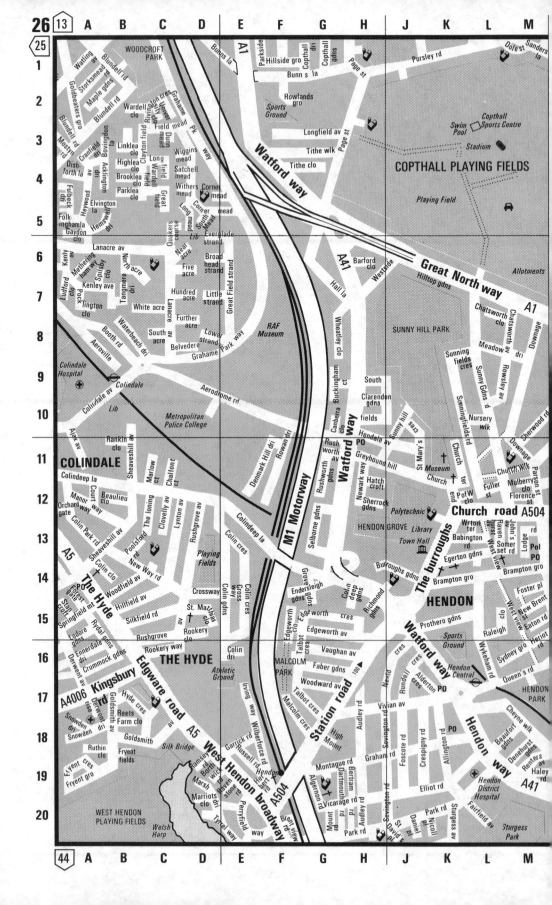

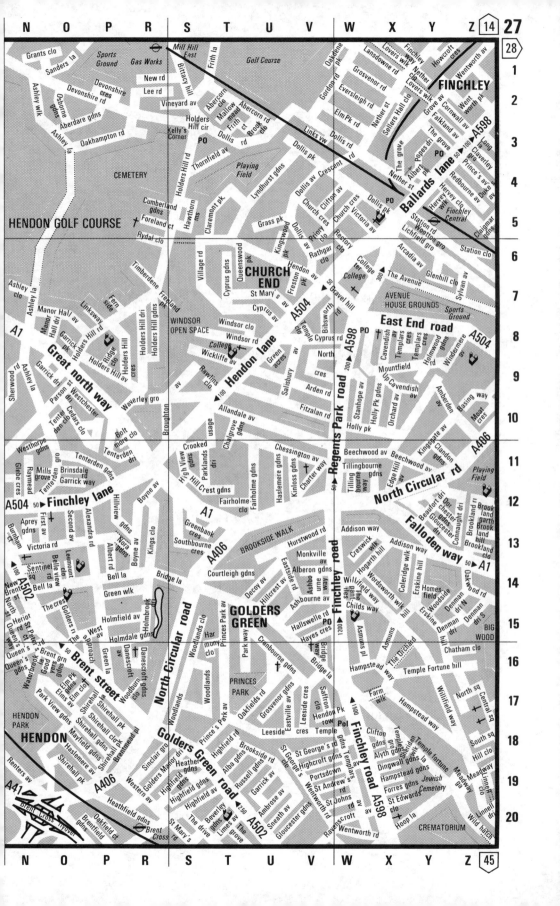

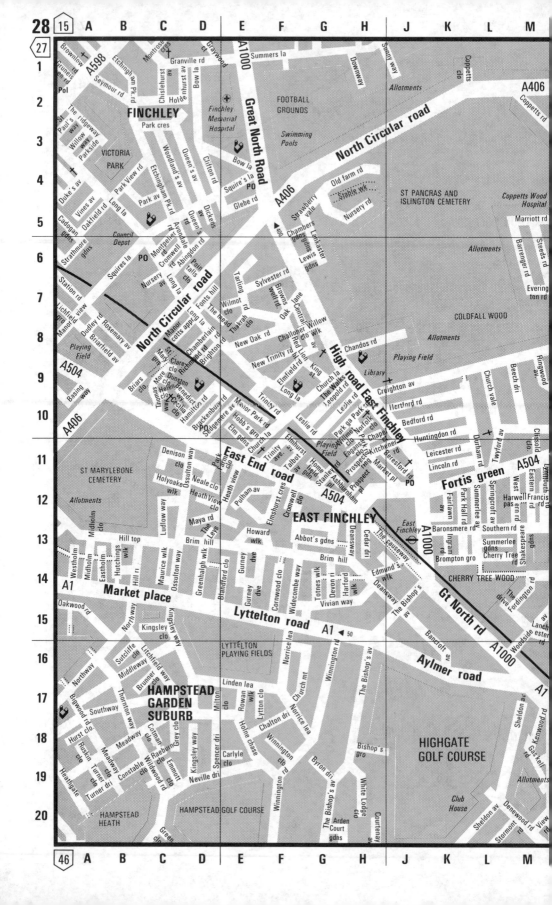

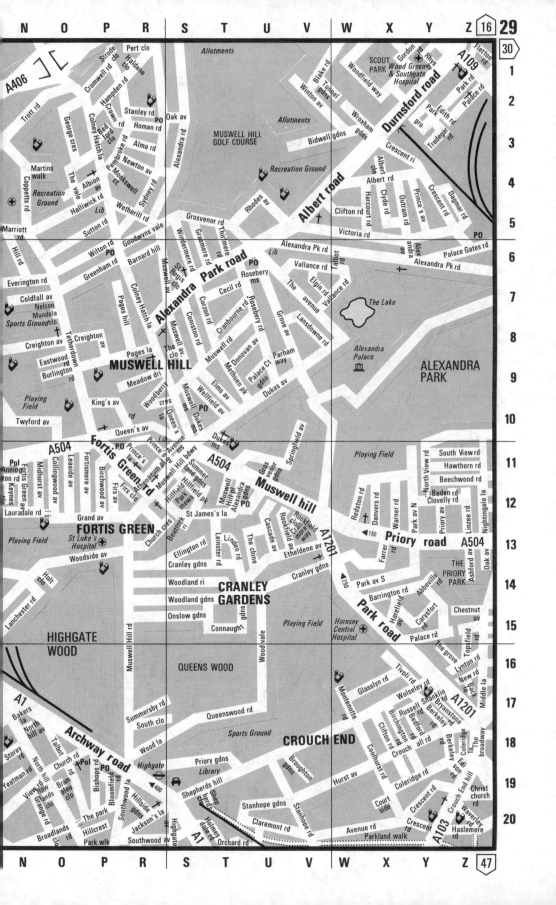

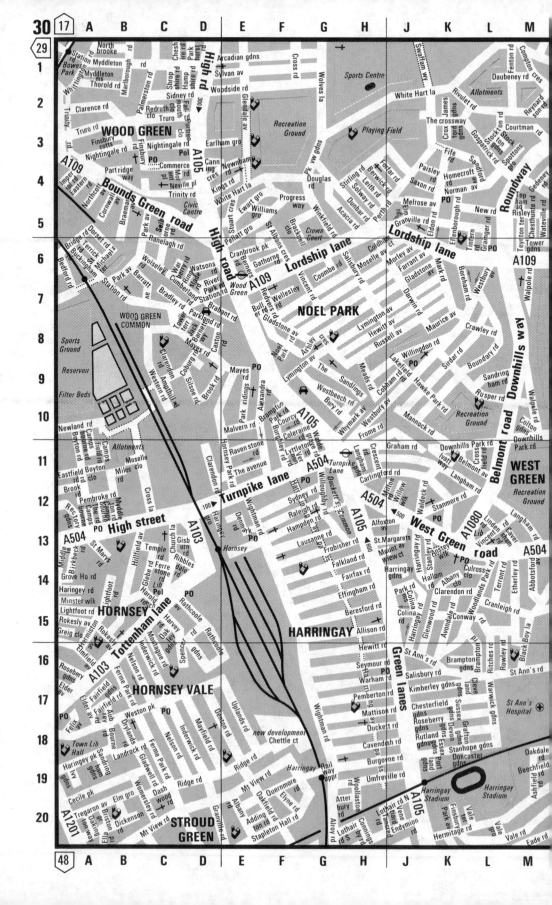

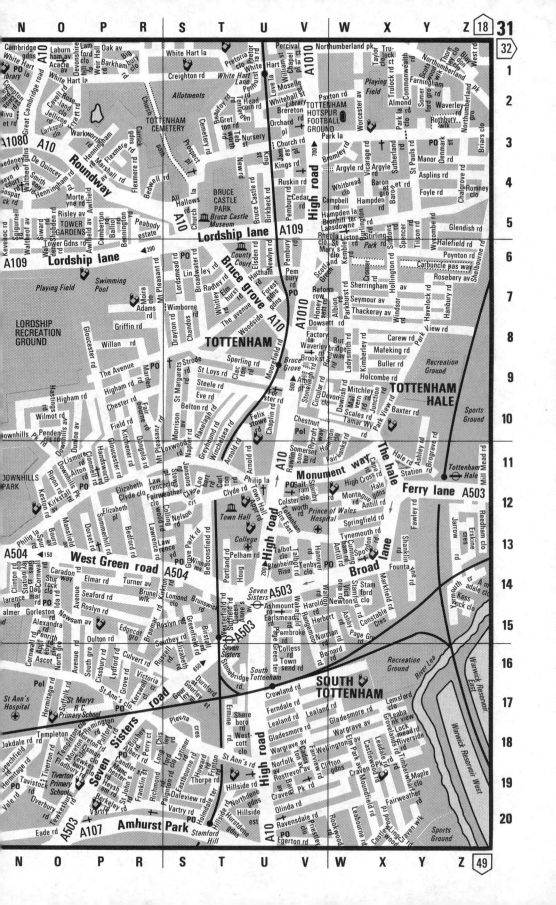

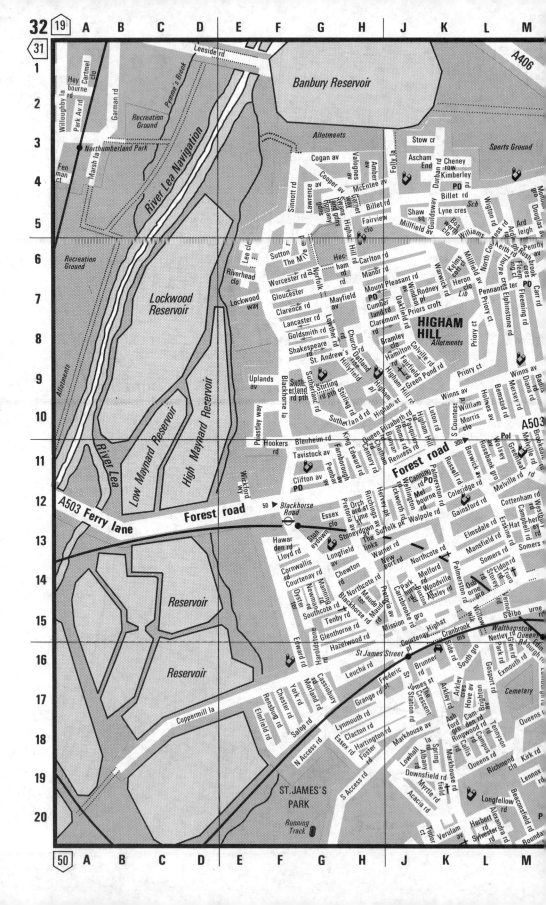

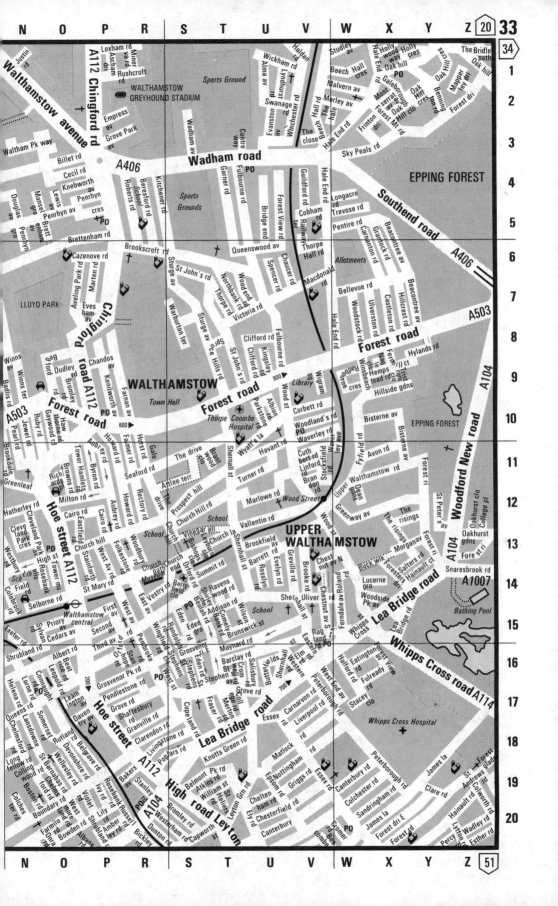

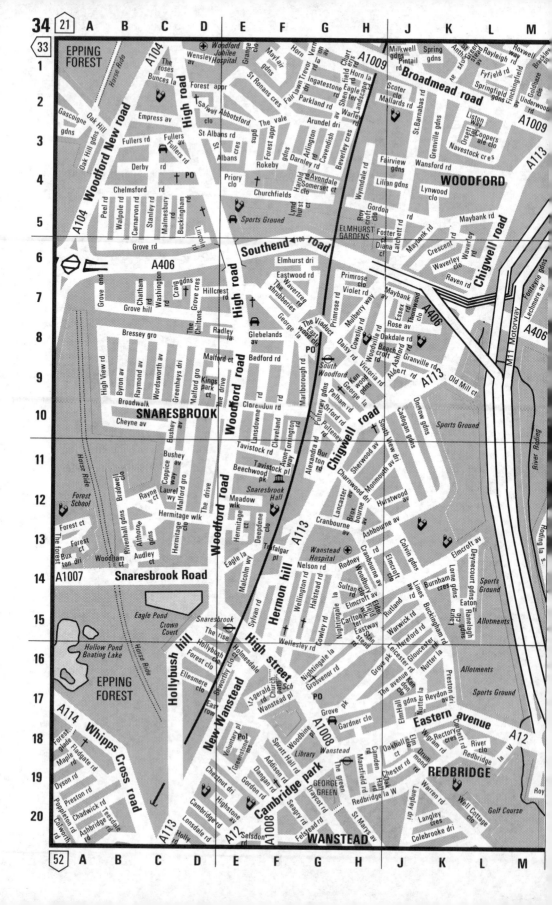

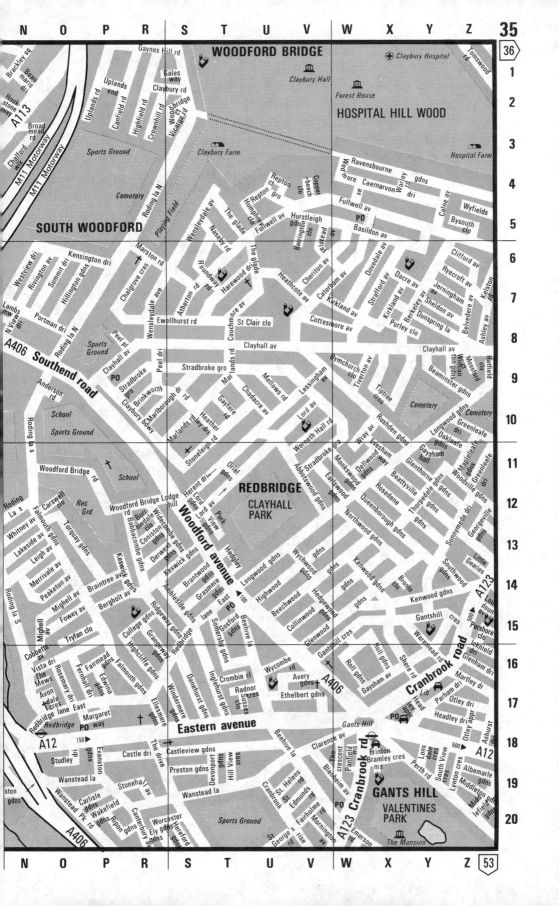

WOODFORD BRIDGE

Claybury Hospital

Claybury Hall

Forest House

HOSPITAL HILL WOOD

Gaynes Hill rd

Tomswood

Brackley sq
Beaumars rd
Uplands rd
Gales way
Claybury rd
Canfield rd
Highfield rd
Crownhill rd
Woodbridge vicarage rd

Hook stone way
A113
Broad mead rd
Chalford walk
M11 Motorway
M11 Motorway

Sports Ground
Claybury Farm
Hospital Farm

Cemetery
Roding la N
Playing Field

SOUTH WOODFORD

Ravensbourne
Wear more la ne
Caernarvon dri
Warley gdns
Calne dri
Wyfields
Bysouth clo

Repton ct
Repton gro
Humphry clo
Copper beech clo
Fullwell av
PO
Basildon av

Wenslendale av
The glade
Naseby rd
Fullwell av
Hurstleigh gdns
Barringham
Eastead

Westview dri
Rivington av
Summit dri
Kensington dri
Marston rd
Chalgrove cres
Wenslevdale av
Roundway
Atherton rd
Harewood dri
The glade
Heathcote av
Cheriton av
Caterham av
Dovedale av
Dacre av
Clifford av
Strafford av
Jerningham av
Ryecroft av
Kelston
Belvedere av
Ashley av
Sheldon av

Lambs N View mw
Portman dri
Roding la N
Ewellhurst rd
Couchmore av
St Clair clo
Cottesmore av
Kirkland av
Kirkland av
Purley clo
Dunspring la

A406 **Southend road**
Sports Ground
Peel pl
Clayhall av
PO
Peel dri
Stradbroke gro
Clayhall av
Stradbroke gro
Marlands rd
Mellows rd
Lessingham
Tiverton rd
Dymchurch clo
Clayhall av
Hatfield clo
Mossford
Beaminster gdns

Anderson rd
Brinkworth
Claybury bdwy
Marlborough rd
Gaylere rd
Chadacre av
Lord av
Werneth Hall rd
Wray av
Tiptree cres
Rushden gdns
Cemetery
Cemetery
Greenleafe

School
Sports Ground
Heather rd
Marlands rd
Henley dri
Stoneleigh rd
Stradbroke gro
Monkswood
Evesham way
Dellwood way
Longwood gdns
Oakleafe gdns
Greenleafe dri
Woodville gdns

Woodford Bridge rd
School
Oriel gdns
Herent dri
Lord av
Park View
Abbotswood gdns
Earlswood
Monkswood gdns
Beattyville
Rosedene
Queenborough gdns
Thorpedale gdns
Glenthorne gdns
Gaysham hall
Maple leafe
Greenleafe dri
Sunnymede dri
Georgeville gdns

REDBRIDGE
CLAYHALL PARK

Roding La s
Carswell clo
Rec Grd
Woodford Bridge Lodge hill
Bowdle clo
Widecombe gdns
Coniston gdns
Derwent gdns
Keswick gdns
Brantwood gdns
Grasmere gdns
Hedgley
Longwood gdns
Wychwood gdns
Highwood
Kenwood gdns
Bronte
Southwood
Little Gearies
A123

Whitney gdns
Falmouth gdns
Lakeside av
Leigh av
Torquay gdns
Babbacombe gdns
Keswick gdns
Woodford avenue
Arbleside gdns
East PO
Beechwood
Collinwood
Hedgewood
Kenwood gdns
Gantshill cres
Pershore clo
Lou doun Icknield dri
Glenham dri

Merrivale av
Mighell av
Fowey av
Braintree av
Bergholt av
Ridgeway gdns
Gosford gdns
Somersby gdns
Glenwood
Gantshill cres
Warnead rd
Gantshill

Peaketon av
Roding La S
Mighell av
Tryfan clo
College gdns
Grangeway
Redbridge
Beehive la
Gantshill cres
Roll gdns
Shere rd

Cobbetts av
Vista dri
The Mews
Avon dale cres
Rosemary dri
Fairmead gdns
Fernhall dri
Edwina gdns
Highcliffe gdns
Falmouth gdns
Crombie ct
Inglehurst gdns
Danehurst gdns
Wycombe rd
Avery gdns
Radnor cres
Sussex rd
A406
Roll gdns
Gaysham av
Cranbrook road
Lib
Martley dr
Parham dri
Otley dri

Redbridge lane East
Windermere gdns
Ethelbert gdns
Head
PO
Otley appr
Ashurst

A12
Margaret way
Ellesmere gdns
Redbridge PO
Eastern avenue
Gants Hill
Clarence av
Frinton
Head
Lonsdale cres
South View cres
A12

150
Castle dri
Castleview gdns
Beehive la
The crescent
Cranbrook rd
Bramley cres
Perth rd
Lynton cres
Albemarle gdns
Middleton gdns
Middleton

Studley
Evanston gdns
Preston gdns
Hill View cres
Devonport rd
Blenheim av
Panfield
A123 **Cranbrook rd**
GANTS HILL
VALENTINES PARK

Wanstead la
Stoneha'l av
Wanstead la
Cranbrook
St Helens
Edmunds
Fairholme
PO

ston gdns
Carlisle gdns
Wanstead Pk Wakefield gdns
Ripon gdns
Canterbury gdns
Ely gdns
Worcester gdns
Hereford gdns
St George's rise
Mornington
A123 Emerson
The Mansion

A406
Sports Ground

1 2 3 4 5 6 7 8 9 10 11 12 13 14 15 16 17 18 19 20

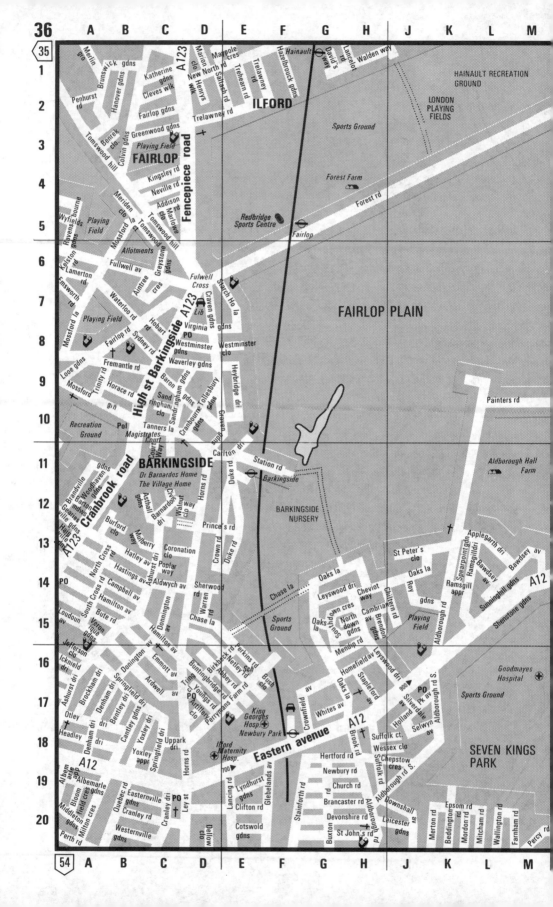

A B C D E F G H J K L M

1 2 3 4 5 6 7 8 9 10 11 12 13 14 15 16 17 18 19 20

35

Merlin gro
Brunswick gdns
A123
Katherine gdns
Marion rd
Marple cres
New North rd
Saltash rd
Treheam rd
Hazelbruck gdns
Trelawney rd
Hainault
David's way
Lancelot
Walden way

ILFORD

HAINAULT RECREATION GROUND

Penhurst rd
Hanover gdns
Cleves wlk
New Henrys wlk
Trelawney rd

LONDON PLAYING FIELDS

Benick gdns
Greenwood gdns
Fairlop gdns
Colvin gdns

Tomswood hill

FAIRLOP

Playing Field
Kingsley rd
Neville rd
Addison rd
Marlowe rd

Fencepiece road

Sports Ground

Forest Farm

Meriden clo
Mossford la
Tomswood la
Greystone
Aintree rd

Wyfields gdns
Ravens bourne gdns
Kelston rd
Lamerton rd
Fullwell av
Allotments
cres
Fulwell Cross

Forest rd

Emsworth rd
Waterloo rd
Hobart rd
Craven gdns
Lib
Virginia gdns

Switch Ho la

Fairlop

Redbridge Sports Centre

FAIRLOP PLAIN

Mossford la
Playing Field
Fairlop rd
Sydney rd
PO
Westminster gdns
Westminster clo
Waverley gdns

High st Barkingside A123

Mossford gdns
Trinity rd
Horace rd
Baron gdns
Sandringham clo
Cranbourne Tollesbury gdns
Heybridge dri

Loop gdns
Fremantle rd
grn

Sand
rd

Craven rd

Painters rd

Recreation Ground
Pol
Magistrates Court
Tanners la

Supplton
Carlton dri
Station rd
Barkingside

Aldborough Hall Farm

BARKINGSIDE
Dr Barnardos Home
The Village Home

Brandville gdns
Woodhaven gdns
Barton molyns
Gearies ville gdns
Help rd
Burford clo
Asthall gdns
Barnardos dri
Walnut way clo

Horns rd
Duke rd
Prince's rd

BARKINGSIDE NURSERY

St Peter's clo
Oaks la

Applegarth dri
Spearpoint gdn
Ramsgilldri
Bawdsey av
Bawdsey av

A12

Mulberry way
Coronation clo
Poplar way

Crown rd
Duke rd

Oaks la

Ramsgill appr
Sunninghill gdns
Shenstone gdns

North Cross rd
Hatley av
Ashurst rd
Aldwych av

Chase la
Oaks la
Leyswood dri
Cheviot way
Chiltern rd
Roy
gdns
Playing Field

Hastings av
Campbell av
Sherwood rd

Own cres
North down gdns
Cambrian av
Brendon gdns

PO
Hamilton av
Bute rd
Warren rd
Chase la

Sports Ground
Oaks la
Southdown gdns
Mendip rd

Goodmayes Hospital

Loudoun av
Veron ridge
Donnington gdns
Hamilton av

Homefield rd
Stapleford
Leyswood dri

Sports Ground

Jefferson clo
Icknield dri
Ashurst dri
Brockham dri
Donington gdns
Springfield dri
Emmott av
Ardwell
Trine clo
Youngs rd
Buntingbridge rd
Birkbeck rd
Netley rd
Abbey rd
Bush
Perkins rd
Oaks la
Whites av

900 PO
Silverdale av
Holland rd
Selwyn av
Aldborough rd

SEVEN KINGS PARK

Otley dri
Headley dri
Bentley dri
Cantley gdns
Yoxley dri
PO
Griffiten clo
Perrymans Farm rd
King Georges Hosp.
Newbury Park
Crownfield
Eastern avenue
A12
Suffolk ct.
Wessex clo
Suffolk rd S.
Chepstow cres

A12
Alhern
Albemarle gdns
Denham dri
Springfield dri
Yoxley appr
Uppark dri
Horns rd
Ilford Maternity Hosp.
Hertford rd
Newbury rd
Brook rd
Downshall av

Bloom
Middleton gdns
Milton cres
Quebec rd
Easternville gdns
Cranley rd
PO
Ley st
Lancing rd
Clifton rd
Lyndhurst gdns
Glebelands av
Stainforth rd
Church rd
Brancaster rd
Aldborough rd
Epsom rd
Beddington gdns
Mordon rd
Mitcham rd

Perth rd
Westernville gdns
Dellow clo
Cotswold gdns
Buxton rd
St John's rd
Devonshire rd
Leicester gdns
Merton rd
Wallington rd
Farnham rd
Percy rd

A B C D E F G H J K L M

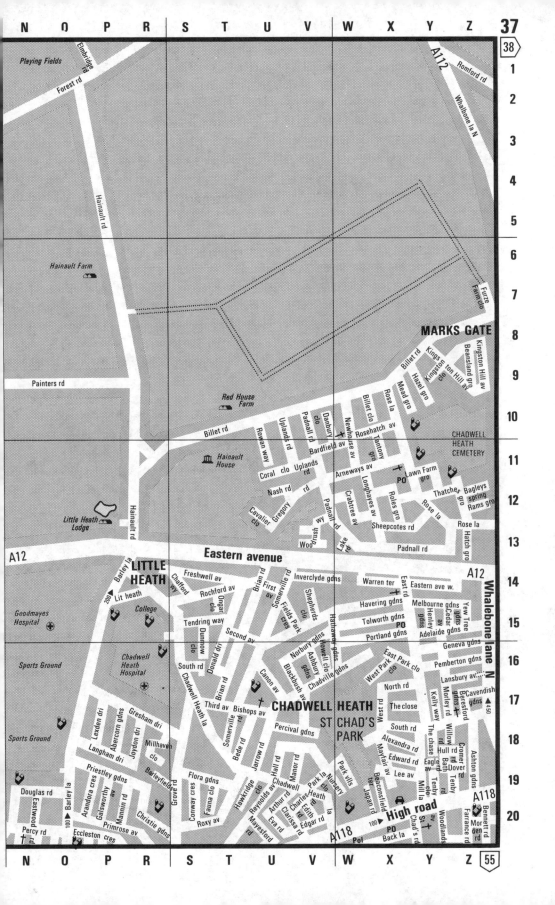

MARKS GATE

CHADWELL HEATH CEMETERY

Playing Fields

Forest rd

Elmbridge rd

Hainault rd

A112

Romford rd

Whalebone la N

Furze Farm clo

Hainault Farm

Painters rd

Red House Farm

Billet rd

Billet rd

Kingston Hill av

Beansland gro

Kingston ton Hill rd

Kingston clo

Hazel gro

Mead gro

Rose la

Billet clo

Danbury clo

Padnall clo

Uplands rd

Rowan way

Bardfield av

Newhouse av

Rosehatch av

Tantony gro

Lawn Farm gro

PO

Thatches gro

Bagleys spring

Rams gro

Hainault House

Coral clo

Nash rd

Uplands rd

Arneways av

Longhayes av

Crabtree av

Roles gro

Rose la

Little Heath Lodge

Cavalier clo

Gregory

Woo

Lake

Padnall rd

Sheepcotes rd

Padnall rd

Rose la

Hatch gro

Hainault rd

A12

Eastern avenue

A12

Whalebone lane N

LITTLE HEATH

Barley la

Lit heath

College

Freshwell av

Chafford wy

Rochford av

Ongar rd

Tendring way

Brian rd

First av

Somerville rd

Fields Park cres

Shepherds clo

Inverclyde gdns

Warren ter

East clo

Eastern ave w.

Havering gdns

Melbourne gdns

Henley gdns

Cedar av

Yew Tree gdns

Goodmayes Hospital

Second av

Dunnow clo

Donald dri

South rd

Norbury gdns

Ashbury gdns

Hathaway gdns

Howell clo

Chadville gdns

Tolworth gdns

Portland gdns

PO

Adelaide gdns

Geneva gdns

Pemberton gdns

Sports Ground

Chadwell Heath Hospital

Brian rd

Chadwell Heath la

Canon av

Blackbush av

West Park clo

East Park clo

North rd

Lansbury av

Cavendish gdns

Beresford rd

Sports Ground

Lexden dri

Abercorn gdns

Gresham dri

Third av

Bishops av

Somerville rd

Percival gdns

CHADWELL HEATH

ST CHAD'S PARK

The close

South rd

West rd

Morley rd

Kelly way

Willow rd

The chase

Hull rd

Cromer rd

Dover rd

Ashton gdns

Tenby rd

Langham dri

Joydon dri

Millhaven clo

Bede rd

Jarrow rd

Hall rd

Manor rd

Alexandra rd

Mayfair rd

Edward rd

Lee av

Bath rd

Tenby clo

Priestley gdns

Barleyfields

Grove rd

Flora gdns

Conway cres

Fauna clo

Hawkridge clo

Reynolds av

Chadwell clo

Arthur rd

Clarissa rd

Edith rd

Edgar rd

Charles rd

Heath la

Park la

Park vlls

Nursery rd

Eagle av

Mill la

Woodlands

Bennett rd

Farrance rd

Douglas rd

Barley la

Arandora cres

Galsworthy av

Mannin rd

Primrose av

Christie gdns

Roxy av

Mayesford rd

Eva rd

High road

Beaconsfield rd

Japan rd

Chad's rd

Morden rd

Percy rd

Eastwood

Eccleston cres

A118

Pol

PO

Back la

St Chad's rd

A118

1 2 3 4 5 6 7 8 9 10 11 12 13 14 15 16 17 18 19 20

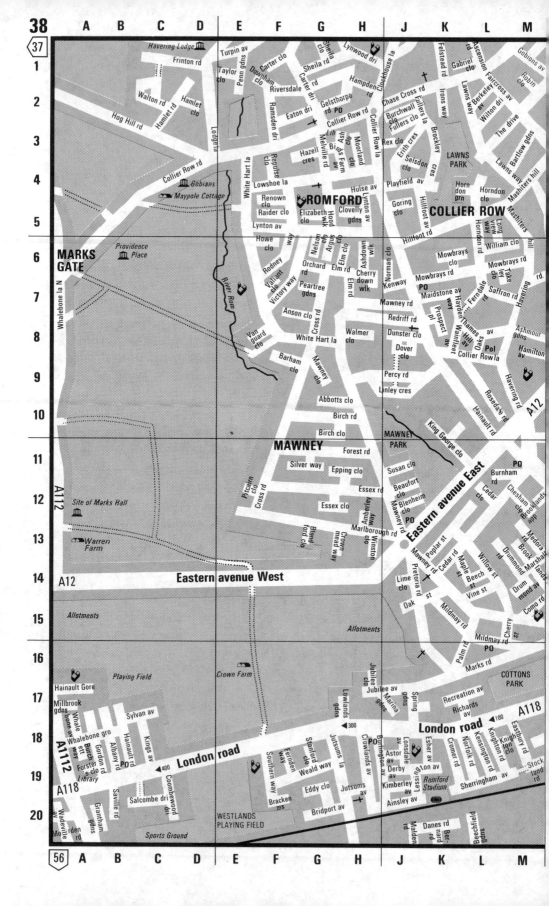

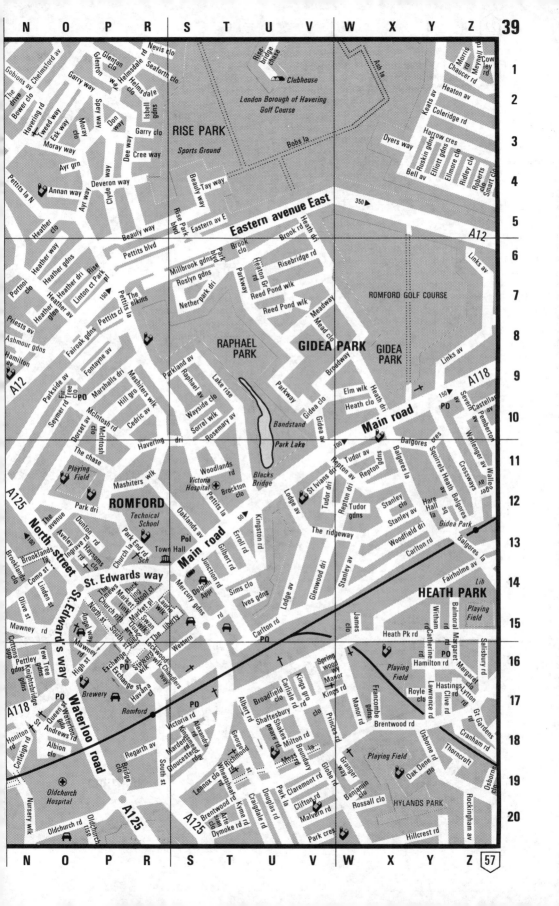

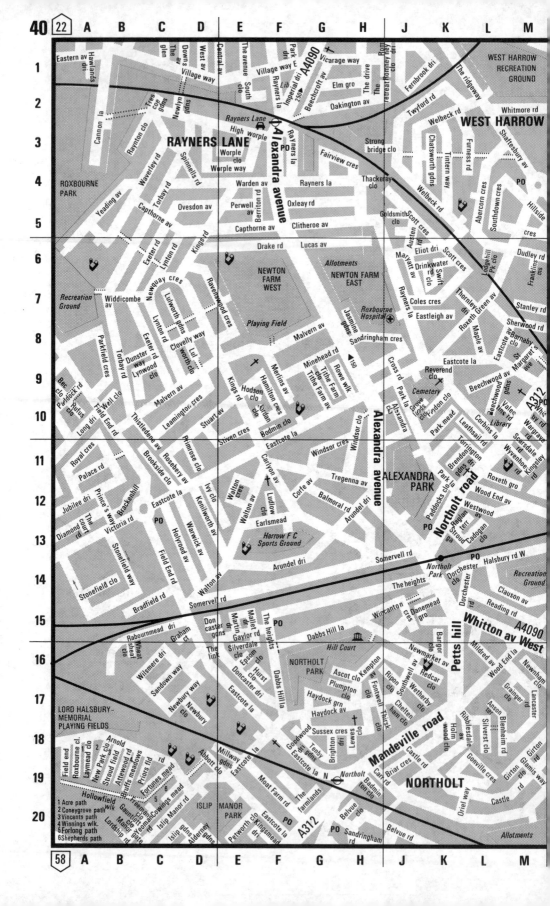

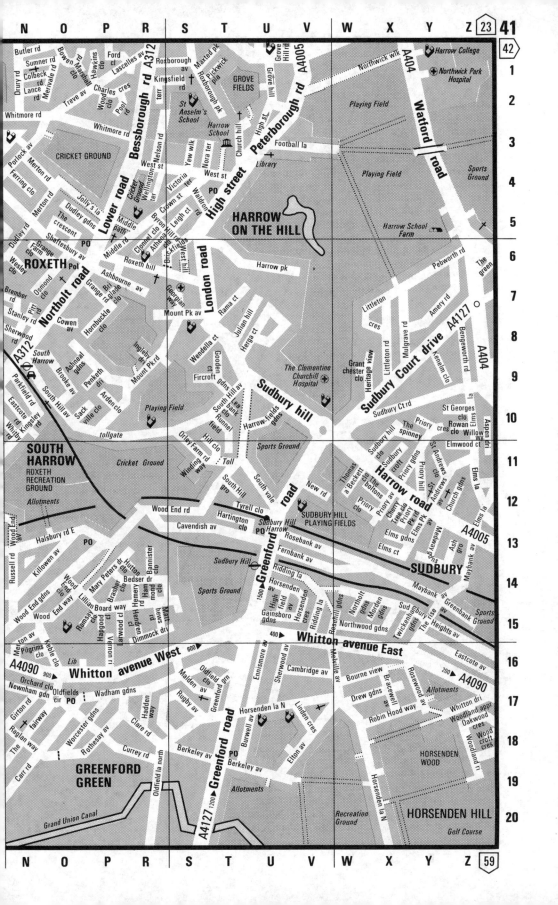

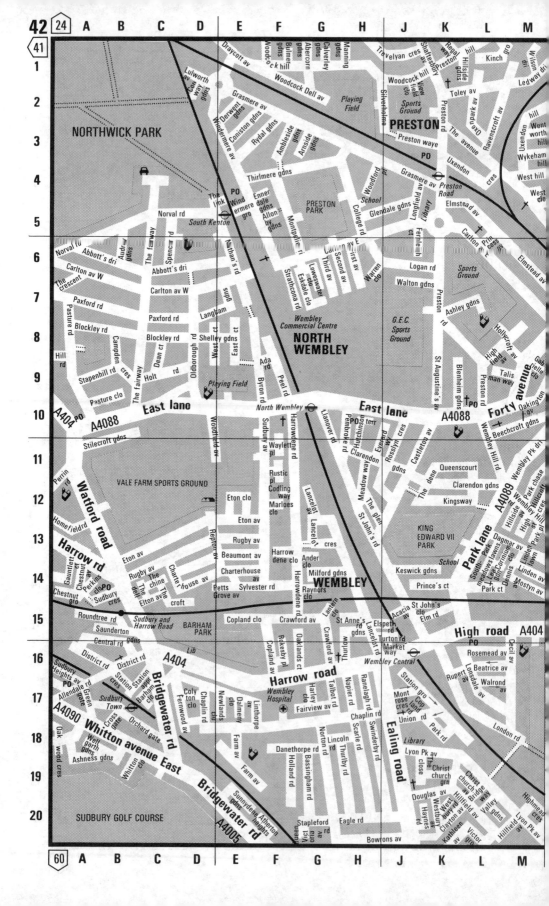

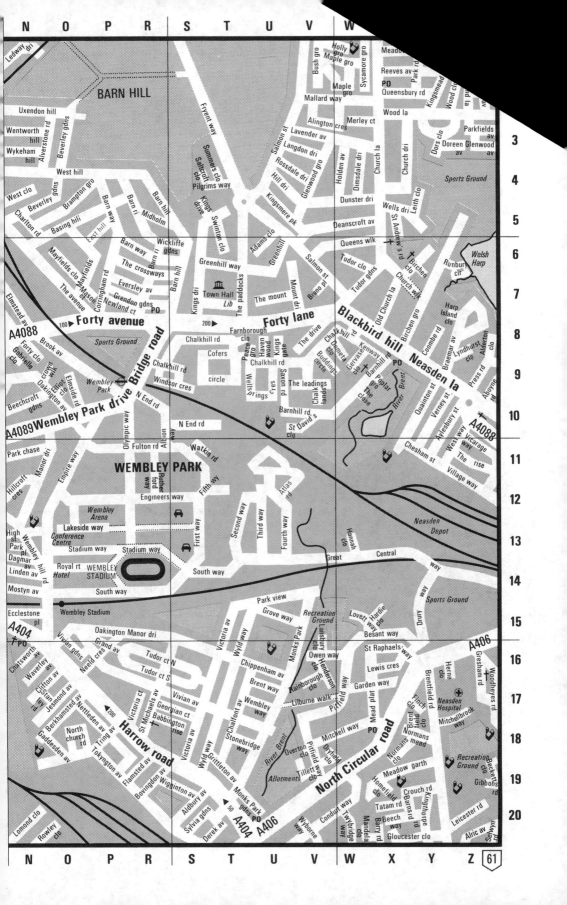

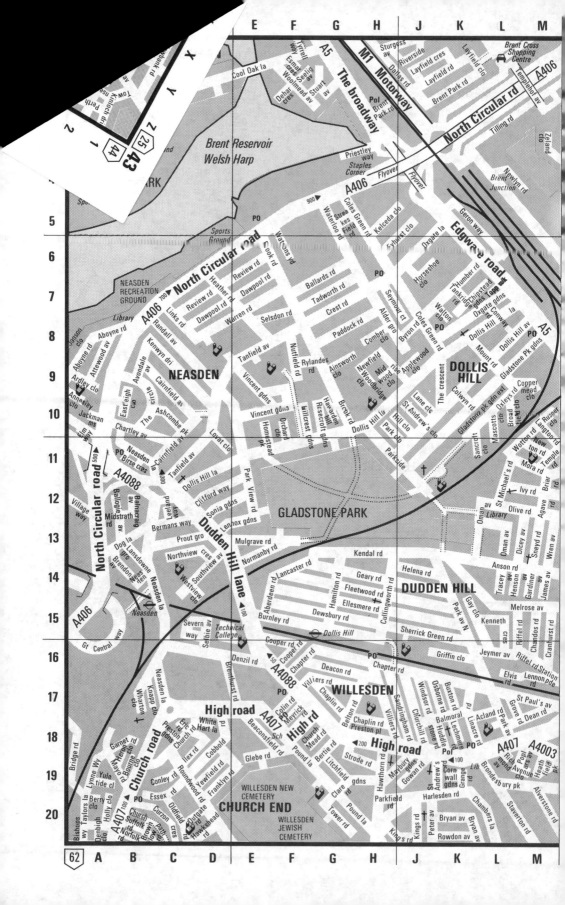

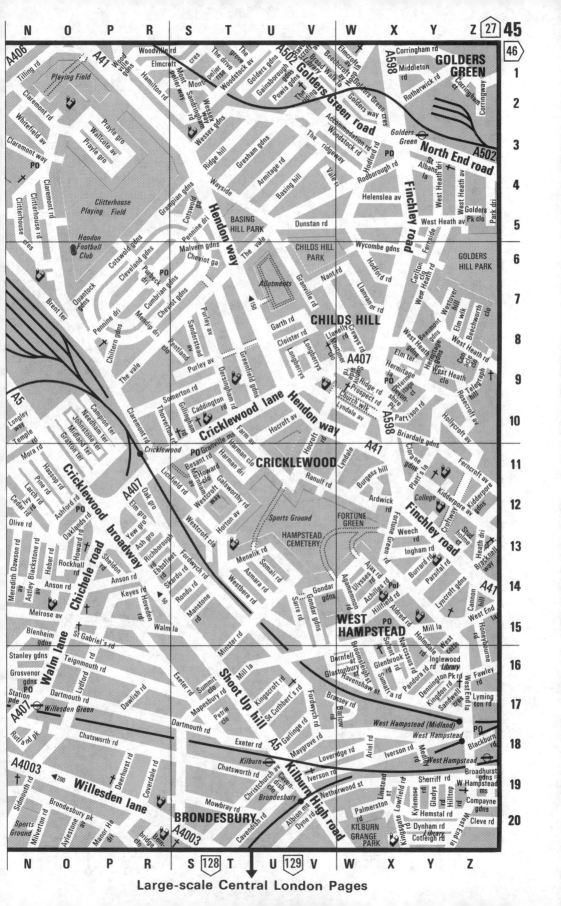

Large-scale Central London Pages

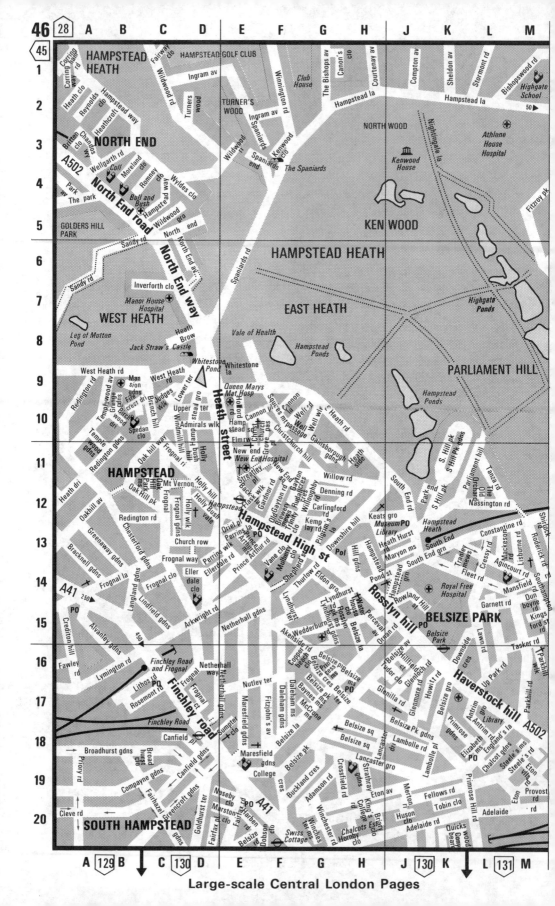

Large-scale Central London Pages

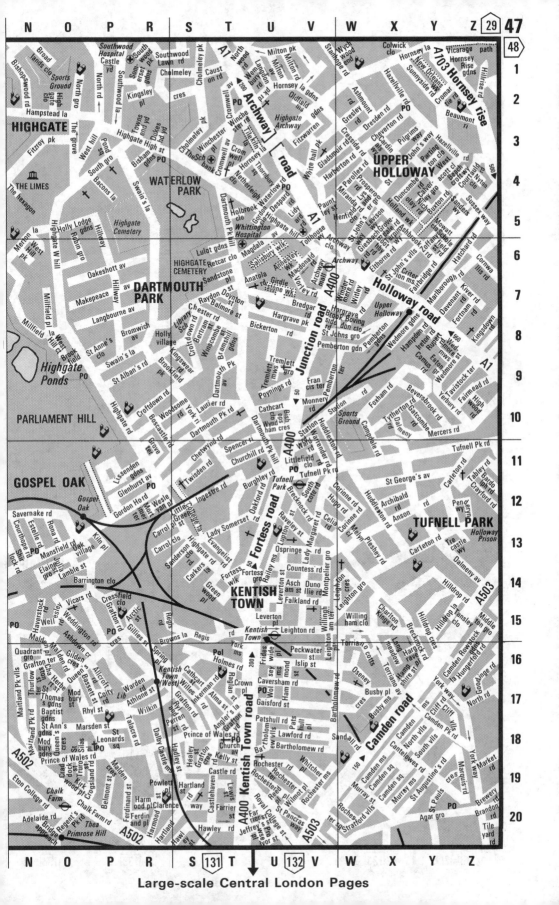

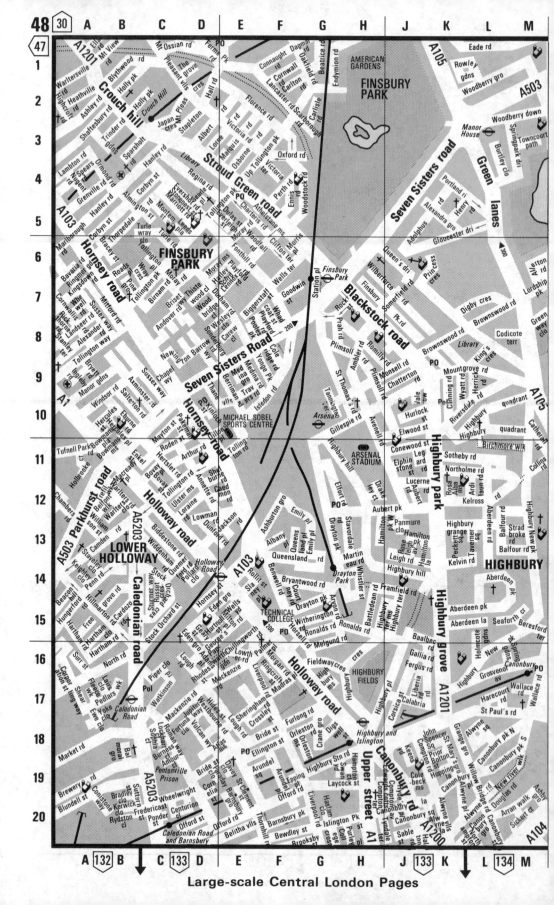

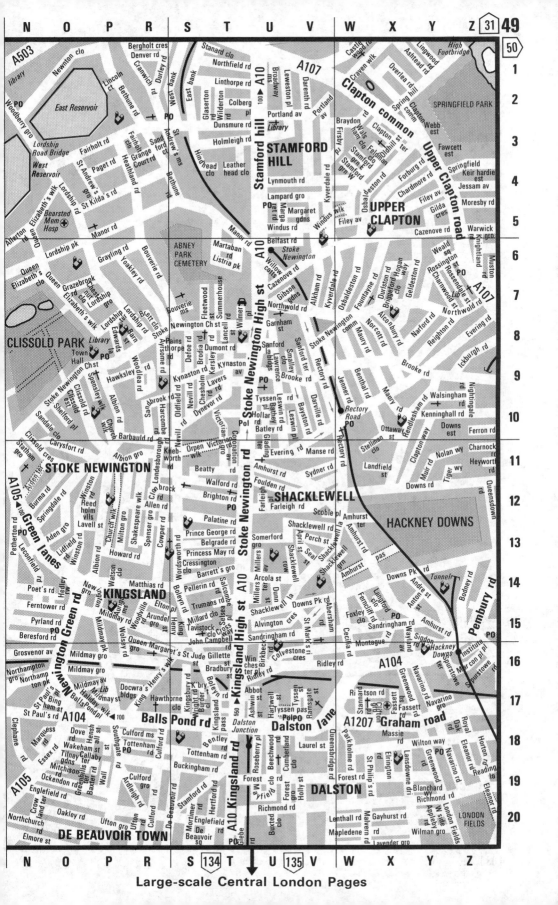

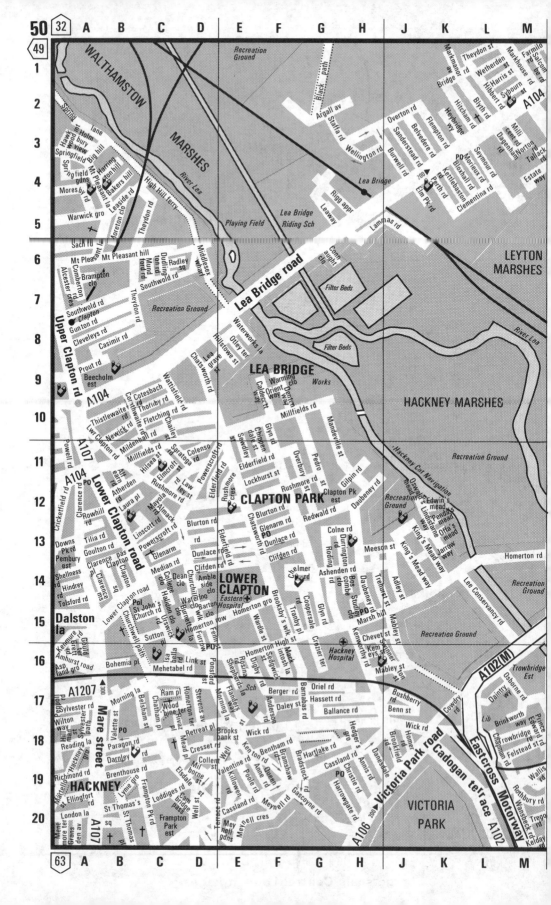

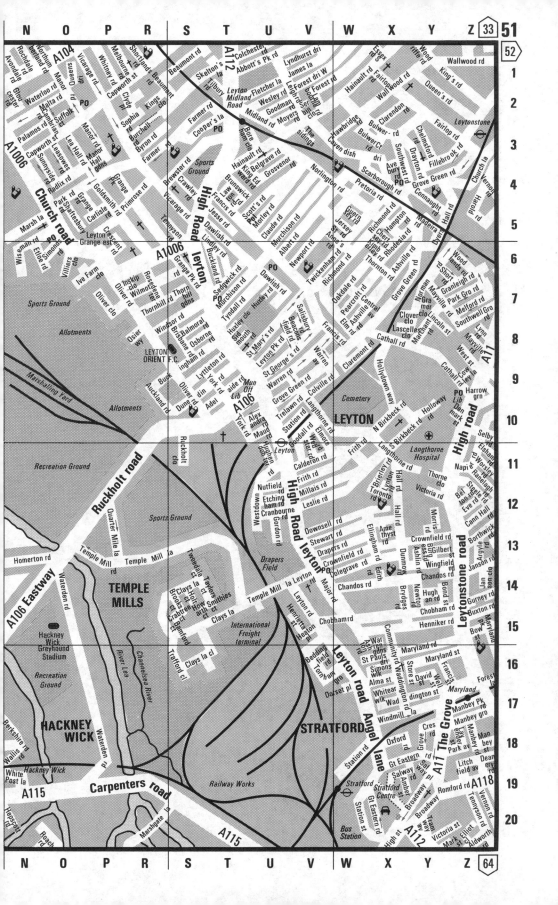

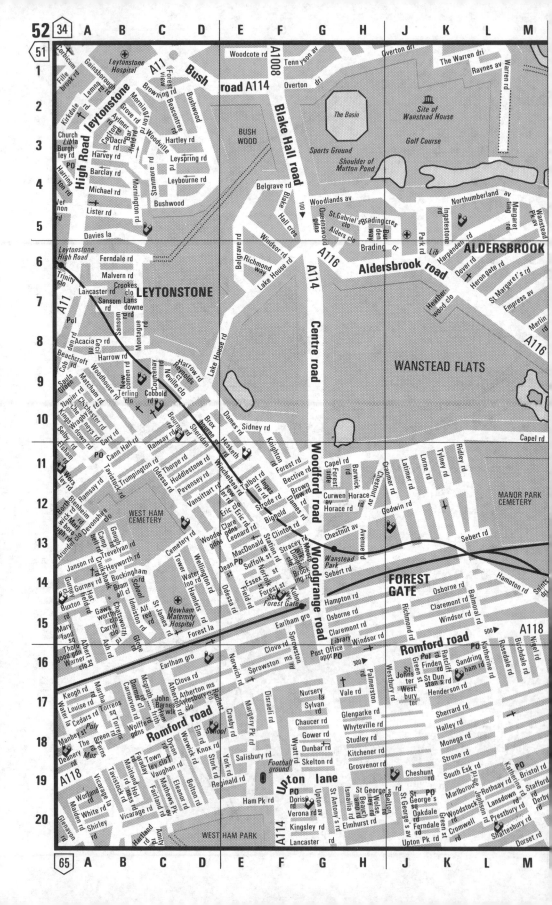

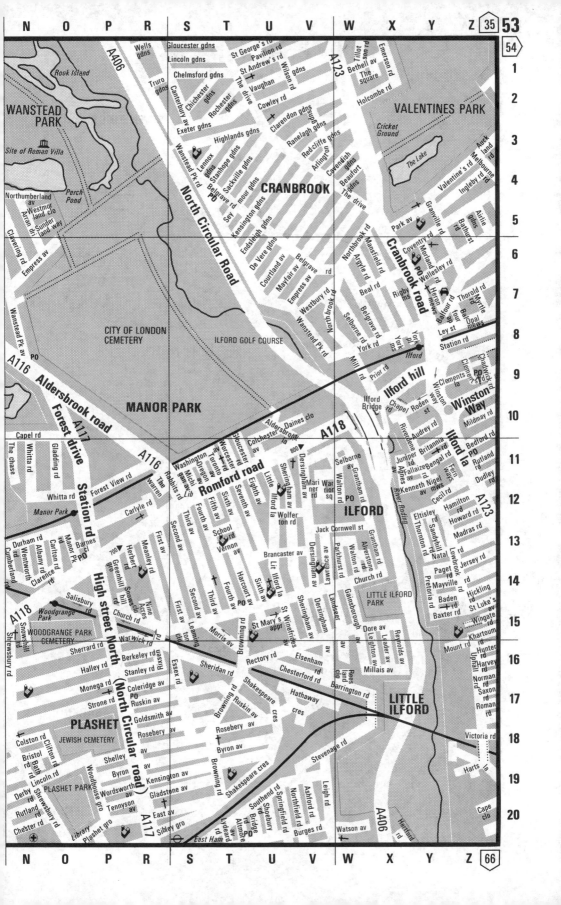

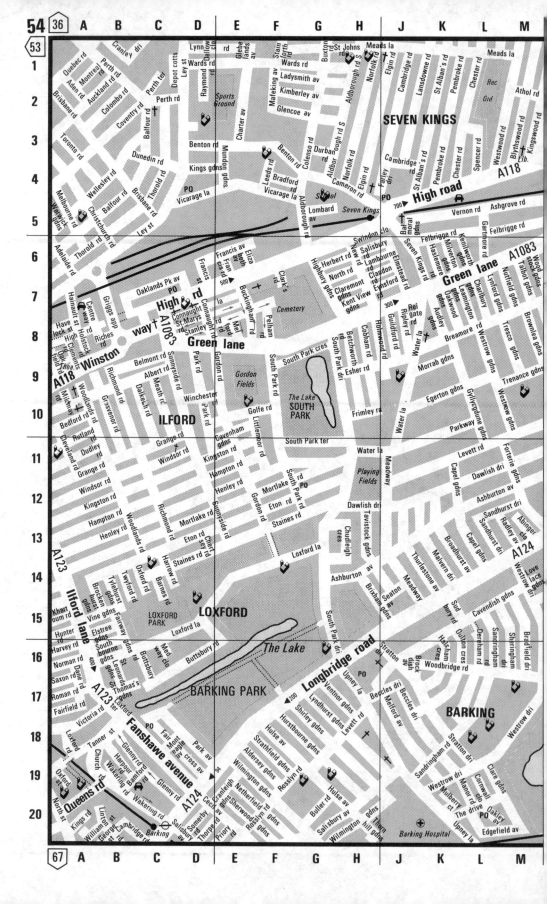

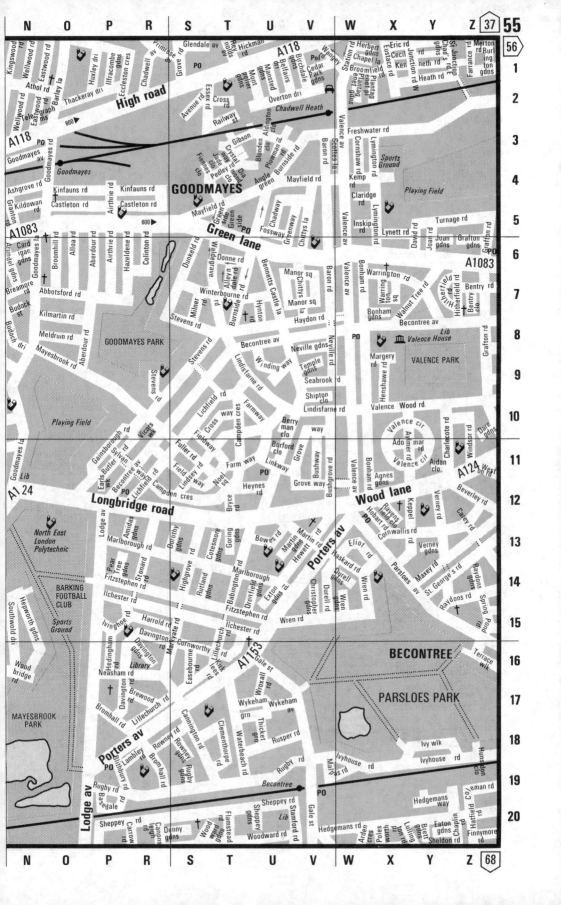

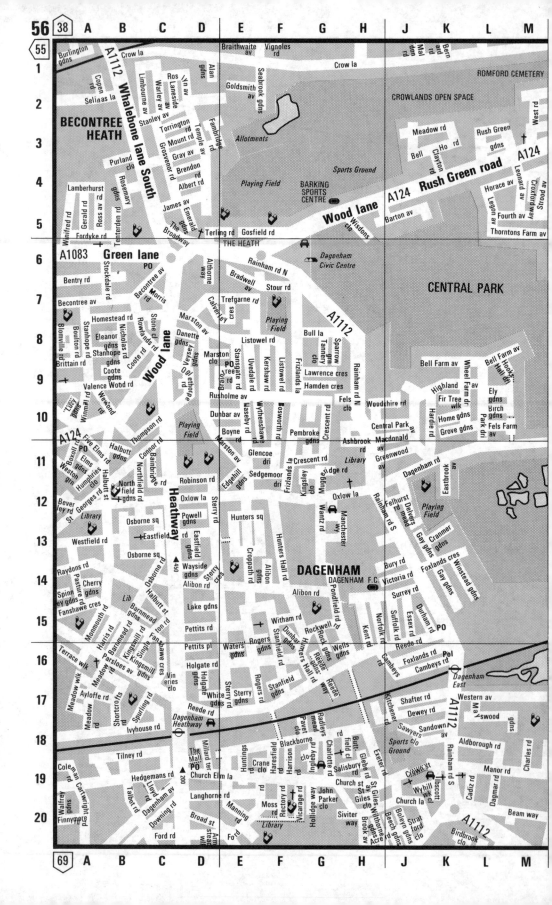

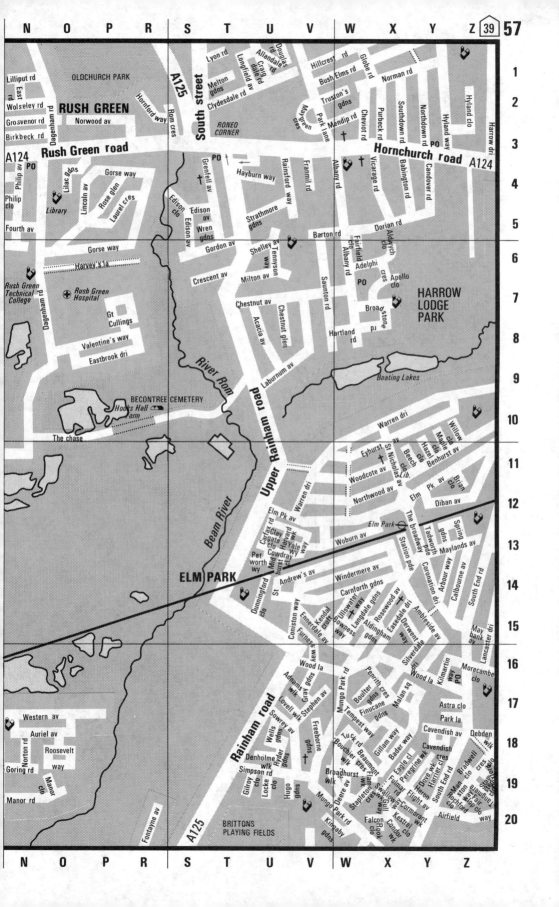

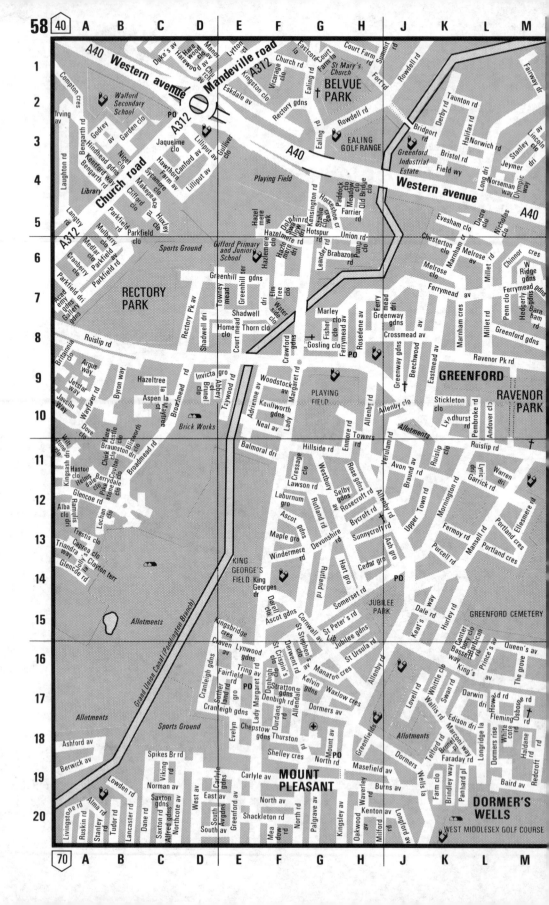

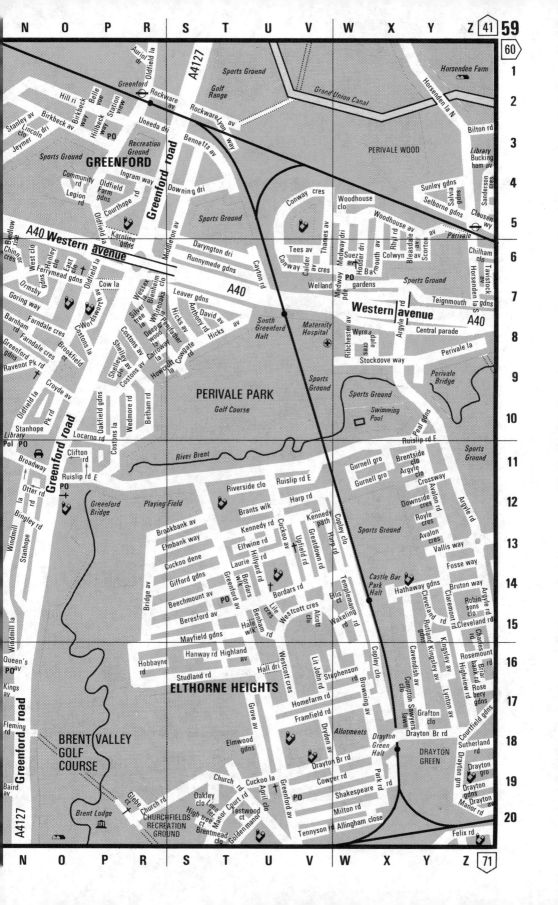

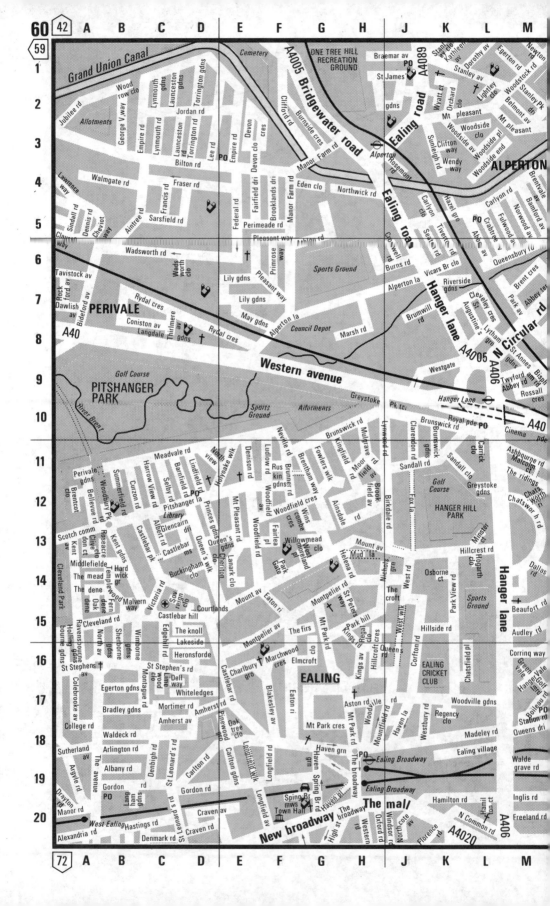

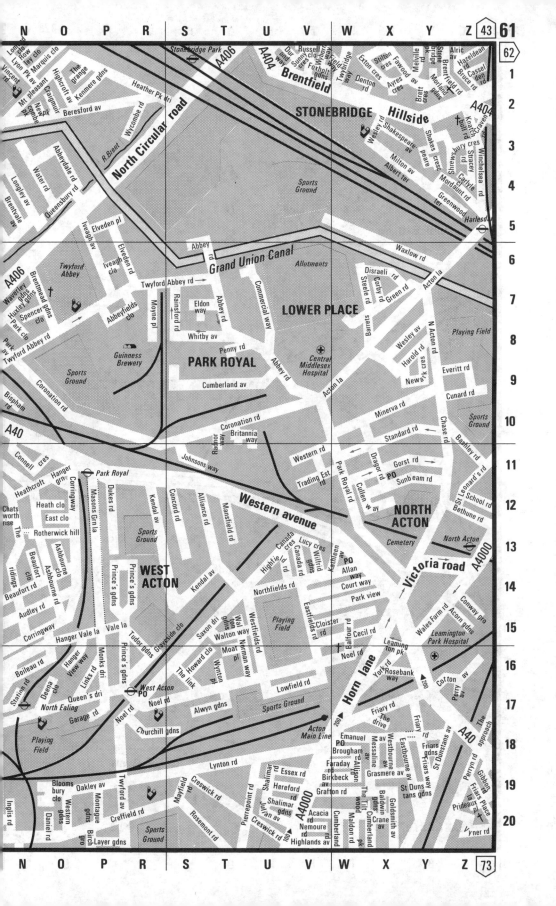

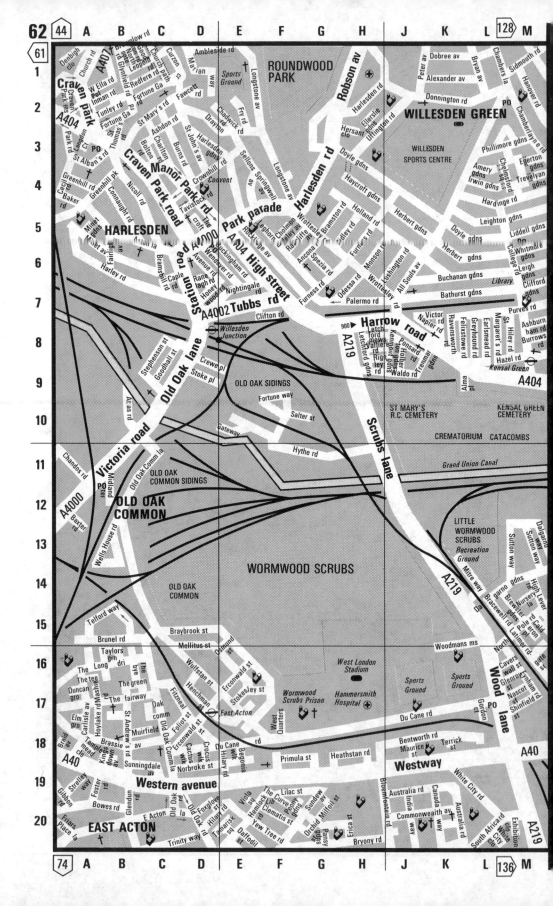

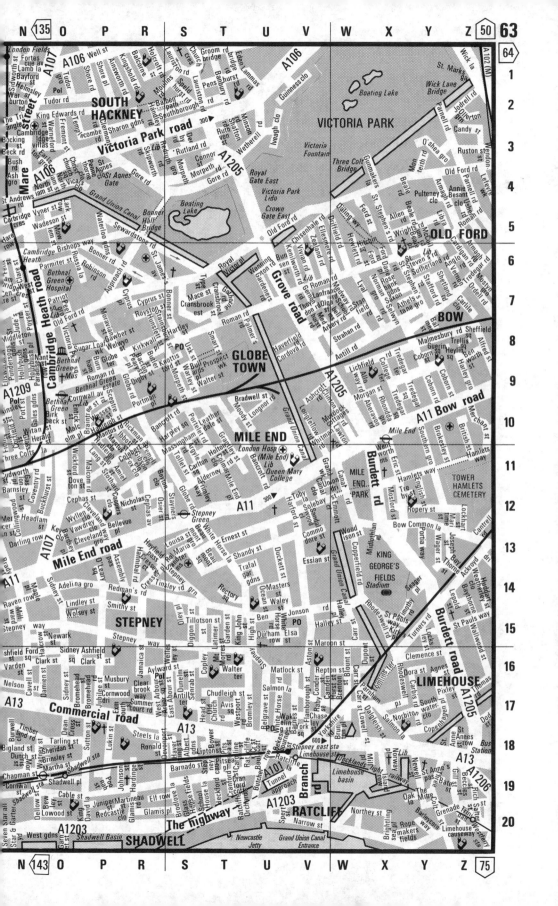

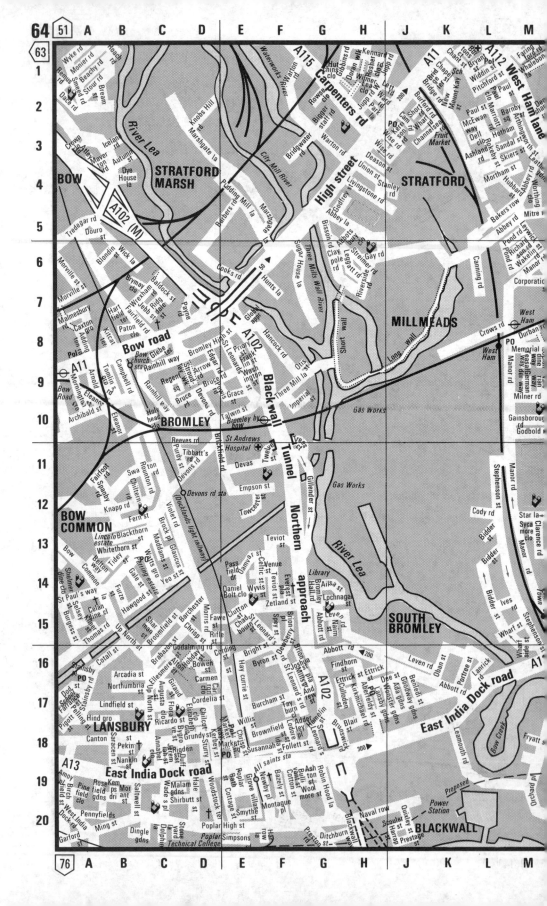

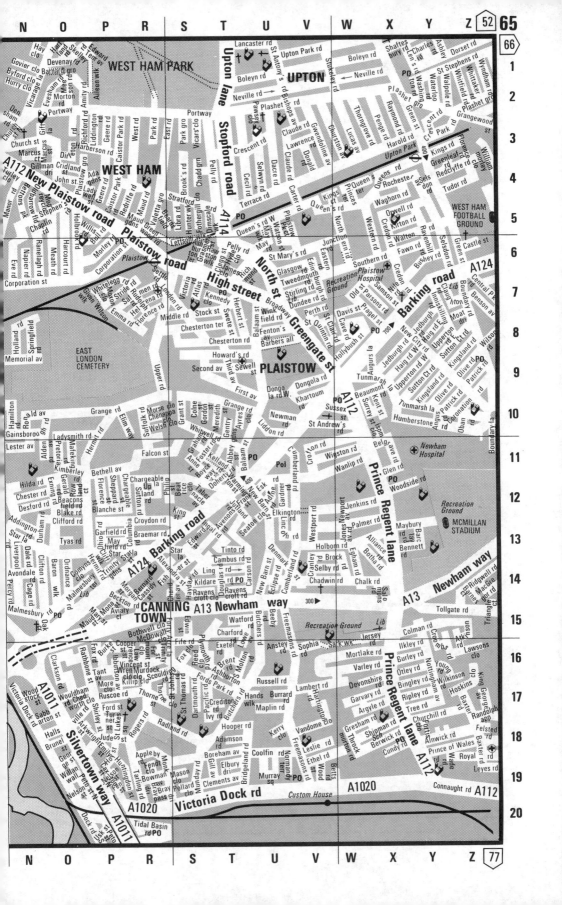

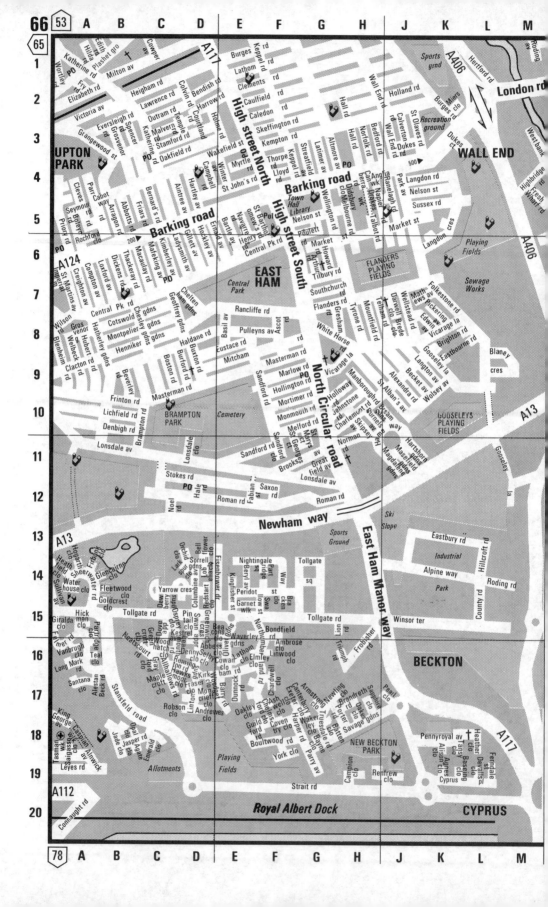

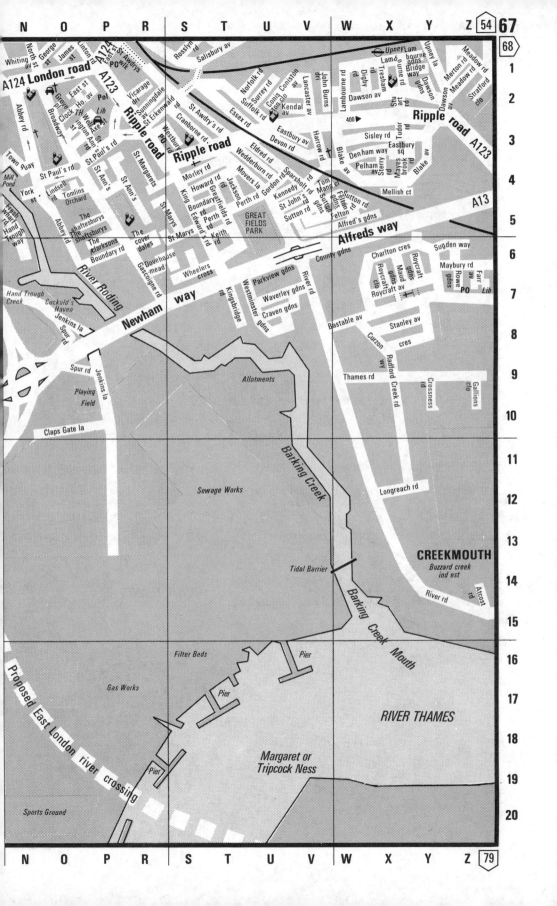

1
2
3
4
5
6
7
8
9
10
11
12
13
14
15
16
17
18
19
20

Whiting st North st George James st
Linton rd St Awdry's wlk
A124 London road A124 East st PO
A123 Vicarage Salisbury av Rosslyn rd
Abbey rd Grove East st Sunningdale dri
Broadway Clock TH Ho av Pol St Erkenwald St Awdry's rd Essex rd Norfolk rd Surrey rd Conis Coniston stan clo Lancaster av John Burns dri Upney Lam Upney la bourne rd Meadow rd Merton rd
Lib Av Ripple road Cranborne rd Suffolk rd Kendal av Lambourne rd Dawson av Tresham Digby Bridge way Dawson gdns Meadow rd Stratford clo
St Paul's rd Ripple road Westbury Eastbury rd Devon rd Harrow rd Dawson av 400 Ripple road A123
Town Quay St Paul's rd St Margarets Morley rd Eldred rd Wedderburn rd Gordon rd Sparsholt rd Tom Mang Sisley rd Tudor Eastbury sq Denham way Blake av Ripple road A123
Mill Pond Lindsell rd St Ann's Howard rd King Greatfields rd Perth rd Kennedy St John's gdns Felton Sutton rd Pelham av Sherry Mayes brook Blake av
York st Tomlins Orchard St Ann's Boundary rd Edward's rd Perth rd Keith rd Sutton rd Felton Alfred's gdns Mellish ct A13
Fresh wharf rd The shaftesburys St Marys GREAT FIELDS PARK Jackson rd Movers la St John's rd
Hand Trough way The shaftesburys The clarksons Boundary rd St Marys Alfreds way
Abbey rd The cover dales Gascoigne rd Dovehouse mead Wheelers cross County gdns Charlton cres Sugden way
River Roding Parkview gdns Maybury rd Roycraft gdns Farr av
Newham way Kingsbridge rd Westminster gdns River rd Roycraft gdns Maud clo Rowe gdns PO Lib
Hand Trough Creek Waverley gdns Craven gdns Roycraft av Stanley av
Cuckold's Haven Bastable av Curzon wy cres
Jenkins la Spur rd Radford Creek rd Crossness rd Gallions clo
Spur rd Jenkins la Allotments Thames rd
Playing Field Longreach rd
Claps Gate la Sewage Works Barking Creek CREEKMOUTH
Buzzard creek ind est
Tidal Barrier River rd Atcost rd
Barking Creek
Mouth
Filter Beds Pier
Proposed East London river crossing Gas Works Pier RIVER THAMES
Pier
Margaret or Tripcock Ness
Sports Ground Pier

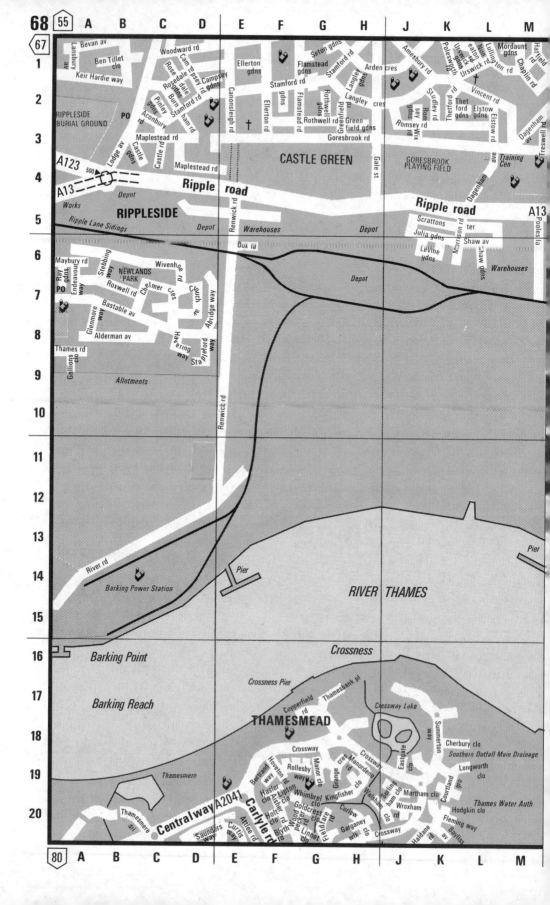

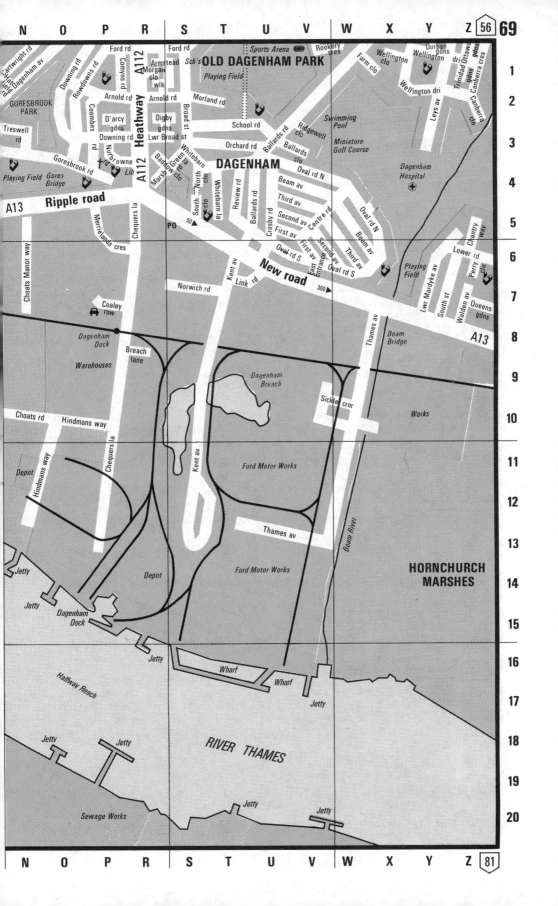

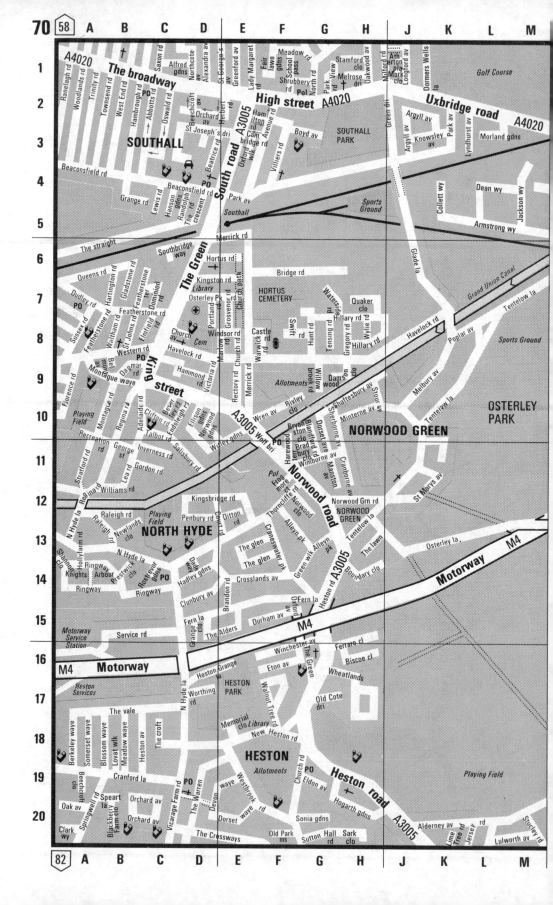

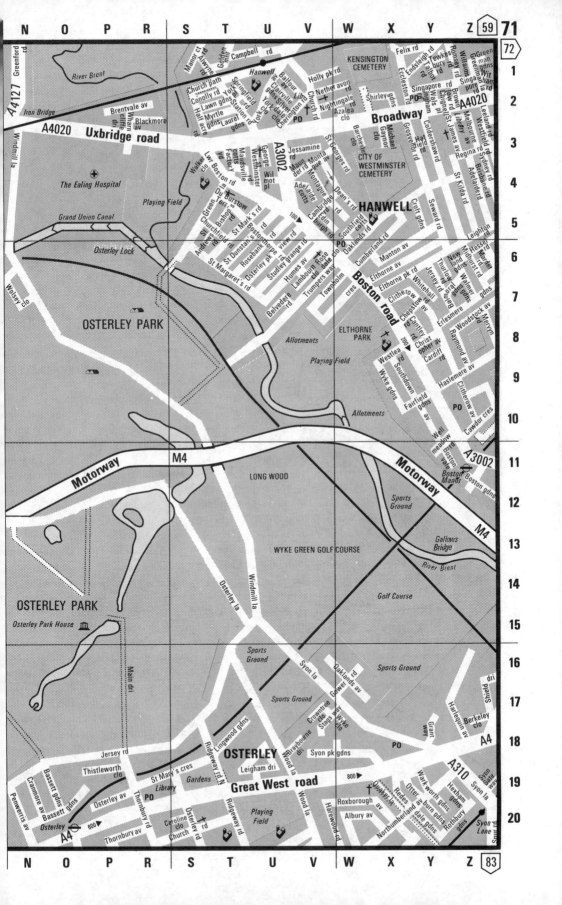

1
2
3
4
5
6
7
8
9
10
11
12
13
14
15
16
17
18
19
20

A4127 Greenford rd

River Brent

Iron Bridge

Brentvale av
Wharn cliffe Blackmore

A4020 **Uxbridge road**

Windmill la

The Ealing Hospital

Playing Field

Grand Union Canal

Osterley Lock

Wolsey clo

OSTERLEY PARK

Church Bath
Conolly rd
Lawn gdns
Myrtle
Laurel gdns

Manor ct
Golden mnr
Alwyne
Campbell rd
Hanwell
Balfour
Carville gdns
Lisard
York st
Springfield
York dale
Church rd

Holly pk rd
Nether avon
Nightingale la
Azalea clo
PO

KENSINGTON
CEMETERY

Felix rd
Endsleigh rd
Talbot rd
Eccleston
Tewkesbury rd
Rosbury rd
Singapore rd
Brown Library

Shirley gdns
Chelmsford

Williams
Wals rd
Chignell rd
St James av
Melbourne av

Green man
Wit rd
Singapore rd

A4020

Broadway

Leeland rd
Westfield rd
Sydney rd
Regina rd

Walker rd
George
Maan Mond
Montana
Wilmot pl
Jessamine
Montague av
Adel cotts
Cambridge gdn
Church rd

CITY OF
WESTMINSTER
CEMETERY

Barclershaw rd
Grosvenor rd
Gaynor
Michael
Hat
Coldershaw rd
Seward rd

St Kilda rd
Adelaide
Brisbane rd
Croft gdns

HANWELL

A3002

Maudsville
Westminster
cotts
Factory

Lwr Boston rd
Du Burstow terr
Green la
Bishop

St Mark's rd
Bostonmore rd
Rosebank rd
Osterley pk view rd
Humes av
Belvedere rd
Studley grange rd
Trumpers way
Lambourn
Rose clo dale
Townholm cres

Andrews rd
St Margaret's rd
St Dunstan's

100

Oaklands rd
Cumberland rd
Manton av
Elthorne av
Elthorne pk rd
Clitherow av
Chepstow rd
Gentrey
Southfield
PO

New land
Thurlow
Jersey rd
Whitehall rd
Hasset gdns
Werter
Walmer gdns
Mid hurst rd
Erlesmere av
Mervin

Boston road

OSTERLEY PARK

ELTHORNE
PARK

Allotments

Playing Field

Allotments

Christopher av
Cardiff rd
Westlea rd
Southdown rd
Wyke gdns
Fairfield gdns

Woodstock av
Raymond av
Haslemere av
Clitherow av
Cawdor cres
PO

Well meadow
A3002
Boston Manor
Boston gdns
A3002

Motorway
M4
LONG WOOD

Motorway
M4

Sports Ground

Osterley Park House

Main dri

Windmill la

Osterley la

WYKE GREEN GOLF COURSE

Gallows Bridge
River Brent

Golf Course

Sports Ground

Sports Ground

Syon la

Oaklands rd
Gower rd

Sports Ground

Shield dri

Sports Ground
Sports Ground
Crowntree clo
Staps way
Wyke clo
Wood la
Grant way
Harlequin av
Berkeley clo
A4

Jersey rd
Thistleworth clo
Bassett gdns
Cranmore av
Penworts av

St Mark's cres
Library
Gardens
Leigham dri
Ridgeway rd
Lingwood gdns

OSTERLEY

Braybourne dri
Syon pk gdns
PO
Warkworth gdns
Otter rd
burn gdns
Hexham gdns
Syon la
A310

Osterley av
Thornbury rd
PO
Caroline clo
Church
Ridgeway rd
Wood la

Great West road
800
Quaker la
Roxborough av
Redes

Syon la way

Osterley
A4
600
Thornbury av

Playing Field
Albury av
Hallowood rd

Northumberland av
dale gdns
Rothbury
gdns
Syon Lane

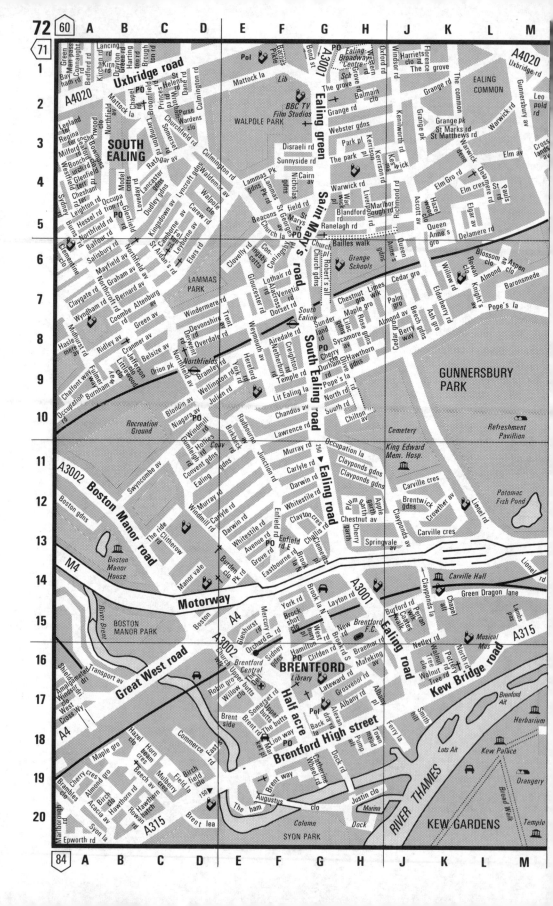

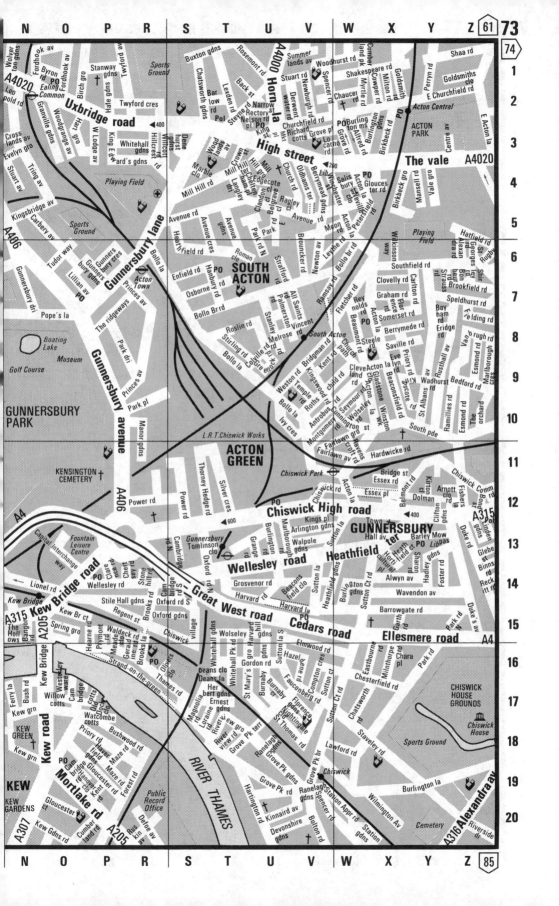

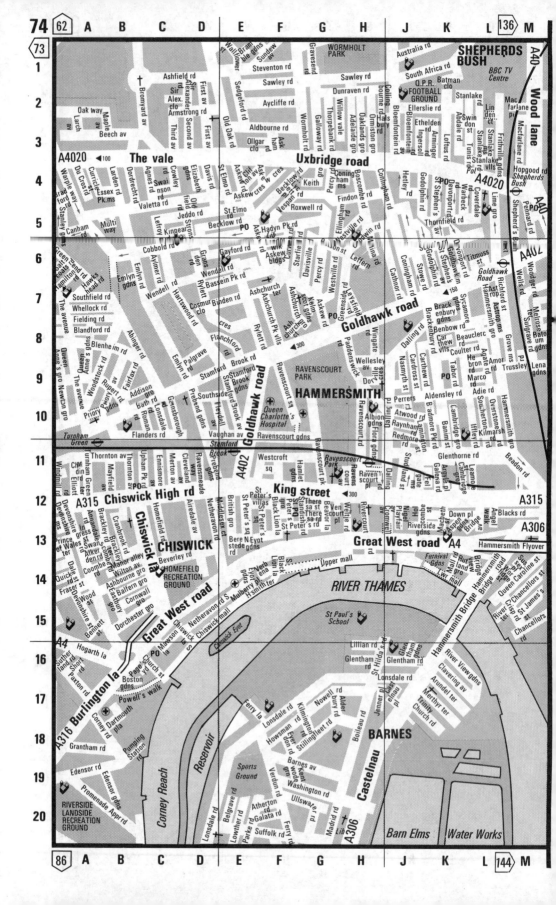

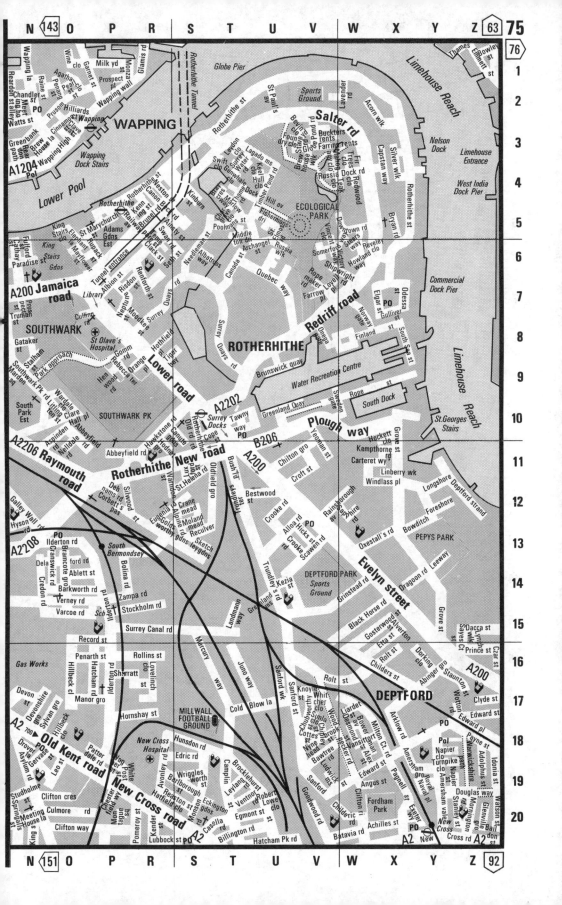

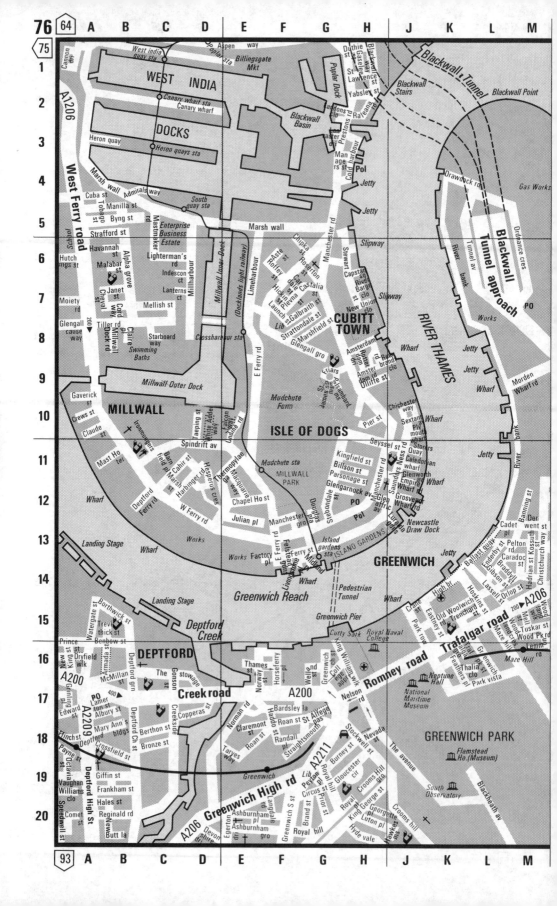

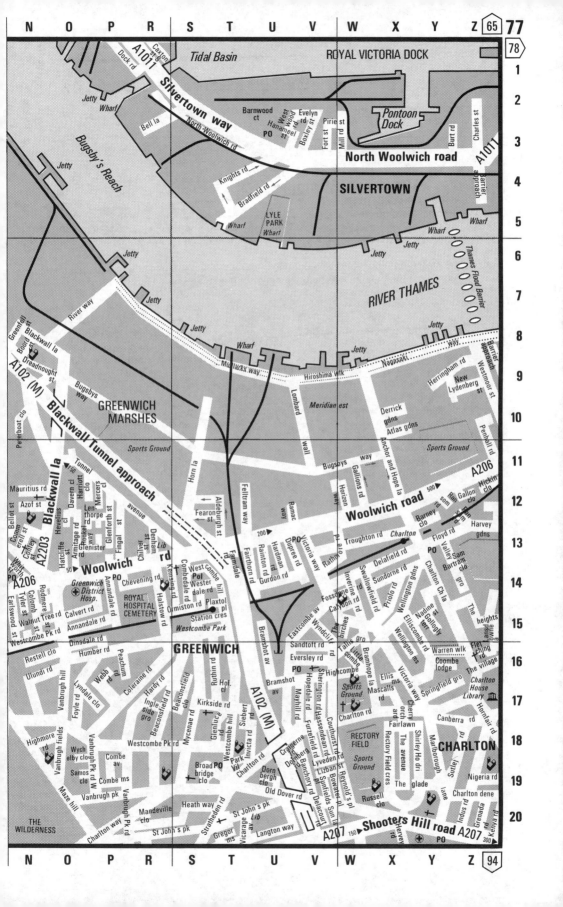

Tidal Basin   ROYAL VICTORIA DOCK

A1011

Caxton st

Dock rd

Silvertown way

Jetty

Wharf

Bell la

North Woolwich rd

PO

Barnwood ct

Hanameel st

West Wood st

Evelyn rd

Boxley st

Pirie st

Fort st

Mill rd

Pontoon Dock

Charles st

Burt rd

North Woolwich road   A1011

Bugsby's Reach

Jetty

Knights rd

Bradfield rd

SILVERTOWN

Barrier approach

Wharf

LYLE PARK Wharf

Wharf

Wharf

Jetty

Jetty

Jetty

Jetty

Thames Flood Barrier

RIVER THAMES

Jetty

River way

Jetty

Greenfell st

Blood rd

Dreadnought st

A102 (M)

Peterboat clo

Blackwall la

Blackwall Tunnel approach

Bugsbys way

GREENWICH MARSHES

Sports Ground

Jetty

Wharf

Mudlarks way

Hiroshima wlk

Nagasaki

way

way

Herringham rd

New Lydenberg st

Westmoor st

Penhall rd

Lombard wall

Meridian est

Derrick gdns

Atlas gdns

Anchor and Hope la

Bugsbys   way

Gallions rd

Horizon

Sports Ground

A206

Mauritius rd

Tunnel

Daven cl

Harriott clo

Mercers cl

avenue

Blackwall la

A2203

Hatcliffe

Hevelius st

Armitage rd

Rocket

Fingal st

Lenthorpe clo

Glenforth st

Glenister st

Chilver st

Denham st

Lib

Horn la

Aldeburgh st

Fearon st

Felltram way

Ramac way

Dupree rd

PO

Rathmore

Troughton rd

Charlton

Woolwich road

Floyd rd

PO

Valley gro

Sam Bartram clo

Barney clo

Ran Gallon clo

Hickin clo

Harvey gdns

500

Azof st

Bellot st

Cumberell st

Chilver st

Woolwich rd

Kemsing rd

Combedale rd

West Combe hill

Westerdale rd

Pol

Plaxtol pl

Station cres

Hardman rd

Rainton rd

Gurdon rd

Fairhorn rd

Victoria way

Delafield rd

Swallowfield rd

Sundorne rd

Inverine rd

Priolo rd

Wellington gdns

Charlton Ch la

Nadine st

Charlton

Bartram

The heights

Insell

Crathie rd

Woolwich

A206

Rodmere st

Colomb st

Tyler st

Earlswood st

Walnut Tree rd

Westcombe Pk rd

Greenwich District Hosp.

ROYAL HOSPITAL CEMETERY

PO

Chevening rd

Halstow rd

Calvert rd

Ormiston rd

Annandale rd

Annandale rd

Dinsdale rd

Humber rd

Eastcombe av

Wyndcliff rd

Fossdene rd

Calydon rd

Birches

Swallowfield rd

Elliscombe rd

Wellington ms

Warren wlk

Coombe lodge

Fletching rd

The village

Sports Ground

Restell clo

Webb rd

Peacham rd

GREENWICH

Bramshot av

Sandtoft rd

Eversley rd

PO

Highcombe

Sherington rd

Hassendean rd

Hopedale rd

Mayhill rd

Tallis gro

Victoria way

Bramhope la

Mascalls rd

Ellis ms

Springfield gro

Charlton House Library

Highmore rd

Vanbrugh fields

Ufundi rd

Foyle rd

Lyndale clo

Coleraine rd

Hardy rd

Beachinsfield clo

Ruthin cl

Hof. cl

Mycenae rd

Kirkside rd

Glenluce rd

Siebert rd

Courthurst rd

Furzefield rd

Lyveden rd

Lizban st

Charlton rd

RECTORY FIELD

Fairlawn

The avenue

Shirley Ho dri

Marlborough

CHARLTON

Canberra rd

Hornfair rd

THE WILDERNESS

Wychelby clo

Samos clo

Combe av

Combe ms

Vanbrugh Pk rd W

Westcombe Pk rd

Westcombe hill

Park Vil

Invicta rd

Broad PO bridge clo

Craterne rd

Dornberg rd

Banchory rd

Bowater pl

Sunfields Sun la

Reynold's pl

Sports Ground

Russell clo

The glade

Nigeria rd

Charlton dene

Maze hill

Vanbrugh pk

Mandeville clo

Charlton way

Charlton Pk rd

Heath way

Stratheden rd

St John's pk

St John's pk

Gregor ms

Vicarage rd

Langton way

Lib

A207

150

Shooters Hill road

A207

PO

Indus rd

Harvey

Granby rd

Grenada rd

Kenilw

Sutlej rd

300

Column numbers (right margin): 1 2 3 4 5 6 7 8 9 10 11 12 13 14 15 16 17 18 19 20

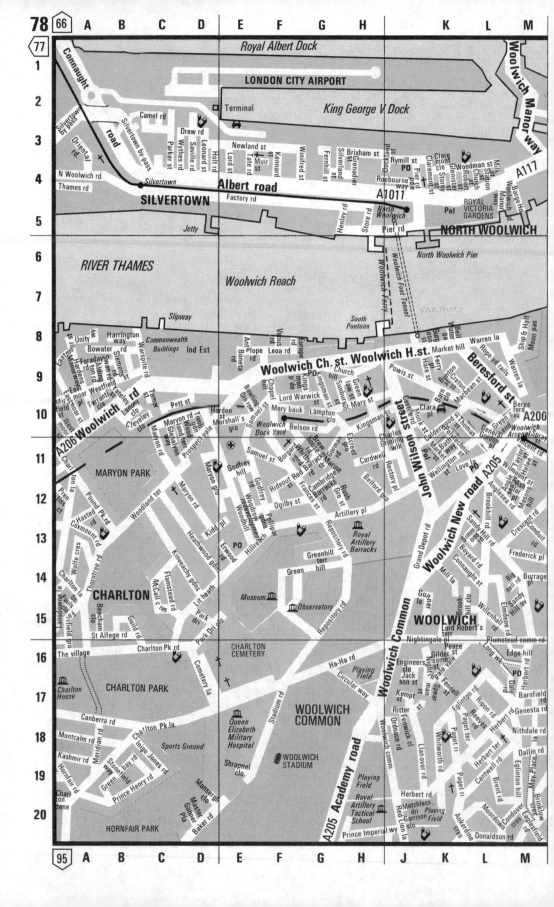

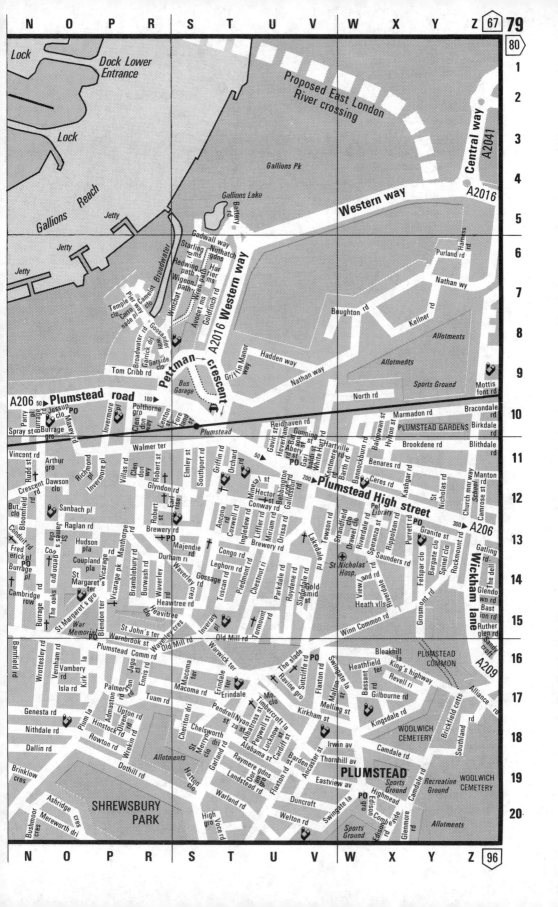

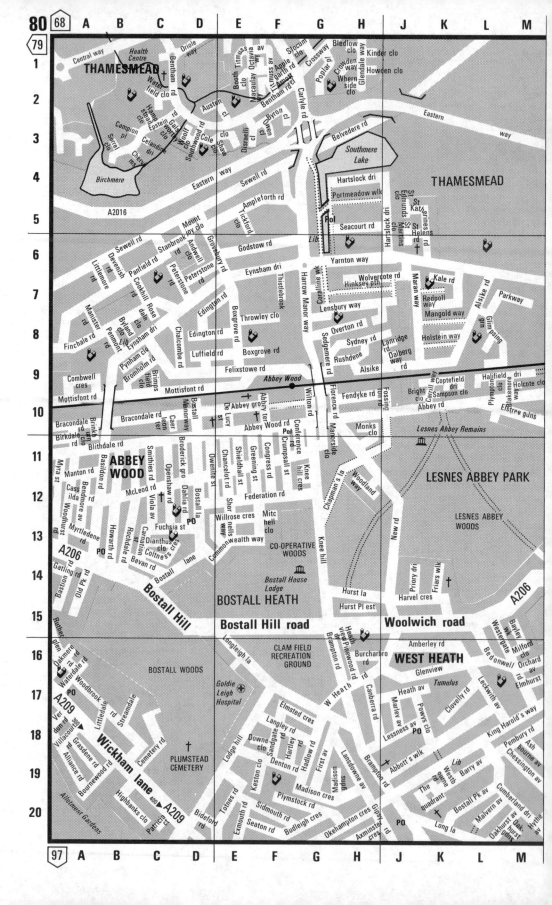

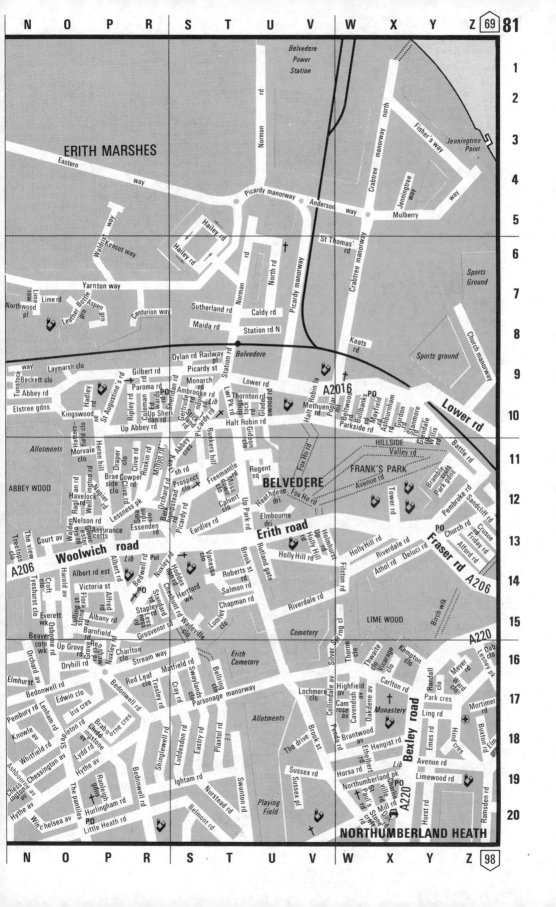

Belvedere Power Station

ERITH MARSHES

Eastern way

Norman rd

Crabtree manorway north

Fisher's way

Jenningtree Point

Picardy manorway

Anderson way

Jenningtree way

way

Hailey rd

Mulberry

Waldric Kencot way

Hailey rd

St Thomas' rd

Crabtree manorway

Sports Ground

Yarnton way

Norman rd

North rd

Picardy manorway

Northwood pl

Lime rd

Leather Bottle gdns

Aspen grn

Centurion way

Sutherland rd

Maida rd

Caldy rd

Maida rd

Station rd N

Keats rd

Sports ground

Church manorway

Tunstock way

Laymarsh clo

Dylan rd

Railway pl

Belvedere

Lower rd

A2016

Lower rd

Beckett clo

Abbey rd

Elstree gdns

Gilbert rd

Picardy st

St Augustine's rd

Hadley rd

Paroma rd

Monarch rd

Ambrooke rd

Coleman

Ripley rd

Up Sheri dan rd

Kingswood

Sheridan rd

Gertrude rd

Park Lib

Lower rd

Thornton rd

Moss rd

Gladed swood rd

Methuen rd

Belmount rd

Poplar rd

PO

Mayfield

Ashburnham

Gordon

Stanmore

Glendale

Lwr Pk rd

Halt Robin la

Robin la

Gulbank's

Willis

Battle rd

Halters field clo

Morvale clo

Heron hill

Diaper

Clive rd

Ruskin rd

Milton rd

Sheridan rd

Abbey cres

Bunkers hill

Gideon rd

Halt Robin rd

Hall rd

Fox Ho rd

Parkside rd

HILLSIDE

Valley rd

Allotments

ABBEY WOOD

Hatters field clo

Ragl an rd

Havelock rd

Brae side rd

Cowper rd

Wellington rd

Napier rd

Lessness pk

Orchard rd

Hampstead rd

Prospect clo

Freemantle rd

Moss down rd

Calvert clo

Regent sq

BELVEDERE

Fox Ho rd

Heathdene dri

Fox Ho rd

FRANK'S PARK

Avenue rd

Bramble Park gdns

Pembroke rd

Sandcliff rd

Nelson rd

Gilbert rd

Assurance cotts

Essenden rd

Park rd

Picardy rd

Eardley rd

Up Park rd

Elmbourne dri

Erith road

Holmhurst rd

Holly Hill

Tower rd

Church rd

PO

Cruse

Alford rd

Friday rd

Woolwich road

Court av

The view

Tree tops clo

Lib

Bedwell rd

Pol

Nuxley rd

Hoddes don rd

Vanessa

Roberts st

Brook rd

Rutland gate

Holly Hill rd

Holly Hill rd

HollyHill rd

Riverdale rd

Athol rd

Deluci rd

Fraser rd

A206

A206

Albert rd est

Albert rd

Cheshunt rd

Hertford wk

Salmon rd

Filston rd

Harold av

Victoria st

Alfred rd

Stapley rd

Standard rd

Chapman rd

Birch wlk

Croft

Tyreshurst clo

Everett wk

Albany rd

Flora rd

Lessness rd

Wadeville clo

Lumley clo

Riverdale rd

LIME WOOD

Osborne rd

Barnfield rd

Grosvenor rd

Cemetery

A220

Beaver cote wk

Up Grove rd

Redshaw rd

Charlton clo

Erith Cemetery

Silver Spring clo

Thorne clo

Thwaite clo

Vicarage

Kempton clo

Meyer rd

Deb clo

Lesney pk

Orchard av

Dryhill rd

Stream way

Matfield rd

Belting rd

Collindale av

Highfield av

Cam rose av

Carlton rd

Randall clo

Ward clo

Elmhurst av

Red Leaf clo

Trosley rd

Cray rd

Lochmere clo

Cavendish

Oakdene av

Park cres

Mortimer rd

Bedonwell rd

Edwin clo

Bedonwell rd

Parsonage manorway

Monastery

Ling rd

Pembury rd

Lenham rd

Iris cres

Allotments

Brantwood rd

Lib

Emes rd

Hind cres

Buxton rd

Knowle av

Stapleton rd

Braborne cres

Shinglewell rd

Luddesdon rd

Eastry rd

Plaxtol rd

The drive

Brook st

Penda rd

Hengist rd

Avenue rd

Whitfield rd

Chessington av

Lydd rd

Ightam rd

Nurstead rd

Swanton rd

Horsa rd

Ethelbert rd

Lib

Limewood rd

Ashbourne av

Chessington av

Hythe av

Ranleigh gdns

Belmont rd

Sussex rd

Sussex pl

Northumberland pk

St Paul's

Mill rd

A220

Hurst rd

Ramsden rd

Hythe av

The pantiles

Hurlingham rd

PO

Little Heath rd

Playing Field

Winchelsea av

Bexley road

Bexley road

NORTHUMBERLAND HEATH

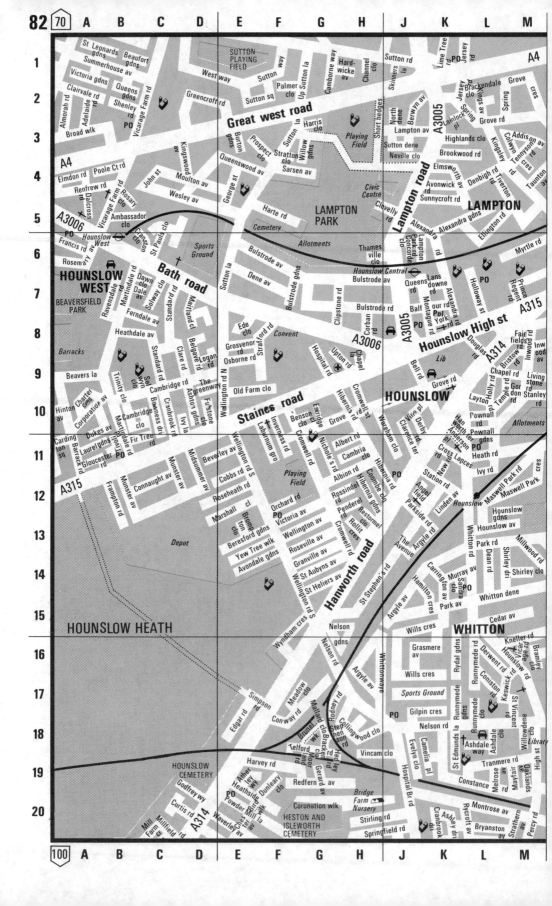

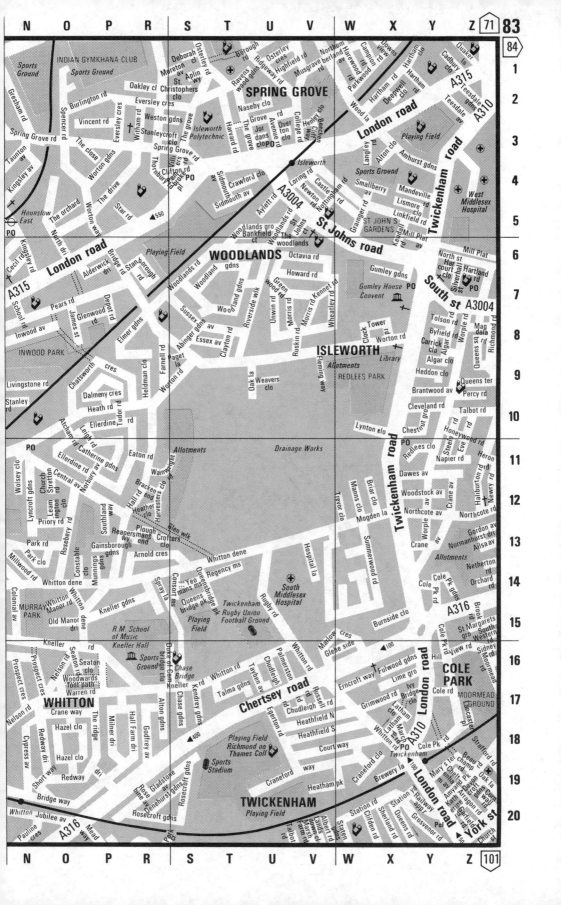

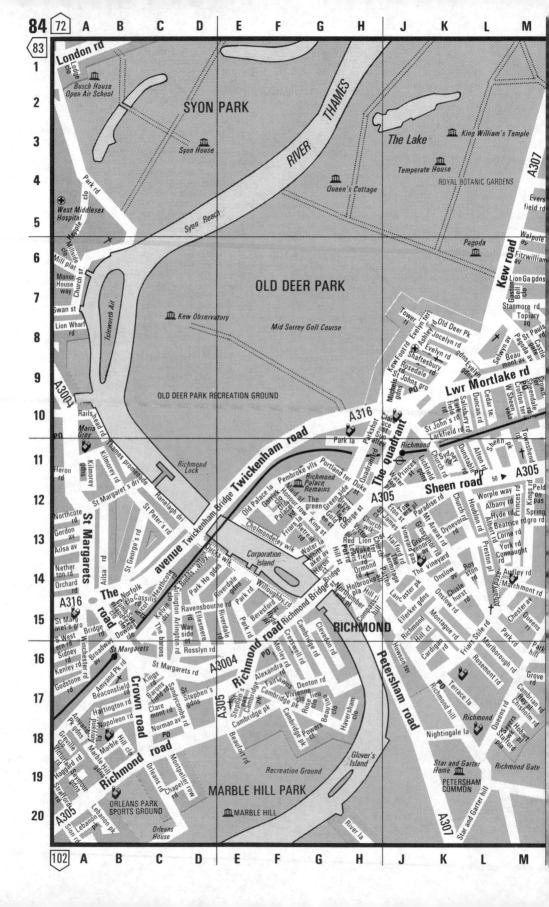

A B C D E F G H J K L M

1
2
3
4
5
6
7
8
9
10
11
12
13
14
15
16
17
18
19
20

London rd

Busch House
Open Air School
Lodge
clo
Park rd
clo
West Middlesex
Hospital
Millside clo
Mill plat
Napthill
Church st
Manor
House
way
Swan st
Lion Wharf
rd
Isleworth Ait

SYON PARK

Syon House

RIVER THAMES

Syon Reach

Kew Observatory

OLD DEER PARK

Mid Surrey Golf Course

Queen's Cottage

The Lake

Temperate House

King William's Temple

ROYAL BOTANIC GARDENS

Pagoda

A307

Evers
field rd

Walpole
av
Kew road
Fitzwilliam
Lion Ga gdns
Gaston
Bell
Stanmore rd
Topiary
sq
St Pauls
Pagoda av
Castle
Beau
mont av

A3004

OLD DEER PARK RECREATION GROUND

Railshead rd
Maria Grey
Thames promenade
Richmond
Lock
Heron
rd
Kilmorey
gdns
Kilmorey
rd
St Margaret's dr
St Peter's rd
Ranelagh dri
St Margarets
Northcote
av
Gordon
av
Ailsa av
Netherton rd
Orchard
rd
St George's rd
Ailsa rd

A316

The
Crown
clo
Cassilis rd
Nicol
Kelvin
Heathcote
The barons
Downes
Arlington rd
Arlington
Ducks wlk
Norfolk
clo
Buttos alley
Park Ho gdns
Ravensbourne rd
Ellesmere rd
Riverdale
gdns
Willoughby rd
Park rd
Riverdale rd

Twickenham Bridge
Twickenham road
avenue Twickenham Bridge

Old Palace la
Garret
clo
Cholmondeley wlk
Corporation
Island

Pembroke vlls
The
green
Old
Palace
yd
Friars
Lane
Friars
Stile
Water la
Baker st
Heron
Wakefield
Ormond
Bridge st
Richmond Bridge

Portland ter
Honour row
King st
Red Lion st
George st
St James
Halford rd
Eton
Paradise rd
Vineyard pas
The vineyard
Onslow
Lancaster pk

Duke
st
Quadrant rd
Parkshot
Park la

A316

The Quadrant

Richmond

Water
la
Princes
Sydney rd
Dunstable
Litchfield
Church rd
Alton rd
Sheen
rd
PO
A305
Worple way
Albany rd
Houblon rd
Hyde rd
Dynevor rd
M Ararat rd
Grosvenor rd
Marchmont rd

Lwr Mortlake rd

St Johns gro
St Johns rd
Salisbury rd
Larkfield rd
Mishitss
gdns
Evelyn rd
Jocelyn rd
Evelyn rd
Shaftesbury
rd
Rosedale
rd
Old Deer Pk
Tower
rd
Kew Foot rd
Ashleigh rd
St Johns
gdns
Clare
Evelyn gdns
Selwin av
Pagoda av
Cedar ter
W Sheen
Crofton ter
Duncan rd
Sheendale
rd

Sheen road

Kings Peld
Princes rd
on pas
Beatrice av
Lorne rd
Spring
gro rd
Preston rd
York rd
Connaught

A305

Netherton rd
Orchard
rd
St Margaret's gro
S West
ern rd
Sidney
rd
Kenley rd
Godstone rd
Winchester rd
Broadway
St Margarets
Anyard Pk rd
Beaconsfield
rd
Hartington rd
Napoleon rd
Amyand
Pk clo
Greville
rd
Haggard rd
Sermon
clo
Victoria
rd
St Margarets rd
Kings
clo
Barons
field rd
St
Stephen's rd
Sandycombe rd
Clare
court rd
Norman av
PO
Montpelier row
Chapel rd
Orleans rd

A3004

Richmond road
Richmond road
Crown road

Stephen's
pass
Cambridge
gdns
Cambridge
gro
Alexandra
rd
Fairlawns
Cambridge pk
Denton rd
Vivienne
clo
Rosebank
Cambridge pk
Beaufort rd
Powers
clo
Beau
lieu
clo
Haversham
clo

Cambridge rd
Morley rd
Creswell rd
Cleveden rd

Richmond
Hill ct
Cardigan rd
Richmond
Hill ct
Friars Stile rd
Montague rd
Rosemont rd
Marlborough rd
Onslow rd
Chisle
hurst
Ellerker gdns
Audley rd
Amberst vlls
Chester av
Queens
rt
Park
hill
Grove
rd
Cambrian rd
Chisholm rd
Queens rd
Hobart
pla
Stafford
pla

Petersham road
Petersham road
Honson ter
Terrace la
Richmond hill
Nightingale la
Richmond
Queens rd

MARBLE HILL PARK

ORLEANS PARK
SPORTS GROUND
Lebanon pk
Orleans
House

Recreation Ground

MARBLE HILL

Glover's
Island

River la

RICHMOND

Star and Garter
Home
PETERSHAM
COMMON

Richmond Gate

A307

Star and Garter hill

A305

Sion rd
Strafford

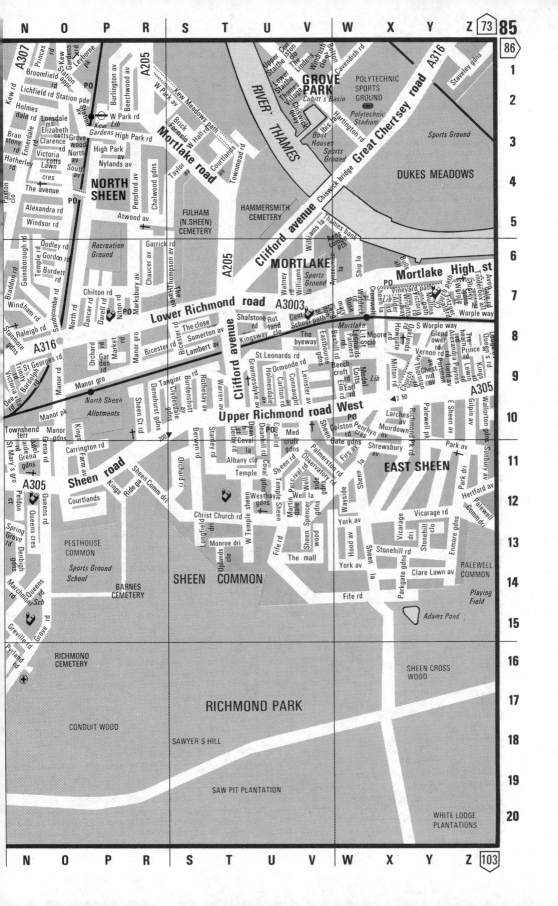

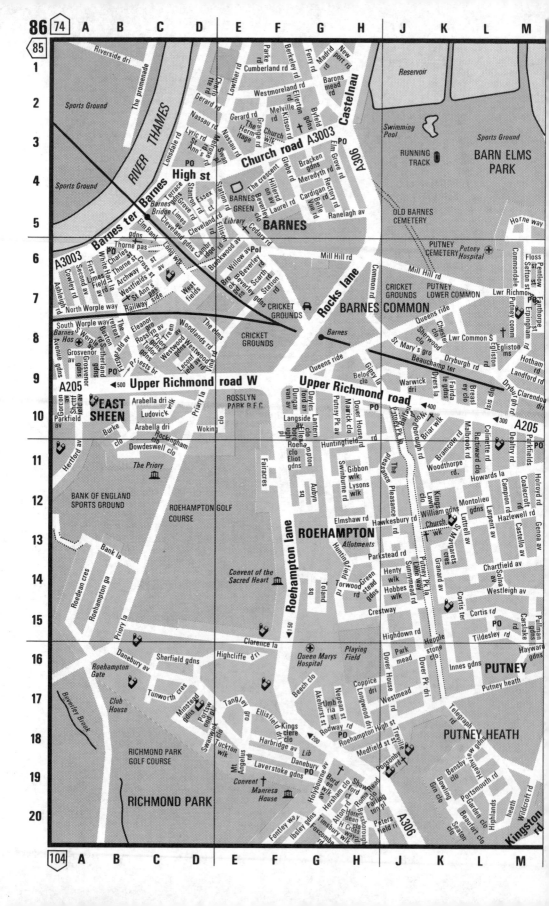

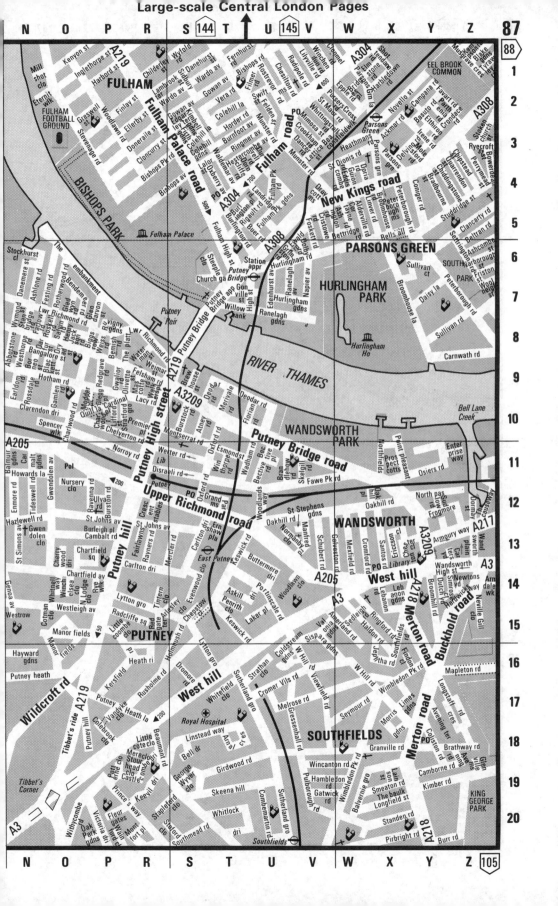

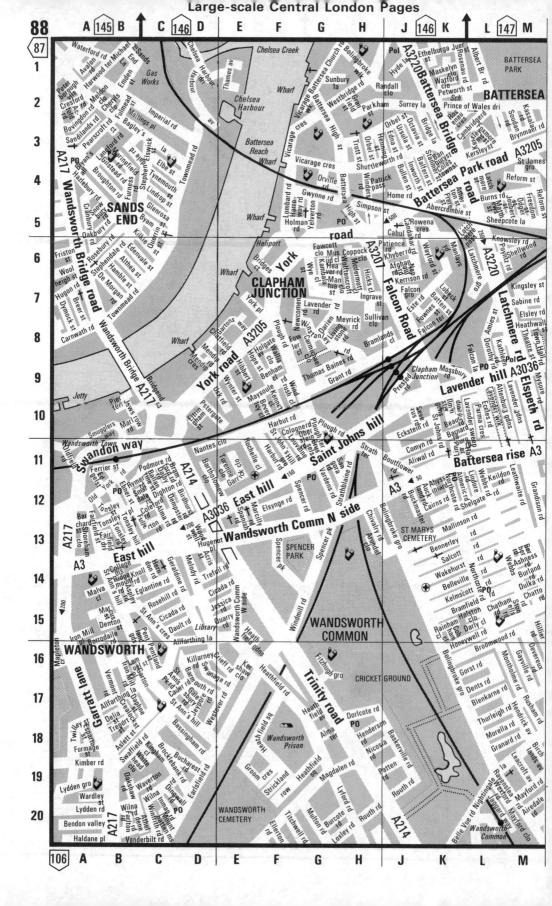

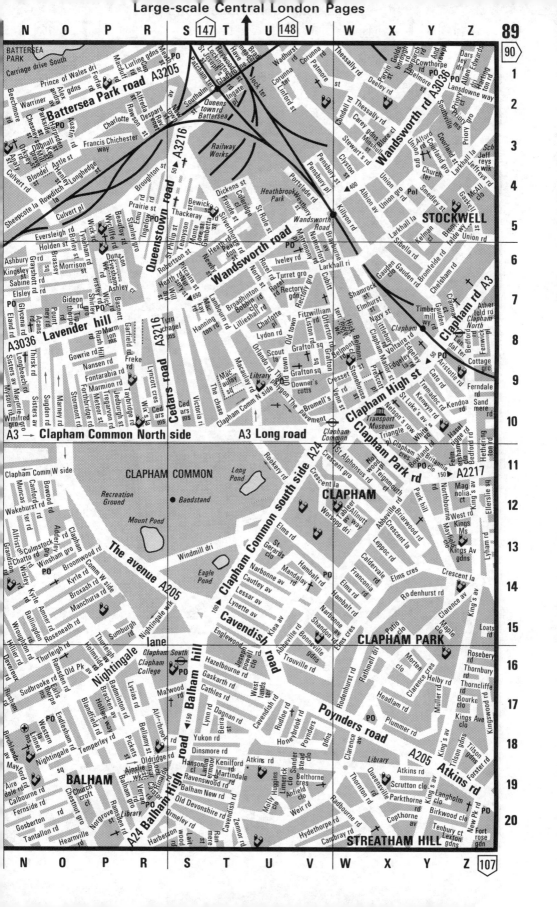

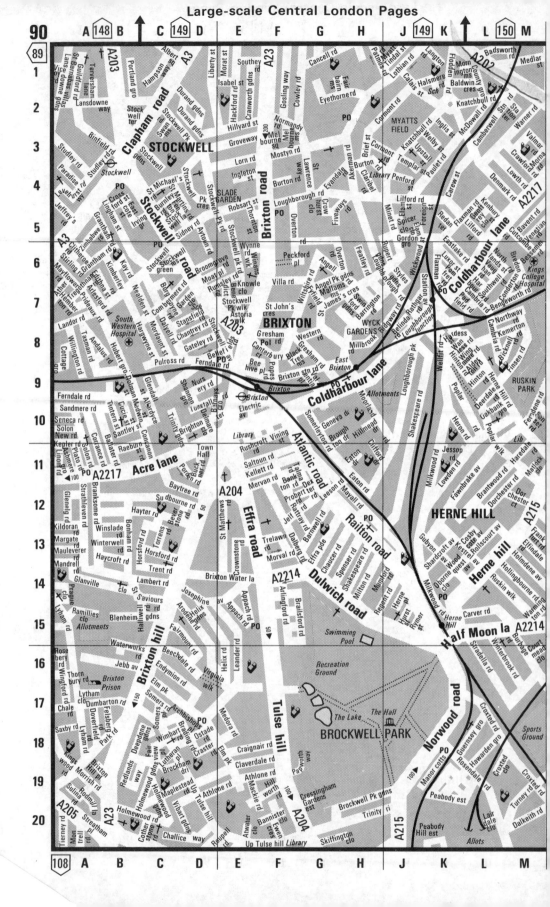

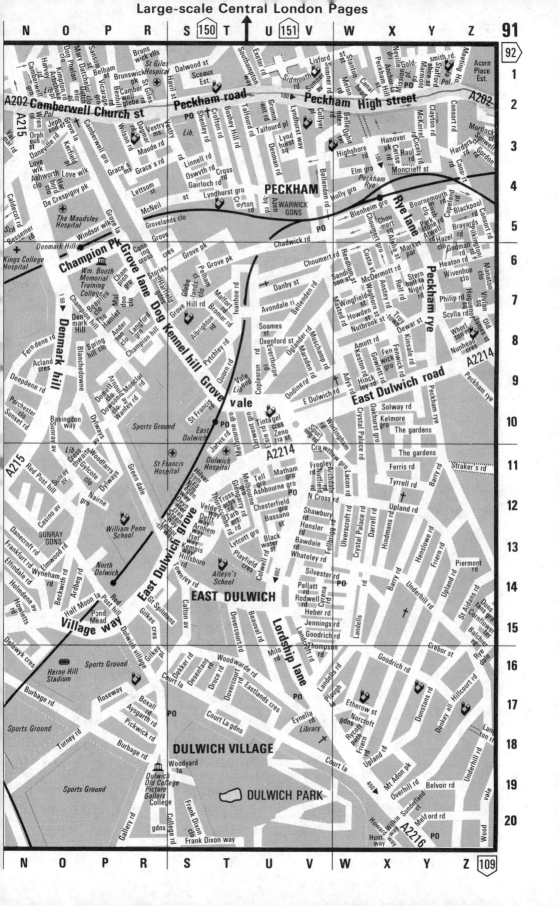

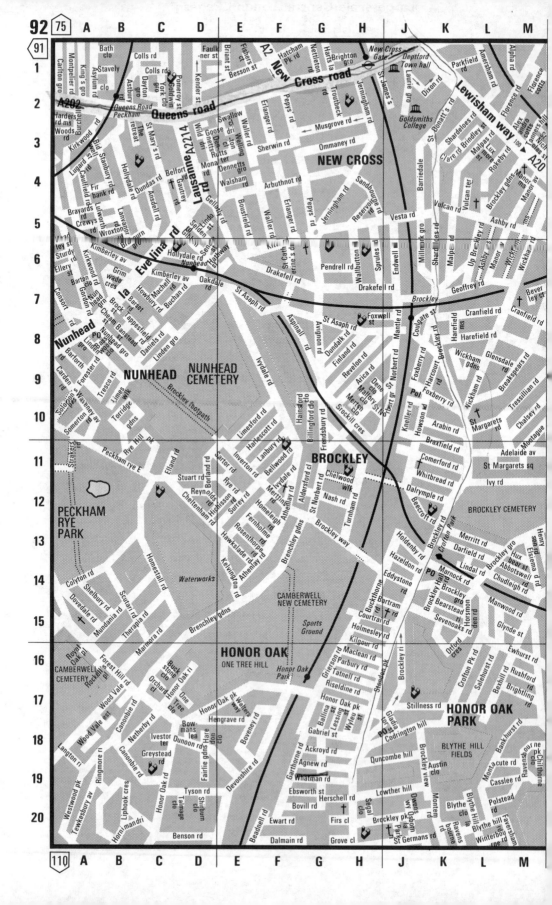

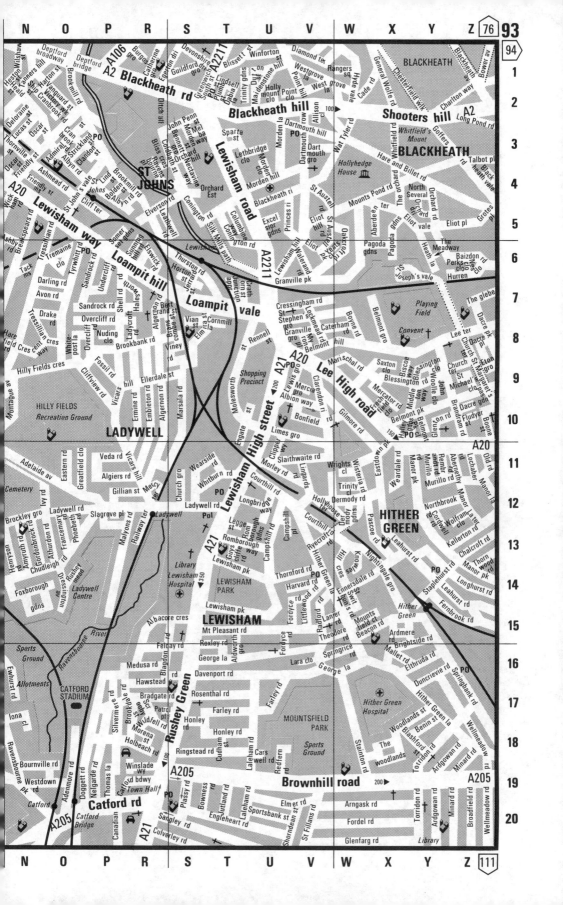

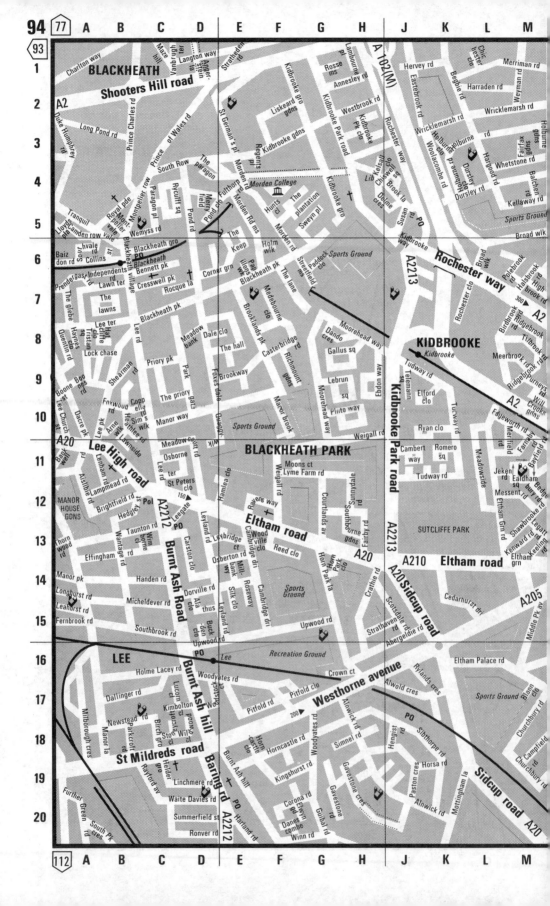

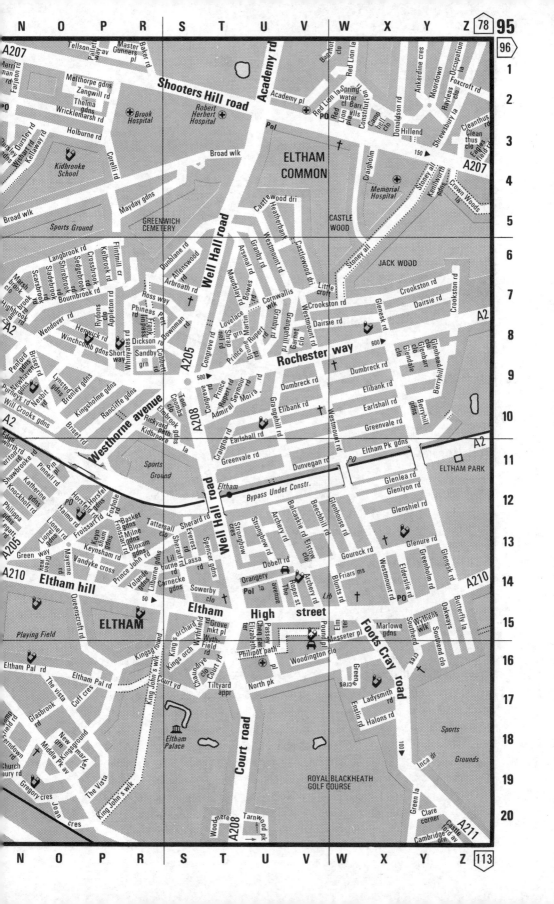

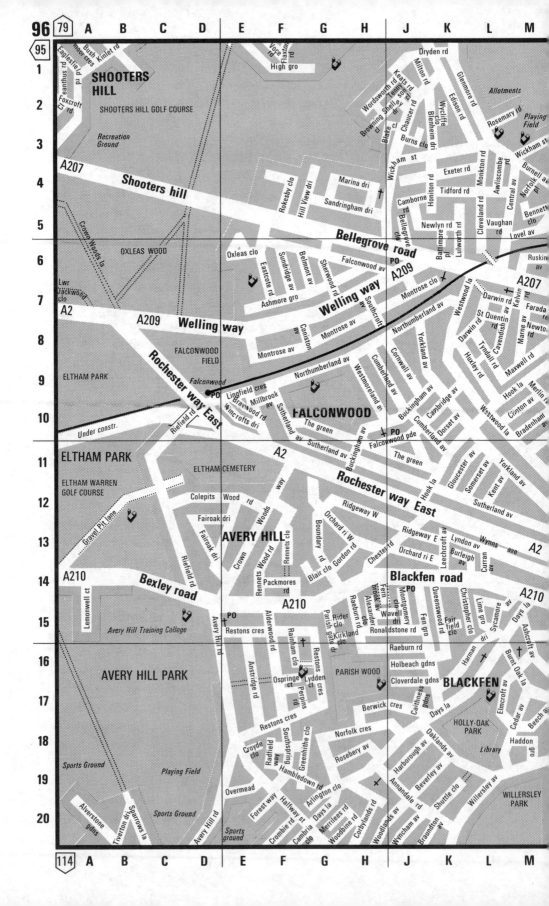

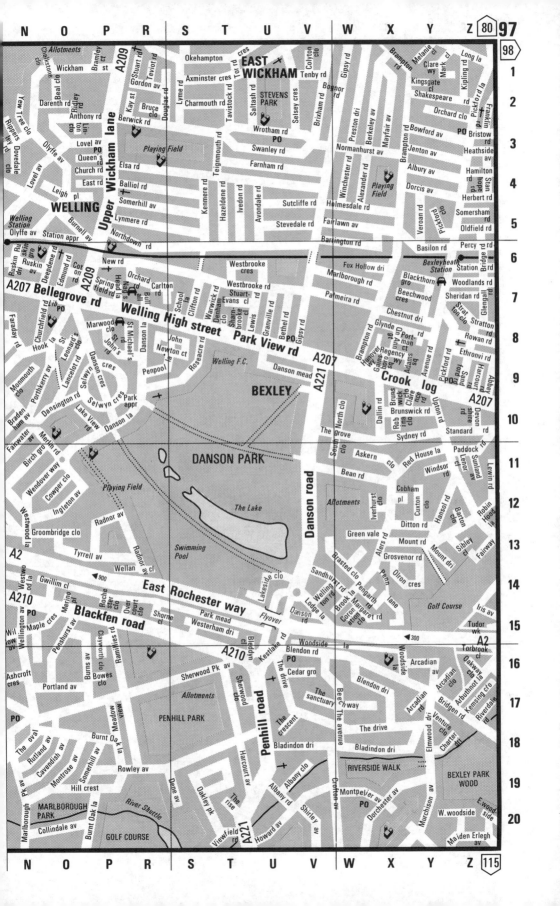

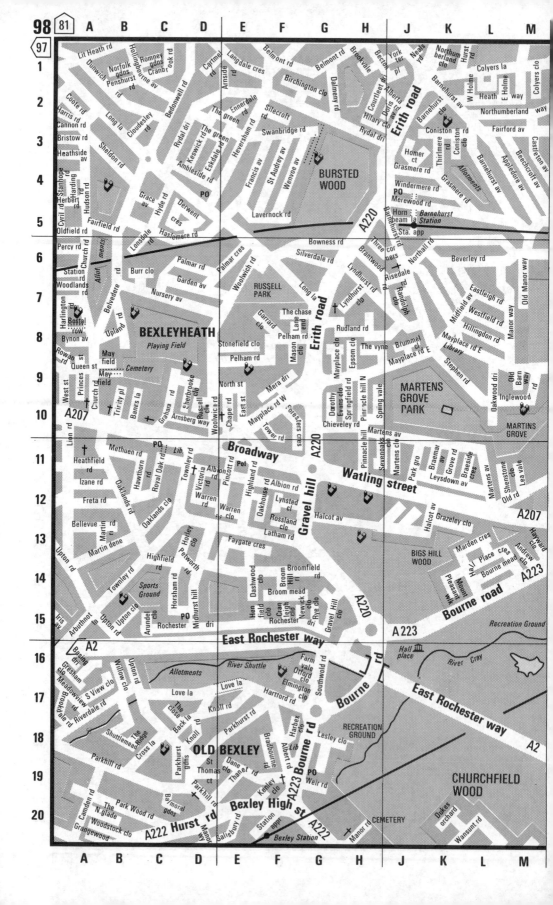

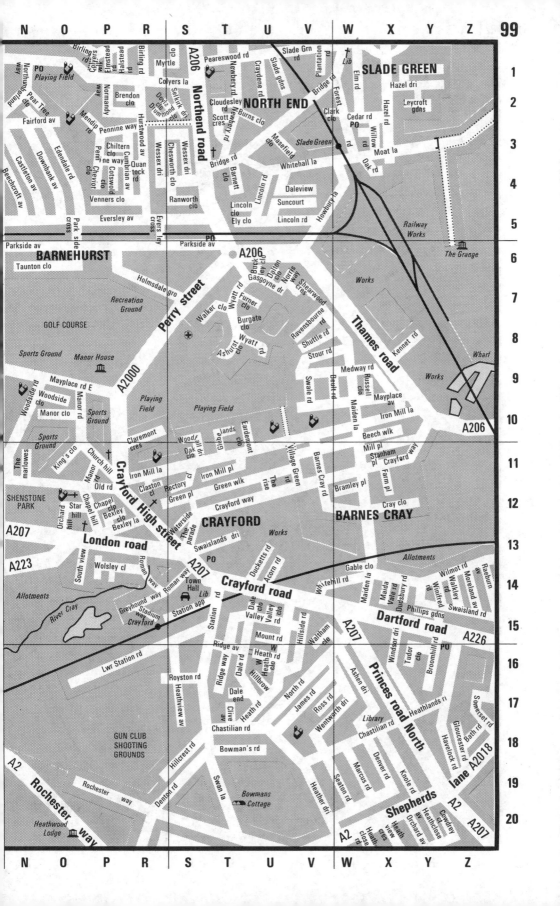

SLADE GREEN

NORTH END

BARNEHURST

Taunton clo

GOLF COURSE

Recreation Ground

Sports Ground

Manor House

Sports Ground

Sports Ground

Playing Field

Playing Field

The marlowes

SHENSTONE PARK

CRAYFORD

Crayford High street

London road

Crayford road

BARNES CRAY

Thames road

Railway Works

The Grange

Works

Works

Wharf

Works

A206

Dartford road A226

Princes road North

Library

Allotments

Allotments

River Cray

GUN CLUB SHOOTING GROUNDS

Rochester way

Heathwood Lodge

Bowmans Cottage

Shepherds

A2

A207

A2018 lane

A2 A207

A207

A223

A2

A2000

A206

A206

Perry street

Birling station rd, Birling rd, Halstead pl, Hurstwood clo

PO Playing Field

Northumbd way

Normandy way

Pear Tree clo

Fairford av

Beechcroft av

Castleton av

Edendale av

Downbank rd

Brendon clo

Mendip rd

Pennine way

Chiltern clo

Pennine way

Pennine clo

Cumbrian av

Cheviot clo

Cotswold clo

Quantock dri

Venners clo

Ranworth clo

Wessex dri

Wessex clo

Chesworth clo

Eversley av

Park side cross

Evers ley cross

PO

Parkside av

Parkside av

Holmsdale gro

Walker clo

Wyatt clo

Burgate clo

Ashurst clo

Wyatt rd

Furner clo

Claremont cres

Woodfall dri

Oak clo

Glebelands clo

Eardemont clo

Village Green

The rise

Gasgoyne dri

Ravensbourne rd

Shuttle rd

Stour rd

Swale rd

Medway rd

Russell clo

Maiden la

Beuff rd

Beech wlk

Mayplace av

Iron Mill la

Mill pl

Stanham pl

Crayford way

Farm pl

Barnes Cray rd

Bramley pl

Cray clo

Buckley clo

Dalton clo

Norris way

Shearwood cres

Kennet rd

Myrtle clo

Peareswood rd

Newbery rd

Craydene rd

Slade gdns

Slade Grn rd

Plantation rd

Lib

Elm rd

Hazel dri

Leycroft gdns

Colyers la

Cloudesley rd

Dolia grn

Diamond clo

Selkirk clo

Scott cres

Burns clo

Bridge rd

Forest rd

Clark clo

PO

Cedar rd

Willow

Hazel rd

Moat la

Oak rd

Howbury la

Masefield clo

Slade Green

Whitehall la

Daleview

Suncourt

Lincoln rd

Barnett clo

Lincoln rd

Lincoln clo

Ely clo

Northend road

Bridge rd

Mayplace rd E

Woodside rd

Woodside clo

Manor clo

Manor rd

Manor rd

Kings clo

Church hill

Old rd

Iron Mill la

Orchard hill

Chapel hill

Star hill

Chapel clo

Bexley clo

Bexley la

Claston cl

Rectory

Green pl

Iron Mill pl

Green wlk

Waterside

The parade

Swaislands dri

Duckerts rd

Acorn rd

Gable clo

Whitehill rd

Wilmot rd

Maida Vale rd

Dudsbury rd

Walkley rd

Winfred rd

Moreland av

Swaisland rd

Raeburn

Phillips gdns

Wolsley cl

Southview

Roman way

Roman way

Town Hall

Lib

Station app

Station rd

Dale clo

Valley rd

Valley rd

Hillside rd

Waltham clo

Maiden la

Windsor dri

Tudor clo

Broomhill rd

Greyhound way

Stadium way

Crayford

Lwr Station rd

Royston rd

Heathview av

Ridge av

Heath rd

Dale av

Hillbrow

Mount rd

North rd

James rd

Ross rd

Wentworth dri

Ashen dri

Heathlands ri

Somerset rd

Gloucester rd

Bath rd

Havelock rd

Heathlands ri

Hillcrest rd

Denton rd

Chastilian rd

Clive av

Heath rd

Dale end

Bowman's rd

Swan la

Bowmans Cottage

Chastilian rd

Heather dri

Seaton rd

Marcus rd

Denver rd

Knole rd

Cowdrey clo

Heathclose

Heath view cres

Orchard av

Heath close rd

Rochester way

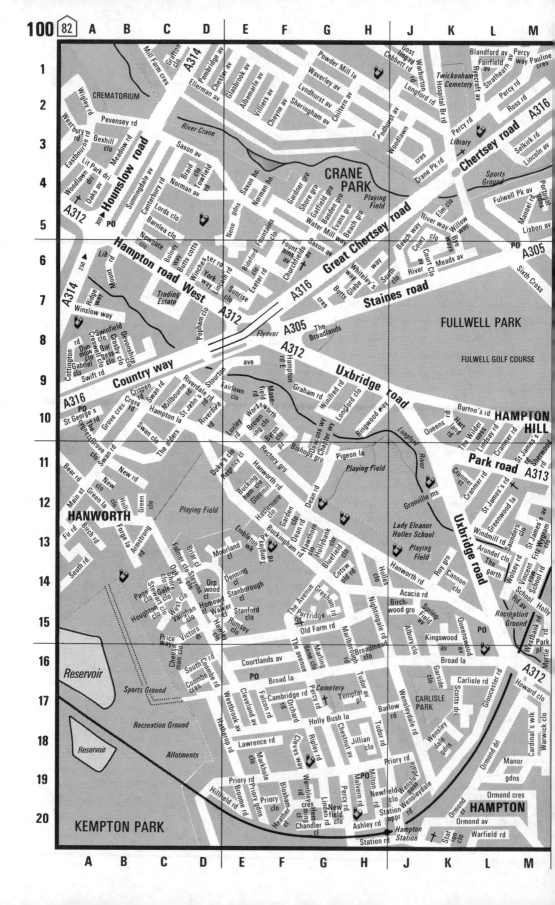

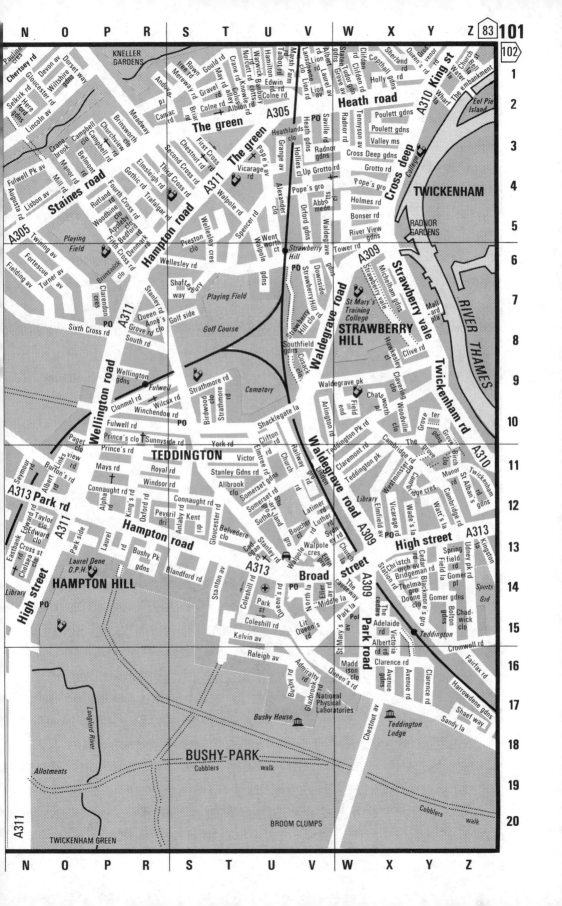

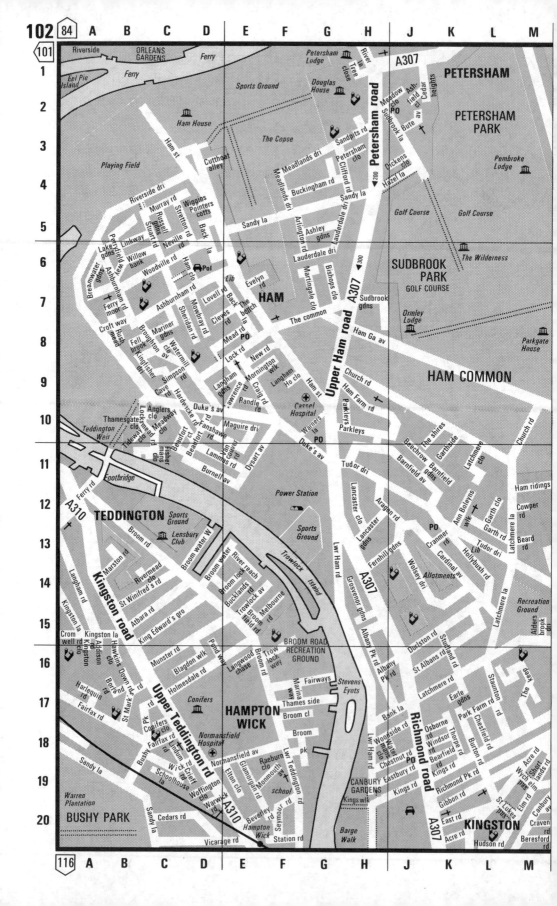

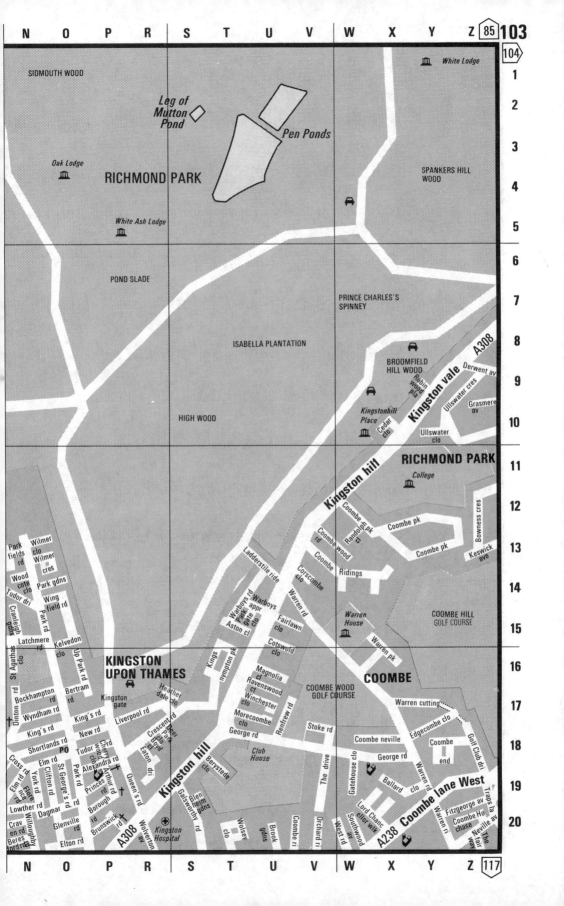

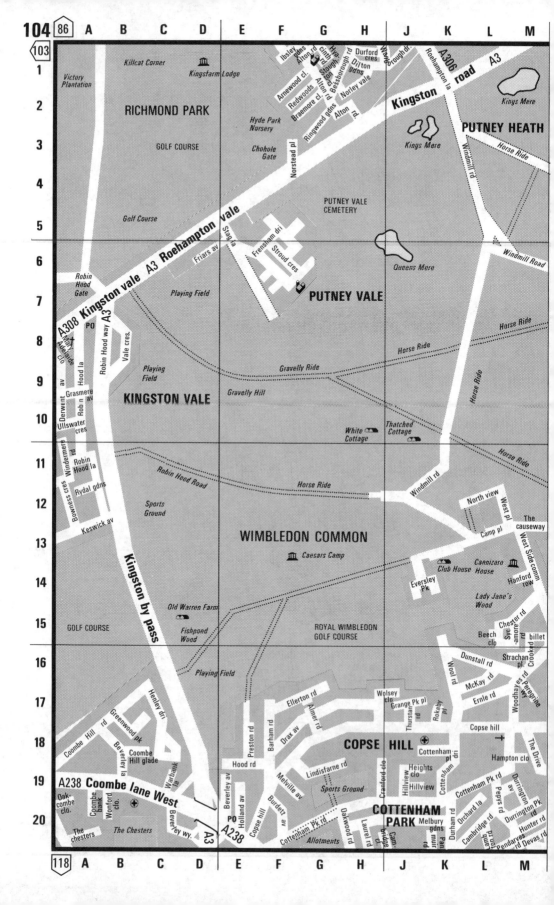

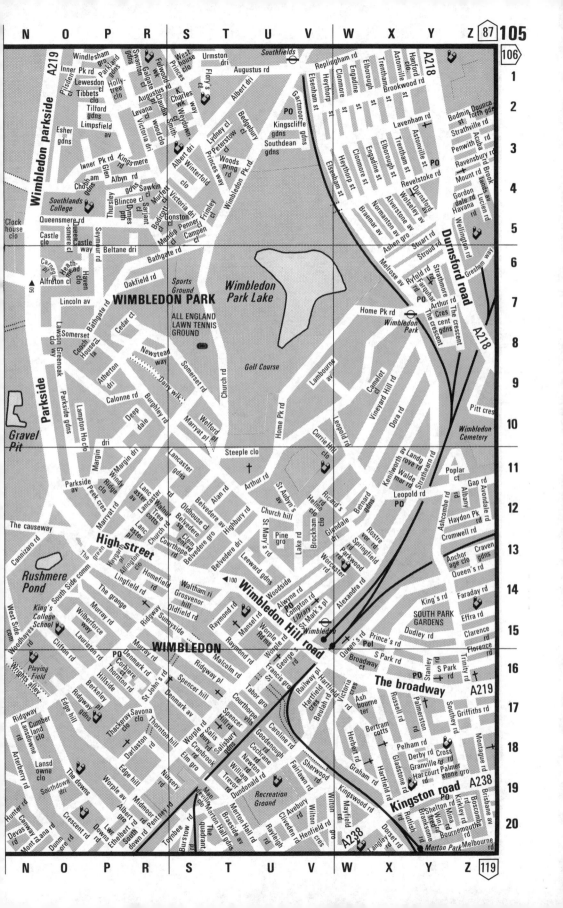

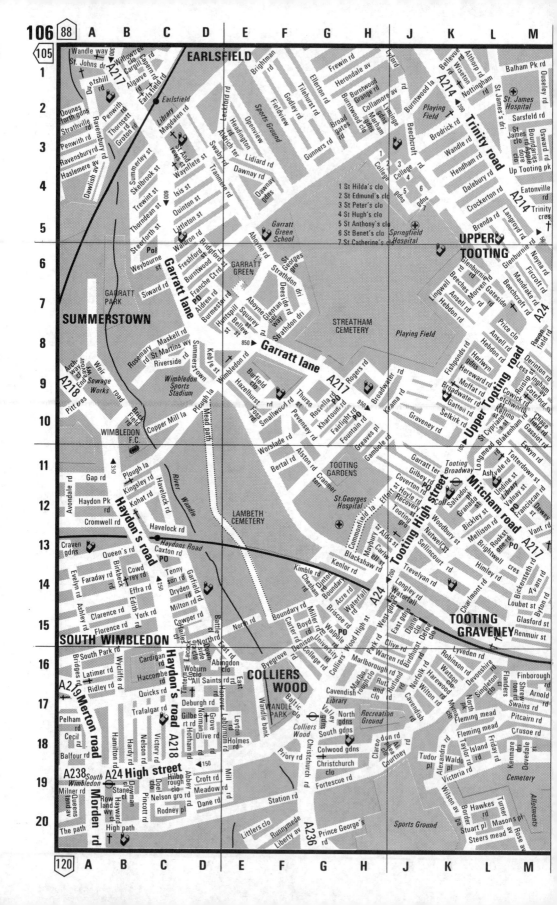

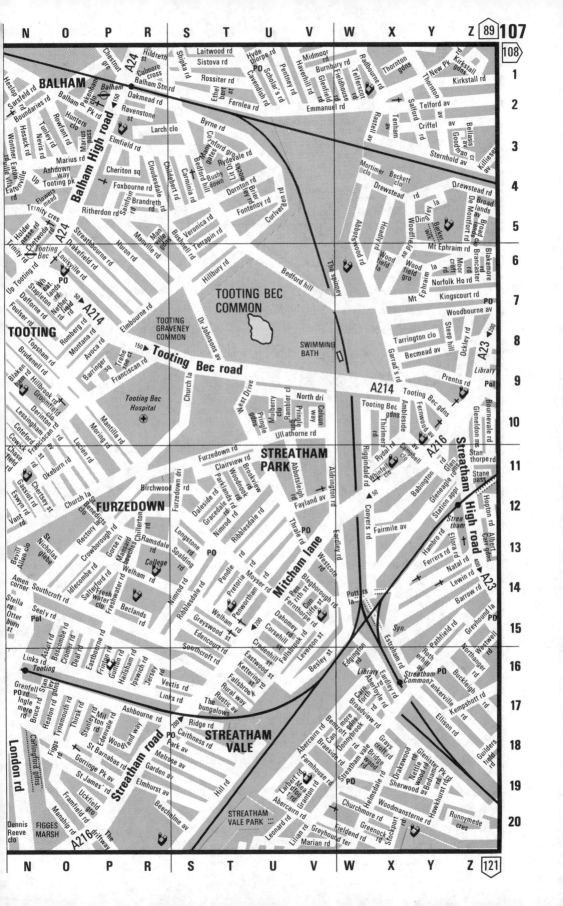

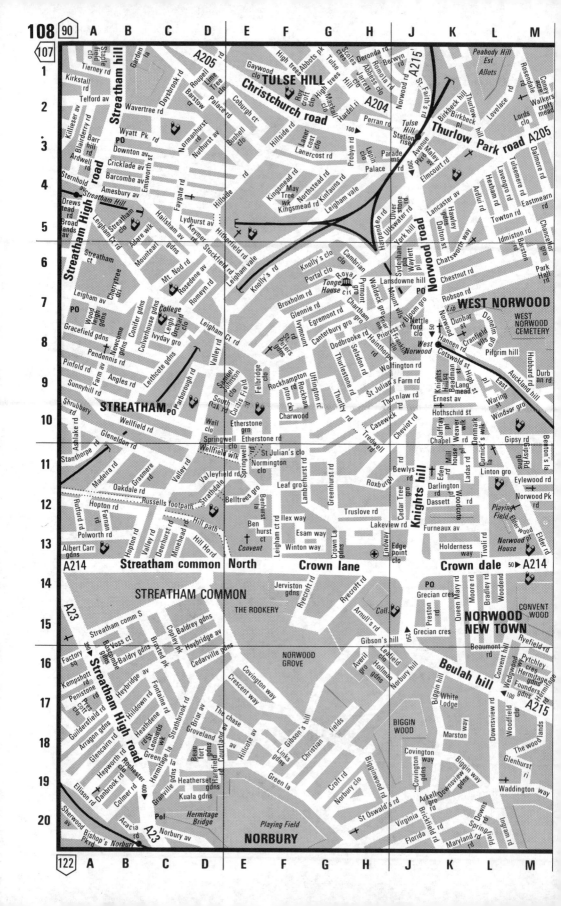

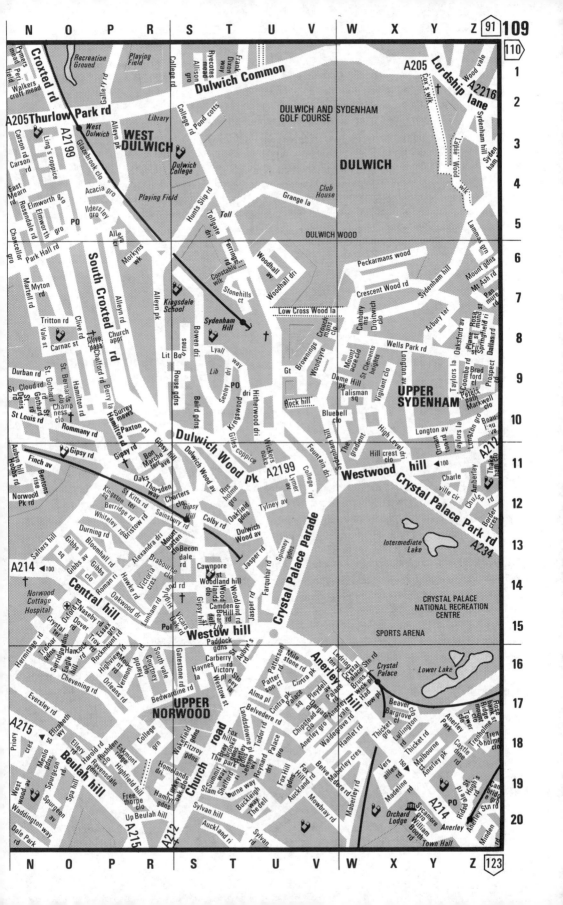

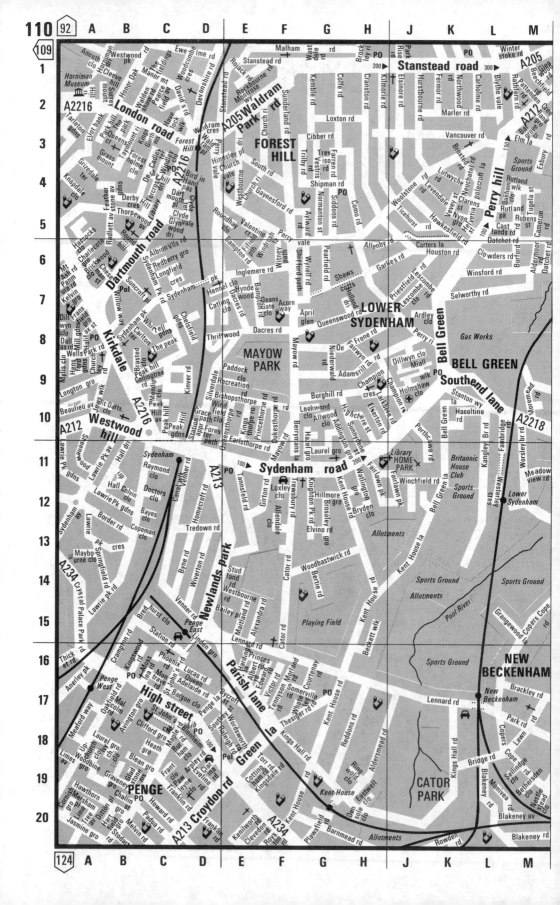

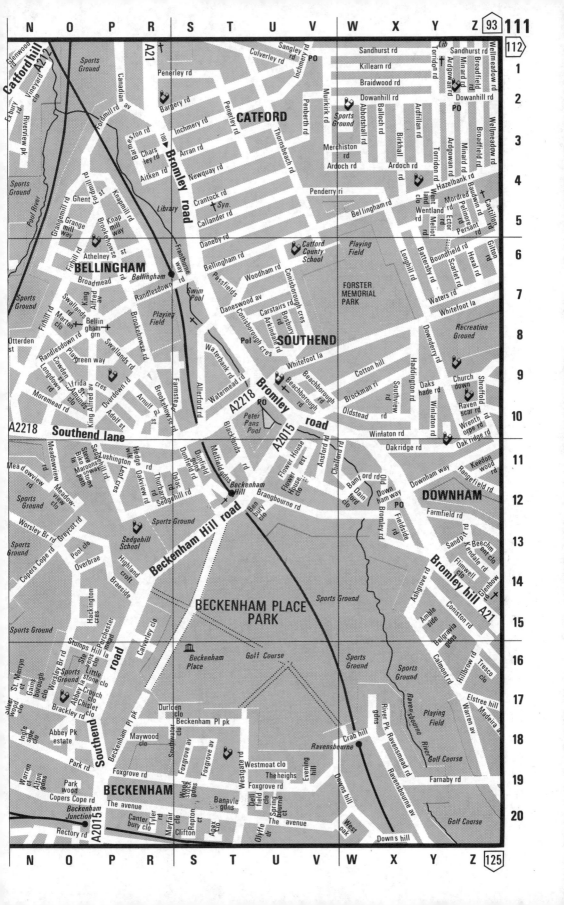

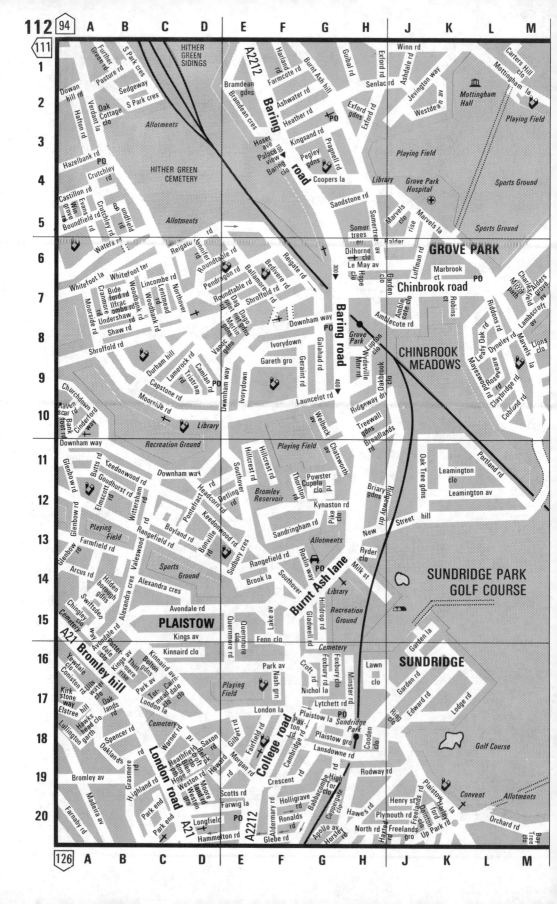

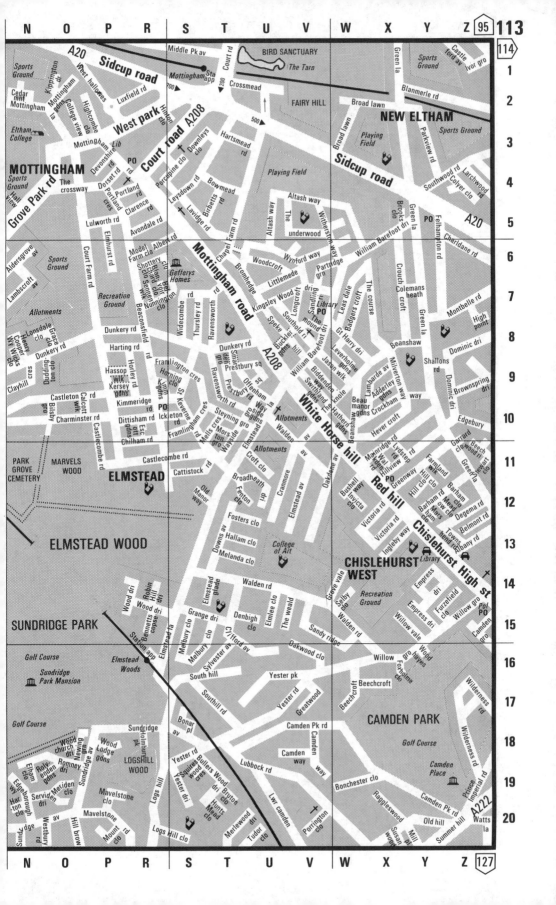

96
113

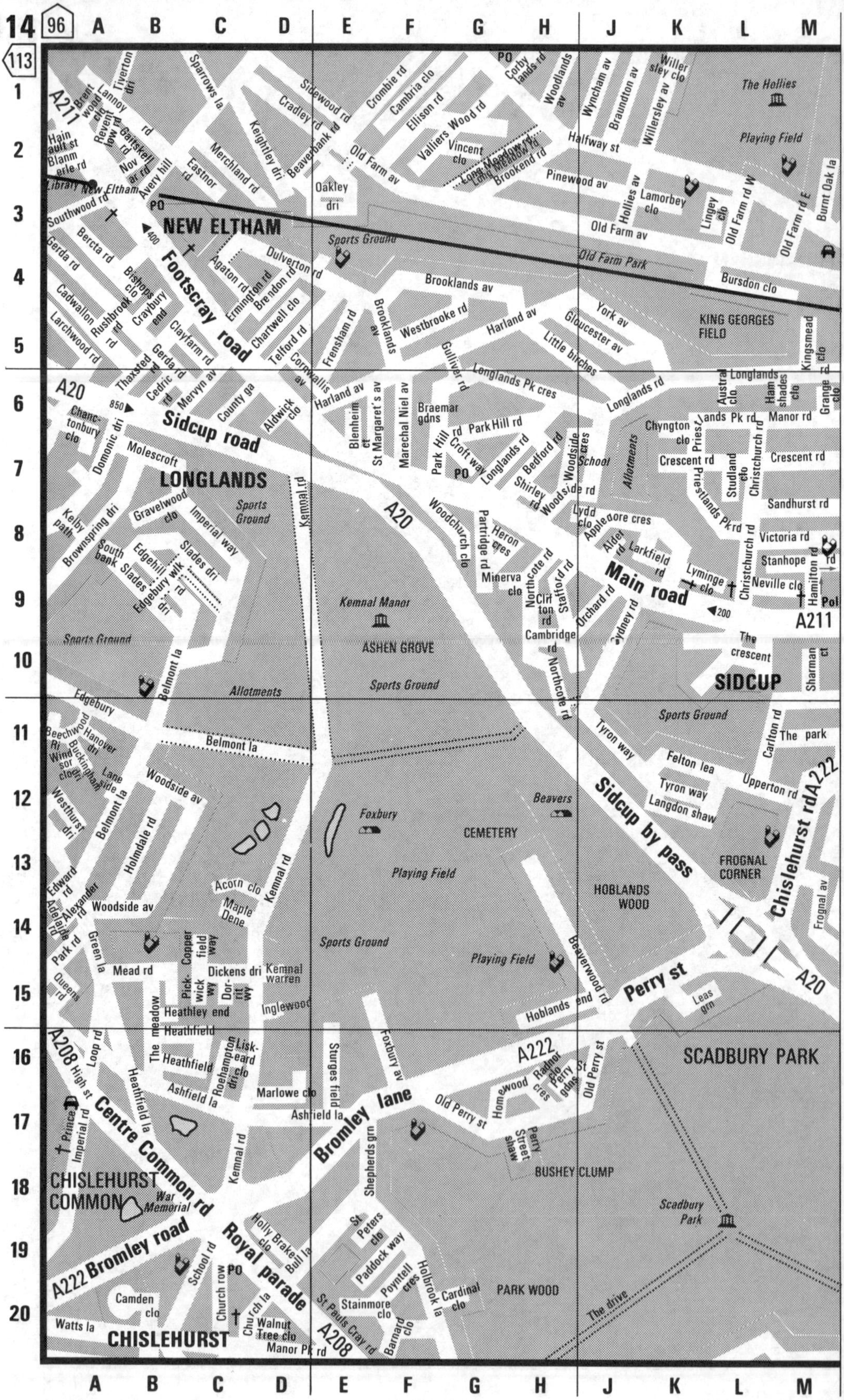
A B C D E F G H J K L M
1 2 3 4 5 6 7 8 9 10 11 12 13 14 15 16 17 18 19 20
NEW ELTHAM
Footscray road
LONGLANDS
Sidcup road
A20
A211
Main road
SIDCUP
Sidcup by pass
Chislehurst rd
A222
FROGNAL CORNER
HOBLANDS WOOD
CEMETERY
Kemnal Manor
ASHEN GROVE
Sports Ground
Playing Field
Allotments
KING GEORGES FIELD
Old Farm Park
The Hollies
SCADBURY PARK
Scadbury Park
BUSHEY CLUMP
PARK WOOD
The drive
Perry st
Bromley lane
Centre Common rd
Royal parade
Bromley road
A208
CHISLEHURST COMMON
War Memorial
CHISLEHURST
Foxbury
Beavers
Halfway st
Old Farm av
Pinewood av
Brooklands av
Westbrooke rd
Harland av
Longlands rd
Longlands Pk cres
Park Hill rd
Woodside rd
Appledore cres
Larkfield rd
Victoria rd
Stanhope rd
Hamilton rd
Neville clo
Crescent rd
Sandhurst rd
Manor rd
Priestlands Pk rd
Christchurch rd
The crescent
Tyron way
Felton lea
Upperton rd
Langdon shaw
The park
Carlton rd
Frognal av
Belmont la
Woodside av
Holmdale rd
Kemnal rd
Imperial way
Gravelwood clo
Brownspring dri
Edgebury
Hoblands end
Beaverwood rd
Old Perry st
Ashfield la
Heathfield la
High st
Watts la
Camden clo
Manor Pk rd
St Pauls Cray rd
Shepherds grn
Foxbury av
Sturges field
Mead rd
Dickens dri
Kemnal warren
Inglewood
Heathley end
Heathfield
Marlowe clo
Burnt Oak la
Bursdon clo
Kingsmead clo
Cambridge rd
Northcote rd
Orchard rd
Sydney rd
Lyminge clo
PO

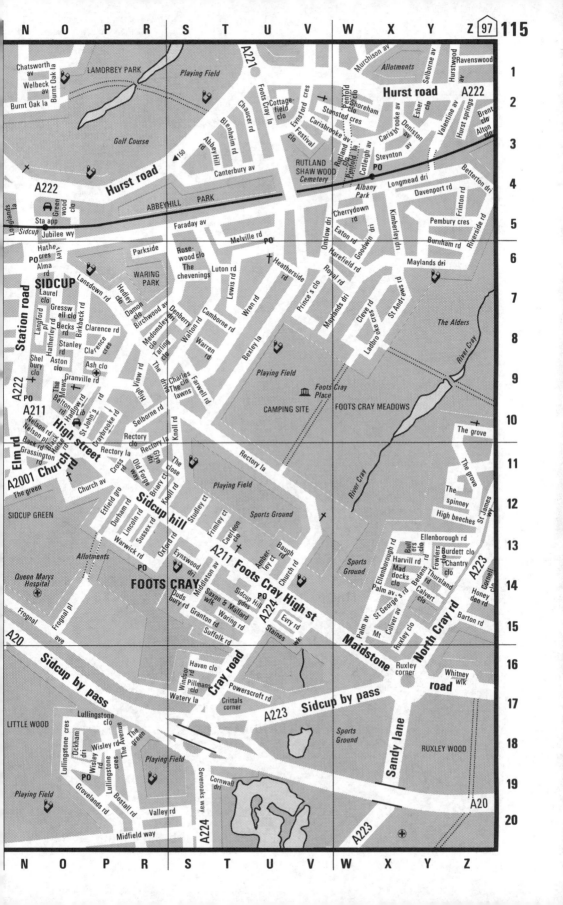

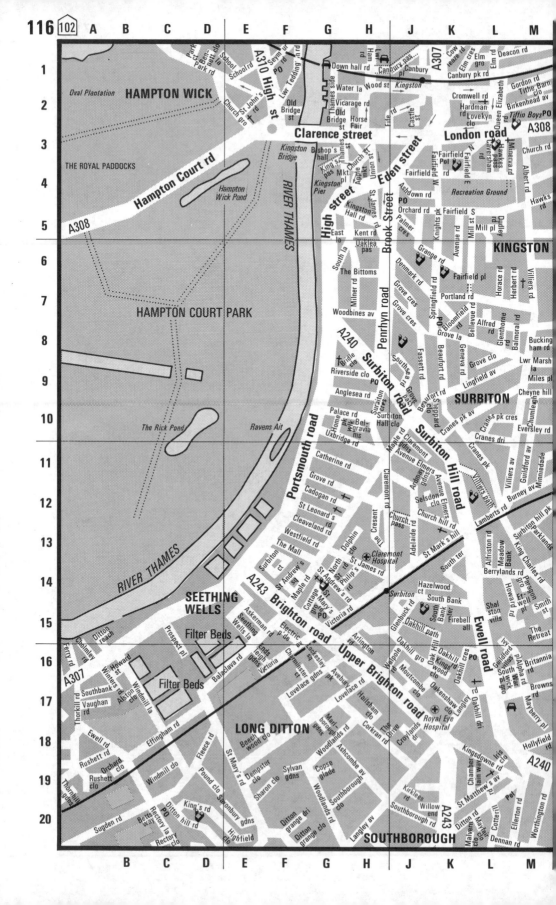

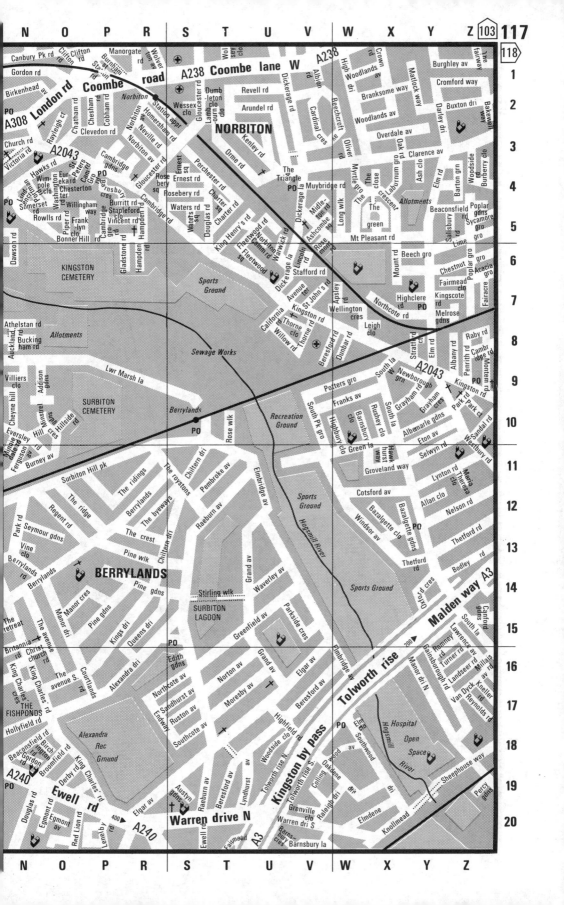

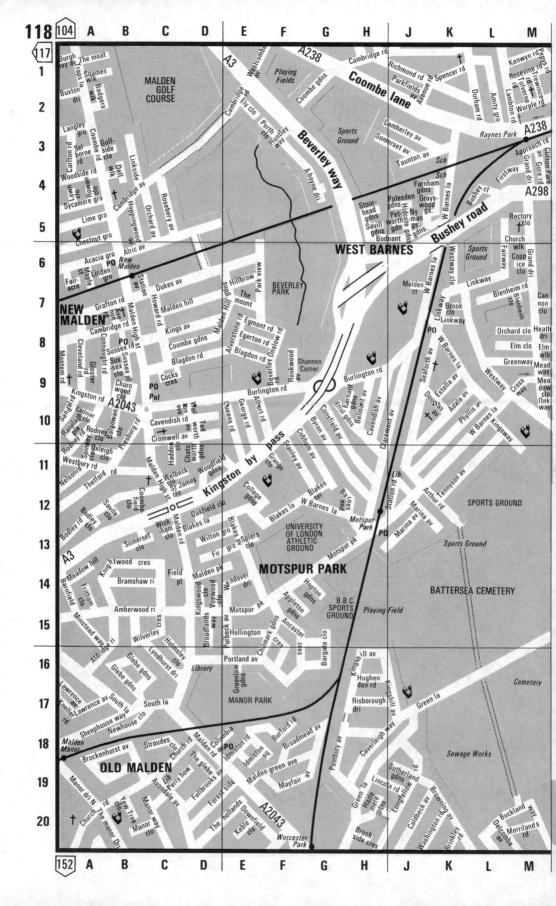

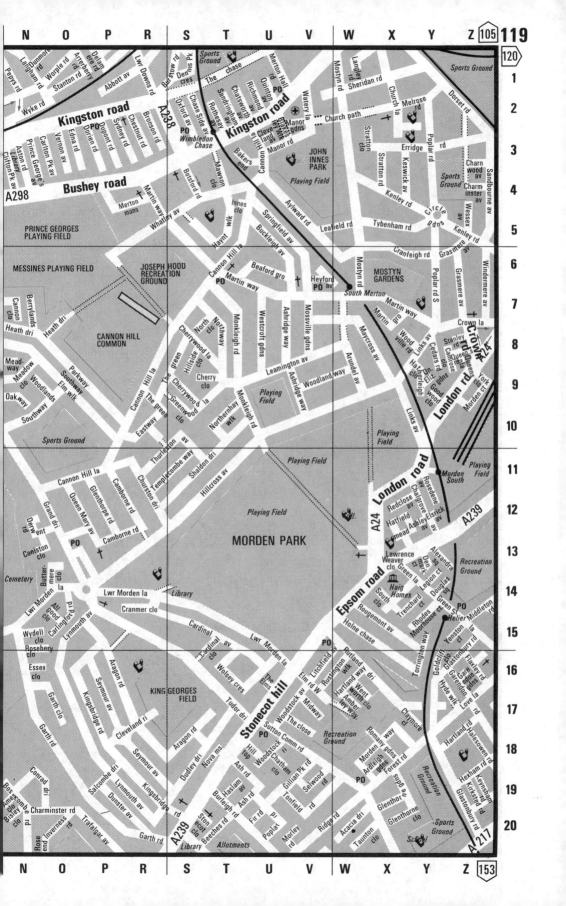

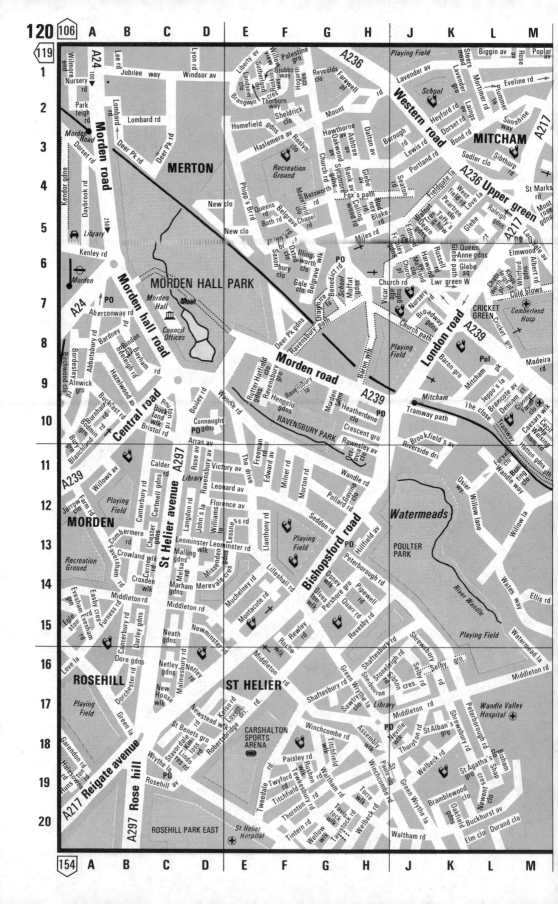

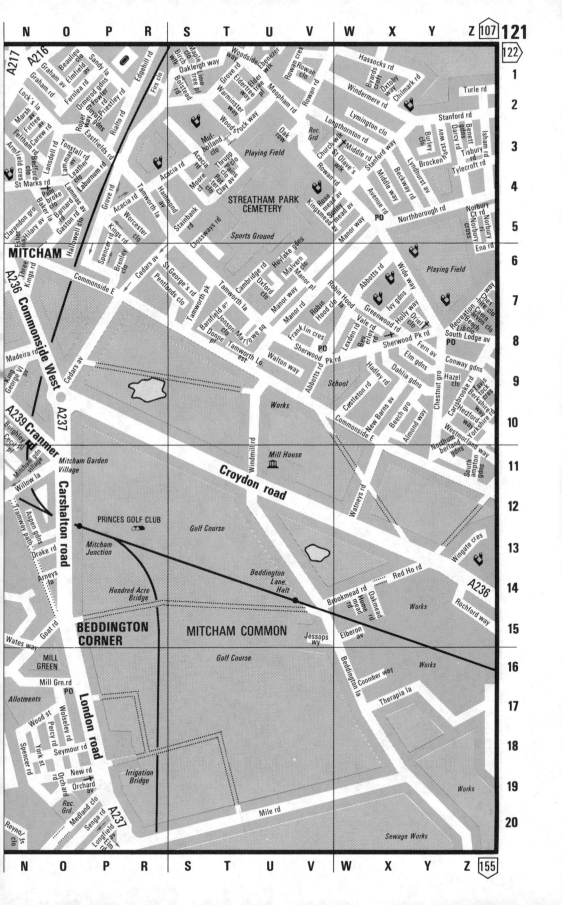

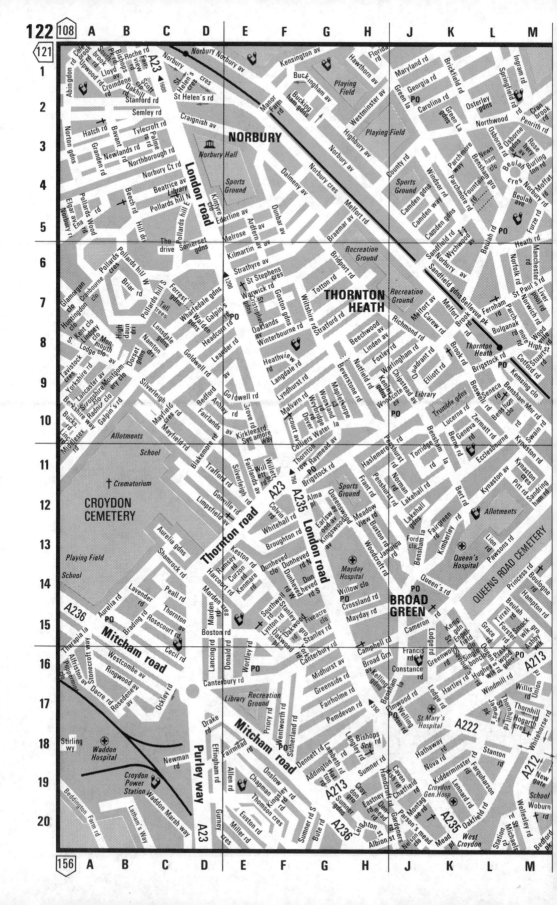

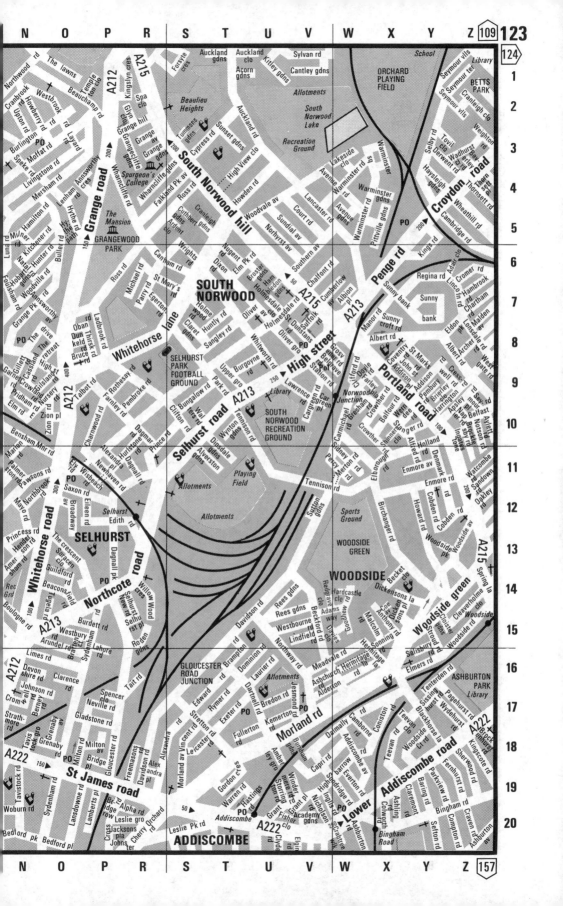

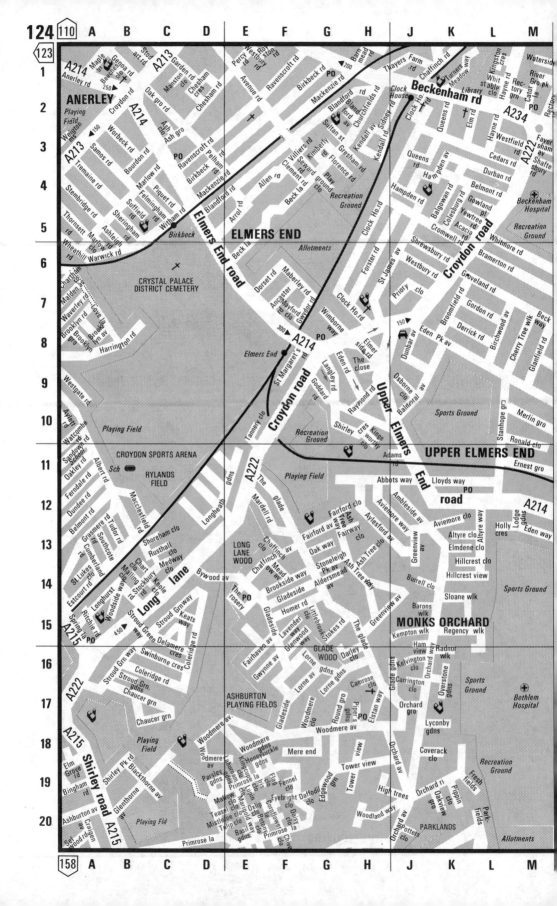

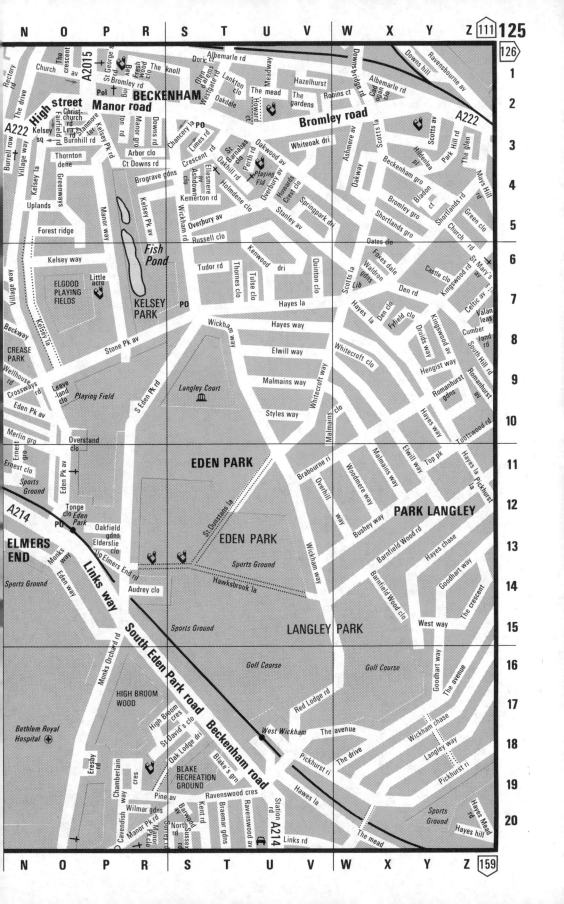

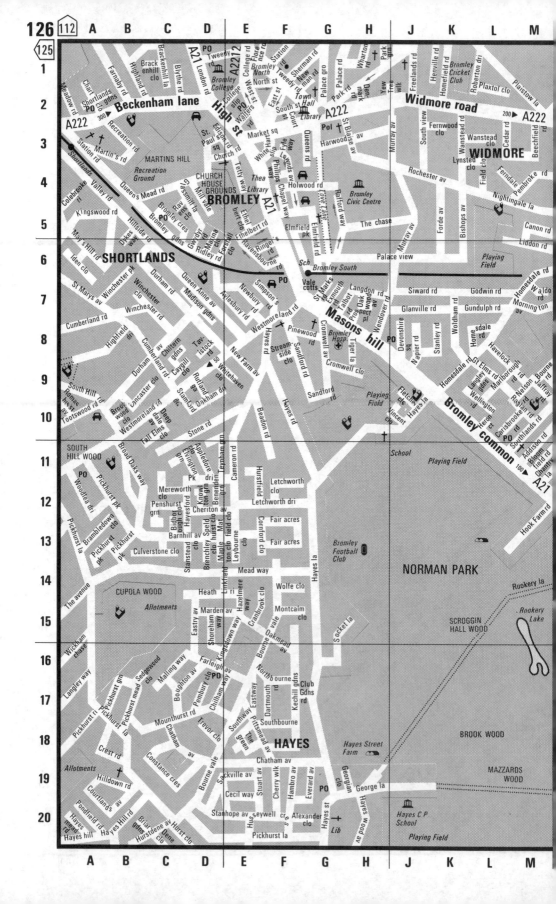

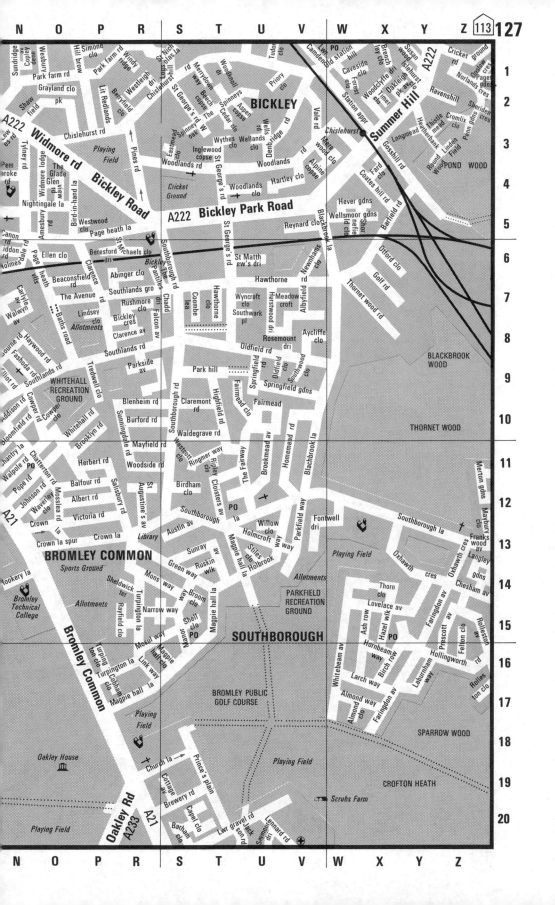

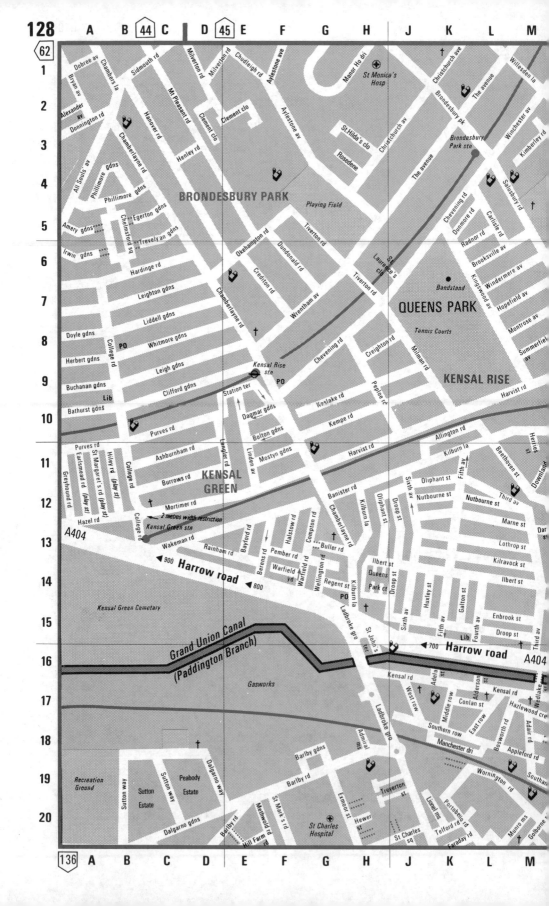

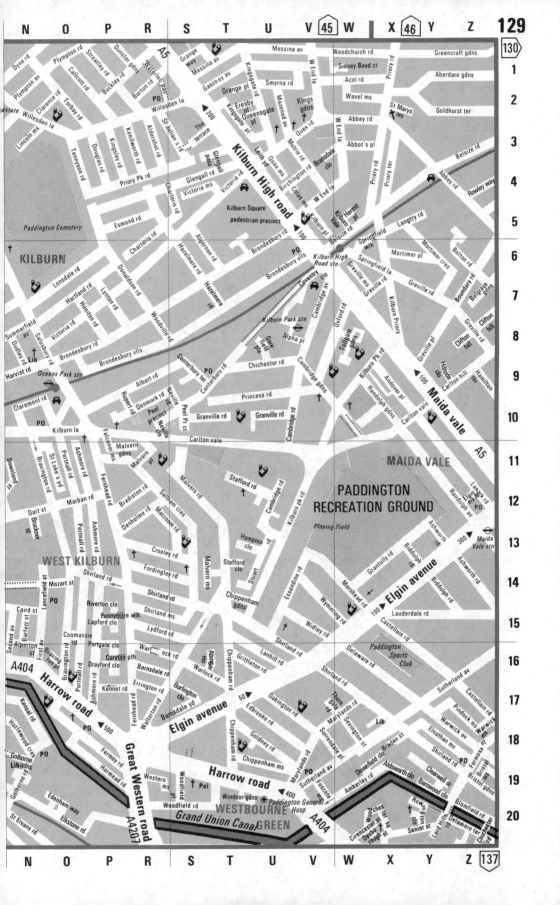

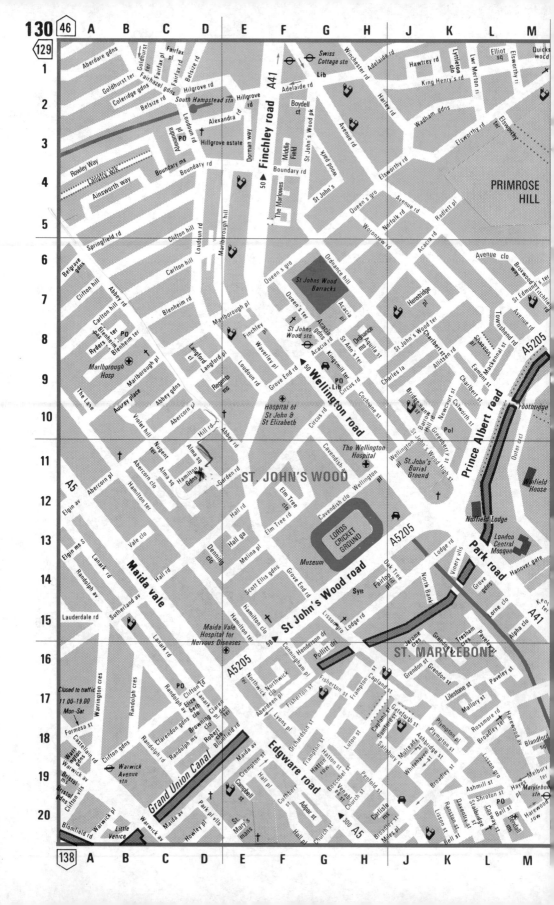

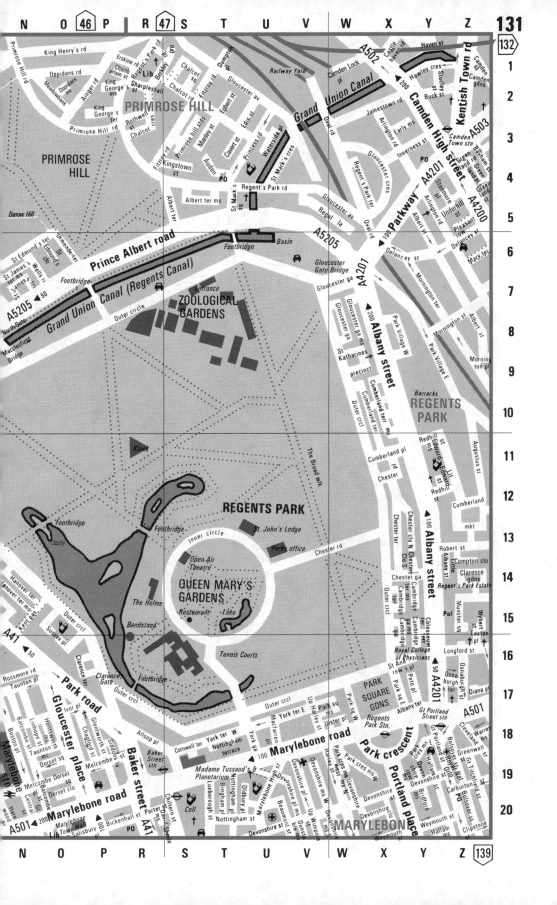

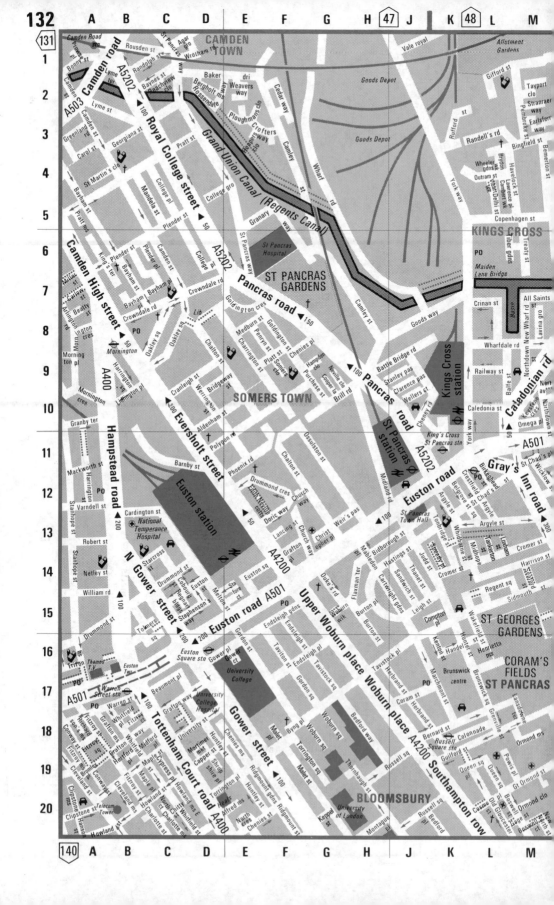

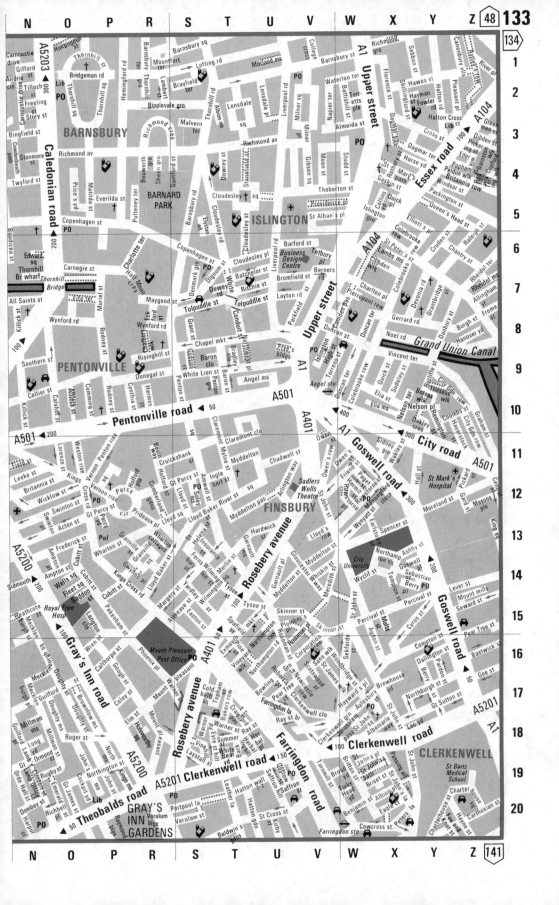

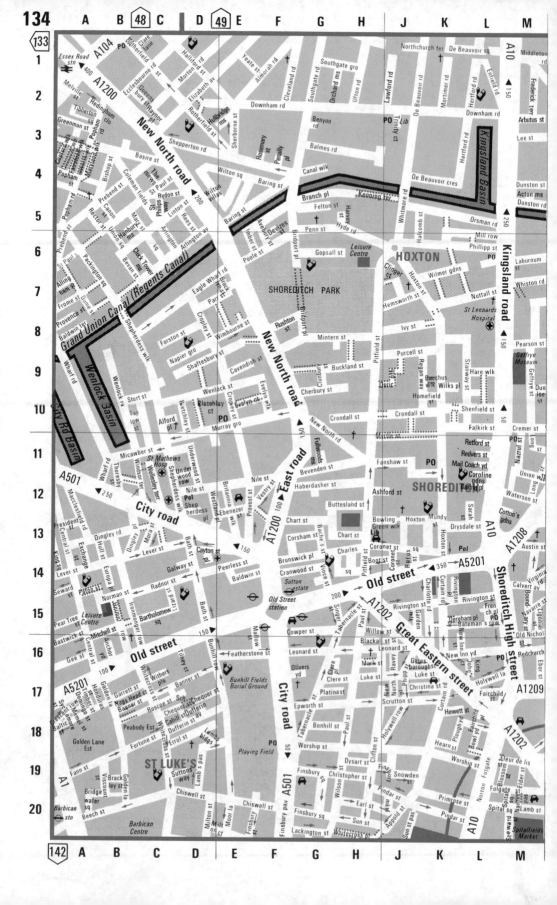

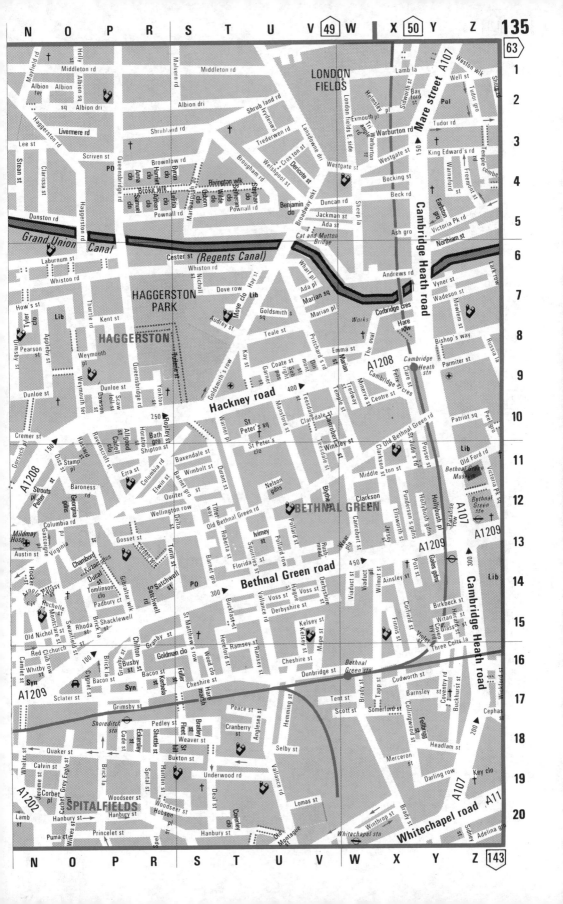

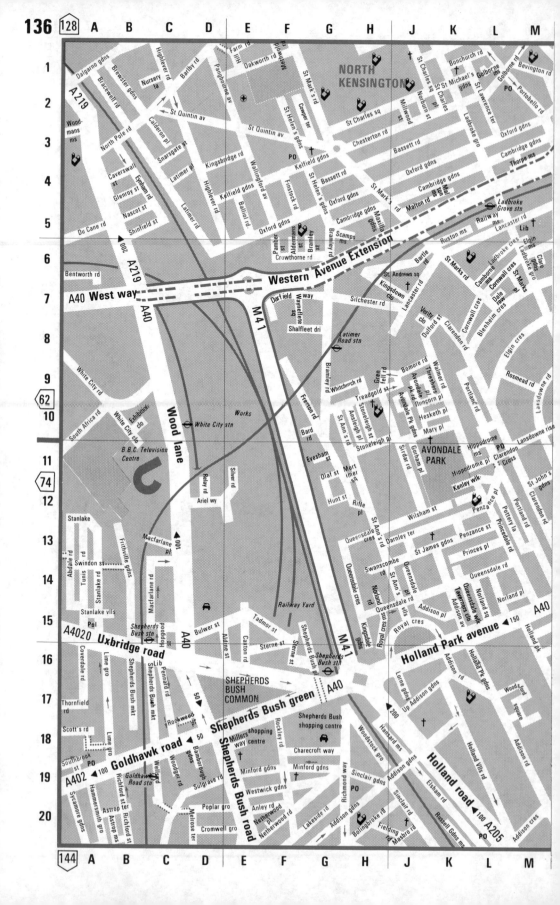

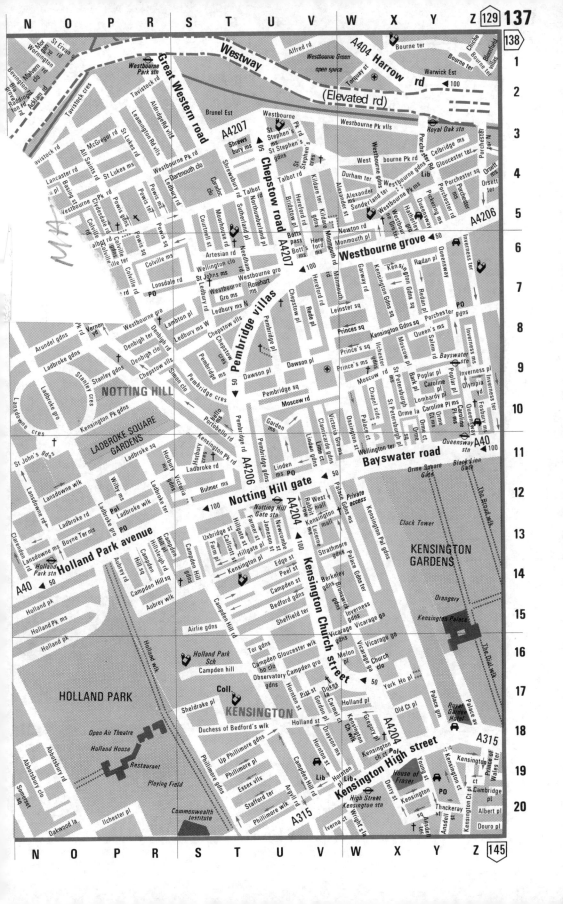

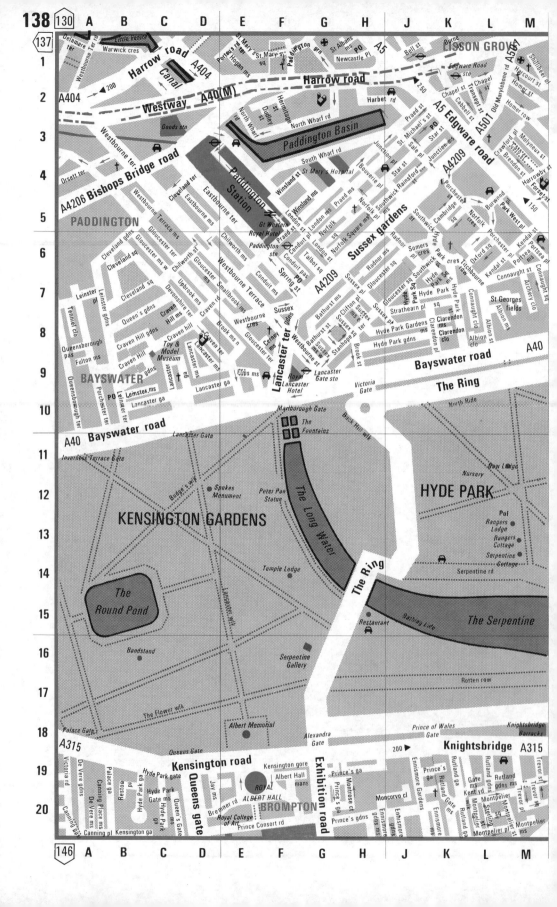

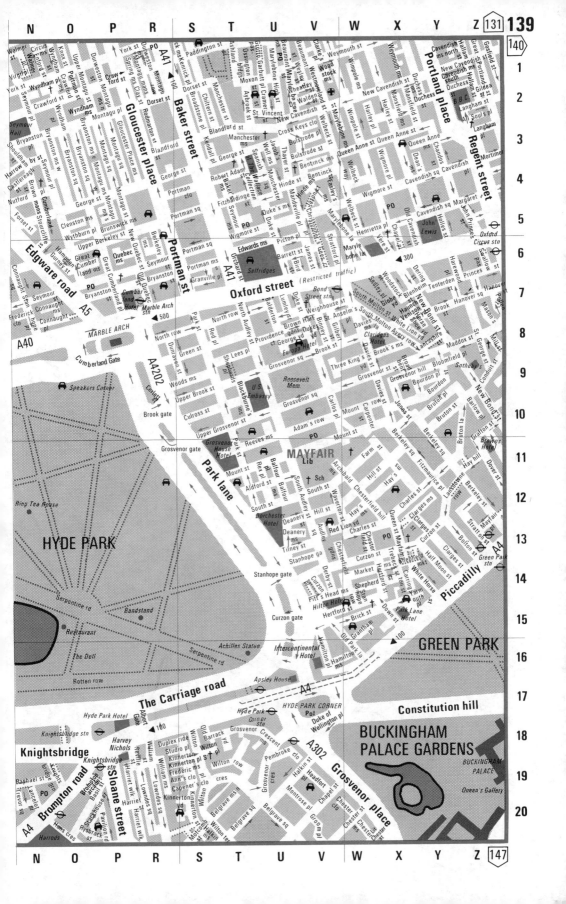

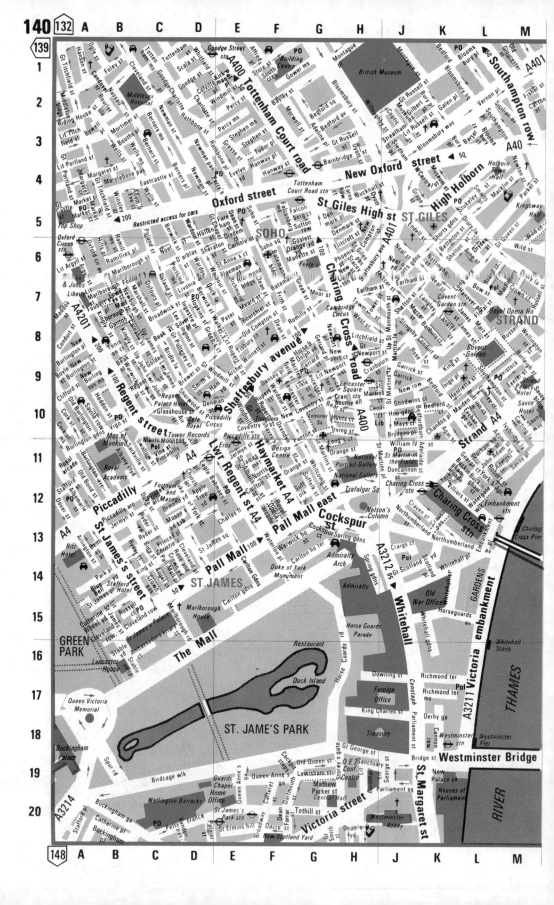

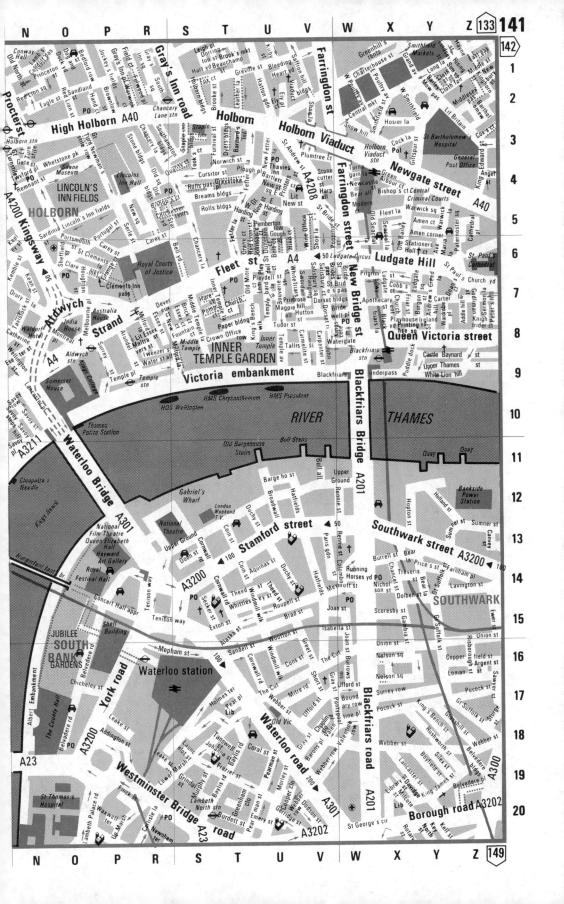

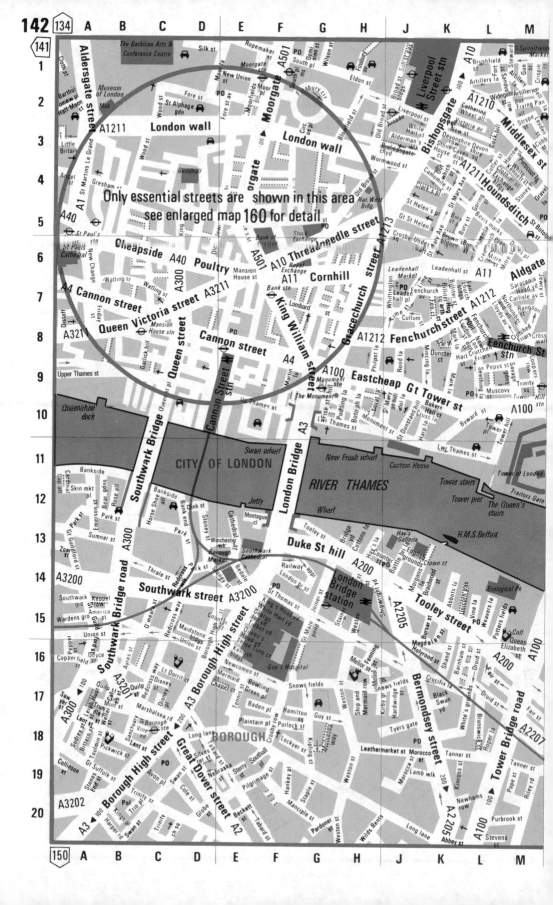

Only essential streets are shown in this area see enlarged map 160 for detail

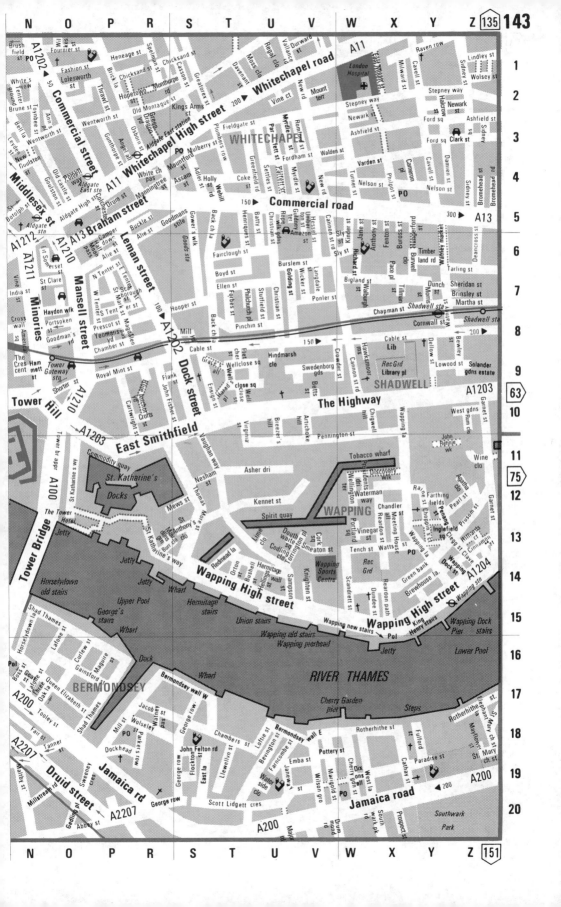

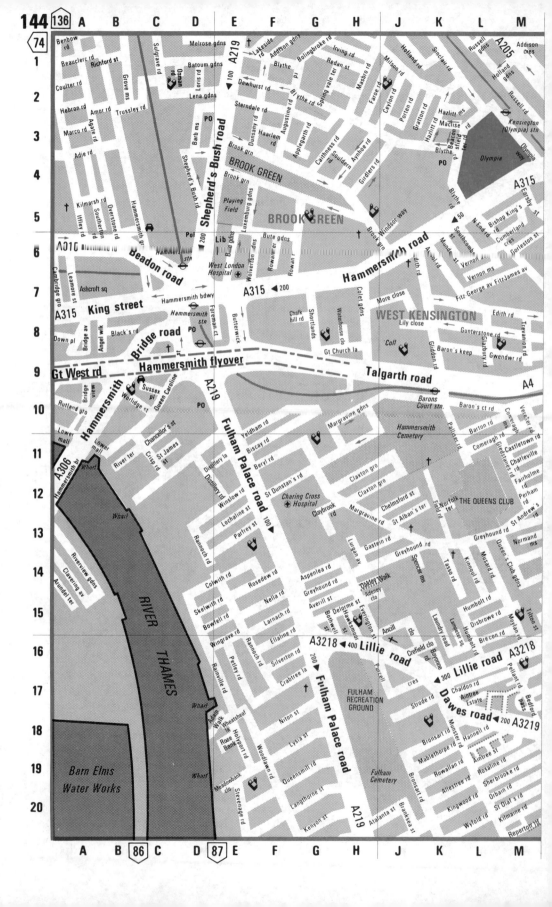

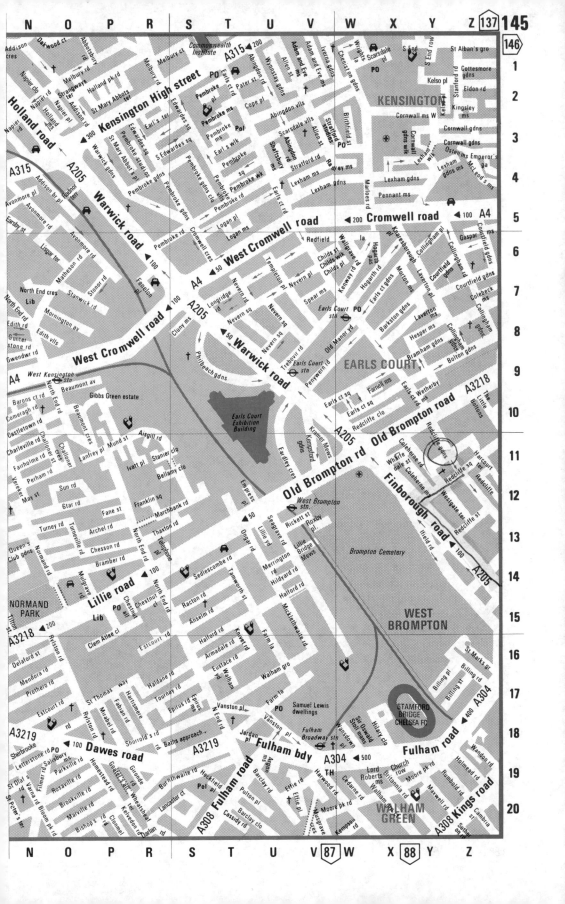

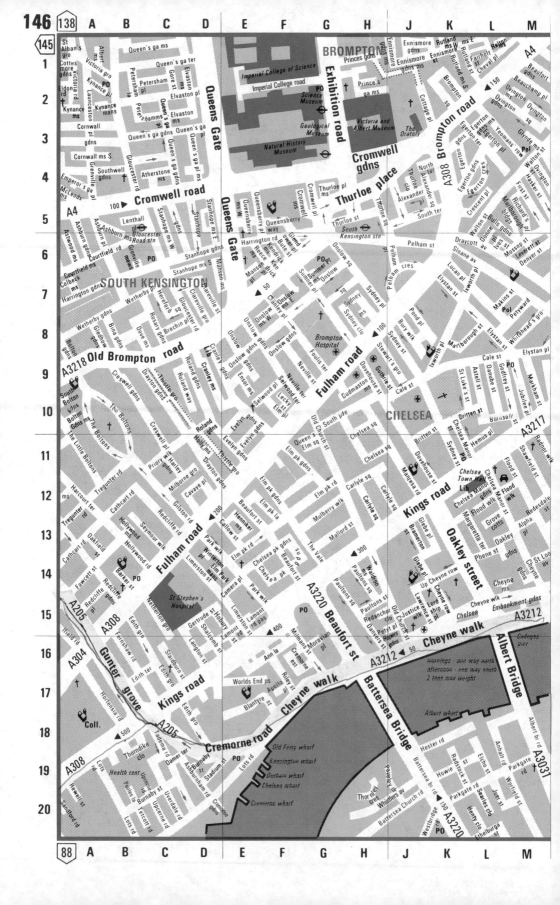

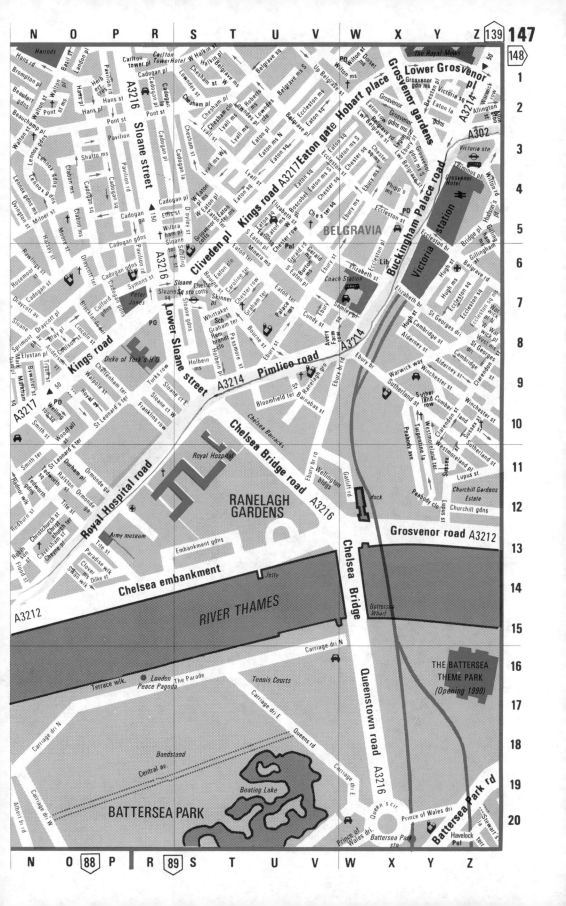

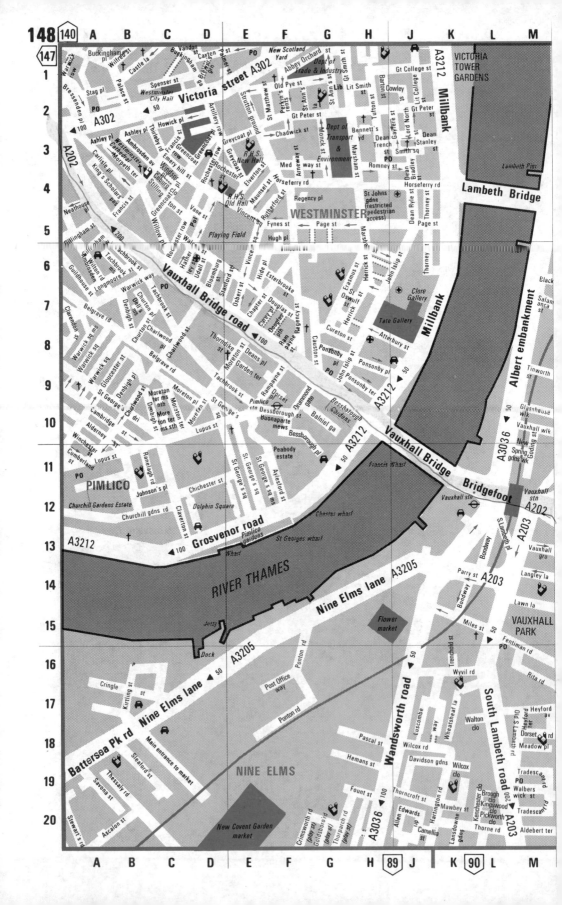

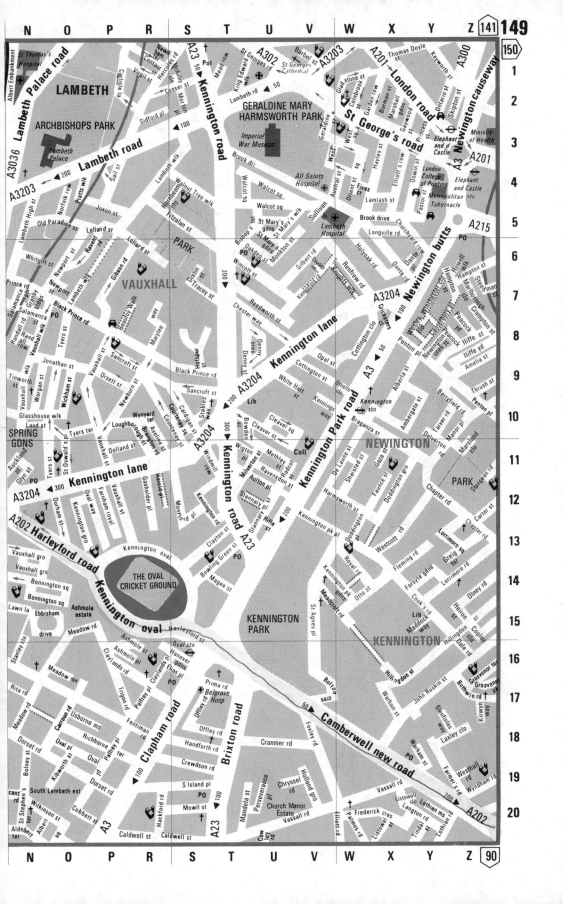

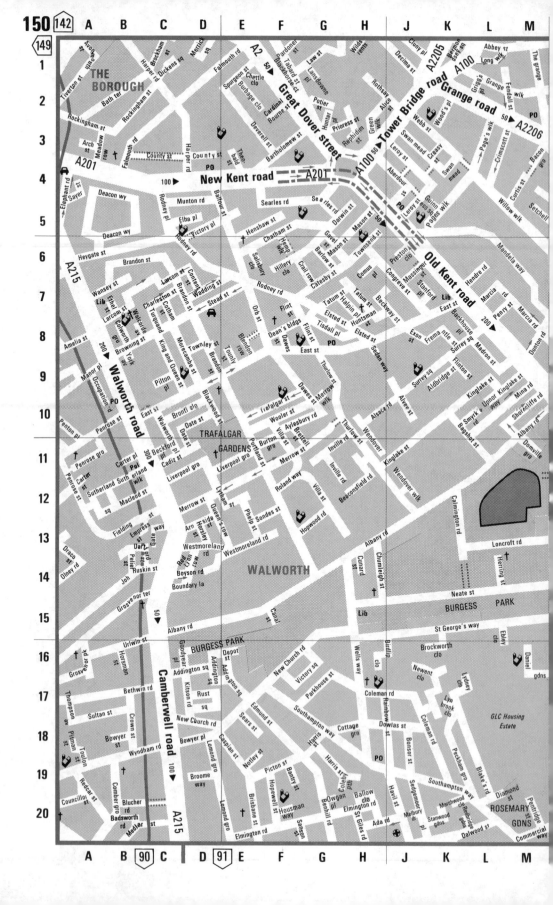

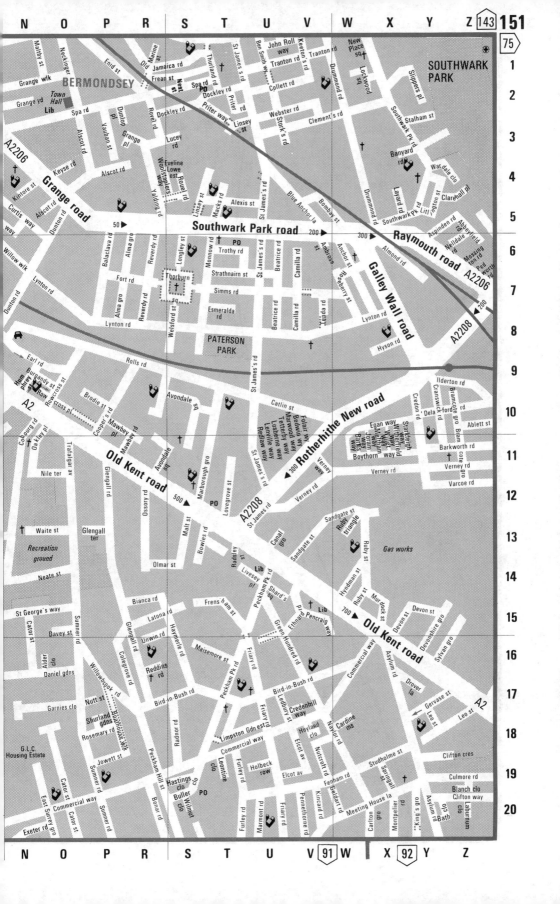

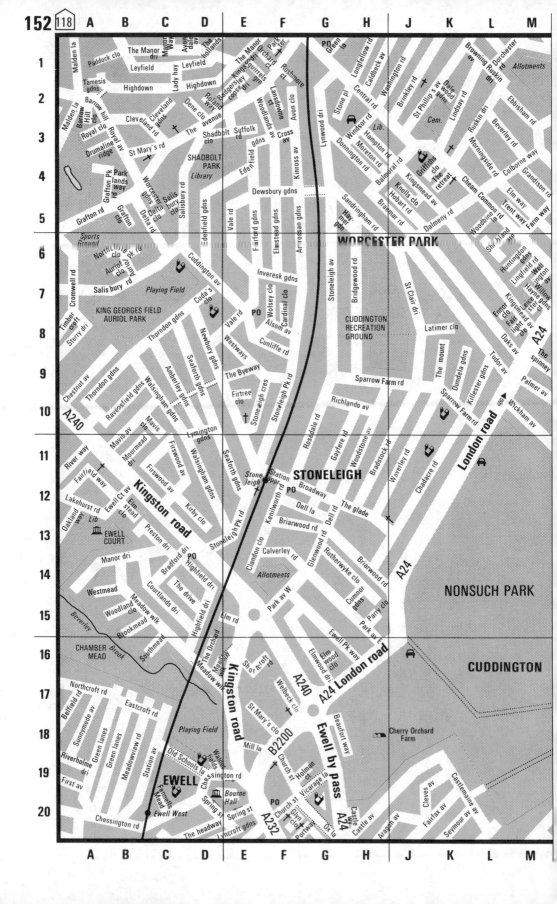

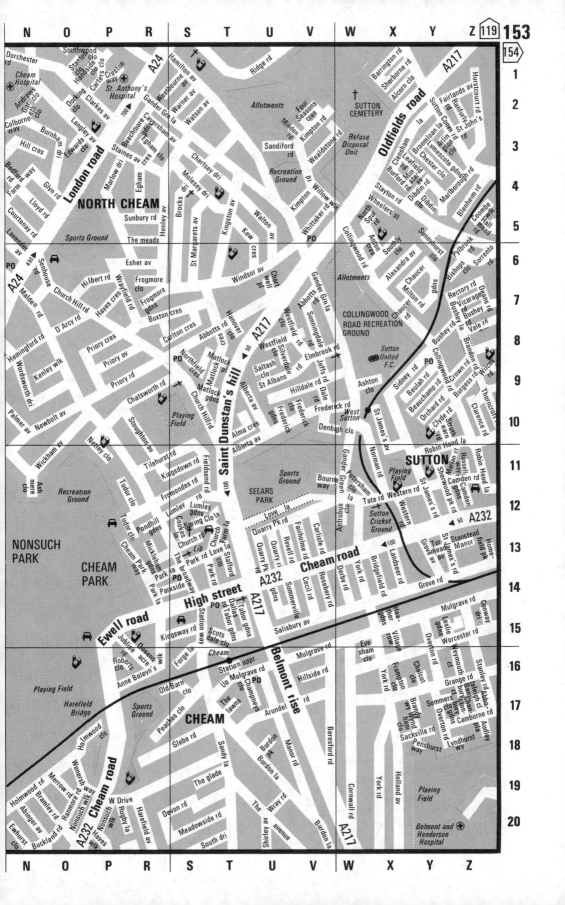

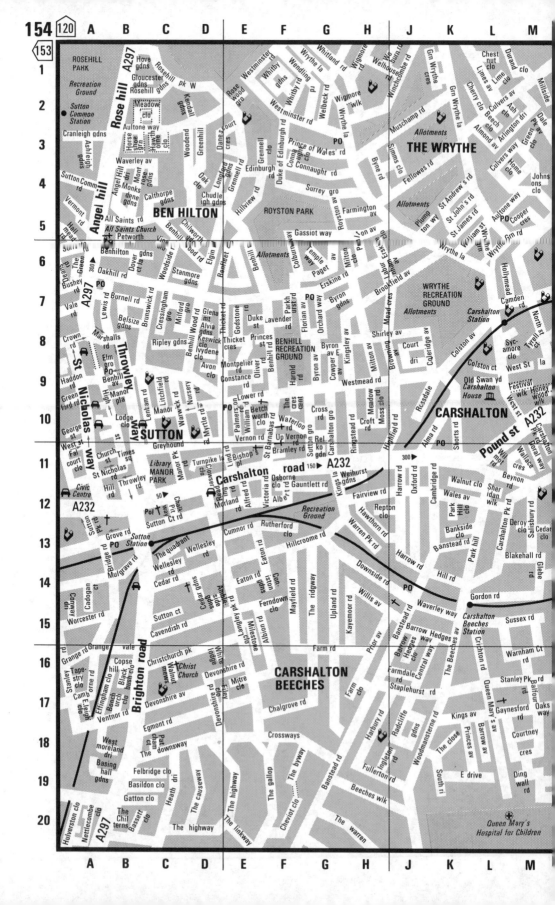

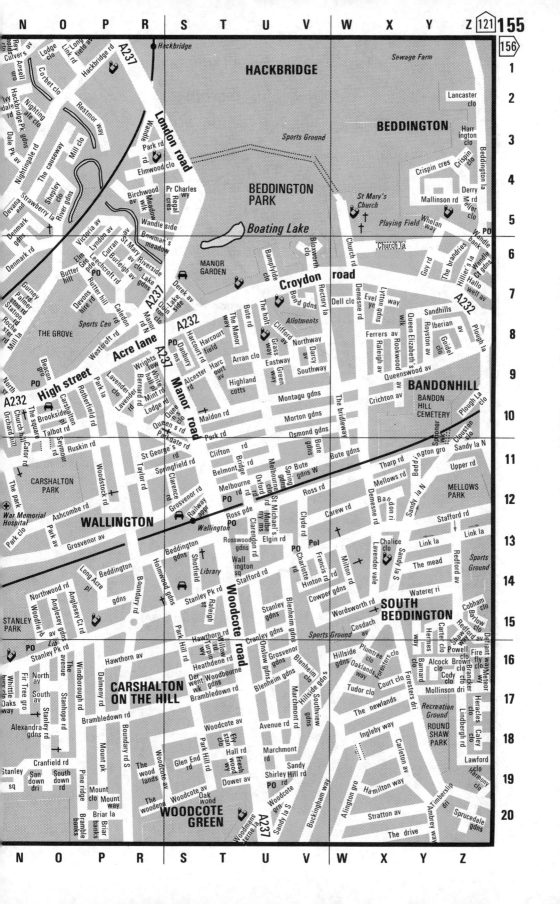

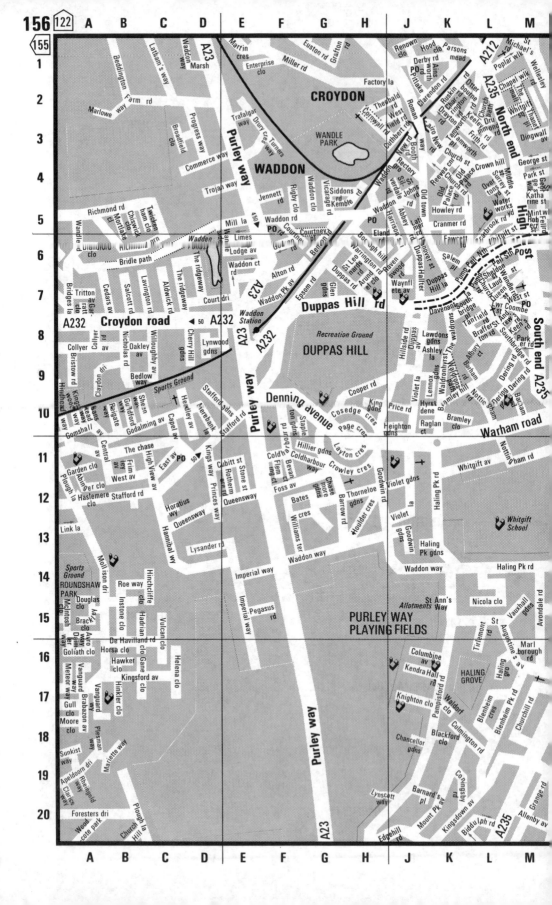

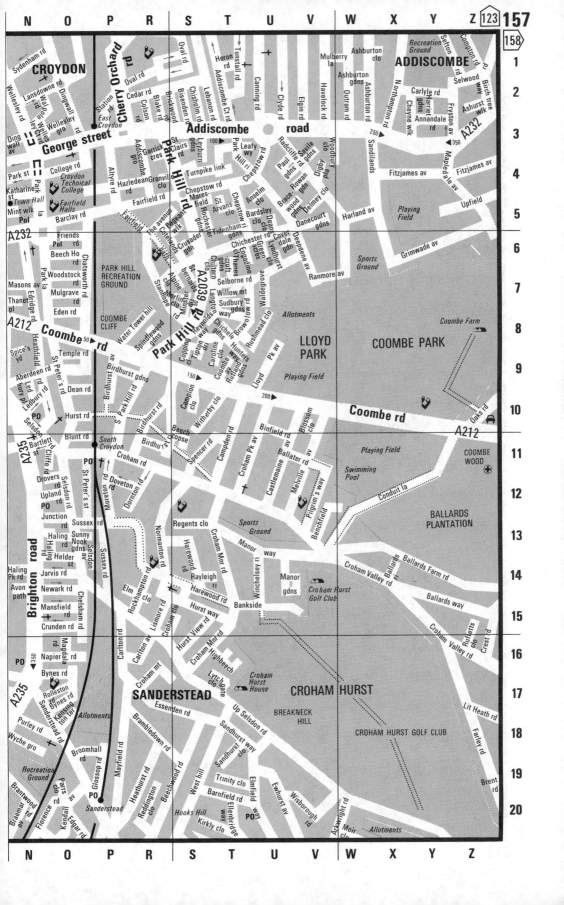

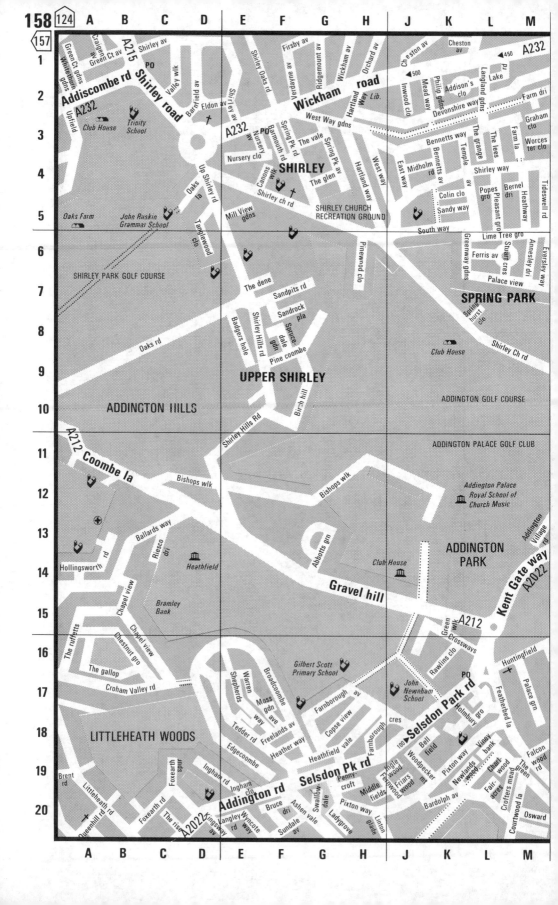

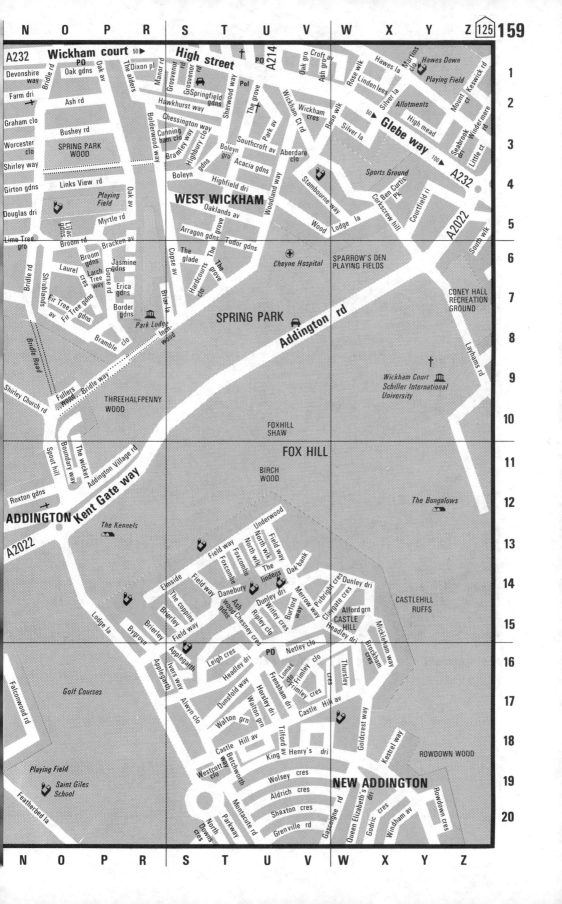

A232 **Wickham court** 50► **High street** A214

Devonshire way
PO
Oak gdns
Oak av
The alders
Dixon pl
Manor rd
Grosvenor rd
Grosvenor rd
Springfield gdns
Sherwood way
Pol
The grove
Oak gro
Croft av
Ash gro
PO
Hawes la
Martins clo
Hawes Down
Playing Field
Rose wlk
Linden lees
Silver la
Mount Keswick rd

Farm dri
Bridle rd
Ash rd
Hawkhurst way
Chessington way
Wickham Cr rd
Park av
Wickham cres
Rose wlk
Silver la
50►
Allotments
High mead
Glebe way
Seabrook dri
Windermere rd

Graham clo
Bushey rd
Cunningham clo
Bramley way
Highbury clo
Boleyn gro
Southcroft av
Acacia gdns
Aberdare clo
100►
A232

Worcester clo
SPRING PARK WOOD
Bolderwood way
Boleyn gdns
Highfield dri
Woodland way
Stambourne way
Sports Ground
Ben Curtis Pk
Corkscrew hill
Courtfield ri
A2022

Shirley way
Links View rd
Oak av
Boleyn
Highfield dri
WEST WICKHAM
Oaklands av
Wood
Lodge la
South wlk

Girton gdns
Playing Field
Lilac gdns
Myrtle rd
Arragon gdns
Tudor gdns

Douglas dri
Broom rd
Bracken av
Copse av
The glade
The grove
Cheyne Hospital
SPARROW'S DEN PLAYING FIELDS

Lime Tree gro
Bridle rd
Laurel
Broom gdns
Jasmine gdns
Larch Tree way
Gorse rd
Erica gdns
Border gdns
Briar la
CONEY HALL RECREATION GROUND

Shrublands
Fir Tree gdns
Fir Tree gdns
Bramble clo
Park Lodge
Inner Wood
SPRING PARK
Addington rd
Layhams rd

Bridle Road
Fullers Wood
Bridle way
THREEHALFPENNY WOOD
Wickham Court Schiller International University

Shirley Church rd
Spout hill
Boundary way
The wicket
Addington Village rd
FOXHILL SHAW

Roxton gdns
The Kennels
FOX HILL
The Bungalows

ADDINGTON Kent Gate way
BIRCH WOOD

A2022
Lodge la
Bygrove
Brierley
The coppins
Elmside
Field way
Field way
Foxcombe
Foxcombe
North wlk
North wlk
Field way
Underwood
The lindens
Oak bank
Merrow way
Pitbright cres
Dunley dri
Claygate cres
CASTLEHILL RUFFS

Brierley
Field way
Danebury
Ash Wood gdns
Chesney cres
Dunley dri
Witley cres
Ripley clo
Burford
Alford grn
CASTLE HILL
Headley dri
Mickleham way
Brockham

Falconwood rd
Golf Courses
Applegarth
Ivers rd
Leigh cres
Headley dri
PO
Frensham dri
Lomas rd
Frimley clo
Frimley cres
Netley clo
Thursley cres
Castle Hill av
Goldcrest way

Applegarth
Alwyn clo
Dunstold way
Horsley dri
Walton grn
Kestrel way
ROWDOWN WOOD

Playing Field
Saint Giles School
Castle Hill av
Betchworth
Tilford av
King Henry's dri
Wolsey cres
Aldrich cres
NEW ADDINGTON
Rowdown cres

Featherbed la
Westcott clo
Montacute rd
North Downs cres
Parkway
Shaxton cres
Grenville rd
Gascoigne rd
Queen Elizabeth's dri
Godric cres
Windham av

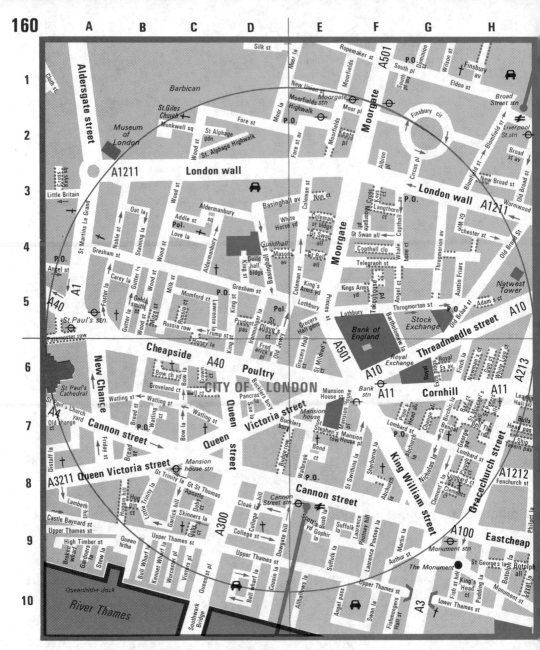

Enlargement of crowded city area for extra clarity

NOTES

The figures and letters before a street name indicate the page number and map square where the name will be found. The figures and letters following a street name indicate the postal district or locality of the entry.

For example **139 T 7 Oxford st W1** will be found on page **139** in square **T7** in the postal district of **W1**.

Abbreviations

Outer districts

Barking **Bark**
Barnet **Barnt**
Beckenham **Becknhm**
Belvedere **Blvdr**
Bexley Heath **Bxly Hth**
Bexley **Bxly**
Borehamwood **Borhm wd**
Brentford **Brentf**
Bromley **Brom**
Buckhurst Hill **Buck Hl**
Carshalton **Carsh**
Chislehurst **Chisl**
Croydon **Croy**
Dagenham **Dgnhm**
Dartford **Drtfrd**
East Molesey **E Molesey**
Edgware **Edg**
Enfield **Enf**
Feltham **Felt**
Greenford **Grnfd**
Hampton **Hampt**
Hornchurch **Hornch**
Hounslow **Hounsl**
Ilford **Ilf**
Isleworth **Islwth**
Kingston **Kingst**
Mitcham **Mitch**
Morden **Mrdn**
New Malden **New Mald**
Northolt **Nthlt**
Orpington **Orp**
Pinner **Pinn**
Rainham **Rainhm**
Richmond **Rich**
Romford **Rom**
Ruislip **Ruis**
Sidcup **Sidcp**
South Croydon **S Croy**
Southall **S'hall**
Stanmore **Stanm**
Surbiton **Surb**
Teddington **Tedd**
Thornton Heath **Thntn Hth**
Twickenham **Twick**
Wallington **Wallgtn**
Watford **Watf**
Wembley **Wemb**
West Wickham **W Wkhm**
Woodford Green **Wdfd Grn**
Worcester Park **Worc Pk**

Streets etc

Alley **all**
Approach **appr**
Arcade **arc**
Avenue **av**
Boulevard **blvd**
Bridge **br**
Broadway **bdwy**
Buildings **bldgs**
Church **ch**
Churchyard **chyd**
Circle **crcl**
Circus **cir**
Close **clo**
Common **comm**
Cottages **cotts**
Court **ct**
Crescent **cres**
Drive **dri**
Embankment **emb**
Estate **est**
Gardens **gdns**
Gate **ga**
Green **grn**
Grove **gro**
House **ho**
Junction **junc**
Lane **la**
Manor **mnr**
Mansions **mans**
Market **mkt**
Mews **ms**
Mount **mt**
Palace **pal**
Parade **pde**
Park **pk**
Passage **pas**
Path **pth**
Place **pl**
Rise **ri**
Road **rd**
Square **sq**
Station **sta**
Street **st**
Terrace **ter**
Villas **vlls**
Walk **wlk**
Yard **yd**

A

66 E 16 Abbess clo E6
108 G 1 Abbess clo SW2
29 Y 14 Abbeville rd N8
89 V 15 Abbeville rd SW4
60 L 5 Abbey av Wemb
58 D 9 Abbey clo SW 2
81 S 11 Abbey cres Erith
130 C 9 Abbey gdns NW8
80 E 10 Abbey gro SE2
115 T 3 Abbey Hill rd Sidcp
111 O 17 Abbey la Becknhm
64 G 5 Abbey la E15
148 F 1 Abbey Orchard st SW1
111 O 18 Abbey Park est Becknhm
67 N 2 Abbey rd Bark
80 K 10 Abbey rd Blvdr
81 N 9 Abbey rd Blvdr
97 Z 9 Abbey rd Bxly Hth
156 J 5 Abbey rd Croy
64 L 5 Abbey rd E15
8 F 17 Abbey rd Enf
36 E 16 Abbey rd Ilf
61 T 5 Abbey rd NW10
61 T 7 Abbey rd NW10
129 Y 4 Abbey rd NW6
130 B 7 Abbey rd NW8
106 D 19 Abbey rd SW19
65 T 11 Abbey st E13
150 L 1 Abbey st SE1
143 O 20 Abbey st SE1
80 F 10 Abbey ter SE2
60 M 7 Abbey ter Wemb
13 S 10 Abbey view NW7
80 F 10 Abbey Wood rd SE2
61 O 3 Abbeydale rd Wemb
75 P 11 Abbeyfield rd SE16
151 Z 5 Abbeyfield rd SE16
61 P 7 Abbeyfields clo NW10
61 P 7 Abbeyfields cres NW10
100 C 16 Abbot clo Hampt
40 D 19 Abbot clo Nthlt
49 T 17 Abbot st E8
129 W 3 Abbot's pl NW6
20 L 14 Abbots cres E4
28 G 13 Abbots gdns N2
142 K 14 Abbots la SE1
108 G 1 Abbots pk SW2
25 W 1 Abbots rd Edg
13 N 20 Abbots rd NW7
124 J 11 Abbots way Becknhm
64 G 5 Abbotsbury clo E15
137 N 19 Abbotsbury clo W14
120 A 8 Abbotsbury rd SW19
137 N 19 Abbotsbury rd W14
30 M 14 Abbotsford av N15
34 E 2 Abbotsford gdns Wdfd Grn
55 O 7 Abbotsford rd Ilf
16 H 12 Abbotshall av N14
111 W 3 Abbotshall rd SE6
153 Z 17 Abbotsleigh clo Sutton
107 V 11 Abbotsleigh rd SW16
87 N 8 Abbotstone rd SW15
92 M 13 Abbotswell rd SE4
35 V 11 Abbotswood gdns Ilf
107 W 5 Abbotswood rd SW16
119 P 1 Abbott av SW20
40 D 18 Abbott clo Grnfd
64 G 15 Abbott rd E14
64 K 16 Abbott rd E14
38 G 9 Abbotts clo Rom
7 X 8 Abbotts cres Enf
42 A 6 Abbotts dri Wemb
42 C 6 Abbotts dri Wemb
158 G 13 Abbotts grn Croy
51 U 1 Abbotts Park rd E10
4 M 16 Abbotts rd Barnt
66 B 5 Abbotts rd E6
25 X 1 Abbotts rd Edg
121 X 6 Abbotts rd Mitch
70 C 2 Abbotts rd S'hall
153 V 7 Abbotts rd Sutton
80 J 19 Abbotts wlk Bxly Hth
101 V 4 Abbottsmede clo Twick
160 F 8 Abchurch la EC4
136 A 14 Abdale rd W12
74 K 3 Abdale rd W12
150 J 4 Abedour st SE1

63 X 10 Aberavon rd E3
107 V 18 Abercairn rd SW16
120 A 7 Aberconway rd SW19
27 T 2 Abercorn clo NW7
130 C 11 Abercorn clo NW8
40 L 4 Abercorn cres Harrow
42 G 1 Abercorn gdns Harrow
37 P 18 Abercorn gdns Rom
130 C 10 Abercorn pl NW8
27 U 2 Abercorn rd NW7
124 D 2 Abercorn rd Stanm
88 K 5 Abercrombie st SW11
159 V 3 Aberdare clo W Wkhm
130 A 1 Aberdare gdns NW6
129 Z 1 Aberdare gdns NW6
27 O 3 Aberdare gdns NW7
9 O 14 Aberdare rd Enf
48 K 15 Aberdeen la N5
48 K 15 Aberdeen pk N5
130 F 17 Aberdeen pl NW8
157 N 9 Aberdeen rd Croy
23 V 8 Aberdeen rd Harrow
18 L 15 Aberdeen rd N18
48 L 13 Aberdeen rd N5
44 E 14 Aberdeen rd NW10
120 F 2 Aberdeen rd SW19
93 X 5 Aberdeen ter SE3
55 P 8 Aberdour rd Ilf
64 H 17 Aberfeldy st E14
107 X 17 Aberfoyle rd SW16
94 J 15 Abergeldie rd SE12
93 Z 11 Abernethy rd SE13
49 V 15 Abersham rd E8
79 U 11 Abery st SE18
106 E 16 Abingdon clo SW19
28 D 6 Abingdon rd N3
122 A 1 Abingdon rd SW16
145 U 1 Abingdon rd W8
148 K 2 Abingdon st SW1
145 U 2 Abingdon vlls W8
153 N 20 Abinger av Sutton
127 P 6 Abinger clo Brom
54 M 13 Abinger clo Ilf
150 A 12 Abinger clo Wallgtn
83 S 8 Abinger gdns Islwth
75 Y 16 Abinger gro SE8
129 S 16 Abinger ms W9
74 B 8 Abinger rd W4
75 O 14 Ablett st SE16
151 Z 10 Ablett st SE16
118 G 4 Aboyne dri SW20
44 B 8 Aboyne rd NW10
43 Z 9 Aboyne rd NW10
106 E 5 Aboyne rd SW17
68 D 7 Abridge way Bark
88 K 12 Abyssinia rd SW11
72 A 20 Acacia av Brentf
57 U 8 Acacia av Hornch
31 O 1 Acacia av N17
42 J 15 Acacia av Wemb
10 G 19 Acacia clo Harrow
119 W 20 Acacia dri Sutton
159 U 4 Acacia gdns W Wkhm
130 G 8 Acacia gdns NW8
118 A 6 Acacia gro New Mald
117 Z 6 Acacia gro New Mald
109 P 4 Acacia gro SE21
130 G 8 Acacia pl NW8
52 A 8 Acacia rd E11
32 J 19 Acacia rd E17
8 C 5 Acacia rd Enf
100 J 14 Acacia rd Hampt
121 R 4 Acacia rd Mitch
30 G 5 Acacia rd N22
130 G 8 Acacia rd NW8
108 B 20 Acacia rd SW16
61 V 20 Acacia rd W3
123 V 20 Academy gdns Croy
58 A 7 Academy gdns Nrthlt
95 U 2 Academy pl SE18
78 G 19 Academy rd SE18
95 U 1 Academy rd SE18
89 N 8 Acans rd SW11
45 W 3 Accommodation rd NW11
88 A 2 Acfold rd SW6
45 W 14 Achilles rd NW6
75 X 20 Achilles st SE14
137 O 1 Acklam rd W10
26 A 4 Acklington dri NW9
87 X 3 Ackmar rd SW6
63 Z 14 Ackroyd dri E3
92 G 18 Ackroyd rd SE23
91 N 8 Acland cres SE5
44 L 17 Acland rd NW2

129 W 1 Acol rd NW6
68 C 3 Aconbury rd Dgnhm
114 C 13 Acorn clo Chisl
20 C 16 Acorn clo E4
7 V 6 Acorn clo Enf
24 C 2 Acorn Clo Stanm
123 T 1 Acorn gdns SE19
61 Z 15 Acorn gdns W3
99 U 14 Acorn rd Drtfrd
75 W 2 Acorn wlk SE16
90 C 11 Acre la SW2
155 R 8 Acre la Wallgtn
40 A 18 Acre pth Nthlt
56 H 20 Acre rd Dgnhm
102 K 20 Acre rd Kingst
106 G 14 Acre rd SW19
88 D 14 Acris st SW18
61 Z 6 Acton la NW10
173 W 4 Acton la W3
73 W 5 Acton la W3
73 W 12 Acton la W4
134 M 3 Acton ms E8
134 M 4 Acton ms E8
133 O 13 Acton st WC1
105 Z 3 Acuba rd SW18
64 J 17 Ada gdns E14
65 P 4 Ada gdns E15
135 V 7 Ada pl E2
150 H 20 Ada rd SE5
42 F 9 Ada rd Wemb
135 V 5 Ada st E8
128 M 18 Adair rd W10
140 B 4 Adam & Eve ct W1
145 V 1 Adam & Eve ms W8
146 C 5 Adam ct SW7
140 L 10 Adam st WC2
144 E 18 Adam wlk SW6
160 H 5 Adam's ct EC2
43 U 6 Adams clo NW9
75 P 5 Adams gdns SE16
48 D 16 Adams pl N7
124 H 11 Adams rd Becknhm
31 R 7 Adams rd N17
139 V 10 Adams row W1
97 Y 9 Adams sq Bxly Hth
65 T 18 Adamson rd E16
46 G 19 Adamson rd NW3
8 B 19 Adamsrill Clo Enf
110 H 9 Adamsrill rd SE26
108 B 5 Adare wlk SW16
113 X 9 Adderley gdns SE9
89 O 13 Adderley gro SW11
23 V 5 Adderley rd Harrow
64 F 18 Adderley st E14
15 S 20 Addington dri N12
110 G 10 Addington gro SE26
158 K 12 Addington pal Croy
158 L 14 Addington pk Croy
159 W 7 Addington rd W Wkhm
122 G 19 Addington rd Croy
65 N 13 Addington rd E16
64 A 8 Addington rd E3
30 E 20 Addington rd N4
158 E 20 Addington rd S Croy
150 D 16 Addington sq SE5
141 P 18 Addington st SE1
158 M 13 Addington Village rd Croy
159 P 11 Addington Village rd Croy
9 S 6 Addis clo Enf
123 W 18 Addiscombe av Croy
24 D 15 Addiscombe clo Harrow
157 T 2 Addiscombe ct Croy
157 R 4 Addiscombe gro Croy
158 A 2 Addiscombe rd Croy
157 U 3 Addiscombe rd Croy
82 M 3 Addison av Hounsl
6 F 18 Addison av N14
136 K 15 Addison av W11
145 N 4 Addison Bridge pl W14
144 M 1 Addison cres W14
136 M 20 Addison cres W14
117 N 9 Addison gdns Surb
144 F 1 Addison gdns W14
136 G 20 Addison gdns W14
74 B 9 Addison gro W4
123 X 9 Addison pl SE25
136 J 15 Addison pl W11
126 M 10 Addison rd Brom
127 N 10 Addison rd Brom
34 F 19 Addison rd E11
33 T 15 Addison rd E17
9 R 6 Addison rd Enf
36 C 5 Addison rd Ilf

123 Y 9 Addison rd SE25
102 A 15 Addison rd Tedd
136 M 18 Addison rd W14
145 O 2 Addison way NW11
27 X 13 Addison way NW11
158 K 2 Addisons clo Croy
141 Y 7 Addle hill EC4
160 C 3 Addle st EC2
118 K 9 Adela av New Mald
128 K 17 Adela st W10
92 M 11 Adelaide av SE4
93 N 11 Adelaide av SE4
8 F 4 Adelaide clo Enf
10 K 13 Adelaide clo Stanm
71 V 4 Adelaide cotts W7
37 Y 15 Adelaide gdns Rom
74 H 3 Adelaide gro W12
114 A 14 Adelaide rd Chisl
51 T 9 Adelaide rd E10
82 A 2 Adelaide rd Hounsl
54 A 6 Adelaide rd Ilf
130 H 1 Adelaide rd NW3
46 M 20 Adelaide rd NW3
47 N 20 Adelaide rd NW3
85 N 11 Adelaide rd Rich
170 B 10 Adelaide rd S'hall
116 J 13 Adelaide rd Surb
101 X 15 Adelaide rd Tedd
71 Z 4 Adelaide rd W13
140 J 11 Adelaide st WC2
63 O 14 Adelina gro E1
135 Z 20 Adelina gro E1
140 G 3 Adeline pl WC1
57 W 6 Adelphi cres Hornch
140 L 11 Adelphi ter WC2
49 O 13 Aden gro N16
9 V 15 Aden rd Enf
54 A 2 Aden rd Ilf
49 N 12 Aden ter N16
144 H 15 Adeney clo W6
93 O 19 Adenmore rd SE6
144 A 3 Adie rd W6
74 L 9 Adie rd W6
65 U 12 Adine rd E13
143 S 4 Adler st E1
50 J 14 Adley st E5
79 P 18 Admaston rd SE18
128 H 18 Admiral ms W10
95 T 9 Admiral Seymour rd SE9
93 O 3 Admiral st SE4
76 B 4 Admirals way E14
46 D 16 Admirals wlk NW3
101 V 16 Admiralty rd Tedd
57 V 17 Adnams wlk Rainhm
111 P 10 Adolf st SE6
48 J 5 Adolphus rd N4
75 Z 19 Adolphus st SE8
55 X 11 Adomar rd Dgnhm
130 G 20 Adpar st W2
58 E 10 Adrienne av S'hall
91 W 9 Adys rd SE15
26 D 9 Aerodrome rd NW4
26 B 8 Aeroville NW9
133 O 10 Affleck st N1
88 J 6 Afghan rd SW11
45 W 14 Agamemnon rd NW6
132 D 1 Agar gro NW1
47 Y 20 Agar gro NW1
140 K 10 Agar st WC2
66 C 18 Agate clo E16
144 A 3 Agate rd W6
74 L 8 Agate rd W6
75 O 2 Agatha clo E1
114 C 4 Agaton rd SE9
44 M 12 Agave rd NW2
133 W 15 Agdon st EC1
46 L 13 Agincourt rd NW3
53 X 11 Agnes av Ilf
66 K 19 Agnes clo E6
55 X 11 Agnes gdns Dgnhm
74 C 4 Agnes rd W3
63 Y 16 Agnes st E14
92 G 18 Agnew rd SE23
8 H 16 Agricola pl Enf
55 Y 11 Aidan clo Dgnhm
65 P 1 Aileen wlk E15
84 A 13 Ailsa av Twick
83 Z 13 Ailsa av Twick
84 B 13 Ailsa rd Twick
64 G 14 Ailsa st E14
131 P 2 Ainger rd NW3
22 H 10 Ainsdale cres Pinn
60 H 13 Ainsdale rd W5
38 J 19 Ainsley av Rom
63 N 9 Ainsley st E2
135 X 14 Ainsley st E2
89 R 19 Ainslie wk SW12
20 C 17 Ainslie Wood cres E4

20 D 15 Ainslie Wood gdns E4
20 C 17 Ainslie Wood rd E4
75 R 5 Ainsty st SE16
44 G 9 Ainsworth clo NW2
156 K 1 Ainsworth rd Croy
63 P 1 Ainsworth rd E9
130 A 4 Ainsworth way NW8
66 C 5 Aintree av E6
36 B 7 Aintree cres Ilf
60 B 5 Aintree rd Grnfd
144 L 18 Aintree st SW6
140 D 10 Air st W1
133 N 2 Airdrie clo N1
74 D 12 Airedale av W2
88 M 20 Airedale rd SW12
89 N 19 Airedale rd SW12
72 F 8 Airedale rd W5
57 Z 20 Airfield way Hornch
53 Z 5 Airlie gdns Ilf
137 S 15 Airlie gdns W8
55 P 5 Airthrie rd Ilf
68 F 20 Aisher rd SE28
94 A 12 Aislibie rd SE12
135 R 5 Aitken clo E8
111 R 4 Aitken rd SE6
26 A 10 Ajax av NW9
45 W 14 Ajax rd NW6
86 G 17 Akehurst st SW15
46 F 15 Akenside rd NW3
116 E 15 Akerman rd Surb
79 T 18 Alabama st SE18
72 F 7 Alacross rd W5
4 D 19 Alan dri Barnt
56 D 1 Alan gdns Rom
105 T 12 Alan rd SW19
94 D 15 Alanthus clo SE12
141 T 16 Alaska st SE1
58 A 12 Alba clo Hay
27 T 18 Alba gdns NW11
137 N 4 Alba pl W11
93 R 15 Albacore cres SE13
10 D 1 Albany clo Bushey
97 U 19 Albany clo Bxly
30 K 14 Albany clo N15
85 U 11 Albany clo SW14
140 B 11 Albany courtyard W1
25 R 2 Albany cres Edg
25 Z 4 Albany ct NW9
9 R 5 Albany Park rd Enf
9 T 4 Albany Park rd Enf
102 H 16 Albany Park rd Kingst
84 L 14 Albany pass Rich
9 U 2 Albany pk Enf
72 H 17 Albany pl Brentf
48 F 13 Albany pl N7
81 P 15 Albany rd Blvdr
72 H 17 Albany rd Brentf
97 U 19 Albany rd Bxly
113 Z 13 Albany rd Chisl
33 O 20 Albany rd E10
53 O 13 Albany rd E12
32 J 18 Albany rd E17
9 S 2 Albany rd Enf
57 W 6 Albany rd Hornch
19 O 17 Albany rd N18
30 E 20 Albany rd N4
117 Y 8 Albany rd New Mald
84 L 12 Albany rd Rich
38 B 18 Albany rd Rom
150 M 10 Albany rd SE1
150 C 15 Albany rd SE17
150 H 13 Albany rd SE5
105 Z 12 Albany rd SW19
60 B 19 Albany rd W13
131 X 8 Albany st NW1
21 P 13 Albany the Wdfd Grn
21 U 4 Albany view Buck Hl
79 T 18 Albatross st SE18
75 S 6 Albatross way SE16
36 A 19 Albemarle appr Ilf
100 E 2 Albemarle av Twick
117 Y 10 Albemarle gdns New Mald
36 A 19 Albemarle gdns Ilf
35 Z 19 Albemarle gdns Ilf
11 R 17 Albemarle pk Stanm
125 X 1 Albemarle rd Becknhm
15 X 2 Albemarle rd Barnt
140 A 12 Albemarle st W1
27 V 14 Alberon gdns NW11
20 B 14 Albert av E4
146 M 16 Albert br SW11
88 L 1 Albert Bridge rd SW11
146 M 18 Albert Bridge rd SW11
147 N 20 Albert Bridge rd SW11

108 A 13 Albert Carr gdns SW16
107 Z 13 Albert Carr gdns SW16
29 X 3 Albert clo N22
20 A 13 Albert cres E4
105 T 2 Albert dri SW19
148 M 8 Albert emb SE1
141 N 17 Albert emb SE1
139 R 17 Albert ga SW1
63 S 18 Albert gdns E1
105 P 20 Albert gro SW20
138 F 19 Albert Hall mans SW7
146 A 1 Albert ms W8
31 U 9 Albert pl N17
27 Y 4 Albert pl N3
137 Z 20 Albert pl W8
5 T 14 Albert rd Barnt
81 P 13 Albert rd Blvdr
127 P 12 Albert rd Brom
98 F 18 Albert rd Bxly
56 D 4 Albert rd Dgnhm
51 U 6 Albert rd E10
78 E 4 Albert rd E16
33 O 16 Albert rd E17
34 J 9 Albert rd E18
101 O 12 Albert rd Hampt
23 N 11 Albert rd Harrow
82 H 11 Albert rd Hounsl
54 C 9 Albert rd Ilf
120 M 6 Albert rd Mitch
31 R 18 Albert rd N15
29 V 5 Albert rd N22
48 D 3 Albert rd N4
118 E 10 Albert rd New Mald
27 P 13 Albert rd NW4
129 R 9 Albert rd NW6
13 S 16 Albert rd NW7
84 L 13 Albert rd Rich
39 T 17 Albert rd Rom
110 E 16 Albert rd SE20
124 B 11 Albert rd SE25
123 Z 8 Albert rd SE25
113 R 6 Albert rd SE9
154 F 12 Albert rd Sutton
101 X 15 Albert rd Tedd
101 V 1 Albert rd Twick
83 V 20 Albert rd Twick
60 C 13 Albert rd W5
81 P 14 Albert Road est Blvdr
52 A 16 Albert sq E15
90 C 1 Albert sq SW8
149 N 20 Albert sq SW8
15 P 15 Albert st N12
131 Z 8 Albert st NW1
131 S 5 Albert ter NW1
61 X 4 Albert ter NW10
131 S 4 Albert Terrace ms NW1
153 U 9 Alberta av Sutton
8 J 19 Alberta rd Enf
98 J 2 Alberta rd Erith
149 X 9 Alberta st SE17
29 O 4 Albion av N10
89 W 4 Albion av SW8
39 O 18 Albion clo Rom
138 L 8 Albion clo W2
135 O 2 Albion dri E8
56 F 14 Albion gdns Dgnhm
74 H 10 Albion gdns W6
49 R 11 Albion gro N16
133 T 2 Albion ms N1
45 V 20 Albion ms NW6
138 L 7 Albion ms W2
133 X 19 Albion pl EC1
160 F 2 Albion pl EC2
123 W 7 Albion pl SE25
98 D 11 Albion rd Bxly Hth
33 U 9 Albion rd E17
82 G 12 Albion rd Hounsl
117 V 1 Albion rd Kingst
49 P 10 Albion rd N16
31 W 7 Albion rd N17
154 E 15 Albion rd Sutton
101 T 2 Albion rd Twick
135 O 1 Albion sq E8
122 H 20 Albion st Croy
75 P 7 Albion st SE16
138 L 8 Albion st W2
135 N 1 Albion ter E8
110 C 6 Albion Vlls rd SE26
93 V 9 Albion way SE13
43 R 10 Albion way Wemb
91 S 8 Albrighton rd SE22
7 U 5 Albuhera clo Enf
97 Y 4 Albury av Bxly Hth
71 W 20 Albury av Islwth
156 L 8 Albury ct CR0

22 A 1 Albury dri Pinn
76 A 17 Albury st SE8
127 V 7 Albyfield Brom
93 P 4 Albyn rd SE8
50 A 6 Alcester cres E5
155 S 9 Alcester rd Wallgtn
155 Y 16 Alcock clo Wallgtn
49 X 8 Alconbury rd E5
153 X 1 Alcorn clo Sutton
59 V 15 Alcott clo W7
56 K 18 Aldborough rd Dgnhm
54 H 1 Aldborough rd Ilf
36 K 15 Aldborough Road north Ilf
54 G 5 Aldborough Road south Ilf
36 K 17 Aldborough Road south Ilf
74 F 3 Aldbourne rd W12
150 J 9 Aldbridge st SE17
43 S 20 Aldbury av Wemb
18 B 3 Aldbury ms N9
148 M 20 Aldebert ter SW8
149 N 20 Aldebert ter SW8
21 T 13 Aldeburgh pl Wdfd Grn
77 T 12 Aldeburgh st SE10
65 N 11 Alden av E15
132 D 10 Aldenham st NW1
74 K 9 Aldensley rd W6
151 O 16 Alder clo SE15
44 H 8 Alder gro NW2
114 J 8 Alder rd Sidcp
85 X 7 Alder rd SW14
89 R 18 Alderbrook rd SW12
74 G 17 Alderbury rd SW13
68 B 8 Alderman av Bark
160 C 4 Aldermanbury EC2
160 C 3 Aldermanbury sq EC2
17 O 13 Aldermans hill N13
136 F 6 Aldermans st W10
142 J 3 Aldermans wlk EC2
112 F 20 Aldermary rd Brom
151 S 9 Alderminster rd SE1
110 M 6 Aldermoor rd SE6
70 K 20 Alderney av Hounsl
40 D 20 Alderney gdns Nthlt
63 T 11 Alderney rd E1
148 A 10 Alderney rd SW1
147 X 8 Alderney rd SW1
20 M 19 Alders av Wdfd Grn
52 G 6 Alders clo E11
12 H 16 Alders clo Edg
12 H 16 Alders rd Edg
100 C 11 Alders the Felt
70 E 15 Alders the Hounsl
17 U 1 Alders the N21
159 R 1 Alders the W Wkhm
8 E 8 Aldersbrook av Enf
102 M 15 Aldersbrook dri Kingst
53 U 10 Aldersbrook la E12
52 H 6 Aldersbrook rd E11
53 O 9 Aldersbrook rd E12
54 F 18 Aldersey gdns Bark
92 F 12 Aldersford clo SE4
142 A 1 Aldersgate st EC1
160 A 1 Aldersgate st EC1
112 M 7 Aldersgrove av SE9
113 N 6 Aldersgrove av SE9
129 R 3 Aldershot rd NW6
124 G 14 Aldersmead av Croy
110 H 18 Aldersmead rd Becknhm
128 L 16 Alderson st W10
43 Z 8 Alderton clo NW10
26 J 17 Alderton cres NW4
123 V 16 Alderton rd Croy
90 L 9 Alderton rd SE24
87 W 5 Alderville rd SW6
83 P 6 Alderwick dri Hounsl
96 F 15 Alderwood rd SE9
139 T 12 Aldford st W1
142 M 6 Aldgate EC3
143 O 5 Aldgate High st E1
136 E 16 Aldine st W12
57 X 15 Aldingham gdns Hornch
55 U 3 Aldington clo Dgnhm
78 A 9 Aldington rd SE18
106 H 13 Aldis st SW17
45 X 15 Aldred rd NW6
106 D 7 Aldren rd SW17
159 U 19 Aldrich cres Croy
106 E 3 Aldrich ter SW18
20 F 19 Aldriche way E4
12 F 9 Aldridge av Edg
9 Z 2 Aldridge av Enf

24 K 6 Aldridge av Stanm
137 R 3 Aldridge rd vlls W11
118 A 16 Aldridge ri New Mald
16 M 3 Aldridge wlk N14
107 V 11 Aldrington rd SW16
129 X 19 Aldsworth clo W9
114 D 6 Aldwick clo SE9
156 C 7 Aldwick rd Croy
93 T 16 Aldworth gro SE13
51 Z 20 Aldworth rd E15
36 C 14 Aldwych av Ilf
57 X 5 Aldwych clo Hornch
141 O 7 Aldwych WC2
97 X 13 Alers rd Bxly Hth
66 B 17 Alestan Beck rd E16
128 A 2 Alexander av NW10
62 K 1 Alexander av NW10
5 U 14 Alexander clo Barnt
126 F 20 Alexander clo Brom
96 H 15 Alexander clo Sidcp
101 U 4 Alexander clo Twick
6 G 16 Alexander ct N14
137 W 4 Alexander ms W2
146 J 4 Alexander pl SW7
97 W 4 Alexander rd Bxly Hth
114 A 14 Alexander rd Chisl
48 A 8 Alexander rd N7
146 J 4 Alexander sq SW7
137 W 4 Alexander st W2
40 F 4 Alexandra av Harrow
29 Y 6 Alexandra av N22
70 D 1 Alexandra av S'hall
153 X 6 Alexandra av SW11
89 O 2 Alexandra av Sutton
73 Z 20 Alexandra av W4
40 J 11 Alexandra clo Harrow
92 M 3 Alexandra cotts SE14
112 B 14 Alexandra cres Brom
112 C 14 Alexandra cres Brom
109 R 13 Alexandra dri SE19
117 R 16 Alexandra dri Surb
82 K 5 Alexandra gdns Hounsl
155 N 18 Alexandra gdns Carsh
29 T 12 Alexandra gdns N10
15 O 18 Alexandra gro N12
48 K 5 Alexandra gro N4
29 W 9 Alexandra palace N22
40 J 11 Alexandra park Harrow
29 Z 9 Alexandra park N22
29 S 7 Alexandra Park rd N22
123 R 19 Alexandra pl Croy
130 C 3 Alexandra pl NW8
130 C 3 Alexandra pl NW8
123 P 11 Alexandra pl SE25
72 G 17 Alexandra rd Brentf
123 R 19 Alexandra rd Croy
51 U 10 Alexandra rd E10
32 L 20 Alexandra rd E17
34 G 11 Alexandra rd E18
66 J 9 Alexandra rd E6
9 T 15 Alexandra rd Enf
82 K 7 Alexandra rd Hounsl
103 P 18 Alexandra rd Kingst
106 K 19 Alexandra rd Mitch
29 S 3 Alexandra rd N10
16 E 20 Alexandra rd N11
31 O 15 Alexandra rd N15
30 F 9 Alexandra rd N8
27 P 13 Alexandra rd NW4
130 D 3 Alexandra rd NW8
85 N 5 Alexandra rd Rich
39 S 18 Alexandra rd Rom
37 X 18 Alexandra rd Rom
110 E 15 Alexandra rd SE26
85 Z 8 Alexandra rd SW14
105 W 14 Alexandra rd SW19
84 F 17 Alexandra rd Twick
73 Z 6 Alexandra rd Twick
119 Y 13 Alexandra sq Mrdn
65 R 14 Alexandra st E16
75 W 18 Alexandra st SE14
60 A 20 Alexandria rd W13
151 T 5 Alexis st SE16
50 B 11 Alfearn rd E5
159 W 15 Alford gro Croy
134 C 10 Alford pl N1
81 Z 13 Alford rd Erith
89 Y 3 Alford rd SW8
30 H 13 Alfoxton av N15
70 C 1 Alfred gdns S'hall
58 C 20 Alfred gdns S'hall
132 E 20 Alfred ms W1
140 E 1 Alfred pl W1
81 P 14 Alfred rd Belvdr
52 C 15 Alfred rd E15
116 L 7 Alfred rd Kingst

123 Y 10 Alfred rd SE25	130 K 8 Allitsen rd NW8	31 O 11 Alton rd N17	128 A 5 Amery gdns NW10
154 E 12 Alfred rd Sutton	89 W 12 Allnutt way SW4	84 L 11 Alton rd Rich	62 L 3 Amery gdns NW10
71 Y 1 Alfred rd W13	55 O 6 Alloa rd Ilf	104 G 1 Alton rd SW15	41 Y 7 Amery rd Harrow
137 U 1 Alfred rd W2	75 U 13 Alloa rd SE8	86 H 19 Alton rd SW15	119 N 19 Ames clo Worc Pk
73 W 3 Alfred rd W3	42 E 5 Allonby gdns Wemb	64 C 16 Alton st E14	108 B 4 Amesbury av SW2
63 Z 8 Alfred st E3	63 W 9 Alloway rd E3	124 K 13 Altyre clo Becknhm	20 D 1 Amesbury dri E4
89 R 2 Alfreda st SW11	131 R 18 Allsop pl NW1	157 P 4 Altyre rd Croy	68 J 1 Amesbury rd
67 W 5 Alfreds gdns Bark	15 P 6 Allum way N20	124 L 12 Altyre way Becknhm	Dgnhm
67 W 5 Alfreds way Bark	110 G 10 Allwood clo SE26	46 B 15 Alvanley gdns NW6	127 O 5 Amesbury rd Brom
105 O 7 Alfreton clo SW19	33 U 1 Alma av E4	123 S 11 Alverston gdns SE25	51 X 13 Amethyst rd E15
122 A 16 Alfriston av Croy	153 T 10 Alma cres Sutton	15 V 2 Alverstone av Barnt	60 C 17 Amherst av W13
22 H 20 Alfriston av Harrow	151 P 6 Alma gro SE1	105 X 5 Alverstone av SW19	60 D 17 Amherst rd W13
116 L 13 Alfriston rd Surb	62 K 9 Alma pl NW10	96 A 20 Alverstone gdns SE9	83 Y 4 Amherst gdns Islwth
89 N 13 Alfriston rd SW11	109 T 17 Alma pl SE19	118 E 8 Alverstone rd	49 W 13 Amhurst pas E8
83 Y 9 Algar clo Islwth	122 G 12 Alma pl Thntn Hth	New Mald	31 R 20 Amhurst pk N16
10 J 17 Algar clo Stanm	154 K 10 Alma rd Carsh	53 W 14 Alverstone rd E12	50 A 16 Amhurst rd E8
83 Y 8 Algar rd Islwth	9 U 12 Alma rd Enf	44 M 20 Alverstone rd NW2	49 Z 15 Amhurst rd E8
106 B 1 Algarve rd SW18	29 R 3 Alma rd N10	43 N 3 Alverstone rd Wemb	49 U 11 Amhurst rd N16
26 G 19 Algernon rd NW4	58 A 20 Alma rd S'hall	75 X 15 Alverton st SE8	49 W 12 Amhurst ter E8
129 S 5 Algernon rd NW6	115 O 6 Alma rd Sidcp	24 B 11 Alveston av Harrow	55 P 13 Amidas gdns Dgnhm
93 R 8 Algernon rd SE13	88 C 12 Alma rd SW18	150 J 9 Alvey st SE17	63 P 11 Amiel st E1
93 P 11 Algiers rd SE13	23 S 3 Alma row Har	154 D 8 Alvia gdns SM1	88 L 8 Amies st SW11
150 J 2 Alice st SE1	130 D 11 Alma sq NW8	49 U 15 Alvington cres E8	118 L 2 Amity gro SW20
24 C 14 Alicia av Harrow	51 X 16 Alma st E15	94 J 17 Alwald cres SE12	65 O 2 Amity rd E15
24 D 14 Alicia clo Harrow	47 T 17 Alma st NW5	73 X 14 Alwyn av W4	89 O 15 Amner rd SW11
24 D 13 Alicia gdns Harrow	88 G 18 Alma ter SW18	159 S 17 Alwyn clo Croy	144 A 2 Amor rd W6
142 R 6 Alington rd E5	50 C 12 Almack rd E5	61 T 17 Alwyne gdns W3	74 I 0 Amroth rd W6
43 V 3 Alington cres NW9	133 W 3 Almeida st N1	48 K 19 Alwyne la N1	91 W 8 Amott rd SE15
155 W 20 Alington gro Wallgtn	104 G 17 Almer rd SW20	48 K 19 Alwyne pl N1	48 C 19 Amour clo N7
66 K 18 Alison clo E6	88 K 12 Almeric rd SW11	48 K 20 Alwyne rd N1	64 A 19 Amoy pl E14
88 J 11 Aliwal rd SW11	48 B 4 Almington st N4	105 V 14 Alwyne rd SW19	80 F 5 Ampleforth rd SE2
74 A 13 Alkerden rd W4	154 L 3 Almond av Carsh	71 S 1 Alwyne rd W7	133 N 13 Ampton pl WC1
49 V 7 Alkham rd N16	72 J 8 Almond av W5	48 L 18 Alwyne sq N1	133 N 14 Ampton st WC1
31 S 4 All Hallows rd N17	72 L 6 Almond av W5	48 K 20 Alwyne vlls N1	110 A 1 Amroth clo SE23
18 H 9 All Saints clo N9	127 W 17 Almond clo Brom	27 X 18 Alyth gdns NW11	76 H 8 Amsterdam rd E14
10 F 19 All Saints ms Stanm	72 A 19 Almond gro Brentf	72 A 17 Amalgamated dri	8 B 17 Amwell clo Enf
154 B 5 All Saints rd Sutton	31 X 2 Almond rd N17	Brentf	133 S 12 Amwell st EC1
106 D 16 All Saints rd SW19	151 X 6 Almond rd SE16	143 V 6 Amazon st E1	84 A 18 Amyand la Twick
137 O 3 All Saints rd W11	127 W 17 Almond way Brom	82 B 5 Ambassador clo	84 A 18 Amyand Park gdns
73 V 7 All Saints rd W3	22 L 8 Almond way Harrow	Hounsl	Twick
132 M 7 All Saints st N1	121 Y 10 Almond way Mitch	140 B 16 Ambassadors ct SW1	84 B 17 Amyand Park rd Twick
133 N 7 All Saints st N1	21 T 9 Almonds av Buck Hl	32 H 4 Amber av E17	83 Z 19 Amyand Park rd Twick
128 A 4 All Souls av NW10	82 A 2 Almorah rd Hounsl	51 X 19 Amber st E15	93 N 13 Amyruth rd SE4
62 J 6 All Souls av NW10	134 F 1 Almorah st N1	27 Z 10 Amberden av N3	89 N 3 Analy st SW11
139 Z 2 All Souls pl W1	66 A 18 Alnwick av E16	149 X 10 Ambergate st SE17	47 U 7 Anatola rd N19
117 Y 12 Allan clo New Mald	120 A 9 Alnwick gro Mrdn	22 D 11 Amberley clo Pinn	118 F 15 Ancaster cres
61 W 13 Allan way W3	65 Y 18 Alnwick rd E16	115 U 13 Amberley ct Sidcp	New Mald
27 I 10 Allandale av N3	94 H 17 Alnwick rd SE12	152 C 9 Amberley gdns	124 F 7 Ancaster rd Becknhm
57 U 1 Allandale rd Hornch	60 F 7 Alperton la Wemb	Epsom	79 V 19 Ancaster st SE18
10 A 7 Allard cres Bushey	129 N 16 Alperton st W10	18 F 4 Amberley gdns Enf	77 X 11 Anchor & Hope la
90 C 10 Allardyce st SW9	130 L 15 Alpha clo NW1	123 U 18 Amberley gro Croy	SE7
101 T 11 Allbrook clo Tedd	76 B6 Alpha gro E14	109 Z 11 Amberley gro SE26	151 W 6 Anchor st SE16
47 P 16 Allcroft rd NW5	129 U 8 Alpha pl NW6	21 Z 5 Amberley rd Buck Hl	105 Z 13 Anchorage clo SW19
148 J 20 Allen Edwards dri	146 M 13 Alpha pl SW3	33 P 20 Amberley rd E10	144 J 15 Ancill clo W6
SW8	123 R 20 Alpha rd Croy	18 F 1 Amberley rd Enf	62 G 6 Ancona rd NW10
89 Z 1 Allen Edwards dri	20 C 11 Alpha rd E4	17 P 9 Amberley rd N13	79 T 12 Ancona rd SE18
SW8	9 W 15 Alpha rd Enf	80 J 16 Amberley rd SE2	90 A 8 Andalus rd SW9
124 E 4 Allen rd Becknhm	18 J 18 Alpha rd N18	129 W 19 Amberley rd W9	42 G 13 Ander clo Wemb
122 E 19 Allen rd Croy	92 M 1 Alpha rd SE14	119 W 17 Amberley way Mrdn	82 K 11 Anderson pl Hounsl
63 X 5 Allen rd E3	116 M 16 Alpha rd Surb	38 H 12 Amberley way Rom	50 F 17 Anderson rd E9
49 R 12 Allen rd N16	101 P 2 Alpha rd Tedd	118 B 15 Amberwood ri	35 O 9 Anderson rd Ilf
145 U 1 Allen st W8	91 X 5 Alpha rd W5	New Mald	147 N 8 Anderson st SW3
156 M 20 Allenby av S Croy	157 S 7 Alpine clo Croy	112 J 7 Amblecote clo SE12	81 V 5 Anderson way Blvdr
58 J 10 Allenby clo Grnfd	127 V 4 Alpine copse Brom	112 J 7 Amblecote rd SE12	91 P 8 Anderton clo SE5
58 H 10 Allenby rd S'hall	75 S 12 Alpine rd SE16	48 H 9 Ambler rd N4	58 L 10 Andover clo Grnfd
110 H 6 Allenby rd SE23	66 K 14 Alpine way E6	124 J 12 Ambleside av	129 X 9 Andover pl NW6
58 G 17 Allendale av S'hall	10 G 8 Alpine wlk Stanm	Becknhm	101 R 2 Andover rd Twick
110 F 12 Allendale clo SE26	61 Z 1 Alric av NW10	57 Y 15 Ambleside av Hornch	49 Y 14 Andre st E8
42 A 17 Allendale rd Grnfd	43 Z 20 Alrick av NW10	107 X 10 Ambleside av SW16	98 M 14 Andrew clo Bxly
9 R 18 Allens rd Enf	30 G 20 Alroy rd N4	111 Y 15 Ambleside Brom	89 Y 1 Andrew pl SW8
95 S 6 Allenswood rd SE9	150 H 10 Alsace rd SE17	50 D 14 Ambleside clo E9	64 G 17 Andrew st E14
22 L 14 Allerford ct Harrow	151 O 5 Alscot rd SE1	9 T 11 Ambleside cres Enf	66 D 17 Andrewes clo E6
111 S 10 Allerford rd SE6	80 H 9 Alsike rd Belvdr	154 D 14 Ambleside gdns	21 Y 7 Andrews clo Buck Hl
48 M 6 Allerton rd N16	152 F 8 Alsom av Worc Pk	Sutton	153 N 2 Andrews clo Worc Pk
49 N 6 Allerton rd N16	116 B 17 Alston clo Surb	42 F 3 Ambleside gdns	135 X 6 Andrews rd E8
144 K 19 Allestree rd SW6	4 E 10 Alston rd Barnt	Wemb	80 D 6 Andwell clo SE2
109 P 5 Alleyn cres SE21	18 M 18 Alston rd N18	35 S 14 Ambleside gdns Ilf	109 V 18 Anerley gro SE19
70 F 13 Alleyn pk S'hall	106 F 11 Alston rd SW17	98 D 4 Ambleside rd	109 W 17 Anerley hill SE19
109 P 3 Alleyn pk SE21	105 U 17 Alt gro SW19	Bxly Hth	109 Y 17 Anerley Park rd
109 P 7 Alleyn rd SE21	18 H 20 Altair clo N17	62 D 1 Ambleside rd NW10	SE20
55 T 7 Alleyndale rd Dgnhm	113 U 5 Altash way SE9	155 Y 20 Ambrey way Wallgtn	110 A 17 Anerley pk SE20
88 B 17 Allfarthing la SW18	72 B 7 Altenburg av W13	81 S 9 Ambrooke rd Belvdr	109 Y 18 Anerley pk SE20
119 O 15 Allgood clo Mrdn	88 L 10 Altenburgh gdns	148 B 3 Ambrosden av SW1	124 A 1 Anerley rd SE20
135 P 10 Allgood st E2	SW11	27 U 20 Ambrose av NW11	109 Y 20 Anerley rd SE20
66 C 16 Allhallows rd E6	22 B 3 Altham rd Pinn	66 F 16 Ambrose clo E6	109 Z 20 Anerley Station rd
65 X 13 Alliance rd E13	88 B 6 Althea st SW6	151 V 6 Ambrose st SE16	SE20
80 A 19 Alliance rd SE18	117 N 7 Altheston rd Kingst	150 A 8 Amelia st SE17	109 V 17 Anerley vale SE19
79 Z 17 Alliance rd SE18	34 B 13 Althorne gdns E18	149 Z 8 Amelia st SE17	89 V 19 Anfield clo SW12
61 S 12 Alliance rd W3	56 D 6 Althorne way Dgnhm	141 Y 5 Amen corner EC4	143 P 3 Angel all E1
59 W 20 Allingham clo W7	106 K 1 Althorp rd SW17	107 N 14 Amen corner SW17	18 H 15 Angel clo N18
134 A 7 Allingham st N1	23 O 16 Althorp rd Harrow	141 Y 5 Amen ct EC4	160 A 4 Angel ct EC1
105 P 13 Allington clo SW19	66 G 4 Altmore av E6	143 N 8 America sq EC3	160 F 5 Angel ct EC2
22 M 15 Allington rd Harrow	53 T 20 Altmore av E6	142 A 15 America st SE1	140 C 14 Angel ct SW1
26 K 18 Allington rd NW4	23 W 2 Alton av Stanm	87 W 15 Amerland rd SW18	154 B 4 Angel Hill dri Sutton
128 K 10 Allington rd W10	115 Z 3 Alton clo Bxly	75 X 18 Amersham gro SE14	154 A 5 Angel hill Sutton
147 Z 2 Allington st SW1	83 X 3 Alton clo Islwth	123 N 13 Amersham rd Croy	51 X 18 Angel la E15
93 V 2 Allison clo SE10	111 N 19 Alton gdns Becknhm	23 S 18 Amersham rd Harrow	133 T 9 Angel ms N1
109 S 1 Allison gro SE21	83 R 17 Alton gdns Twick	18 B 18 Amersham rd N18	90 G 7 Angel Park gdns SW9
30 H 15 Allison rd N8	156 F 7 Alton rd Croy	92 L 1 Amersham rd SE14	160 E 10 Angel pass EC4
61 W 19 Allison rd W3		75 Y 19 Amersham vale SE14	18 J 15 Angel pl N18

9 O 14	Angel rd Enf
23 U 18	Angel rd Harrow
19 O 17	Angel rd N18
142 A 4	Angel st EC1
141 Z 4	Angel st EC1
39 O 15	Angel way Rom
144 B 8	Angel wlk W6
74 L 12	Angel wlk W6
82 K 12	Angelfield Hounsl
190 G 6	Angell rd SW9
94 D 1	Angerstein la SE3
55 U 4	Angle green Dgnhm
102 C 10	Anglers clo Rich
47 T 17	Anglers la NW5
108 B 9	Angles rd SW16
78 M 12	Anglesea av SE18
116 G 9	Anglesea rd Kingst
78 L 12	Anglesea rd SE18
135 U 18	Anglesea st E1
155 O 15	Anglesey Ct rd Carsh
155 O 15	Anglesey gdns Carsh
9 O 13	Anglesey rd Enf
22 G 10	Anglesmede cres Pinn
22 F 10	Anglesmede way Pinn
66 H 4	Anglia wk E6
63 Y 6	Anglo rd E3
25 Z 5	Angus gdns NW9
65 Y 10	Angus rd E13
75 W 19	Angus st SE14
146 L 19	Anhalt rd SW11
78 L 20	Ankerdine cres SE18
95 Y 1	Ankerdine cres SE18
101 S 12	Anlaby rd Tedd
136 E 20	Anley rd W14
11 R 14	Anmer lodge Stanm
24 H 6	Anmersh gro Stanm
146 F 16	Ann la SW10
88 C 17	Ann's Park rd SW18
135 R 4	Anna clo E8
64 C 18	Annabel clo E14
39 O 4	Annan way Rom
157 Y 3	Annandale rd Croy
77 P 14	Annandale rd SE10
96 J 19	Annandale rd Sidcp
74 A 13	Annandale rd W4
102 K 12	Anne Boleyns wlk Kingst
153 R 16	Anne Boleyns wlk Sutton
65 S 11	Anne st E13
25 Z 10	Annesley av NW9
44 A 10	Annesley clo NW10
158 M 6	Annesley dri Croy
94 G 2	Annesley rd SE3
47 U 6	Annestey wlk N19
23 T 7	Annette clo Harrow
48 D 12	Annette rd N7
63 Z 4	Annie Besant clo E3
29 N 11	Annington rd N2
50 H 19	Annis rd E9
139 S 19	Anns clo SW1
143 O 2	Anns pl E1
123 N 7	Annsworthy av Thntn Hth
123 P 4	Annsworthy cres Thntn Hth
92 C 5	Ansdell rd SE15
137 Y 20	Ansdell st W8
137 Y 20	Ansdell ter W8
155 N 1	Ansell gro Carsh
106 K 7	Ansell rd SW17
157 U 4	Anselm clo Croy
22 E 3	Anselm rd Pinn
145 S 15	Anselm rd SW6
111 V 11	Ansford rd Brom
136 H 10	Ansleigh pl W11
38 F 7	Anson clo Rom
47 X 12	Anson rd N7
44 L 14	Anson rd NW2
45 P 14	Anson rd NW2
40 L 17	Anson ter Nthlt
65 U 16	Anstey rd E16
91 X 7	Anstey rd SE15
30 K 13	Anstey wlk N15
96 E 16	Anstridge rd SE9
78 E 8	Antelope rd SE18
13 P 14	Anthony clo NW7
59 S 7	Anthony rd Grnfd
123 X 15	Anthony rd SE25
97 O 2	Anthony rd Welling
143 X 5	Anthony st E1
63 W 8	Antill rd E3
31 W 13	Antill rd N15
63 S 17	Antill ter E1
153 W 6	Anton cres Sutton
49 Y 14	Anton st E8
46 L 17	Antrim gro NW3
46 L 18	Antrim rd NW3
153 W 13	Antrobus clo Sutton
73 V 10	Antrobus rd W4
21 U 19	Anworth clo Wdfd Grn
156 A 19	Apeldoorn dri SM6
111 S 20	Apex clo Becknhm
83 S 1	Aplin way Islwth
112 G 20	Apollo av Brom
57 X 6	Apollo clo Hornch
146 F 17	Apollo pl SW10
141 W 7	Apothecary st EC4
90 E 14	Appach rd SW2
8 E 12	Apple gro Enf
116 H 4	Apple mkt Kingst
140 D 12	Apple Tree yd SW1
20 E 19	Appleby clo E4
31 O 16	Appleby clo N15
101 P 5	Appleby clo Twick
65 R 18	Appleby rd E16
49 Y 20	Appleby rd E8
135 N 8	Appleby st E2
98 L 4	Appledore av Bxly Hth
126 D 11	Appledore clo Brom
25 O 4	Appledore clo Edg
106 L 3	Appledore clo SW17
114 J 8	Appledore cres Sidcp
128 M 18	Appleford rd W10
72 H 12	Applegarth Brentf
159 S 16	Applegarth Croy
36 L 13	Applegarth dri Ilf
80 F 1	Applegarth rd SE28
144 G 3	Applegarth rd W14
118 F 14	Appleton gdns New Mald
95 P 7	Appleton rd SE9
44 J 9	Applewood clo NW2
134 J 20	Appold st EC2
5 S 15	Approach rd Barnt
63 P 7	Approach rd E2
118 M 3	Approach rd SW20
9 N 8	Approach the Enf
27 O 15	Approach the NW4
61 Z 17	Approach the W3
27 N 13	Aprey gdns NW4
59 U 19	April clo W7
110 F 7	April glen SE23
49 V 13	April st E8
22 M 15	Apsley clo Harrow
32 K 14	Apsley rd E17
117 W 7	Apsley rd New Mald
123 Z 9	Apsley rd SE25
130 H 8	Aquila st NW8
141 T 14	Aquinas st SE1
86 C 10	Arabella dri SW15
20 H 2	Arabia clo E4
92 K 10	Arabin rd SE4
152 H 20	Aragon av Epsom
102 H 12	Aragon rd Kingst
119 P 16	Aragon rd Mrdn
11 S 14	Aran dri Stanm
37 O 19	Arandora cres Brom
63 V 7	Arbery rd E3
125 R 3	Arbor clo Becknhm
20 K 11	Arbor rd E4
9 T 12	Arbour rd Enf
63 R 17	Arbour sq E1
57 Y 14	Arbour way Hornch
95 S 7	Arbroath rd SE9
109 Y 8	Arbury ter SE26
98 A 15	Arbuthnot la Bxly
97 Z 16	Arbuthnot la Bxly
92 F 4	Arbuthnot rd SE14
134 M 2	Arbutus st E8
39 R 11	Arcade pl Rom
142 J 2	Arcade the EC2
27 X 6	Arcadia av N3
64 B 16	Arcadia st E14
97 Y 16	Arcadian av Bxly
97 Y 16	Arcadian clo Bxly
30 E 1	Arcadian gdns N22
97 Y 17	Arcadian rd Bxly
150 A 3	Arch st SE1
75 U 6	Archangel st SE16
149 O 2	Archbishops pk SE11
90 D 17	Archbishops pl SW2
91 V 11	Archdale rd SE22
145 P 13	Archer rd SE25
123 Z 8	Archer rd SE25
140 E 9	Archer st W1
23 W 9	Archery clo Harrow
138 M 7	Archery clo W2
95 U 12	Archery rd SE9
139 W 11	Archibald ms W1
47 X 12	Archibald rd N7
64 A 10	Archibald st E3
47 V 6	Archway clo N19
106 A 9	Archway clo SW19
47 V 6	Archway mall N19
29 O 18	Archway rd N6
47 U 3	Archway rd N6
86 B 7	Archway st SW13
49 U 14	Arcola st E8
47 R 15	Arctic st NW5
112 A 14	Arcus rd Brom
91 O 14	Ardbeg rd SE24
10 G 2	Arden clo Bushey
41 P 10	Arden clo Harrow
28 G 20	Arden Court gdns N2
68 H 1	Arden cres Dgnhm
55 W 20	Arden cres Dgnhm
27 V 9	Arden rd N3
122 E 5	Ardfern av SW16
111 Y 3	Ardfillan rd SE6
93 Y 19	Ardgowan rd SE6
111 Y 3	Ardgowan rd SE6
48 L 12	Ardilaun rd N5
119 X 19	Ardleigh gdns Sutton
32 L 5	Ardleigh rd E17
49 P 18	Ardleigh rd N1
32 M 5	Ardleigh ter E17
44 A 9	Ardley clo NW10
110 J 7	Ardlui rd SE23
108 L 4	Ardlui rd SE27
116 J 12	Ardmay gdns Surb
93 X 15	Ardmere rd SE13
21 W 4	Ardmore la Buck Hl
111 W 4	Ardoch rd SE6
152 F 5	Ardrossan gdns Worc Pk
36 C 17	Ardwell av Ilf
108 A 3	Ardwell rd SW2
45 X 12	Ardwick rd NW2
50 G 2	Argall av E10
141 Z 16	Argent st SE1
145 U 19	Argon ms SW6
38 G 6	Argus clo Rom
58 A 9	Argus way Nthlt
82 H 17	Argyle av Hounsl
82 J 15	Argyle av Hounsl
59 Y 11	Argyle clo W13
74 K 11	Argyle pl W6
4 A 13	Argyle rd Barnt
63 S 11	Argyle rd E1
51 Z 13	Argyle rd E15
59 X 8	Argyle rd Grnfd
22 J 17	Argyle rd Harrow
82 K 13	Argyle rd Hounsl
53 W 6	Argyle rd Ilf
14 M 16	Argyle rd N12
15 N 17	Argyle rd N12
31 W 4	Argyle rd N17
18 L 13	Argyle rd N18
60 A 19	Argyle rd W13
59 Z 12	Argyle rd W13
132 L 12	Argyle sq WC1
132 L 13	Argyle st WC1
70 J 2	Argyll gdns Edg
25 T 7	Argyll gdns Edg
137 U 20	Argyll rd W8
140 A 6	Argyll st W1
92 H 9	Arica rd SE4
45 X 18	Ariel rd NW6
136 D 12	Ariel way W12
89 Y 9	Aristotle rd SW4
108 J 19	Arkell gro SE19
111 U 8	Arkindale rd SE6
32 K 17	Arkley cres E17
32 K 17	Arkley rd E17
75 X 17	Arklow rd SE14
46 D 15	Arkwright rd NW3
157 V 20	Arkwright rd S Croy
65 P 18	Arkwright st E16
90 A 7	Arlesford rd SW9
87 S 14	Arlesley clo SW15
90 F 15	Arlingford rd SW2
134 D 6	Arlington av N1
96 G 19	Arlington clo Sidcp
153 Y 3	Arlington clo Sutton
84 C 14	Arlington clo Twick
154 L 3	Arlington dri Carsh
53 V 3	Arlington gdns Ilf
73 V 13	Arlington gdns W4
14 K 11	Arlington N12
34 G 3	Arlington rd Wdfd Grn
16 G 6	Arlington rd N14
132 A 8	Arlington rd NW1
131 Y 5	Arlington rd NW1
102 F 5	Arlington rd Rich
116 H 15	Arlington rd Surb
101 V 10	Arlington rd Tedd
84 C 15	Arlington rd Twick
60 B 18	Arlington rd W13
134 C 6	Arlington sq N1
140 A 13	Arlington st SW1
133 U 12	Arlington way EC1
17 U 6	Arlow rd N21
31 Z 14	Armadale clo N15
145 T 16	Armadale rd SW6
63 Y 4	Armagh rd E3
121 N 3	Armfield cres Mitch
8 B 6	Armfield rd Enf
74 K 3	Arminger rd W12
45 U 4	Armitage rd NW11
77 O 13	Armitage rd SE10
87 Y 13	Armoury way SW18
56 D 20	Armstead wlk Dgnhm
69 R 1	Armstead wlk Dgnhm
20 M 19	Armstrong av Wdfd Grn
66 G 17	Armstrong clo E6
5 T 12	Armstrong cres Barnt
77 Y 12	Armstrong gdns SE7
100 B 13	Armstrong rd Felt
74 D 2	Armstrong rd W3
70 L 5	Armstrong wy S'hall
87 T 18	Arnal cres SW 18
87 Z 14	Arndale wlk SW18
140 L 6	Arne st WC2
94 B 10	Arne wlk SE3
148 E 3	Arneway st SW1
37 W 11	Arneways av Rom
104 F 2	Arnewood clo SW15
121 N 14	Arneys la Mitch
93 W 19	Arngask rd SE6
91 S 13	Arnhem way SE22
9 Z 2	Arnold av Enf
135 N 14	Arnold cir E2
25 N 20	Arnold clo Harrow
83 R 13	Arnold cres Islwth
17 U 15	Arnold gdns N13
69 P 2	Arnold rd Dgnhm
69 R 2	Arnold rd Dgnhm
64 A 9	Arnold rd E3
31 T 11	Arnold rd N15
40 B 18	Arnold rd Nthlt
106 M 17	Arnold rd SW17
16 K 12	Arnos gro N14
16 J 15	Arnos rd N11
80 F 1	Arnott clo SE28
73 Y 12	Arnott clo W4
91 P 9	Arnould av SE5
98 D 10	Arnsberg way Bxly Hth
42 G 3	Arnside gdns Wemb
98 E 2	Arnside rd Bxly Hth
150 D 13	Arnside st SE17
111 R 10	Arnulf st SE6
108 H 15	Arnulls rd SW16
90 D 15	Arodene rd SW2
110 D 19	Arpley rd SE20
159 S 5	Arragon gdns W Wkhm
108 A 18	Arragon gdns SW16
66 B 5	Arragon rd E6
83 Z 20	Arragon rd Twick
155 T 8	Arran cl Wallgtn
53 N 5	Arran dri E12
111 S 3	Arran rd SE6
48 M 20	Arran wlk
120 D 10	Arras av Mrdn
124 E 5	Arrol rd Becknhm
64 D 9	Arrow rd E3
95 T 6	Arsenal rd SE9
105 N 18	Arterberry rd SW20
39 T 20	Artesian clo Hornch
137 T 6	Artesian rd W2
64 M 3	Arthingworth st E15
79 O 11	Arthur gro SE18
66 G 6	Arthur rd E6
103 P 19	Arthur rd Kingst
48 D 11	Arthur rd N7
18 F 7	Arthur rd N9
118 K 12	Arthur rd New Mald
37 U 19	Arthur rd Rom
105 Y 7	Arthur rd SW19
160 F 9	Arthur st EC4
143 V 10	Artichoke hill E1
91 O 2	Artichoke pl SE5
36 D 17	Artillery clo Ilf
142 L 1	Artillery la E1
142 M 2	Artillery pas E1
78 H 12	Artillery pl SE18
148 D 2	Artillery row SW1
119 W 9	Arundel av Mrdn
98 C 15	Arundel clo Bxly
156 H 7	Arundel clo Croy
52 A 13	Arundel clo E15
100 L 13	Arundel clo Hampt
88 H 13	Arundel clo SW18
34 G 2	Arundel dri Wdfd Grn
40 F 14	Arundel dri Harrow
25 Y 2	Arundel gdns Edg
55 N 6	Arundel gdns Ilf

17 U 7 Arundel gdns N21
137 N 8 Arundel gdns W11
49 R 15 Arundel gro N16
48 F 19 Arundel pl N1
5 X 12 Arundel rd Barnt
123 O 15 Arundel rd Croy
117 U 2 Arundel rd Kingst
153 U 17 Arundel rd Sutton
48 F 19 Arundel sq N1
141 P 8 Arundel st WC2
144 A 14 Arundel ter SW13
74 K 17 Arundel ter SW13
48 G 15 Arvon rd N5
148 B 20 Ascalon st SW8
38 L 1 Ascension rd Rom
33 P 1 Ascham dri E4
32 J 3 Ascham end E17
47 V 14 Ascham st NW5
40 G 16 Ascot clo Nthlt
9 P 1 Ascot gdns Enf
58 F 15 Ascot gdns S'hall
66 F 8 Ascot rd E6
31 O 16 Ascot rd N15
18 L 13 Ascot rd N18
107 N 15 Ascot rd SW17
72 J 5 Ascott av W5
Ash clo Cranh
117 Y 3 Ash clo New Mald
38 G 3 Ash clo Rom
124 C 3 Ash clo SE20
115 P 9 Ash clo Sidcp
10 K 20 Ash clo Stanm
135 X 5 Ash gro E8
18 D 2 Ash gro Enf
17 X 12 Ash gro N13
45 R 13 Ash gro NW2
58 J 13 Ash gro S'hall
124 C 3 Ash gro SE 20
159 V 1 Ash gro W Wckm
72 K 8 Ash gro W5
41 Y 13 Ash gro Wemb
39 W 1 Ash la Rom
159 O 2 Ash rd Croy
52 B 15 Ash rd E5
119 T 19 Ash rd Sutton
127 X 15 Ash row Brom
124 H 13 Ash Tree clo Croy
25 X 15 Ash Tree dell NW9
124 G 12 Ash Tree way Croy
124 H 14 Ash Tree way Croy
81 N 19 Ashbourne av Bxly Hth
41 R 7 Ashbourne av Harrow
34 H 13 Ashbourne av E18
107 R 17 Ashbourne av Mitch
15 Z 7 Ashbourne av N20
27 V 14 Ashbourne av NW11
15 O 14 Ashbourne clo N12
61 O 13 Ashbourne clo W5
12 L 17 Ashbourne gro NW7
91 U 12 Ashbourne gro SE22
74 B 14 Ashbourne gro W4
60 M 11 Ashbourne rd W5
61 O 14 Ashbourne rd W5
105 W 17 Ashbourne ter SW19
27 V 14 Ashbourne way NW11
24 E 19 Ashbridge clo Harrow
34 A 20 Ashbridge rd E11
130 K 18 Ashbridge st NW8
56 H 10 Ashbrook rd Dgnhm
47 X 5 Ashbrook rd N19
146 A 5 Ashburn gdns SW7
146 B 5 Ashburn ms SW7
146 A 5 Ashburn pl SW7
23 W 20 Ashburnham av Harrow
23 X 20 Ashburnham gdns Harrow
76 E 20 Ashburnham gro SE10
28 G 12 Ashburnham pl N2
76 E 20 Ashburnham pl SE10
128 C 11 Ashburnham rd NW10
146 D 19 Ashburnham rd SW10
62 M 8 Ashburnham rd NW10
81 X 10 Ashburnham rd Erith
102 C 7 Ashburnham rd Rich
123 Z 20 Ashburton av Croy
54 H 14 Ashburton av Ilf
157 W 1 Ashburton clo Croy
157 W 2 Ashburton gdns Croy
48 F 13 Ashburton gro N7
157 W 2 Ashburton rd Croy
123 W 20 Ashburton rd Croy

65 T 17 Ashburton rd E16
65 S 4 Ashburton ter E13
37 V 16 Ashbury gdns Rom
89 N 6 Ashbury rd SW11
48 M 20 Ashby gro N1
92 L 6 Ashby ms SE4
31 W 15 Ashby rd N15
92 L 5 Ashby rd SE4
93 N 5 Ashby st Croy
133 X 13 Ashby st EC1
122 M 15 Ashby wlk Croy
74 F 8 Ashchurch ct W12
74 F 7 Ashchurch gro W12
74 F 8 Ashchurch Park vlls W12
74 F 7 Ashchurch ter W12
116 G 18 Ashcombe av Surb
12 B 14 Ashcombe gdns Edg
44 C 10 Ashcombe pk NW2
155 O 12 Ashcombe rd Carsh
105 Y 12 Ashcombe rd SW19
117 V 5 Ashcombe sq New Mald
87 Z 6 Ashcombe st SW6
96 M 15 Ashcroft av Sidcp
97 N 16 Ashcroft cres Sidcp
63 V 9 Ashcroft rd E3
144 A 7 Ashcroft sq W6
82 L 18 Ashdale clo Twick
10 K 19 Ashdale gro Stanm
112 J 1 Ashdale rd SE12
82 L 18 Ashdale way Twick
21 V 19 Ashdon clo Wdfd Grn
62 C 3 Ashdon rd NW10
125 S 4 Ashdown clo Becknhm
47 O 15 Ashdown cres NW5
9 O 10 Ashdown rd Enf
116 J 4 Ashdown rd Kingst
107 O 3 Ashdown way SW17
38 H 6 Ashdown wlk Rom
99 W 16 Ashen dri Drtfrd
105 X 5 Ashen gro SW19
158 G 20 Ashen vale S Croy
50 G 14 Ashenden rd E5
143 U 11 Asher dri E1
102 J 2 Ashfield clo Rich
114 C 17 Ashfield la Chisl
16 J 6 Ashfield pde N14
16 G 11 Ashfield rd N14
30 M 19 Ashfield rd N4
74 C 1 Ashfield rd W3
63 P 16 Ashfield st E1
143 W 3 Ashfield st E1
29 Z 14 Ashford av N8
58 A 18 Ashford clo Hay
9 R 8 Ashford cres Enf
32 K 18 Ashford gro E17
34 J 8 Ashford rd E18
53 V 20 Ashford rd E6
45 O 12 Ashford rd NW2
134 J 12 Ashgrove rd Brom
111 Y 14 Ashgrove rd Brom
54 L 5 Ashgrove rd Ilf
55 N 4 Ashgrove rd Ilf
87 W 5 Ashington rd SW6
108 A 10 Ashlake rd SW16
139 T 1 Ashland pl W1
64 L 3 Ashland rd E15
78 M 12 Ashlar pl SE18
154 A 3 Ashleigh gdns Sutton
124 B 5 Ashleigh rd SE20
86 A 7 Ashleigh rd SW14
35 Z 8 Ashley av Ilf
119 Y 12 Ashley av Mrdn
27 N 1 Ashley clo NW4
30 G 8 Ashley cres N22
89 P 7 Ashley cres SW11
82 K 20 Ashley dri Twick
17 Z 14 Ashley gdns N13
102 G 5 Ashley gdns Rich
42 K 7 Ashley gdns Wemb
156 J 8 Ashley la Croy
27 N 7 Ashley la NW4
148 B 3 Ashley pl SW1
20 A 18 Ashley rd E4
65 Y 1 Ashley rd E7
9 P 10 Ashley rd Enf
100 H 20 Ashley rd Hampt
31 Y 11 Ashley rd N17
48 A 2 Ashley rd N19
84 K 8 Ashley rd Rich
106 A 15 Ashley rd SW19
122 D 10 Ashley rd Thntn Hth
27 N 2 Ashley wlk NW7
51 Y 13 Ashlin rd E15
123 X 20 Ashling rd Croy
87 N 6 Ashlone rd SW15

6 H 18 Ashmead N14
93 O 4 Ashmead rd SE8
125 W 3 Ashmere av Becknhm
153 N 12 Ashmere clo Sutton
90 A 11 Ashmere gro SW4
130 L 19 Ashmill st NW1
149 O 15 Ashmole est SW8
149 R 16 Ashmole pl SW8
149 R 16 Ashmole st SW8
96 F 7 Ashmore gro Welling
129 O 11 Ashmore rd W9
31 U 14 Ashmount rd N15
47 W 2 Ashmount rd N19
38 M 8 Ashmour gdns Rom
39 N 8 Ashmour gdns Rom
41 O 9 Ashneal gdns Harrow
42 A 19 Ashness gdns Grnfd
88 M 13 Ashness rd SW11
24 E 19 Ashridge clo Harrow
79 O 20 Ashridge cres SE18
16 M 15 Ashridge gdns N13
17 N 16 Ashridge gdns N13
22 B 13 Ashridge gdns Pinn
119 U 8 Ashridge way Mrdn
49 X 1 Ashtead rd E5
153 W 9 Ashton clo Sutton
82 D 10 Ashton gdns Hounsl
37 Z 19 Ashton gdns Rom
51 X 16 Ashton rd E15
64 G 19 Ashton st E14
120 H 3 Ashtree way Mitch
123 V 17 Ashurch rd Croy
99 T 8 Ashurst clo Drtfrd
36 C 14 Ashurst dri Ilf
35 Z 18 Ashurst dri Ilf
6 A 15 Ashurst rd Barnt
5 Z 17 Ashurst rd Barnt
16 X 17 Ashurst rd N12
157 Z 2 Ashurst wlk Croy
106 L 11 Ashvale rd SW17
51 W 8 Ashville rd E11
112 F 2 Ashwater rd SE12
66 F 17 Ashwell clo E6
49 T 17 Ashwin st E8
159 T 15 Ashwood gdns Croy
20 K 11 Ashwood rd E4
91 N 4 Ashworth clo SE5
129 Y 13 Ashworth rd W9
97 X 11 Askern clo Bxly Hth
74 F 6 Askew bldgs W12
74 E 4 Askew cres W12
74 E 4 Askew rd W12
74 E 5 Askew rd W12
74 G 7 Askew rd W12
74 F 3 Askham rd W12
87 T 14 Askill dri SW15
88 B 18 Aslett st SW18
45 U 14 Asmara rd NW2
27 X 15 Asmuns hill NW11
27 W 15 Asmuns pl NW11
72 M 6 Aspen clo W5
127 U 3 Aspen copse Brom
41 Z 10 Aspen dri Harrow
121 N 12 Aspen gdns Mitch
74 K 13 Aspen gdns W6
81 P 7 Aspen grn Blvdr
58 C 10 Aspen la Nthlt
76 E 1 Aspen way E14
144 G 14 Aspenlea rd W6
92 F 8 Aspinall rd SE4
75 O 10 Aspinden rd SE16
151 Y 5 Aspinden rd SE16
50 A 16 Aspland gro E8
88 B 14 Aspley rd SW18
31 Y 4 Asplins rd N17
143 S 4 Assam st E1
63 P 13 Assembly pas E1
120 H 18 Assembly wlk Carsh
81 P 13 Assurance cotts Blvdr
23 R 5 Astall clo Harrow
92 B 1 Astbury rd SE15
76 F 6 Aste st E14
146 L 9 Astell st SW3
36 C 12 Astle gdns Ilf
89 O 3 Astle st SW11
45 N 14 Astley av NW2
133 Z 1 Astleys row N1
24 E 20 Aston av Harrow
103 T 15 Aston clo Kingst
115 O 9 Aston clo Sidcp
119 N 3 Aston rd SW20
60 H 17 Aston rd W5
63 V 16 Aston st E14
105 Y 3 Astonville st SW18
38 J 18 Astor av Rom
90 E 7 Astoria wlk SW9
57 Y 17 Astra clo Hornch
136 B 20 Astrop ms W6
74 L 7 Astrop ms W6

136 B 20 Astrop ter W6
74 L 7 Astrop ter W6
146 A 6 Astwood ms SW5
92 A 1 Asylum rd SE15
75 N 19 Asylum rd SE15
151 X 16 Asylum rd SE15
144 J 20 Atalanta st SW6
102 C 15 Atbara rd Tedd
83 O 10 Atcham rd Hounsl
67 Z 14 Atcost rd Bark
88 B 20 Atheldene rd SW18
111 P 6 Athelney st SE6
117 N 8 Athelstan rd Kingst
63 X 7 Athelstane gro E3
48 F 5 Athelstane ms N4
23 R 8 Athelstone rd Harrow
41 R 5 Athena clo Harrow
29 R 11 Athenaeum pl N20
15 S 6 Athenaeum rd N20
92 F 13 Athenlay rd SE15
50 B 12 Atherden rd E5
90 A 7 Atherfold rd SW9
89 Z 7 Atherfold rd SW9
146 C 4 Atherstone ms SW7
105 P 9 Atherton dri SW19
42 F 20 Atherton heights Wemb
Atherton pk SW19
70 J 1 Atherton pl S'hall
52 C 17 Atherton rd E7
35 S 7 Atherton rd Ilf
74 F 20 Atherton rd SW13
88 K 5 Atherton st SW11
60 G 6 Athlon rd Wemb
90 D 19 Athlone rd SW2
47 R 17 Athlone st NW5
81 X 14 Athol rd Erith
54 M 2 Athol rd Ilf
55 N 1 Athol rd Ilf
8 E 18 Athole gdns Enf
93 O 13 Athurdon rd SE4
33 S 19 Atkins rd E10
89 Z 19 Atkins rd SW12
65 Z 15 Atkinson rd E16
90 F 11 Atlantic rd SW9
77 X 10 Atlas gdns SE7
48 D 18 Atlas ms N7
65 S 7 Atlas rd E13
62 B 10 Atlas rd NW10
43 U 12 Atlas rd Wemb
64 A 3 Atley rd E3
87 S 10 Atney rd SW15
30 G 19 Atterbury rd N4
148 H 8 Atterbury st SW1
44 A 9 Attewood av NW10
40 B 19 Attewood rd Nthlt
68 F 20 Attlee rd SE28
33 S 11 Attlee ter E17
133 S 15 Attneave st WC1
90 E 20 Atwater clo SW2
91 Y 5 Atwell rd SE15
85 R 5 Atwood av Rich
74 J 10 Atwood rd W6
78 G 3 Auberon st E16
48 H 12 Aubert pk N5
48 J 12 Aubert rd N5
130 B 10 Aubrey pl NW8
33 P 11 Aubrey rd E17
30 B 18 Aubrey rd N8
137 P 14 Aubrey rd W8
137 R 15 Aubrey wlk W8
109 N 11 Aubyn hill SE27
86 G 12 Aubyn sq SW15
123 U 1 Auckland clo SE19
123 T 1 Auckland gdns SE19
108 M 9 Auckland hill SE27
51 R 9 Auckland rd E10
54 A 2 Auckland rd Ilf
53 Z 3 Auckland rd Ilf
117 N 8 Auckland rd Kingst
123 T 3 Auckland rd SE19
109 V 19 Auckland rd SE19
88 J 12 Auckland rd SE19
109 T 20 Auckland ri SE19
149 N 11 Auckland st SE11
131 T 3 Auden pl NW1
131 T 4 Auden pl NW1
125 R 14 Audley clo Becknhm
34 C 14 Audley ct E18
54 K 8 Audley gdns Ilf
153 Z 18 Audley pl Sutton
7 V 8 Audley rd Enf
26 H 18 Audley rd NW4
84 M 14 Audley rd Rich
60 M 15 Audley rd W5
61 N 14 Audley rd W5
139 V 13 Audley sq W1
42 B 6 Audrey gdns Wemb
53 Y 10 Audrey rd Ilf
135 T 8 Audrey st E2

65 X 9	Augurs la E13
101 N 4	Augusta rd Twick
64 C 17	Augusta st E14
22 M 6	Augustine rd Harrow
144 F 3	Augustine rd W14
72 F 20	Augustus clo Brentf
105 R 2	Augustus rd SW19
105 T 1	Augustus rd SW19
131 Z 11	Augustus st NW1
151 R 13	Aulay st SE1
149 U 12	Aulton rd E17
154 L 5	Aultone way Carsh
154 B 2	Aultone way Sutton
122 C 13	Aurelia gdns Croy
122 A 15	Aurelia rd Croy
57 O 18	Auriel av Dgnhm
49 R 15	Auriga ms N1
152 B 6	Auriol clo Worc Pk
59 R 1	Auriol dri Grnfd
152 B 6	Auriol Park rd Worc Pk
144 K 6	Auriol rd W14
13 O 11	Austell gdns NW7
80 E 2	Austen clo SE28
40 J 6	Austen rd Harrow
127 S 13	Austin av Brom
92 K 19	Austin clo SE23
160 G 5	Austin friars EC2
89 O 3	Austin rd SW11
134 M 14	Austin st E2
114 L 6	Austral clo Sidcp
149 W 4	Austral st SE11
74 J 1	Australia rd W12
62 J 19	Australia rd W12
117 S 19	Austyn gdns Surb
8 L 7	Autumn clo Enf
64 B 3	Autumn st E3
7 U 7	Avalon clo Enf
59 Y 13	Avalon cres W13
88 A 1	Avalon rd SW6
59 Y 12	Avalon rd W13
106 M 14	Avarn rd SW17
141 Y 6	Ave Maria la EC4
116 G 16	Avebury pk Surb
51 X 3	Avebury rd E11
105 V 19	Avebury rd SW19
134 F 5	Avebury st N1
39 O 13	Aveley rd Rom
149 R 10	Aveline st SE11
33 O 7	Aveling Park rd E17
48 H 10	Avenell rd N5
87 Z 18	Avening rd SW18
87 Y 17	Avening ter SW18
65 T 12	Avenons rd E13
6 H 19	Avenue clo N14
44 M 19	Avenue clo NW2
130 L 6	Avenue clo NW8
73 S 5	Avenue cres W3
116 J 11	Avenue elmers Surb
116 K 12	Avenue elmers Surb
123 W 5	Avenue gdns SE25
86 A 8	Avenue gdns SW14
101 X 16	Avenue gdns Tedd
73 T 5	Avenue gdns W3
29 S 11	Avenue ms N10
108 J 3	Avenue Park rd SE27
81 W 11	Avenue rd Blvdr
72 E 13	Avenue rd Brentf
97 Y 9	Avenue rd Bxly Hth
52 H 13	Avenue rd E7
81 Y 19	Avenue rd Erith
83 U 3	Avenue rd Islwth
116 K 6	Avenue rd Kingst
15 R 14	Avenue rd N12
16 H 1	Avenue rd N14
6 H 19	Avenue rd N14
31 O 16	Avenue rd N15
29 W 20	Avenue rd N6
118 B 7	Avenue rd New Mald
62 D 6	Avenue rd NW10
130 J 4	Avenue rd NW8
22 A 9	Avenue rd Pinn
55 S 2	Avenue rd Rom
70 F 2	Avenue rd S'hall
110 D 20	Avenue rd SE20
124 E 2	Avenue rd SE20
123 V 4	Avenue rd SE25
121 X 4	Avenue rd SW16
118 J 2	Avenue rd SW20
101 X 16	Avenue rd Tedd
71 Y 1	Avenue rd W13
73 S 5	Avenue rd W3
155 U 18	Avenue rd Wallgtn
21 Z 18	Avenue rd Wdfd Grn
117 O 16	Avenue South the Surb
117 V 7	Avenue ter New Mald
4 E 13	Avenue the Barnt
111 U 20	Avenue the Becknhm
127 O 7	Avenue the Brom
97 W 18	Avenue the Bxly
155 O 16	Avenue the Carsh
157 R 5	Avenue the Croy
34 J 17	Avenue the E11
20 J 19	Avenue the E4
142 K 9	Avenue the EC3
100 F 14	Avenue the Hampt
23 V 4	Avenue the Harrow
82 J 13	Avenue the Hounsl
29 V 7	Avenue the N10
16 D 15	Avenue the N11
31 P 9	Avenue the N17
27 X 7	Avenue the N3
30 E 11	Avenue the N8
128 J 4	Avenue the NW6
115 R 18	Avenue the Orp
22 E 19	Avenue the Pinn
22 G 1	Avenue the Pinn
85 N 4	Avenue the Rich
39 O 12	Avenue the Rom
76 J 19	Avenue the SE10
77 X 18	Avenue the SE7
95 U 14	Avenue the SE9
117 O 15	Avenue the Surb
153 U 20	Avenue the Sutton
89 P 13	Avenue the SW4
84 C 14	Avenue the Twick
126 A 14	Avenue the W Wkhm
125 W 18	Avenue the W Wkhm
60 A 19	Avenue the W13
74 A 9	Avenue the W4
42 K 3	Avenue the Wemb
43 O 7	Avenue the Wemb
152 D 3	Avenue the Worc Pk
108 H 16	Averil gro SW16
144 G 15	Averill st W6
147 W 8	Avery Farm row SW1
35 V 16	Avery gdns Ilf
96 B 16	Avery Hill pk SE9
96 D 20	Avery Hill rd SE9
114 B 2	Avery hill Sidcp
139 X 8	Avery row W1
65 P 15	Aviary clo E16
124 K 12	Aviemore clo Becknhm
124 J 12	Aviemore way Becknhm
92 G 8	Avignon rd SE4
110 B 17	Avington gro SE20
63 T 17	Avis sq E1
107 P 8	Avoca rd SW17
79 S 8	Avocet ms SE28
154 D 8	Avon clo Sutton
152 F 2	Avon clo Worc Pk
22 D 3	Avon mews Pinn
142 C 19	Avon pl SE1
157 N 14	Avon pth S Croy
33 X 11	Avon rd E17
58 J 11	Avon rd Grnfd
93 O 7	Avon rd N4
34 F 11	Avon way E18
15 Y 4	Avondale av Barnt
15 N 17	Avondale av N12
44 B 9	Avondale av NW2
118 C 19	Avondale av Worc Pk
9 V 11	Avondale cres Enf
35 O 17	Avondale cres Ilf
34 G 4	Avondale ct E18
82 E 14	Avondale gdns Hounsl
136 J 10	Avondale Park gdns W11
136 J 9	Avondale Park rd W11
136 K 11	Avondale pk W11
112 C 15	Avondale rd Brom
65 N 14	Avondale rd E16
51 N 1	Avondale rd E17
23 W 9	Avondale rd Harrow
17 U 9	Avondale rd N13
30 K 15	Avondale rd N15
28 C 5	Avondale rd N3
156 M 15	Avondale rd S Croy
113 R 5	Avondale rd SE9
85 Z 7	Avondale rd SW14
106 A 12	Avondale rd SW19
105 Z 12	Avondale rd SW19
97 U 5	Avondale rd Welling
91 U 7	Avondale rd SE15
151 S 10	Avondale sq SE1
151 S 11	Avondale sq SE1
75 R 19	Avonley rd SE14
145 N 4	Avonmore pl W14
145 N 5	Avonmore rd W14
150 A 1	Avonmouth st SE1
82 K 4	Avonwick rd Hounsl
20 H 16	Avril way E4
156 A 15	Avro way Wallgtn
31 P 5	Awlfield av N17
96 L 4	Awliscombe rd Welling
67 P 3	Axe st Bark
25 R 4	Axholme av Edg
80 H 20	Axminster cres Welling
97 S 1	Axminster cres Welling
48 B 9	Axminster rd N7
139 T 2	Aybrook st W1
127 V 8	Aycliffe clo Brom
74 F 2	Aycliffe rd W12
52 D 17	Aylesbury clo E7
126 E 7	Aylesbury rd Brom
133 W 17	Aylesbury st EC1
43 Y 10	Aylesbury st NW10
124 H 13	Aylesford av Becknhm
148 F 11	Aylesford st SW1
128 F 2	Aylestone av NW6
45 O 20	Aylestone av NW6
83 U 5	Aylett rd Islwth
124 A 10	Aylett rd SE25
123 Z 10	Aylett rd SE25
8 K 18	Ayley croft Enf
10 L 12	Aylmer clo Stanm
10 K 13	Aylmer dri Stanm
55 X 11	Aylmer rd Dgnhm
52 B 2	Aylmer rd E11
28 K 16	Aylmer rd N2
74 C 6	Aylmer rd W12
56 A 17	Ayloffe rd Dgnhm
110 G 5	Aylward rd SE23
119 V 5	Aylward rd SW20
63 R 16	Aylward st E1
10 L 13	Aylwards ri Stanm
144 H 3	Aynhoe rd W14
85 V 6	Aynscombe la SW14
85 W 6	Aynscombe pth SW14
39 O 4	Ayr grn Rom
39 O 4	Ayr way Rom
65 T 10	Ayres clo E13
61 X 1	Ayres cres NW10
142 B 16	Ayres st SE1
49 R 8	Aysrome rd N16
91 P 17	Aysgarth rd SE21
90 D 5	Aytoun rd SW9
71 W 2	Azalea clo W7
91 U 4	Azenby st SE15
77 N 12	Azof st SE10

B

48 J 15	Baalbec rd N5
35 P 12	Babbacombe gdns Ilf
112 G 19	Babbacombe rd Brom
43 R 18	Babbington ri Wemb
55 T 14	Babington rd Dgnhm
57 X 4	Babington rd Hornch
26 K 13	Babington rd NW4
107 Y 11	Babington rd SW16
140 E 12	Babmaes st SW1
134 G 13	Baches st N1
143 T 5	Back Church la E1
133 T 18	Back hill EC1
72 G 18	Back la Brentf
98 C 18	Back la Bxly
25 V 5	Back la Edg
29 Z 17	Back la N8
46 E 12	Back la NW3
102 D 5	Back la Rich
37 X 20	Back la Rom
115 N 10	Back rd Sidcp
73 T 2	Back st W3
150 K 8	Backhouse pl SE17
150 M 3	Bacon gro SE1
25 P 3	Bacon la Edg
135 R 16	Bacon st E2
47 P 4	Bacons la N6
63 R 8	Bacton st E2
69 S 4	Baddow clo Dgnhm
142 F 17	Baden pl SE1
53 Y 14	Baden rd Ilf
29 Z 12	Baden rd N8
57 X 18	Bader way Rainhm
7 X 12	Badgers clo Enf
23 R 19	Badgers clo Harrow
152 E 2	Badgers copse Worc Pk
14 F 4	Badgers croft N20
113 W 7	Badgers croft SE9
158 E 8	Badgers hole Croy
118 A 2	Badgers wlk New Mald
33 N 9	Badlis rd E17
40 H 19	Badminton clo Nthlt
23 S 13	Badminton clo Har
89 P 17	Badminton rd SW12
150 B 20	Badsworth rd SE5
90 L 1	Badsworth rd SE5
88 B 3	Bagleys la SW6
37 Z 12	Bagleys spring Rom
95 W 1	Bagshot clo SE18
18 F 1	Bagshot rd Enf
150 K 10	Bagshot st SE17
75 Z 20	Baildon st SE8
110 E 15	Bailey pl SE26
72 H 5	Bailles wlk W5
56 C 11	Bainbridge rd Dgnhm
140 G 4	Bainbridge st WC1
58 M 19	Baird av S'hall
25 V 18	Baird clo NW9
109 S 10	Baird gdns SE21
8 L 4	Baird rd Enf
94 A 6	Baizdon rd SE3
93 Z 6	Baizdon rd SE3
132 D 2	Baker dri NW1
121 N 4	Baker la Mitch
62 A 4	Baker rd NW10
78 D 20	Baker rd SE18
95 R 1	Baker rd SE18
8 D 6	Baker st Enf
131 R 19	Baker st NW1
139 S 2	Baker st W1
33 R 19	Bakers av E17
119 T 3	Bakers end SW20
50 B 4	Bakers hill E5
29 N 17	Bakers la N6
72 G 1	Bakers la W5
139 T 4	Bakers ms W1
64 L 5	Bakers row E15
133 T 17	Bakers row EC1
117 Z 2	Bakewell way New Mald
65 U 11	Balaam st E13
16 K 8	Balaams la N14
151 P 6	Balaclava rd SE1
116 D 16	Balaclava rd Surb
63 S 2	Balbenpath E9
95 V 12	Balcaskie rd SE9
94 M 4	Balchen rd SE3
91 Z 15	Balchier rd SE22
131 N 18	Balcombe st NW1
63 R 1	Balcorne st E9
112 J 5	Balder ri SE12
139 U 7	Balderton st W1
64 C 7	Baldock st E3
108 B 16	Baldry gdns SW16
90 K 2	Baldwin cres SE5
61 X 19	Baldwin gdns W3
134 E 14	Baldwin st EC1
134 A 8	Baldwin ter N1
133 S 20	Baldwins gdns EC1
132 L 9	Balfe st N1
74 B 14	Balfern gro W4
88 J 4	Balfern st SW11
53 Z 7	Balfour appr Ilf
71 V 2	Balfour av W7
15 Z 11	Balfour gro N20
18 K 10	Balfour ms N9
139 U 12	Balfour ms W1
86 J 10	Balfour pl SW15
139 U 11	Balfour pl W1
127 P 11	Balfour rd Brom
154 M 17	Balfour rd Carsh
23 R 16	Balfour rd Harrow
82 J 7	Balfour rd Hounsl
54 C 3	Balfour rd Ilf
53 Z 7	Balfour rd Ilf
48 M 13	Balfour rd N5
123 X 10	Balfour rd SE25
106 A 18	Balfour rd SW19
72 A 6	Balfour rd W13
61 W 15	Balfour rd W3
150 D 5	Balfour st SE17
20 J 6	Balgonie rd E4
39 Y 11	Balgores cres Rom
39 X 11	Balgores la Rom
39 Y 12	Balgores sq Rom
118 B 10	Balgowan clo New Mald
124 K 4	Balgowan rd Becknhm
79 X 11	Balgowan st SE18
89 H 19	Balham gro SW12
107 P 3	Balham High rd SW17
89 R 20	Balham High rd SW12
89 S 17	Balham hill SW12
89 S 19	Balham New rd SW12
106 M 1	Balham Park rd SW12

107 O 2　Balham Park rd SW12
18 L 8　Balham rd N9
107 R 1　Balham Station rd SW12
160 H 7　Ball ct EC3
112 E 7　Ballamore rd Brom
50 G 17　Ballance rd E9
88 C 11　Ballantyne st SW18
103 X 19　Ballard clo Kingst
69 V 3　Ballards clo Dgnhm
157 Y 14　Ballards Farm rd Croy
27 Y 4　Ballards la N3
69 U 3　Ballards rd Dgnhm
44 G 7　Ballards rd NW2
157 X 14　Ballards ri S Croy
158 C 13　Ballards way Croy
157 Y 15　Ballards way S Croy
76 L 13　Ballast quay SE10
157 U 11　Ballater rd S Croy
90 B 11　Ballater rd SW2
92 G 17　Ballina st SE23
89 N 15　Ballingdon rd SW11
20 K 14　Balliol av E4
31 P 5　Balliol rd N17
136 E 5　Balliol rd W10
97 R 4　Balliol rd Welling
111 X 3　Balloch rd SE6
44 B 11　Ballogie av NW10
150 H 20　Ballow clo SE5
49 O 17　Balls Pond pl N1
49 R 17　Balls Pond rd N1
72 H 2　Balmain clo W5
63 Y 8　Balmer st E3
134 G 3　Balmes rd N1
124 J 9　Balmoral av Becknhm
98 C 20　Balmoral gdns Bxly
54 J 5　Balmoral gdns Ilf
71 Y 7　Balmoral gdns W13
48 B 18　Balmoral gro N7
51 S 8　Balmoral rd E10
52 L 14　Balmoral rd E7
40 G 12　Balmoral rd Harrow
116 L 8　Balmoral rd Kingst
44 K 17　Balmoral rd NW2
39 Y 15　Balmoral rd Rom
152 H 4　Balmoral rd Worc Pk
6 B 16　Balmore cres Barnt
47 T 7　Balmore st N19
87 N 11　Balmuir gdns SW15
44 B 12　Balnacraig av NW10
148 G 10　Balniel ga SW1
106 F 17　Baltic clo SW19
134 A 18　Baltic st EC1
96 K 5　Baltimore pl Welling
87 W 19　Balvernie gro SW18
136 D 18　Bamborough gdns W12
60 M 5　Bamford av Wemb
51 S 15　Bamford ct E15
54 B 19　Bamford rd Bark
111 W 12　Bamford rd Brom
155 U 6　Bamfylde clo Wallgtn
110 E 6　Bampton rd SE23
111 T 20　Banavie gdns Becknhm
101 U 2　Banbury cotts Twick
153 Z 17　Banbury ct Sutton
140 K 8　Banbury ct WC2
63 T 1　Banbury rd E9
88 K 4　Banbury st SW11
77 V 19　Banchory rd SE3
21 T 9　Bancroft av Buck Hl
28 K 15　Bancroft av N2
22 M 5　Bancroft gdns Harrow
63 U 11　Bancroft rd E1
23 N 6　Bancroft rd Har
155 X 12　Bandon ri Wallgtn
87 O 8　Bangalore st SW15
40 K 15　Bangor clo Nrthlt
73 N 15　Bangor rd Brentf
74 K 10　Banim st W6
128 G 12　Banister rd NW10
120 G 4　Bank av Mitch
142 D 12　Bank end SE1
102 J 17　Bank la Kingst
86 B 13　Bank la SW15
47 S 3　Bank the N6
83 U 5　Bankfield ct Islwth
112 A 10　Bankfoot rd Brom
92 L 18　Bankhurst rd SE6
98 B 10　Banks la Bxly Hth
154 K 13　Bankside clo Carsh
7 X 7　Bankside Enf
157 T 15　Bankside S Croy
142 A 11　Bankside SE1
90 F 12　Bankton rd SW2
94 A 11　Bankwell rd SE13

134 B 18　Banner st EC1
76 M 12　Banning st SE10
41 R 13　Bannister clo Grnfd
90 F 20　Bannister clo SW2
79 W 11　Bannockburn rd SE18
18 C 10　Banstead gdns N9
154 K 13　Banstead rd Carsh
92 B 8　Banstead st SE15
156 A 10　Banstead way Wallgtn
12 G 20　Banstock rd Edg
8 M 9　Banton clo Enf
150 F 19　Bantry st SE5
150 X 3　Banyard rd SE16
47 O 17　Baptist gdns NW5
144 D 3　Barb ms W6
49 R 10　Barbauld rd N16
149 V 1　Barbel st SE1
17 U 3　Barber clo N21
65 U 8　Barbers all E13
64 E 5　Barbers rd E15
58 L 15　Barbican rd Grnfd
18 J 11　Barbot clo N9
88 A 13　Barchard st SW18
71 W 3　Barchester clo W7
23 R 6　Barchester rd Harrow
64 D 15　Barchester st E14
145 T 20　Barclay clo SW6
21 T 14　Barclay oval Wdfd Grn
157 O 5　Barclay rd Croy
52 B 4　Barclay rd E11
65 Y 13　Barclay rd E13
33 T 16　Barclay rd E17
18 B 19　Barclay rd N18
145 U 19　Barclay rd SW6
108 B 4　Barcombe av SW2
136 G 10　Bard rd W10
79 U 19　Barden st SE18
37 V 11　Bardfield av Rom
120 B 8　Bardney rd Mrdn
158 K 20　Bardolph av Croy
47 Z 12　Bardolph rd N7
85 N 9　Bardolph rd Rich
63 O 13　Bardsey pl E1
157 T 5　Bardsley clo Croy
76 F 17　Bardsley la SE10
129 N 15　Barfett st W10
15 Y 8　Barfield av N20
127 X 5　Barfield rd Brom
52 B 3　Barfield rd E11
136 F 7　Barfield way W10
26 H 6　Barford clo NW4
133 U 6　Barford st N1
92 A 8　Barforth rd SE15
118 G 16　Bargate clo New Mald
79 Y 13　Bargate clo SE18
78 M 4　Barge House rd E16
141 U 11　Barge House st SE1
111 S 2　Bargery rd SE6
109 X 17　Bargrove clo SE19
110 M 3　Bargrove cres SE6
127 S 20　Barham clo Brom
113 Z 12　Barham clo Chisl
38 F 9　Barham clo Rom
42 C 17　Barham clo Wemb
113 Y 12　Barham clo Chisl
156 L 9　Barham rd CR2
156 M 10　Barham rd S Croy
104 F 18　Barham rd SW20
112 F 4　Baring clo SE12
5 U 12　Baring rd Barnt
123 Y 19　Baring rd Croy
94 D 19　Baring rd SE12
112 F 2　Baring rd SE12
134 E 5　Baring st N1
146 B 14　Barker st SW10
31 P 1　Barkham rd N17
54 E 17　Barking pk Bark
65 R 13　Barking rd E16
66 F 4　Barking rd E6
151 W 11　Barkis way SE16
145 X 7　Barkston gdns SW5
75 O 14　Barkworth rd SE16
151 Y 11　Barkworth rd SE16
75 R 19　Barlborough st SE14
128 G 18　Barlby gdns W10
128 F 19　Barlby rd W10
55 O 2　Barley la Ilf
37 P 14　Barley la Rom
141 Y 2　Barley Mow pass EC1
73 Y 13　Barley Mow pass W4
63 Y 20　Barleycorn way E14
37 R 19　Barleyfields Rom
155 Z 15　Barlow clo Wallgtn
139 Z 10　Barlow pl W1
100 J 17　Barlow rd Hampt

45 V 17　Barlow rd NW6
73 T 2　Barlow rd W3
150 G 6　Barlow st SE17
111 R 3　Barmeston rd SE6
22 L 6　Barmor clo Harrow
59 X 6　Barmouth av Grnfd
158 F 3　Barmouth rd Croy
88 D 17　Barmouth rd SW18
78 K 9　Barn clo SE18
11 R 20　Barn cres Stanm
144 A 19　Barn Elms Water Works SW13
43 R 5　Barn Hill Wemb
43 S 7　Barn hill Wemb
43 R 5　Barn ri Wemb
43 R 6　Barn ri Wemb
49 P 8　Barn st N16
43 P 5　Barn way Wemb
43 R 6　Barn way Wemb
50 G 17　Barnabas rd E9
40 M 8　Barnaby clo Harrow
114 F 20　Barnard clo Chisl
155 Y 16　Barnard clo Wallgtn
118 G 9　Barnard gdns New Mald
65 O 1　Barnard gro E15
29 R 6　Barnard hill N10
9 N 9　Barnard rd Enf
121 O 4　Barnard rd Mitch
88 K 10　Barnard rd SW11
156 J 19　Barnard's pl S Croy
36 C 12　Barnardo dri Ilf
63 S 19　Barnardo st E1
141 T 3　Barnards Inn EC4
64 L 2　Barnby sq E15
64 L 2　Barnby st E15
132 C 11　Barnby st NW1
98 K 2　Barnehurst av Bxly Hth
98 L 4　Barnehurst av Bxly Hth
98 K 2　Barnehurst clo Erith
98 J 5　Barnehurst rd Bxly Hth
74 F 19　Barnes av SW13
53 O 13　Barnes clo E12
99 V 11　Barnes Cray rd Drtfrd
65 Z 14　Barnes ct E16
118 H 12　Barnes end New Mald
86 C 4　Barnes High st SW13
72 F 1　Barnes pickle W5
54 C 14　Barnes rd Ilf
19 P 13　Barnes rd N18
63 V 18　Barnes st E14
86 B 5　Barnes ter SW13
13 T 1　Barnet Ga la Barnt
135 S 13　Barnet gro E2
4 J 14　Barnet hill Barnt
4 K 17　Barnet la Barnt
11 X 1　Barnet la Brhm Wd
14 G 5　Barnet la N20
12 L 7　Barnet way NW7
99 T 4　Barnett clo Erith
77 Y 12　Barney clo SE7
158 D 2　Barnfield av Croy
102 J 11　Barnfield av Kingst
121 T 7　Barnfield av Mitch
102 K 11　Barnfield gdns Rich
118 A 14　Barnfield New Mald
76 C 11　Barnfield pl E14
81 P 15　Barnfield rd Blvdr
25 U 5　Barnfield rd Edg
157 T 20　Barnfield rd S Croy
79 N 16　Barnfield rd SE18
60 C 11　Barnfield rd W5
125 X 14　Barnfield Wood clo W Wkhm
125 X 13　Barnfield Wood rd Becknhm
58 M 7　Barnham rd Grnfd
59 N 8　Barnham rd Grnfd
142 K 16　Barnham st SE1
126 C 13　Barnhill av Brom
43 W 9　Barnhill rd Wemb
100 C 5　Barnlea clo Felt
56 C 15　Barnmead gdns Dgnhm
110 G 20　Barnmead rd Becknhm
56 B 15　Barnmead rd Dgnhm
43 X 20　Barns rd NW10
117 W 10　Barnsbury clo New Mald
117 U 20　Barnsbury cres Surb
48 E 19　Barnsbury gro N7
117 V 20　Barnsbury la Surb
48 F 20　Barnsbury pk N1
133 S 5　Barnsbury rd N1

133 S 1　Barnsbury sq N1
133 V 1　Barnsbury st N1
133 R 1　Barnsbury ter N1
129 R 16　Barnsdale rd W9
129 S 17　Barnsdale yd W9
63 N 12　Barnsley st E1
135 X 17　Barnsley st E1
133 Z 4　Barnston wlk N1
90 G 13　Barnwell rd SW2
129 Y 19　Barnwood clo W9
77 U 3　Barnwood ct E16
133 T 9　Baron clo N1
36 C 9　Baron gdns Ilf
120 K 8　Baron gro Mitch
55 V 3　Baron rd Dgnhm
133 T 9　Baron st N1
65 O 14　Baron wlk E16
120 H 9　Baron wlk Mitch
135 O 12　Baroness rd E2
31 X 4　Baronet gro N17
31 X 4　Baronet rd N17
144 L 10　Barons Court rd W14
145 N 10　Barons Court rd W14
5 W 18　Barons ga Barnt
144 K 8　Barons keep W14
23 U 12　Barons mead Harrow
141 V 18　Barons pl SE1
84 C 15　Barons the Twick
124 J 14　Barons wlk Croy
84 C 17　Baronsfield rd Twick
86 G 2　Baronsmead rd SW13
72 M 7　Baronsmede W5
28 K 13　Baronsmere rd N2
76 G 13　Barque st E14
95 W 2　Barr vlls SE18
82 A 11　Barrack rd Hounsl
23 R 9　Barrat way Harrow
30 B 6　Barratt av N22
28 M 6　Barrenger rd N10
33 U 13　Barrett rd E17
139 U 6　Barrett st W1
61 X 7　Barretts Green rd NW10
49 T 13　Barretts gro N16
92 J 4　Barriedale SE14
77 Z 9　Barrier appr SE7
107 P 9　Barringer sq SW17
35 V 5　Barrington clo Ilf
47 O 14　Barrington clo NW5
97 W 6　Barrington rd Bxly Hth
53 W 17　Barrington rd E12
29 X 14　Barrington rd N8
153 X 1　Barrington rd Sutton
90 H 7　Barrington rd SW9
132 M 20　Barrington rd WC1
154 L 18　Barrow av Carsh
17 W 10　Barrow clo N21
154 J 15　Barrow Hedges clo Carsh
154 J 15　Barrow Hedges way Carsh
152 A 2　Barrow Hill clo Worc Pk
130 J 10　Barrow Hill rd NW8
152 A 2　Barrow hill Worc Pk
22 A 8　Barrow Point av Pinn
22 A 6　Barrow Point la Pinn
156 G 12　Barrow rd Croy
107 Z 14　Barrow rd SW16
22 B 8　Barrowdene clo Pinn
17 W 9　Barrowell grn N21
19 O 11　Barrowfield clo N9
73 X 15　Barrowgate rd W4
80 L 19　Barry av Bxly Hth
31 V 19　Barry av N15
66 E 17　Barry rd E6
43 X 20　Barry rd NW10
91 X 14　Barry rd SE22
92 B 7　Barset rd SE15
110 C 17　Barson clo SE20
108 M 6　Barston rd SE27
108 D 2　Barstow cres SW2
140 L 3　Barter st WC1
79 N 13　Barth rd SE18
88 D 12　Bartholomew clo SW18
141 Z 2　Bartholomew clo EC1
160 F 5　Bartholomew la EC2
142 A 2　Bartholomew pl EC1
47 V 18　Bartholomew rd NW5
134 C 15　Bartholomew sq EC1
150 F 3　Bartholomew st SE1
47 U 18　Bartholomew vlls NW5
66 E 5　Bartle av E6
136 J 6　Bartle rd W11

150 H 7	Beckway st SE17
91 O 14	Beckwith rd SE24
107 R 14	Beclands rd SW17
24 B 15	Becmead av Harrow
107 Y 8	Becmead av SW16
109 S 13	Becondale rd SE19
56 A 7	Becontree av Dgnhm
55 T 8	Becontree av Dgnhm
87 U 11	Bective pl SW15
52 F 11	Bective rd E7
87 U 11	Bective rd SW15
98 H 1	Becton pl Erith
7 Y 4	Bedale rd Enf
142 E 14	Bedale st SE1
51 V 16	Beddingfield rd E15
122 A 19	Beddington Farm rd Croy
156 C 2	Beddington Farm rd Croy
155 P 14	Beddington gdns Carsh
155 Y 11	Beddington gro Wallgtn
155 Z 3	Beddington la Wallgtn
121 W 16	Beddington la Croy
155 U 4	Beddington pk Wallgtn
36 K 20	Beddington rd Ilf
37 T 18	Bede rd Rom
115 Y 14	Bedens rd Sidcp
4 J 15	Bedford av Barnt
140 G 2	Bedford av WC1
121 N 4	Bedford clo Mitch
29 P 3	Bedford clo N10
140 K 10	Bedford ct WC2
137 U 15	Bedford gdns W8
107 V 6	Bedford hill SW16
144 M 17	Bedford pass SW9
122 M 20	Bedford pk Croy
123 O 20	Bedford pl Croy
140 K 1	Bedford pl WC1
132 K 20	Bedford pl WC1
33 O 8	Bedford rd E17
34 E 8	Bedford rd E18
66 H 3	Bedford rd E6
23 N 17	Bedford rd Harrow
54 A 10	Bedford rd Ilf
53 Z 10	Bedford rd Ilf
31 R 13	Bedford rd N15
28 J 10	Bedford rd N2
30 A 6	Bedford rd N22
29 Y 17	Bedford rd N8
18 M 1	Bedford rd N9
19 N 2	Bedford rd N9
13 N 9	Bedford rd NW7
114 H 7	Bedford rd Sidcp
89 Z 8	Bedford rd SW9
101 P 5	Bedford rd Twick
72 A 1	Bedford rd W13
73 Z 9	Bedford rd W4
153 N 4	Bedford rd Worc Pk
141 O 1	Bedford row WC1
140 G 2	Bedford sq WC1
140 K 9	Bedford st WC2
132 H 18	Bedford way WC1
140 J 10	Bedfordbury WC2
105 T 2	Bedgebury gdns SW19
94 M 11	Bedgebury rd SE9
112 F 6	Bedivere rd Brom
98 C 2	Bedonwell rd Bxly Hth
81 N 16	Bedonwell rd Blvdr
81 R 17	Bedonwell rd Blvdr
80 M 16	Bedonwell rd SE2
41 P 14	Bedser clo Grnfd
109 R 17	Bedwardine rd SE 19
81 R 14	Bedwell rd Blvdr
31 R 4	Bedwell rd N17
151 V 10	Bedwin way SE16
65 U 15	Beeby rd E16
72 B 19	Beech av Brentf
21 V 8	Beech av Buck HI
15 X 6	Beech av N20
96 M 17	Beech av Sidcp
74 B 3	Beech av W3
154 L 2	Beech clo Carsh
8 L 20	Beech clo Enf
57 X 11	Beech clo Hornch
121 Z 8	Beech clo Mitch
86 G 17	Beech clo SW15
104 L 15	Beech clo SW19
127 T 2	Beech copse Brom
157 S 10	Beech copse S Croy
28 L 9	Beech dri N2
56 J 20	Beech gdns Dgnhm
72 J 8	Beech gdns W5
121 X 10	Beech gro Mitch
117 Y 6	Beech gro New Mald
33 W 1	Beech Hall cres E4
20 J 20	Beech Hall rd E4
33 V 3	Beech Hall rd E4
5 S 5	Beech Hill av Barnt
5 U 4	Beech hill Barnt
5 V 7	Beech Hill pk Barnt
157 O 6	Beech House rd Croy
21 U 9	Beech la Buck HI
15 U 15	Beech lawns N12
17 N 19	Beech rd N11
122 B 4	Beech rd SW16
134 A 20	Beech st EC1
38 L 14	Beech st Rom
11 S 17	Beech Tree clo Stanm
21 O 4	Beech Tree glade E4
15 X 15	Beech Vale clo N12
43 X 20	Beech way NW10
100 J 5	Beech way Twick
99 X 10	Beech wlk Drtford
12 M 18	Beech wlk NW7
40 G 2	Beechcroft av Harrow
98 M 4	Beechcroft av Bxly Hth
117 W 2	Beechcroft av New Mald
45 V 1	Beechcroft av NW11
70 D 2	Beechcroft av S'hall
113 W 17	Beechcroft Chisl
70 A 19	Beechcroft clo Hounsl
42 M 10	Beechcroft gdns Wemb
43 N 10	Beechcroft gdns Wemb
34 H 8	Beechcroft rd E18
85 W 9	Beechcroft rd SW14
106 J 3	Beechcroft rd SW17
17 R 8	Beechdale N21
90 D 16	Beechdale rd SW2
83 V 3	Beechen Cliff way Islwth
22 D 11	Beechen gro Pinn
154 K 16	Beeches Avenue the Carsh
124 B 1	Beeches clo SE20
119 T 20	Beeches rd Sutton
106 K 6	Beeches rd SW 17
154 H 19	Beeches rd SW17
38 L 20	Beechfield gdns Rom
126 M 3	Beechfield rd Brom
31 N 18	Beechfield rd N4
110 M 1	Beechfield rd SE6
95 V 12	Beechhill rd SE9
111 Z 13	Beechmont clo Brom
153 R 3	Beechmore gdns Sutton
89 N 2	Beechmore rd SW11
59 S 14	Beechmount av W7
107 R 19	Beecholme av Mitch
50 A 9	Beecholme est
102 J 11	Beechrow Rich
97 W 17	Beechway Bxly
122 H 8	Beechwood av Thntn Hth
40 L 9	Beechwood av Harrow
58 J 8	Beechwood av Grnfd
27 W 11	Beechwood av N3
85 P 2	Beechwood av Rich
12 M 16	Beechwood clo NW7
116 F 18	Beechwood clo Surb
97 Y 7	Beechwood cres Bxly Hth
21 P 17	Beechwood dri Wdfd Grn
40 L 9	Beechwood gdns Harrow
35 U 14	Beechwood gdns Ilf
34 E 11	Beechwood pk E18
157 R 19	Beechwood rd S Croy
49 U 18	Beechwood rd E8
29 Y 11	Beechwood rd N8
45 Z 8	Beechworth clo NW3
92 J 12	Beecroft rd SE4
35 T 15	Beehive la Ilf
90 F 9	Beehive pl SW9
120 B 8	Beeleigh rd Mrdn
147 Y 2	Beeston pl SW1
5 U 18	Beeston rd Barnt
11 T 1	Beethoven rd Borhm Wd
128 L 11	Beethoven st W10
22 G 3	Beeton clo Pinn
94 K 2	Begbie rd SE3
152 E 16	Beggars hill Epsom
62 E 18	Begonia wlk W12
89 T 17	Beira st SW12
63 U 18	Bekesbourne st E1
112 D 18	Belcroft clo Brom
55 U 1	Belfairs dri Rom
49 U 6	Belfast rd N16
123 Z 10	Belfast rd SE25
48 B 12	Belfont wlk N7
78 H 12	Belford gro SE18
92 C 4	Belfort rd SE15
49 T 13	Belgrade rd N16
6 H 15	Belgrave clo N14
73 U 4	Belgrave clo W3
6 J 15	Belgrave gdns N14
130 A 6	Belgrave gdns NW8
129 Z 7	Belgrave gdns NW8
11 S 15	Belgrave gdns Stanm
139 S 20	Belgrave Mews north SW1
147 U 1	Belgrave Mews south SW1
147 T 1	Belgrave Mews west SW1
147 U 3	Belgrave pl SW1
51 U 3	Belgrave rd E10
52 F 4	Belgrave rd E11
65 X 11	Belgrave rd E13
33 O 18	Belgrave rd E17
82 D 8	Belgrave rd Hounsl
53 T 4	Belgrave rd Ilf
120 F 5	Belgrave rd Mitch
123 V 8	Belgrave rd SE25
148 C 8	Belgrave pk SE13
147 Z 6	Belgrave rd SW1
74 E 20	Belgrave rd SW13
139 T 20	Belgrave sq SW1
147 U 1	Belgrave sq SW1
63 U 17	Belgrave st E1
21 S 11	Belgrave ter Wdfd Grn
120 G 6	Belgrave wlk Mitch
147 W 2	Belgrave yd SW1
111 Y 15	Belgravia gdns Brom
116 H 10	Belgravia ms Kingst
132 K 12	Belgravia st WC1
91 P 1	Belham st SE5
90 J 8	Belinda rd SW9
48 E 20	Belitha vlls N1
39 Y 4	Bell av Rom
87 B 18	Bell dri SW18
56 K 9	Bell Farm av Dgnhm
158 K 18	Bell field Croy
110 K 9	Bell Green la SE26
110 J 12	Bell grn SE26
110 K 8	Bell grn SE26
110 K 8	Bell grn SE26
56 K 3	Bell House rd Rom
160 H 7	Bell Inn yd EC3
142 M 2	Bell la E1
143 N 3	Bell la E1
77 R 2	Bell la E16
9 U 4	Bell la Enf
27 N 14	Bell la NW4
101 Z 1	Bell la Twick
8 C 7	Bell rd Enf
82 J 9	Bell rd Hounsl
138 J 1	Bell st NW1
130 K 20	Bell st NW1
78 K 8	Bell Water ga SE18
160 D 10	Bell Wharf la EC4
141 S 6	Bell yd WC2
145 R 11	Bellamy clo SW5
24 B 5	Bellamy dri Stanm
20 E 20	Bellamy rd E4
89 R 18	Bellamy rd SW12
107 Z 3	Bellasis av SW2
27 O 14	Belle View rd NW4
88 K 20	Belle Vue rd SW17
90 D 8	Bellefields rd SW9
96 J 5	Bellegrove clo Welling
96 G 5	Bellegrove rd Welling
97 O 7	Bellegrove rd Welling
91 V 4	Bellenden rd SE15
20 B 7	Bellestaines E4
88 K 14	Belleville rd SW11
59 P 2	Bellevue Grnfd
10 C 5	Bellevue la Bushey
122 L 7	Bellevue pk Thntn Hth
63 P 13	Bellevue pl E1
98 A 13	Bellevue rd Bxly Hth
33 W 7	Bellevue rd E17
116 K 8	Bellevue rd Kingst
16 B 16	Bellevue rd N11
86 G 5	Bellevue rd SW13
106 K 1	Bellevue rd SW17
60 A 12	Bellevue rd W13
106 E 7	Bellew st SW17
10 B 20	Bellfield av Harrow
152 A 18	Bellfield rd Epsom
66 D 14	Bellflower clo E6
111 P 8	Bellingham grn SE6
111 S 6	Bellingham rd SE6
77 N 12	Bellot st SE10
81 T 16	Bellring clo Blvdr
87 X 5	Bells all SW6
4 D 14	Bells hill Barnt
108 E 12	Belltrees gro SW16
92 F 11	Bellwood rd SE15
118 H 10	Belmont av New Mald
6 A 14	Belmont av Barnt
5 Z 17	Belmont av Barnt
17 O 15	Belmont av N13
30 L 11	Belmont av N17
18 L 5	Belmont av N9
70 B 9	Belmont av S'hall
96 F 6	Belmont av Welling
60 M 2	Belmont av Wemb
24 A 6	Belmont cir Harrow
21 U 13	Belmont clo Wdfd Grn
6 A 14	Belmont clo Barnt
89 W 8	Belmont clo SW4
93 X 8	Belmont gro SE13
93 V 8	Belmont hill SE13
114 B 10	Belmont la Chisl
24 D 3	Belmont la Stanm
93 Y 10	Belmont Park clo SE13
33 S 19	Belmont Park rd E10
93 X 10	Belmont pk SE13
124 L 4	Belmont rd Becknhm
113 Z 12	Belmont rd Chisl
98 F 1	Belmont rd Erith
81 S 20	Belmont rd Erith
23 X 10	Belmont rd Harrow
54 C 9	Belmont rd Ilf
30 L 12	Belmont rd N17
124 A 13	Belmont rd SE25
89 W 8	Belmont rd SW4
101 P 3	Belmont rd Twick
73 X 12	Belmont rd W4
155 T 11	Belmont rd Wallgtn
153 U 16	Belmont ri Sutton
47 P 19	Belmont st NW1
89 Y 2	Belmore st SW8
86 H 9	Beloe clo SW15
50 C 17	Belsham st E9
17 R 19	Belsize av N13
46 J 16	Belsize av NW3
72 C 8	Belsize av W13
46 G 16	Belsize cres NW3
154 B 7	Belsize gdns Sutton
46 K 17	Belsize gro NW3
46 F 18	Belsize la NW3
46 G 16	Belsize ms NW3
46 J 17	Belsize Park gdns NW3
46 G 17	Belsize Park ms NW3
46 G 16	Belsize pl NW3
23 P 1	Belsize rd Harrow
130 C 2	Belsize rd NW6
130 D 1	Belsize rd NW6
46 E 20	Belsize rd NW6
129 Z 3	Belsize rd NW6
46 H 18	Belsize sq NW3
46 G 17	Belsize ter NW3
78 F 10	Belson rd SE18
105 P 6	Beltane dri SW19
89 V 19	Belthorn cres SW12
51 Z 12	Belton rd E11
52 J 20	Belton rd E7
31 S 10	Belton rd N17
44 G 17	Belton rd NW2
115 O 9	Belton rd Sidcp
64 A 14	Belton way E3
87 Z 5	Beltran rd SW6
81 W 10	Beltwood rd Blvdr
35 Z 8	Belvedere av Ilf
105 T 12	Belvedere av SW19
141 Z 19	Belvedere bldgs SE1
101 T 13	Belvedere clo Tedd
105 T 13	Belvedere dri SW19
105 S 13	Belvedere gro SW19
26 C 8	Belvedere NW9
141 Z 19	Belvedere pl SE1
98 B 7	Belvedere rd Bxly Hth
50 J 3	Belvedere rd E10
141 O 18	Belvedere rd SE1
109 U 17	Belvedere rd SE19
80 H 3	Belvedere rd SE2
71 U 7	Belvedere rd W7
105 S 12	Belvedere sq SW19
24 K 19	Belvedere way Harrow
113 R 6	Belvoir clo SE9
91 Y 19	Belvoir rd SE22
40 H 20	Belvue clo Nthlt
58 H 2	Belvue pk Nthlt

40 J 20	Belvue rd Nthlt
45 R 20	Bembridge clo NW6
132 M 3	Bemerton st N1
87 P 8	Bemish rd SW15
32 L 9	Bemsted rd E17
159 X 4	Ben Curtis pk Wkhm
91 P 2	Ben Hill rd SE5
63 U 15	Ben Jonson rd E1
151 U 1	Ben Smith way SE16
68 B 1	Ben Tillet clo Bark
79 X 11	Benares rd SE18
144 A 1	Benbow rd W6
74 K 8	Benbow rd W6
76 B 15	Benbow st SE8
111 U 12	Benbury clo Brom
102 E 7	Bench the Rich
157 V 13	Benchfield S Croy
107 W 17	Bencroft rd NW6
130 M 20	Bendall ms NW1
87 O 7	Bendemeer rd SW15
66 D 2	Bendish rd E6
80 A 12	Bendmore av SE2
88 A 20	Bendon valley SW18
120 G 7	Benedict rd Mitch
90 E 7	Benedict rd SW9
28 C 9	Benedict way N2
126 D 12	Benenden grn Brom
121 Z 3	Benett gdns SW16
154 D 6	Benfleet clo Sutton
160 G 7	Bengal ct EC3
53 Y 11	Bengal rd Ilf
23 R 7	Bengarth dri Harrow
58 A 3	Bengarth rd Nthlt
41 Z 8	Bengeworth rd Harrow
90 L 7	Bengeworth rd SE5
11 N 15	Benhale clo Stanm
88 F 9	Benham clo SW11
59 U 15	Benham rd W7
154 B 9	Benhill av Sutton
150 G 20	Benhill rd SE5
154 E 6	Benhill rd Sutton
154 C 5	Benhill Wood rd Sutton
154 B 6	Benhilton gdns Sutton
57 Y 11	Benhurst av Hornch
108 E 12	Benhurst ct SW16
93 Y 18	Benin st SE13
18 M 13	Benjafield clo N18
135 V 4	Benjamin clo E8
39 W 19	Benjamin clo Hornch
133 W 20	Benjamin st EC1
64 J 16	Benledi st E14
50 J 17	Benn st E9
88 K 13	Bennerley rd SW11
140 A 13	Bennet st SW1
116 D 1	Bennett clo Kingst
96 M 5	Bennett clo Welling
93 S 3	Bennett gro SE13
94 C 6	Bennett pk SE3
65 X 13	Bennett rd E13
37 Z 20	Bennett rd Rom
74 A 15	Bennett st W4
158 K 4	Bennetts av Croy
59 S 3	Bennetts av Grnfd
55 U 7	Bennetts Castle la Dgnhm
113 R 15	Bennetts copse Chisl
158 K 3	Bennetts way Croy
148 H 3	Bennetts wd SW1
13 N 19	Benningholme rd Edg
33 Y 2	Bennington rd Wdfd Grn
31 P 5	Bennington rd N17
36 B 3	Benrek clo Ilf
86 K 19	Bensby clo SW15
122 L 10	Bensham clo Thntn Hth
122 L 3	Bensham gro Thntn Hth
122 J 10	Bensham la Thntn Hth
122 M 9	Bensham Manor rd Thntn Hth
123 N 10	Bensham Manor rd Thntn Hth
15 Y 11	Bensley clo N11
65 Z 7	Benson av E6
82 G 10	Benson clo Hounsl
156 G 6	Benson rd Croy
92 D 20	Benson rd SE23
49 W 9	Benthal rd N16
50 F 18	Bentham rd E9
80 C 1	Bentham rd SE28
68 C 20	Bentham rd SE28
139 V 3	Bentinck ms W1
139 V 4	Bentinck st W1
36 B 17	Bentley dri Ilf
10 G 12	Bentley priory Stanm
49 S 18	Bentley rd N1
21 S 9	Bentley way Wdfd Grn
10 K 17	Bentley way Stanm
54 D 3	Benton rd Ilf
108 M 11	Bentons la SE27
109 N 11	Bentons ri SE27
55 Z 7	Bentry clo Dgnhm
56 A 7	Bentry rd Dgnhm
55 Z 7	Bentry rd Dgnhm
136 A 6	Bentworth rd W12
62 J 18	Bentworth rd W12
48 F 14	Benwell rd N7
63 Z 8	Benworth st E3
134 G 3	Benyon rd N1
88 M 13	Berber rd SW11
114 A 4	Bercta rd SE9
128 F 13	Berens rd NW10
15 Y 8	Beresford av N20
117 T 19	Beresford av Surb
84 F 15	Beresford av Twick
59 S 15	Beresford av W7
61 P 2	Beresford av Wemb
127 P 6	Beresford dri BR1
21 Y 13	Beresford dri Buck Hl
82 E 13	Beresford gdns Hounsl
8 D 14	Beresford gdns Enf
37 Z 17	Beresford gdns Rom
117 V 8	Beresford rd New Mald
33 R 4	Beresford rd E17
20 M 4	Beresford rd E4
23 O 16	Beresford rd Harrow
102 M 20	Beresford rd Kingst
103 N 20	Beresford rd Kingst
28 J 11	Beresford rd N2
49 N 15	Beresford rd N5
30 H 15	Beresford rd N8
153 V 18	Beresford rd Sutton
78 M 10	Beresford sq SE18
78 L 9	Beresford st SE18
48 M 15	Beresford ter N5
74 E 13	Berestede rd W6
50 F 17	Berger rd E9
35 P 14	Bergholt av Ilf
49 R 1	Bergholt cres N16
132 D 2	Bergholt way NW1
97 X 2	Berkeley av Bxly Hth
41 S 18	Berkeley av Grnfd
35 Y 7	Berkeley av Ilf
38 L 2	Berkeley av Rom
71 Z 18	Berkeley clo Brentf
16 G 1	Berkeley ct N14
18 A 2	Berkeley gdns N21
137 V 14	Berkeley gdns W8
139 R 5	Berkeley ms W1
105 P 17	Berkeley pl SW19
53 R 16	Berkeley rd E12
31 P 19	Berkeley rd N15
29 Y 17	Berkeley rd N8
25 P 14	Berkeley rd NW9
86 F 1	Berkeley rd SW13
139 Y 11	Berkeley sq W1
139 Z 12	Berkeley st W1
70 A 18	Berkeley waye Hounsl
81 R 12	Berkhampstead rd Blvdr
43 O 18	Berkhamsted av Wemb
5 U 18	Berkley cres Barnt
131 S 1	Berkley gro NW1
131 R 1	Berkley rd NW1
17 S 20	Berkshire gdns N13
18 M 17	Berkshire gdns N18
51 N 17	Berkshire rd E9
122 A 10	Berkshire way Mitch
121 Z 10	Berkshire way Mitch
44 C 13	Bermans way NW10
150 K 1	Bermondsey sq SE1
142 J 17	Bermondsey st SE1
143 R 16	Bermondsey Wall west SE16
143 U 18	Bermondsey Wall east SE16
72 B 7	Bernard av W13
65 R 14	Bernard Cassidy st E16
105 W 12	Bernard gdns SW19
31 V 15	Bernard rd N15
56 K 1	Bernard rd Rom
38 K 20	Bernard rd Rom
155 K 9	Bernard rd Wallgtn
132 K 18	Bernard st WC1
11 R 19	Bernays clo Stanm
90 D 9	Bernays gro SW9
122 K 10	Berne rd Thntn Hth
158 M 4	Bernel dri Croy
140 C 2	Berners ms W1
140 D 4	Berners pl W1
133 V 6	Berners rd N1
30 E 6	Berners rd N22
140 C 3	Berners st W1
123 N 17	Berney rd Croy
25 O 15	Bernville way NW9
21 N 11	Bernwell rd E4
25 R 3	Berridge grn Edg
109 P 12	Berridge rd SE19
48 E 9	Berriman rd N7
40 E 5	Berriton rd Harrow
17 W 4	Berry clo N21
44 A 20	Berry clo NW10
11 V 13	Berry hill Stanm
109 P 9	Berry la SE27
133 X 14	Berry pl EC1
133 X 16	Berry st EC1
72 J 8	Berry way W5
58 B 11	Berrydale Grnfd
127 R 2	Berryfield clo BR1
33 S 14	Berryfield clo E17
149 Y 10	Berryfield rd SE17
95 Y 10	Berryhill gdns SE9
95 Y 9	Berryhill SE9
116 L 13	Berrylands rd Surb
117 N 13	Berrylands rd Surb
117 R 12	Berrylands Surb
119 N 7	Berrylands SE20
55 V 10	Berryman clo Dgnhm
110 F 10	Berrymans la SE26
73 V 4	Berrymead gdns W3
73 X 8	Berrymede rd W4
122 K 12	Bert rd Thntn Hth
8 J 14	Bert way Enf
106 F 11	Bertal rd SW17
76 C 18	Berthon st SE8
44 G 18	Bertie rd NW10
110 G 14	Bertie rd SE26
105 X 18	Bertram cotts SW19
8 J 14	Bertram rd Enf
103 O 17	Bertram rd Kingst
26 H 19	Bertram rd NW4
47 S 8	Bertram rd N19
93 R 7	Bertrand st SE13
68 F 19	Bertrand way SE28
58 A 19	Berwick av Hay
10 J 20	Berwick clo Stanm
96 H 17	Berwick cres Sidcp
65 X 18	Berwick rd E16
30 H 4	Berwick rd N22
97 R 3	Berwick rd Welling
140 C 5	Berwick st W1
82 J 2	Berwyn av Hounsl
85 S 10	Berwyn rd Rich
108 J 1	Berwyn rd SE21
66 E 14	Beryl av E6
144 F 11	Beryl rd W6
103 T 18	Berystede clo Kingst
45 S 11	Besant rd NW2
43 W 15	Besant way NW10
107 V 16	Besley st SW16
148 G 10	Bessborough gdns SW1
148 F 9	Bessborough ms SW1
148 F 10	Bessborough pl SW1
104 G 1	Bessborough rd SW15
86 H 20	Bessborough rd SW15
41 R 3	Bessborough rd Harrow
148 F 10	Bessborough st SW1
148 G 10	Bessborough way SW1
90 M 6	Bessemer rd SE5
91 N 5	Bessemer rd SE5
92 E 1	Besson st SE14
75 T 12	Bestwood st SE8
154 F 10	Betchworth clo Sutton
54 H 8	Betchworth rd Ilf
159 T 18	Betchworth way Croy
59 R 10	Betham rd Grnfd
23 T 14	Bethecar rd Harrow
97 U 8	Bethel rd Welling
65 P 11	Bethell av E16
53 W 1	Bethell av Ilf
110 M 19	Bethersden clo Becknhm
135 U 14	Bethnal Green rd E2
135 Z 11	Bethnal Green museum E2
15 Z 14	Bethune av N11
49 S 4	Bethune rd N16
61 Z 12	Bethune rd NW10
150 C 17	Bethwin rd SE5
149 Z 17	Bethwin rd SE5
22 G 13	Betjemin clo Harrow
124 E 20	Betony clo CR0
20 M 13	Betoyne av E4
16 F 14	Betstyle rd N11
115 Z 4	Betterton dri Sidcp
140 K 5	Betterton st WC2
65 N 4	Bettons pk E15
87 W 5	Bettridge rd SW6
65 V 19	Betts rd E16
143 V 9	Betts st E1
116 B 20	Betts way Surb
122 M 4	Beulah av Thntn Hth
12 E 10	Beulah clo Edg
122 M 4	Beulah cres Thntn Hth
122 L 14	Beulah gro Croy
108 K 16	Beulah hill SE19
33 T 14	Beulah rd E17
153 Y 9	Beulah rd Sutton
105 V 17	Beulah rd SW19
122 L 5	Beulah rd Thntn Hth
99 W 9	Beult rd Drtfrd
68 A 1	Bevan av Bark
156 F 11	Bevan ct Croy
5 Z 13	Bevan rd Barnt
80 C 14	Bevan rd SE2
134 B 6	Bevan st N1
134 G 12	Bevenden st N1
82 D 11	Beverley av Hounsl
96 J 19	Beverley av Sidcp
104 E 19	Beverley av SW20
17 Y 6	Beverley clo N21
88 F 10	Beverley clo SW11
86 F 5	Beverley clo SW13
34 H 3	Beverley cres Wdfd Grn
16 H 2	Beverley ct N14
92 M 7	Beverley ct SE4
25 R 9	Beverley dri Edg
27 T 20	Beverley gdns NW11
23 Y 5	Beverley gdns Stanm
86 E 7	Beverley gdns SW13
43 O 3	Beverley gdns Wemb
104 B 18	Beverley la Kingst
118 F 7	Beverley pk New Mald
118 F 9	Beverley rd New Mald
98 K 6	Beverley rd Bxly Hth
56 A 12	Beverley rd Dgnhm
55 Z 12	Beverley rd Dgnhm
20 K 19	Beverley rd E4
66 B 9	Beverley rd E6
102 E 20	Beverley rd Kingst
121 W 8	Beverley rd Mitch
70 C 10	Beverley rd S'hall
123 Z 3	Beverley rd SE20
86 E 6	Beverley rd SW13
74 C 14	Beverley rd W4
152 L 3	Beverley rd Worc Pk
104 C 20	Beverley way New Mald
118 G 3	Beverley way SW20
47 Y 10	Beversbrook rd N19
122 H 9	Beverstone rd Thntn Hth
90 C 12	Beverstone rd SW2
107 N 13	Bevill Allen clo SW17
75 V 3	Bevin clo SE16
133 R 11	Bevin way WC1
125 P 1	Bevington rd Becknhm
136 M 1	Bevington rd W10
137 N 2	Bevington rd W10
143 U 18	Bevington st SE16
142 L 5	Bevis marks EC3
7 N 14	Bewcastle gdns Enf
48 F 20	Bewdley st N1
89 S 4	Bewick st SW8
63 O 19	Bewley st E1
143 Z 8	Bewley st E1
108 J 11	Bewleys rd SE27
100 A 3	Bexhill clo Felt
16 J 17	Bexhill rd N11
92 L 17	Bexhill rd SE4
85 W 8	Bexhill rd SW14
99 P 12	Bexley clo Dartford
18 B 11	Bexley gdns N9
98 E 20	Bexley High st Bxly
99 P 12	Bexley la Drtford
115 U 8	Bexley la Sidcp
96 C 14	Bexley rd SE9
154 L 11	Beynon rd Carsh
151 R 14	Bianca st SE15
27 V 8	Bibsworth rd N3
85 S 8	Bicester rd Rich
131 P 20	Bickenhall st W1
106 M 14	Bickersteth rd SW17
47 U 8	Bickerton rd N19
127 R 8	Bickley cres Brom
127 U 5	Bickley Park rd Brom

Ref	Name
127 P 4	Bickley rd Brom
33 R 20	Bickley rd E10
106 K 13	Bickley st SW17
90 M 8	Bicknell rd SE5
8 F 5	Bicknoller rd Enf
126 C 12	Bidborough clo Brom
132 H 13	Bidborough st WC1
113 V 9	Biddenden way SE9
64 L 14	Bidder st E16
48 C 13	Biddestone rd N7
156 L 20	Biddulph rd S Croy
129 Y 14	Biddulph rd W9
60 A 7	Bideford av Grnfd
25 O 5	Bideford clo Edg
100 E 6	Bideford clo Felt
18 E 2	Bideford gdns Enf
112 B 7	Bideford rd Brom
9 X 3	Bideford rd Enf
80 D 20	Bideford rd Welling
29 V 3	Bidwell gdns N11
92 A 3	Bidwell st SE15
50 A 3	Big hill E5
31 R 1	Bigbury clo N17
64 G 2	Biggerstaff rd E15
48 E 7	Biggerstaff st N4
120 L 1	Biggin av Mitch
108 K 17	Biggin hill SE19
108 K 19	Biggin way SE19
108 H 19	Bigginwood rd SW16
87 O 8	Biggs row SW15
63 N 18	Bigland st E1
78 M 14	Bignell rd SE18
52 F 13	Bignold rd E7
28 A 17	Bigwood rd NW11
37 W 10	Billet clo Rom
32 H 5	Billet rd E17
33 O 3	Billet rd E17
37 T 10	Billet rd Rom
145 Y 17	Billing pl SW10
145 Z 16	Billing rd SW10
145 Y 17	Billing st SW10
92 G 10	Billingford clo SE4
76 G 16	Billingsgate st SE10
75 T 20	Billington rd SE14
142 K 7	Billiter sq EC3
142 K 7	Billiter st EC3
70 G 11	Billson st E14
113 O 10	Bilsby gro SE9
60 D 3	Bilton rd Grnfd
59 Z 3	Bilton rd Grnfd
9 X 4	Bilton way Enf
146 B 8	Bina gdns SW5
7 R 12	Bincote rd Enf
74 E 7	Binden rd W12
120 B 8	Bindon gdns Mrdn
157 U 10	Binfield rd S Croy
90 A 3	Binfield rd SW4
132 M 3	Bingfield st N1
133 N 3	Bingfield st N1
131 T 19	Bingham pl W1
123 Y 20	Bingham rd Croy
49 O 17	Bingham st N1
65 X 17	Bingley rd E16
59 N 12	Bingley rd Grnfd
139 V 8	Binney st W1
73 Z 13	Binns rd W4
10 H 17	Binyon cres Stanm
113 T 5	Birbetts rd SE9
17 Y 12	Birch av N13
72 B 19	Birch clo Brentf
38 G 10	Birch clo Rom
91 Y 5	Birch clo SE15
101 Y 11	Birch clo Tedd
56 L 10	Birch gdns Dgnhm
94 C 18	Birch gro SE12
73 O 2	Birch gro W3
61 P 20	Birch gro W3
97 N 11	Birch gro Welling
158 G 10	Birch hill Croy
22 L 1	Birch pk Harrow
100 A 13	Birch rd Felt
38 G 10	Birch rd Rom
127 X 16	Birch row Brom
157 Z 2	Birch Tree way Croy
81 Y 15	Birch wlk Erith
121 S 1	Birch wlk Mitch
123 X 12	Birchanger rd SE25
55 V 1	Birchdale gdns Rom
52 M 15	Birchdale rd E7
43 X 6	Birchen clo NW9
43 X 8	Birchen gro NW9
7 P 19	Birches the N21
77 W 15	Birches the SE7
72 D 19	Birchfield clo Brentf
64 A 19	Birchfield st E14
160 G 7	Birchin la EC3
98 F 1	Birchington clo Bxly Hth
29 X 17	Birchington rd N8
129 V 4	Birchington rd NW6
117 O 18	Birchington rd Surb
88 M 18	Birchlands av SW12
89 N 18	Birchlands av SW12
48 L 11	Birchmore wlk N5
124 L 8	Birchwood av Becknhm
155 R 4	Birchwood av Wallgtn
29 P 11	Birchwood av N10
115 R 7	Birchwood av Sidcp
25 V 8	Birchwood ct Edg
17 V 16	Birchwood ct N13
46 B 10	Birchwood dri NW3
100 J 15	Birchwood gro Hampt
107 R 11	Birchwood rd SW17
110 D 4	Bird in the Hand pass SE23
139 V 6	Bird st W1
82 E 20	Bird wlk Twick
151 R 17	Bird-in-Bush rd SE15
127 O 4	Bird-in-Hand la Brom
56 K 20	Birdbrook clo Dgnhm
69 X 1	Birdbrook clo Dgnhm
94 M 8	Birdbrook rd SE3
140 C 19	Birdcage wlk SW1
127 S 12	Birdham clo Brom
157 P 9	Birdhurst av S Croy
157 P 9	Birdhurst gdns S Croy
157 R 10	Birdhurst rd S Croy
88 C 12	Birdhurst rd SW18
106 J 16	Birdhurst rd SW19
157 R 11	Birdhurst ri S Croy
150 J 15	Birdlip clo SE15
38 G 3	Birds Farm av Rom
59 O 3	Birkbeck av Grnfd
61 W 19	Birkbeck av W3
21 R 9	Birkbeck gdns Wdfd Grn
73 X 4	Birkbeck gro W3
108 K 2	Birkbeck hill SE21
108 K 2	Birkbeck pl SE21
124 D 4	Birkbeck rd Becknhm
49 U 16	Birkbeck rd E8
8 B 5	Birkbeck rd Enf
36 D 16	Birkbeck rd Ilf
15 O 17	Birkbeck rd N12
31 U 5	Birkbeck rd N17
30 A 13	Birkbeck rd N8
13 S 16	Birkbeck rd NW7
57 N 3	Birkbeck rd Rom
115 O 8	Birkbeck rd Sidcp
106 B 14	Birkbeck rd SW19
73 X 3	Birkbeck rd W3
72 E 10	Birkbeck rd W5
63 O 10	Birkbeck st E2
135 Y 14	Birkbeck st E2
59 O 3	Birkbeck way Grnfd
22 H 10	Birkdale av Pinn
80 A 11	Birkdale av SE2
79 Z 10	Birkdale rd SE2
60 J 12	Birkdale rd W5
116 M 2	Birkenhead av Kingst
117 N 2	Birkenhead av Kingst
111 X 3	Birkhall rd SE6
89 Y 20	Birkwood clo SW12
15 R 8	Birley rd N20
89 O 5	Birley st SW11
99 R 1	Birling rd Erith
48 C 7	Birnam rd N4
44 B 11	Birse cres NW10
31 T 15	Birstall rd N15
144 F 11	Biscay rd W6
70 H 16	Biscoe clo Hounsl
93 X 9	Biscoe way SE13
157 S 2	Bisenden rd Croy
120 L 18	Bisham clo Carsh
47 R 3	Bisham gdns N6
7 V 7	Bishop Craven clo Enf
23 W 6	Bishop Ken rd Harrow
144 L 5	Bishop Kings rd W14
16 D 4	Bishop rd N14
134 B 4	Bishop st N1
154 E 11	Bishop's pl Sutton
126 K 5	Bishops av Brom
65 U 2	Bishops av E13
37 T 17	Bishops av Rom
87 R 4	Bishops av Welling
46 G 2	Bishops av the N2
28 H 16	Bishops av the N2
138 B 4	Bishops Bridge rd W2
4 A 20	Bishops clo Barnt
33 S 13	Bishops clo E17
8 M 9	Bishops clo Enf
47 U 10	Bishops clo N19
102 G 6	Bishops clo Rich
114 B 4	Bishops clo SE9
153 Z 6	Bishops clo Sutton
141 X 4	Bishops ct EC4
141 R 4	Bishops ct WC2
100 G 11	Bishops gro Hampt
28 H 18	Bishops gro N2
116 G 3	Bishops hall Kingst
108 A 20	Bishops Park rd SW16
122 B 1	Bishops Park rd SW16
87 R 4	Bishops Park rd SW6
87 O 4	Bishops pk SW6
122 H 18	Bishops rd Croy
29 P 19	Bishops rd N6
145 O 20	Bishops rd SW6
87 U 1	Bishops rd W7
71 T 5	Bishops rd W7
149 T 5	Bishops ter SE11
63 O 6	Bishops way E2
135 Y 8	Bishops way E2
44 A 20	Bishops way NW10
158 G 12	Bishops wlk Croy
120 G 13	Bishopsford rd Mrdn
142 J 3	Bishopsgate chyd EC2
142 K 3	Bishopsgate EC2
110 E 9	Bishopsthorpe rd SE26
46 M 1	Bishopswood rd N6
47 N 2	Bishopswood rd N6
119 N 20	Bisley clo Worc Pk
61 N 9	Bispham rd NW10
60 M 9	Bispham rd Wemb
64 G 5	Bisson rd E15
33 X 10	Bisterne av E17
14 B 18	Bittacy clo NW7
14 C 19	Bittacy hill NW7
27 S 2	Bittacy hill NW7
14 B 19	Bittacy hill pk NW7
14 B 18	Bittacy Park av NW7
14 D 20	Bittacy rd NW7
14 A 19	Bittacy ri NW7
142 A 18	Bittern st SE1
116 H 6	Bittoms the Kingst
70 E 9	Bixley clo S'hall
30 M 16	Black Boy la N15
135 N 19	Black Eagle st E1
150 F 1	Black Horse ct SE1
75 W 15	Black Horse rd SE8
115 O 10	Black Horse rd Sidcp
74 F 12	Black Lion la W6
143 S 2	Black Lion yd E1
149 O 7	Black Prince rd SE11
50 G 2	Black pth E10
142 K 17	Black Swan yd SE1
90 G 9	Black Tree ms SW9
134 H 16	Blackall st EC2
70 B 20	Blackberry Farm clo Hounsl
43 W 8	Blackbird hill NW9
56 F 18	Blackborne rd Dgnhm
127 V 5	Blackbrook la Brom
45 Z 18	Blackburn rd NW6
139 T 10	Blackburnes ms W1
37 V 17	Blackbush av Rom
154 B 16	Blackbush clo Sutton
87 O 8	Blackett st SW15
96 J 14	Blackfen rd Sidcp
97 P 15	Blackfen rd Sidcp
156 K 18	Blackford clo S Croy
141 W 10	Blackfriars br EC4
141 X 8	Blackfriars rd EC4
141 W 17	Blackfriars rd SE1
141 V 9	Blackfriars underpass EC4
93 Z 1	Blackheath av SE10
94 C 6	Blackheath gro SE3
93 T 2	Blackheath hill SE10
94 E 7	Blackheath pk SE3
93 R 2	Blackheath rd SE10
93 U 4	Blackheath ri SE13
93 Z 4	Blackheath vale SE3
94 B 6	Blackheath village SE3
123 Y 17	Blackhorse la Croy
32 F 9	Blackhorse la E17
32 G 14	Blackhorse rd E17
111 T 10	Blacklands rd SE6
147 O 7	Blacklands ter SW3
71 R 2	Blackmore av S'hall
101 Y 14	Blackmores gro Tedd
91 Z 5	Blackpool rd SE15
144 B 8	Blacks rd W6
74 M 12	Blacks rd W6
134 L 2	Blackshaw pl N1
106 H 13	Blackshaw rd SW17
48 H 7	Blackstock rd N4
45 N 14	Blackstone rd NW2
124 B 19	Blackthorn av Croy
97 Y 7	Blackthorn gro Bxly Hth
64 B 13	Blackthorn st E3
20 K 13	Blackthorne dri E4
77 N 8	Blackwall la SE10
77 O 12	Blackwall la SE10
64 F 9	Blackwall tunnel northern appr E14
76 K 1	Blackwall tunnel E14
77 P 1	Blackwall tunnel1 appr SE10
76 H 1	Blackwall way E14
64 H 20	Blackwall way E14
91 U 13	Blackwater st SE22
23 P 2	Blackwell clo Harrow
12 C 12	Blackwell gdns Edg
150 D 10	Blackwood st SE17
97 V 18	Bladindon dri Bxly
125 Y 4	Bladon ct Brom
22 K 18	Bladon gdns Harrow
16 J 8	Blagdens clo N14
16 J 7	Blagdens la N14
118 E 8	Blagdon ho New Mald
118 E 8	Blagdon rd Mald Mald
93 R 16	Blagdon rd SE13
102 D 16	Blagdon wlk Tedd
137 N 2	Blagrove rd W10
44 A 2	Blair av NW9
96 G 14	Blair clo Sidcp
64 H 18	Blair st E14
108 A 3	Blairderry rd SW2
67 W 4	Blake av Bark
87 Z 1	Blake gdns SW6
52 F 5	Blake Hall cres E11
52 F 3	Blake Hall rd E11
157 R 2	Blake rd Croy
65 O 12	Blake rd E16
120 H 5	Blake rd Mitch
16 J 20	Blake rd N11
29 V 2	Blake rd N11
154 M 13	Blakehall rd Carsh
122 D 11	Blakemore rd Thntn Hth
107 Z 6	Blakemore rd SW16
80 L 9	Blakemore way Blvdr
110 M 20	Blakeney av Becknhm
15 P 6	Blakeney clo N20
110 L 19	Blakeney rd Becknhm
106 L 10	Blakenham rd SW17
107 N 9	Blakenham rd SW17
118 E 13	Blakes av New Mald
125 T 19	Blakes grn W Wkhm
118 D 13	Blakes la New Mald
150 L 19	Blakes rd SE15
118 G 12	Blakes ter New Mald
60 F 17	Blakesley av W5
119 U 3	Blakesley wlk SW20
18 C 3	Blakesware gdns N9
151 Z 19	Blanch clo SE15
113 R 6	Blanchard clo SE9
49 V 19	Blanchard way E16
65 P 12	Blanche st E16
91 O 8	Blanchedowne SE5
120 A 11	Blanchland rd Mrdn
89 P 17	Blandfield rd SW12
124 G 2	Blandford av Becknhm
100 L 1	Blandford av Twick
156 A 6	Blandford clo Croy
28 E 14	Blandford clo N2
38 G 13	Blandford clo Rom
20 F 3	Blandford cres E4
124 D 5	Blandford rd Becknhm
70 G 10	Blandford rd S'hall
101 S 14	Blandford rd Tedd
74 A 8	Blandford rd W4
72 H 5	Blandford rd W5
130 M 18	Blandford sq NW1
139 T 3	Blandford st W1
66 L 9	Blaney cres E6
114 A 2	Blanmerle rd SE9
113 Y 2	Blanmerle rd SE9
94 M 17	Blann clo SE9
146 E 18	Blantyre st SW10
93 Y 18	Blashford st SE 13
23 U 14	Blawith rd Harrow
31 Z 1	Blaydon clo N17
79 X 16	Blean gro SE20
110 B 18	Blean gro SE20
59 X 6	Bleasdale av Grnfd
97 U 15	Bleddyn clo Bxly
80 H 1	Bledlow clo SE2
59 N 6	Bledlow ri Grnfd
141 U 1	Bleeding Heart yd EC1

107 V 14	Blegborough rd SW16	
97 W 17	Blendon dri Bxly	
112 D 19	Blendon pth Brom	
97 V 16	Blendon rd Bxly	
150 E 9	Blendon rd SE17	
150 E 8	Blendon row SE17	
79 P 15	Blendon ter SE18	
35 V 19	Blenheim av Ilf	
17 Y 4	Blenheim clo N21	
59 R 7	Blenheim clo Nrthlt	
38 J 12	Blenheim clo Rom	
118 L 7	Blenheim clo SW20	
155 V 16	Blenheim clo Wallgtn	
156 L 17	Blenheim cres S Croy	
136 L 7	Blenheim cres W11	
137 N 6	Blenheim cres W11	
114 E 6	Blenheim ct Sidcp	
96 K 3	Blenheim dri Welling	
103 S 19	Blenheim gdns Kingst	
155 V 15	Blenheim gdns Wallgtn	
45 N 15	Blenheim gdns NW2	
90 B 15	Blenheim gdns SW2	
42 K 9	Blenheim gdns Wemb	
91 W 5	Blenheim gro SE15	
156 L 17	Blenheim Park rd S Croy	
130 B 8	Blenheim pas NW8	
4 C 13	Blenheim rd Barnt	
127 R 9	Blenheim rd Brom	
52 A 12	Blenheim rd E15	
32 G 10	Blenheim rd E17	
66 A 8	Blenheim rd E6	
40 L 18	Blenheim rd Grnfd	
22 J 17	Blenheim rd Harrow	
22 L 18	Blenheim rd Harrow	
30 E 8	Blenheim rd N22	
130 C 7	Blenheim rd NW8	
110 C 18	Blenheim rd SE20	
115 T 3	Blenheim rd Sidcp	
153 Z 4	Blenheim rd Sutton	
118 L 7	Blenheim rd SW20	
74 B 8	Blenheim rd W4	
31 V 14	Blenheim ri N15	
139 X 7	Blenheim st W1	
130 B 8	Blenheim ter NW8	
88 L 17	Blenkarne rd SW11	
25 V 4	Blessbury rd Edg	
93 X 9	Blessington clo SE13	
93 X 9	Blessington rd SE13	
134 C 10	Bletchely st N1	
134 D 10	Bletchley ct N1	
105 P 4	Blincoe clo SW19	
93 R 3	Bliss cres SE13	
93 T 1	Blissett st SE10	
58 B 10	Blisworth clo Grnfd	
55 P 19	Blithbury rd Dgnhm	
80 B 11	Blithdale rd SE2	
79 Z 11	Blithdale rd SE2	
145 W 3	Blithfield st W8	
42 A 8	Blockley rd Wemb	
74 J 3	Bloemfontein av W12	
62 H 19	Bloemfontein rd W12	
74 J 3	Bloemfontein rd W12	
130 E 18	Blomfield rd W9	
129 Z 20	Blomfield rd W9	
160 H 2	Blomfield st EC2	
142 H 3	Blomfield st EC2	
137 Z 1	Blomfield vlls W2	
56 A 8	Blomville rd Dgnhm	
89 N 4	Blondel st SW11	
72 C 10	Blondin av W5	
64 B 6	Blondin st E3	
108 J 7	Bloom gro SE27	
145 N 20	Bloom Park rd SW6	
148 D 6	Bloomburg st SW1	
36 A 19	Bloomfield cres Ilf	
139 Y 8	Bloomfield pl W1	
126 M 11	Bloomfield rd Brom	
127 N 10	Bloomfield rd Brom	
116 K 8	Bloomfield rd Kingst	
29 P 19	Bloomfield rd N6	
79 N 13	Bloomfield rd SE18	
147 U 9	Bloomfield ter SW1	
109 P 13	Bloomhall rd SE19	
61 O 19	Bloomsbury clo W5	
22 E 9	Bloomsbury ct Pinn	
140 L 3	Bloomsbury ct WC1	
140 L 1	Bloomsbury pl WC1	
140 K 1	Bloomsbury sq WC1	
140 H 2	Bloomsbury st WC1	
140 K 3	Bloomsbury way WC1	
89 X 3	Blore clo SW8	
157 V 10	Blossom clo S Croy	
72 L 6	Blossom clo W5	
7 X 5	Blossom la Enf	
134 M 19	Blossom st E1	
70 B 18	Blossom waye Hounsl	
63 W 16	Blount st E14	
50 K 4	Bloxhall rd E10	
100 F 19	Bloxham cres Hampt	
95 R 13	Bloxham gdns SE9	
155 V 6	Bloxworth clo Wallgtn	
150 B 20	Blucher rd SE5	
91 X 1	Blue Anchor la SE15	
151 V 5	Blue Anchor la SE16	
143 R 10	Blue Anchor yd E1	
140 B 14	Blue Bell yd SW1	
109 V 10	Bluebell clo SE26	
100 G 13	Bluefield clo Hampt	
21 N 9	Bluehouse rd E4	
26 A 3	Blundell rd Edg	
25 Z 4	Blundell rd Edg	
48 A 20	Blundell st N7	
55 U 3	Blunden clo Dgnhm	
157 O 11	Blunt rd S Croy	
95 W 14	Blunts st SE9	
50 D 13	Blurton rd E5	
50 L 2	Blyth rd E17	
68 F 20	Blyth rd SE28	
92 K 19	Blythe clo SE6	
92 L 19	Blythe Hill la SE6	
92 L 20	Blythe hill SE6	
126 C 1	Blythe rd Brom	
144 F 1	Blythe rd W14	
144 K 3	Blythe rd W14	
135 V 12	Blythe st E2	
110 L 2	Blythe vale SE6	
54 M 3	Blythswood rd Ilf	
48 B 1	Blythwood rd N4	
133 N 6	Boadicea st N1	
80 M 9	Boarers Manor way Blvdr	
151 P 18	Boathouse wlk SE15	
89 U 7	Bobbin clo SW4	
39 U 3	Bobs la Rom	
103 N 17	Bockhampton rd Kingst	
135 X 4	Bocking st E8	
63 N 3	Bocking st E8	
8 C 9	Bodiam clo Enf	
107 Y 19	Bodiam rd SW16	
105 R 5	Bodicott clo SW19	
118 A 13	Bodley clo New Mald	
117 Z 13	Bodley rd New Mald	
40 E 10	Bodmin clo Nthlt	
120 A 10	Bodmin gro Mrdn	
105 Z 2	Bodmin st SW18	
118 H 5	Bodnant gdns New Mald	
49 Z 14	Bodney rd E5	
97 V 2	Bognor rd Welling	
50 B 16	Bohemia pl E8	
5 Y 19	Bohun gro Barnt	
74 H 18	Boileau rd SW13	
60 M 17	Boileau rd W5	
61 N 16	Boileau rd W5	
93 P 4	Bolden st SE8	
159 R 3	Bolderwood way W Wckm	
8 M 5	Boleyn av Enf	
159 S 4	Boleyn gdns W Wckm	
56 J 20	Boleyn gdns Dgnhm	
159 T 3	Boleyn gro BR4	
66 A 5	Boleyn rd E6	
65 W 1	Boleyn rd E7	
49 S 14	Boleyn rd N16	
5 P 12	Boleyn way Barnt	
75 P 14	Boleyn rd SE16	
88 K 16	Bolingbroke gro SW11	
144 G 1	Bolingbroke rd W14	
136 H 20	Bolingbroke rd W14	
88 H 1	Bolingbroke wlk SW11	
73 T 7	Bollo Br rd W3	
73 R 6	Bollo la W3	
73 V 10	Bollo la W4	
149 N 18	Bolney st SW8	
100 C 6	Bolney way Felt	
131 Z 20	Bolsover st W1	
121 S 2	Bolstead rd Mitch	
141 U 6	Bolt ct EC4	
27 P 11	Boltmore clo NW4	
149 V 17	Bolton cres SE5	
146 A 10	Bolton Gardens ms SW5	
112 C 16	Bolton gdns Brom	
128 F 10	Bolton gdns NW10	
146 A 8	Bolton gdns SW5	
101 Y 15	Bolton gdns Tedd	
52 D 19	Bolton rd E15	
18 G 16	Bolton rd N18	
62 C 3	Bolton rd NW10	
129 Z 6	Bolton rd NW8	
73 V 20	Bolton rd W4	
85 W 1	Bolton rd W1	
139 Z 13	Bolton st W1	
146 B 10	Boltons the SW10	
41 X 12	Boltons the Wemb	
151 V 5	Bombay st SE16	
136 J 8	Bomore rd W11	
109 R 11	Bon Marche ter SE27	
113 S 18	Bonar pl Chisl	
151 R 20	Bonar rd SE15	
113 W 19	Bonchester clo Chisl	
154 B 17	Bonchurch clo Sutton	
136 K 1	Bonchurch rd W10	
72 A 4	Bonchurch rd W13	
160 E 7	Bond ct EC4	
155 V 7	Bond gdns Wallgtn	
120 K 3	Bond rd Mitch	
51 Y 14	Bond st E15	
	Bond st W1	
	see under	
	New & Old Bond St	
73 Z 12	Bond st W4	
72 G 1	Bond st W5	
66 F 15	Bondfield rd E6	
148 K 14	Bondway SW8	
78 E 8	Boneta rd SE18	
93 V 10	Bonfield rd SE13	
55 W 7	Bonham rd Dgnhm	
90 B 13	Bonham rd SW2	
73 Y 7	Bonheur rd W4	
134 G 18	Bonhill st EC2	
22 K 3	Boniface gdns Harrow	
22 K 2	Boniface wlk Harrow	
117 O 5	Bonner Hill rd Kingst	
63 P 6	Bonner rd E2	
63 S 7	Bonner st E2	
23 X 17	Bonnersfield clo Harrow	
23 X 17	Bonnersfield la Harrow	
23 Z 17	Bonnersfield la Harrow	
89 V 15	Bonneville gdns SW4	
149 N 14	Bonnington sq SW8	
132 A 1	Bonny st NW1	
101 W 5	Bonser rd Twick	
150 J 18	Bonsor st SE5	
112 D 13	Bonville rd Brom	
18 K 16	Booker rd N18	
94 A 9	Boone st SE13	
93 Z 10	Boone st SE13	
94 A 9	Boones rd SE13	
77 N 8	Boord st SE10	
134 H 14	Boot st N1	
80 E 2	Booth clo SE28	
156 J 3	Booth rd Croy	
26 B 8	Booth rd NW9	
25 Z 6	Booth rd NW9	
47 X 6	Boothby rd N19	
140 B 3	Booths pl W1	
59 U 14	Bordars rd W7	
59 T 14	Bordars wlk W7	
18 B 1	Borden av Enf	
86 G 19	Borden wlk SW15	
109 Z 12	Border rd SE26	
106 K 20	Border ga Mitch	
159 P 7	Border gdns Croy	
110 B 13	Border rd SE26	
120 A 9	Bordesley rd Mrdn	
65 T 18	Boreham av E16	
51 T 3	Boreham clo E11	
30 K 6	Boreham rd N22	
78 F 11	Borgard rd SE18	
92 D 11	Borland rd SE15	
102 B 17	Borland rd Tedd	
87 N 9	Borneo st SW15	
142 B 19	Borough High st SE1	
156 H 6	Borough hill Croy	
83 T 1	Borough rd Islwth	
103 P 19	Borough rd Kingst	
120 J 3	Borough rd Mitch	
142 A 19	Borough rd SE1	
141 Y 20	Borough rd SE1	
149 Z 10	Borrett rd SE17	
88 B 15	Borrodaile rd SW18	
23 Y 8	Borrowdale av Harrow	
35 H 12	Borrowdale clo Ilf	
52 A 12	Borthwick rd E15	
51 Z 13	Borthwick rd E15	
26 D 19	Borthwick rd NW9	
76 B 15	Borthwick st SE8	
32 K 11	Borwick av E17	
111 U 8	Bosbury rd SE6	
47 R 10	Boscastle rd NW5	
147 V 4	Boscobel pl SW1	
130 G 19	Boscobel st NW8	
33 V 20	Boscombe av E10	
50 H 14	Boscombe clo E5	
108 B 16	Boscombe gdns SW16	
119 N 19	Boscombe rd Worc Pk	
107 O 15	Boscombe rd SW17	
105 Z 19	Boscombe rd SW19	
74 H 4	Boscombe rd W12	
20 F 7	Bosgrove E4	
143 N 16	Boss st SE1	
98 A 8	Bostal row Bxly Hth	
80 E 14	Bostall heath SE2	
80 F 15	Bostall Hill rd SE2	
80 C 15	Bostall hill SE2	
80 F 14	Bostall House lodge SE2	
80 D 12	Bostall la SE2	
80 D 10	Bostall manorway SE2	
80 L 20	Bostall Park av Bxly Hth	
115 P 19	Bostall rd Orp	
72 A 12	Boston gdns Brentf	
71 Z 12	Boston gdns Brentf	
74 B 16	Boston gdns W4	
72 B 13	Boston Manor ho Brentf	
72 B 12	Boston Manor rd Brentf	
72 D 15	Boston Park rd Brentf	
131 N 18	Boston pl NW1	
122 D 15	Boston rd Croy	
33 N 19	Boston rd E17	
66 C 9	Boston rd E6	
25 V 2	Boston rd Edg	
71 X 7	Boston rd W7	
135 S 9	Boston st E2	
71 Y 11	Boston vale W7	
71 U 5	Bostonthorpe rd W7	
132 M 20	Boswell ct WC1	
122 L 9	Boswell rd Thntn Hth	
132 M 20	Boswell st WC1	
32 K 5	Bosworth clo E17	
4 M 12	Bosworth rd Barnt	
56 F 10	Bosworth rd Dgnhm	
16 L 18	Bosworth rd N11	
128 L 18	Bosworth rd W10	
20 K 9	Boteley clo E4	
65 X 13	Botha rd E13	
65 R 15	Bothwell clo E16	
144 G 15	Bothwell st W6	
160 H 9	Botolph all EC3	
142 H 10	Botolph la EC3	
119 S 4	Botsford rd SW20	
137 V 6	Botts ms W2	
137 U 6	Botts pass W2	
101 V 13	Boucher clo Tedd	
57 W 18	Bouchier wlk Rainhm	
126 C 17	Boughton av Brom	
79 W 7	Boughton rd SE18	
63 U 18	Boulcott st E1	
122 M 14	Boulogne rd Croy	
123 N 14	Boulogne rd Croy	
57 X 17	Boulter gdns Rainhm	
56 A 8	Boulton rd Dgnhm	
66 F 18	Boultwood rd E6	
18 M 7	Bounces la N9	
19 P 8	Bounces rd N9	
106 M 3	Boundaries rd SW12	
107 N 2	Boundaries rd SW12	
117 S 5	Boundary clo Kingst	
70 H 14	Boundary clo S'hall	
65 Z 11	Boundary la E13	
150 C 14	Boundary la SE17	
130 C 4	Boundary ms NW8	
67 P 6	Boundary rd Bark	
67 S 5	Boundary rd Bark	
65 Z 7	Boundary rd E13	
33 O 19	Boundary rd E17	
30 L 8	Boundary rd N22	
9 P 20	Boundary rd N9	
130 D 4	Boundary rd NW8	
39 V 18	Boundary rd Rom	
96 G 13	Boundary rd Sidcp	
106 F 15	Boundary rd SW19	
106 G 14	Boundary rd SW19	
155 R 14	Boundary rd Wallgtn	
155 R 18	Boundary Road south Wallgtn	
141 W 17	Boundary row SE1	
134 M 15	Boundary st E2	
159 O 11	Boundary way Croy	
112 A 5	Boundfield rd SE6	
111 Y 6	Boundfield rd SE6	

30 B 4	Bounds Green rd N22
16 J 19	Bounds Green rd N11
140 E 7	Bourchier st W1
139 X 9	Bourdon pl W1
124 B 3	Bourdon rd SE20
139 Y 9	Bourdon st W1
89 Z 17	Bourke clo SW2
140 B 2	Bourlet clo W1
5 U 18	Bourn av Barnt
31 O 13	Bourn av N15
95 O 7	Bournbrook rd SE3
16 M 7	Bourne av N14
44 B 19	Bourne clo NW10
20 E 15	Bourne gdns E4
17 S 9	Bourne hill N13
98 L 14	Bourne mead Bxly
126 M 9	Bourne rd Brom
127 N 8	Bourne rd Brom
98 K 15	Bourne rd Bxly
52 C 10	Bourne rd E7
30 B 18	Bourne rd N8
147 S 7	Bourne st SW1
137 X 1	Bourne ter W2
16 L 6	Bourne the N14
17 O 8	Bourne the N14
126 D 19	Bourne vale Brom
41 W 16	Bourne way Grnfd
153 V 12	Bourne way Sutton
91 X 4	Bournemouth rd SE 15
105 Z 20	Bournemouth rd SW19
107 Z 10	Bournevale rd SW16
80 A 19	Bournewood rd SW2
93 N 18	Bournville rd SE6
5 Z 10	Bournwell clo Barnt
92 E 5	Bousfield rd SE14
88 J 11	Boutflower rd SW11
24 H 20	Bouverie gdns Harrow
49 S 7	Bouverie ms N16
138 H 4	Bouverie pl W2
23 O 20	Bouverie rd Harrow
49 R 6	Bouverie rd N16
141 U 7	Bouverie st EC4
9 R 3	Bouverie rd Enf
48 C 11	Bovay pl N7
48 C 11	Bovay st N7
92 E 18	Boveney rd SE23
92 G 20	Bovill rd SE23
43 R 19	Bovingdon av Wemb
47 W 8	Bovingdon clo N19
26 A 3	Bovingdon la NW9
88 A 3	Bovingdon rd SW6
160 B 6	Bow Church yd EC4
64 A 13	Bow Common la E3
63 Y 13	Bow Common la E3
160 C 7	Bow la EC4
28 D 1	Bow la N12
64 C 8	Bow rd E3
63 Y 10	Bow rd E3
51 Z 15	Bow st E15
140 L 7	Bow st WC2
25 X 16	Bowater clo NW9
77 W 19	Bowater pl SE3
78 B 8	Bowater st SE18
33 O 20	Bowden rd E17
149 T 10	Bowden st SE11
75 X 12	Bowditch SE8
109 S 8	Bowen dri SE21
41 O 1	Bowen rd Harrow
23 O 20	Bowen rd Harrow
64 D 16	Bowen st E14
93 Z 1	Bower av SE10
39 N 2	Bower clo Rom
63 T 18	Bower st E1
87 Z 3	Bowerdean st SW6
75 W 18	Bowerman av SE14
97 P 16	Bowes clo Sidcp
55 U 13	Bowes rd Dgnhm
16 G 15	Bowes rd N11
16 L 16	Bowes rd N13
17 P 17	Bowes rd N13
62 A 20	Bowes rd W3
144 E 15	Bowfell rd W6
97 Y 3	Bowford av Bxly Hth
89 Y 11	Bowland rd SW4
21 Z 17	Bowland rd Wdfd Grn
151 S 13	Bowles rd SE1
109 U 13	Bowley clo SE19
75 Z 1	Bowley st E14
86 K 19	Bowling Green clo SW15
133 U 17	Bowling Green la EC1
142 E 17	Bowling Green pl SE1
78 E 9	Bowling Green row SE 18
149 T 13	Bowling Green st SE11
134 H 12	Bowling Green wlk N1
11 N 16	Bowls clo Stanm
65 R 19	Bowman av E16
72 A 3	Bowmans clo W13
92 D 18	Bowmans lea SE23
155 R 6	Bowmans meadow Wallgtn
48 A 11	Bowmans ms N7
48 B 11	Bowmans ms N7
99 T 18	Bowmans rd Drtford
113 T 4	Bowmead SE9
104 A 12	Bowness cres SW15
103 Z 12	Bowness cres SW15
82 C 10	Bowness dri Hounsl
98 G 6	Bowness rd Bxly Hth
93 S 19	Bowness rd SE6
57 W 15	Bowness way Hornch
9 T 8	Bowood rd Enf
89 O 12	Bowood rd SW11
42 H 20	Bowrons av Wemb
150 D 18	Bowyer pl SE5
150 B 18	Bowyer st SE5
56 A 11	Boxall rd Dgnhm
91 R 17	Boxall rd SE21
80 F 8	Boxgrove rd SE2
120 D 10	Boxley rd Mrdn
77 V 3	Boxley st E16
24 A 13	Boxmoor rd Harrow
23 O 3	Boxtree la Harrow
133 R 4	Boxworth gr N1
78 L 13	Boyard rd SE18
65 T 12	Boyce way E13
25 W 18	Boycroft av NW9
70 G 3	Boyd av S'hall
103 R 18	Boyd clo Kingst
106 F 15	Boyd rd SW19
143 T 7	Boyd st E1
130 F 2	Boydell ct NW8
141 Y 19	Boyfield st SE1
112 C 13	Boyland rd Brom
10 M 18	Boyle av Stanm
140 A 9	Boyle st W1
27 R 13	Boyne av NW4
56 E 10	Boyne rd Dgnhm
93 W 8	Boyne rd SE13
137 O 13	Boyne Terrace ms W1
12 G 8	Boyseland ct Edg
150 D 14	Boyston rd SE17
151 X 11	Boythorn way SE16
63 R 12	Boyton clo E1
30 A 11	Boyton clo N8
30 A 11	Boyton rd N8
30 D 7	Brabant rd N22
156 A 17	Brabazon av Wallgtn
58 G 6	Brabazon rd Grnfd
64 C 16	Brabazon st E14
92 B 6	Brabourn gro SE15
109 R 14	Brabourne clo SE19
81 P 18	Brabourne cres Bxly Hth
125 V 11	Brabourne ri Becknhm
41 X 17	Bracewell av Grnfd
136 A 2	Bracewell rd W10
62 L 14	Bracewell rd W10
157 V 5	Bracewood gdns Croy
48 B 6	Bracey st N4
159 P 6	Bracken av Croy
89 P 17	Bracken av SW12
66 F 15	Bracken clo E6
83 R 11	Bracken end Islwth
86 G 4	Bracken gdns SW13
38 F 20	Bracken ms Rom
20 G 7	Bracken the E4
74 K 7	Brackenbury gdns W6
28 D 10	Brackenbury rd N2
74 K 8	Brackenbury rd W6
82 L 2	Brackendale clo Hounsl
17 R 7	Brackendale N21
126 C 1	Brackenhill clo Brom
126 C 1	Brackenhill la Brom
40 B 12	Brackenhill Ruis
18 C 2	Brackens the Enf
156 A 15	Brackley clo Croy
111 O 17	Brackley rd Becknhm
74 B 12	Brackley rd W4
35 N 1	Brackley sq Ilf
34 M 1	Brackley sq Wdfd Grn
134 B 19	Brackley st EC1
74 B 13	Brackley ter W4
30 F 5	Bracknell clo N22
46 A 13	Bracknell gdns NW3
45 Z 13	Bracknell way NW3
80 C 10	Bracondale rd SE2
79 Z 10	Bracondale rd SE2
141 U 15	Brad st SE1
98 F 18	Bradbourne rd Bxly
87 Y 4	Bradbourne st SW6
70 G 11	Bradbury clo S'hall
49 T 16	Bradbury st N16
85 N 7	Braddon rd Rich
76 L 13	Braddyll st SE10
129 X 18	Braden st W9
96 M 10	Bradenham av Welling
97 N 10	Bradenham av Welling
24 A 12	Bradenham rd Harrow
54 M 16	Bradfield dri Bark
77 T 4	Bradfield rd E16
40 C 15	Bradfield rd Ruis
152 C 14	Bradford dri Epsom
54 F 4	Bradford rd Ilf
109 Z 9	Bradford rd SE26
74 A 4	Bradford rd W3
93 R 17	Bradgate rd SE6
52 H 5	Brading cres E11
52 H 6	Brading cres E11
122 B 15	Brading rd Croy
90 D 18	Brading rd SW2
129 R 12	Bradiston rd W9
48 B 20	Bradley clo N7
60 B 17	Bradley gdns W13
9 X 1	Bradley rd Enf
30 C 7	Bradley rd N22
108 L 14	Bradley rd SE19
133 T 9	Bradleys clo N1
89 U 1	Bradmead SW8
74 K 10	Bradmore Park rd W6
50 G 19	Bradstock rd E9
152 H 11	Bradstock rd Epsom
56 E 6	Bradwell av Dgnhm
34 B 12	Bradwell clo E18
57 Z 19	Bradwell clo Hornch
18 K 14	Bradwell ms N18
63 U 9	Bradwell st E1
63 N 14	Brady st E1
135 X 20	Brady st E1
122 G 5	Braemar av Thntn Hth
98 K 11	Braemar av Bxly Hth
30 B 5	Braemar av N22
43 Y 8	Braemar av NW10
157 N 20	Braemar av S Croy
105 X 5	Braemar av SW19
60 J 1	Braemar av Wemb
125 T 20	Braemar gdns W Wkhm
25 Z 6	Braemar gdns NW9
114 F 6	Braemar gdns Sidcp
72 H 16	Braemar rd Brentf
65 R 13	Braemar rd E13
31 R 15	Braemar rd N13
152 J 5	Braemar rd Worc Pk
104 F 2	Braemore clo SW15
54 K 8	Braemore rd Ilf
105 T 20	Braeside av SW19
111 P 14	Braeside Beckhm
81 P 11	Braeside clo Blvdr
98 L 11	Braeside cres Bxly Hth
107 V 18	Braeside rd SW16
156 L 8	Brafferton rd Croy
149 W 10	Braganza st SE17
143 P 5	Braham st E1
62 A 18	Braid av W3
100 C 4	Braid clo Felt
111 X 2	Braidwood rd SE6
142 K 14	Braidwood st SE1
90 G 15	Brailsford rd SW2
35 P 14	Braintree av Ilf
56 E 9	Braintree rd Dgnhm
63 P 10	Braintree st E2
56 E 1	Braithwaite av Rom
24 E 5	Braithwaite gdns Stanm
29 O 19	Bramalea clo N6
15 V 18	Bramber rd N12
145 P 14	Bramber rd W14
155 O 20	Bramble banks Carsh
159 P 8	Bramble clo Croy
24 H 4	Bramble clo Stanm
122 C 6	Bramble gdns SW16
174 E 1	Bramble gdns W12
79 P 14	Bramblebury rd SE18
81 Y 11	Bramblecroft Erith
126 A 13	Brambledown clo Brom
155 P 17	Brambledown rd Carsh
157 R 18	Brambledown rd S Croy
72 A 19	Brambles clo Brentf
120 K 20	Bramblewood clo Carsh
20 L 14	Bramblings the E4
120 L 9	Bramcote av Mitch
75 O 13	Bramcote gro SE16
151 Z 10	Bramcote rd SW15
86 K 11	Bramcote rd SW15
112 E 2	Bramdean cres SE12
112 E 2	Bramdean gdns SE12
124 L 6	Bramerton rd Beck
146 J 13	Bramerton st SW3
88 L 15	Bramfield rd SW11
16 K 7	Bramford ct N14
88 C 11	Bramford rd SW18
145 Y 8	Bramham gdns SW5
77 W 16	Bramhope la SE7
88 H 8	Bramlands clo SW11
32 J 8	Bramley clo E17
6 D 17	Bramley clo N14
156 K 10	Bramley clo S Croy
82 M 16	Bramley clo Twick
35 X 18	Bramley cres Ilf
97 P 1	Bramley ct Welling
156 K 10	Bramley hill S Croy
99 W 12	Bramley pl Drtfrd
6 J 14	Bramley rd Enf
6 D 17	Bramley rd N14
154 F 11	Bramley rd Sutton
153 N 19	Bramley rd Sutton
136 G 9	Bramley rd W11
72 D 9	Bramley rd W5
136 G 6	Bramley st W10
159 S 3	Bramley way W Wkhm
52 B 14	Brammel clo E15
50 A 6	Brampton clo E5
30 K 16	Brampton gdns N15
24 A 13	Brampton gro Harrow
23 Z 12	Brampton gro Harrow
26 K 14	Brampton gro NW4
43 O 4	Brampton gro Wemb
30 F 10	Brampton Park rd N8
80 H 19	Brampton rd Bxly Hth
97 X 1	Brampton rd Bxly Hth
123 T 16	Brampton rd Croy
66 C 10	Brampton rd E6
30 L 16	Brampton rd N15
25 R 15	Brampton rd NW9
80 G 16	Brampton rd SE2
50 F 19	Bramshaw rd E9
118 B 14	Bramshaw ri New Mald
47 T 8	Bramshill gdns NW5
62 C 6	Bramshill rd NW10
77 U 15	Bramshot av SE7
62 G 5	Bramston rd NW10
53 U 13	Brancaster av E12
36 G 19	Brancaster rd Ilf
107 Z 6	Brancaster rd SW16
21 S 9	Brancepeth gdns Buck Hl
46 C 10	Branch hill NW3
134 G 4	Branch pl N1
63 V 19	Branch rd E14
155 Z 16	Brancker clo Wallgtn
24 F 10	Brancker rd Harrow
76 G 20	Brand st SE10
87 V 11	Brandlehow rd SW15
33 V 12	Brandon rd E17
47 Z 20	Brandon rd N7
70 E 14	Brandon rd S'hall
153 Z 8	Brandon rd Sutton
150 B 6	Brandon st SE17
150 C 7	Brandon st SE17
93 V 10	Brandram rd SE13
66 H 17	Brandreth rd E6
107 R 4	Brandreth rd SW17
155 Z 6	Brandries the Wallgtn
36 A 12	Brandville gdns Ilf
153 X 17	Brandy way Sutton
111 U 12	Brangbourne rd Brom
149 R 10	Brangton rd SE11
120 E 1	Brangwyn cres SW19
144 J 20	Branksea st SW6
18 F 18	Branksome av N18
105 Y 20	Branksome rd SW19
90 A 12	Branksome rd SW2
24 L 18	Branksome way Harrow
117 X 2	Branksome way New Mald

17 S 3 Branscombe gdns N21
93 R 8 Branscombe st SE13
129 V 3 Bransdale clo NW6
24 M 3 Bransgrove rd Edg
85 N 3 Branstone rd Rich
59 U 12 Brants wlk W7
81 W 18 Brantwood av Erith
83 Y 9 Brantwood av Islwth
33 S 11 Brantwood clo E17
6 M 15 Brantwood gdns Enf
35 S 14 Brantwood gdns Ilf
98 H 6 Brantwood rd Bxly Hth
18 L 20 Brantwood rd N17
157 N 20 Brantwood rd S Croy
90 L 12 Brantwood rd SE24
41 P 14 Brasher clo Grnfd
45 W 17 Brassey rd NW6
89 O 6 Brassey sq SW11
62 B 18 Brassie av W3
97 W 13 Brasted clo Bxly Hth
110 B 9 Brasted clo SE26
87 Z 18 Brathway rd SW18
135 S 18 Bratley st E1
123 O 15 Bratten ct Croy
58 J 11 Braund av Grnfd
114 J 1 Braundton av Sidcp
96 K 20 Braundton av Sidcp
58 C 11 Braunston dri Grnfd
129 O 16 Bravington pl W9
129 O 11 Bravington rd W9
129 O 16 Bravington rd W9
92 K 11 Braxfield rd SE4
108 C 15 Braxted pk SW16
75 T 4 Bray cres SE16
65 R 19 Bray dri E16
65 R 19 Bray pass E16
147 O 8 Bray pl SW3
14 C 18 Bray rd NW7
92 A 5 Brayards rd SE15
91 Z 5 Brayards rd SE15
71 U 18 Braybourne dri Islwth
62 D 15 Braybrook st W12
109 T 18 Braybrooke gdns SE19
89 V 5 Brayburne av SW4
49 W 2 Braydon rd N16
133 S 2 Brayfield ter N1
6 L 14 Brayton gdns Enf
96 E 10 Braywood rd SE9
69 R 8 Breach la Dgnhm
160 B 7 Bread st EC4
92 M 9 Breakspears rd SE4
93 N 6 Breakspears rd SE4
66 J 10 Bream gdns E6
64 A 2 Bream st E3
104 G 2 Breamore clo SW15
54 K 8 Breamore rd Ilf
55 N 7 Breamore rd Ilf
141 S 4 Breams bldgs EC4
102 A 7 Breamwater gdns Rich
86 L 9 Breasley clo SW15
146 C 8 Brechin pl SW7
47 Y 15 Brecknock rd N7
9 O 13 Brecon rd Enf
144 L 16 Brecon rd W6
66 J 8 Brede clo E6
47 V 7 Bredgar rd N19
110 B 15 Bredhurst clo SE20
123 U 17 Bredon rd Croy
90 M 6 Bredon rd SE5
88 A 7 Breer st SW6
143 U 10 Breezers hill E1
41 N 7 Brember rd Harrow
138 D 20 Bremner rd SW7
126 D 13 Brenchley clo Brom
127 X 1 Brenchley clo Chisl
92 D 15 Brenchley gdns SE23
106 L 5 Brenda rd SW17
44 A 14 Brendon av NW10
99 P 2 Brendon clo Erith
40 K 11 Brendon gdns Harrow
36 H 15 Brendon gdns Ilf
56 D 4 Brendon rd Dgnhm
114 D 4 Brendon rd SE9
138 M 4 Brendon st W1
18 D 2 Brendon way Enf
121 P 6 Brenley clo Mitch
95 O 9 Brenley gdns SE9
115 Z 2 Brent clo Bxly
60 M 7 Brent cres NW10
27 O 16 Brent grn NW4
72 D 20 Brent Lea Brentf
44 H 2 Brent Park rd NW4
4 J 18 Brent pl Barnt
72 E 18 Brent rd Brentf
158 A 19 Brent rd CR2
65 T 16 Brent rd E16
157 Z 19 Brent rd S Croy
78 L 19 Brent rd SE18
72 E 17 Brent side Brentf
27 O 16 Brent st NW4
26 F 20 Brent View rd NW9
72 G 19 Brent way Brentf
14 K 19 Brent way N3
43 U 17 Brent way Wemb
60 A 12 Brentcot clo W13
43 X 18 Brentfield clo NW10
27 P 20 Brentfield gdns NW11
61 V 1 Brentfield NW10
61 Y 1 Brentfield rd NW10
43 Y 17 Brentfield rd NW10
72 G 18 Brentford High st Brentf
60 F 11 Brentham way W5
50 B 19 Brenthouse rd E9
44 D 16 Brenthurst rd NW10
59 T 20 Brentmead clo W7
61 N 7 Brentmead gdns NW10
27 P 18 Brentmead pl NW11
63 W 17 Brenton st E14
59 Y 11 Brentside clo W13
71 P 2 Brentvale av S'hall
60 M 4 Brentvale av Wemb
61 N 5 Brentvale av Wemb
72 J 12 Brentwick gdns Brentf
114 A 1 Brentwood clo SE9
39 X 18 Brentwood rd Rom
31 V 2 Brereton rd N17
148 A 2 Bressenden pl SW1
34 B 8 Bressey gro E18
49 R 7 Brett clo N16
61 Y 2 Brett cres NW10
55 Y 20 Brett gdns Dgnhm
50 A 16 Brett rd E8
150 F 10 Brettell st SE17
33 O 5 Brettenham av E17
33 O 5 Brettenham rd E17
18 M 13 Brettenham rd N18
18 L 13 Brettenham Road east N18
140 D 9 Brewer st W1
148 D 1 Brewers grn SW1
84 G 12 Brewers la Rich
83 X 19 Brewery la Twick
127 S 19 Brewery rd Brom
47 Z 19 Brewery rd N1
48 A 19 Brewery rd N7
79 R 13 Brewery rd SE18
143 Y 14 Brewhouse la E1
78 G 11 Brewhouse rd SE18
87 S 9 Brewhouse st SW15
75 V 3 Brewhouse wlk SE16
133 X 17 Brewhouse yd EC1
55 R 17 Brewood rd Dgnhm
136 A 1 Brewster gdns W10
62 M 14 Brewster gdns W10
51 S 4 Brewster rd E10
57 Y 11 Brian clo Hornch
37 U 14 Brian rd Rom
92 E 1 Briant st SE14
22 C 6 Briants clo Pinn
108 D 17 Briar av SW16
155 P 20 Briar banks Carsh
100 D 14 Briar clo Hampt
83 W 12 Briar clo Islwth
17 Z 11 Briar clo N13
40 J 19 Briar cres Nthlt
126 B 20 Briar gdns Brom
155 P 20 Briar la Carsh
159 R 7 Briar la Croy
24 D 17 Briar rd Harrow
44 M 11 Briar rd NW2
122 B 7 Briar rd SW16
101 S 2 Briar rd Twick
25 W 2 Briar wlk Edg
86 K 10 Briar wlk SW15
59 Z 16 Briarbank rd W13
45 X 10 Briardale gdns NW3
31 Z 3 Briars clo N17
28 B 9 Briars clo N2
25 W 18 Briarwood clo NW9
152 F 13 Briarwood rd Epsom
89 X 12 Briarwood rd SW4
46 H 20 Briary clo NW3
115 R 12 Briary ct Sidcp
112 H 12 Briary gdns Brom
18 F 12 Briary la N9
141 S 8 Brick ct EC4
85 S 3 Brick Farm clo Rich
143 P 2 Brick la E1
8 L 9 Brick la Enf
9 O 9 Brick la Enf
24 G 3 Brick la Stanm
24 G 3 Brick la Stanm
139 W 15 Brick st W1
106 B 10 Brick-Field rd SW19
79 Y 18 Brickfield cotts SE18
122 K 1 Brickfield rd Thntn Hth
64 D 10 Brickfield rd E3
41 S 6 Brickfields Harrow
157 S 2 Brickwood rd Croy
141 W 6 Bride la EC4
48 D 19 Bride st N7
141 W 7 Bridewell pl EC4
131 Y 19 Bridford ms W1
47 N 20 Bridge appr NW3
144 A 8 Bridge av W6
74 L 14 Bridge av W6
59 R 14 Bridge av W7
9 N 8 Bridge clo Enf
39 P 19 Bridge clo Rom
88 F 6 Bridge ct SW11
33 U 5 Bridge end E17
17 Y 3 Bridge ga N21
27 R 14 Bridge la NW11
88 J 3 Bridge la SW11
123 P 18 Bridge pl Croy
147 Y 6 Bridge pl SW1
110 L 18 Bridge rd Becknhm
97 Z 6 Bridge rd Bxly Hth
64 K 2 Bridge rd E15
50 K 2 Bridge rd E17
53 T 20 Bridge rd E6
99 T 3 Bridge rd Erith
99 V 1 Bridge rd Erith
83 P 6 Bridge rd Hounsl
30 A 6 Bridge rd N22
18 K 10 Bridge rd N9
44 A 19 Bridge rd NW10
70 E 5 Bridge rd S'hall
154 B 14 Bridge rd Sutton
84 A 15 Bridge rd Twick
155 T 11 Bridge rd Wallgtn
43 R 9 Bridge rd Wemb
123 P 19 Bridge row Croy
22 A 11 Bridge st Pinn
84 G 14 Bridge st Rich
140 K 18 Bridge st SW1
73 X 11 Bridge st W4
64 K 1 Bridge ter E15
23 U 11 Bridge the Harrow
144 A 9 Bridge view W6
16 G 12 Bridge way N11
27 V 16 Bridge way NW11
83 O 19 Bridge way Twick
142 H 13 Bridge yd SE1
153 X 14 Bridgefield rd Sutton
148 L 12 Bridgefoot SE1
65 T 18 Bridgeland rd E16
133 O 2 Bridgeman rd N1
101 X 14 Bridgeman rd Tedd
130 J 9 Bridgeman st NW8
97 Y 17 Bridgen rd Bxly
88 C 9 Bridgend rd SW18
8 H 5 Bridgenhall rd Enf
156 A 7 Bridges la Croy
87 W 2 Bridges pl SW 6
10 H 17 Bridges rd Stanm
106 A 16 Bridges rd SW19
105 Z 16 Bridges rd SW19
74 L 13 Bridgeview W6
24 L 7 Bridgewater gdns Edg
42 D 19 Bridgewater rd Wemb
42 C 17 Bridgewater rd Grnfd
134 A 20 Bridgewater sq EC1
67 Y 1 Bridgeway Bark
132 D 9 Bridgeway st NW1
42 L 19 Bridgeway Wemb
152 H 7 Bridgewood rd Worc Pk
107 X 18 Bridgewood rd SW16
106 D 6 Bridgford st SW18
73 V 8 Bridgman rd W4
64 F 3 Bridgwater rd E15
140 C 9 Bridle la W1
156 B 6 Bridle pth Croy
159 O 1 Bridle rd Croy
159 P 9 Bridleway Croy
155 W 10 Bridleway the Wallgtn
18 M 2 Bridlington rd N9
19 N 3 Bridlington rd N9
38 G 20 Bridport av Rom
134 F 6 Bridport pl N1
134 F 8 Bridport pl N1
58 K 3 Bridport rd Grnfd
18 E 18 Bridport rd N18
122 G 6 Bridport rd Thntn Hth
75 O 18 Bridson st SE15
137 U 5 Bridstow pl W2
90 H 3 Brief st SE5
19 R 6 Brierley av N9
123 Y 9 Brierley clo SE25
159 R 15 Brierley Croy
51 X 12 Brierley rd E11
107 T 4 Brierley rd SW12
76 H 12 Brig st E14
8 A 5 Brigadier av Enf
7 Y 3 Brigadier hill Enf
49 X 7 Briggeford clo E5
80 J 10 Bright clo Blvdr
64 E 16 Bright st E14
94 B 12 Brightfield rd SE12
92 M 17 Brightling rd SE4
63 X 20 Brightlingsea pl E14
106 E 1 Brightman rd SW18
32 L 17 Brighton av E17
40 G 18 Brighton dri Nthlt
92 H 1 Brighton gro SE14
66 K 8 Brighton rd E6
49 T 12 Brighton rd N16
28 D 8 Brighton rd N2
157 N 14 Brighton rd S Croy
116 F 15 Brighton rd Surb
154 B 17 Brighton rd Sutton
90 D 10 Brighton ter SW9
93 X 15 Brightside rd SE13
9 U 5 Brightside the Enf
106 L 13 Brightwell cres SW17
41 P 7 Briglade clo Harrow
122 L 9 Brigstock rd Thntn Hth
81 T 10 Brigstock rd Blvdr
132 G 10 Brill rd NW1
28 D 13 Brim hill N2
80 C 9 Brimpsfield clo SE2
9 W 7 Brimsdown av Enf
92 L 3 Brindley st SE14
58 K 19 Brindley way S'hall
20 A 10 Brindwood rd E4
19 Z 10 Brindwood rd E4
25 S 9 Brinkburn clo Edg
80 A 10 Brinkburn clo SE2
25 R 9 Brinkburn gdns Edg
152 J 2 Brinkley rd Worc Pk
78 M 20 Brinklow cres SE18
79 N 19 Brinklow cres SE18
35 R 9 Brinkworth rd Ilf
50 M 17 Brinkworth way E9
27 O 11 Brinsdale rd NW4
23 P 7 Brinsley rd Harrow
63 O 18 Brinsley st E1
143 Z 7 Brinsley st E1
101 P 2 Brinsworth clo Twick
105 Z 20 Brisbane av SW19
51 S 8 Brisbane rd E10
54 A 2 Brisbane rd Ilf
71 Z 4 Brisbane rd W13
150 E 20 Brisbane st SE5
106 G 15 Briscoe rd SW19
95 N 8 Briset rd SE9
133 W 19 Briset st EC1
48 C 7 Briset way N7
86 L 19 Bristol gdns SW15
130 A 19 Bristol gdns W9
129 Z 19 Bristol gdns W9
130 A 19 Bristol ms W9
129 Z 19 Bristol ms W9
53 N 18 Bristol rd E12
52 M 19 Bristol rd E7
58 K 3 Bristol rd Grnfd
120 C 10 Bristol rd Mrdn
30 B 20 Briston gro N8
98 A 3 Bristow rd Bxly Hth
97 Z 3 Bristow rd Bxly Hth
156 A 9 Bristow rd Croy
82 M 9 Bristow rd Hounsl
109 R 12 Bristow rd SE19
58 A 8 Britannia clo Nthlt
89 Y 11 Britannia clo SW4
53 Y 11 Britannia rd Ilf
15 S 12 Britannia rd N12
116 M 16 Britannia rd Surb
117 N 16 Britannia rd Surb
145 X 19 Britannia rd SW6
133 Z 4 Britannia row N1
133 N 12 Britannia st WC1
61 T 10 Britannia way NW10
134 E 12 Britannia wlk N1
74 E 12 British gro W4
21 O 7 British Legion rd E4
140 H 2 British Museum WC1
63 Z 10 British st E3
56 A 9 Brittain rd Dgnhm
46 A 3 Britten clo NW11
146 J 10 Britten st SW3
133 W 19 Britton st EC1

145 O 19 Brookville rd SW6
94 E 9 Brookway SE3
86 E 6 Brookwood av SW13
126 B 10 Brookwood clo BR2
82 K 4 Brookwood rd
　Hounsl
105 X 1 Brookwood rd SW18
127 S 14 Broom clo Brom
102 F 17 Broom clo Tedd
159 P 6 Broom gdns Croy
98 F 14 Broom Hill ri
　Bxly Hth
102 E 14 Broom lock Tedd
98 F 14 Broom mead
　Bxly Hth
102 F 18 Broom pk Tedd
159 O 6 Broom rd Croy
102 B 13 Broom rd Tedd
102 D 14 Broom water Tedd
102 D 13 Broom Water west
　Tedd
100 E 19 Broome rd Hampt
150 D 19 Broome way SE5
17 P 15 Broomfield av N13
32 L 20 Broomfield E17
17 O 14 Broomfield ho N13
17 R 15 Broomfield la N13
17 N 14 Broomfield pk N13
98 F 14 Broomfield rd
　Bxly Hth
124 K 7 Broomfield rd Beck
17 O 17 Broomfield rd N13
85 N 1 Broomfield rd Rich
55 W 1 Broomfield rd Rom
117 O 18 Broomfield rd Surb
102 E 15 Broomfield rd Tedd
72 C 2 Broomfield rd W13
64 C 15 Broomfield st E14
25 P 4 Broomgrove gdns
　Edg
90 D 6 Broomgrove rd SW9
157 O 18 Broomhall rd S Croy
21 S 18 Broomhill rd
　Wdfd Grn
21 S 20 Broomhill rd
　Wdfd Grn
99 Y 16 Broomhill rd Drtfrd
55 O 6 Broomhill rd Ilf
87 Y 14 Broomhill rd SW18
87 X 7 Broomhouse la SW6
87 X 5 Broomhouse rd SW6
153 Y 3 Broomloan la Sutton
45 W 16 Broomsleigh st NW6
88 L 16 Broomwood rd
　SW11
89 P 13 Broomwood rd SW4
110 G 12 Broseley gro SE26
148 L 19 Brough clo SW8
148 K 19 Brough st SW8
135 T 3 Brougham rd E8
61 W 18 Brougham rd W3
27 R 10 Broughton av N3
102 C 8 Broughton av Rich
90 G 11 Broughton dri SW9
29 V 18 Broughton gdns N6
122 F 13 Broughton rd
　Thntn Hth
88 B 4 Broughton rd SW6
72 C 1 Broughton rd W13
89 R 4 Broughton st SW8
73 V 6 Brouncker rd W3
155 Z 16 Brown clo Wallgtn
139 V 7 Brown Hart gdns W1
64 E 18 Brownfield st E14
93 V 19 Brownhill rd SE6
118 K 19 Browning av
　Worc Pk
154 J 8 Browning av Sutton
59 W 17 Browning av W7
100 E 10 Browning clo Hampt
130 D 18 Browning clo W9
96 H 2 Browning clo Well
52 C 2 Browning rd E11
53 T 18 Browning rd E12
8 A 2 Browning rd Enf
150 B 8 Browning st SE17
54 M 8 Brownlea gdns Ilf
133 O 17 Brownlow ms WC1
157 T 8 Brownlow rd Croy
52 G 12 Brownlow rd E7
135 R 3 Brownlow rd E8
16 M 18 Brownlow rd N11
28 A 1 Brownlow rd N3
62 B 1 Brownlow rd NW10
44 B 20 Brownlow rd NW10
71 Y 2 Brownlow rd W13
141 P 2 Brownlow st WC1
142 K 5 Browns bldgs EC3
47 R 15 Browns la NW5
33 O 11 Browns rd E17

116 M 17 Browns rd Surb
139 N 4 Browns st W1
114 A 8 Brownspring dri SE9
113 Z 9 Brownspring dri SE9
28 F 7 Brownswell rd N2
48 K 8 Brownswood rd N4
89 P 14 Broxash rd SW11
34 H 12 Broxbourne av E18
52 D 10 Broxbourne st E7
108 F 7 Broxholm rd SE27
110 K 3 Broxted rd SE6
130 M 7 Broxwood way NW8
31 T 5 Bruce Castle
　museum N17
31 T 4 Bruce Castle pk
　N17
31 U 5 Bruce Castle rd N17
97 R 2 Bruce clo Welling
158 F 20 Bruce dri S Croy
15 Y 12 Bruce gdns N20
31 T 6 Bruce gro N17
4 F 12 Bruce rd Barnt
64 C 9 Bruce rd E3
64 D 9 Bruce rd E3
23 T 8 Bruce rd Harrow
107 N 17 Bruce rd Mitch
61 Z 1 Bruce rd NW10
123 O 8 Bruce rd SE25
129 N 13 Bruckner st W10
107 N 8 Brudenell rd SW17
40 B 19 Bruffs meadow Nthlt
98 J 8 Brummel clo Bxly Hth
60 J 7 Brumwell rd Wemb
143 N 2 Brune st E1
58 D 9 Brunel clo Nthlt
58 K 18 Brunel pl S'hall
75 R 5 Brunel rd SE16
62 B 15 Brunel rd W3
65 O 18 Brunel st E16
31 R 14 Brunel wlk N15
28 C 17 Brunner clo NW11
32 J 16 Brunner rd E17
60 F 11 Brunner rd W5
43 V 7 Bruno pl NW9
16 B 11 Brunswick av N11
97 X 9 Brunswick clo
　Bxly Hth
22 C 20 Brunswick clo Pinn
16 B 11 Brunswick cres N11
142 L 18 Brunswick ct SE1
36 B 1 Brunswick gdns Ilf
60 K 10 Brunswick gdns W5
137 W 15 Brunswick gdns W8
16 B 12 Brunswick gro N11
139 P 5 Brunswick ms W1
16 B 9 Brunswick Park gdns
　N11
16 B 8 Brunswick Park rd N11
91 P 1 Brunswick pk SE5
134 F 14 Brunswick pl N1
109 W 16 Brunswick pl SE19
75 V 9 Brunswick quay SE16
97 X 10 Brunswick rd
　Bxly Hth
51 T 4 Brunswick rd E10
103 P 20 Brunswick rd Kingst
31 S 14 Brunswick rd N15
154 C 7 Brunswick rd Sutton
60 K 10 Brunswick rd W5
8 G 20 Brunswick sq N17
132 L 17 Brunswick sq WC1
33 T 15 Brunswick st E17
91 R 1 Brunswick vlls SE5
16 E 13 Brunswick way N11
63 W 18 Brunton pl E14
142 L 1 Brushfield st E1
143 N 1 Brushfield st E1
88 G 11 Brussels st SW11
113 T 19 Bruton clo Chisl
139 Y 10 Bruton la W1
139 Y 9 Bruton pl W1
120 C 10 Bruton rd Mrdn
139 Y 10 Bruton st W1
59 Z 14 Bruton way W13
128 A 1 Bryan av NW10
44 K 20 Bryan clo S'hall
62 L 1 Bryan rd NW10
75 X 5 Bryan rd SE16
88 A 4 Bryans all SW6
82 L 20 Bryanston av Twick
70 F 10 Bryanston clo S'hall
139 O 3 Bryanston Mews east
　W1
139 O 3 Bryanston Mews west
　W1
139 N 3 Bryanston pl W1
139 O 4 Bryanston sq W1
139 R 6 Bryanston st W1
29 Y 17 Bryanstone rd N8
4 J 19 Bryant clo Barnt

64 L 1 Bryant st E15
48 F 14 Bryantwood rd N7
55 T 12 Bryce rd Dgnhm
16 J 12 Brycedale cres N14
110 H 12 Bryden clo SE26
140 J 10 Brydges pl WC2
51 X 14 Brydges rd E15
132 L 4 Brydon wlk N1
48 A 9 Bryett rd N7
64 B 6 Brymay clo E3
8 J 13 Bryn-y-Mawr rd Enf
88 M 3 Brynmaer rd SW11
23 W 10 Bryon rd Harrow
62 H 20 Bryony rd W12
92 C 7 Buchan rd SE15
128 A 9 Buchanan gdns
　NW10
62 K 7 Buchanan gdns
　NW10
88 D 19 Bucharest rd SW18
138 H 10 Buck Hill wlk W2
25 X 16 Buck la NW9
131 Y 2 Buck st NW1
33 W 13 Buck wlk E17
94 D 15 Buckden clo SE12
120 B 10 Buckfast rd Mrdn
135 T 14 Buckfast st E2
87 Y 16 Buckhold rd SW18
120 L 20 Buckhurst av Carsh
63 O 12 Buckhurst st E1
135 Y 17 Buckhurst st E1
140 L 12 Buckingham arc
　WC2
122 G 1 Buckingham av
　Thntn Hth
96 H 11 Buckingham av
　Welling
59 Z 3 Buckingham av
　Grnfd
15 R 3 Buckingham av N20
100 E 12 Buckingham clo
　Hampt
8 E 8 Buckingham clo Enf
60 D 14 Buckingham clo W5
26 G 9 Buckingham ct NW4
148 C 1 Buckingham ga SW1
122 F 2 Buckingham gdns
　Thntn Hth
24 L 3 Buckingham gdns
　Edg
140 A 19 Buckingham pal
　SW1
139 Z 19 Buckingham pal
　SW1
139 X 18 Buckingham Palace
　gdns SW1
147 X 6 Buckingham Palace
　rd SW1
62 E 6 Buckingham rd
　NW10
100 F 13 Buckingham rd
　Hampt
116 M 8 Buckingham rd
　Kingst
117 N 8 Buckingham rd
　Kingst
23 R 15 Buckingham rd
　Harrow
51 R 9 Buckingham rd E10
34 K 15 Buckingham rd E11
52 B 14 Buckingham rd E15
34 C 5 Buckingham rd E18
24 M 2 Buckingham rd Edg
25 N 1 Buckingham rd Edg
54 E 7 Buckingham rd Ilf
122 A 10 Buckingham rd Mitch
49 S 19 Buckingham rd N1
30 A 6 Buckingham rd N22
102 F 4 Buckingham rd Rich
140 L 11 Buckingham st WC2
155 V 20 Buckingham way
　Wallgtn
46 F 19 Buckland cres NW3
51 T 6 Buckland rd E10
153 N 20 Buckland rd Sutton
134 G 9 Buckland st N1
118 M 20 Buckland way
　Worc Pk
120 C 10 Buckland wlk Mrdn
102 E 14 Bucklands rd Tedd
143 R 5 Buckle st E1
119 U 5 Buckleigh av SW20
107 Z 16 Buckleigh rd SW16
109 T 19 Buckleigh way SE19
113 U 8 Buckler gdns SE9
160 D 7 Bucklersbury EC4
99 U 6 Buckley clo Drtfrd
129 P 2 Buckley rd NW6
88 J 12 Buckmaster rd
　SW11

140 H 4 Bucknall st WC2
90 D 11 Buckner rd SW2
20 K 9 Buckrell rd E4
18 K 18 Buckstone rd N18
75 V 3 Buckters rents SE16
92 H 14 Buckthorne rd SE4
43 V 9 Buddings crcl Wemb
84 D 14 Budds all Twick
160 D 7 Budge row EC4
80 F 20 Budleigh cres
　Welling
55 N 7 Budoch ct Ilf
55 N 8 Budoch dri Ilf
87 U 5 Buer rd SW6
77 V 11 Bugsbys way SE7
122 L 7 Bulganak rd
　Thntn Hth
148 H 7 Bulinga st SW1
141 V 12 Bull all SE1
97 R 7 Bull all Welling
140 L 9 Bull Inn ct WC2
114 D 19 Bull la Chisl
56 G 8 Bull la Dgnhm
18 E 19 Bull la N18
65 P 5 Bull rd E15
160 B 9 Bull Wharf la EC4
63 S 9 Bullards pl E1
81 W 10 Bullbanks rd Blvdr
88 J 4 Bullen st SW11
151 S 19 Buller clo SE15
54 G 20 Buller rd Bark
31 X 9 Buller rd N17
30 E 7 Buller rd N22
128 G 13 Buller rd NW10
123 O 6 Buller rd Thntn Hth
115 X 13 Bullers clo Sidcp
113 S 18 Bullers Wood dri
　Chisl
12 D 10 Bullescroft rd Edg
64 G 19 Bullivant st E14
85 X 6 Bulls all SW14
146 L 5 Bulls gdns SW3
160 H 7 Bulls Head pas EC3
42 F 1 Bulmer gdns Harrow
137 S 12 Bulmer ms W11
82 F 6 Bulstrode av Hounsl
82 F 7 Bulstrode gdns
　Hounsl
139 V 3 Bulstrode pl W1
82 H 7 Bulstrode rd Hounsl
139 V 3 Bulstrode st W1
51 W 3 Bulwer Court rd E11
5 P 14 Bulwer gdns Barnt
5 O 14 Bulwer rd Barnt
51 X 3 Bulwer rd E11
18 E 15 Bulwer rd N18
136 D 15 Bulwer st W12
34 C 1 Bunces la Wdfd Grn
143 Y 7 Bunch st E1
123 S 9 Bungalow rd SE25
107 S 17 Bungalows the
　SW16
134 D 16 Bunhill row EC1
81 S 11 Bunkers hill Blvdr
26 O 1 Bunns la NW7
13 O 19 Bunns la NW7
63 U 6 Bunsen st E3
120 M 11 Bunting clo Mitch
36 D 16 Buntingbridge rd Ilf
78 K 9 Bunton st SE18
32 J 10 Bunyan rd E17
148 F 10 Buonaparte ms
　SW1
150 E 2 Burbage clo SE1
150 E 2 Burbage clo SE1
90 M 15 Burbage rd SE24
91 N 17 Burbage rd SE24
117 Z 4 Burberry clo
　New Mald
31 W 8 Burbridge way N17
64 F 17 Burcham st E14
80 H 16 Burcharbro rd SE2
51 R 3 Burchell rd E10
92 A 3 Burchell rd SE15
38 A 18 Burchett way Rom
38 J 2 Burchwall clo Rom
88 G 20 Burcote rd SW18
72 E 14 Burden clo Brentf
52 H 5 Burden way E11
85 S 9 Burdenshott av Rich
49 S 17 Burder clo N1
104 F 20 Burdett av SW20
115 Y 13 Burdett clo Sidcp
123 P 15 Burdett rd Croy
63 Y 15 Burdett rd E14
85 O 6 Burdett rd Rich
141 T 20 Burdett st SE1
153 V 20 Burdon la Sutton
153 U 18 Burdon pk Sutton
106 E 9 Burfield clo SW17

55 U 11 Burford clo Dgnhm
36 B 12 Burford clo Ilf
17 S 10 Burford gdns N13
72 J 15 Burford rd Brentf
127 R 10 Burford rd Brom
64 J 2 Burford rd E15
66 C 9 Burford rd E6
110 M 6 Burford rd SE6
153 X 4 Burford rd Sutton
118 F 18 Burford rd Worc Pk
159 V 15 Burford way Croy
151 N 9 Burgandy st SE1
99 T 8 Burgate clo Drtfrd
150 E 2 Burge st SE1
150 F 3 Burge st SE1
66 E 1 Burges rd E6
66 K 2 Burges rd E6
53 V 20 Burges rd E6
25 X 18 Burgess av NW9
100 B 8 Burgess clo Felt
45 W 11 Burgess hill NW2
51 Y 13 Burgess rd E15
153 Z 9 Burgess rd Sutton
64 A 15 Burgess st E14
133 Z 8 Burgh st N1
110 G 9 Burghill rd SE26
118 A 1 Burghley av New Mald
117 Y 1 Burghley av New Mald
52 A 3 Burghley rd E11
30 F 10 Burghley rd N8
47 T 11 Burghley rd NW5
105 R 9 Burghley rd SW19
121 N 10 Burgley pl Mitch
141 Y 7 Burgon st EC4
93 R 1 Burgos gro SE10
30 H 19 Burgoyne rd N4
123 T 8 Burgoyne rd SE25
90 C 7 Burgoyne rd SW9
110 C 18 Burham clo SE20
22 B 7 Burhill gro Pinn
86 B 10 Burke clo SW15
65 P 16 Burke st E16
88 M 14 Burland rd SW11
96 K 13 Burleigh av Sidcp
155 P 6 Burleigh av Wallgtn
16 G 6 Burleigh gdns N14
87 P 13 Burleigh pl SW15
8 E 14 Burleigh rd Enf
119 T 19 Burleigh rd Sutton
140 M 8 Burleigh st WC2
8 B 12 Burleigh way Enf
20 A 17 Burley clo E4
121 Y 3 Burley clo SW16
65 X 16 Burley rd E16
140 A 11 Burlington arc W1
85 P 2 Burlington av Rich
38 H 18 Burlington av Rom
129 S 17 Burlington clo W9
56 A 1 Burlington gdns Rom
55 Z 1 Burlington gdns Rom
140 A 11 Burlington gdns W1
73 X 3 Burlington gdns W3
73 W 14 Burlington gdns W4
74 A 17 Burlington la W4
73 Y 19 Burlington la W4
73 W 3 Burlington ms W3
87 T 5 Burlington pl SW 6
118 E 9 Burlington rd New Mald
122 M 4 Burlington rd Thntn Hth
123 N 3 Burlington rd Thntn Hth
8 A 5 Burlington rd Enf
83 O 2 Burlington rd Islwth
29 O 9 Burlington rd N10
31 X 5 Burlington rd N17
87 T 5 Burlington rd SW6
73 U 13 Burlington rd W4
15 Y 4 Burlington ri Barnt
49 N 12 Burma rd N16
149 X 2 Burman st SE1
106 D 7 Burmester rd SW17
19 P 11 Burn side N9
73 U 17 Burnaby cres W4
73 U 16 Burnaby gdns W4
66 M 19 Burnaby st E6
146 B 20 Burnaby st SW10
146 D 19 Burnaby st SW10
15 N 19 Burnbrae clo N12
107 V 1 Burnbury rd SW12
9 R 10 Burncroft av Enf
138 K 1 Burne st NW1
102 D 11 Burnell av Rich
96 M 4 Burnell av Well
97 O 5 Burnell av Welling
24 F 7 Burnell gdns Stanm
154 B 7 Burnell rd Sutton
66 H 10 Burnels av E6
48 C 19 Burness clo N7
50 D 15 Burnett clo E9
149 N 10 Burnett st SE11
116 L 12 Burney av Surb
117 N 11 Burney av Surb
76 G 19 Burney st SE10
87 T 3 Burnfoot av SW6
8 E 4 Burnham clo Enf
34 K 14 Burnham cres E11
27 N 13 Burnham ct NW4
153 O 3 Burnham dri Worc Pk
68 C 2 Burnham rd Dgnhm
19 X 17 Burnham rd E4
120 A 10 Burnham rd Mrdn
38 L 11 Burnham rd Rom
115 Y 5 Burnham rd Sidcp
63 P 8 Burnham st E2
117 P 1 Burnham st Kingst
72 A 9 Burnham way W13
125 O 3 Burnhill rd Becknhm
44 E 15 Burnley rd NW10
90 C 4 Burnley rd SW9
58 J 19 Burns av S'hall
97 O 16 Burns av Sidcp
99 T 2 Burns clo Erith
96 J 3 Burns clo Welling
62 C 3 Burns rd NW10
88 L 4 Burns rd SW11
72 A 5 Burns rd W13
60 J 6 Burns rd Wemb
146 L 10 Burnsall st SW3
4 L 13 Burnside clo Barnt
83 X 15 Burnside clo Twick
60 G 3 Burnside cres Wemb
55 U 3 Burnside rd Dgnhm
94 E19 Burnt Ash hill SE12
112 G 1 Burnt Ash hill SE12
112 G 14 Burnt Ash la Brom
94 C 14 Burnt Ash rd SE12
25 S 3 Burnt Oak bdwy Edg
25 U 3 Burnt Oak fields Edg
96 L 16 Burnt Oak la Sidcp
114 M 3 Burnt Oak la Sidcp
97 P 18 Burnt Oak la Sidcp
145 R 19 Burnthwaite rd SW6
100 H 2 Burntwood clo SW18
106 H 2 Burntwood Grange rd SW18
106 D 6 Burntwood la SW17
143 X 5 Buross st E1
98 B 6 Burr clo Bxly Hth
87 Y 20 Burr rd SW18
79 O 10 Burrage gro SE18
78 M 14 Burrage pl SE18
79 N 14 Burrage pl SE18
79 O 10 Burrage rd SE18
65 U 17 Burrard rd E16
45 Y 14 Burrard rd NW6
124 J 14 Burrell clo Becknhm
12 G 8 Burrell clo Edg
125 N 3 Burrell row Becknhm
141 X 13 Burrell st SE1
117 P 4 Burritt rd Kingst
26 J 13 Burroughs gdns NW4
26 J 13 Burroughs the NW4
141 W 16 Burrows ms SE1
128 C 12 Burrows rd NW10
62 M 8 Burrows rd NW10
142 K 15 Bursar st SE1
114 L 4 Bursdon clo Sidcp
9 S 13 Bursland rd Enf
143 U 6 Burslem st E1
87 S 10 Burstock rd SW15
87 P 12 Burston rd SW15
119 S 1 Burstow rd SW20
105 S 20 Burstow rd SW20
77 Y 3 Burt rd E16
48 L 3 Burtley clo N4
82 E 3 Burton gdns Hounsl
150 F 11 Burton gro SE17
147 V 6 Burton ms SW1
132 H 15 Burton pl WC1
34 G 11 Burton rd E18
102 L 18 Burton rd Kingst
129 R 2 Burton rd NW6
90 F 4 Burton rd SW9
90 H 4 Burton rd SW9
132 H 15 Burton st WC1
14 B 13 Burtonhole la NW7
64 L 1 Burtons ct E15
100 K 10 Burtons rd Hampt
101 O 11 Burtons rd Hampt
79 R 14 Burwash rd SE18
41 T 18 Burwell av Grnfd
63 N 18 Burwell clo E1
143 X 6 Burwell clo E1
50 J 3 Burwell rd E10
138 L 5 Burwood pl W2
142 K 5 Bury ct EC3
120 A 10 Bury gro Mrdn
18 G 4 Bury Hall vlls N9
140 K 2 Bury pl WC1
56 J 14 Bury rd Dgnhm
21 N 2 Bury rd E4
30 G 10 Bury rd N22
142 K 5 Bury st EC3
18 K 5 Bury st N9
140 C 13 Bury st SW1
18 D 4 Bury st west N9
146 J 8 Bury wlk SW3
47 X 17 Busby ms NW5
47 X 17 Busby pl NW5
135 P 16 Busby st E2
36 F 16 Bush clo Ilf
57 V 1 Bush Elms rd Hornch
43 V 1 Bush gro NW9
25 V 20 Bush gro NW9
24 F 4 Bush gro Stanm
8 B 18 Bush hill Enf
17 Y 2 Bush hill N21
24 M 19 Bush Hill rd Harrow
18 B 2 Bush Hill rd N21
160 E 9 Bush la EC4
52 D 1 Bush rd E11
63 N 3 Bush rd E8
135 W 5 Bush rd E8
73 N 17 Bush rd Rich
75 T 11 Bush rd SE8
50 J 17 Bushberry rd E9
108 E 3 Bushell clo SW2
10 B 8 Bushell gro Bushey
143 T 14 Bushell st E1
113 W 12 Bushell way Chisl
34 C 10 Bushey av E18
118 L 4 Bushey ct SW20
91 T 2 Bushey Hill rd SE5
153 Z 7 Bushey la Sutton
101 S 18 Bushey pk Tedd
159 O 3 Bushey rd Croy
65 Y 6 Bushey rd E13
31 R 18 Bushey rd N15
154 A 7 Bushey rd Sutton
153 Y 8 Bushey rd Sutton
118 K 5 Bushey rd SW20
119 P 4 Bushey rd SW20
125 W 13 Bushey way Becknhm
12 E 8 Bushfield clo Edg
12 F 8 Bushfield cres Edg
55 V 11 Bushgrove rd Dgnhm
96 A 1 Bushmoor cres SE18
79 N 20 Bushmoor cres SE18
107 S 5 Bushnell rd SW17
55 V 11 Bushway Dgnhm
52 D 2 Bushwood E11
73 P 18 Bushwood rd Rich
8 G 15 Bushy Hill pk Enf
101 U 17 Bushy House Tedd
101 R 13 Bushy Park gdns Tedd
102 B 18 Bushy Park rd Tedd
101 V 16 Bushy rd Tedd
63 U 19 Butcher row E14
65 T 17 Butchers rd E16
102 J 2 Bute av Rich
155 V 11 Bute Gardens west Wallgtn
144 F 6 Bute gdns W6
155 V 11 Bute gdns Wallgtn
122 G 20 Bute rd Croy
36 B 15 Bute rd Ilf
155 U 7 Bute rd Wallgtn
146 F 6 Bute st SW7
23 R 20 Butler av Harrow
55 P 11 Butler rd Dgnhm
41 N 1 Butler rd Harrow
23 P 20 Butler rd Harrow
63 R 8 Butler st E2
155 O 7 Butter hill Carsh
155 P 7 Butter hill Wallgtn
33 U 16 Butterfields E17
95 Z 15 Butterfly la SE9
119 N 14 Buttermere clo Mrdn
87 U 13 Buttermere dri SW15
144 E 8 Butterwick W6
134 G 12 Buttesland st N1
56 H 18 Buttfield clo Dgnhm
79 N 12 Buttmarsh clo SE18
100 C 6 Butts cotts Felt
100 G 7 Butts cres Felt
112 A 11 Butts rd Brom
72 F 18 Butts the Brentf
54 C 16 Buttsbury rd Ilf
49 U 20 Buxted clo E8
15 X 16 Buxted rd N12
92 C 16 Buxton clo SE23
153 R 7 Buxton cres Sutton
34 A 14 Buxton dri E11
118 A 2 Buxton dri New Mald
117 Z 2 Buxton dri New Mald
73 S 1 Buxton gdns W3
52 A 15 Buxton rd E15
51 Z 15 Buxton rd E15
32 J 14 Buxton rd E17
20 K 3 Buxton rd E4
66 D 9 Buxton rd E6
81 Z 18 Buxton rd Erith
54 G 1 Buxton rd Ilf
36 G 20 Buxton rd Ilf
47 Y 5 Buxton rd N19
44 K 17 Buxton rd NW2
86 B 8 Buxton rd SW13
122 H 13 Buxton rd Thntn Hth
135 R 18 Buxton st E1
88 C 5 Byam st SW6
121 X 1 Byards croft SW16
58 H 13 Bycroft rd S'hall
110 E 17 Bycroft st SE20
7 X 10 Bycullah av Enf
7 V 9 Bycullah rd Enf
62 B 16 Bye the W3
23 U 5 Bye Way the Harrow
100 K 5 Bye ways Twick
106 F 16 Byegrove rd SW19
152 E 9 Byeway the Epsom
85 V 8 Byeway the SW14
117 R 12 Byeways the Surb
86 G 3 Byfeld gdns SW13
83 Y 8 Byfield rd Islwth
65 N 1 Byford clo E15
159 R 15 Bygrove Croy
64 C 18 Bygrove st E14
17 O 1 Byland clo N21
80 B 8 Byland clo SE2
154 H 4 Byne rd Carsh
110 D 14 Byne rd SE26
157 O 17 Bynes rd S Croy
132 F 18 Byng pl WC1
4 C 11 Byng rd Barnt
76 B 5 Byng st E14
98 A 8 Bynon av Bxly Hth
107 T 2 Byrne rd SW12
53 P 19 Byron av E12
34 B 9 Byron av E18
118 G 10 Byron av New Mald
25 T 11 Byron av NW9
154 G 9 Byron av Sutton
154 G 9 Byron Avenue east Sutton
135 S 4 Byron clo E8
100 F 10 Byron clo Hampt
80 F 3 Byron clo SE18
7 X 9 Byron ct Enf
28 G 19 Byron dri N2
154 G 7 Byron gdns Sutton
41 R 5 Byron Hill rd Harrow
51 R 3 Byron rd E10
33 P 11 Byron rd E17
23 T 18 Byron rd Harrow
44 J 8 Byron rd NW2
13 T 16 Byron rd NW7
73 O 1 Byron rd W5
42 F 9 Byron rd Wemb
64 F 16 Byron st E14
19 O 1 Byron terr N9
58 B 9 Byron way Nthlt
35 Z 5 Bysouth clo Ilf
106 M 14 Byton rd SW17
142 L 10 Byward st EC3
147 N 9 Bywater st SW3
154 F 19 Byway the Sutton
140 A 3 Bywell pl W1
124 D 14 Bywood av Croy

C

138 K 2 Cabbell st NW1
143 X 8 Cable st E1
66 B 5 Cabot way E6
88 J 5 Cabul rd SW11
62 D 18 Cactus wlk W12
5 W 17 Caddington clo Barnt
45 S 10 Caddington rd NW2
23 W 1 Caddis clo Stanm
93 W2 Cade rd SE10
76 L 13 Cadeb pl SE10
135 P 11 Cadell clo E2
88 C 17 Cader rd SW18
56 L 19 Cadiz rd Dgnhm
150 C 11 Cadiz st SE17

110 C 3	Cadley ter SE23
118 A 10	Cadmer clo New Mald
125 X 2	Cadogan clo Becknhm
40 L 13	Cadogan clo Harrow
101 U 13	Cadogan clo Tedd
154 A 14	Cadogan ct Sutton
147 P 5	Cadogan ga SW3
34 J 10	Cadogan gdns E18
7 S 18	Cadogan gdns N21
28 A 5	Cadogan gdns N3
147 P 6	Cadogan gdns SW3
147 R 2	Cadogan la SW1
147 S 3	Cadogan la SW1
147 R 1	Cadogan pl SW1
116 G 12	Cadogan rd Surb
147 O 4	Cadogan sq SW1
147 N 7	Cadogan st SW3
50 K 18	Cadogan ter E9
31 V 18	Cadoxton av N15
114 A 4	Cadwallon rd SE9
48 E 12	Caedmon rd N7
115 T 13	Caerleon clo Sidcp
80 C 10	Caerleon ter SE2
121 Z 7	Caernarvon clo Mitch
35 W 4	Caernarvon dri Ilf
134 M 11	Caesar st E2
104 F 13	Caesars clo SW19
120 M 10	Caesars wlk Mitch
76 C 11	Cahir st E14
129 N 15	Caird st W10
72 G 4	Cairn av W5
10 J 19	Cairn way Stanm
112 C 17	Cairndale clo Brom
44 C 11	Cairnfield av NW2
88 K 12	Cairns rd SW11
156 J 3	Cairo New rd Croy
33 O 12	Cairo rd E17
65 P 3	Caistor Park rd E15
65 P 4	Caistor pk E15
89 R 19	Caistor rd SW12
96 J 17	Caithness gdns Sidcp
107 S 18	Caithness rd Mitch
144 G 3	Caithness rd W14
48 K 17	Calabria rd N5
90 J 1	Calais st SE5
57 Z 14	Calbourne av Hornch
89 N 19	Calbourne rd SW12
113 O 10	Calcott wlk SE9
118 J 19	Caldbeck av Worc Pk
91 N 4	Caldecot rd SE5
10 E 1	Caldecote gdns Bushey
10 G 1	Caldecote la Bushey
50 F 9	Caldecott way E5
59 V 6	Calder av Grnfd
8 D 12	Calder clo Enf
25 O 9	Calder gdns Edg
120 C 11	Calder rd Mrdn
136 C 3	Calderon pl W10
62 M 15	Calderon pl W10
51 V 11	Calderon rd E11
89 W 13	Caldervale rd SW4
78 K 10	Calderwood st SE18
150 E 16	Caldew st SE5
149 R 20	Caldwell st SW9
81 U 7	Caldy rd Blvdr
146 J 9	Cale st SW3
142 B 17	Caleb st SE1
66 F 2	Caledon rd E6
155 P 7	Caledon rd Wallgtn
132 L 10	Caledonia st N1
132 M 9	Caledonian rd N1
133 N 4	Caledonian rd N1
48 C 15	Caledonian rd N7
76 J 11	Caledonian wharf E14
155 Z 18	Caley clo Wallgtn
10 C 7	California la Bushey
117 U 7	California rd New Mald
49 O 18	Callaby ter N1
111 S 5	Callander rd SE6
17 W 15	Callard av N13
129 O 1	Callcott rd NW6
137 T 13	Callcott st W8
32 L 18	Callis rd E17
146 E 13	Callow st SW3
150 K 13	Calmington rd SE5
111 Y 16	Calmont rd Brom
35 Y 4	Calne av Ilf
105 P 9	Calonne rd SW19
133 O 10	Calshot st N1
7 W 12	Calshot way Enf
154 C 4	Calthorpe gdns Sutton
11 Y 15	Calthorpe gdns Edg
133 P 16	Calthorpe st WC1
91 S 14	Calton av SE21
5 S 19	Calton rd Barnt
111 R 16	Calverley clo Becknhm
56 D 7	Calverley cres Dgnhm
42 G 1	Calverley gdns Harrow
152 F 14	Calverley rd Epsom
134 M 14	Calvert av E2
81 T 12	Calvert clo Blvdr
115 Y 14	Calvert clo Sidcp
4 D 10	Calvert rd Barnt
77 O 14	Calvert rd SE10
66 J 3	Calverton rd E6
135 N 18	Calvin st E1
77 W 14	Calydon rd SE7
64 J 3	Cam rd E15
101 R 2	Camac rd Twick
87 P 13	Cambalt rd SW15
118 J 3	Camberley av SW20
8 D 15	Camberley ave Enf
8 D 15	Camberley clo Enf
94 J 11	Cambert way SE3
132 L4	Cambert wlk N1
91 P 3	Camberwell Church st SE5
91 P 2	Camberwell glebe SE5
91 N 1	Camberwell grn SE5
91 P 2	Camberwell gro SE5
149 W 18	Camberwell New rd SE5
91 N 2	Camberwell pas SE5
150 C 17	Camberwell rd SE5
90 L 2	Camberwell Station rd SE5
56 K 16	Cambeys rd Dgnhm
72 C 5	Camborne av W13
136 L 6	Camborne ms W11
123 W 18	Camborne rd Croy
119 P 12	Camborne rd Mrdn
115 T 8	Camborne rd Sidcp
154 A 16	Camborne rd Sutton
153 Z 17	Camborne rd Sutton
87 Y 19	Camborne rd SW18
96 J 4	Camborne rd Welling
82 G 1	Camborne way Hounsl
19 S 4	Cambourne av N9
89 W 20	Cambray rd SW12
82 H 11	Cambria clo Hounsl
114 F 1	Cambria clo Sidcp
96 F 20	Cambria clo Sidcp
90 L 7	Cambria rd SE5
145 Z 20	Cambria st SW6
36 H 15	Cambrian av Ilf
108 H 6	Cambrian clo SE27
51 N 2	Cambrian rd E10
84 M 17	Cambrian rd Rich
118 B 4	Cambridge av New Mald
96 K 10	Cambridge av Welling
41 V 16	Cambridge av Grnfd
129 V 7	Cambridge av NW6
78 G 12	Cambridge Barracks rd SE18
140 G 7	Cambridge cir WC2
82 C 10	Cambridge clo Hounsl
104 J 20	Cambridge clo SW20
104 J 20	Cambridge clo SW20
73 O 17	Cambridge cotts Rich
63 N 7	Cambridge cres E2
135 W 9	Cambridge cres E2
101 X 11	Cambridge cres Tedd
94 E 13	Cambridge dri SE12
131 X 15	Cambridge ga NW1
131 Y 15	Cambridge Gate ms NW1
136 K 4	Cambridge gdns W10
117 P 3	Cambridge gdns Kingst
129 V 9	Cambridge gdns NW6
8 K 9	Cambridge gdns Enf
31 N 1	Cambridge gdns N17
18 A 2	Cambridge gdns N21
95 Y 20	Cambridge grn SE9
109 Z 19	Cambridge gro SE20
144 A 7	Cambridge gro W6
74 K 10	Cambridge gro W6
117 P 4	Cambridge Grove rd Kingst
117 P 5	Cambridge Grove rd Kingst
63 O 9	Cambridge Heath rd E2
135 Y 5	Cambridge Heath rd E2
63 N 3	Cambridge Lodge vlls E9
50 D 19	Cambridge pass E9
34 F 19	Cambridge pk E11
84 E 17	Cambridge pk Twick
137 Z 19	Cambridge pl W8
118 B 8	Cambridge rd New Mald
22 J 16	Cambridge rd Harrow
117 Z 8	Cambridge rd New Mald
54 B 20	Cambridge rd Bark
112 F 18	Cambridge rd Brom
154 K 11	Cambridge rd Carsh
34 D 20	Cambridge rd E11
20 K 5	Cambridge rd E4
100 F 17	Cambridge rd Hampt
82 C 9	Cambridge rd Hounsl
54 J 1	Cambridge rd Ilf
117 R 5	Cambridge rd Kingst
121 U 6	Cambridge rd Mitch
129 U 12	Cambridge rd NW6
129 V 10	Cambridge rd NW6
73 O 19	Cambridge rd Rich
70 E 3	Cambridge rd S'hall
123 Z 5	Cambridge rd SE20
114 H 10	Cambridge rd Sidcp
88 L 3	Cambridge rd SW11
86 D 6	Cambridge rd SW13
118 H 1	Cambridge rd SW20
104 L 20	Cambridge rd SW20
101 X 11	Cambridge rd Tedd
84 G 15	Cambridge rd Twick
71 V 5	Cambridge rd W7
73 S 13	Cambridge Road north W4
73 S 14	Cambridge Road south W4
79 N 14	Cambridge row SE18
138 K 5	Cambridge sq W2
148 A 10	Cambridge st SW1
147 Y 8	Cambridge st SW1
18 F 3	Cambridge ter Enf
131 X 14	Cambridge ter NW1
131 Y 14	Cambridge Terrace ms NW1
65 T 13	Cambstone rd E16
79 X 19	Camdale rd SE18
91 U 1	Camden av SE5
114 B 20	Camden clo Chisl
122 J 4	Camden gdns Thntn Hth
131 Z 1	Camden gdns NW1
153 Z 12	Camden gdns Sutton
113 Z 15	Camden gro Chisl
151 N 20	Camden gro SE15
132 A 6	Camden High st NW1
131 Y 2	Camden High st NW1
109 T 15	Camden Hill rd SE19
47 Z 16	Camden la N7
131 W 1	Camden Lock pl NW1
47 X 18	Camden ms NW1
113 Y 20	Camden Park rd Chisl
47 Y 18	Camden Park rd NW1
133 V 8	Camden pas N1
113 X 17	Camden pk Chisl
113 Y 19	Camden pl Chisl
98 A 20	Camden rd Bxly
154 L 7	Camden rd Carsh
34 H 18	Camden rd E11
32 K 18	Camden rd E17
48 B 13	Camden rd N7
47 X 18	Camden rd N7
132 A 2	Camden rd NW1
153 Z 11	Camden rd Sutton
94 A 5	Camden row SE3
47 X 19	Camden sq NW1
132 A 2	Camden st NW1
131 Z 1	Camden st NW1
122 J 5	Camden way Thntn Hth
113 V 18	Camden way Chisl
133 X 7	Camden wlk N1
63 W 17	Camdenhurst st E14
78 B 2	Camel rd E16
82 J 18	Camelia pl Twick
148 J 20	Camellia st SW8
79 R 7	Camelot clo SE18
105 X 9	Camelot clo SW19
146 E 14	Camera pl SW10
19 N 15	Cameron clo N18
15 U 8	Cameron clo N20
15 V 8	Cameron clo N20
143 X 4	Cameron pl E1
126 E 11	Cameron rd Brom
122 J 15	Cameron rd Croy
54 H 4	Cameron rd Ilf
110 M 5	Cameron rd SE6
66 L 19	Cameron st E6
151 V 6	Camilla rd SE16
112 D 9	Camlan rd Brom
135 N 16	Camlet st E2
4 L 8	Camlet way Barnt
5 R 5	Camlet way Barnt
132 E 5	Camley st NW1
142 K 4	Camomile st EC3
104 L 13	Camp rd SW19
104 L 12	Camp view SW19
87 Y 2	Campana rd SW6
36 B 14	Campbell av Ilf
95 X 3	Campbell clo SE18
101 O 3	Campbell clo Twick
12 C 15	Campbell Croft Edg
122 H 15	Campbell rd Croy
52 A 13	Campbell rd E15
32 M 12	Campbell rd E17
64 B 9	Campbell rd E3
66 D 4	Campbell rd E6
31 W 4	Campbell rd N17
101 P 3	Campbell rd Twick
71 T 1	Campbell rd W7
130 E 19	Campbell st W2
47 W 10	Campdale rd N7
105 S 5	Campden clo SW19
42 B 8	Campden cres Wemb
55 T 10	Campden cres Dgnhm
137 V 16	Campden gro W8
137 S 14	Campden Hill gdns W8
137 R 13	Campden Hill pl W11
137 T 15	Campden Hill rd W8
137 R 14	Campden Hill sq W8
137 S 16	Campden hill W8
137 U 16	Campden House clo W8
157 T 11	Campden rd S Croy
137 U 14	Campden st W8
143 O 6	Camperdown st E1
94 M 18	Campfield rd SE9
95 N 18	Campfield rd SE9
66 H 19	Campion clo E6
25 N 19	Campion clo Harrow
157 S 10	Campion clo S Croy
80 B 3	Campion pl SE28
83 W 1	Campion rd Islwth
86 L 12	Campion rd SW15
45 P 10	Campion ter NW2
24 J 14	Campion rd Harrow
75 T 19	Camplin st SE14
30 A 11	Campsbourne rd N8
30 B 12	Campsbourne the N8
68 D 2	Campsey gdns Dgnhm
68 D 1	Campsey rd Dgnhm
30 A 10	Campsfield rd N8
93 U 13	Campshill pl SE13
93 U 13	Campshill rd SE13
32 L 18	Campus rd E17
24 L 6	Camrose av Edg
25 R 2	Camrose av Edg
81 W 17	Camrose av Erith
119 Y 9	Camrose clo SW19
79 Z 12	Camrose st SE2
33 U 18	Canada av N18
61 U 13	Canada cres W3
61 U 13	Canada rd W3
75 T 6	Canada st SE16
62 K 20	Canada way W12
111 P 2	Canadian av SE6
93 P 20	Canadian av SE6
63 V 11	Canal clo E1
151 U 13	Canal gro SE15
91 W 1	Canal head SE15
63 W 12	Canal rd E3
150 E 15	Canal st SE5
134 G 3	Canal wlk N1
110 D 12	Canal wlk SE26
76 B 2	Canary wharf E14
69 Z 2	Canberra clo Dgnhm
26 G 10	Canberra clo NW9
69 Z 1	Canberra cres Dgnhm
80 H 17	Canberra rd Bxly Hth
66 H 4	Canberra rd E6
78 A 17	Canberra rd SE7
77 Y 18	Canberra rd SE7
102 M 19	Canbury av Kingst
109 W 8	Canbury ms SE26
116 K 1	Canbury Park rd Kingst
117 N 1	Canbury Park rd Kingst
116 H 1	Canbury pas Kingst

140 F 19 Carteret st SW1
75 W 11 Carteret way SE8
8 L 7 Carterhatch la Enf
9 N 8 Carterhatch la Enf
9 P 8 Carterhatch rd Enf
153 P 2 Carters clo Worc Pk
112 M 1 Carters Hill clo SE9
110 J 5 Carters la SE23
87 Y 13 Carters yd SW18
74 J 8 Carthew rd W6
74 K 8 Carthew vlls W6
133 Z 20 Carthusian st EC1
140 M 10 Carting la WC2
32 A 1 Cartmel clo N17
98 D 1 Cartmel rd Bxly Hth
120 C 12 Cartmell gdns Mrdn
132 H 14 Cartwright gdns WC1
56 A 19 Cartwright rd Dgnhm
69 N 1 Cartwright rd Dgnhm
143 P 10 Cartwright st E1
90 L 15 Carver rd SE24
47 Y 4 Carverley gro N19
72 J 12 Carville cres Brentf
52 B 10 Cary rd E11
49 O 11 Carysfort rd N16
29 Y 15 Carysfort rd N8
29 U 12 Cascade av N10
75 T 20 Casella rd SE14
108 H 10 Casewick rd SE27
50 B 8 Casimir rd E5
91 O 12 Casino av SE24
135 Y 17 Caslon pl E1
150 E 18 Caspian st SE5
66 A 18 Caspian wlk E16
61 Z 1 Casselden rd NW10
145 U 20 Cassidy rd SW5
80 A 12 Cassilda rd SE2
84 C 14 Cassilis rd Twick
32 G 17 Cassiobury rd E17
123 N 9 Cassland rd Thntn Hth
50 H 19 Cassland rd E9
92 L 19 Casslee rd SE6
143 S 1 Casson st E1
76 G 7 Castalia st E14
130 A 18 Castellain rd W9
129 X 15 Castellain rd W9
39 Z 10 Castellan av Rom
23 W 1 Castellane clo Stanm
86 M 13 Castello av SW15
74 J 17 Castelnau pl SW13
74 H 18 Castelnau SW13
86 H 2 Castelnau SW13
94 F 8 Casterbridge rd SE3
78 J 10 Castile rd SE18
112 A 4 Castillon rd SE6
111 Z 5 Castillon rd SE6
110 L 5 Castlands rd SE6
20 K 17 Castle av E4
152 H 20 Castle av Epsom
141 Z 9 Castle Baynard st EC4
125 Y 7 Castle clo BR2
105 O 5 Castle clo SW19
160 G 7 Castle clo EC3
35 R 18 Castle dri Ilf
68 B 3 Castle gdns Dgnhm
159 U 18 Castle Hill av Croy
148 B 1 Castle la SW1
47 R 19 Castle ms NW5
68 C 4 Castle rd Dgnhm
9 V 4 Castle rd Enf
83 V 4 Castle rd Islwth
15 S 17 Castle rd N12
40 J 19 Castle rd Nthlt
47 T 19 Castle rd NW1
70 E 8 Castle rd S'hall
65 Z 6 Castle st E6
116 J 2 Castle st Kingst
152 H 20 Castle way Epsom
105 O 5 Castle way SW19
47 P 1 Castle yd N6
60 C 15 Castlebar hill W5
60 C 13 Castlebar ms W5
60 B 13 Castlebar pk W5
60 E 16 Castlebar rd W5
87 R 19 Castlecombe dri SW19
113 P 11 Castlecombe rd SE9
109 Z 1 Castledine rd SE20
113 Z 1 Castleford av SE9
95 Z 20 Castleford av SE9
84 M 9 Castlegate Rich
47 S 19 Castlehaven rd NW1
131 X 1 Castlehaven rd NW1
8 C 17 Castleleigh ct Enf
152 K 19 Castlemaine av Epsom
157 U 11 Castlemaine S Croy

139 N 3 Castlereagh st W1
98 M 3 Castleton av Bxly Hth
99 N 4 Castleton av Bxly Hth
42 J 12 Castleton av Wemb
33 X 7 Castleton rd E17
55 O 4 Castleton rd Ilf
121 W 9 Castleton rd Mitch
113 O 10 Castleton rd SE9
144 M 11 Castletown rd W14
145 N 10 Castletown rd W14
35 S 18 Castlewew gdns Ilf
95 V 4 Castlewood dri SE9
5 V 12 Castlewood rd Barnt
49 W 1 Castlewood rd E5
31 X 20 Castlewood rd N16
135 V 5 Cat & Mutton br E8
6 A 17 Cat hill Barnt
5 X 18 Cat hill Barnt
35 V 7 Caterham av Ilf
93 V 8 Caterham rd SE13
150 G 7 Catesby st SE17
93 P 19 Catford bdwy SE6
111 N 1 Catford hill SE6
93 P 19 Catford rd SE6
51 X 8 Cathall rd E11
51 Y 9 Cathall rd E11
75 N 6 Cathay st SE16
143 X 18 Cathay st SE16
47 U 10 Cathcart hill N19
146 A 13 Cathcart rd SW10
47 S 16 Cathcart st NW5
141 Z 5 Cathedral pl EC4
142 E 13 Cathedral st SE1
48 M 10 Catherall rd N5
6 H 17 Catherine ct N14
83 P 11 Catherine gdns Hounsl
93 R 1 Catherine gro SE10
140 B 20 Catherine pl SW1
39 Y 16 Catherine rd Rom
116 G 11 Catherine rd Surb
141 N 8 Catherine st WC2
142 K 2 Catherine Wheel all EC2
72 G 19 Catherine Wheel rd Brentf
140 B 15 Catherine Wheel yd SW1
89 T 17 Cathles rd SW12
74 J 7 Cathnor rd W12
9 V 1 Catistield rd Enf
151 U 10 Catlin st SE16
110 D 7 Catling clo SE23
89 Y 9 Cato rd SW4
138 M 3 Cato st W1
91 V 1 Caton st SE15
124 M 1 Cator la Becknhm
110 J 19 Cator pk Becknhm
155 N 11 Cator rd Carsh
110 F 15 Cator rd SE26
151 O 17 Cator st SE15
10 A 5 Catsey woods Bushey
113 S 11 Cattistock rd SE9
140 M 2 Catton st WC1
66 E 2 Caulfield rd E6
92 A 4 Caulfield rd SE15
155 O 4 Causeway the Carsh
28 H 13 Causeway the N2
154 D 19 Causeway the Sutton
87 Z 12 Causeway the SW16
104 M 12 Causeway the SW19
105 N 12 Causeway the SW19
101 W 14 Causeway the Tedd
19 O 3 Causeyware rd N9
47 T 1 Causton rd N6
148 G 8 Causton st SW1
89 T 14 Cautley av SW4
37 T 12 Cavalier clo Rom
146 O 12 Cavaye pl SW10
65 W 8 Cave rd E13
102 C 9 Cave rd Rich
7 U 8 Cavell dri Enf
31 O 2 Cavell rd N17
63 N 16 Cavell st E1
143 Y 4 Cavell st E1
34 G 3 Cavendish av Wdfd Grn
118 H 10 Cavendish av New Mald
96 M 8 Cavendish av Welling
81 W 17 Cavendish av Erith
41 T 13 Cavendish av Harrow
57 Y 18 Cavendish av Hornch
27 X 8 Cavendish av N3
130 G 11 Cavendish av NW8
97 N 18 Cavendish av Sidcp
59 Y 16 Cavendish av W13
130 G 12 Cavendish clo NW8

45 U 19 Cavendish clo NW8
57 Y 18 Cavendish cres Hornchurch
142 K 3 Cavendish ct EC2
51 V 3 Cavendish dri E11
12 A 19 Cavendish dri Edg
54 L 15 Cavendish gdns Bark
53 W 3 Cavendish gdns Ilf
37 Z 17 Cavendish gdns Rom
139 Y 1 Cavendish mews north W1
139 Y 1 Cavendish mews south W1
139 Y 3 Cavendish pl W1
118 C 10 Cavendish rd New Mald
4 A 12 Cavendish rd Barnt
122 J 19 Cavendish rd Croy
20 H 20 Cavendish rd E4
19 N 16 Cavendish rd N18
30 H 18 Cavendish rd N4
45 U 19 Cavendish rd NW6
154 C 15 Cavendish rd Sutton
107 T 1 Cavendish rd SW12
89 T 17 Cavendish rd SW12
106 H 17 Cavendish rd SW19
106 J 17 Cavendish rd SW19
85 W 1 Cavendish rd W4
139 Y 4 Cavendish sq W1
134 E 9 Cavendish st N1
125 P 20 Cavendish way W Wkhm
54 E 10 Cavenham gdns Ilf
118 H 18 Caverleigh way Worc Pk
17 T 10 Caversham av N13
153 R 2 Caversham av Sutton
30 L 13 Caversham rd N15
47 U 17 Caversham rd NW5
147 N 13 Caversham st SW3
136 B 4 Caverswall st W12
62 L 16 Caverswall st W12
131 T 3 Cavert st NW1
127 W 1 Caveside clo Chisl
71 Z 10 Cawdor cres W7
109 T 14 Cawnpore st SE19
64 A 7 Caxton gro E3
30 D 8 Caxton rd N22
106 C 13 Caxton rd SW19
136 E 16 Caxton rd W12
148 D 1 Caxton st SW1
65 P 19 Caxton Street north E16
77 R 1 Caxton Street south E16
126 C 9 Caygill clo Brom
134 D 13 Cayton rd EC1
59 U 7 Cayton rd Grnfd
134 D 13 Cayton st EC1
33 O 6 Cazenove rd E17
49 Y 5 Cazenove rd N16
54 D 20 Cecil av Bark
8 G 14 Cecil av Enf
42 M 16 Cecil av Wemb
4 C 10 Cecil ct Barnt
140 H 10 Cecil ct WC2
22 D 13 Cecil pk Pinn
120 M 9 Cecil pl Mitch
121 N 11 Cecil pl Mitch
122 C 16 Cecil rd Croy
52 A 8 Cecil rd E11
65 T 4 Cecil rd E13
33 O 3 Cecil rd E17
8 B 14 Cecil rd Enf
7 Z 13 Cecil rd Enf
23 S 10 Cecil rd Harrow
83 N 6 Cecil rd Hounsl
53 Y 12 Cecil rd Ilf
29 T 7 Cecil rd N10
16 F 5 Cecil rd N14
62 A 4 Cecil rd NW10
25 Z 11 Cecil rd NW9
55 X 1 Cecil rd Rom
153 V 14 Cecil rd Sutton
106 A 18 Cecil rd SW19
61 W 15 Cecil rd W3
126 E 19 Cecil way Brom
30 A 19 Cecile pk N8
28 C 10 Cecilia clo N2
49 W 15 Cecilia rd E8
15 W 1 Cedar av Barnt
9 P 8 Cedar av Enf
37 Y 15 Cedar av Rom
96 M 17 Cedar av Sidcp
82 M 15 Cedar av Twick
127 T 2 Cedar clo Brom
38 L 12 Cedar clo Rom
154 M 12 Cedar clo SM5
103 X 10 Cedar clo SW15
127 T 3 Cedar copse Brom

105 P 8 Cedar ct SW19
28 H 13 Cedar dri N2
154 D 14 Cedar gdns Sutton
97 V 16 Cedar gro Bxly
58 H 14 Cedar gro S'hall
72 J 7 Cedar gro W5
102 J 1 Cedar heights Rich
14 F 17 Cedar Lawn av Barnt
113 N 2 Cedar mt SE9
55 V 1 Cedar Park gdns Rom
8 A 3 Cedar Park rd Enf
126 L 3 Cedar rd Brom
7 X 4 Cedar rd Enf
99 W 2 Cedar rd Erith
31 V 4 Cedar rd N17
45 N 12 Cedar rd NW2
38 K 14 Cedar rd Rom
154 C 14 Cedar rd Sutton
101 Y 13 Cedar rd Tedd
16 C 2 Cedar ri N14
84 L 10 Cedar ter Rich
108 J 12 Cedar Tree gro SE27
132 F 2 Cedar way NW1
89 R 10 Cedar's ms SW4
89 S 10 Cedar's rd SW4
94 K 14 Cedarhurst dri SE9
145 W 19 Cedarne rd SW6
156 B 7 Cedars av Croy
33 O 15 Cedars av E17
121 P 8 Cedars av Mitch
27 O 10 Cedars clo NW4
18 E 7 Cedars ct N9
124 L 3 Cedars rd Becknhm
156 B 7 Cedars rd Croy
52 A 18 Cedars rd E15
102 C 20 Cedars rd Kingst
119 Y 8 Cedars rd Mrdn
17 W 7 Cedars rd N21
18 K 9 Cedars rd N9
86 F 5 Cedars rd SW13
73 V 15 Cedars rd W4
21 T 6 Cedars the Buck Hl
101 X 15 Cedars the Tedd
108 D 16 Cedarville gdns SW16
39 R 10 Cedric av Rom
114 B 6 Cedric rd SE9
80 B 4 Celadine dri SE28
64 A 15 Celandine clo E14
80 C 3 Celandine dri SE28
64 M 9 Celandine way E15
137 Y 3 Celbridge ms W2
47 V 12 Celia rd N19
126 A 7 Celtic av Brom
125 Z 7 Celtic av Brom
64 F 13 Celtic st E14
78 D 17 Cemetery la SE7
52 D 13 Cemetery rd E7
31 T 3 Cemetery rd N17
80 C 19 Cemetery rd SE2
45 Z 8 Cenacle clo NW3
149 R 1 Centaur st SE1
9 X 13 Centenary rd Enf
51 X 7 Central av E11
8 M 8 Central av Enf
9 N 8 Central av Enf
83 O 12 Central av Hounsl
28 F 7 Central av N12
18 F 10 Central av N9
22 D 19 Central av Pinn
147 R 19 Central av SW1
156 B 11 Central av Wallgtn
96 M 4 Central av Welling
109 P 14 Central hill SE19
141 W 2 Central mkts EC1
56 H 10 Central Park av Dgnhm
66 F 6 Central Park rd E6
65 Z 7 Central Park rd E6
59 Y 8 Central pde Grnfd
56 L 7 Central pk Rom
120 B 10 Central rd Mrdn
42 B 15 Central rd Wemb
152 H 2 Central rd Worc Pk
85 V 7 Central School pth SW14
27 Z 17 Central sq NW11
134 A 16 Central st EC1
133 Z 12 Central st EC1
154 J 16 Central way Carsh
80 A 1 Central way SE28
68 C 20 Central way SE28
79 Z 3 Central way SE28
73 Y 3 Centre av W3
114 B 17 Centre Common rd Chisl
69 V 5 Centre rd Dgnhm
78 H 13 Centre rd SE18
63 N 7 Centre st E2

119 V 18	Chatham clo Sutton
50 C 17	Chatham pl E9
34 C 7	Chatham rd E17
32 H 11	Chatham rd E17
117 O 2	Chatham rd Kingst
88 L 15	Chatham rd SW11
150 F 5	Chatham st SE17
60 K 16	Chatsfield pl W5
112 G 11	Chatsworth av Brom
26 L 8	Chatsworth av NW4
115 N 1	Chatsworth av Sidcp
119 T 2	Chatsworth av SW20
43 N 16	Chatsworth av Wemb
26 L 8	Chatsworth clo NW4
83 P 9	Chatsworth cres Hounsl
18 J 1	Chatsworth dri Enf
8 K 20	Chatsworth dri Eng
118 D 11	Chatsworth gdns New Mald
40 K 4	Chatsworth gdns Harrow
73 S 2	Chatsworth gdns W3
101 X 9	Chatsworth pl Tedd
157 O 7	Chatsworth rd Croy
52 B 15	Chatsworth rd E15
50 D 9	Chatsworth rd E5
45 O 18	Chatsworth rd NW2
153 R 9	Chatsworth rd Sutton
73 W 17	Chatsworth rd W4
60 M 12	Chatsworth ri W5
60 M 12	Chatsworth ri W5
108 K 6	Chatsworth way SE2
127 N 11	Chatterton rd Brom
48 J 9	Chatterton rd N4
88 M 14	Chatto rd SW11
89 N 13	Chatto rd SW11
85 R 6	Chaucer av Rich
16 J 16	Chaucer clo N11
153 Y 6	Chaucer gdns Sutton
124 C 17	Chaucer grn Croy
34 E 18	Chaucer rd E11
33 U 7	Chaucer rd E17
52 G 18	Chaucer rd E7
39 Z 1	Chaucer rd Rom
90 G 14	Chaucer rd SE24
115 T 2	Chaucer rd Sidcp
153 X 7	Chaucer rd Sutton
73 W 2	Chaucer rd W3
96 J 2	Chaucer rd Welling
18 J 10	Chauncey clo N9
95 T 16	Chaundrye clo SE9
152 L 4	Cheam Common rd Worc Pk
153 P 14	Cheam Park Sutton
153 R 13	Cheam Park way Sutton
153 P 20	Cheam rd Sutton
92 B 7	Cheam st SE15
142 B 6	Cheapside EC2
160 B 6	Cheapside EC2
18 A 14	Cheapside N13
18 C 12	Cheddington rd N18
65 P 17	Chedworth clo E16
100 D 15	Cheeseman clo Hampt
111 W 11	Chelford rd Brom
68 C 7	Chelmer cres Bark
50 F 14	Chelmer rd E9
39 O 1	Chelmsford av Rom
66 F 18	Chelmsford clo E6
53 S 1	Chelmsford gdns Ilf
51 Y 3	Chelmsford rd E11
33 N 18	Chelmsford rd E17
34 B 4	Chelmsford rd E18
16 H 4	Chelmsford rd N14
128 B 5	Chelmsford sq NW10
62 L 4	Chelmsford sq NW10
144 J 12	Chelmsford st
147 W 13	Chelsea br SW1
147 U 11	Chelsea Bridge rd SW1
25 O 7	Chelsea clo Edg
101 N 13	Chelsea clo Hampt
147 R 14	Chelsea emb SW3
146 L 15	Chelsea Embankment gdns SW3
88 D 1	Chelsea Harbour dri SW10
146 K 12	Chelsea Manor gdns SW3
146 L 12	Chelsea Manor st SW3
146 F 14	Chelsea Park gdns SW3
146 H 10	Chelsea sq SW3
19 S 2	Chelsfield av N9
110 D 8	Chelsfield gdns SE26
157 O 15	Chelsham rd S Croy
89 Y 7	Chelsham rd SW4
79 S 18	Chelsworth clo SE18
83 Y 19	Cheltenham av Twick
40 J 17	Cheltenham clo Nthlt
66 D 7	Cheltenham gdns E6
24 J 13	Cheltenham pl Harrow
73 T 4	Cheltenham pl W3
33 U 19	Cheltenham rd E10
92 D 12	Cheltenham rd SE15
147 P 9	Cheltenham ter SW3
87 P 10	Chelverton rd SW15
85 R 4	Chelwood gdns Rich
15 U 7	Chelwood N20
92 G 11	Chelwood wlk SE4
65 R 10	Chenappa clo E13
10 J 17	Chenduit way Stanm
132 J 10	Cheney rd NW1
32 K 4	Cheney row E17
52 A 10	Cheneys rd E11
132 E 18	Chenies ms WC1
132 F 8	Chenies pl NW1
132 E 20	Chenies st WC1
145 W 1	Cheniston gdns W8
145 X 1	Cheniston gdns W8
87 S 15	Chepstow clo SW15
36 J 19	Chepstow cres Ilf
137 T 8	Chepstow cres W11
58 F 18	Chepstow gdns S'hall
137 U 7	Chepstow pl W2
157 S 4	Chepstow rd Croy
137 U 4	Chepstow rd W2
71 X 7	Chepstow rd W7
157 T 5	Chepstow ri Croy
137 R 9	Chepstow vlls W11
134 D 18	Chequer st EC1
69 R 5	Chequers la Dgnhm
95 U 15	Chequers par SE9
17 X 15	Chequers way N13
68 K 18	Cherbury clo SE28
134 G 9	Cherbury st N1
71 V 2	Cherington rd W7
126 D 12	Cheriton av Brom
35 V 6	Cheriton av Ilf
60 E 14	Cheriton clo W5
79 S 18	Cheriton dri SE18
107 P 4	Cheriton sq SW17
154 L 2	Cherry clo Carsh
119 S 9	Cherry clo Mrdn
72 G 8	Cherry clo W5
72 A 19	Cherry cres Brentf
143 W 19	Cherry Garden st SE16
72 H 13	Cherry garth Brentf
56 A 14	Cherry gdns Dgnhm
5 O 20	Cherry hill Barnt
156 D 8	Cherry Hill gdns Croy
157 P 1	Cherry orchard Croy
123 R 20	Cherry Orchard rd Croy
77 X 17	Cherry orchard SE7
9 R 3	Cherry rd Enf
38 M 15	Cherry st Rom
41 X 12	Cherry Tree clo Wemb
28 L 13	Cherry Tree rd N2
21 Z 13	Cherry Tree ri Buck Hl
124 M 8	Cherry Tree wlk Becknhm
28 L 14	Cherry Tree wood N2
126 F 19	Cherry wlk Brom
20 A 12	Cherrydown av E4
19 Z 11	Cherrydown av E4
20 A 11	Cherrydown clo E4
19 Z 11	Cherrydown clo E4
115 W 5	Cherrydown rd Sidcp
38 H 7	Cherrydown wlk Rom
108 B 7	Cherrytree dri SW16
11 O 18	Cherrytree way Stanm
103 P 18	Cherrywood clo Kingst
87 O 13	Cherrywood dri SW15
119 S 8	Cherrywood la Mrdn
153 T 4	Chertsey dri Sutton
51 X 5	Chertsey rd E11
54 D 13	Chertsey rd Ilf
100 L 3	Chertsey rd Twick
101 N 1	Chertsey rd Twick
83 U 17	Chertsey rd Twick
73 P 14	Chertsey rd W4
107 N 12	Chertsey st SW17
80 B 4	Chervil ms SE28
88 B 2	Cheryls clo SW6
110 A 6	Cheseman st SE26
102 L 18	Chesfield rd Kingst
127 Z 14	Chesham av Brom
38 M 12	Chesham clo Rom
147 S 2	Chesham clo SW1
124 D 1	Chesham cres SE20
147 S 2	Chesham pl SW1
117 P 2	Chesham rd Kingst
124 D 2	Chesham rd SE20
106 F 13	Chesham rd SW19
43 Y 11	Chesham st NW10
147 S 1	Chesham st SW1
147 S 3	Chesham st SW1
72 A 4	Chesham ter W13
121 Z 7	Cheshire clo Mitch
30 C 1	Cheshire rd N22
17 P 20	Cheshire rd N22
135 S 16	Cheshire st E2
49 S 9	Chesholm rd N16
81 R 14	Cheshunt av Blvdr
52 J 19	Cheshunt rd E7
87 U 1	Chesilton rd SW6
66 C 8	Chesley gdns E6
159 U 15	Chesney cres Croy
89 N 2	Chesney st SW11
31 W 10	Chesnut rd N17
80 M 19	Chessington av Bxly Hth
81 N 19	Chessington av Bxly Hth
81 O 19	Chessington av Bxly Hth
27 V 11	Chessington av N3
22 E 14	Chessington ct Pinn
152 B 20	Chessington rd Epsom
159 S 3	Chessington way W Wckm
145 P 13	Chesson rd W14
82 E 20	Chester av Hounsl
84 M 15	Chester av Rich
100 D 1	Chester av Twick
153 Y 3	Chester clo Sutton
139 W 20	Chester clo SW1
86 K 8	Chester clo SW13
131 X 13	Chester Close north NW1
131 X 13	Chester Close south NW1
147 S 6	Chester cotts SW1
22 H 17	Chester dri Harrow
131 X 14	Chester ga NW1
9 N 19	Chester gdns Enf
120 C 13	Chester gdns Mrdn
139 W 20	Chester ms SW1
131 X 11	Chester pl NW1
34 J 19	Chester rd E11
65 N 12	Chester rd E16
32 F 17	Chester rd E17
53 N 20	Chester rd E7
54 L 2	Chester rd Ilf
31 P 9	Chester rd N17
47 S 7	Chester rd N19
19 N 7	Chester rd N9
131 V 13	Chester rd NW1
96 H 13	Chester rd Sidcp
104 M 15	Chester rd SW19
147 T 7	Chester row SW1
147 U 5	Chester row SW1
147 V 4	Chester sq SW1
147 W 3	Chester Square ms SW1
139 W 20	Chester st SW1
131 X 13	Chester ter NW1
149 T 7	Chester way SE11
148 G 12	Chester wharf SW1
139 W 13	Chesterfield gdns W1
30 K 17	Chesterfield gdns N4
91 U 12	Chesterfield gro SE22
139 W 12	Chesterfield hill W1
4 B 18	Chesterfield rd Barnt
33 U 20	Chesterfield rd E10
9 V 1	Chesterfield rd Enf
14 L 18	Chesterfield rd N3
73 W 17	Chesterfield rd W4
139 W 13	Chesterfield st W1
75 P 20	Chesterfield way SE15
93 X 1	Chesterfield wlk SE10
46 B 13	Chesterford gdns NW3
53 U 17	Chesterford rd E12
104 A 20	Chesters the New Mald
58 K 6	Chesterton clo Grnfd
87 X 13	Chesterton clo SW18
65 T 8	Chesterton rd E13
136 H 3	Chesterton rd W10
65 S 8	Chesterton ter E13
117 O 4	Chesterton ter Kingst
30 M 5	Chesthunte rd N17
145 R 15	Chestnut all SW6
72 H 12	Chestnut av Brentf
52 G 13	Chestnut av E7
11 Y 19	Chestnut av Edg
152 A 9	Chestnut av Epsom
100 G 18	Chestnut av Hampt
57 U 7	Chestnut av Hornch
29 Z 15	Chestnut av N8
33 V 14	Chestnut av SE17
85 Y 9	Chestnut av SW14
101 W 18	Chestnut av Tedd
42 A 14	Chestnut av Wemb
33 V 13	Chestnut Avenue north E17
154 L 1	Chestnut clo Carsh
6 J 18	Chestnut clo N14
49 O 6	Chestnut clo N16
97 X 8	Chestnut dri Bxly Hth
34 E 19	Chestnut dri E11
23 V 3	Chestnut dri Harrow
22 A 19	Chestnut dri Pinn
57 U 8	Chestnut glen Hornch
118 A 5	Chestnut gro New Mald
117 Z 6	Chestnut gro New Mald
5 Z 18	Chestnut gro Barnt
83 Y 10	Chestnut gro Islwth
121 Y 9	Chestnut gro Mitch
158 B 16	Chestnut gro S Croy
107 P 1	Chestnut gro SW12
72 G 7	Chestnut gro W5
89 O 19	Chestnut gro W5
42 A 14	Chestnut gro Wemb
14 C 5	Chestnut la N20
102 J 18	Chestnut rd Kingst
108 K 6	Chestnut rd SE27
119 R 3	Chestnut rd SW20
101 S 3	Chestnut rd Twick
79 U 14	Chestnut ri SE18
21 S 16	Chestnut wlk Wdfd Grn
158 K 1	Cheston av CR0
158 J 1	Cheston av Croy
99 S 3	Cheswrth clo Erith
150 E 2	Chettle clo SE1
30 E 18	Chettle ct N8
107 N 5	Chetwode rd SW17
15 Z 5	Chetwynd av Barnt
47 S 11	Chetwynd rd NW5
146 L 1	Cheval pl SW7
76 A 7	Cheval st E14
128 G 9	Chevening rd NW6
77 R 14	Chevening rd SE10
109 O 16	Chevening rd SE19
115 S 6	Chevenings the Sidcp
47 X 3	Cheverton rd N19
50 H 15	Chevet st E9
99 P 4	Cheviot clo Bxly Hth
8 B 9	Cheviot clo Enf
154 F 20	Cheviot clo Sutton
45 S 6	Cheviot ga NW2
45 R 7	Cheviot gdns NW2
57 W 2	Cheviot rd Hornch
108 J 10	Cheviot rd SE27
60 B 5	Cheviot way Grnfd
36 H 14	Cheviot way Ilf
32 H 14	Chewton rd E17
34 B 10	Cheyne av E18
100 F 2	Cheyne av Twick
146 M 14	Cheyne gdns SW3
116 M 9	Cheyne hill Surb
117 N 10	Cheyne hill Surb
146 L 14	Cheyne ms SW3
147 O 13	Cheyne pl SW3
146 K 15	Cheyne row SW3
157 X 3	Cheyne wlk Croy
7 V 16	Cheyne wlk N21
26 M 18	Cheyne wlk NW4
146 F 17	Cheyne wlk SW10
146 K 16	Cheyne wlk SW3
146 L 15	Cheyne wlk SW3
24 J 1	Cheyneys av Edg
11 V 19	Cheyneys av Edg
157 T 8	Chichele gdns Croy
45 P 13	Chichele rd NW2
22 M 2	Chicheley gdns Harrow
23 N 3	Chicheley rd Harrow
141 O 16	Chicheley st SE1
94 L 1	Chichester clo SE3
24 L 10	Chichester ct Stanm
53 S 2	Chichester gdns Ilf
157 U 6	Chichester rd Croy
52 A 10	Chichester rd E11
18 J 5	Chichester rd N9
129 U 9	Chichester rd NW6

129 Z 20	Chichester rd W9
141 R 5	Chichester rents WC2
148 D 11	Chichester st SW1
76 J 10	Chichester way E14
143 R 1	Chicksand st E1
14 L 11	Chiddingfold N12
81 P 18	Chiddingstone av Bxly Hth
87 Y 4	Chiddingstone st SW6
98 G 10	Chieveley rd Bxly Hth
71 Y 2	Chignell pl W13
143 X 10	Chigwell hill E1
34 H 10	Chigwell rd E18
64 D 18	Chilcot clo E14
145 V 6	Child's pl SW5
145 V 6	Child's st SW5
27 W 15	Child's way NW11
145 V 6	Child's wlk SW5
107 S 4	Childebert rd SW17
75 W 20	Childeric rd SE14
87 R 1	Childerley st SW6
75 X 16	Childers st SE8
59 Z 6	Chilham clo Grnfd
113 R 10	Chilham rd SE9
126 D 17	Chilham way Brom
107 P 13	Chillerton rd SW17
48 E 16	Chillingworth rd N7
118 F 15	Chilmark gdns New Mald
121 X 2	Chilmark rd SW16
100 G 2	Chiltern av Twick
99 P 3	Chiltern clo Bxly Hth
157 T 6	Chiltern clo Croy
7 R 14	Chiltern dene Enf
117 R 13	Chiltern dri Surb
126 C 8	Chiltern gdns Brom
45 P 8	Chiltern gdns NW2
64 B 12	Chiltern rd E3
36 J 14	Chiltern rd Ilf
135 R 15	Chiltern st E2
131 S 19	Chiltern st W1
139 S 2	Chiltern st W1
21 T 12	Chiltern way Wdfd Grn
154 B 20	Chilterns, the Sutton
92 M 18	Chilthorne clo SE6
10 B 1	Chilton av Bushey
72 G 10	Chilton av W5
75 U 11	Chilton gro SE8
12 C 19	Chilton rd Edg
85 P 7	Chilton rd Rich
135 R 15	Chilton st E2
34 D 8	Chiltons The E18
77 R 13	Chilver st SE10
154 D 5	Chilworth gdns Sutton
138 E 6	Chilworth ms W2
138 C 6	Chilworth st W2
17 U 15	Chimes av N13
112 J 7	Chinbrook rd SE12
29 U 13	Chine the N10
7 X 18	Chine the N21
42 C 14	Chine the Wemb
20 M 11	Chingdale rd E4
21 N 11	Chingdale rd E4
20 C 9	Chingford av E4
21 O 14	Chingford la Wdfd Grn
20 B 16	Chingford Mount rd E4
20 B 19	Chingford rd E4
33 P 2	Chingford rd E4
112 A 15	Chingley clo Brom
58 M 6	Chinnor cres Grnfd
59 N 6	Chinnor cres Grnfd
76 F 6	Chipka st E14
75 V 18	Chipley st SE14
50 F 10	Chippendale st E5
43 U 16	Chippenham av Wemb
129 U 15	Chippenham gdns W9
129 U 19	Chippenham ms W9
129 T 18	Chippenham rd W9
122 J 9	Chipstead av Thntn Hth
109 V 18	Chipstead clo SE19
44 L 7	Chipstead gdns NW2
87 Y 3	Chipstead st SW6
58 B 11	Chirk clo Grnfd
63 V 5	Chisenhale rd E3
157 S 2	Chisholm rd Croy
84 M 17	Chisholm rd Rich
28 C 2	Chislehurst av N12
113 Z 14	Chislehurst High st Chisl
127 S 1	Chislehurst rd Chisl
84 K 14	Chislehurst rd Rich
114 M 13	Chislehurst rd Sidcp
31 R 18	Chisley rd N15
94 H 4	Chiswell sq SE3
134 E 20	Chiswell st EC1
85 V 4	Chiswick br W4
156 B 5	Chiswick clo Croy
73 Z 11	Chiswick Common rd W4
22 E 10	Chiswick ct Pinn
74 B 12	Chiswick High rd W4
73 U 12	Chiswick High rd W4
74 C 13	Chiswick la NW4
74 D 15	Chiswick la SW4
74 D 15	Chiswick mall W4
85 V 2	Chiswick quay W4
18 L 8	Chiswick rd N9
73 V 12	Chiswick rd W4
73 S 15	Chiswick village W4
132 C 20	Chitty st W1
55 V 5	Chittys la Dgnhm
88 H 13	Chivalry rd SW11
124 F 20	Chive clo CR0
20 E 13	Chivers rd E4
68 F 11	Choats Manor way Dgnhm
69 N 10	Choats rd Dgnhm
105 O 4	Chobham gdns SW19
51 W 15	Chobham rd E15
47 S 1	Cholmeley cres N6
47 S 1	Cholmeley pk N6
116 A 16	Cholmley rd Surb
62 F 5	Cholmondeley av NW10
84 F 13	Cholmondeley wlk Rich
143 Y 13	Choppins ct E1
91 X 5	Choumert gro SE15
91 V 6	Choumert rd SE15
91 X 5	Choumert sq SE15
64 D 15	Chrisp st E14
64 E 18	Chrisp st E14
85 S 12	Christ Church rd SW14
24 B 12	Christchurch av Harrow
42 L 19	Christchurch av Wemb
23 Z 12	Christchurch av Harrow
15 P 19	Christchurch av N12
128 J 3	Christchurch av NW6
45 U 19	Christchurch av NW6
101 X 13	Christchurch av Tedd
106 G 19	Christchurch clo SW19
23 Z 12	Christchurch gdns Harrow
42 K 19	Christchurch grn Wemb
46 F 10	Christchurch hill NW3
4 F 10	Christchurch la Barnt
4 F 10	Christchurch pas Barnt
46 F 10	Christchurch pas NW3
154 C 16	Christchurch pk Sutton
106 G 19	Christchurch rd SW19
114 L 8	Christchurch rd Sidcp
125 O 2	Christchurch rd Becknhm
54 A 5	Christchurch rd Ilf
29 Z 19	Christchurch rd N8
117 N 16	Christchurch rd Surb
108 E 2	Christchurch rd SW2
63 O 4	Christchurch sq E9
147 N 13	Christchurch rd SW3
147 O 13	Christchurch ter SW3
76 M 14	Christchurch way SE10
108 G 18	Christian fields SW16
143 U 7	Christian st E1
37 R 20	Christie gdns Rom
50 H 19	Christie rd E9
134 J 17	Christina st EC2
71 Y 8	Christopher av W7
96 K 15	Christopher clo Sidcp
55 V 14	Christopher gdns Dgnhm
132 G 13	Christopher pl NW1
134 G 19	Christopher st EC2
149 U 19	Chryssel rd SW9
75 V 17	Chubworthy st SE14
54 H 13	Chudleigh cres Ilf
154 D 4	Chudleigh gdns Sutton
128 E 1	Chudleigh rd NW6
92 M 14	Chudleigh rd SE4
93 N 13	Chudleigh rd SE4
83 V 17	Chudleigh rd Twick
63 T 17	Chudleigh st E1
109 Z 12	Chulsa rd SE26
150 H 14	Chumleigh st SE5
116 M 10	Chumleigh Surb
109 P 8	Church appr SE21
125 O 1	Church av Becknhm
20 K 18	Church av E4
58 D 1	Church av Nthlt
47 T 18	Church av NW1
22 D 19	Church av Pinn
70 D 8	Church av S'hall
115 P 11	Church av Sidcp
85 Y 9	Church av SW14
12 J 18	Church clo Edg
15 X 11	Church clo N20
137 W 16	Church clo W8
63 S 1	Church cres E9
29 R 13	Church cres N10
15 W 10	Church cres N20
27 V 5	Church cres N3
141 T 7	Church ct WC2
22 G 18	Church dri Harrow
43 X 3	Church dri NW9
33 R 14	Church end E17
26 K 11	Church end NW4
141 X 7	Church entry EC4
153 T 13	Church Farm la Sutton
87 S 6	Church ga SW6
72 G 6	Church gdns W5
41 Y 12	Church gdns Wemb
113 E 2	Church gro Kingst
93 S 12	Church gro SE13
155 N 10	Church hill Carsh
156 B 20	Church hill Croy
99 P 11	Church hill Drtfrd
33 P 13	Church hill E17
41 T 3	Church hill Harrow
17 R 2	Church hill N21
16 A 5	Church Hill rd Barnt
5 W 20	Church Hill rd Barnt
16 X 1	Church Hill rd Barnt
33 S 12	Church Hill rd E17
116 J 12	Church Hill rd Surb
153 S 10	Church Hill rd Sutton
78 H 9	Church hill SE18
105 U 12	Church hill SW19
127 R 18	Church la Brom
114 D 20	Church la Chisl
56 J 20	Church la Dgnhm
52 A 3	Church la E11
51 Z 4	Church la E11
33 T 13	Church la E17
8 B 12	Church la Enf
23 V 6	Church la Harrow
31 S 4	Church la N17
25 X 18	Church la N17
28 G 9	Church la N2
30 C 13	Church la N8
18 H 8	Church la N9
44 B 18	Church la NW9
43 W 4	Church la NW9
22 C 11	Church la Pinn
107 O 12	Church la SW17
119 X 2	Church la SW19
101 W 13	Church la Tedd
72 F 5	Church la W5
155 X 6	Church la Wallgtn
149 U 20	Church Manor est SW9
79 Z 12	Church Manor way SE2
81 Z 8	Church Manor way Erith
44 G 18	Church Mead rd NW10
28 F 17	Church mt N2
116 J 12	Church pas Surb
120 J 6	Church pl Mitch
140 D 11	Church pl SW1
72 G 6	Church pl W5
156 L 2	Church pth Croy
33 R 14	Church pth E17
120 J 8	Church pth Mitch
15 P 13	Church pth N12
31 R 3	Church pth N17
44 B 20	Church pth NW10
39 P 14	Church pth Rom
70 E 7	Church pth S'hall
85 Y 7	Church pth SW14
119 W 2	Church pth SW19
71 S 2	Church pth W4
73 W 8	Church pth W4
126 E 3	Church rd Brom
125 Y 5	Church rd Brom
21 V 5	Church rd Buck Hl
98 A 9	Church rd Bxly Hth
156 K 4	Church rd Croy
156 K 7	Church rd Croy
159 N 10	Church rd Croy
51 N 3	Church rd E10
53 W 14	Church rd E12
32 G 8	Church rd E17
9 S 18	Church rd Enf
81 Y 13	Church rd Erith
70 F 19	Church rd Hounsl
36 G 19	Church rd Ilf
71 S 20	Church rd Islwth
116 M 3	Church rd Kingst
117 N 3	Church rd Kingst
120 G 4	Church rd Mitch
31 U 3	Church rd N17
29 O 18	Church rd N6
58 B 4	Church rd Nthlt
44 C 18	Church rd NW10
26 M 12	Church rd NW4
84 K 12	Church rd Rich
102 M 10	Church rd Rich
70 E 8	Church rd S'hall
109 S 20	Church rd SE19
115 O 11	Church rd Sidcp
115 V 13	Church rd Sidcp
11 P 16	Church rd Stanm
153 S 13	Church rd Sutton
86 F 3	Church rd SW13
105 R 13	Church rd SW19
101 U 11	Church rd Tedd
73 V 4	Church rd W3
59 T 19	Church rd W7
71 V 2	Church rd W7
155 W 5	Church rd Wallgtn
97 P 4	Church rd Welling
118 C 18	Church rd Worc Pk
110 F 2	Church ri SE23
114 C 20	Church row Chisl
46 C 13	Church row NW 3
145 X 19	Church row SW6
156 K 4	Church st Croy
56 H 19	Church st Dgnhm
65 N 3	Church st E15
78 L 4	Church st E16
152 T 10	Church st Epsom
84 A 7	Church st Islwth
116 H 3	Church st Kingst
18 C 6	Church st N9
130 H 20	Church st NW8
76 G 17	Church st SE10
154 B 11	Church st Sutton
101 Z 1	Church st Twick
83 Z 20	Church st Twick
130 G 20	Church st W2
74 C 16	Church st W4
65 N 3	Church Street north E15
83 O 11	Church Stretton rd Hounsl
26 L 11	Church ter NW4
84 H 13	Church ter Rich
93 Y 9	Church ter SE13
89 Y 4	Church ter SW8
28 L 9	Church vale N2
110 E 4	Church vale SE23
12 D 19	Church way Edg
15 V 10	Church way N20
72 E 16	Church wlk Brentf
49 P 13	Church wlk N16
45 W 9	Church wlk NW2
26 M 11	Church wlk NW4
43 X 7	Church wlk NW9
84 H 12	Church wlk Rich
86 F 3	Church wlk SW13
86 K 13	Church wlk SW15
121 V 3	Church wlk SW16
118 M 5	Church wlk SW20
8 D 10	Churchbury clo Enf
8 C 12	Churchbury la Enf
8 D 8	Churchbury rd Enf
94 M 17	Churchbury rd SE9
95 N 19	Churchbury rd SE9
89 P 19	Churchcroft clo SW12
112 A 9	Churchdown Brom
111 Z 9	Churchdown Brom
15 S 18	Churchfield av Tedd
22 M 13	Churchfield clo Harrow
97 N 8	Churchfield rd Welling
72 C 3	Churchfield rd W13
73 V 3	Churchfield rd W3
71 S 5	Churchfield rd W7
100 F 6	Churchfields av Felt
34 F 4	Churchfields E18
124 H 2	Churchfields rd Becknhm

24 A 19 Churchill av Harrow
148 A 12 Churchill Garden's est SW1
148 B 12 Churchill Gardens rd SW1
147 Z 12 Churchill gdns SW1
61 R 18 Churchill gdns W3
23 U 13 Churchill pl Harrow
65 Y 17 Churchill rd E16
12 A 20 Churchill rd Edg
44 J 18 Churchill rd NW2
47 T 11 Churchill rd NW5
156 M 17 Churchill rd S Croy
20 B 12 Churchill ter E4
50 D 14 Churchill wlk E9
110 A 9 Churchley rd SE26
5 W 20 Churchmead clo Barnt
107 W 20 Churchmore rd SW16
101 P 3 Churchview rd Twick
132 F 12 Churchway NW1
50 B 15 Churchwell pth E9
149 X 5 Churchyard row SE11
65 V 3 Churston av E13
119 R 12 Churston dri Mrdn
16 H 20 Churston gdns N11
148 B 7 Churton pl SW1
148 B 8 Churton st SW1
114 K 6 Chyngton clo Sidcp
110 G 3 Cibber rd SE23
88 C 15 Cicada rd SW18
91 X 3 Cicely rd SE15
112 A 10 Cinderford way Brom
60 M 10 Cinema pde W5
75 O 3 Cinnamon st E1
143 Z 13 Cinnamon st E1
109 V 16 Cintra pk SE19
119 Y 5 Circle gdns SW19
44 C 10 Circle the NW2
12 L 18 Circle the NW7
31 V 9 Circular rd N17
78 H 16 Circular way SE18
139 N 1 Circus ms W1
160 G 2 Circus pl EC2
130 G 10 Circus rd NW8
76 G 19 Circus st SE10
129 X 20 Cirencester st W2
31 P 16 Cissbury rd N15
14 K 15 Cissbury Ring north N12
14 K 16 Cissbury Ring south N12
133 Y 10 City Garden row N1
134 C 12 City rd EC1
133 Y 11 City rd EC1
36 C 12 Civic way Ilf
147 O 4 Clabon ms SW1
75 R 6 Clack st SE16
32 H 18 Clacton rd E17
66 A 9 Clacton rd E6
31 U 9 Clacton rd N17
27 Z 5 Claigmar gdns N3
15 P 12 Claire ct N12
22 E 2 Claire ct Pinn
76 B 8 Claire pl E14
82 A 2 Clairvale rd Hounsl
107 T 11 Clairview rd SW16
71 U 2 Clairville gdns W7
10 G 18 Clamp hill Stanm
87 Z 5 Clancarty rd SW6
152 E 14 Clandon clo Epsom
73 U 4 Clandon clo W3
27 Y 11 Clandon gdns N3
54 H 7 Clandon rd Ilf
93 O 3 Clandon st SE8
137 V 10 Clanricarde gdns W2
89 R 11 Clapham comm SW4
89 N 11 Clapham Common West side SW4
89 P 10 Clapham Common North side SW4
89 U 12 Clapham Common South side SW4
89 X 11 Clapham cres SW4
89 X 9 Clapham High st SW4
89 X 8 Clapham Manor st SW4
89 X 10 Clapham Park rd SW4
90 C 2 Clapham rd SW9
149 R 18 Clapham rd SW9
89 Y 8 Clapham rd SW9
67 O 10 Claps Gate la Bark
49 W 2 Clapton comm E5
50 G 12 Clapton Park est E5
50 B 14 Clapton pas E5
50 B 14 Clapton sq E5
49 X 3 Clapton ter N16
49 X 11 Clapton way E5
78 J 10 Clara pl SE18
28 C 9 Clare clo N2
95 Y 20 Clare corner SE9
54 L 19 Clare gdns Bark
52 E 13 Clare gdns E7
11 R 17 Clare gdns Stanm
136 M 6 Clare gdns W11
75 O 10 Clare Hall pl SE16
134 B 1 Clare la N1
85 Y 14 Clare Lawn av SW14
141 O 6 Clare mkt WC2
33 Y 19 Clare rd E11
41 R 18 Clare rd Grnfd
82 C 9 Clare rd Hounsl
44 G 19 Clare rd NW10
92 K 3 Clare rd SE14
63 N 7 Clare st E2
135 X 9 Clare st E2
97 Y 1 Clare way Bxly Hth
135 V 10 Claredale st E2
151 Y 4 Clarehall pl SE16
118 H 10 Claremont av New Mald
24 K 16 Claremont av Harrow
78 K 3 Claremont clo E16
133 T 11 Claremont clo N1
99 R 10 Claremont cres Drtfrd
54 G 7 Claremont gdns Ilf
116 J 10 Claremont gdns Surb
21 Y 18 Claremont gro Wdfd Grn
27 T 5 Claremont pk N3
5 T 2 Claremont rd Barnt
127 S 10 Claremont rd Brom
123 Y 19 Claremont rd Croy
51 W 9 Claremont rd E11
32 J 8 Claremont rd E17
52 K 15 Claremont rd E7
23 U 8 Claremont rd Harrow
39 V 19 Claremont rd Hornch
29 U 20 Claremont rd N6
45 N 2 Claremont rd NW2
116 H 11 Claremont rd Surb
101 W 11 Claremont rd Tedd
84 C 17 Claremont rd Twick
59 Y 14 Claremont rd W13
129 N 10 Claremont rd W9
133 S 10 Claremont sq N1
78 K 4 Claremont st E16
18 J 18 Claremont st N18
76 E 18 Claremont st SE10
45 N 3 Claremont way NW2
117 Y 3 Clarence av New Mald
127 R 8 Clarence av Brom
35 V 18 Clarence av Ilf
89 Y 14 Clarence av SW4
10 G 3 Clarence clo Bushey
115 P 8 Clarence cres Sidcp
89 Y 16 Clarence cres SW4
131 P 16 Clarence ga NW1
131 Z 14 Clarence gdns NW1
86 E 15 Clarence la SW15
50 A 14 Clarence ms E5
132 J 9 Clarence pas NW1
50 A 14 Clarence pl E5
127 P 7 Clarence rd Brom
97 X 9 Clarence rd Bxly Hth
123 O 16 Clarence rd Croy
53 N 14 Clarence rd E12
64 M 13 Clarence rd E16
32 F 7 Clarence rd E17
50 A 12 Clarence rd E5
9 P 18 Clarence rd Enf
31 N 14 Clarence rd N15
30 A 2 Clarence rd N22
129 O 2 Clarence rd NW6
85 O 3 Clarence rd Rich
113 R 5 Clarence rd SE9
115 P 8 Clarence rd Sidcp
153 Z 10 Clarence rd Sutton
106 A 15 Clarence rd SW19
105 Z 15 Clarence rd SW19
101 X 16 Clarence rd Tedd
73 P 14 Clarence rd W4
155 S 12 Clarence rd Wallgtn
116 H 3 Clarence st Kingst
84 J 10 Clarence st Rich
82 J 10 Clarence ter Hounsl
131 O 16 Clarence ter NW1
47 R 20 Clarence way NW1
138 K 8 Clarendon clo W2
101 P 7 Clarendon cres Twick
136 L 11 Clarendon cross W11
86 M 9 Clarendon dri SW15
87 N 10 Clarendon dri SW15
42 H 11 Clarendon gdns Wemb
26 H 9 Clarendon gdns NW4
53 V 2 Clarendon gdns Ilf
130 C 18 Clarendon gdns W9
121 N 5 Clarendon gro Mitch
138 K 8 Clarendon ms W2
138 K 8 Clarendon pl W2
156 K 2 Clarendon rd Croy
51 X 2 Clarendon rd E11
33 R 18 Clarendon rd E17
34 E 10 Clarendon rd E18
23 T 19 Clarendon rd Harrow
30 K 14 Clarendon rd N15
18 K 18 Clarendon rd N18
30 C 9 Clarendon rd N22
30 D 11 Clarendon rd N8
106 H 18 Clarendon rd SW19
136 K 8 Clarendon rd W11
137 N 13 Clarendon rd W11
60 J 10 Clarendon rd W5
155 U 13 Clarendon rd Wallgtn
93 V 9 Clarendon ri SE13
148 A 8 Clarendon st SW1
147 Y 10 Clarendon st SW1
130 D 17 Clarendon ter W9
17 Z 1 Clarendon way N21
110 K 4 Clarens st SE6
123 S 7 Claret gdns SE25
146 D 7 Clareville gro SW7
146 D 7 Clareville st SW7
139 X 12 Clarges ms W1
139 Y 13 Clarges st W1
90 H 4 Claribel rd SW9
156 A 20 Clarice way SM6
55 W 4 Claridge rd Dgnhm
110 D 19 Clarins rd SE20
37 U 20 Clarissa rd Rom
135 N 4 Clarissa st E8
99 W 2 Clark clo Erith
63 O 16 Clark st E1
143 Z 3 Clark st E1
70 A 20 Clark way Hounsl
139 V 1 Clarke's pl W1
153 P 2 Clarkes av Worc Pk
10 B 3 Clarks mead Bushey
75 O 6 Clarks orchard SE16
143 Z 18 Clarks orchard SE16
142 J 4 Clarks pl EC3
54 F 7 Clarks rd Ilf
65 O 16 Clarkson rd E2
135 W 12 Clarkson st E2
67 P 6 Clarksons the Bark
99 R 11 Claston clo Drtfd
51 U 5 Claude rd E10
65 U 4 Claude rd E13
91 Z 7 Claude rd SE15
76 A 10 Claude st E14
105 R 2 Claudia pl SW19
65 Y 7 Claughton rd E13
60 A 5 Clausen way Grnfd
59 Z 5 Clausen wy Grnfd
40 L 14 Clauson av Grnfd
75 O 3 Clave st E1
143 Z 13 Clave st E1
90 E 19 Claverdale rd SW2
144 A 14 Clavering av SW13
74 K 16 Clavering av SW13
101 X 9 Clavering clo Twick
53 N 6 Clavering rd E12
27 Z 4 Claverley gro N3
148 C 12 Claverton st SW1
144 H 11 Claxton gro W6
121 T 4 Clay av Mitch
8 E 3 Clay hill Enf
10 F 3 Clay la Bushey
12 B 7 Clay la Edg
139 R 2 Clay st W1
112 M 9 Claybridge rd SE12
144 G 13 Claybrook rd W6
35 R 10 Claybury bdwy Ilf
35 V 1 Claybury Hall Wdfd Grn
35 R 2 Claybury rd Wdfd Grn
156 B 9 Claydon dri CR0
114 B 5 Clayfarm rd SE9
57 V 13 Claygate clo Hornch
159 W 15 Claygate cres Croy
72 A 7 Claygate rd W13
35 T 8 Clayhall av Ilf
113 N 9 Clayhill cres SE9
149 R 16 Claylands pl SW8
119 X 17 Claymore clo Sutton
64 G 6 Claypole rd E15
72 J 13 Clayponds av Brentf
72 H 11 Clayponds gdns W5
72 K 14 Clayponds la Brentf
51 S 16 Clays la clo E15
51 T 14 Clays la E15
42 K 20 Clayton av Wemb
72 G 13 Clayton cres Brentf
26 B 3 Clayton field NW9
83 T 8 Clayton rd Islwth
56 K 4 Clayton rd Rom
91 Y 2 Clayton rd SE15
149 T 13 Clayton st SE11
58 B 14 Clayton ter Hay
97 P 15 Clayworth clo Sidcup
95 Z 3 Cleanthus clo SE18
96 A 2 Cleanthus rd SE18
95 Z 2 Cleanthus rd SE18
63 R 17 Clearbrook way E1
129 Y 19 Clearwell dri W9
116 G 12 Cleaveland rd Surb
149 U 10 Cleaver sq SE11
149 U 10 Cleaver st SE11
123 Z 14 Cleaverholme clo SE25
110 B 1 Cleeve hill SE23
65 T 6 Clegg st E13
143 Y 13 Clegg st E13
145 O 15 Clem Attlee ct SW6
62 F 20 Clematis st W12
63 Y 16 Clemence st E14
128 E 2 Clement clo NW6
124 F 4 Clement rd Becknhm
105 S 13 Clement rd SW19
55 T 18 Clementhorpe rd Dgnhm
50 K 5 Clementina rd E10
72 A 6 Clementine clo W13
65 T 19 Clements av E16
141 P 6 Clements Inn pass WC2
160 G 8 Clements la EC3
72 G 13 Clements pl Brentf
66 E 2 Clements rd E6
54 A 9 Clements rd Ilf
53 Z 9 Clements rd Ilf
151 V 3 Clements rd SE16
79 P 11 Clendon way SE18
79 R 10 Clendon way SE18
153 X 3 Clensham la Sutton
139 O 5 Clenston ms W1
49 N 18 Clephane rd N1
134 G 16 Clere pl EC2
134 G 17 Clere st EC2
133 V 17 Clerkenwell clo EC1
133 V 17 Clerkenwell grn EC1
133 W 17 Clerkenwell rd EC1
63 P 2 Clermont rd E9
46 A 20 Cleve rd NW6
45 Z 20 Cleve rd NW6
115 W 7 Cleve rd Sidcp
117 P 3 Clevedon rd Kingst
110 E 20 Clevedon rd SE20
84 G 15 Clevedon rd Twick
100 E 17 Cleveland av Hampt
119 U 3 Cleveland av SW20
74 C 11 Cleveland av W4
86 C 5 Cleveland gdns SW13
30 L 17 Cleveland gdns N4
45 P 6 Cleveland gdns NW2
138 B 6 Cleveland gdns W2
152 C 2 Cleveland gdns Worc
63 P 12 Cleveland gro E1
132 B 19 Cleveland ms W1
33 N 13 Cleveland Park av E17
33 N 13 Cleveland Park cres E17
60 A 14 Cleveland Park W13
140 D 13 Cleveland pl SW1
118 A 8 Cleveland rd New Mald
152 C 3 Cleveland rd Worc Pk
34 F 10 Cleveland rd E18
54 A 11 Cleveland rd Ilf
83 Y 10 Cleveland rd Islwth
134 F 2 Cleveland rd N1
86 D 5 Cleveland rd SW13
60 B 15 Cleveland rd W13
59 Y 15 Cleveland rd W13
73 W 9 Cleveland rd W4
96 L 5 Cleveland rd Welling
119 R 17 Cleveland ri Mrdn
140 B 15 Cleveland row SW1
138 B 7 Cleveland sq W2
132 A 19 Cleveland st W1
131 Z 18 Cleveland st W1
138 C 4 Cleveland ter W2
63 P 12 Cleveland way E1
78 B 10 Cleveley clo SE7
60 K 7 Cleveley cres W5
50 A 8 Cleveleys rd E5

152 J 19	Cleves av Epsom
66 A 4	Cleves rd E6
102 D 7	Cleves rd Rich
100 F 18	Cleves way Hampt
36 C 2	Cleves wlk Ilf
23 P 5	Clewer cres Harrow
72 G 16	Clifden rd Brentf
50 D 14	Clifden rd E5
101 W 1	Clifden rd Twick
83 X 20	Clifden rd Twick
47 Y 17	Cliff rd NW1
93 P 4	Cliff ter SW4
47 Z 17	Cliff vlls NW1
65 P 13	Cliff wlk E16
157 O 11	Cliffe rd S Croy
113 T 15	Clifford av Chisl
35 Z 6	Clifford av Ilf
85 U 6	Clifford av SW14
155 U 8	Clifford av Wallgtn
58 B 5	Clifford clo Nthlt
90 H 11	Clifford dri SW9
128 C 9	Clifford gdns NW10
62 M 7	Clifford gdns NW10
110 C 18	Clifford gro SE20
5 O 12	Clifford rd Barnt
65 O 13	Clifford rd E16
33 U 8	Clifford rd E17
102 H 4	Clifford rd Rich
123 W 9	Clifford rd SE25
19 R 1	Clifford rd W9
60 F 3	Clifford rd Wemb
140 A 9	Clifford st W1
44 D 12	Clifford way NW1
93 O 9	Cliffview rd SE13
32 G 12	Clifton av E17
27 V 4	Clifton av N3
24 C 7	Clifton av Stanm
74 E 4	Clifton av W12
43 N 17	Clifton av Wemb
151 Z 18	Clifton cres SE15
6 M 15	Clifton gdns Enf
31 W 18	Clifton gdns N15
27 X 18	Clifton gdns NW11
73 Y 12	Clifton gdns W4
130 B 18	Clifton gdns W9
49 X 17	Clifton gro E8
130 C 5	Clifton hill NW8
129 Y 8	Clifton hill NW8
119 N 3	Clifton Park av SW20
138 H 7	Clifton pl W2
53 O 18	Clifton rd E12
65 N 13	Clifton rd E16
59 O 11	Clifton rd Grnfd
24 L 15	Clifton rd Harrow
39 V 19	Clifton rd Hornch
36 E 20	Clifton rd Ilf
83 S 4	Clifton rd Islwth
117 O 1	Clifton rd Kingst
103 O 19	Clifton rd Kingst
29 W 5	Clifton rd N22
28 D 4	Clifton rd N3
29 X 18	Clifton rd N8
62 F 7	Clifton rd NW10
70 C 10	Clifton rd S'hall
123 S 10	Clifton rd SE25
114 H 9	Clifton rd Sidcp
105 O 15	Clifton rd SW19
101 U 10	Clifton rd Tedd
130 D 17	Clifton rd W9
155 T 11	Clifton rd Wallgtn
97 S 7	Clifton rd Welling
75 W 19	Clifton ri SE14
134 H 19	Clifton st EC2
48 F 6	Clifton ter N4
130 A 20	Clifton vlls W9
75 O 20	Clifton way SE15
151 Z 20	Clifton way SE15
60 K 3	Clifton way Wemb
16 H 19	Cline rd N11
134 J 6	Clinger ct N1
142 D 12	Clink st SE1
96 M 9	Clinton av Welling
63 V 9	Clinton rd E3
52 F 13	Clinton rd E7
31 N 14	Clinton rd N15
93 U 11	Clipper wy SE13
82 G 8	Clipstone rd Hounsl
132 A 20	Clipstone st W1
131 Z 20	Clipstone st W1
28 M 10	Clissold clo N2
49 N 11	Clissold cres N16
49 O 9	Clissold est N16
49 N 8	Clissold pk N16
49 O 9	Clissold rd N16
40 G 5	Clitheroe av Harrow
90 A 6	Clitheroe rd SW9
71 X 7	Clitherow av W7
72 C 13	Clitherow rd Brentf
45 N 5	Clitterhouse cres NW2
45 N 5	Clitterhouse rd NW2
99 T 17	Clive av Drtfrd
18 J 19	Clive av N18
109 O 8	Clive pass SE21
81 P 12	Clive rd Blvdr
8 J 14	Clive rd Enf
39 Y 17	Clive rd Rom
109 O 8	Clive rd SE21
106 J 15	Clive rd SW19
101 X 8	Clive rd Twick
8 J 15	Clive way Enf
15 P 14	Cliveden clo N12
147 S 6	Cliveden pl SW1
105 U 20	Cliveden rd SW19
60 A 13	Clivedon ct W13
20 L 17	Clivedon rd E4
160 D 8	Cloak la EC4
124 H 5	Clock House rd Becknhm
149 Y 6	Clock pl SE17
134 C 6	Clock Tower ms N1
83 X 8	Clock Tower rd Islwth
67 O 2	Clockhouse av Bark
105 N 5	Clockhouse clo SW19
38 H 2	Clockhouse la Rom
12 J 16	Cloister gdns Edg
123 Z 14	Cloister gdns SE25
45 U 8	Cloister rd NW2
61 V 15	Cloister rd W3
127 T 12	Cloisters av Brom
49 R 12	Clonbrock rd N16
87 R 3	Cloncurry st SW6
145 P 20	Clonmel rd SW6
87 W 1	Clonmel rd SW6
101 P 10	Clonmel rd Tedd
31 P 11	Clonmell rd N17
105 W 2	Clonmore st SW18
41 R 5	Clonnel clo Harrow
45 X 11	Clorane gdns NW3
6 A 18	Close the Barnt
124 H 9	Close the Becknhm
98 C 17	Close the Bxly
154 K 18	Close the Carsh
33 V 3	Close the E4
23 N 8	Close the Harrow
83 P 3	Close the Islwth
120 K 10	Close the Mitch
29 S 8	Close the N10
16 K 8	Close the N14
14 H 7	Close the N20
117 X 4	Close the New Mald
85 S 7	Close the Rich
37 X 17	Close the Rom
115 R 11	Close the Sidcp
119 V 17	Close the Sutton
42 J 18	Close the Wemb
43 W 10	Close the Wemb
141 Y 1	Cloth ct EC1
141 Y 2	Cloth fair EC1
142 A 1	Cloth st EC1
160 A 1	Cloth st EC1
142 L 4	Clothier st E1
107 R 4	Cloudesdale rd SW17
133 T 6	Cloudesley pl N1
98 C 2	Cloudesley rd Bxly Hth
99 T 2	Cloudesley rd Erith
133 T 5	Cloudesley rd N1
133 T 4	Cloudesley sq N1
133 T 5	Cloudesley st N1
155 Z 10	Clouston clo Wallgtn
52 F 16	Clova rd E7
26 C 12	Clovelly av NW9
18 D 3	Clovelly gdns Enf
38 H 5	Clovelly gdns Rom
80 K 17	Clovelly rd Bxly Hth
29 Y 12	Clovelly rd N8
73 X 7	Clovelly rd W4
72 E 6	Clovelly rd W5
40 D 8	Clovelly way Harrow
51 X 8	Clover clo E11
147 O 13	Clover ms SW3
96 J 16	Cloverdale gdns Sidcp
110 L 6	Clowders rd SE6
154 D 11	Clowser clo SM1
11 V 20	Cloyster wood Edg
126 G 17	Club Gardens rd Brom
135 N 16	Club row E2
70 D 14	Clunbury av S'hall
145 S 8	Cluny ms SW5
150 J 1	Cluny pl SE1
64 E 15	Clutton st E14
8 H 13	Clydach rd Enf
31 S 12	Clyde cir N15
51 P 2	Clyde pl E10
157 U 2	Clyde rd Croy
123 U 20	Clyde rd Croy
77 T 2	Clyde rd E16
31 T 12	Clyde rd N15
29 X 4	Clyde rd N22
153 Y 10	Clyde rd Sutton
155 V 13	Clyde rd Wallgtn
75 Z 17	Clyde st SE8
110 D 4	Clyde ter SE23
110 D 5	Clyde vale SE23
39 P 4	Clyde way Rom
24 G 9	Clydesdale av Stanm
9 S 16	Clydesdale Enf
85 S 10	Clydesdale gdns Rich
57 T 2	Clydesdale rd Hornch
137 P 5	Clydesdale rd W11
89 W 3	Clyston st SW8
86 M 12	Coalecroft rd SW15
69 R 7	Coaley row Dgnhm
135 U 8	Coate st E2
127 X 4	Coates Hill rd Brom
11 T 2	Coates rd Borehm Wd
72 J 15	Coates wlk Brentf
142 M 3	Cobb st E1
95 R 8	Cobbett rd SE9
100 J 1	Cobbett rd Twick
149 O 20	Cobbett st SW8
35 O 15	Cobbetts av Ilf
52 C 9	Cobbold rd E11
44 D 18	Cobbold rd NW10
74 C 6	Cobbold rd W12
141 X 7	Cobbs ct EC4
82 E 12	Cobbs rd Hounsl
52 A 8	Cobden rd E11
123 Y 12	Cobden rd SE25
18 F 10	Cobham av New Mald
127 P 16	Cobham clo Brom
88 K 15	Cobham clo SW11
155 Z 15	Cobham clo Wallgtn
97 X 12	Cobham pl Bxly Hth
33 V 5	Cobham rd E17
54 H 8	Cobham rd Ilf
117 P 2	Cobham rd Kingst
30 J 9	Cobham rd N22
112 M 10	Cobland rd SE12
63 Y 9	Coborn rd E3
63 Y 8	Coborn st E3
63 Y 9	Coborn st E3
151 N 11	Cobourg rd SE5
132 C 14	Cobourg st NW1
148 C 4	Coburg clo SW1
30 D 9	Coburg rd N22
108 E 2	Coburgh st SW12
105 U 18	Cochrane rd SW19
130 H 10	Cochrane st NW8
142 L 3	Cock hill E1
141 X 3	Cock la EC1
6 A 14	Cockfosters pde Barnt
6 A 13	Cockfosters rd Barnt
5 X 4	Cockfosters rd Barnt
140 F 19	Cockpit steps SW1
133 O 19	Cockpit yd WC1
118 C 9	Cocks cres New Mald
140 G 13	Cockspur ct SW1
140 H 13	Cockspur st SW1
135 P 18	Code st E1
48 L 7	Codicote terr N4
143 U 13	Codling clo E1
42 F 12	Codling way Wemb
92 J 18	Codrington hill SE23
137 N 7	Codrington ms W11
24 H 11	Cody clo Harrow
155 Z 17	Cody clo Wallgtn
64 L 12	Cody rd E16
43 T 9	Cofers crcl Wemb
32 G 3	Cogan av E17
141 T 13	Coin st SE1
47 P 17	Coity rd NW5
143 T 4	Coke st E1
129 V 4	Colas ms NW6
146 A 7	Colbeck ms SW7
41 N 1	Colbeck rd Harrow
49 T 2	Colberg pl N16
152 M 3	Colborne way Worc Pk
153 N 2	Colborne way Worc Pk
154 F 6	Colburn way Sutton
109 T 13	Colby rd SE19
53 U 10	Colchester av E12
51 T 1	Colchester rd E10
33 N 20	Colchester rd E17
25 W 2	Colchester rd Edg
143 P 5	Colchester st E1
75 T 17	Cold Blow la SE14
120 M 7	Cold blows Mitch
76 H 4	Cold harbour E14
133 S 17	Coldbath sq EC1
71 Y 3	Coldershaw rd W13
29 N 7	Coldfall av N10
30 H 6	Coldham ct N22
9 V 1	Coldham gro Enf
90 H 9	Coldharbour la SW9
156 F 11	Coldharbour rd Croy
156 G 11	Coldharbour way Croy
42 F 13	Colding way Wemb
87 V 16	Coldstream gdns SW18
80 D 3	Cole clo SE18
83 Y 14	Cole Park gdns Twick
83 Y 15	Cole Park rd Twick
83 Y 18	Cole Park rd Twick
83 Y 17	Cole rd Twick
142 D 19	Cole st SE1
48 J 19	Colebeck ms N1
145 Z 7	Colebeck ms SW5
63 R 11	Colebert av E1
87 P 17	Colebrook clo SW15
122 A1	Colebrook rd SW16
126 A 4	Colebrook ri Brom
16 F 17	Colebrook way N11
60 A 17	Colebrooke av W13
34 K 20	Colebrooke dri E11
133 X 7	Colebrooke row N1
150 G 19	Coleby pth SE5
24 D 4	Coledale dri Stanm
88 C 12	Coleford rd SW18
51 W 13	Colegrave rd E15
151 R 16	Colegrove rd SE15
145 Y 12	Coleherne ms SW10
145 X 11	Coleherne rd SW10
87 S 3	Colehill gdns SW6
87 S 3	Colehill la SW6
134 B 4	Coleman fields N1
81 R 10	Coleman rd Blvdr
56 A 19	Coleman rd Dgnhm
55 Z 19	Coleman rd Dgnhm
150 H 17	Coleman rd SE5
150 K 18	Coleman rd SE5
160 E 4	Coleman st EC2
142 E 5	Coleman st EC2
160 E 3	Coleman Street bldgs EC2
113 X 7	Colemans heath SE9
50 D 11	Colenso rd E5
54 G 4	Colenso rd Ilf
96 D 12	Colepits Wood rd SE9
30 F 10	Coleraine rd N8
77 R 16	Coleraine rd SE3
53 R 17	Coleridge av E12
154 K 8	Coleridge av Sutton
89 T 4	Coleridge clo SW8
130 B 2	Coleridge gdns NW6
29 Z 18	Coleridge la N8
124 C 16	Coleridge rd Croy
32 L 12	Coleridge rd E17
15 P 7	Coleridge rd N12
48 F 8	Coleridge rd N4
29 X 19	Coleridge rd N8
39 Y 3	Coleridge rd Rom
27 X 14	Coleridge wlk NW11
40 K 7	Coles cres Harrow
44 H 5	Coles Green rd NW2
10 A 5	Coles grn Bushey
124 K 5	Colesburg rd Becknhm
101 U 15	Coleshill rd Tedd
88 K 4	Colestown st SW11
144 H 7	Colet gdns W14
133 P 17	Coley st WC1
110 G 1	Colfe rd SE23
158 K 4	Colin clo Croy
26 B 14	Colin clo NW9
26 E 15	Colin cres NW9
26 E 16	Colin dri NW9
26 E 15	Colin gdns NW9
26 A 13	Colin Park rd NW9
44 F 17	Colin rd NW10
30 J 14	Colina ms N15
30 J 15	Colina rd N15
25 Z 11	Colindale av NW9
26 H 14	Colindeep gdns NW4
26 F 13	Colindeep la NW9
86 L 10	Colinette rd SW15
55 R 6	Colinton rd Ilf
87 Y 18	Coliston rd SW18
106 H 3	Collamore av SW18
22 L 17	Collapit clo Harrow
76 G 16	College appr SE10
23 T 4	College av Harrow
50 C 14	College clo E9
23 U 2	College clo Harrow
46 F 19	College cres NW3
133 V 1	College cross N1

Ref	Name
118 E 12	College gdns New Mald
20 D 4	College gdns E4
35 R 15	College gdns Ilf
18 H 16	College gdns N18
91 S 20	College gdns SE21
106 H 4	College gdns SW17
109 R 18	College grn SE19
132 D 5	College gro NW1
160 D 8	College hill EC4
23 U 3	College Hill rd Harrow
23 V 4	College Hill rd Harrow
47 S 12	College la NW5
88 B 14	College ms SW18
18 F 20	College Park rd N17
33 Z 12	College pl E17
132 C 4	College pl NW1
126 E 1	College rd Brom
112 F 18	College rd Brom
157 O 4	College rd Croy
33 T 17	College rd E17
8 B 8	College rd Enf
23 T 3	College rd Harrow
23 U 19	College rd Harrow
83 V 3	College rd Islwth
18 F 20	College rd N17
17 U 8	College rd N21
128 B 8	College rd NW10
62 M 6	College rd NW10
109 S 1	College rd SE21
91 S 20	College rd SE21
106 G 16	College rd SW19
60 A 18	College rd W13
42 H 5	College rd Wemb
126 E 2	College slip Brom
160 D 9	College st EC4
63 X 8	College ter E3
27 W 6	College ter N3
113 O 3	College view SE9
50 D 18	Collent st E9
31 U 16	Colless rd N15
151 U 2	Collett rd SE16
70 K 4	Collett wy S'hall
25 P 7	Collier dri Edg
38 H 3	Collier Row la Rom
38 C 4	Collier Row rd Rom
133 N 9	Collier st N1
122 G 10	Colliers Water la Thntn Hth
106 G 16	Colliers Wood High st SW19
74 J 2	Collinbourne rd W12
81 V 17	Collindale av Erith
97 O 20	Collindale av Sidcp
145 Z 7	Collingham gdns SW5
145 Y 6	Collingham pl SW5
110 C 9	Collingtree rd SE26
29 O 11	Collingwood av N10
117 V 18	Collingwood av Surb
82 H 18	Collingwood clo Twick
153 W 5	Collingwood rd Sutton
33 N 18	Collingwood rd E17
120 G 5	Collingwood rd Mitch
31 S 12	Collingwood rd N15
63 N 12	Collingwood st E1
135 X 17	Collingwood st E1
24 K 7	Collins av Stanm
48 M 11	Collins rd N5
94 B 6	Collins st SE3
133 X 5	Collins yd N1
142 A 19	Collinson st SE1
9 P 12	Collinwood av Enf
35 U 15	Collinwood gdns Ilf
92 C 1	Colls rd SE15
156 A 8	Collyer av Croy
91 V 2	Collyer pl SE15
156 A 8	Collyer rd CR0
156 A 8	Collyer rd Croy
65 Y 15	Colman rd E16
63 T 11	Colmar clo E1
23 P 3	Colmer pl Harrow
108 B 19	Colmer rd SW16
9 R 14	Colmore rd Enf
149 W 2	Colnbrook st SE1
50 H 13	Colne rd E5
18 A 3	Colne rd N21
101 U 2	Colne rd Twick
65 S 10	Colne st E13
29 P 2	Colney Hatch la N10
15 Y 18	Colney Hatch la N11
16 A 20	Colney Hatch rd N11
88 G 10	Cologne rd SW11
77 N 14	Colomb st SE10
54 B 2	Colombo rd Ilf
141 W 15	Colombo st SE1
7 V 10	Colonels wlk Enf
83 N 15	Colonial av Twick
132 K 18	Colonnade WC1
131 Y 15	Colosseum ter NW1
157 R 2	Colson rd Croy
107 V 10	Colson way SW16
31 V 12	Colsterworth rd N15
154 K 8	Colston av Carsh
154 L 9	Colston ct Carsh
53 N 18	Colston rd E7
85 W 10	Colston rd SW14
80 C 13	Coltness cres SE2
30 M 10	Colton gdns N17
23 U 14	Colton rd Harrow
118 E 18	Columbia av Worc Pk
25 S 4	Columbia av Edg
65 R 13	Columbia rd E13
135 P 12	Columbia rd E2
66 D 15	Columbine av E6
156 J 16	Columbine av S Croy
93 T 5	Columbine way SE13
101 T 2	Colus all Twick
49 U 16	Colvestone cres E8
137 P 6	Colville gdns W11
137 R 6	Colville ms W11
140 D 2	Colville pl W1
51 V 9	Colville rd E11
32 J 8	Colville rd E17
18 L 4	Colville rd N9
137 P 5	Colville rd W11
137 R 7	Colville rd W11
73 U 8	Colville rd W3
137 O 6	Colville sq W11
137 O 5	Colville Square ms W11
137 P 6	Colville ter W11
34 J 13	Colvin gdns E11
20 H 11	Colvin gdns E4
36 B 3	Colvin gdns Ilf
66 D 2	Colvin rd E6
122 F 12	Colvin rd Thntn Hth
91 U 14	Colwell rd SE22
47 X 1	Colwick clo N6
144 E 14	Colwith rd W6
106 G 16	Colwood gdns SW19
150 B 8	Colworth gro SE17
123 X 20	Colworth rd Croy
34 A 20	Colworth rd E11
33 Z 19	Colworth rd E11
59 X 6	Colwyn av Grnfd
82 M 3	Colwyn cres Hounsl
44 K 9	Colwyn rd NW2
113 Z 4	Colyer clo SE9
98 M 1	Colyers clo Erith
98 L 1	Colyers la Erith
99 S 1	Colyers la Erith
99 P 1	Colyers wlk Erith
97 V 1	Colyton clo Welling
42 D 17	Colyton clo Wemb
92 A 14	Colyton rd SE22
18 H 17	Colyton way N18
77 P 19	Combe av SE3
77 P 19	Combe ms SE3
103 V 17	Combe Wood Golf course Kingst
77 S 14	Combedale rd SE10
87 T 20	Combemartin rd SW18
44 H 8	Comber clo NW2
150 B 20	Comber gro SE5
90 C 7	Combermere rd SW9
50 A 6	Comberton rd E5
79 X 20	Combeside SE18
38 C 19	Combewood dri Rom
80 A 9	Combwell cres SE2
33 T 15	Comely Bank rd E17
144 M 10	Comeragh ms W14
144 L 11	Comeragh rd W14
145 N 10	Comeragh rd W14
92 K 11	Comerford rd SE4
76 A 20	Comet st SE8
72 C 18	Commerce rd Brentf
30 D 4	Commerce rd N22
63 O 17	Commercial rd E1
143 U 5	Commercial rd E1
18 F 19	Commercial rd N18
143 O 2	Commercial st E1
150 M 20	Commercial way SE15
151 T 18	Commercial way SE15
61 U 7	Commercial way NW10
77 N 13	Commerell st SE10
143 P 11	Commodity quay E1
63 V 13	Commodore st E1
10 D 11	Common rd Stanm
86 H 7	Common rd SW13
102 F 7	Common the Rich
10 H 9	Common the Stanm
72 K 2	Common the W5
86 M 6	Commondale SW15
106 H 13	Commonfield la SW17
121 P 7	Commonside east Mitch
121 N 8	Commonside west Mitch
137 S 20	Commonwealth institute W8
62 K 20	Commonwealth av W12
31 X 1	Commonwealth rd N17
80 E 13	Commonwealth way SE2
51 X 16	Community rd E15
59 P 4	Community rd Grnfd
38 M 15	Como rd Rom
110 H 5	Como rd SE23
39 N 14	Como st Rom
84 H 15	Compass hill Rich
46 B 19	Compayne gdns NW6
45 Z 19	Compayne gdns NW6
66 A 6	Compton av E6
48 J 19	Compton av N1
46 J 1	Compton av N6
131 Z 14	Compton clo NW1
59 Y 17	Compton clo W13
31 N 2	Compton cres N17
58 A 1	Compton cres Nthlt
73 V 17	Compton cres W4
132 K 15	Compton pl WC1
157 Z 1	Compton rd Croy
123 Z 20	Compton rd Croy
48 K 19	Compton rd N1
17 V 5	Compton rd N21
128 G 13	Compton rd NW10
105 V 14	Compton rd SW19
22 D 16	Compton ri Pinn
133 X 16	Compton st EC1
48 H 19	Compton ter N1
7 V 4	Comreddy clo Enf
150 H 6	Comus pl SE17
47 X 9	Comus rd N19
88 J 11	Comyn rd SW11
65 O 14	Comyns clo E16
69 P 1	Comyns rd Dgnhm
10 A 6	Comyns the Bushey
90 B 10	Concanon rd SW2
141 P 14	Concert Hall appr SE1
82 J 6	Concord clo Hounsl
9 O 18	Concord rd Enf
61 S 12	Concord rd W3
89 W 2	Condell rd SW8
63 V 17	Conder st E14
90 L 7	Conderton rd SE5
57 X 20	Condor wlk Hornch
78 M 20	Condover cres SE18
4 D 20	Conduct rd Barnt
140 K 8	Conduit WC2
9 V 20	Conduit la Enf
19 U 2	Conduit la N9
157 X 12	Conduit la S Croy
138 F 7	Conduit ms W2
138 F 6	Conduit pas W2
138 G 6	Conduit pl W2
78 M 13	Conduit rd SE18
79 N 13	Conduit rd SE18
140 A 8	Conduit st W1
139 Z 9	Conduit st W1
43 V 20	Conduit way NW10
48 J 11	Conewood st N5
108 M 1	Coney acre SE21
20 M 7	Coney Burrows E4
40 A 18	Coneygrove pth Nthlt
80 G 10	Conference rd SE2
79 N 13	Congleton gro SE18
79 T 13	Congo rd SE18
80 F 11	Congress rd SE2
95 S 8	Congreve rd SE9
150 J 7	Congreve st SE17
7 Y 9	Conical corner Enf
8 D 20	Conifer gdns Enf
108 B 8	Conifer gdns SW16
102 C 18	Conifers clo Tedd
87 X 4	Coniger rd SW6
74 H 4	Coningham ms W12
74 J 6	Coningham rd W12
72 F 6	Coningsby cotts W5
20 D 18	Coningsby gdns E4
30 H 20	Coningsby rd N4
156 K 19	Coningsby rd S Croy
72 F 6	Coningsby rd W5
93 T 5	Conington rd SE13
6 H 17	Conisbee ct N14
111 U 7	Conisborough cres SE6
17 Z 12	Coniscliffe rd N13
67 U 2	Coniston av Bark
60 B 8	Coniston av Grnfd
96 G 8	Coniston av Welling
67 U 2	Coniston clo Bark
98 K 3	Coniston clo Bxly Hth
119 N 13	Coniston clo Mrdn
15 S 11	Coniston clo N20
85 U 1	Coniston clo W4
42 E 3	Coniston gdns Wemb
154 F 14	Coniston gdns Sutton
35 R 12	Coniston gdns Ilf
19 P 6	Coniston gdns N9
25 Y 16	Coniston gdns NW9
112 A 17	Coniston rd Brom
111 Y 15	Coniston rd Brom
98 K 3	Coniston rd Bxly Hth
123 X 17	Coniston rd Croy
29 S 7	Coniston rd N10
18 J 20	Coniston rd N17
82 L 17	Coniston rd Twick
57 V 15	Coniston way Hornch
48 A 20	Conistone way N7
128 L 17	Conlan st W10
44 C 19	Conley rd NW10
77 N 13	Conley st SE10
16 A 5	Connaught av Barnt
20 J 2	Connaught av E4
8 F 9	Connaught av Enf
82 C 12	Connaught av Hounsl
85 V 9	Connaught av SW14
50 G 6	Connaught clo E10
8 F 10	Connaught clo Enf
154 F 3	Connaught clo Sutton
138 L 7	Connaught clo W2
27 Z 13	Connaught dri NW11
29 T 15	Connaught gdns N10
17 W 15	Connaught gdns N13
139 N 7	Connaught ms W2
139 N 7	Connaught pl W2
118 B 8	Connaught rd New Mald
23 W 5	Connaught rd Harrow
4 D 20	Connaught rd Barnt
51 Y 4	Connaught rd E11
66 A 20	Connaught rd E16
78 B 3	Connaught rd E16
65 Z 20	Connaught rd E16
33 N 16	Connaught rd E17
20 L 4	Connaught rd E4
54 D 8	Connaught rd Ilf
48 F 1	Connaught rd N4
62 B 5	Connaught rd NW10
84 L 13	Connaught rd Rich
154 G 4	Connaught rd Sutton
101 S 12	Connaught rd Tedd
72 A 1	Connaught rd W13
138 M 7	Connaught sq W2
139 N 6	Connaught sq W2
78 L 14	Connaught st SE18
138 M 6	Connaught st W2
17 X 14	Connaught way N13
60 N 11	Connell cres W5
61 N 11	Connell cres W5
20 K 10	Connington cres E4
9 S 2	Connop rd Enf
56 C 11	Connor rd Dgnhm
63 S 3	Connor st E9
71 S 2	Conolly rd W7
119 N 19	Conrad dri Worc Pk
141 U 16	Cons st SE1
118 G 9	Consfield av New Mald
83 S 14	Consort ms Islwth
92 A 7	Consort rd SE15
91 Z 2	Consort rd SE15
91 Z 5	Consort rd SE15
83 O 13	Constable clo Hounsl
28 B 19	Constable clo NW11
31 X 15	Constable cres N15
25 O 6	Constable gdns Edg
126 C 19	Constance cres Brom
122 J 16	Constance rd Croy
18 D 1	Constance rd Enf
154 E 9	Constance rd Sutton
82 L 19	Constance rd Twick
78 C 3	Constance st E16
46 L 13	Constantine rd NW3
139 Y 17	Constitution hill SW1
95 W 2	Constitution ri SE18
150 C 7	Content st SE17
72 D 11	Convent gdns W5
108 L 16	Convent hill SE19
108 L 16	Convent hill SE19
10 L 19	Conway clo Stanm

100 B 9 Country way Felt
15 O 1 County ga Barnt
114 C 6 County ga SE9
67 V 6 County gdns Bark
90 L 1 County gro SE5
141 N 18 County Hall the SE1
66 L 15 County rd E6
122 J 4 County rd Thntn Hth
150 C 3 County st SE1
150 D 3 County st SE1
79 O 14 Coupland pla SE18
30 F 10 Courcy rd N8
89 Y 3 Courland gro SW8
89 Y 3 Courland st SW8
113 X 7 Course the St9
81 N 13 Court av Blvdr
100 J 6 Court Clo av Twick
24 H 12 Court clo Harrow
155 X 17 Court clo Wallgtn
125 R 3 Court Downs rd
Becknhm
156 D 7 Court dri Croy
11 X 14 Court dri Stanm
154 J 8 Court dri Sutton
58 G 1 Court Farm la Nthlt
58 H 1 Court Farm rd Nthlt
113 O 6 Court Farm rd SE9
14 M 18 Court House gdns
N3
91 T 17 Court La gdns SE21
91 V 18 Court la SE21
58 E 8 Court mead Nthlt
70 E 13 Court rd S'hall
123 V 5 Court rd SE25
113 S 3 Court rd SE9
95 U 17 Court rd SE9
126 F 3 Court st Brom
40 A 13 Court the Ruislip
36 C 11 Court way Ilf
26 B 12 Court way NW9
83 W 18 Court way Twick
61 W 14 Court way W3
21 Y 16 Court way Wdfd Grn
95 S 17 Court yd SE9
95 T 16 Court yd SE9
47 Z 4 Courtauld rd N19
22 L 2 Courtenay av Harrow
23 N 6 Courtenay av Harrow
46 H 1 Courtenay av N6
28 H 20 Courtenay av N6
23 N 7 Courtenay gdns
Harrow
23 N 6 Courtenay gdns Har
32 J 15 Courtenay pl E17
153 N 5 Courtenay rd
Worc Pk
52 C 9 Courtenay rd E11
32 G 14 Courtenay rd E17
110 G 16 Courtenay rd SE20
149 S 10 Courtenay sq SE11
149 S 10 Courtenay st SE11
23 W 17 Courtfield av Harrow
23 X 16 Courtfield cres
Harrow
145 Y 6 Courtfield gdns SW5
145 Z 6 Courtfield gdns SW5
59 Z 17 Courtfield gdns W13
146 A 6 Courtfield rd SW7
159 Y 5 Courtfield ri
W Wckm
93 U 12 Courthill rd SE13
59 P 5 Courthope rd Grnfd
47 N 13 Courthope rd NW3
105 R 13 Courthope rd SW19
105 T 17 Courthope vlls SE19
14 M 17 Courthouse rd N12
126 A 20 Courtland av Brom
21 P 8 Courtland av E4
53 U 6 Courtland av Ilf
12 M 9 Courtland av NW7
13 N 9 Courtland av NW7
108 D 18 Courtland av SW16
68 K 19 Courtland gro SE28
66 D 2 Courtland rd E6
100 E 16 Courtlands av Hampt
85 T 3 Courtlands av Rich
94 G 12 Courtlands av SE12
152 C 14 Courtlands dri Epsom
117 P 16 Courtlands rd Surb
117 P 17 Courtlands rd Surb
85 P 12 Courtlands Rich
60 D 15 Courtlands W5
98 H 2 Courtleet dri Erith
5 T 3 Courtleigh av Barnt
27 T 14 Courtleigh gdns
NW11
30 M 2 Courtman rd N17
90 M 16 Courtmead clo SE24
137 S 5 Courtnell st W2
109 R 16 Courtney clo SE19

154 M 18 Courtney cres Carsh
156 G 5 Courtney pl Croy
156 F 5 Courtney rd Croy
48 F 14 Courtney rd N7
106 J 18 Courtney rd SW19
92 H 15 Courtrai rd SE23
29 X 19 Courtside N8
158 M 20 Courtswood la Croy
160 D 10 Cousin la EC4
77 W 18 Couthurst rd SE3
85 U 11 Coval gdns SW14
85 T 10 Coval la SW14
85 U 10 Coval rd SW14
140 L 8 Covent gdn WC2
137 N 6 Covent gdns W11
66 F 18 Coventry clo E6
129 V 7 Coventry clo NW6
63 N 12 Coventry rd E1
135 Y 15 Coventry rd E1
135 Y 17 Coventry rd E1
54 B 3 Coventry rd Ilf
53 Y 5 Coventry rd Ilf
123 X 8 Coventry rd SE25
140 E 10 Coventry st W1
124 J 18 Coverack clo Croy
16 F 1 Coverack clo N14
6 F 20 Coverack clo N14
11 P 15 Coverdale clo Stanm
157 U 6 Coverdale gdn Croy
45 R 19 Coverdale rd NW2
136 A 16 Coverdale rd W12
74 L 4 Coverdale rd W12
67 R 6 Coverdales the Bark
135 T 20 Coverley clo E1
5 S 7 Covert way Barnt
106 J 11 Coverton rd SW17
108 J 19 Covington gdns
SW16
108 E 16 Covington way
SW16
108 J 18 Covington way
SW16
59 P 7 Cow la Grnfd
66 E 16 Cowan clo E6
150 J 13 Cowan st SE5
25 N 13 Cowbridge rd
Harrow
133 X 20 Cowcross st EC1
111 O 9 Cowden st SE6
133 N 3 Cowdenbeath pth N1
57 V 13 Cowdray way Hornch
8 D 9 Cowdrey clo Eng
99 Z 20 Cowdrey ct Drtfd
106 B 14 Cowdrey rd SW19
50 K 17 Cowdry rd E9
41 O 8 Cowen av Harrow
59 S 8 Cowgate rd Grnfd
106 M 9 Cowick rd SW17
107 N 10 Cowick rd SW17
40 C 19 Cowings mead Nthlt
9 R 13 Cowland av Enf
116 K 1 Cowleaze rd Kingst
51 Z 9 Cowley la E11
34 G 15 Cowley rd E11
53 U 2 Cowley rd Ilf
39 Z 1 Cowley rd Rom
86 A 7 Cowley rd SW14
90 F 2 Cowley rd SW14
149 U 20 Cowley rd SW14
74 C 4 Cowley rd W3
148 J 1 Cowley st W1
66 C 1 Cowper av E6
154 G 9 Cowper av Sutton
127 O 10 Cowper clo Brom
97 O 12 Cowper clo Welling
155 V 14 Cowper gdns
Wallgtn
6 F 19 Cowper gdns N14
81 P 11 Cowper rd Blvdr
127 N 10 Cowper rd Brom
102 M 12 Cowper rd Kingst
16 E 5 Cowper rd N14
49 R 13 Cowper rd N16
18 J 18 Cowper rd N18
106 D 15 Cowper rd SW19
73 X 2 Cowper rd W3
59 V 19 Cowper rd W7
134 G 15 Cowper st EC2
136 F 2 Cowper ter W10
34 H 8 Cowper rd E18
89 Y 1 Cowthorpe rd SW8
141 Z 3 Cox's ct EC1
78 A 13 Coxmount rd SE7
109 Y 2 Coxs wlk SE21
79 T 13 Coxwell rd SE18
111 W 18 Crab hill Becknhm
37 W 12 Crabtree av Rom
60 L 5 Crabtree av Wemb
51 S 15 Crabtree ct E15
144 F 17 Crabtree la SW6

81 W 7 Crabtree Manor way
Blvdr
81 X 4 Crabtree Manorway
north Blvdr
8 G 13 Craddock rd Enf
47 O 19 Craddock st NW5
114 D 2 Cradley rd SE9
34 C 7 Craig gdns E18
18 M 15 Craig Park rd N18
102 E 9 Craig rd Rich
57 U 1 Craigdale rd Hornch
39 U 20 Craigdale rd Hornch
158 A 1 Craigen av Croy
124 A 20 Craigen av Croy
77 U 18 Craigerne rd SE5
95 X 3 Craigholm SE18
61 O 2 Craigmuir pk Wemb
90 E 18 Craignair rd SW2
122 D 2 Craignish av SW16
140 J 13 Craigs ct SW1
95 T 11 Craigton rd SE9
11 U 17 Craigwell clo Stanm
11 T 16 Craigwell dri Stanm
150 F 6 Crail row SE17
139 U 2 Cramer st W1
110 B 16 Crampton rd SE20
149 Z 8 Crampton st SE17
58 A 6 Cranberry clo Nthlt
135 T 18 Cranberry st E1
70 H 11 Cranborne av S'hall
67 S 3 Cranborne rd Bark
140 H 9 Cranbourn st WC2
140 H 9 Cranbourne all WC2
34 H 13 Cranbourne av E11
122 A 7 Cranbourne clo SW16
27 U 16 Cranbourne gdns
NW11
36 D 10 Cranbourne gdns Ilf
51 U 12 Cranbourne rd E15
29 T 8 Cranbourne rd N10
126 E 15 Cranbrook clo Brom
82 K 20 Cranbrook dri Twick
63 S 7 Cranbrook est E2
32 K 15 Cranbrook ms E17
30 E 6 Cranbrook pk N22
98 C 1 Cranbrook rd
Bxly Hth
122 M 2 Cranbrook rd
Thntn Hth
5 V 20 Cranbrook rd Barnt
82 C 10 Cranbrook rd Hounsl
36 A 12 Cranbrook rd Ilf
35 X 17 Cranbrook rd Ilf
53 X 6 Cranbrook rd Ilf
95 N 7 Cranbrook rd SE8
93 O 2 Cranbrook rd SE8
105 S 18 Cranbrook rd SW19
74 B 13 Cranbrook rd W4
35 U 19 Cranbrook rise Ilf
63 T 7 Cranbrook st E2
88 A 5 Cranbury rd SW6
83 Y 13 Crane av Islwth
61 X 20 Crane av W3
56 F 19 Crane clo Dgnhm
141 U 5 Crane ct EC4
48 G 18 Crane gro N7
75 S 12 Crane mead SE16
100 J 4 Crane Park rd Twick
100 G 4 Crane pk Twick
101 T 1 Crane rd Twick
76 J 15 Crane st SE10
83 O 17 Crane way Twick
101 O 3 Cranebrook Twick
83 W 19 Craneford clo Twick
83 U 19 Craneford way Twick
116 K 10 Cranes dri Surb
116 K 10 Cranes Park av Surb
116 L 10 Cranes Park cres Surb
116 K 11 Cranes pk Surb
70 F 13 Craneswater pk
S'hall
26 A 3 Cranfield dri NW9
155 O 19 Cranfield rd Carsh
92 M 7 Cranfield rd SE4
108 L 8 Cranfield vlls SE27
17 O 16 Cranford av N13
104 H 19 Cranford clo SW20
63 T 19 Cranford cotts E1
70 B 19 Cranford la Hounsl
63 T 19 Cranford st E1
39 Z 18 Cranham rd Hornch
44 M 15 Cranhurst rd NW2
98 F 15 Cranleigh clo Bxly
123 Z 2 Cranleigh clo SE20
154 A 3 Cranleigh gdns
Sutton
24 J 16 Cranleigh gdns
Harrow
103 N 15 Cranleigh gdns
Kingst

54 E 19 Cranleigh gdns Bark
7 T 17 Cranleigh gdns N21
58 D 17 Cranleigh gdns S'hall
123 S 5 Cranleigh gdns SE25
30 L 14 Cranleigh rd N15
119 X 6 Cranleigh rd SW19
132 C 9 Cranleigh st NW1
54 C 1 Cranley dri Ilf
36 C 20 Cranley dri Ilf
155 U 15 Cranley gdns
Wallgtn
29 S 14 Cranley gdns N10
29 V 14 Cranley gdns N10
17 R 10 Cranley gdns N13
146 D 9 Cranley gdns SW7
146 D 9 Cranley ms SW7
146 F 7 Cranley pl SW7
65 V 14 Cranley rd E13
36 B 20 Cranley rd Ilf
89 Y 7 Cranmar ct SW4
72 B 8 Cranmer av W13
119 R 14 Cranmer clo Mrdn
24 E 1 Cranmer clo Stanm
100 K 11 Cranmer ct Hampt
120 L 9 Cranmer Farm clo
Mitch
56 K 13 Cranmer gdns
Dgnhm
156 K 5 Cranmer rd Croy
52 J 11 Cranmer rd E7
12 E 10 Cranmer rd Edg
100 L 11 Cranmer rd Hampt
102 K 13 Cranmer rd Kingst
121 N 10 Cranmer rd Mitch
149 W 8 Cranmer rd SW9
106 G 11 Cranmer ter SW17
71 N 19 Cranmore av Islwth
112 B 7 Cranmore rd Brom
113 V 11 Cranmore rd Chisl
29 V 12 Cranmore way N10
82 B 5 Cranston clo Hounsl
20 D 18 Cranston gdns E4
110 H 2 Cranston rd SE23
75 O 13 Cranswick rd SE16
151 Y 10 Cranswick rd SE16
111 S 4 Crantock rd SE6
18 A 1 Cranwich av N21
49 R 1 Cranwich rd N16
134 F 14 Cranwood st EC1
20 J 6 Cranworth cres E4
90 E 2 Cranworth gdns
SW9
90 D 18 Craster rd SW2
94 H 14 Crathie rd SE12
93 T 7 Crathorn st SE13
58 E 16 Craven av S'hall
60 D 20 Craven av W5
67 U 7 Craven gdns Bark
36 D 7 Craven gdns Ilf
106 A 13 Craven gdns SW19
105 Z 13 Craven gdns SW19
138 C 9 Craven Hill gdns W2
138 C 8 Craven Hill ms W2
138 D 8 Craven hill W2
62 A 2 Craven Park ms
NW10
31 V 19 Craven Park rd N15
62 C 4 Craven Park rd NW10
140 K 12 Craven pas WC2
123 Z 20 Craven rd Croy
102 M 20 Craven rd Kingst
103 N 20 Craven rd Kingst
61 Z 3 Craven rd NW10
138 D 7 Craven rd W2
60 D 20 Craven rd W5
140 K 12 Craven st WC2
138 D 8 Craven ter W2
49 W 1 Craven wlk E5
31 Y 20 Craven wlk N16
42 G 15 Crawford av Wemb
83 T 4 Crawford clo Islwth
17 W 10 Crawford gdns N13
58 F 8 Crawford gdns Nthlt
139 O 1 Crawford ms W1
133 T 17 Crawford pas EC1
138 L 3 Crawford pl W1
90 M 3 Crawford rd SE5
139 N 2 Crawford st W1
51 S 4 Crawley rd E10
18 E 3 Crawley rd Enf
30 L 7 Crawley rd N22
91 V 11 Crawthew gro SE22
99 X 12 Cray clo Drtfrd
81 S 17 Cray rd Blvdr
115 T 16 Cray rd Sidcp
115 P 10 Craybrooke rd Sidcp
114 B 5 Craybury end SE9
99 U 1 Craydene rd Erith
99 R 12 Crayford High st
Drtfrd

156 H 11	Crowley cres Croy
64 A 3	Crown clo E3
13 S 7	Crown clo NW7
160 C 6	Crown ct EC2
94 G 16	Crown ct SE12
140 M 7	Crown ct WC2
108 L 14	Crown dale SE19
156 L 4	Crown hill Croy
62 D 4	Crown Hill rd NW10
127 O 13	Crown la Brom
119 Z 7	Crown la Mrdn
16 H 5	Crown la N14
108 G 14	Crown la SW16
108 G 13	Crown Lane gdns SW16
127 O 13	Crown Lane spur Brom
141 T 8	Crown Office row EC4
140 C 14	Crown pas SW1
47 T 17	Crown pl NW5
8 M 14	Crown rd Enf
36 D 13	Crown rd Ilf
119 Z 8	Crown rd Mrdn
29 P 2	Crown rd N10
117 X 1	Crown rd New Mald
154 A 8	Crown rd Sutton
153 Z 9	Crown rd Sutton
84 C 17	Crown rd Twick
56 J 19	Crown st Dgnhm
41 S 4	Crown st Harrow
150 B 18	Crown st SE5
73 T 3	Crown st W3
84 M 9	Crown ter Rich
43 O 8	Crown wlk Wemb
95 Z 4	Crown Woods la SE18
96 F 12	Crown Woods way SE9
132 B 8	Crowndale rd NW1
36 F 17	Crownfield av Ilf
51 W 13	Crownfield rd E15
35 R 3	Crownhill rd Wdfd Grn
38 H 13	Crownmead way Rom
90 E 13	Crownstone rd SW2
71 V 17	Crowntree clo Islwth
96 A 5	Crownwoods la SE9
64 L 8	Crows rd E15
24 F 6	Crowshott av Stanm
72 K 12	Crowther av Brentf
123 X 10	Crowther rd SE25
25 O 9	Croxden clo Edg
120 C 14	Croxden wlk Mrdn
30 K 3	Croxford gdns N22
56 M 4	Croxford way Rom
129 R 13	Croxley rd W9
90 L 19	Croxted clo SE21
109 N 2	Croxted rd SE21
90 L 18	Croxted rd SE24
59 O 9	Croyde av Grnfd
96 E 18	Croyde clo Sidcp
122 H 19	Croydon gro Croy
124 L 6	Croydon rd Becknhm
156 B 8	Croydon rd Croy
65 R 12	Croydon rd E13
121 T 11	Croydon rd Mitch
110 D 20	Croydon rd SE20
123 Z 4	Croydon rd SE20
155 V 7	Croydon rd Wallgtn
18 J 5	Croyland rd N9
116 J 18	Croylands dri Surb
129 P 16	Croyton pth W9
50 G 16	Crozier ter E9
142 K 17	Crucifix la SE1
133 Y 6	Cruden st N1
52 B 14	Cruikshank rd E15
133 R 11	Cruikshank st WC1
26 B 16	Crummock gdns NW9
80 F 11	Crumpsall st SE2
25 R 17	Crundale av NW9
157 O 15	Crunden rd S Croy
157 S 6	Crusader gdn Croy
106 M 18	Crusoe rd Mitch
142 L 8	Crutched friars EC3
112 A 4	Crutchley rd SE6
109 U 12	Crystal ct SE19
109 V 13	Crystal Palace pde SE19
109 Y 12	Crystal Palace pk SE26
91 W 10	Crystal Palace rd SE22
109 W 16	Crystal Palace Station rd SE19
109 O 15	Crystal ter SE19
55 T 4	Crystal way Dgnhm
23 W 15	Crystal way Harrow
9 O 9	Cuba dri Enf
76 A 4	Cuba st E14
156 E 11	Cubitt st Croy
133 O 14	Cubitt st WC1
89 V 7	Cubitt ter SW4
59 U 13	Cuckoo av W7
59 S 13	Cuckoo dene W7
19 P 2	Cuckoo Hall la N9
59 T 19	Cuckoo la W7
152 D 7	Cudas clo Epsom
152 D 6	Cuddington av Worc Pk
93 T 18	Cudham st SE6
63 N 11	Cudworth st E1
135 X 16	Cudworth st E1
95 P 17	Cuff cres SE9
147 O 7	Culford gdns SW3
49 R 19	Culford gro N1
49 R 18	Culford ms N1
134 J 2	Culford rd N1
49 R 18	Culford rd N1
7 N 13	Culgaith gdns Enf
61 W 12	Cullen way NW10
75 O 7	Culling rd SE16
143 Z 20	Culling rd SE16
23 X 13	Cullington clo Harrow
44 H 15	Cullingworth rd NW10
7 V 9	Culloden rd Enf
64 H 17	Culloden st E14
142 J 7	Cullum st EC3
156 K 18	Culmington rd S Croy
72 D 3	Culmington rd W13
107 R 1	Culmore cross SW12
75 O 20	Culmore rd SE15
151 Z 19	Culmore rd SE15
89 O 13	Culmstock rd SW11
133 S 7	Culpepper st N1
30 L 14	Culross clo N15
139 S 9	Culross st W1
24 F 8	Culver gro Stanm
108 C 8	Culverhouse gdns SW16
11 N 14	Culverlands clo Stanm
93 R 20	Culverley rd SE6
111 U 1	Culverley rd SE6
154 L 2	Culvers av Carsh
155 N 1	Culvers av Carsh
154 L 3	Culvers way Carsh
89 O 5	Culvert pl SW11
31 R 16	Culvert rd N15
89 N 4	Culvert rd SW11
126 C 13	Culvestone clo Brom
130 K 10	Culworth st NW8
96 K 10	Cumberland av Welling
61 T 9	Cumberland av NW10
84 B 15	Cumberland clo Twick
105 N 18	Cumberland clo SW20
49 U 18	Cumberland clo E8
144 M 5	Cumberland cres W14
80 M 20	Cumberland dri Hth Hth
133 R 12	Cumberland gdns WC1
27 R 4	Cumberland gdns NW4
139 N 5	Cumberland mans W1
131 Z 12	Cumberland mkt NW1
73 W 1	Cumberland pk W3
61 X 20	Cumberland pk W3
131 X 12	Cumberland pl NW1
86 E 1	Cumberland rd SW13
22 K 15	Cumberland rd Harrow
24 N 11	Cumberland rd Stanm
126 C 8	Cumberland rd Brom
125 Z 8	Cumberland rd Brom
53 N 14	Cumberland rd E12
65 V 11	Cumberland rd E13
32 H 7	Cumberland rd E17
30 D 6	Cumberland rd N22
19 P 7	Cumberland rd N9
73 O 20	Cumberland rd Rich
124 A 13	Cumberland rd SE25
61 W 20	Cumberland rd W3
71 W 6	Cumberland rd W7
148 A 11	Cumberland st SW1
147 Y 10	Cumberland st SW1
131 W 10	Cumberland ter NW1
131 X 10	Cumberland Terrace ms NW1
123 W 7	Cumberlow av SE25
31 P 5	Cumberton rd N17
99 R 4	Cumbrian av Bxly Hth
45 R 7	Cumbrian gdns NW2
133 O 9	Cumming st N1
152 H 15	Cumnor gdns Epsom
154 E 13	Cumnor rd Sutton
61 Z 9	Cunard rd NW10
150 H 14	Cunard st SE5
65 X 18	Cundy rd E16
147 V 7	Cundy st SW1
152 F 8	Cunliffe rd Worc Pk
107 V 14	Cunliffe st SW16
159 S 3	Cunningham clo W Wckm
23 P 15	Cunningham pk Harrow
130 F 16	Cunningham pl NW8
31 W 13	Cunningham rd N15
73 W 10	Cunnington st W4
89 R 1	Cupar rd SW11
112 G 12	Cupola clo Brom
148 G 8	Cureton st SW1
68 H 20	Curlew clo SE28
143 O 16	Curlew st SE1
107 U 5	Curlverden rd SW12
108 L 11	Curnicks la SE27
96 L 14	Curran av Sidcp
155 P 6	Curran av Wallgtn
41 P 18	Currey rd Grnfd
74 A 4	Curricle st W3
105 V 10	Currie Hill clo SW19
14 C 18	Curry ri NW7
141 S 4	Cursitor st EC4
134 K 14	Curtain rd EC2
6 L 15	Curthwaite gdns Enf
108 E 9	Curtis Field rd SW16
82 D 20	Curtis rd Hounsl
150 M 4	Curtis st SE1
151 N 5	Curtis way SE1
68 E 20	Curtis way SE28
62 F 20	Curve the W12
52 G 12	Curwen av E7
74 F 6	Curwen rd W12
9 U 17	Curzon av Enf
23 Y 5	Curzon av Stanm
67 X 8	Curzon cres Bark
62 C 1	Curzon cres NW10
44 C 20	Curzon cres NW10
139 V 14	Curzon pl W1
29 S 7	Curzon rd N10
122 E 14	Curzon rd Thntn Hth
60 B 12	Curzon rd W5
139 W 13	Curzon st W1
101 V 8	Cusack clo Twick
81 Z 13	Cusoe rd Erith
141 U 17	Cut the SE1
90 M 5	Cutcombe rd SE5
156 J 3	Cuthbert rd Croy
33 V 11	Cuthbert rd E17
18 K 15	Cuthbert rd N18
130 F 20	Cuthbert st W2
142 L 4	Cutler st E1
102 D 3	Cutthroat all Rich
97 X 12	Cuxton clo Bxly Hth
135 O 16	Cygnet st E2
100 A 10	Cygnets the Felt
133 P 9	Cynthia st N1
83 N 18	Cypress av Twick
132 C 19	Cypress pl W1
23 P 7	Cypress rd Harrow
123 T 3	Cypress rd SE25
27 U 7	Cyprus av N3
27 T 6	Cyprus gdns N3
63 P 7	Cyprus pl E6
66 K 19	Cyprus pl E6
27 V 8	Cyprus rd N3
18 G 7	Cyprus rd N9
63 R 7	Cyprus st E2
91 V 14	Cyrena rd SE22
98 A 5	Cyril rd Bxly Hth
133 X 15	Cyrus st EC1
75 Z 16	Czar st SE8

D

140 D 6	D'arblay st W1
24 H 14	D'arcy dri Harrow
69 P 2	D'arcy gdns Dgnhm
24 J 13	D'arcy gdns Harrow
153 O 8	D'arcy rd Sutton
147 S 5	D'Oyley st SW1
40 G 15	Dabbs Hill la Grnfrd
93 T 2	Dabia la SE10
75 Z 15	Dacca st SE8
64 A 2	Dace rd E3
35 X 7	Dacre av Ilf
58 L 5	Dacre clo Grnfd
93 Z 10	Dacre gdn SE13
94 A 10	Dacre pk SE13
93 Z 7	Dacre pk SE13
93 Z 8	Dacre pl SE13
122 A 17	Dacre rd Croy
52 B 3	Dacre rd E11
65 U 4	Dacre rd E13
140 F 20	Dacre st SW1
110 E 7	Dacres rd SE23
70 D 14	Dade way S'hall
124 G 19	Daffodil clo CRO
74 E 1	Daffodil st W12
62 E 20	Daffodil st W12
107 N 7	Dafforne rd SW17
56 C 20	Dagenham av Dgnhm
68 L 4	Dagenham av Dgnhm
68 M 3	Dagenham av Dgnhm
69 N 1	Dagenham av Dgnhm
56 J 11	Dagenham rd Dgnhm
50 M 3	Dagenham rd E10
57 N 8	Dagenham rd Rom
42 L 13	Dagmar av Wemb
43 N 13	Dagmar av Wemb
128 E 10	Dagmar gdns NW10
133 X 3	Dagmar pas N1
56 L 19	Dagmar rd Dgnhm
103 O 19	Dagmar rd Kingst
13 O 14	Dagmar rd N22
29 Y 4	Dagmar rd N22
48 F 1	Dagmar rd N4
70 C 9	Dagmar rd S'hall
123 R 10	Dagmar rd SE25
91 R 3	Dagmar rd SE5
133 X 3	Dagmar ter N1
123 P 13	Dagnall pk SE25
123 R 11	Dagnall rd SE25
89 N 3	Dagnall st SW11
89 T 17	Dagnan rd SW12
112 E 8	Dagonet gdns Brom
112 E 7	Dagonet rd Brom
121 X 9	Dahlia gdns Mitch
80 D 12	Dahlia rd SE2
107 U 15	Dahomey rd SW16
156 A 15	Daimler way Wallgtn
53 V 10	Daines clo E12
111 W 12	Dainford clo Brom
112 K 19	Dainton clo Brom
23 Z 13	Daintry clo Harrow
50 L 17	Daintry way E9
95 Y 7	Dairsie rd SE9
105 R 9	Dairy wlk SW19
124 F 20	Daisy clo CR0
87 Y 7	Daisy la SW6
34 H 8	Daisy rd E18
90 F 13	Dalberg rd SW2
80 J 9	Dalberg way SE2
88 C 11	Dalby rd SW18
47 R 18	Dalby st NW5
82 A 5	Dalcross rd Hounsl
24 M 6	Dale av Edg
25 N 7	Dale av Edg
82 C 7	Dale av Hounsl
5 N 20	Dale clo Barnt
99 U 14	Dale clo Drtfrd
94 D 8	Dale clo SE3
99 U 17	Dale end Drtfrd
21 V 13	Dale gdns Wdfd Grn
16 F 12	Dale Green rd N11
154 M 3	Dale Park av Carsh
155 N 3	Dale Park av Carsh
109 N 20	Dale Park rd SE19
99 U 16	Dale rd Drtfrd
65 N 14	Dale rd E16
58 K 15	Dale rd Grnfd
47 O 15	Dale rd NW5
78 M 17	Dale rd SE17
149 Z 16	Dale rd SE5
153 V 9	Dale rd Sutton
136 L 6	Dale row W11
74 A 14	Dale st W4
20 H 9	Dale View av E4
20 G 8	Dale View cres E4
20 H 9	Dale View gdns E4
106 K 4	Dalebury rd SW17
46 F 17	Daleham gdns NW3
46 F 17	Daleham ms NW3
107 S 12	Daleside rd SW16

99 V 4	Daleview Erith
31 S 19	Daleview rd N15
152 K 2	Dalewood gdns Worc Pk
50 F 17	Daley st E9
136 A 1	Dalgarno gdns W10
128 C 20	Dalgarno gdns W10
62 L 14	Dalgarno gdns W10
128 D 19	Dalgarno way W10
62 M 12	Dalgarno way W10
63 X 17	Dalgleish st E14
63 W 5	Daling way E3
11 W 17	Dalkeith gro Stanm
54 C 10	Dalkeith rd Ilf
90 M 20	Dalkeith rd SE21
44 H 1	Dalkeith rd NW4
110 A 8	Dallas rd SE26
109 Z 8	Dallas rd SE26
153 T 14	Dallas rd Sutton
60 M 14	Dallas rd W5
97 X 10	Dallin rd Bxly Hth
78 M 18	Dallin rd SE18
79 N 18	Dallin rd SE18
74 J 8	Dalling rd W6
94 B 17	Dallinger rd SE12
133 X 16	Dallington st EC1
92 F20	Dalmain rd SE23
123 W 17	Dalmally rd Croy
47 Z 14	Dalmeny av N7
122 F 4	Dalmeny av SW16
42 E 17	Dalmeny clo Wemb
83 P 9	Dalmeny cres Hounsl
5 S 20	Dalmeny rd Barnt
98 G 2	Dalmeny rd Bxly Hth
155 P 17	Dalmeny rd Carsh
47 X 10	Dalmeny rd N7
152 K 5	Dalmeny rd Worc Pk
108 M 3	Dalmore rd SE21
92 J 12	Dalrymple rd SE4
24 J 6	Dalston gdns Stanm
50 A 15	Dalston la E8
49 V 18	Dalston la E8
120 H 3	Dalton av Mitch
99 U 6	Dalton clo Drtfrd
108 K 5	Dalton st SE27
91 S 1	Dalwood st SE27
150 L 20	Dalwood st SE5
90 C 8	Dalyell rd SW9
146 C 19	Damer ter SW10
52 F 12	Dames rd E7
63 N 17	Damien st E1
143 Y 4	Damien st E1
115 R 7	Damon clo Sidcp
70 H 9	Damsonwood clo S'hall
108 B 19	Danbrook rd SW16
37 V 10	Danbury clo Rom
155 S 8	Danbury ms Wallgtn
133 Y 8	Danbury st N1
21 Y 20	Danbury way Wdfd Grn
91 U 7	Danby st SE15
85 P 7	Dancer rd Rich
87 V 3	Dancer rd SW6
94 G 8	Dando cres SE3
98 E 19	Dane clo Bxly
63 X 6	Dane pl E3
54 A 16	Dane rd Ilf
19 P 13	Dane rd N18
58 C 20	Dane rd S'hall
106 D 20	Dane rd SW19
72 D 2	Dane rd W13
86 B 16	Danebury av SW15
159 U 14	Danebury Croy
111 S 5	Daneby rd SE6
91 N 13	Danecroft rd SE24
35 S 17	Danehurst gdns Ilf
87 S 1	Danehurst st SW6
5 Z 20	Daneland Barnt
40 K 15	Danemead gro Nthlt
87 N 7	Danemere st SW15
23 S 11	Danes ga Harrow
38 K 20	Danes rd Rom
94 F 20	Danescombe SE12
154 D 3	Danescourt cres Sutton
157 V 5	Danescourt gdns Croy
27 R 16	Danescroft av NW4
27 R 16	Danescroft gdns NW4
50 H 18	Danesdale rd E9
111 T 7	Daneswood av SE6
42 F 18	Danethorpe rd Wemb
56 D 8	Danette gdns Dgnhm
91 N 3	Daneville rd SE5
34 E 19	Dangan rd E11
64 E 14	Daniel Bolt clo E14
106 J 15	Daniel clo SW17

150 M 16	Daniel gdns SE15
151 O 17	Daniel gdns SE15
26 J 20	Daniel pl NW4
61 O 20	Daniel rd W5
92 C 8	Daniels rd SE15
140 F 9	Dansey pl W1
97 O 9	Dansington rd Welling
97 O 9	Danson cres Welling
97 P 10	Danson la Welling
97 V 9	Danson mead Welling
97 U 15	Danson rd Bxly
97 V 12	Danson rd Bxly Hth
149 Y 12	Danson rd SE17
149 X 6	Dante pl SE11
149 X 6	Dante rd SE11
146 L 9	Danube st SW3
29 W 12	Danvers rd N8
146 H 15	Danvers st SW3
20 G 10	Daphne gdns E4
88 B 17	Daphne st SW18
155 V 8	Darcy av Wallgtn
121 Z 3	Darcy rd SW16
55 Z 10	Dare gdns Dgnhm
85 P 7	Darell rd Rich
49 V 2	Darenth rd N16
97 O 2	Darenth rd Welling
92 K 13	Darfield rd SE4
87 O 8	Darfur st SW15
109 V 17	Dargate clo SE19
88 G 8	Darien rd SW11
145 R 20	Darlan rd SW6
105 R 18	Darlaston rd SW19
124 H 16	Darley clo Croy
117 Y 3	Darley dri New Mald
18 G 4	Darley rd N9
93 O 7	Darling rd SE4
63 N 13	Darling row E1
135 Y 19	Darling row E1
108 K 12	Darlington rd SE27
88 L 15	Darly clo SW11
50 B 19	Darnley rd E9
34 G 4	Darnley rd Wdfd Grn
136 J 13	Darnley ter W11
91 X 13	Darrell rd SE22
89 Z 1	Darsley dri SW8
129 N 12	Dart st W10
19 R 1	Dartford av N9
99 Y 15	Dartford rd Drtfrd
150 B 13	Dartford st SE17
137 S 4	Dartmouth clo W2
93 V 3	Dartmouth gro SE10
93 V 3	Dartmouth hill SE10
47 T 9	Dartmouth Park av NW5
47 T 5	Dartmouth Park hill NW5
47 S 10	Dartmouth Park rd NW5
110 D 4	Dartmouth pl SE23
74 B 18	Dartmouth pl W4
126 F 17	Dartmouth rd Brom
65 S 17	Dartmouth rd E16
45 O 17	Dartmouth rd NW2
26 G 19	Dartmouth rd NW4
110 C 5	Dartmouth rd SE26
93 V 3	Dartmouth row SE10
140 F 19	Dartmouth st SW1
123 U 17	Dartnell rd Croy
49 V 10	Darville rd N16
66 J 7	Darwell clo E6
58 L 17	Darwin dri S'hall
30 J 7	Darwin rd N22
72 F 12	Darwin rd W5
96 L 8	Darwin rd Welling
150 G 5	Darwin st SE17
59 T 6	Daryngton dri Grnfd
98 E 14	Dashwood clo Bxly Hth
30 C 19	Dashwood rd N8
108 K 12	Dassett rd SE27
91 O 2	Datchelor pl SE5
110 L 6	Datchet rd SE6
150 D 10	Date st SE17
50 H 12	Daubeney rd E5
30 L 2	Daubeney rd N17
88 C 15	Dault rd SW18
156 J 7	Davenant rd Croy
47 Z 7	Davenant rd N19
143 T 2	Davenant st E1
93 T 16	Davenport rd SE6
115 Y 4	Davenport rd Sidcp
23 W 1	Daventer dri Stanm
33 O 17	Daventry av E17
130 K 20	Daventry st NW1
77 O 12	Davern clo SE10
48 E 19	Davey clo N7
151 O 15	Davey st SE15
59 T 8	David av Grnfd

131 S 20	David ms W1
55 X 6	David rd Dgnhm
51 Y 16	David st E15
141 X 19	Davidge st SE1
110 C 2	Davids rd SE23
36 G 1	Davids way Ilf
148 J 18	Davidson gdns SW8
123 U 15	Davidson rd Croy
52 A 5	Davies la E11
139 W 8	Davies ms W9
139 W 9	Davies st W1
55 R 16	Davington gdns Dgnhm
55 R 15	Davington rd Dgnhm
74 D 4	Davis rd W3
65 W 7	Davis st E13
74 G 6	Davisville rd W12
83 X 11	Dawes av Islwth
144 K 17	Dawes rd SW6
145 P 18	Dawes rd SW6
150 F 8	Dawes st SE17
150 G 9	Dawes st SE17
60 A 7	Dawlish av Grnfd
16 M 14	Dawlish av N13
17 N 15	Dawlish av N13
106 A 4	Dawlish av SW18
54 H 12	Dawlish dri Ilf
22 B 17	Dawlish dri Pinn
51 T 5	Dawlish rd E10
31 W 9	Dawlish rd N17
45 P 17	Dawlish rd NW2
82 B 7	Dawn clo Hounsl
106 E 4	Dawnay gdns SW18
106 E 3	Dawnay rd SW18
44 E 7	Dawpool rd NW2
13 T 16	Daws la NW7
67 W 2	Dawson av Bark
67 Y 2	Dawson av Bark
67 Y 2	Dawson gdns Bark
137 U 9	Dawson pl W2
45 N 13	Dawson rd NW2
117 N 6	Dawson rd Surb
135 O 9	Dawson st E2
120 A 4	Daybrook rd SW19
86 G 9	Daylesford av SW15
96 G 20	Days la Sidcp
108 C 2	Daysbrook rd SW2
92 C 1	Dayton gro SE15
134 K 4	De Beauvoir cres N1
134 J 2	De Beauvoir rd N1
49 R 20	De Beauvoir rd N1
134 K 1	De Beauvoir sq N1
49 S 20	De Beauvoir sq N1
6 D 20	De Bohun av N14
91 O 4	De Crespigny pk SE5
110 H 8	De Frene rd SE26
156 B 16	De Havilland rd Croy
25 S 8	De Havilland rd Edg
149 W 11	De Laune st SE17
80 E 10	De Lucy st SE2
107 Z 5	De Montford rd SW16
88 B 7	De Morgan rd SW6
31 O 4	De Quincey rd N17
53 T 5	De Vere gdns Ilf
138 A 19	De Vere gdns W8
138 A 20	De Vere ms W8
139 V 2	De Walden st W1
116 M 1	Deacon rd Kingst
44 G 16	Deacon rd NW2
150 B 4	Deacon way SE17
100 G 11	Deacons way Hampt
107 O 15	Deal rd SW17
135 S 19	Deal st E1
86 L 10	Dealtry rd SW15
148 J 4	Dean Bradley st SW1
50 D 14	Dean clo E9
42 C 9	Dean ct Wemb
24 K 8	Dean dri Stanm
140 F 20	Dean Farrar st SW1
33 W 12	Dean gdns E17
157 O 9	Dean rd Croy
100 F 13	Dean rd Hampt
82 L 14	Dean rd Hounsl
44 M 17	Dean rd NW2
148 J 4	Dean Ryle st SW1
52 E 14	Dean st E7
140 F 7	Dean st W1
148 J 3	Dean Stanley st SW1
148 J 3	Dean Trench st SW1
12 K 20	Dean wlk Edg
70 L 4	Dean wy S'hall
141 Y 7	Dean's ct EC4
140 H 20	Dean's yd SW1
63 O 17	Deancross st E1
143 Z 6	Deancross st E1
139 U 13	Deanery ms W1
52 A 19	Deanery rd E15
51 Z 18	Deanery rd E15

139 U 13	Deanery st W1
85 T 10	Deanhill ct SW14
85 U 10	Deanhill rd SW14
150 F 8	Deans bldgs SE17
157 U 5	Deans clo Croy
12 H 20	Deans clo Edg
73 T 16	Deans clo W4
12 K 16	Deans dri Edg
12 H 18	Deans la Edg
73 T 16	Deans la W4
139 X 4	Deans ms W1
148 E 8	Deans pl SW1
154 A 6	Deans rd Sutton
153 Z 7	Deans rd Sutton
71 W 4	Deans rd W7
12 G 17	Deans way Edg
25 U 1	Deansbrook clo Edg
25 S 2	Deansbrook rd Edg
12 H 20	Deansbrook rd Edg
13 N 20	Deansbrook rd Edg
43 W 5	Deanscroft av W5
28 G 13	Deansway N2
18 C 10	Deansway N9
120 J 5	Dearn gdns Mitch
10 L 17	Dearne clo Stanm
64 H 3	Deason st E15
57 Z 18	Debden wlk Hornch
75 P 12	Debnams rd SE16
83 S 1	Deborah clo Islwth
81 Z 16	Debrabant clo Erith
106 D 17	Deburgh rd SW19
150 J 1	Decima st SE1
27 U 14	Decoy av NW11
85 N 9	Dee rd Rich
64 J 16	Dee st E14
39 P 3	Dee way Rom
89 X 2	Deeley rd SW8
61 O 17	Deena clo W3
126 C 10	Deepdale av Brom
105 R 10	Deepdale SW19
157 V 7	Deepdene av Croy
34 F 13	Deepdene clo E11
7 W 20	Deepdene ct N21
90 C 18	Deepdene gdns SW2
91 N 9	Deepdene rd SE5
97 O 6	Deepdene rd Welling
83 X 2	Deepwell clo Islwth
59 R 8	Deepwood la Grnfd
103 R 18	Deer Park clo Kingst
120 C 3	Deer Park rd SW19
108 H 1	Deerbrook rd SE24
90 L 9	Deerdale rd SE24
57 W 19	Deere av Rainhm
45 P 19	Deerhurst rd NW2
108 C 13	Deerhurst rd SW16
106 F 7	Deeside rd SW17
155 Z 16	Defiant way Wallgtn
73 R 20	Defoe av Rich
106 J 15	Defoe clo SW17
49 S 8	Defoe rd N16
113 Y 12	Degema rd Chisl
44 F 2	Dehar cres NW9
91 S 16	Dekker rd SE21
118 L 20	Delacombe av Worc Pk
77 V 20	Delacourt rd SE3
77 X 13	Delafield rd SE7
75 O 13	Delaford rd SE16
151 Y 10	Delaford rd SE16
145 N 16	Delaford st SW6
124 C 15	Delamere cres Croy
12 K 18	Delamere gdns NW7
119 P 1	Delamere rd SW20
72 L 4	Delamere rd W5
138 A 1	Delamere ter W2
129 Y 20	Delamere ter W2
131 X 6	Delancey st NW1
129 W 9	Delaware rd W9
91 N 16	Delawyk cres SE24
91 S 12	Delft way SE22
18 G 1	Delhi rd Enf
132 L 5	Delhi st N1
88 B 18	Delia st SW18
64 L 3	Dell clo E15
155 W 7	Dell clo Wallgtn
21 U 11	Dell clo Wdfd Grn
152 F 12	Dell la Epsom
9 P 2	Dell rd Enf
152 G 12	Dell rd Epsom
72 E 16	Dell the Brentf
109 U 19	Dell the SE19
79 Z 14	Dell the SE2
21 U 11	Dell the Wdfd Grn
42 C 14	Dell the Wemb
60 C 17	Dell way W13
118 B 4	Dell wlk New Mald
148 B 7	Dell's ms SW1
111 U 20	Dellfield clo Becknhm
4 C 16	Dellors clo Barnt

Ref	Name
54 D 1	Dellow clo
36 D 20	Dellow clo Ilf
63 N 20	Dellow st E1
143 Y 8	Dellow st E1
35 X 11	Dellwood gdns Ilf
90 D 10	Delmare clo SW19
94 J 4	Delme cres SE3
157 V 5	Delmey clo Croy
93 N 2	Deloraine st SE8
144 H 15	Delorme st W6
152 C 5	Delta clo Worc Pk
152 C 5	Delta rd Worc Pk
135 S 12	Delta st E2
81 Y 13	Deluci rd Erith
56 J 12	Delversmead Dgnhm
149 Y 10	Delverton rd SE17
87 X 3	Delvino rd SW6
155 W 7	Demesne rd Wallgtn
43 V 9	Demeta clo Wemb
116 E 19	Dempster clo Surb
88 C 12	Dempster rd SW18
125 X 7	Den clo Becknhm
125 X 7	Den rd Brom
115 S 8	Denberry dri Sidcp
113 T 15	Denbigh clo Chisl
62 A 1	Denbigh clo NW10
44 A 20	Denbigh clo NW10
58 F 17	Denbigh clo S'hall
153 V 10	Denbigh clo Sutton
137 R 8	Denbigh clo W11
85 N 14	Denbigh gdns Rich
148 B 9	Denbigh pl SW1
66 B 10	Denbigh rd E6
82 L 4	Denbigh rd Hounsl
58 F 17	Denbigh rd S'hall
137 R 8	Denbigh rd W11
60 C 19	Denbigh rd W13
148 C 10	Denbigh st SW1
137 R 8	Denbigh ter W11
127 U 3	Denbridge rd Brom
82 E 7	Dene av Hounsl
97 S 19	Dene av Sidcp
126 C 20	Dene clo Brom
92 H 9	Dene clo SE4
152 D 2	Dene clo Worc Pk
11 S 16	Dene gdns Stanm
16 A 7	Dene rd N11
158 E 7	Dene the Croy
60 A 14	Dene the W13
42 J 12	Dene the Wemb
5 S 17	Dene wood Barnt
26 M 19	Denehurst gdns NW4
83 R 19	Denehurst gdns Twick
21 U 13	Denehurst gdns Wdfd Grn
85 R 10	Denehurst gdns Rich
73 S 3	Denehurst gdns W3
28 M 20	Denewood rd N6
120 L 9	Denham clo Mitch
97 T 8	Denham clo Welling
36 A 18	Denham dri Ilf
15 Y 10	Denham rd N20
77 R 13	Denham st SE10
67 W 3	Denham way Bark
57 U 18	Denholme wlk Rainhm
129 R 12	Denhome rd W9
28 C 11	Denison clo N2
106 F 16	Denison rd SW19
60 E 11	Denison rd W5
115 Y 3	Deniston av Bxly
17 S 4	Denleigh gdns N21
27 Z 15	Denman dri NW11
27 Z 14	Denman Drive north NW11
27 Z 15	Denman Drive south NW11
91 U 3	Denman rd SE15
140 E 9	Denman st W1
105 S 17	Denmark av SW19
119 Y 13	Denmark ct Mrdn
155 N 5	Denmark gdns Carsh
133 S 7	Denmark gro N1
26 E 11	Denmark Hill dri NW9
91 O 8	Denmark hill SE5
140 G 5	Denmark pl WC2
126 H 2	Denmark rd Brom
155 N 6	Denmark rd Carsh
60 C 20	Denmark rd Grnfd
116 J 6	Denmark rd Kingst
30 E 12	Denmark rd N8
129 R 9	Denmark rd NW6
123 Y 11	Denmark rd SE25
90 L 4	Denmark rd SE5
105 R 16	Denmark rd SW19
101 R 6	Denmark rd Twick
51 Y 10	Denmark st E11
65 U 13	Denmark st E13
31 Y 3	Denmark st N17
140 H 5	Denmark st WC2
108 L 10	Denmark wlk SE27
122 H 19	Denmead rd Croy
116 L 20	Dennan rd Surb
135 P 5	Denne ter E8
20 B 8	Denner rd E4
122 G 18	Dennett rd Croy
92 D 3	Dennetts dri SE14
92 E 4	Dennetts gro SE14
156 G 10	Denning av Croy
100 E 14	Denning clo Hampt
130 D 14	Denning clo NW8
46 G 12	Denning rd NW3
45 Y 16	Dennington Park rd NW6
42 L 14	Dennis av Wemb
11 R 15	Dennis gdns Stanm
11 O 12	Dennis la Stanm
119 S 1	Dennis Park cres SW2
60 A 5	Dennis rd Grnfd
107 N 20	Dennis Reeve clo Mitch
66 D 16	Denny clo E6
149 U 8	Denny cres SE11
55 S 20	Denny gdns Dgnhm
18 M 5	Denny rd N9
149 T 8	Denny st SE11
64 M 2	Densham rd E15
65 N 3	Densham rd E15
110 H 20	Densole clo Becknhm
19 P 10	Densworth gro N9
99 S 19	Denton rd Drtfrd
18 F 14	Denton rd N18
30 E 17	Denton rd N8
61 W 2	Denton rd NW10
84 G 17	Denton rd Twick
80 F 19	Denton rd Welling
88 B 15	Denton st SW18
50 F 9	Denton way E5
88 L 17	Dents rd SW11
99 X 19	Denver rd Drtfrd
49 R 1	Denver rd N16
146 M 6	Denyer st SW3
44 E 16	Denzil rd NW10
87 U 9	Deodar rd SW15
54 C 1	Depot cotts Ilf
83 P 7	Depot rd Hounsl
150 E 16	Depot st SE5
93 O 1	Deptford bdwy SE8
93 O 1	Deptford br SE8
76 B 17	Deptford Church st SE
76 B 12	Deptford Ferry rd E14
76 B 16	Deptford grn SE8
76 A 18	Deptford High st SE8
75 Y 12	Deptford strand SE8
23 P 5	Derby av Harrow
15 P 17	Derby av N12
38 J 19	Derby av N9
140 K 17	Derby ga SW1
110 B 4	Derby Hill cres SE23
110 C 4	Derby hill SE23
156 J 1	Derby rd Croy
34 B 4	Derby rd E18
52 M 20	Derby rd E7
53 N 19	Derby rd E7
63 S 3	Derby rd E9
9 P 17	Derby rd Enf
58 K 2	Derby rd Grnfd
82 K 10	Derby rd Hounsl
30 K 13	Derby rd N15
19 O 16	Derby rd N18
117 O 18	Derby rd Surb
153 W 14	Derby rd Sutton
85 T 10	Derby rd SW14
105 Y 18	Derby rd SW19
139 V 14	Derby rd W1
135 U 14	Derbyshire st E2
134 K 15	Dereham pl EC2
54 L 16	Dereham rd Bark
155 S 7	Derek av Wallgtn
43 S 20	Derek av Wemb
135 V 4	Dericote st E8
156 L 9	Dering pl Croy
156 M 9	Dering rd Croy
139 X 6	Dering st W1
106 M 8	Derinton rd SW17
107 N 10	Derinton rd SW17
93 W 12	Dermody gdns SE13
93 W 12	Dermody rd SE13
108 H 1	Deronda rd SE24
154 M 12	Deroy clo Carsh
77 X 10	Derrick gdns SE7
124 L 8	Derrick rd Becknhm
155 Z 4	Derry rd Wallgtn
137 X 19	Derry st W8
53 V 13	Dersingham av E12
53 V 14	Dersingham av E12
53 V 16	Dersingham av E12
45 T 9	Dersingham rd NW2
15 Y 5	Derwent av Barnt
18 A 17	Derwent av N18
12 L 18	Derwent av NW7
26 A 16	Derwent av NW9
104 A 10	Derwent av SW15
103 Z 9	Derwent av SW15
98 D 5	Derwent cres Bxly Hth
15 S 11	Derwent cres N20
24 E 7	Derwent cres Stanm
35 R 13	Derwent gdns Ilf
42 E 2	Derwent gdns Wemb
91 T 10	Derwent gro SE22
119 N 12	Derwent rd Mrdn
17 P 11	Derwent rd N13
58 F 16	Derwent rd S'hall
123 Y 3	Derwent rd SE20
82 L 16	Derwent rd Twick
72 C 8	Derwent rd W5
26 A 17	Derwent ri NW9
76 M 12	Derwent st SE10
57 Y 15	Derwent way Hornch
155 S 17	Derwent wlk Wallgtn
73 V 2	Derwentwater rd W3
129 X 20	Desborough st W2
91 S 16	Desenfans rd SE21
65 N 12	Desford rd E16
75 W 17	Desmond st SE14
47 U 4	Despard rd N19
112 E 12	Detling rd Brom
66 L 19	Devalls clo E6
155 N 5	Devana end Carsh
65 O 1	Devaney rd E15
104 M 20	Devas rd SW20
105 N 20	Devas rd SW20
64 F 11	Devas st E3
80 B 6	Devenish rd SE2
91 S 12	Deventer cres SE22
150 E 3	Deverell st SE1
141 R 7	Devereux ct WC2
88 M 16	Devereux rd SW11
39 P 4	Deveron way Rom
134 F 5	Devizes st N1
101 O 1	Devon av Twick
21 V 7	Devon clo Buck Hl
60 E 3	Devon clo Grnfd
31 W 9	Devon clo N17
60 E 3	Devon cres Grnfd
30 K 18	Devon gdns N4
67 U 3	Devon rd Bark
153 S 19	Devon rd Sutton
28 G 14	Devon ri N2
75 N 17	Devon st SE15
151 X 15	Devon st SE15
70 E 19	Devon way Hounsl
83 Z 19	Devoncroft gdns Twick
17 Y 19	Devonia gdns N18
133 X 7	Devonia rd N1
35 T 19	Devonport gdns Ilf
74 K 4	Devonport rd W12
63 R 18	Devonport st E1
64 C 11	Devons rd E3
154 C 17	Devonshire av Sutton
52 A 13	Devonshire clo E15
100 B 8	Devonshire clo Felt
17 S 12	Devonshire clo N13
131 X 20	Devonshire clo W1
27 P 1	Devonshire cres NW7
17 Y 19	Devonshire ct N17
76 D 20	Devonshire dri SE10
93 S 1	Devonshire dri SE10
17 Z 2	Devonshire gdns N21
17 Z 20	Devonshire gdns N17
73 U 20	Devonshire gdns W4
75 N 17	Devonshire gro SE15
151 Y 16	Devonshire gro SE15
17 Y 19	Devonshire Hill la
18 A 20	Devonshire Hill la N17
31 O 1	Devonshire Hill la N17
131 V 19	Devonshire Mews west W1
131 W 20	Devonshire Mews south W1
131 X 20	Devonshire Mews north W1
74 A 13	Devonshire ms W4
45 X 9	Devonshire pl NW2
131 V 19	Devonshire pl W1
131 V 19	Devonshire Place ms W1
23 O 18	Devonshire rd Harrow
155 O 7	Devonshire rd Wallgtn
97 Z 10	Devonshire rd Bxly Hth
123 N 16	Devonshire rd Croy
65 W 19	Devonshire rd E16
33 O 18	Devonshire rd E17
36 G 20	Devonshire rd Ilf
17 Z 20	Devonshire rd N17
19 P 6	Devonshire rd N9
27 O 2	Devonshire rd NW7
22 D 3	Devonshire rd Pinn
58 G 13	Devonshire rd S'hall
110 D 2	Devonshire rd SE23
92 E 19	Devonshire rd SE23
113 P 4	Devonshire rd SE9
154 D 16	Devonshire rd Sutton
106 L 16	Devonshire rd SW19
74 A 13	Devonshire rd W4
72 D 8	Devonshire rd W5
142 K 3	Devonshire row EC2
131 Y 19	Devonshire Row ms W1
126 J 8	Devonshire sq Brom
142 L 3	Devonshire sq EC2
131 X 19	Devonshire st W1
74 A 15	Devonshire st W4
138 C 7	Devonshire ter W2
158 K 2	Devonshire way Croy
159 N 1	Devonshire way Croy
91 X 8	Dewar st SE15
66 C 15	Dewberry gdns E6
56 J 18	Dewey rd Dgnhm
133 S 7	Dewey rd N1
106 M 12	Dewey st SW17
144 F 2	Dewhurst rd W14
22 C 19	Dewsbury clo Pinn
152 F 4	Dewsbury gdns Worc Pk
44 G 15	Dewsbury rd NW10
4 B 19	Dexter rd Barnt
90 G 12	Dexter rd SE24
31 N 4	Deyncourt rd N17
34 L 14	Deynecourt gdns E11
140 E 5	Diadem ct W1
55 T 4	Diamond clo Dgnhm
40 A 13	Diamond rd Pinn
150 L 19	Diamond st SE15
93 V 1	Diamond ter SE10
34 H 6	Diana clo E18
131 Z 19	Diana pl NW1
32 M 9	Diana rd E17
80 C 13	Dianthus clo SE2
57 Y 12	Diban av Hornch
133 Z 3	Dibden st N1
153 Y 4	Dibdin clo Sutton
153 Y 4	Dibdin rd Sutton
44 L 13	Dicey av NW2
28 D 5	Dickens av N3
102 J 3	Dickens clo Rich
114 C 14	Dickens dri Chisl
18 E 16	Dickens la N18
66 B 6	Dickens rd E6
150 C 1	Dickens sq SE1
89 T 4	Dickens st SW8
30 B 20	Dickenson rd N8
123 X 14	Dickensons la SE25
123 X 15	Dickensons pl SE25
117 V 4	Dickerage la New Mald
117 V 2	Dickerage rd Kingst
95 R 8	Dickson rd SE9
66 G 4	Didsbury clo E6
48 K 7	Digby cres N4
69 R 2	Digby gdns Dgnhm
157 V 4	Digby pl Croy
67 W 1	Digby rd Bark
50 F 16	Digby rd E9
63 R 9	Digby st E2
63 S 15	Diggon st E1
88 C 12	Dighton rd SW18
133 S 6	Dignum st N1
48 G 18	Digswell st N7
112 H 6	Dilhorne clo SE12
147 P 14	Dilke st SW3
48 D 11	Dillon pl N7
110 A 7	Dillwyn clo SE26
110 J 8	Dillwyn clo SE26
104 H 1	Dilton gdns SW15
41 R 15	Dimmock dri Grnfd
52 F 14	Dimond clo E7
18 J 1	Dimsdale dri Enf
43 W 4	Dimsdale dri NW9
65 S 5	Dimsdale wlk E13
64 B 20	Dingle gdns E14
107 X 5	Dingley la SW16
134 B 13	Dingley pl EC1
134 B 13	Dingley rd EC1
156 M 3	Dingwall av Croy

157 N 3 Dingwall av Croy
27 X 19 Dingwall gdns NW11
154 M 19 Dingwall rd Carsh
157 O 2 Dingwall rd Croy
88 C 19 Dingwall rd SW18
135 V 9 Dinmont st E2
5 O 18 Dinsdale gdns Barnt
123 T 10 Dinsdale gdns SE25
77 O 15 Dinsdale rd SE3
89 S 18 Dinsmore rd SW12
103 N 17 Dinton rd Kingst
106 G 14 Dinton rd SW19
65 O 3 Dirleton rd E15
144 L 15 Disbrowe rd W6
143 W 11 Discovery wlk E1
26 A 4 Dishforth la NW9
142 C 17 Disney pl SE1
142 C 17 Disney st SE1
9 S 6 Dison clo Enf
80 E 3 Disraeli clo SE28
52 F 17 Disraeli rd E7
61 X 6 Disraeli rd NW10
87 R 11 Disraeli rd SW15
72 F 3 Disraeli rd W5
135 O 11 Diss st E2
142 A 8 Distaff la EC4
160 A 8 Distaff la EC4
144 L 11 Distillery la W6
144 D 12 Distillery rd W6
149 S 7 Distin st SE11
42 B 16 District rd Wemb
93 R 2 Ditch all SE10
64 G 20 Ditchburn st E14
113 R 10 Dittisham rd SE9
116 F 20 Ditton Grange clo Surb
116 F 20 Ditton Grange dri Surb
116 C 20 Ditton Hill rd Surb
110 A 20 Ditton pl SE20
97 Y 13 Ditton rd Bxly Hth
70 E 13 Ditton rd S'hall
116 K 20 Ditton rd Surb
116 A 15 Ditton reach Surb
159 R 1 Dixon pl W Wckm
92 K 1 Dixon rd SE14
123 T 6 Dixon st SE25
143 W 19 Dixons all SE16
23 Z 7 Dobbin clo Harrow
95 U 13 Dobell rd SE9
128 A 1 Dobree av NW10
62 K 1 Dobree av NW10
46 F 20 Dobson clo NW6
160 C 9 Doby ct EC4
75 U 5 Dock Hill av SE16
72 H 18 Dock rd Brentf
77 P 1 Dock rd E16
65 P 20 Dock rd E16
143 S 9 Dock st E1
143 P 18 Dockhead SE1
78 J 3 Dockland st E16
151 S 2 Dockley rd SE16
110 C 12 Doctors clo SE26
49 R 17 Docwras bldgs N1
64 A 17 Dod st E14
63 Z 17 Dod st E14
108 H 8 Dodbrooke rd SE27
149 X 12 Doddington gro SE17
149 W 13 Doddington pl SE17
141 V 20 Dodson st SE1
106 C 19 Doel clo SW19
141 P 1 Dog and Duck yd WC1
91 S 8 Dog Kennel hill SE22
44 B 13 Dog la NW10
93 O 19 Dogget rd SE6
5 W 19 Doggets clo Barnt
65 T 11 Doherty rd E13
141 X 14 Dolben st SE1
87 V 6 Dolby rd SW6
26 M 1 Dole st NW7
149 P 11 Dolland st SE11
27 V 4 Dollis av N3
4 E 20 Dollis Brook wlk Barnt
44 L 8 Dollis Hill av NW2
44 H 10 Dollis Hill la NW2
27 V 3 Dollis pk N3
27 T 3 Dollis rd NW7
4 H 18 Dollis Valley way Barnt
73 Y 12 Dolman rd W4
90 B 9 Dolman st SW4
39 S 14 Dolphin appr Rom
116 G 13 Dolphin clo Surb
64 C 20 Dolphin la E14
58 F 5 Dolphin rd Nthlt
148 D 12 Dolphin sq SW1
133 N 20 Dombey st WC1

109 V 9 Dome Hill pk SE26
91 P 9 Domett clo SE5
134 A 17 Domingo st EC1
123 U 16 Dominion rd Croy
70 C 7 Dominion rd S'hall
142 G 1 Dominion st EC2
160 G 1 Dominion st EC2
114 A 7 Domonic dri SE9
113 Z 8 Domonic dri SE9
15 T 8 Domville clo N20
150 M 11 Domville gro SE5
91 O 1 Don Phelan clo SE5
39 P 3 Don way Rom
37 T 16 Donald dri Rom
122 E 16 Donald rd Croy
65 V 4 Donald rd E13
129 P 6 Donaldson rd NW6
78 L 20 Donaldson rd SE18
95 X 2 Donaldson rd SE18
40 E 17 Doncaster dri Nthlt
40 D 15 Doncaster gdns Nthlt
30 L 19 Doncaster gdns N4
18 M 3 Doncaster rd N9
133 R 9 Donegal st N1
87 P 3 Doneraile st SW6
65 V 9 Dongola rd E13
31 V 11 Dongola rd N17
65 U 9 Dongola Road west E13
36 C 15 Donington av Ilf
91 Y 17 Donkey all SE22
8 K 8 Donkey la Enf
121 T 8 Donne pl Mitch
146 L 5 Donne pl SW3
55 T 6 Donne rd Dgnhm
24 K 1 Donnefield av Edg
128 A 3 Donnington rd NW10
24 G 18 Donnington rd Harrow
152 H 3 Donnington rd Worc Pk
62 K 2 Donnington rd NW10
107 W 18 Donnybrook rd SW16
29 T 8 Donovan av N10
141 S 13 Doon st SE1
101 X 14 Doone clo Tedd
105 X 10 Dora rd SW19
63 Y 16 Dora st E14
154 M 11 Doral way Carsh
79 U 19 Doran gro SE18
64 H 1 Doran wlk E15
22 L 20 Dorchester av Harrow
97 X 19 Dorchester av Bxly
17 Y 13 Dorchester av N13
40 L 14 Dorchester clo Nthlt
16 F 2 Dorchester ct N14
90 M 12 Dorchester ct SE24
27 Y 12 Dorchester gdns NW11
20 B 14 Dorchester gdns E4
74 B 15 Dorchester gro W4
152 L 1 Dorchester rd Worc Pk
153 N 1 Dorchester rd Worc Pk
120 B 17 Dorchester rd Mrdn
40 L 14 Dorchester rd Nthlt
90 L 12 Dorchester rd SE24
24 M 18 Dorchester way Harrow
25 N 17 Dorchester way Harrow
97 Y 4 Dorcis av Bxly Hth
74 B 4 Dordrecht rd W3
53 W 15 Dore av E12
120 B 16 Dore gdns Mrdn
43 Y 3 Doria av NW9
87 W 4 Doria rd SW6
57 X 5 Dorian rd Hornch
57 X 5 Dorian rd Hornch
125 S 1 Doric ct Becknhm
132 F 13 Doric way NW1
119 P 3 Dorien rd SW20
98 J 2 Doris av Erith
52 F 20 Doris rd E7
153 O 2 Dorking clo Worc Pk
75 Y 16 Dorking clo SE8
88 H 17 Dorlcote rd SW18
130 E 4 Dorman way NW8
87 Z 12 Dormans clo SW18
4 B 18 Dormer clo Barnt
52 B 17 Dormer clo E15
58 G 17 Dormers av S'hall
58 L 18 Dormers ri S'hall

58 J 19 Dormers Wells la S'hall
70 K 1 Dormers Wells la S'hall
77 U 19 Dornberg rd SE3
77 U 19 Dornbergh clo SE3
87 T 4 Dorncliffe rd SW6
45 W 16 Dornfell st NW6
157 P 12 Dornton rd S Croy
107 T 4 Dornton rd SW12
60 L 1 Dorothy av Wemb
98 G 10 Dorothy Evans clo Bxly Hth
55 S 13 Dorothy gdns Dgnhm
88 L 8 Dorothy rd SW11
141 T 1 Dorrington st EC1
18 F 15 Dorrit ms N18
114 C 15 Dorrit way Chisl
43 Y 3 Dors clo NW9
39 O 10 Dorset av Rom
70 G 10 Dorset av S'hall
96 K 10 Dorset av Welling
141 V 7 Dorset bldgs EC4
131 O 19 Dorset clo NW1
12 A 20 Dorset dri Edg
11 Z 20 Dorset dri Edg
122 B 8 Dorset gdns Mitch
141 W 7 Dorset ms EC4
51 W 17 Dorset pl E15
148 F 9 Dorset pl SW1
124 E 6 Dorset rd Becknhm
52 M 20 Dorset rd E7
65 Z 1 Dorset rd E7
23 O 18 Dorset rd Harrow
120 K 3 Dorset rd Mitch
31 P 13 Dorset rd N15
30 A 6 Dorset rd N22
113 P 4 Dorset rd SE9
120 A 3 Dorset rd SW19
105 X 20 Dorset rd SW19
119 Z 2 Dorset rd SW19
148 M 18 Dorset rd SW8
149 P 19 Dorset rd SW8
72 F 7 Dorset rd W5
141 V 7 Dorset ri EC4
131 O 18 Dorset sq NW1
148 M 18 Dorset st Sch SW8
139 S 1 Dorset st W1
70 E 20 Dorset way Hounsl
101 O 1 Dorset way Twick
74 H 9 Dorville cres W6
94 D 14 Dorville rd SE12
79 P 19 Dothill rd SE18
133 N 1 Doughty ms WC1
133 O 17 Doughty st WC1
118 K 9 Douglas av New Mald
32 M 5 Douglas av E17
33 N 4 Douglas av E17
42 K 19 Douglas av Wemb
156 A 14 Douglas clo Croy
10 M 17 Douglas clo Stanm
159 N 5 Douglas dri Croy
102 G 1 Douglas ho Rich
76 G 12 Douglas pl E14
148 F 8 Douglas pth SW1
65 T 14 Douglas rd E16
20 M 4 Douglas rd E4
21 N 4 Douglas rd E4
39 U 19 Douglas rd Hornch
82 L 8 Douglas rd Hounsl
57 U 1 Douglas rd Hounsl
37 N 19 Douglas rd Ilf
117 T 5 Douglas rd Kingst
48 L 19 Douglas rd N1
30 G 4 Douglas rd N22
129 P 3 Douglas rd NW6
117 N 19 Douglas rd Surb
97 R 2 Douglas rd Welling
119 Y 14 Douglas sq Mrdn
148 F 7 Douglas st SW1
75 Z 19 Douglas way SE8
106 A 2 Dounesforth gdns SW18
105 Z 2 Dounesforth gdns SW18
137 Z 20 Douro pl W8
64 A 5 Douro st E3
143 V 13 Douthwaite sq E1
66 C 15 Dove appr E6
58 A 10 Dove clo Nthlt
20 A 8 Dove House gdns E4
146 B 8 Dove ms SW5
22 F 2 Dove pk Pinn
49 O 18 Dove rd N1
135 T 7 Dove row E2
57 Y 19 Dove wlk Hornch
35 X 6 Dovedale av Ilf
97 N 3 Dovedale clo Welling
24 E 18 Dovedale rd Harrow

92 A 15 Dovedale rd SE22
106 M 19 Dovedale ri Mitch
67 R 6 Dovehouse mead Bark
146 J 11 Dovehouse st SW3
38 J 8 Dover clo Rom
154 B 6 Dover Court la Sutton
86 H 10 Dover House rd SW15
86 K 16 Dover Park dri SW15
52 K 6 Dover rd E12
19 P 9 Dover rd N9
37 Z 19 Dover rd Rom
109 O 15 Dover rd SE19
140 A 12 Dover st W1
139 Z 11 Dover st W1
122 G 10 Dovercourt av Thntn Hth
11 W 16 Dovercourt gdns Stanm
91 T 15 Dovercourt rd SE22
90 B 17 Doverfield rd SW2
17 W 14 Doveridge gdns N13
157 P 12 Doveton rd S Croy
63 P 12 Doveton st E1
112 A 2 Dowanhill rd SE6
111 X 2 Dowanhill rd SE6
88 B 11 Dowdeswell clo SW15
10 L 18 Dowding pl Stanm
155 T 19 Dower av Wallgtn
160 D 9 Dowgate hill EC4
129 N 11 Dowland st W10
150 J 18 Dowlas st SE5
106 B 19 Dowman clo SW19
116 G 1 Down Hall rd Kingst
144 A 8 Down pl W6
74 K 12 Down pl W6
102 B 16 Down rd Tedd
139 X 15 Down st W1
26 M 8 Downage NW4
99 O 4 Downbank av Bxly Hth
111 Y 8 Downderry rd Brom
80 F 18 Downe clo Welling
89 V 9 Downer's cotts SW4
84 B 15 Downes clo Twick
17 T 5 Downes ct N21
129 W 18 Downfield clo W9
118 E 20 Downfield Worc Pk
38 F 2 Downham rd N1
134 E 2 Downham rd N1
112 A 11 Downham way Brom
111 Y 11 Downham way Brom
31 O 10 Downhills av N17
30 L 11 Downhills Park rd N17
31 O 11 Downhills Park rd N17
30 M 9 Downhills way N17
12 L 17 Downhurst av NW7
23 O 10 Downing clo Harrow
59 S 4 Downing dri Grnfd
56 C 20 Downing rd Dgnhm
69 O 1 Downing rd Dgnhm
140 J 16 Downing st SW1
15 R 4 Downland clo N20
128 M 11 Downland st W10
113 T 3 Downleys clo SE9
95 S 8 Downman rd SE9
133 T 4 Downrey st N1
113 T 13 Downs av Chisl
22 D 20 Downs av Pinn
125 W 1 Downs Bridge rd Becknhm
49 Y 10 Downs est E5
111 W 20 Downs hill Becknhm
125 X 1 Downs hill Becknhm
50 A 13 Downs Park rd E5
49 X 14 Downs Park rd E8
125 R 2 Downs rd Becknhm
49 Y 12 Downs rd E5
8 F 15 Downs rd Enf
108 L 20 Downs rd Thntn Hth
105 O 19 Downs the SW20
83 X 1 Downs view Islwth
51 V 12 Downsell rd E15
31 V 8 Downsett rd N17
32 J 19 Downsfield rd E17
36 J 19 Downshall av Ilf
46 G 13 Downshire hill NW3
106 D 16 Downside clo SW19
46 K 16 Downside cres NW3
59 Y 12 Downside cres W13
154 H 14 Downside rd Sutton
101 V 6 Downside Twick
108 K 19 Downsview gdns SE19
108 L 17 Downsview rd SE19
154 C 18 Downsway the Sutton
108 B 3 Downton av SW2

75 W 5	Downtown rd SE16
28 H 1	Downway N12
91 P 10	Dowson clo SE5
142 B 16	Doyce st SE1
99 R 2	Doyle clo Erith
128 A 8	Doyle gdns NW10
62 H 3	Doyle gdns NW10
123 X 9	Doyle rd SE25
47 T 1	Doynton st N19
107 S 8	Dr Johnson av SW17
150 A 13	Draco st SE17
120 G 7	Dragmire la Mitch
75 X 14	Dragoon rd SE8
61 X 11	Dragor rd NW10
122 D 17	Drake rd Croy
121 N 13	Drake rd Croy
40 F 6	Drake rd Harrow
93 O 8	Drake rd SE4
8 B 6	Drake st Enf
92 F 6	Drakefell rd SE14
107 O 6	Drakefield rd SW17
48 H 12	Drakeley ct N5
66 H 5	Drakes wlk E6
107 X 18	Drakewood rd SW16
81 P 11	Draper clo Blvdr
51 V 13	Drapers rd E15
7 V 8	Drapers rd Enf
151 T 4	Drappers rd SE16
76 K 4	Drawdock rd SE10
79 W 13	Drawell clo SE18
104 F 18	Drax av SW20
105 T 14	Draxmont appr SW19
34 G 19	Draycott rd E11
24 B 18	Draycott av Harrow
146 K 6	Draycott av SW3
147 N 7	Draycott av SW3
24 C 18	Draycott clo Harrow
87 V 4	Draycott ms SW6
87 V 4	Draycott ms SW6
147 N 7	Draycott pl SW3
147 O 6	Draycott ter SW3
129 P 16	Drayford clo W9
137 V 18	Drayson ms W8
59 Z 20	Drayton av W13
59 V 19	Drayton Bridge rd W7
17 W 2	Drayton gdns N21
146 B 9	Drayton gdns SW10
59 Z 19	Drayton gdns W13
72 B 1	Drayton Green rd W13
59 Z 19	Drayton grn W13
59 Z 19	Drayton gro W13
48 G 15	Drayton pk N5
156 K 2	Drayton rd Croy
51 X 3	Drayton rd E11
31 S 8	Drayton rd N17
62 E 3	Drayton rd NW10
60 A 19	Drayton rd W13
24 C 17	Drayton way Harrow
77 O 9	Dreadnought st SE10
47 X 2	Dresden rd N19
93 O 14	Dressington av SE4
14 D 19	Drew av NW7
41 W 17	Drew gdns Grnfd
78 D 3	Drew rd E16
108 A 5	Drewstead rd SW16
107 X 4	Drewstead rd SW16
63 W 5	Driffield rd E3
107 P 20	Driftway the Mitch
40 K 6	Drinkwater rd Harrow
54 L 20	Drive the Bark
4 E 12	Drive the Barnt
5 P 20	Drive the Barnt
125 N 2	Drive the Becknhm
21 Y 3	Drive the Buck HI
97 W 18	Drive the Bxly
114 J 19	Drive the Chisl
33 S 11	Drive the E17
34 E 9	Drive the E18
20 K 3	Drive the E4
12 E 15	Drive the Edg
8 C 7	Drive the Enf
152 C 14	Drive the Epsom
81 V 18	Drive the Erith
40 H 2	Drive the Harrow
22 H 20	Drive the Harrow
35 R 18	Drive the Ilf
53 T 2	Drive the Ilf
83 P 4	Drive the Islwth
103 V 19	Drive the Kingst
120 E 11	Drive the Mrdn
16 H 20	Drive the N11
14 L 20	Drive the N3
28 L 14	Drive the N6
27 S 20	Drive the NW11
45 T 1	Drive the NW11
38 L 3	Drive the Rom
39 N 2	Drive the Rom
115 R 9	Drive the Sidcp
116 J 18	Drive the Surb
122 C 6	Drive the SW16
104 M 18	Drive the SW20
123 N 8	Drive the Thntn Hth
125 W 18	Drive the W Wkhm
61 X 17	Drive the W3
155 X 20	Drive the Wallgtn
43 V 8	Drive the Wemb
109 X 8	Droitwich clo SE26
23 V 1	Dromey gdns Harrow
87 S 16	Dromore rd SW15
55 T 14	Dronfield gdns Dgnhm
128 J 14	Droop st W10
128 M 15	Droop st W10
75 N 18	Drover la SE15
151 Y 17	Drover la SE15
157 N 12	Drovers rd S Croy
91 T 16	Druce rd SE21
142 L 16	Druid st SE1
143 O 19	Druid st SE1
125 Y 8	Druids way Brom
143 P 5	Drum st E1
152 A 3	Drumaline ridge Worc Pk
38 M 14	Drummond av Rom
99 R 2	Drummond clo Erith
132 E 12	Drummond cres NW1
23 W 2	Drummond dri Stanm
148 F 10	Drummond ga SW1
148 F 10	Drummond ga SW1
156 L 2	Drummond rd Croy
34 K 18	Drummond rd E11
38 L 13	Drummond rd Rom
151 W 1	Drummond rd SE16
143 W 20	Drummond rd SE16
132 C 14	Drummond st NW1
21 W 8	Drummonds the Buck HI
156 F 3	Drury cres CR0
140 L 5	Drury la WC2
41 N 2	Drury rd Harrow
23 N 20	Drury rd Harrow
43 X 15	Drury way NW10
87 O 8	Dryad st SE15
25 R 10	Dryburgh gdns NW9
86 M 9	Dryburgh rd SW15
59 V 18	Dryden av W7
149 V 6	Dryden ct SE11
8 F 19	Dryden rd Enf
23 W 6	Dryden rd Harrow
106 C 14	Dryden rd SW19
96 K 1	Dryden rd Welling
140 L 6	Dryden st WC2
43 V 18	Dryfield clo NW10
12 J 19	Dryfield rd Edg
76 A 16	Dryfield wlk SE8
81 O 16	Dryhill rd Blvdr
30 B 18	Drylands rd N8
20 E 1	Drysdale av E4
93 T 3	Drysdale st SE13
134 L 13	Drysdale st N1
71 T 4	Du Burstow ter W7
136 A 5	Du Cane rd W12
62 E 18	Du Cane rd W12
11 U 18	Du Cros dri Stanm
74 A 4	Du Cros rd W3
135 P 14	Ducal st E2
135 P 14	Ducat st E2
139 X 2	Duchess ms W1
137 T 18	Duchess of Bedford's wlk W8
139 Y 2	Duchess st W1
5 U 2	Duchy rd Barnt
141 T 12	Duchy st SE1
90 B 10	Ducie st SW4
140 D 7	Duck la W1
30 H 18	Duckett rd N4
63 U 13	Duckett st E1
99 T 13	Ducketts rd Drtfrd
39 P 14	Duckling Stool ct Rom
84 D 13	Ducks wlk Twick
44 E 14	Dudden Hill la NW10
113 N 9	Duddington clo SE9
24 D 10	Dudley av Harrow
119 S 18	Dudley dri Mrdn
41 O 5	Dudley gdns Harrow
72 C 5	Dudley gdns W13
33 O 9	Dudley rd E17
40 M 6	Dudley rd Harrow
41 N 5	Dudley rd Harrow
54 A 11	Dudley rd Ilf
53 Z 11	Dudley rd Ilf
116 L 5	Dudley rd Kingst
28 A 8	Dudley rd N3
129 N 8	Dudley rd NW6
85 O 6	Dudley rd Rich
70 A 7	Dudley rd S'hall
105 Y 15	Dudley rd SW19
138 F 2	Dudley st W2
50 C 6	Dudlington rd E5
146 H 9	Dudmaston ms SW3
99 X 14	Dudsbury rd Drtfrd
115 S 14	Dudsbury rd Sidcp
64 C 18	Duff st E14
134 D 17	Dufferin av EC1
134 D 18	Dufferin st EC1
23 W 16	Duffield clo Harrow
88 K 7	Duffield st SW11
140 C 7	Dufours pl W1
76 C 18	Dugald st SE8
94 A 2	Duke Humphrey rd SE3
93 Z 2	Duke Humphrey rd SE3
83 R 16	Duke of Cambridge clo Twick
154 F 4	Duke of Edinburgh rd Sutton
139 V 17	Duke of Wellington pl SW1
140 D 12	Duke of York st SW1
36 E 13	Duke rd Ilf
73 Z 13	Duke rd W4
84 H 12	Duke st Rich
154 E 8	Duke st Sutton
140 C 12	Duke st SW1
139 U 7	Duke st W1
142 G 13	Duke Street hill SE1
142 M 6	Duke's pl EC3
11 Z 18	Dukes av Edg
22 F 20	Dukes av Harrow
23 T 12	Dukes av Harrow
82 A 10	Dukes av Hounsl
102 D 10	Dukes av Kingst
102 G 11	Dukes av Kingst
29 U 9	Dukes av N10
28 A 4	Dukes av N3
27 Z 4	Dukes av N3
118 C 7	Dukes av New Mald
58 C 1	Dukes av Nthlt
73 Z 15	Dukes av W4
100 D 11	Dukes clo Hampt
66 K 3	Dukes ct E6
47 R 3	Dukes Head yd N6
137 V 17	Dukes la W8
29 T 10	Dukes ms N10
139 U 4	Dukes ms W1
98 K 20	Dukes orchard Bxly
66 J 3	Dukes rd E6
61 P 12	Dukes rd W3
132 G 14	Dukes rd WC1
110 F 10	Dukesthorpe rd SE26
48 E 5	Dulas st N4
136 J 8	Dulford st W11
88 M 14	Dulka rd SW11
114 D 4	Dulverton rd SE9
109 T 1	Dulwich comm SE21
91 U 19	Dulwich pk SE21
90 G 14	Dulwich rd SE24
91 P 15	Dulwich village SE21
109 S 11	Dulwich Wood av SE19
109 T 11	Dulwich Wood pk SE19
90 B 17	Dumbarton rd SW2
117 T 2	Dumbleton clo Kingst
95 V 9	Dumbreck rd SE9
49 T 8	Dumont rd N16
131 T 1	Dumpton pl NW1
124 J 8	Dunbar av Becknhm
56 E 10	Dunbar av Dgnhm
122 F 5	Dunbar av SW16
56 F 15	Dunbar gdns Dgnhm
52 G 18	Dunbar rd E7
30 H 5	Dunbar rd N22
117 W 8	Dunbar rd New Mald
108 L 7	Dunbar st SE27
95 S 6	Dunblane rd SE9
46 M 14	Dunboyne rd NW3
135 V 16	Dunbridge st E2
5 P 15	Duncan clo Barnt
62 A 17	Duncan gro W3
135 V 4	Duncan rd E8
84 L 10	Duncan rd Rich
133 V 8	Duncan st N1
133 W 9	Duncan ter N1
140 J 11	Duncannon st WC2
63 N 18	Dunch st E1
143 Y 7	Dunch st E1
92 J 18	Duncombe hill SE23
47 X 4	Duncombe rd N19
93 Y 16	Duncrievie rd SE13
79 U 20	Duncroft SE18
92 G 8	Dundalk rd SE4
92 C 4	Dundas rd SE15
65 V 7	Dundee rd E13
124 A 12	Dundee rd SE25
143 X 15	Dundee st E1
152 K 9	Dundela gdns Worc Pk
128 F 6	Dundonald rd NW10
105 U 19	Dundonald rd SW19
51 S 9	Dunedin rd E10
54 C 3	Dunedin rd N7
108 K 7	Dunelm gro SE27
63 S 17	Dunelm st E1
111 S 11	Dunfield gdns SE6
111 S 11	Dunfield rd SE6
48 D 13	Dunford rd N7
86 F 9	Dungarvan av SW15
122 F 13	Dunheved clo Thntn Hth
122 F 14	Dunheved Rd west Thntn Hth
122 F 13	Dunheved Road north Thntn Hth
122 G 14	Dunheved Road south Thntn Hth
18 G 10	Dunholme grn N9
18 G 12	Dunholme la N9
18 G 12	Dunholme rd N9
143 S 1	Dunk st E1
55 S 6	Dunkeld rd Dgnhm
123 O 8	Dunkeld rd SE25
113 O 8	Dunkeld rd SE9
108 L 9	Dunkirk st SE27
50 D 13	Dunlace rd E5
82 F 19	Dunleary clo Hounsl
159 W 14	Dunley dri Croy
31 O 10	Dunloe av N17
134 M 9	Dunloe st E2
135 P 9	Dunloe st E2
151 P 3	Dunlop pl SE16
128 K 5	Dunmore rd NW6
119 N 1	Dunmore rd SW20
105 O 20	Dunmore rd SW20
100 A 8	Dunmow clo Felt
37 S 15	Dunmow clo Rom
51 X 13	Dunmow rd E15
51 X 13	Dunmow rd E15
134 A 3	Dunmow wlk N1
26 C 3	Dunn mead NW9
49 U 14	Dunn st E8
57 U 14	Dunningford clo Hornch
66 E 17	Dunnock rd E6
47 V 14	Dunollie rd NW5
92 D 18	Dunoon rd SE23
7 U 8	Dunraven dri Enf
74 H 2	Dunraven rd W12
139 S 8	Dunraven st W1
144 E 3	Dunsany rd W14
159 T 17	Dunsfold way Croy
49 T 3	Dunsmure rd N16
35 Y 8	Dunspring la Ilf
131 V 20	Dunstable ms W1
84 K 11	Dunstable rd Rich
104 L 16	Dunstall rd SW20
45 V 5	Dunstall rd NW11
91 Z 15	Dunstans gro SE22
91 Y 17	Dunstans rd SE22
119 P 19	Dunster av Mrdn
4 D 15	Dunster clo Barnt
38 J 7	Dunster clo Rom
142 K 8	Dunster ct EC3
43 W 4	Dunster dri NW9
129 P 1	Dunster gdns NW6
40 B 9	Dunster way Harrow
28 C 9	Dunston clo N2
135 N 5	Dunston rd E8
89 P 6	Dunston rd SW11
134 M 4	Dunston st E8
33 R 20	Dunton rd E10
39 O 13	Dunton rd Rom
150 M 8	Dunton rd SE1
151 O 5	Dunton rd SE1
106 A 1	Duntshill rd SW18
95 V 11	Dunvegan rd SE9
98 B 2	Dunwich rd Bxly Hth
139 R 18	Duplex ride SW1
119 P 3	Dupont rd SW20
63 X 16	Dupont st E14
156 J 8	Duppas av Croy
156 K 7	Duppas Hill la Croy
156 G 7	Duppas Hill rd Croy
156 J 7	Duppas Hill ter Croy
156 H 7	Duppas rd Croy
77 U 13	Dupree rd SE7
120 L 20	Durand clo Carsh
154 M 1	Durand clo Carsh
90 D 2	Durand gdns SW9
61 U 1	Durand way NW10
135 S 11	Durant st E2
9 S 13	Durants Park av Enf

94 H 9	Ebdon way SE3
134 E 13	Ebenezer st N1
121 U 1	Ebenezer wlk SW16
150 L 15	Ebley clo SE15
88 B 12	Ebner st SW18
134 M 16	Ebor st E2
24 F 19	Ebrington rd Harrow
92 G 19	Ebsworth st SE23
48 B 10	Eburne rd N7
147 W 9	Ebury br SW1
147 V 11	Ebury Bridge rd SW1
147 W 4	Ebury Mews east SW1
147 W 5	Ebury ms SW1
147 V 7	Ebury sq SW1
147 V 6	Ebury st SW1
88 L 9	Eccles rd SW11
17 S 16	Ecclesbourne clo N13
17 S 16	Ecclesbourne gdns N13
122 L 11	Ecclesbourne rd Thntn Hth
134 B 2	Ecclesbourne rd N1
147 Y 5	Eccleston br SW1
5 Y 15	Eccleston clo Barnt
37 O 20	Eccleston cres Rom
55 P 1	Eccleston cres Rom
147 V 2	Eccleston ms SW1
147 W 6	Eccleston pl SW1
71 X 2	Eccleston rd W13
147 Z 7	Eccleston sq SW1
147 Z 7	Eccleston Square ms SW1
147 X 5	Eccleston st SW1
42 K 15	Ecclestone ms Wemb
43 N 15	Ecclestone pl Wemb
20 D 6	Echo Heights E4
135 P 18	Eckersley st E1
133 R 7	Eckford st N1
75 S 19	Eckington gdns SE16
88 J 10	Eckstein rd SW11
65 U 14	Eclipse rd E13
111 Y 5	Ector rd SE6
129 U 18	Edbrooke rd W9
87 W 4	Eddiscombe rd SW6
38 G 19	Eddy clo Rom
92 J 14	Eddystone rd SE4
100 E 8	Ede clo Hounsl
60 F 4	Eden clo Wemb
33 S 15	Eden gro E17
48 D 15	Eden gro N7
124 K 8	Eden Park av Becknhm
125 O 11	Eden Park av Becknhm
125 T 13	Eden pk Becknhm
124 G 8	Eden rd Becknhm
157 O 8	Eden rd Croy
33 S 15	Eden rd E17
108 K 11	Eden rd SE27
116 J 9	Eden st Kingst
124 M 12	Eden way Becknhm
125 O 14	Eden way Becknhm
63 T 1	Edenbridge rd E9
18 E 1	Edenbridge rd Enf
107 T 15	Edencourt rd SW16
99 O 4	Edendale rd Bxly Hth
152 E 4	Edenfield gdns Worc Pk
87 U 7	Edenhurst av SW6
74 B 19	Edensor gdns W4
74 A 19	Edensor rd W4
107 P 18	Edenvale rd Mitch
88 C 6	Edenvale st SW6
133 Z 4	Eder wlk N1
122 E 5	Ederline av SW16
64 D 8	Edgar rd E3
64 D 9	Edgar rd E3
82 E 18	Edgar rd Hounsl
37 V 20	Edgar rd Rom
157 O 20	Edgar rd Rom
87 S 2	Edgarley ter SW6
27 X 11	Edge Hill av N3
78 M 16	Edge Hill SE18
105 O 17	Edge hill SW19
108 J 13	Edge Point clo SE27
137 U 14	Edge st W8
113 N 19	Edgeborough way Chisl
114 A 10	Edgebury Chisl
113 Z 10	Edgebury Chisl
114 B 9	Edgebury wlk Chisl
103 X 18	Edgecombe clo Kingst
158 E 18	Edgecoombe S Croy
31 R 15	Edgecot gro N15
73 U 4	Edgecote W3
54 L 20	Edgefield av Bark
56 E 12	Edgehill gdns Dgnhm
114 B 9	Edgehill rd Chisl
121 R 1	Edgehill rd Mitch

156 H 20	Edgehill rd S Croy
60 C 15	Edgehill rd W13
88 A 11	Edgel st SW18
89 X 8	Edgeley la SW4
89 X 8	Edgeley rd SW4
124 G 19	Edgewood grn Croy
26 G 15	Edgeworth av NW4
26 F 15	Edgeworth clo NW4
26 G 15	Edgeworth cres NW4
5 X 13	Edgeworth rd Barnt
94 L 10	Edgeworth rd SE9
95 N 11	Edgeworth rd SE9
107 W 16	Edgington rd SW16
12 C 20	Edgware High st Edg
12 A 18	Edgware rd Edg
44 K 5	Edgware rd NW2
26 C 17	Edgware rd NW9
25 W 9	Edgware rd NW9
130 F 19	Edgware rd W2
138 K 3	Edgware rd W2
139 N 6	Edgware rd W2
12 B 12	Edgware way Edg
11 U 4	Edgware way Edg
12 C 16	Edgwarebury gdns Edg
11 X 3	Edgwarebury house Borhm Wd
11 Y 3	Edgwarebury la Borhm Wd
12 B 12	Edgwarebury la Edg
12 B 8	Edgwarebury la Edg
12 C 14	Edgwarebury la Edg
12 A 10	Edgwarebury pk Edg
65 V 7	Edinburgh rd E13
32 M 16	Edinburgh rd E17
18 L 15	Edinburgh rd N18
154 E 4	Edinburgh rd Sutton
71 V 5	Edinburgh rd W7
9 P 10	Edington rd Enf
80 D 7	Edington rd SE2
131 U 2	Edis st NW1
57 T 4	Edison av Hornch
57 S 4	Edison clo Hornch
58 K 17	Edison dri S'hall
79 X 20	Edison gro SE18
126 D 3	Edison rd Brom
29 Z 19	Edison rd N8
79 Y 20	Edison rd SE18
96 K 2	Edison rd Welling
117 S 16	Edith gdns Surb
146 B 15	Edith gro SW10
51 X 14	Edith rd E15
66 A 1	Edith rd E6
29 Y 2	Edith rd N11
37 V 20	Edith rd Rom
123 P 12	Edith rd SE25
106 B 15	Edith rd SW19
144 J 6	Edith rd W14
145 N 8	Edith rd W14
113 R 7	Edith st E25
146 B 17	Edith ter SW10
145 O 8	Edith vlls W14
90 B 7	Edithna st SW9
120 J 5	Edmund rd Mitch
97 O 6	Edmund rd Welling
150 F 18	Edmund st SE5
28 H 14	Edmunds wlk N2
119 O 3	Edna rd SW20
88 J 3	Edna st SW11
75 S 18	Edrick rd SE14
12 G 20	Edrick rd Edg
12 G 20	Edrick wlk Edg
157 N 7	Edridge rd Croy
20 C 18	Edward av E4
120 F 11	Edward av Mrdn
101 N 13	Edward clo Hampt
18 H 3	Edward clo N9
5 T 16	Edward gro Barnt
131 Y 11	Edward ms NW1
75 Z 17	Edward pl SE8
5 T 16	Edward rd Barnt
112 J 17	Edward rd Brom
114 A 13	Edward rd Chisl
123 T 16	Edward rd Croy
32 G 16	Edward rd E17
101 N 12	Edward rd Hampt
23 N 11	Edward rd Harrow
37 X 18	Edward rd Rom
110 F 16	Edward rd SE20
133 N 6	Edward sq N1
65 S 13	Edward st E16
76 A 17	Edward st SE8
75 Z 17	Edward st SE8
65 O 1	Edward Temme av E15
145 R 3	Edwards sq W8
153 O 3	Edwards clo Worc Pk
48 H 19	Edwards cotts N1
49 P 8	Edwards la N16

139 T 6	Edwards ms W1
81 R 9	Edwards rd Blvdr
133 N 6	Edwards sq N1
66 K 8	Edwin av E6
81 O 17	Edwin clo Bxly Hth
12 K 20	Edwin rd Edg
101 U 1	Edwin rd Twick
65 S 15	Edwin st E16
50 K 12	Edwin's mead E9
35 P 16	Edwina gdns Ilf
4 A 18	Edwyn clo Barnt
145 U 19	Effie pl SW6
145 U 19	Effie rd SW6
154 B 17	Effingham clo Sutton
122 D 18	Effingham rd Croy
30 H 14	Effingham rd N8
94 B 13	Effingham rd SE12
116 C 18	Effingham rd Surb
106 J 12	Effort st SW17
90 G 13	Effra pde SW2
106 B 14	Effra rd SW19
105 Z 14	Effra rd SW19
90 E 13	Effra rd SW2
151 W 10	Egan way SE16
131 T 3	Egbert pl NW1
131 T 2	Egbert st NW1
146 L 4	Egerton cres SW3
76 E 20	Egerton dri SE10
93 S 1	Egerton dri SE10
54 K 10	Egerton gdns Ilf
146 L 3	Egerton Gdns ms SW3
128 C 5	Egerton gdns NW10
62 M 3	Egerton gdns NW10
26 K 13	Egerton gdns NW4
146 K 4	Egerton gdns SW3
60 B 17	Egerton gdns W13
146 L 3	Egerton pl SW3
31 U 20	Egerton rd N16
118 E 8	Egerton rd New Mald
123 R 7	Egerton rd SE25
83 U 17	Egerton rd Twick
60 L 1	Egerton rd Wemb
146 K 3	Egerton ter SW3
153 R 3	Egham clo Sutton
153 R 4	Egham cres Sutton
65 W 14	Egham rd E13
88 C 14	Eglantine rd SW18
120 A 15	Egleston rd Mrdn
20 K 2	Eglington rd E4
78 M 19	Eglinton hill SE18
78 K 17	Eglinton rd SE18
86 L 8	Egliston ms SW15
86 L 8	Egliston rd SW15
117 O 20	Egmont av Surb
118 E 7	Egmont rd New Mald
117 O 20	Egmont rd Surb
154 C 18	Egmont rd Sutton
75 T 20	Egmont st SE14
108 G 7	Egremont rd SE27
53 U 11	Eighth av E12
123 P 12	Eileen rd SE25
66 D 14	Eisenhower dri E6
47 N 14	Elaine gro NW5
90 J 5	Elam clo SE5
90 J 5	Elam st SE5
156 H 5	Eland rd Croy
89 N 7	Eland rd SW11
150 C 5	Eland rd SW17
88 C 4	Elbe st SW6
121 W 15	Elberon av Croy
123 X 11	Elborough rd SE25
105 X 2	Elborough st SW18
65 T 19	Elbury dri E16
146 L 19	Elcho st SW11
151 V 18	Elcot av SE15
30 A 17	Elder av N8
108 M 13	Elder rd SE27
134 M 19	Elder st E1
72 K 7	Elderberry rd W5
50 D 12	Elderfield rd E5
34 H 15	Elderfield wlk E11
125 P 13	Elderslie clo Becknhm
95 X 14	Elderslie rd SE9
110 H 10	Elderton rd SE26
121 U 1	Eldertree pl Mitch
121 T 2	Eldertree way Mitch
158 D 2	Eldon av Croy
70 G 19	Eldon av Hounsl
46 G 14	Eldon gro NW3
123 Z 8	Eldon pk SE25
32 L 14	Eldon rd E17
30 K 5	Eldon rd N22
19 O 7	Eldon rd N9
146 A 2	Eldon rd W8
145 Z 2	Eldon rd W8
160 G 1	Eldon st EC2
142 H 1	Eldon st EC2
61 S 7	Eldon way NW10
67 U 3	Eldred rd Bark

14 B 15	Eleanor cres NW7
4 B 18	Eleanor gdns Barnt
56 A 8	Eleanor gdns Dgnhm
86 C 8	Eleanor gro SW13
52 D 19	Eleanor rd E15
49 Z 18	Eleanor rd E8
17 N 20	Eleanor rd N11
64 A 9	Eleanor st E3
64 B 10	Eleanor st E3
90 E 10	Electric av SW9
116 F 15	Electric pde Surb
149 Y 3	Elephant and Castle SE1
75 O 5	Elephant la SE16
143 Z 17	Elephant rd SE17
150 A 4	Elephant rd SE17
72 D 6	Elers rd W13
19 R 16	Eley rd N18
63 R 19	Elf row E1
101 V 13	Elfin gro Tedd
90 M 13	Elfindale rd SE24
91 N 14	Elfindale rd SE24
94 J 9	Elford clo SE3
48 G 12	Elford rd N5
111 O 9	Elfrida cres SE6
59 T 13	Elfwine rd W7
117 R 19	Elgar av Surb
122 A 5	Elgar av SW16
72 K 5	Elgar av W5
11 S 2	Elgar clo Borehm Wd
75 W 7	Elgar st SE16
24 A 8	Elgin av Harrow
130 A 12	Elgin av W9
129 T 17	Elgin av W9
136 L 8	Elgin cres W11
137 N 7	Elgin cres W11
129 Z 12	Elgin Mews north W9
130 A 13	Elgin Mews south W9
136 M 5	Elgin ms W11
157 V 2	Elgin rd Croy
123 V 20	Elgin rd Croy
54 J 1	Elgin rd Ilf
29 V 7	Elgin rd N22
154 D 6	Elgin rd Sutton
155 U 13	Elgin rd Wallgtn
113 N 19	Elham clo Chisl
133 W 10	Elia st N1
149 S 16	Elias pl SE11
95 V 10	Elibank rd SE9
65 P 10	Elim way E13
110 A 3	Eliot bank SE23
40 J 6	Eliot dri Harrow
86 F 11	Eliot gdns SW15
93 V 5	Eliot hill SE13
93 V 5	Eliot pk SE13
93 Y 5	Eliot pl SE3
55 W 13	Eliot rd Dgnhm
93 X 5	Eliot vale SE3
7 X 10	Elizabeth av Enf
54 E 6	Elizabeth av Ilf
134 D 2	Elizabeth av N1
147 X 7	Elizabeth br SW1
4 B 12	Elizabeth clo Barnt
64 D 17	Elizabeth clo E14
38 G 5	Elizabeth clo Rom
130 D 17	Elizabeth clo W9
31 R 12	Elizabeth Clyde clo N15
85 O 2	Elizabeth cotts Rich
11 T 18	Elizabeth gdns Stanm
74 D 4	Elizabeth gdns W3
46 L 18	Elizabeth ms NW3
31 P 12	Elizabeth pl N15
66 A 2	Elizabeth rd E6
31 S 16	Elizabeth rd N15
19 O 3	Elizabeth ride N9
147 W 6	Elizabeth st SW1
95 U 15	Elizabeth ter SE9
109 O 18	Elizabeth wy SE19
65 U 12	Elizabeth rd E13
39 P 7	Elkins the Rom
129 O 20	Elkstone rd W10
30 B 20	Ella rd N8
144 F 15	Ellaline rd W6
19 N 15	Ellanby cres N18
92 C 11	Elland rd SE15
22 A 16	Ellement clo Pinn
127 O 6	Ellen clo Brom
19 P 10	Ellen ct N9
143 T 7	Ellen st E1
86 F 10	Ellenborough pl SW15
115 Y 13	Ellenborough rd Sidcp
30 K 5	Ellenborough rd N22
157 T 20	Ellenbridge way S Croy
101 V 14	Elleray rd Tedd
87 P 2	Ellerby st SW6

198 Ell–Eme

46 D 14 Ellerdale clo NW3
46 D 14 Ellerdale rd NW3
93 R 9 Ellerdale st SE13
83 O 11 Ellerdine rd Hounsl
84 J 15 Ellerker gdns Rich
62 H 2 Ellerslie gdns NW10
74 J 2 Ellerslie rd W12
89 Z 12 Ellerslie sq SW4
68 E 1 Ellerton gdns Dgnhm
68 F 2 Ellerton rd Dgnhm
116 M 20 Ellerton rd Surb
86 F 2 Ellerton rd SW13
88 F 20 Ellerton rd SW13
106 G 1 Ellerton rd SW18
104 G 17 Ellerton rd SW20
109 O 18 Ellery rd SE19
92 A 6 Ellery st SE15
125 S 4 Ellesmere av Becknhm
12 K 10 Ellesmere av NW7
34 D 16 Ellesmere clo E11
35 R 17 Ellesmere gdns Ilf
4 G 16 Ellesmere gro Barnt
63 V 5 Ellesmere rd E3
58 M 12 Ellesmere rd Grnfd
44 G 15 Ellesmere rd NW10
84 D 15 Ellesmere rd Twick
77 T 2 Ellesmere rd W4
73 X 15 Ellesmere rd W4
64 C 17 Ellesmere st E14
50 A 19 Ellingfort rd E8
51 X 13 Ellingham rd E15
74 G 5 Ellingham rd W12
82 L 5 Ellington rd Hounsl
29 S 13 Ellington rd N10
48 F 18 Ellington st N7
51 Z 20 Elliot clo E15
43 O 9 Elliot clo Wemb
126 M 9 Elliot rd Brom
127 N 9 Elliot rd Brom
26 K 19 Elliot rd NW4
130 L 1 Elliot sq NW3
39 Y 4 Elliott gdns Rom
122 K 9 Elliott rd Thntn Hth
10 M 18 Elliott rd Stanm
149 W 20 Elliott rd SW9
74 A 11 Elliott rd W4
149 X 4 Elliotts row SE11
59 W 14 Ellis ct W7
59 W 14 Ellis ct W7
77 X 16 Ellis ms SE7
120 M 14 Ellis rd Mitch
147 R 4 Ellis st SW1
77 Y 15 Elliscombe rd SE7
86 F 17 Ellisfield dri SW15
70 D 10 Ellison gdns S'hall
114 F 2 Ellison rd Sidcp
86 E 5 Ellison rd SW13
108 A 19 Ellison rd SW16
107 Y 18 Ellison rd SW16
39 Y 4 Ellmore clo Rom
107 Y 13 Ellora rd SW16
63 N 9 Ellsworth st E2
135 X 12 Ellsworth st E2
72 L 4 Elm av W5
86 C 5 Elm Bank gdns SW13
120 L 20 Elm clo Carsh
34 J 18 Elm clo E11
22 J 19 Elm clo Harrow
27 O 17 Elm clo NW4
38 G 6 Elm clo Rom
157 P 14 Elm clo S Croy
117 W 17 Elm clo Surb
118 M 8 Elm clo SW20
100 K 5 Elm clo Twick
116 K 1 Elm cres Kingst
72 K 4 Elm cres W5
22 J 18 Elm dri Harrow
8 A 2 Elm gdns Enf
121 X 6 Elm gdns Mitch
28 E 10 Elm gdns N2
62 A 17 Elm grn W3
81 Z 18 Elm gro Erith
40 G 2 Elm gro Harrow
116 L 1 Elm gro Kingst
30 B 19 Elm gro N8
45 R 12 Elm gro NW2
91 W 4 Elm gro SE15
154 B 9 Elm gro Sutton
105 S 18 Elm gro SW19
21 R 17 Elm gro Wdfd Grn
155 P 6 Elm Grove pde Wallgtn
124 A 18 Elm Grove rd Croy
86 G 4 Elm Grove rd SW13
34 J 18 Elm Hall gdns E11
110 M 3 Elm la SE6
57 Y 12 Elm Park av Hornch
31 W 18 Elm Park av N15
27 O 17 Elm Park gdns NW4
146 F 11 Elm Park gdns SW10
146 F 12 Elm Park la SW3
146 D 14 Elm Park mans SW10
50 J 4 Elm Park rd E10
17 X 4 Elm Park rd N21
27 W 2 Elm Park rd N3
123 T 6 Elm Park rd SE25
146 E 14 Elm Park rd SW3
11 P 17 Elm pk Stanm
90 C 17 Elm pk SW2
90 E 18 Elm pk SW2
146 F 10 Elm pl SW7
4 G 14 Elm rd Barnt
124 L 2 Elm rd Becknhm
51 W 8 Elm rd E11
33 V 16 Elm rd E17
52 D 18 Elm rd E7
152 E 15 Elm rd Epsom
99 W 1 Elm rd Erith
116 L 1 Elm rd Kingst
102 M 19 Elm rd Kingst
103 O 18 Elm rd Kingst
30 J 5 Elm rd N22
117 Y 4 Elm rd New Mald
38 G 7 Elm rd Rom
114 M 2 Elm rd Sidcp
85 W 9 Elm rd SW14
123 N 10 Elm rd Thntn Hth
121 P 20 Elm rd Wallgtn
42 K 15 Elm rd Wemb
119 V 16 Elm Road west Sutton
46 E 10 Elm row NW3
133 P 17 Elm st WC1
23 R 3 Elm ter Harrow
45 X 9 Elm ter NW2
95 W 15 Elm ter SE9
11 P 17 Elm ter Stanm
58 F 7 Elm Tree clo Nthlt
130 F 12 Elm Tree clo NW8
130 F 13 Elm Tree rd NW8
16 B 20 Elm way N11
44 A 10 Elm way NW10
152 M 4 Elm way Worc Pk
45 Z 8 Elm wlk NW3
39 W 9 Elm wlk Rom
118 M 8 Elm wlk SW20
119 O 9 Elm wlk SW20
31 P 14 Elmar rd N15
4 A 15 Elmbank av Brentf
17 O 2 Elmbank gdns N14
59 S 13 Elmbank way W7
81 U 12 Elmbourne dri Blvdr
107 R 7 Elmbourne rd SW17
117 W 16 Elmbridge av Surb
37 P 1 Elmbridge rd Ilf
95 S10 Elmbrook gdns SE9
153 V 8 Elmbrook rd Sutton
108 K 3 Elmcourt rd SE27
34 H 14 Elmcroft av E11
9 N 20 Elmcroft av Enf
45 W 1 Elmcroft av NW11
96 L 17 Elmcroft av Sidcp
34 J 13 Elmcroft clo E11
60 G 16 Elmcroft clo W5
22 H 11 Elmcroft cres Harrow
45 R 1 Elmcroft cres NW11
25 P 14 Elmcroft gdns NW9
50 C 11 Elmcroft st E5
17 R 17 Elmdale rd N13
124 K 13 Elmdene clo Becknhm
78 M 15 Elmdene rd SE18
117 X 20 Elmdene Surb
82 A 4 Elmdon rd Hounsl
7 P 11 Elmer clo Enf
25 R 1 Elmer gdns Edg
83 R 8 Elmer gdns Islwth
93 U 19 Elmer rd SE6
124 H 8 Elmer Side rd Becknhm
124 D 5 Elmers End rd Becknhm
123 Y 16 Elmers rd SE25
121 O 1 Elmfield av Mitch
30 A 16 Elmfield av N8
101 X 12 Elmfield av Tedd
126 F 5 Elmfield pk Brom
126 G 5 Elmfield rd Brom
32 E 17 Elmfield rd E17
20 J 7 Elmfield rd E4
28 F 9 Elmfield rd N2
70 C 8 Elmfield rd S'hall
107 P 3 Elmfield rd SW17
157 U 19 Elmfield way S Croy
12 J 15 Elmgate gdns Edg
23 X 16 Elmgrove cres Harrow
23 X 15 Elmgrove gdns Harrow
72 K 4 Elmgrove rd W5
107 R 19 Elmhurst av Mitch
28 F 11 Elmhurst av N2
80 M 17 Elmhurst Blvdr
81 N 17 Elmhurst Blvdr
34 F 6 Elmhurst dri E18
52 H 20 Elmhurst rd E7
31 T 7 Elmhurst rd N17
113 P 6 Elmhurst rd SE9
89 X 7 Elmhurst st SW4
98 F 17 Elmington clo Bxly
150 E 20 Elmington rd SE5
150 H 20 Elmington rd SE5
93 S 8 Elmira st SE13
113 U 15 Elmlee clo Chisl
66 E 15 Elmley clo E6
79 S 12 Elmley st SE18
51 V 10 Elmore rd E11
9 S 4 Elmore rd Enf
49 N 20 Elmore st N1
29 T 9 Elms av N10
27 O 17 Elms av NW4
89 X 14 Elms cres SW4
41 X 13 Elms ct Wemb
56 A 11 Elms gdns Dgnhm
41 X 13 Elms gdns Wemb
41 Z 10 Elms la Harrow
41 Z 12 Elms la Wemb
138 E 9 Elms ms W2
41 Y 12 Elms Park av Wemb
10 G 20 Elms rd Harrow
23 S 2 Elms rd Harrow
89 U 13 Elms rd SW4
86 D 8 Elms the SW13
7 Z 20 Elmscott gdns N21
112 A 12 Elmscott rd Brom
32 L 13 Elmsdale rd E17
86 H 13 Elmshaw rd SW15
28 F 12 Elmshurst cres N2
159 S 14 Elmside Croy
43 O 9 Elmside rd Wemb
24 C 13 Elmsleigh av Harrow
101 R 4 Elmsleigh rd Twick
113 V 12 Elmstead av Chisl
42 K 5 Elmstead av Wemb
43 N 7 Elmstead av Wemb
152 B 12 Elmstead clo Epsom
14 K 8 Elmstead clo N20
80 F 17 Elmstead cres Bxly Hth
152 F 5 Elmstead gdns Worc Pk
113 T 14 Elmstead glade Chisl
113 U 10 Elmstead la Chisl
99 P 1 Elmstead rd Erith
54 J 7 Elmstead rd Ilf
87 W 1 Elmstone rd SW6
82 K 4 Elmsworth av Hounsl
101 U 11 Elmtree rd Tedd
24 A 18 Elmwood av Harrow
17 O 15 Elmwood av N13
152 G 16 Elmwood clo Epsom
155 R 4 Elmwood clo Wallgtn
25 W 13 Elmwood cres NW9
41 Z 11 Elmwood ct Wemb
97 Y 18 Elmwood dri Bxly
152 G 16 Elmwood dri Epsom
59 T 18 Elmwood gdns W7
122 J 17 Elmwood rd Croy
120 M 6 Elmwood rd Mitch
91 O 14 Elmwood rd SE24
73 V 16 Elmwood rd W4
109 N 4 Elmworth gro SE21
109 N 5 Elmworth gro SE21
129 Y 18 Elnathan ms W9
32 L 7 Elphinstone rd E17
48 J 11 Elphinstone st N5
49 X 18 Elrington rd E8
97 R 4 Elsa rd Welling
63 U 15 Elsa st E1
50 D 18 Elsdale st E9
31 U 6 Elsden rd N17
53 V 16 Elsenham rd E12
105 V 2 Elsenham st SW18
52 A 11 Elsham rd E11
51 Z 11 Elsham rd E11
136 K 19 Elsham rd W14
91 U 10 Elsie rd SE22
17 Z 3 Elsiedene rd N21
92 M 13 Elsiemaud rd SE4
110 J 2 Elsinore rd SE23
88 M 7 Elsley rd SW11
89 N 7 Elsley rd SW11
82 D 8 Elsma ter Hounsl
88 M 9 Elspeth rd SW11
42 J 15 Elspeth rd Wemb
119 Y 12 Elsrick av Mrdn
124 H 17 Elstan way Croy
150 G 8 Elsted st SE17
95 V 13 Elstow clo SE9
68 L 2 Elstow gdns Dgnhm
68 L 3 Elstow rd Dgnhm
80 M 10 Elstree gdns Blvdr
81 N 10 Elstree gdns Blvdr
54 B 15 Elstree gdns Ilf
19 N 7 Elstree gdns N9
112 A 17 Elstree hill Brom
111 Z 17 Elstree hill Brom
11 T 2 Elstree Hill south Borhm Wd
11 S 5 Elstree rd Borhm Wd
10 E 3 Elstree rd Bushey
93 R 6 Elswick rd SE13
88 C 3 Elswick st SW6
130 J 4 Elsworthy rd NW3
130 L 1 Elsworthy ri NW3
130 L 3 Elsworthy ter NW3
88 F 12 Elsynge rd SW18
95 V 4 Eltham comm SE18
94 L 12 Eltham Green rd SE9
94 M 13 Eltham grn SE9
95 T 14 Eltham High st SE9
95 N 14 Eltham hill SE9
95 S 18 Eltham pal SE9
94 L 16 Eltham Palace rd SE9
95 N 16 Eltham Palace rd SE9
95 X 11 Eltham Park gdns SE9
96 A 11 Eltham pk SE9
94 F 12 Eltham rd SE12
150 E 8 Eltham st SE17
87 Y 2 Elthiron rd SW6
71 X 6 Elthorne av W7
71 X 6 Elthorne Park rd W7
25 Y 20 Elthorne rd NW9
25 Y 19 Elthorne way NW9
93 Y 16 Elthruda rd SE13
53 Y 12 Eltisley rd Ilf
4 J 17 Elton av Barnt
41 V 18 Elton av Grnfd
42 C 14 Elton av Wemb
102 E 19 Elton clo Kingst
49 R 14 Elton pl N16
103 O 20 Elton rd Kingst
88 D 10 Eltringham st SW18
146 C 2 Elvaston ms SW7
146 C 2 Elvaston pl SW7
61 P 5 Elveden pl NW10
61 P 6 Elveden rd NW10
17 N 18 Elvendon rd N13
93 R 5 Elverson rd SE8
148 E 4 Elverton st SW1
126 C 11 Elvington grn Brom
26 A 4 Elvington la NW9
110 G 13 Elvino rd SE26
44 L 16 Elvis rd NW2
125 U 8 Elwill way Becknhm
135 R 12 Elwin st E2
48 J 10 Elwood st N5
94 F 19 Elwyn gdns SE12
9 T 5 Ely clo Erith
118 E 2 Ely clo New Mald
56 L 9 Ely gdns Dgnhm
35 R 20 Ely gdns Ilf
141 U 2 Ely pl EC1
123 O 11 Ely rd Croy
33 U 20 Ely rd E10
30 F 19 Elyne rd N4
155 T 18 Elystan clo Wallgtn
146 M 8 Elystan pl SW3
147 N 8 Elystan pl SW3
146 K 7 Elystan st SW3
133 S 5 Elystan wk N1
61 W 18 Emanuel av W3
143 V 19 Emba st SE16
147 S 13 Embankment gdns SW3
140 L 13 Embankment pl WC2
87 O 6 Embankment the SW15
101 Z 1 Embankment the Twick
93 R 10 Embleton rd SE13
100 E 13 Embleton wlk Hampt
10 L 14 Embry clo Stanm
10 M 18 Embry dri Stanm
10 L 15 Embry way Stanm
88 B 2 Emden st SW6
66 C 18 Emerald clo E16
56 D 5 Emerald gdns Dgnhm
133 O 19 Emerald st WC1
24 M 20 Emerson gdns Harrow
35 W 20 Emerson rd Ilf
53 X 1 Emerson rd Ilf
142 A 12 Emerson st SE1
148 C 3 Emery Hill st SW1

141 T 20 Emery st SE1
81 Y 18 Emes rd Erith
48 G 13 Emily pl N7
65 P 18 Emily st E16
74 C 6 Emlyn gdns W12
74 B 6 Emlyn rd W12
65 P 8 Emma rd E13
135 V 8 Emma st E2
107 V 2 Emmanuel rd SW12
75 Z 1 Emmett st E14
36 C 16 Emmott av Ilf
63 V 12 Emmott clo E1
28 C 19 Emmott clo NW11
146 A 4 Emperors SW7
145 Z 4 Emperors ga SW7
18 A 19 Empire av N18
17 Y 18 Empire av N18
60 E 3 Empire rd Grnfd
43 O 11 Empire way Wemb
76 J 11 Empire Wharf rd E14
34 C 2 Empress av Wfdf Grn
52 M 7 Empress av E12
53 N 7 Empress av E12
33 P 2 Empress av E4
53 V 7 Empress av Ilf
113 Y 14 Empress dri Chisl
145 U 12 Empress pl SW5
150 B 13 Empress st SE17
64 F 12 Empson st E3
19 O 5 Emsworth clo N9
36 A 7 Emsworth rd Ilf
108 C 4 Emsworth st SW2
89 R 5 Emu rd SW8
122 A 5 Ena rd SW16
121 Z 6 Ena rd SW16
128 L 15 Enbrook st W10
68 A 7 Endeavour way Bark
121 X 16 Endeavour way Croy
106 A 9 Endeavour way SW19
140 J 5 Endell st WC2
76 L 13 Enderby st SE10
23 S 6 Enderley rd Harrow
26 G 14 Endersleigh gdns NW4
20 F 8 Endlebury rd E4
89 O 17 Endlesham rd SW12
53 U 5 Endsleigh gdns Ilf
116 E 16 Endsleigh gdns Surb
132 F 15 Endsleigh gdns WC1
132 F 16 Endsleigh pl WC1
70 D 10 Endsleigh rd S'hall
71 Y 1 Endsleigh rd W13
132 F 15 Endsleigh st WC1
46 E 7 Endway NW3
117 R 17 Endway Surb
92 J 6 Endwell rd SE4
48 G 2 Endymion rd N4
30 J 20 Endymion rd N4
90 C 16 Endymion rd SW2
6 M 12 Enfield cres Enf
72 F 13 Enfield rd Brentf
6 L 12 Enfield rd Enf
7 O 12 Enfield rd Enf
134 L 1 Enfield rd N1
73 S 6 Enfield rd W3
72 F 13 Enfield Road east Brentf
139 N 1 Enford st W1
157 T 6 Engadine clo Croy
105 W 2 Engadine st SW18
93 T 10 Engate st SE13
14 A 19 Engel pk NW7
78 J 16 Engineer clo SE18
43 R 12 Engineers way Wemb
46 L 18 Englands la NW3
122 K 15 Englefield clo Croy
7 T 10 Englefield clo Enf
49 N 19 Englefield rd N1
93 T 20 Engleheart rd SE6
89 T 15 Englewood rd SW12
142 J 13 English grounds SE1
142 J 13 English Grounds SE1
63 Y 12 English st E3
151 P 1 Enid st SE16
48 B 11 Enkel st N7
123 Y 11 Enmore av SE25
85 Z 13 Enmore gdns SW14
58 H 10 Enmore rd S'hall
123 Y 11 Enmore rd SE25
87 N 12 Enmore rd SW15
57 V 15 Enmore av Hornch
24 D 9 Ennerdale av Stanm
26 A 16 Ennerdale dri NW9
25 Z 16 Ennerdale dri NW9
42 E 4 Ennerdale gdns Wemb
98 E 2 Ennerdale rd Bxly Hth

85 N 3 Ennerdale rd Rich
93 W 14 Ennersdale rd SE13
48 F 4 Ennis rd N4
79 R 16 Ennis rd SE18
41 U 16 Ennismore av Grnfd
74 C 11 Ennismore av W4
138 H 20 Ennismore Gardens ms SW7
146 J 1 Ennismore Gardens ms SW7
146 J 1 Ennismore gdns SW7
138 K 20 Ennismore gdns SW7
146 J 1 Ennismore ms SW7
138 K 20 Ennismore ms SW7
146 K 1 Ennismore st SW7
146 J 1 Ennismore ter SW7
152 L 8 Ennor ct Worc Pk
17 X 10 Ensign dri N13
143 T 9 Ensign st E1
95 W 17 Enslin rd SE9
146 E 9 Ensor ms SW7
9 V 11 Enstone rd Enf
156 E 1 Enterprise clo CR0
87 Z 11 Enterprise way SW18
63 O 10 Entick st E2
145 S 17 Epirus ms SW6
145 S 17 Epirus rd SW6
38 H 11 Epping clo Rom
21 U 3 Epping forest Buck HI
21 U 8 Epping New rd Buck HI
48 F 19 Epping pl N1
87 W 2 Epple rd SW6
98 H 9 Epsom clo Bxly Hth
40 E 16 Epsom clo Nthlt
156 G 7 Epsom rd Croy
33 U 19 Epsom rd E10
36 K 20 Epsom rd Ilf
119 W 14 Epsom rd Mrdn
80 C 3 Epstein rd SE28
72 A 20 Epworth rd Brentf
134 G 17 Epworth st EC2
148 H 6 Erasmus st SW1
62 D 18 Erconwald st W12
129 T 2 Eresby pl NW6
125 P 19 Eresby rd W Wkhm
52 E 12 Eric clo E7
52 E 13 Eric rd E7
44 C 18 Eric rd NW10
55 X 1 Eric rd Rom
63 X 11 Eric rd E3
159 P 7 Erica gdns Croy
62 H 20 Erica st W12
87 X 13 Ericsson clo SW18
73 Y 8 Eridge rd W4
79 T 17 Erindale SE18
79 T 17 Erindale ter SE18
38 J 3 Erith cres Rom
81 O 3 Erith marshes Blvdr
81 U 13 Erith rd Blvdr
98 G 8 Erith rd Bxly Hth
98 J 3 Erith rd Erith
92 F 2 Erlanger rd SE14
71 Y 7 Erlesmere gdns W13
31 T 17 Ermine rd N15
93 R 10 Ermine rd SE13
8 J 16 Ermine side Enf
114 C 4 Ermington rd SE9
66 D 5 Ernald av E6
83 W 17 Erncroft way Twick
108 K 9 Ernest av SE27
125 N 11 Ernest clo Becknhm
73 T 17 Ernest gdns W4
124 M 11 Ernest gro Becknhm
125 N 11 Ernest gro Becknhm
65 O 13 Ernest rd E16
117 S 4 Ernest rd Kingst
117 S 3 Ernest sq Kingst
63 U 13 Ernest st E1
104 L 17 Ernle rd SW20
87 T 13 Ernshaw pla SW15
86 M 7 Erpingham rd SW15
119 Y 3 Erridge rd S19
129 R 17 Errington rd W9
118 G 10 Errol gdns New Mald
134 D 18 Errol st EC1
39 T 13 Erroll rd Rom
154 H 6 Erskine clo Sutton
31 Z 13 Erskine cres N15
27 Y 15 Erskine hill NW11
131 R 1 Erskine ms NW3
32 L 12 Erskine rd E17
131 R 1 Erskine rd NW3
154 G 7 Erskine rd Sutton
78 E 13 Erwood rd SE7
108 G 13 Esam way SW16

113 R 10 Escott gdns SE9
78 H 11 Escreet gro SE18
129 U 14 Esendine rd W9
38 K 18 Esher av Rom
153 R 6 Esher av Sutton
115 Y 2 Esher clo Bxly
105 O 3 Esher gdns SW19
121 N 5 Esher ms Mitch
54 H 9 Esher rd Ilf
65 U 12 Esk rd E13
39 O 3 Esk way Rom
58 E 2 Eskdale av Nthlt
42 G 7 Eskdale clo Wemb
98 D 4 Eskdale rd Bxly Hth
109 P 18 Eskmont ridge SE19
44 F 1 Esmar cres NW9
151 T 8 Esmeralda rd SE1
129 P 5 Esmond rd NW6
73 Z 10 Esmond rd W4
87 T 11 Esmond st SW15
88 A 18 Esparto st SW18
81 R 13 Essenden rd Blvdr
157 R 17 Essenden rd S Croy
83 T 8 Essex av Islwth
32 G 12 Essex clo E17
119 N 16 Essex clo Mrdn
38 G 12 Essex clo Rom
86 D 4 Essex ct SW13
141 S 7 Essex ct WC2
30 K 18 Essex gdns N4
109 P 15 Essex gro SE19
74 B 4 Essex Park ms W3
15 N 20 Essex pk N3
73 X 12 Essex pl W4
67 T 3 Essex rd Bark
56 J 15 Essex rd Dgnhm
33 V 19 Essex rd E10
53 S 16 Essex rd E12
32 H 18 Essex rd E17
34 J 7 Essex rd E18
20 M 5 Essex rd E4
8 B 15 Essex rd Enf
49 N 18 Essex rd N1
133 Y 4 Essex rd N1
44 C 19 Essex rd NW10
38 H 12 Essex rd Rom
55 S 2 Essex rd Rom
61 U 19 Essex rd W3
73 X 11 Essex rd W4
51 X 1 Essex Road south E11
52 E 14 Essex st E7
141 R 8 Essex st WC2
137 U 19 Essex vlls W8
63 V 13 Essian st E1
25 N 9 Essoldo way NW9
50 M 4 Estate way E10
124 A 14 Estcourt rd SE25
145 N 17 Estcourt rd SW6
88 J 7 Este rd SW11
118 K 9 Estella av New Mald
47 N 13 Estelle rd NW3
148 F 6 Esterbrooke st SW1
17 U 2 Esther clo N21
33 Z 20 Esther rd E11
107 X 15 Estreham rd SW16
82 G 10 Estridge clo Hounsl
106 M 10 Eswyn rd SW17
107 N 12 Eswyn rd SW17
28 B 1 Etchingham Park rd N3
51 U 12 Etchingham rd E15
115 P 12 Etfield gro Sidcp
65 V 19 Ethel rd E16
150 B 7 Ethel st SE17
126 E 5 Ethelbert clo Brom
35 V 17 Ethelbert gdns Ilf
126 E 5 Ethelbert rd Brom
81 W 19 Ethelbert rd Erith
105 P 20 Ethelbert rd SW20
107 T 2 Ethelbert st SW12
88 K 1 Ethelburga st SW11
146 L 20 Ethelburga st SW11
74 J 3 Ethelden rd W12
29 U 13 Etheldene av N10
30 L 14 Etherley rd N15
91 W 17 Etherow st SE22
108 E 10 Etherstone grn SW16
108 E 10 Etherstone rd SW16
151 V 15 Ethnard rd SE15
97 Z 8 Ethronvi rd Bxly Hth
51 N 6 Etloe rd E10
70 F 16 Eton av Hounsl
15 R 20 Eton av N12
117 Y 10 Eton av New Mald
46 H 19 Eton av NW3
42 E 13 Eton av Wemb
47 N 19 Eton College rd NW3
42 E 12 Eton ct Wemb

25 R 12 Eton gro NW9
93 Z 8 Eton gro SE13
54 D 13 Eton rd Ilf
46 M 19 Eton rd NW3
84 J 12 Eton st Rich
46 M 19 Eton vlls NW3
50 H 11 Etropol rd E5
75 X 15 Etta st SE8
64 H 16 Ettrick st E14
116 M 14 Etwell pl Surb
75 R 12 Eugenia rd SE16
117 O 4 Eureka rd Kingst
134 B 14 Europa pl EC1
78 F 8 Europe rd SE18
66 E 8 Eustace rd E6
55 X 1 Eustace rd Rom
145 T 16 Eustace rd SW6
122 E 20 Euston rd Croy
156 G 1 Euston rd Croy
132 E 15 Euston rd NW1
132 E 14 Euston sq NW1
132 D 14 Euston st NW1
132 D 13 Euston sta NW1
37 U 20 Eva rd Rom
90 G 4 Evandale rd SW9
47 T 13 Evangelist rd NW5
100 G 5 Evans gro Felt
112 A 5 Evans rd SE6
33 U 2 Evanston av E4
35 P 18 Evanston gdns Ilf
51 Z 12 Eve rd E11
65 N 6 Eve rd E15
83 Z 11 Eve rd Islwth
31 T 9 Eve rd N17
92 C 6 Evelina rd SE15
110 D 19 Evelina rd SE20
120 L 2 Eveline rd Mitch
25 X 12 Evelyn av NW9
82 J 18 Evelyn clo Twick
134 E 10 Evelyn ct N1
22 A 2 Evelyn dri Pinn
84 L 9 Evelyn gdns Rich
146 E 10 Evelyn gdns SW7
58 E 18 Evelyn gro S'hall
73 N 3 Evelyn gro W5
5 Z 15 Evelyn rd Barnt
77 V 2 Evelyn rd E16
33 U 14 Evelyn rd E17
102 E 6 Evelyn rd Rich
84 K 8 Evelyn rd Rich
106 A 14 Evelyn rd SW19
73 X 9 Evelyn rd W4
75 W 13 Evelyn st SE8
84 J 8 Evelyn ter Rich
155 X 7 Evelyn way Wallgtn
134 E 10 Evelyn wlk N1
140 E 4 Evelyn yd W1
111 V 19 Evening hill Becknhm
87 S 14 Evenwood clo SW15
16 G 19 Everard av Brom
42 H 11 Everard way Wemb
74 F 18 Everdon rd SW13
64 F 14 Everest pla E14
95 S 13 Everest rd SE9
81 O 15 Everett wk Blvdr
26 D 5 Everglade strand NW9
133 P 5 Everilda st N1
49 U 11 Evering rd N16
28 M 7 Everington rd N10
29 N 6 Everington rd N10
144 H 15 Everington st W6
61 Z 9 Everitt rd NW10
48 E 5 Everleigh st N4
13 N 20 Eversfield gdns NW7
84 M 4 Eversfield rd Rich
85 N 4 Eversfield rd Rich
132 C 10 Eversholt st NW1
48 C 4 Evershot rd N4
5 R 18 Eversleigh rd Barnt
66 B 3 Eversleigh rd E6
27 W 2 Eversleigh rd N3
89 O 5 Eversleigh rd SW11
99 P 5 Eversley av Bxly Hth
43 P 7 Eversley av Wemb
7 P 19 Eversley clo N21
83 R 2 Eversley cres Islwth
7 S 19 Eversley cres N21
99 R 5 Eversley cross Bxly Hth
7 R 19 Eversley mt N21
17 R 1 Eversley Park rd N21
7 R 20 Eversley Park rd N21
104 J 14 Eversley pk SW19
109 O 17 Eversley rd SE19
77 V 16 Eversley rd SE7
116 M 10 Eversley rd Surb
117 N 10 Eversley rd Surb
158 M 6 Eversley way Croy
91 U 8 Everthorpe rd SE15

24 L 10 Everton dri Stanm
123 W 19 Everton rd Croy
33 P 7 Evesham av E17
58 K 5 Evesham clo Grnfd
153 W 16 Evesham clo Sutton
120 A 14 Evesham grn Mrdn
65 O 2 Evesham rd E15
120 A 15 Evesham rd Mrdn
16 J 18 Evesham rd N11
136 G 11 Evesham st W11
35 X 11 Evesham way Ilf
89 P 6 Evesham wlk SW11
115 U 15 Evry rd Sidcp
21 X 18 Ewanrigg ter Wdfd Grn
30 E 5 Ewart gro N22
92 F 20 Ewart rd SE23
48 A 18 Ewe clo N7
152 G 18 Ewell By-pass Epsom
152 B 12 Ewell Court av Epsom
152 G 16 Ewell Park way Epsom
116 A 18 Ewell rd Surb
117 P 20 Ewell rd Surb
153 P 15 Ewell rd Sutton
35 S 8 Ewellhurst rd Ilf
110 D 1 Ewelme rd SE23
90 F 20 Ewen cres SW2
141 Z 15 Ewer st SE1
157 U 20 Ewhurst av S Croy
153 N 20 Ewhurst clo Sutton
92 M 16 Ewhurst rd SE4
93 N 16 Ewhurst rd SE4
110 M 4 Exbury rd SE6
93 U 5 Excelsior gdns SE13
117 O 4 Excelsior rd Kings
142 L 4 Exchange bldgs E1
140 L 10 Exchange ct WC2
134 A 14 Exchange st EC1
39 P 16 Exchange st Rom
66 F 17 Exeter clo E6
53 S 2 Exeter gdns Ilf
123 T 17 Exeter rd Croy
56 H 19 Exeter rd Dgnhm
65 T 16 Exeter rd E16
33 N 15 Exeter rd E17
9 T 12 Exeter rd Enf
100 F 7 Exeter rd Felt
40 C 6 Exeter rd Harrow
16 E 3 Exeter rd N14
19 O 9 Exeter rd N9
45 S 17 Exeter rd NW2
151 N 20 Exeter rd SE15
91 U 1 Exeter rd SE5
96 K 4 Exeter rd Welling
140 M 9 Exeter st WC2
141 N 9 Exeter st WC2
75 X 20 Exeter way SE14
112 H 2 Exford gdns SE12
112 H 2 Exford rd SE12
136 B 10 Exhibition clo W12
62 M 20 Exhibition clo W12
138 G 19 Exhibition rd SW7
146 G 2 Exhibition rd SW7
128 H 20 Exmoor st W10
133 T 16 Exmouth mkt EC1
126 G 7 Exmouth rd Brom
32 L 16 Exmouth rd E17
80 E 20 Exmouth rd Welling
63 P 17 Exmouth st E1
65 O 12 Exon st SE17
150 J 8 Exon st SE17
61 X 2 Exton cres NW10
55 U 14 Exton gdns Dgnhm
141 T 15 Exton st SE1
124 F 20 Eyebright clo CR0
57 W 11 Eyhurst av Hornch
44 H 6 Eyhurst clo NW2
108 M 11 Eylewood rd SE27
91 V 17 Eynella rd SE22
136 B 4 Eynham rd W10
62 M 17 Eynham rd W12
115 V 2 Eynsford cres Bxly
54 J 7 Eynsford rd Ilf
80 F 6 Eynsham dri SE2
115 S 13 Eynswood dri Sidcp
74 E 14 Eyot gdns W6
133 S 18 Eyre Street hill EC1
90 G 2 Eythorne rd SW9
135 P 11 Ezra st E2

F

26 G 16 Faber gdns NW4
145 P 17 Fabian rd SW6
66 F 12 Fabian st E6
156 H 2 Factory la Croy
31 V 8 Factory la N17
76 F 13 Factory pl E14
78 E 4 Factory rd E16
108 A 16 Factory sq SW16
71 T 3 Factory yd W7
126 F 13 Fair acres Brom
142 M 16 Fair st SE1
143 N 19 Fair st SE1
118 A 6 Fairacre New Mald
117 Z 7 Fairacre New Mald
158 L 19 Fairacres Croy
86 F 11 Fairacres SW15
90 H 2 Fairbairn grn SW9
31 W 11 Fairbanks rd N17
31 R 10 Fairbourne rd N17
47 Y 7 Fairbridge rd N19
17 T 18 Fairbrook clo N13
17 T 18 Fairbrook rd N13
94 H 13 Fairby rd SE12
134 L 17 Fairchild st EC2
143 T 6 Fairclough st E1
54 C 18 Faircross av Bark
38 L 2 Faircross av Rom
86 K 9 Fairdale gdns SW15
152 J 20 Fairfax av Epsom
94 M 3 Fairfax gdns SE3
130 C 1 Fairfax pl NW6
30 H 14 Fairfax rd N8
130 C 1 Fairfax rd NW6
46 E 20 Fairfax rd NW6
102 C 18 Fairfax rd Tedd
101 Z 16 Fairfax rd Tedd
74 B 9 Fairfax rd W4
12 E 20 Fairfield av Edg
25 S 1 Fairfield av Edg
26 L 20 Fairfield av NW4
100 L 1 Fairfield av Twick
9 U 16 Fairfield clo Enf
57 W 6 Fairfield clo Hornch
15 S 14 Fairfield clo N12
96 K 15 Fairfield clo Sidcp
12 E 20 Fairfield cres Edg
157 R 5 Fairfield Croy
60 E 4 Fairfield dri Grnfd
23 N 10 Fairfield dri Harrow
88 B 13 Fairfield dri SW18
116 K 3 Fairfield east Kingst
30 B 17 Fairfield gdns N8
71 Y 10 Fairfield gdns W7
78 A 15 Fairfield gro SE7
116 K 3 Fairfield north Kingst
116 K 6 Fairfield pl Kingst
157 R 5 Fairfield pth Croy
125 O 2 Fairfield rd Beckhm
112 E 18 Fairfield rd Bxly Hth
98 B 5 Fairfield rd Bxly Hth
32 J 8 Fairfield rd E17
64 B 7 Fairfield rd E3
54 A 17 Fairfield rd Ilf
116 J 4 Fairfield rd Kingst
18 K 15 Fairfield rd N18
30 B 17 Fairfield rd N8
58 E 16 Fairfield rd S'hall
21 S 19 Fairfield rd Wdfd Grn
116 K 5 Fairfield south Kingst
88 A 11 Fairfield st SW18
4 L 17 Fairfield way Barnt
152 A 12 Fairfield way Epsom
116 K 4 Fairfield west Kingst
25 W 15 Fairfields clo NW9
25 W 14 Fairfields cres NW9
82 M 8 Fairfields rd Hounsl
64 B 11 Fairfoot rd E3
98 M 2 Fairford av Bxly Hth
99 N 2 Fairford av Bxly Hth
124 G 13 Fairford clo Becknhm
152 E 5 Fairford gdns Worc Pk
5 Y 10 Fairgreen Barnt
5 Z 11 Fairgreen ct Barnt
5 Y 11 Fairgreen east Barnt
124 E 16 Fairhaven av Croy
130 C 2 Fairhazel gdns NW6
46 C 20 Fairhazel gdns NW6
39 Y 14 Fairholme av Rom
27 T 12 Fairholme clo N3
27 U 12 Fairholme gdns N3
122 G 17 Fairholme rd Croy
23 V 17 Fairholme rd Harrow
35 V 20 Fairholme rd Ilf
153 V 13 Fairholme rd Sutton
145 N 11 Fairholme rd W14
49 P 3 Fairholt clo N16
49 P 3 Fairholt rd N16
146 L 1 Fairholt st SW7
52 C 19 Fairland rd E15
122 D 10 Fairlands av Thntn Hth
21 U 7 Fairlands av Buck Hl
153 Z 2 Fairlands av Sutton
97 W 5 Fairlawn av Bxly Hth
28 K 12 Fairlawn av N2
73 W 11 Fairlawn av W4
100 E 9 Fairlawn clo Felt
103 U 15 Fairlawn clo Kingst
6 J 20 Fairlawn clo N14
34 F 2 Fairlawn dri Wdfd Grn
70 F 1 Fairlawn gdns S'hall
73 W 10 Fairlawn gro W4
110 J 12 Fairlawn pk SE26
105 V 19 Fairlawn rd SW19
77 X 18 Fairlawn SE7
87 R 13 Fairlawns SW15
84 F 17 Fairlawns Twick
60 F 13 Fairlea pl W5
92 D 19 Fairlie gdns SE23
21 T 20 Fairlight av Wdfd Grn
20 J 8 Fairlight av E4
62 B 6 Fairlight av NW10
152 L 8 Fairlight clo Worc Pk
20 J 8 Fairlight clo E4
106 H 10 Fairlight rd SW17
57 Z 19 Fairlop clo Hornch
36 C 2 Fairlop gdns Ilf
130 H 14 Fairlop pl NW8
36 H 7 Fairlop plain Ilf
51 X 2 Fairlop rd E11
36 B 8 Fairlop rd Ilf
127 U 10 Fairmead Brom
117 Z 7 Fairmead clo New Mald
127 U 10 Fairmead clo Brom
12 H 11 Fairmead cres Edg
35 P 16 Fairmead gdns Ilf
122 E 18 Fairmead rd Croy
47 Z 9 Fairmead rd N19
117 T 20 Fairmead Surb
107 X 12 Fairmile the SW16
90 D 15 Fairmount rd SW2
96 D 13 Fairoak dri SE9
39 O 8 Fairoak gdns Rom
10 C 0 Fairseat clo Bushey
134 A 3 Fairstead wlk N1
77 T 13 Fairthorn rd SE7
42 G 17 Fairview av Wemb
32 H 5 Fairview clo E17
40 G 3 Fairview cres Harrow
34 J 4 Fairview gdns Wdfd Grn
90 C 18 Fairview pl SW2
7 T 6 Fairview rd Enf
31 V 18 Fairview rd N15
154 H 12 Fairview rd Sutton
122 B 1 Fairview rd SW16
12 C 14 Fairview way Edg
97 N 10 Fairwater av Welling
25 T 10 Fairway av NW9
97 Z 13 Fairway Bxly Hth
124 H 13 Fairway clo Croy
46 C 1 Fairway clo NW11
58 M 2 Fairway dri Grnfd
54 B 15 Fairway gdns Ilf
118 L 6 Fairway SW20
117 Z 1 Fairway the New Mald
5 O 19 Fairway the Barnt
127 T 11 Fairway the Brom
103 Z 20 Fairway the Kingst
18 A 11 Fairway the N13
17 Z 10 Fairway the N13
6 F 19 Fairway the N14
41 N 17 Fairway the Nthlt
12 L 9 Fairway the NW7
62 B 17 Fairway the W3
42 C 5 Fairway the Wemb
21 Z 16 Fairway Wdfd Grn
24 J 7 Fairways Stanm
102 G 16 Fairways Tedd
31 R 12 Fairweather clo N15
31 X 19 Fairweather rd N16
110 H 8 Fairwyn rd SE26
127 R 7 Falcon av Brom
9 T 18 Falcon cres Enf
88 J 7 Falcon gro SW11
88 L 8 Falcon la SW11
88 J 7 Falcon rd Enf
100 F 17 Falcon rd Hampt
88 J 7 Falcon rd SW11
65 R 11 Falcon st E13
88 K 8 Falcon ter SW11
76 D 10 Falcon way E14
24 K 18 Falcon way Harrow
57 X 20 Falcon way Hornch
140 G 5 Falconberg ct W1
140 F 5 Falconberg ms W1
129 P 11 Falconer ms W9
96 H 6 Falconwood av Welling
96 J 10 Falconwood pde Welling
158 M 18 Falconwood rd Croy
159 N 17 Falconwood rd Croy
154 A 11 Falcourt clo Sutton
134 L 10 Falkirk st N1
16 D 13 Falkland av N11
27 Y 3 Falkland av N3
123 S 4 Falkland Park av SE25
4 E 10 Falkland rd Barnt
30 H 14 Falkland rd N8
47 V 14 Falkland rd NW5
53 X 11 Fallaize av Ilf
27 Y 13 Fallesden way NW11
15 R 20 Fallow Court av N12
10 L 12 Fallowfield ct Stanm
10 K 12 Fallowfield Stanm
107 T 17 Fallsbrook rd SW16
33 P 10 Falmer rd E17
8 F 14 Falmer rd Enf
31 N 15 Falmer rd N15
20 L 17 Falmouth av E4
30 C 2 Falmouth clo N22
35 N 2 Falmouth gdns Wdfd Grn
35 P 16 Falmouth gdns Ilf
150 B 3 Falmouth rd SE1
150 E 1 Falmouth rd SE1
51 Y 16 Falmouth st E15
56 D 3 Fambridge rd Dgnhm
110 L 10 Fambridge rd SE26
145 P 12 Fane st W14
134 A 19 Fann st EC1
134 J 11 Fanshaw st N1
54 C 18 Fanshawe av Bark
56 A 15 Fanshawe cres Dgnhm
102 D 10 Fanshawe rd Rich
86 M 7 Fanthorpe st SW15
115 S 5 Faraday av Sidcp
48 D 19 Faraday clo N7
52 B 19 Faraday rd E15
58 K 18 Faraday rd S'hall
78 B 9 Faraday rd SE18
106 A 14 Faraday rd SW19
105 Z 14 Faraday rd SW19
128 L 20 Faraday rd W10
61 W 18 Faraday rd W3
96 M 7 Faraday rd Well
97 N 8 Faraday rd Welling
127 X 3 Fard clo Brom
140 E 5 Fareham st W1
120 G 2 Farewell pl Mitch
127 X 16 Faringdon av Brom
64 M 1 Faringford rd E15
95 N 1 Farjeon rd SE3
126 D 16 Farleigh av Brom
49 U 12 Farleigh pl N16
49 V 12 Farleigh rd N16
54 J 4 Farley dri Ilf
123 X 9 Farley pl SE25
157 Z 18 Farley rd S Croy
93 T 17 Farley rd SE6
86 H 19 Farlington pl SW15
87 N 8 Farlow rd SW15
88 B 20 Farlton rd SW18
22 G 20 Farm av Harrow
45 T 10 Farm av NW2
108 A 9 Farm av SW16
42 E 18 Farm av Wemb
21 Y 12 Farm clo Buck Hl
69 W 1 Farm clo Dgnhm
58 K 19 Farm clo S'hall
154 H 16 Farm clo Sutton
158 M 2 Farm dri Croy
159 N 2 Farm dri Croy
158 M 3 Farm la Croy
6 C 20 Farm la N14
145 V 16 Farm la SW6
99 X 11 Farm pl Drtfrd
137 S 13 Farm pl W8
12 G 17 Farm rd Edg
120 A 12 Farm rd Mrdn
17 X 5 Farm rd N21
154 G 16 Farm rd Sutton
139 W 11 Farm st W1
98 G 16 Farm vale Bxly
21 Y 13 Farm way Buck Hl
152 M 5 Farm way Worc Pk
153 N 4 Farm way Worc Pk
27 X 17 Farm wlk NW11
112 F 1 Farmcote rd SE12
154 J 16 Farmdale rd Carsh
77 T 14 Farmdale rd SE10
51 R 3 Farmer rd E10
137 T 13 Farmer st W8

134 F 20	Finsbury pavement EC2
48 J 3	Finsbury pk N4
30 B 3	Finsbury pk N22
134 G 20	Finsbury sq EC2
134 E 20	Finsbury st EC2
90 M 9	Finsen rd SE5
136 F 4	Finstock rd W10
57 W 17	Finucane gdns Rainhm
10 B 7	Finucane ri Bushey
118 E 13	Fir gro New Mald
100 A 13	Fir rd Felt
119 U 20	Fir rd Sutton
109 Z 8	Fir st SE26
39 O 9	Fir Tree clo Rom
159 O 7	Fir Tree gdns Croy
155 N 18	Fir Tree rd Carsh
82 C 11	Fir Tree rd Hounsl
56 K 10	Fir Tree wlk Dgnhm
8 C 11	Fir Tree wlk Enf
75 W 3	Fir Trees clo SE16
66 B 14	Firbank clo E16
92 B 4	Firbank rd SE15
41 S 9	Fircroft gdns Harrow
106 M 6	Fircroft rd SW17
116 K 15	Firebell all surb
40 D 10	Theclest url NW3
155 Z 16	Firefly clo Wallgtn
111 O 7	Firhill rd SE6
29 P 12	Firs av N10
16 A 19	Firs av N11
85 W 11	Firs av SW14
29 P 12	Firs clo N10
92 G 20	Firs clo SE23
17 Y 3	Firs la N21
18 B 6	Firs Park av N21
18 A 6	Firs Park gdns N21
15 U 6	Firs the N20
60 F 15	Firs the W5
21 S 15	Firs wlk Wdfd Grn
158 F 1	Firsby av Croy
49 W 3	Firsby rd N16
17 Y 10	Firscroft N13
69 V 5	First av Dgnhm
53 R 13	First av E12
65 T 10	First av E13
33 P 14	First av E17
8 G 18	First av Enf
152 A 19	First av Epsom
19 P 15	First av N18
27 N 13	First av NW4
37 V 14	First av Rom
86 A 7	First av SW14
129 N 16	First av W10
74 D 2	First av W3
74 D 3	First av W3
80 G 19	First av Welling
42 H 6	First av Wemb
101 S 3	First Cross rd Twick
146 M 4	First st SW3
118 L 4	Firstway SW20
152 C 11	Firswood av Epsom
152 C 12	Firswood av Epsom
87 S 3	Firth gdns SW6
121 N 2	Firtree av Mitch
152 E 10	Firtree clo Epsom
142 G 10	Fish Street hill EC3
160 G 10	Fish Street hill EC3
123 U 20	Fisher clo Croy
58 G 8	Fisher clo Grnfd
23 X 6	Fisher rd Harrow
65 R 14	Fisher st E16
140 M 2	Fisher st WC1
81 X 3	Fisher's way Blvdr
102 C 11	Fishermans clo Rich
75 U 5	Fishermans dri SE16
92 E 1	Fishers ct SE14
73 Z 12	Fishers la W4
130 F 17	Fisherton st NW8
160 F 10	Fishmongers Hall st EC4
106 K 8	Fishponds rd SW17
100 M 13	Fitz Wygram clo Hampt
27 V 10	Fitzalan rd N3
149 S 3	Fitzalan st SE11
103 Z 19	Fitzgeorge av Kingst
144 L 7	Fitzgeorge av W14
86 B 9	Fitzgerald av SW14
34 F 17	Fitzgerald rd E11
85 Y 7	Fitzgerald rd SW14
139 T 4	Fitzhardinge st W1
88 H 16	Fitzhugh gro SW18
157 Z 4	Fitzjames av Croy
144 M 6	Fitzjames av W14
4 H 14	Fitzjohn av Barnt
46 F 17	Fitzjohn's av NW3
139 X 12	Fitzmaurice pl W1
62 D 17	Fitzneal st W12
132 B 18	Fitzroy ct W1
109 S 18	Fitzroy gdns SE19
132 A 19	Fitzroy ms W1
46 M 5	Fitzroy pk N6
47 N 3	Fitzroy pk N6
131 T 2	Fitzroy rd NW1
132 A 18	Fitzroy sq W1
132 B 19	Fitzroy st W1
55 T 15	Fitzstephen rd Dgnhm
47 V 3	Fitzwarren gdns N19
84 M 6	Fitzwilliam av Rich
89 V 7	Fitzwilliam rd SW4
26 C 6	Five acre NW9
56 A 11	Five Elms rd Dgnhm
149 W 4	Fives ct SE11
90 G 5	Fiveways rd SW9
31 O 19	Fladbury rd N15
34 A 18	Fladgate rd E11
124 F 19	Flag clo CRO
23 Z 18	Flambard rd Harrow
63 V 17	Flamborough st E14
57 W 19	Flamingo Hornch
68 G 1	Flamstead gdns Dgnhm
68 F 2	Flamstead rd Dgnhm
55 T 20	Flamstead rd Dgnhm
78 C 14	Flamstead rd SE7
43 P 19	Flamsted av Wemb
74 E 8	Flanchford rd W12
106 L 17	Flanders cres SW17
66 G 7	Flanders rd E6
74 C 10	Flanders rd W4
50 E 17	Flanders way E9
143 R 9	Flank st E1
46 E 12	Flask wlk NW3
119 Z 16	Flaxley rd Mrdn
140 E 6	Flaxman ct W1
90 L 5	Flaxman rd SE5
132 H 14	Flaxman ter WC1
96 F 1	Flaxton rd SE18
79 U 19	Flaxton rd SE18
10 J 16	Flecker clo Stanm
116 D 19	Fleece rd Surb
48 A 17	Fleece wlk N7
32 L 6	Fleeming clo E17
32 M 7	Fleeming rd E17
141 X 5	Fleet la EC4
46 K 14	Fleet rd NW3
133 O 14	Fleet sq WC1
141 T 6	Fleet st EC4
135 S 18	Fleet Street hill E1
66 B 14	Fleetwood clo E16
117 T 6	Fleetwood rd New Mald
44 H 15	Fleetwood rd NW10
117 T 6	Fleetwood sq New Mald
49 S 7	Fleetwood st N16
156 F 11	Fleming ct Croy
106 L 18	Fleming mead Mitch
58 M 17	Fleming rd S'hall
149 X 13	Fleming rd SE17
83 V 9	Fleming way Islwth
68 K 20	Fleming way SE28
50 K 3	Flempton rd E10
126 J 9	Fletcher clo Brom
51 U 1	Fletcher la E10
73 W 7	Fletcher rd W4
143 T 8	Fletcher st E1
50 C 10	Fletching rd E5
77 Z 16	Fletching rd SE7
29 Z 1	Fletton rd N11
134 M 19	Fleur De Lis st E1
87 P 20	Fleur gates SW19
31 R 4	Flexmere rd N17
111 Z 13	Flimwell clo Brom
150 G 8	Flint st SE17
95 P 6	Flintmill ct SE9
150 K 9	Flinton st SE17
140 H 5	Flitcroft st WC2
143 S 19	Flockton st SE16
90 K 1	Flodden rd SE5
146 L 11	Flood st SW3
146 K 12	Flood wlk SW3
64 C 17	Flora clo E14
37 S 19	Flora gdns Rom
74 H 10	Flora gdns W6
81 P 14	Flora st Blvdr
140 L 7	Floral st WC2
7 Y 11	Florence av Enf
120 D 12	Florence av Mrdn
92 M 1	Florence cotts SE14
7 Y 10	Florence dri Enf
73 V 17	Florence gdns W4
124 G 4	Florence rd Becknhm
126 F 1	Florence rd Brom
65 R 7	Florence rd E13
65 Z 3	Florence rd E6
103 N 19	Florence rd Kingst
48 E 2	Florence rd N4
157 N 20	Florence rd S Croy
70 A 9	Florence rd S'hall
92 M 2	Florence rd SE14
80 G 10	Florence rd SE2
106 A 15	Florence rd SW19
73 X 7	Florence rd W4
72 J 1	Florence rd W5
60 J 20	Florence rd W5
65 P 12	Florence st E16
133 X 2	Florence st N1
26 L 12	Florence st NW4
92 M 1	Florence ter SE14
154 F 7	Florian av Sutton
87 U 10	Florian rd SW15
10 C 7	Florida clo Bushey
122 H 1	Florida rd Thntn Hth
108 J 20	Florida rd Thntn Hth
135 T 13	Florida st E2
24 C 4	Floriston clo Stanm
24 C 4	Floriston gdns Stanm
105 S 1	Florys ct SW19
86 M 6	Floss st SW15
111 V 12	Flower House clo SE6
111 V 11	Flower House est SE6
12 D 10	Fl... la NW1
107 O 4	Flowers ms SW17
77 Y 13	Floyd rd SE7
93 Z 10	Fludyer st SE13
151 V 10	Folair SE16
140 B 1	Foley st W1
134 M 20	Folgate sq E1
134 L 20	Folgate st E1
62 C 18	Foliot st W12
33 R 13	Folkestone rd E17
66 K 7	Folkestone rd E6
18 K 14	Folkestone rd N18
26 A 5	Folkingham la NW9
14 H 17	Folkington corner N12
64 F 18	Follett st E14
5 T 11	Folly ho Barnt
32 J 3	Folly la E17
76 H 6	Folly wall E14
108 C 17	Fontaine rd SW16
89 P 9	Fontarabia rd SW11
57 R 20	Fontayne av Rainhm
39 P 9	Fontayne av Rom
107 U 4	Fontenoy rd SW12
34 M 6	Fonteyne gdns Ilf
48 E 6	Fonthill rd N4
86 F 20	Fontley way SW15
28 D 7	Fonts hill N2
23 T 1	Fontwell clo Harrow
40 H 17	Fontwell clo Nthlt
127 V 12	Fontwell dri Brom
41 V 3	Football la Harrow
115 V 15	Foots Cray High st Sidcp
115 U 3	Foots Cray la Sidcp
115 U 9	Foots Cray pl Sidcp
114 B 4	Foots Cray rd SE9
95 X 15	Foots Cray rd SE9
143 T 8	Forbes st E1
49 X 4	Forburg rd N16
122 J 13	Ford clo Thntn Hth
41 P 1	Ford clo Harrow
21 V 20	Ford end Wdfd Grn
56 C 20	Ford rd Dgnhm
69 P 1	Ford rd Dgnhm
69 S 1	Ford rd Dgnhm
63 X 6	Ford rd E3
68 N 16	Ford sq E1
143 Y 3	Ford sq E1
63 X 5	Ford st
65 P 17	Ford st E16
126 K 5	Forde av Brom
93 W 20	Forde rd SE6
5 V 12	Fordham clo Barnt
5 W 13	Fordham rd Barnt
143 V 3	Fordham st E1
73 O 1	Fordhook av W5
129 R 14	Fordingley rd W9
28 M 14	Fordington rd N6
111 O 3	Fordmill rd SE6
17 X 5	Fords gro N21
65 T 17	Fords Park rd E16
45 S 13	Fordwych rd NW2
93 U 16	Fordyce rd SE13
56 A 5	Fordyke rd Dgnhm
142 D 2	Fore st EC2
160 D 2	Fore st EC2
18 J 13	Fore st N18
18 J 17	Fore st N18
160 E 2	Fore Street av EC2
90 J 5	Foreign st SE5
27 R 5	Foreland ct NW4
79 S 10	Foreland st SE18
144 D 7	Foreman ct W6
75 Y 12	Foreshore SE8
34 D 1	Forest appr Wdfd Grn
20 M 2	Forest appr E4
127 W 1	Forest clo BR7
34 D 16	Forest clo E11
21 U 12	Forest clo Wdfd Grn
34 A 13	Forest ct E11
21 P 6	Forest ct E4
53 O 10	Forest dri E12
33 Z 2	Forest dri Wdfd Grn
33 X 20	Forest Drive east E11
51 V 1	Forest Drive west E11
21 Z 12	Forest edge Buck Hl
26 A 14	Forest ga NW9
31 U 7	Forest gdns N17
34 A 18	Forest glade E11
33 Z 18	Forest glade E11
20 M 17	Forest glade E4
49 U 19	Forest gro E8
92 B 16	Forest Hill rd SE22
35 W 1	Forest ho Wdfd Grn
52 D 15	Forest la E15
51 Z 16	Forest la E15
51 Z 16	Forest la E15
33 X 2	Forest Mount rd Wdfd Grn
51 V 1	Forest rd E11
33 X 20	Forest rd E11
32 C 13	Forest rd E17
33 O 10	Forest rd E17
52 F 11	Forest rd E7
49 T 19	Forest rd E8
99 W 2	Forest rd Erith
36 H 4	Forest rd Ilf
19 N 5	Forest rd N9
73 P 19	Forest rd Rich
38 H 11	Forest rd Rom
119 X 18	Forest rd Sutton
21 S 11	Forest rd Wdfd Grn
33 Y 11	Forest ri E17
33 Z 13	Forest ri E17
125 O 5	Forest ridge Becknhm
21 X 5	Forest side Buck Hl
21 O 3	Forest side E4
52 G 11	Forest side E7
118 D 19	Forest side Worc Pk
52 F 15	Forest st E7
34 A 13	Forest the E11
33 X 16	Forest View av E10
52 C 1	Forest view E11
20 K 1	Forest view E4
53 P 12	Forest View rd E12
33 U 4	Forest View rd E17
96 E 20	Forest way Sidcp
21 U 12	Forest way Wdfd Grn
21 W 13	Forest way Wdfd Grn
16 K 13	Forestdale N14
92 A 9	Forester rd SE15
155 X 16	Foresters clo Wallgtn
98 F 10	Foresters cres Bxly Hth
33 X 14	Foresters dri E17
156 A 20	Foresters dri Wallgtn
155 Y 17	Foresters dri Wallgtn
110 B 4	Forestholme clo SE23
30 H 4	Forfar rd N22
89 P 1	Forfar rd SW11
100 B 13	Forge la Felt
153 S 16	Forge la Sutton
40 C 20	Forlong pth Nthlt
24 D 10	Formby av Stanm
130 A 18	Formosa st W9
129 Z 18	Formosa st W9
65 P 16	Formunt clo E16
10 J 18	Fornums acre Stanm
27 X 19	Forres gdns NW11
122 C 7	Forrest gdns SW16
110 D 10	Forrester pth SE26
139 N 5	Forset st W1
126 E 6	Forstall clo Brom
111 W 7	Forster Memorial pk SE6
124 H 6	Forster rd Bcknhm
122 L 15	Forster rd Croy
31 U 9	Forster rd N17
89 Z 18	Forster rd SW2
134 C 8	Forston st N1
123 S 1	Forsyte cres SE19
149 X 14	Forsyth gdns SE17
58 H 2	Fort rd Nthlt
151 R 7	Fort rd SE1
142 L 1	Fort st E1
77 V 3	Fort st E16
54 L 11	Forterie gdns Ilf
63 N 1	Fortescue av E8
101 N 6	Fortescue av Twick

43 S 2	Fryent way NW9
142 M 2	Frying Pan all E1
157 Z 3	Fryston av Croy
80 C 13	Fuchsia st SE2
26 A 4	Fulbeck dri NW9
22 M 8	Fulbeck way Harrow
33 T 4	Fulbourne rd E17
47 V 11	Fulbrook rd N19
75 N 6	Fulford st SE16
143 Y 18	Fulford st SE16
145 T 18	Fulham bdwy SW6
87 T 5	Fulham High st SW6
144 H 18	Fulham Palace rd SW6
87 R 3	Fulham Palace rd SW6
144 E 11	Fulham Palace rd W6
87 P 5	Fulham Palace SW6
87 U 5	Fulham Park gdns SW6
87 U 4	Fulham Park rd SW6
146 G 9	Fulham rd SW3
145 T 19	Fulham rd SW6
87 U 3	Fulham rd SW6
118 D 19	Fullbrooks av Worc Pk
55 S 11	Fuller rd Dgnhm
135 S 16	Fuller st E2
26 L 12	Fuller st NW4
01 ? ?	Fullers av Wdfd Grn
38 J 3	Fullers clo Rom
38 J 2	Fullers la Rom
34 B 3	Fullers rd E18
159 O 9	Fullers wood Croy
154 H 18	Fullerton rd Carsh
123 U 17	Fullerton rd SE5
88 C 13	Fullerton rd SW18
35 W 4	Fullwell av Ilf
36 B 6	Fullwell av Ilf
100 K 8	Fullwell pk Twick
134 G 11	Fullwoods ms N1
57 X 19	Fulmar rd Hornch
88 B 2	Fulmead st SW6
100 C 14	Fulmer clo Hampt
66 A 16	Fulmer rd E16
72 A 9	Fulmer way W13
33 W 16	Fulready rd E10
82 D 10	Fulstone clo Hounsl
94 E 5	Fulthorp rd SE3
138 A 9	Fulton ms W2
43 R 11	Fulton rd Wemb
100 L 4	Fulwell Park av Twick
101 N 4	Fulwell Park av Twick
101 P 10	Fulwell rd Tedd
60 L 5	Fulwood av Wemb
83 X 16	Fulwood gdns Twick
141 R 2	Fulwood pl WC1
105 R 1	Fulwood wlk SW19
22 H 1	Furham fields Pinn
151 T 20	Furley st SE15
121 P 18	Furlong clo Mitch
48 F 18	Furlong rd N7
40 C 19	Furlongs wlk Grnfd
88 A 18	Furmage st SW18
108 K 12	Furneaux av SE27
99 T 7	Furner clo Drtfrd
40 L 3	Furness rd Harrow
120 B 15	Furness rd Mrdn
62 G 7	Furness rd NW10
88 B 4	Furness rd SW6
57 V 15	Furness way Hornch
141 T 3	Furnival st EC4
50 D 15	Furrow la E9
14 L 19	Fursby av N3
26 D 8	Further acre NW9
112 A 1	Further Green rd SE6
94 A 20	Further Green rd SE6
37 Z 7	Furze Farm clo Rom
122 M 5	Furze rd Thntn Hth
64 B 14	Furze st E3
107 S 12	Furzedown dri SW17
107 T 11	Furzedown rd SW17
113 Z 14	Furzefield clo Chisl
77 V 18	Furzefield rd SE3
126 F 3	Fyfe way Brom
125 Y 8	Fyfield clo BR2
33 W 11	Fyfield rd E17
8 C 12	Fyfield rd Enf
90 G 7	Fyfield rd SW9
34 L 1	Fyfield rd Wdfd Grn
148 F 5	Fynes st SW1

G

99 W 13	Gable clo Dartford
22 G 3	Gable clo Pinn
100 A 9	Gabriel clo Felt
38 K 1	Gabriel clo Rom
92 G 18	Gabriel st SE23
42 M 9	Gabrielle clo Wemb
43 N 9	Gabrielle clo Wemb
43 O 18	Gaddesden av Wemb
79 T 5	Gadwall way SE18
65 N 14	Gage rd E16
132 M 20	Gage st WC1
133 S 4	Gainford st N1
41 U 15	Gainsboro gdns Grnfd
97 X 9	Gainsboro sq Bxly Hth
55 P 11	Gainsborough Dgnhm
53 W 14	Gainsborough av E12
111 N 16	Gainsborough clo Becknhm
15 N 17	Gainsborough ct N12
46 G 11	Gainsborough gdns NW3
25 O 7	Gainsborough gdns Edg
83 P 13	Gainsborough gdns Islwth
45 U 1	Gainsborough gdns NW11
85 N 6	Gainsborough rd Rich
15 O 16	Gainsborough rd N12
117 Y 15	Gainsborough rd New Mald
52 A 1	Gainsborough rd E11
64 M 10	Gainsborough rd E15
65 N 10	Gainsborough rd E15
74 C 10	Gainsborough rd W4
32 K 13	Gainsford rd E17
143 O 17	Gainsford st SE1
122 K 13	Gairgreen Thntn Hth
91 S 4	Gairloch rd SE5
47 U 17	Gaisford st NW5
114 B 2	Gaitskell rd SE9
112 G 8	Galahad rd Brom
74 F 20	Galata rd SW13
91 Z 7	Galatea sq SE15
76 F 7	Galbraith st E14
5 P 12	Galdana av Barnt
100 C 14	Gale clo Hampt
120 F 6	Gale clo Mitch
68 H 4	Gale st Dgnhm
55 V 20	Gale st Dgnhm
64 B 14	Gale st E3
33 X 2	Galeborough av Wdfd Grn
140 K 2	Galen pl WC1
74 K 11	Galena rd W6
63 N 10	Gales gdns E2
135 Y 14	Gales gdns E8
35 S 1	Gales way Wdfd Grn
88 D 17	Galesbury rd SW18
105 R 1	Galgate clo SW19
15 Y 6	Gallants Farm rd Barnt
58 A 7	Gallery gdns Nrthlt
109 P 2	Gallery rd SE21
91 R 20	Gallery rd SE21
75 N 12	Galley Wall rd SE16
151 W 6	Galley Wall rd SE16
48 J 16	Gallia rd N5
9 N 20	Galliard av Enf
18 K 4	Galliard rd N9
18 L 1	Galliard rd N9
67 Z 10	Gallions clo Bark
77 W 11	Gallions rd SE7
77 Y 12	Gallon clo SE7
158 B 16	Gallop the S Croy
154 F 19	Gallop the Sutton
79 U 12	Gallosson rd SE18
74 G 2	Galloway rd W12
7 R 20	Gallus clo N21
94 G 8	Gallus sq SE3
122 B 10	Galpin's rd Thntn Hth
37 P 20	Galsworthy av Rom
103 S 19	Galsworthy rd Kingst
45 T 12	Galsworthy rd NW2
128 K 15	Galton st W10
6 A 14	Galva clo Barnt
87 W 13	Galveston rd SW15
134 C 14	Galway st EC1
89 T 5	Gambetta st SW8
141 X 15	Gambia st SE1
106 H 11	Gambole rd SW17
5 Z 12	Games rd Barnet
87 O 9	Gamlen rd SW15
153 W 13	Gander Green la Sutton
156 B 16	Gane clo Croy
140 B 7	Ganton st W1
35 V 15	Gantshill cres Ilford
106 A 11	Gap rd SW19
105 Z 11	Gap rd SW19
61 O 17	Garage rd
139 U 1	Garbutt pl W1
133 Y 12	Gard st EC1
98 D 6	Garden av Bxly Hth
107 R 19	Garden av Mitch
12 C 19	Garden city Edg
19 Z 17	Garden clo E4
100 F 13	Garden clo Hampt
58 B 3	Garden clo Nthlt
112 H 6	Garden clo SE12
86 K 20	Garden clo SW15
90 D 7	Garden clo SW9
156 A 11	Garden clo Wallgtn
14 M 15	Garden ct N12
112 J 15	Garden la Brom
108 B 1	Garden la SW2
137 U 10	Garden ms W2
112 J 17	Garden rd Brom
130 E 11	Garden rd NW8
85 P 9	Garden rd Rich
124 C 1	Garden rd SE20
149 X 2	Garden row SE1
63 T 15	Garden st E1
148 U 10	Garden ter SW1
43 X 17	Garden way NW10
134 J 15	Garden wlk EC2
122 J 19	Gardeners rd Croy
63 U 7	Gardeners rd E3
18 E 1	Gardenia rd Enf
125 V 2	Gardens the Becknhm
22 M 18	Gardens the Harrow
23 N 19	Gardens the Harrow
22 E 18	Gardens the Pinn
91 X 10	Gardens the SE22
44 M 14	Gardiner av NW2
34 H 18	Gardner clo E11
100 F 4	Gardner gro Felt
65 U 12	Gardner rd E13
46 F 12	Gardnor rd NW3
119 Z 16	Garendon gdns Mrdn
120 A 18	Garendon rd Mrdn
119 Z 16	Garendon rd Mrdn
153 N 2	Gareth clo Worc pk
112 F 9	Gareth gro Brom
65 P 13	Garfield rd E13
20 L 4	Garfield rd E4
9 R 16	Garfield rd Enf
89 P 8	Garfield rd SW11
106 D 14	Garfield rd SW19
83 Z 20	Garfield rd Twick
64 A 20	Garford st E14
68 H 20	Garganey wlk SE28
79 U 11	Garibaldi st SE18
79 T 19	Garland rd SE18
24 J 4	Garland rd Stanm
160 B 8	Garlick hill EC4
142 C 9	Garlick hill EC4
110 J 6	Garlie's rd SE23
45 U 18	Garlinge rd NW2
32 B 2	Garman rd N17
133 T 13	Garnault ms EC1
133 U 14	Garnault pl EC1
8 H 4	Garnault rd Enf
33 T 4	Garner rd E17
143 Z 10	Garner st E1
135 U 9	Garner st E2
44 A 18	Garnet rd NW10
123 N 9	Garnet rd Thntn Hth
75 O 1	Garnet st E1
63 O 20	Garnet st E1
66 E 15	Garnet wlk E6
95 V 8	Garnett clo SE9
46 L 14	Garnett rd NW3
32 G 4	Garnett way E17
49 U 7	Garnham st N16
151 O 17	Garnies clo SE15
107 X 8	Garrads rd SW16
98 F 8	Garrard clo Bxly Hth
113 Z 10	Garrard clo Chisl
156 A 7	Garratt clo Croy
106 G 9	Garratt la SW17
88 B 18	Garratt la SW18
12 D 20	Garratt rd Edgw
25 R 1	Garratt rd Edgw
106 J 11	Garratt ter SW17
134 B 17	Garrett st EC1
10 B 2	Garretts rd Bushey
27 U 19	Garrick av NW11
84 F 12	Garrick cl Rich
88 E 11	Garrick clo SW18
157 R 3	Garrick cres Croy
27 N 9	Garrick dri NW4
79 R 9	Garrick dri SE18
27 O 8	Garrick pk NW4
58 L 12	Garrick rd Grnfd
26 E 18	Garrick rd NW9
85 R 6	Garrick rd Rich
140 J 9	Garrick st WC2
27 O 12	Garrick way NW4
140 J 9	Garrick yd WC2
78 J 20	Garrison clo SE18
39 R 3	Garry clo Rom
39 O 2	Garry way Rom
100 K 16	Garside clo Hampt
79 R 9	Garside clo SE18
102 L 12	Garth clo Kingst
119 O 17	Garth clo Mrdn
100 L 14	Garth Hampt
102 L 13	Garth rd Kingstn
119 O 18	Garth rd Mrdn
45 U 8	Garth rd NW2
73 X 15	Garth rd W4
25 N 18	Garth the Harrow
15 V 20	Garth way N12
92 F 18	Garthorne rd SE23
102 K 11	Garthside Rich
105 V 2	Gartmoor gdns SW19
54 L 5	Gartmore rd Ilf
88 B 16	Garton pl SW18
88 E 8	Gartons way SW11
144 K 14	Garvan clo W6
65 ? ?	Garvary rd E16
137 W 7	Garway rd W2
34 A 2	Gascoigne gdns Wdfd Grn
135 N 12	Gascoigne pl E2
67 R 6	Gascoigne rd Bark
159 W 20	Gascoigne rd Croy
129 T 1	Gascony av NW6
99 U 6	Gascoyne dri Drtfrd
50 G 19	Gascoyne rd E9
76 H 1	Gaselee st E14
149 R 12	Gasholder pl SE11
25 V 6	Gaskarth rd Edg
89 T 17	Gaskarth rd SW12
28 M 18	Gaskell rd N6
89 Z 5	Gaskell st SW4
133 X 4	Gaskin st N1
106 M 10	Gassiot rd SW17
107 N 11	Gassiot rd SW17
154 G 5	Gassiot way Sutton
144 H 13	Gastein rd W6
84 L 7	Gaston Bell clo Rich
63 N 11	Gaston pl E2
121 O 5	Gaston rd Mitch
75 N 8	Gataker st SE16
151 X 2	Gataker st SE16
47 Y 10	Gatcombe rd N19
138 L 19	Gate ms SW7
18 K 14	Gate rd N18
141 N 3	Gate st WC2
130 J 17	Gateforth st NW8
103 W 19	Gatehouse clo Kingst
90 D 8	Gateley rd SW9
134 J 16	Gatesborough st EC2
106 L 7	Gateside rd SW17
109 S 16	Gatestone rd SE19
62 E 10	Gateway NW10
150 C 13	Gateway SE17
100 G 5	Gatfield gro Felt
63 T 7	Gathorne rd E2
30 F 6	Gathorne rd N22
147 W 11	Gatliff rd SW1
80 A 14	Gatling rd SE2
79 Z 13	Gatling rd SE2
91 U 1	Gatonby st SE15
154 C 19	Gatton clo Sutton
106 K 9	Gatton rd SW17
17 V 1	Gatward clo N21
18 F 8	Gatward grn N9
87 V 19	Gatwick rd SW18
89 X 6	Gauden clo SW4
89 X 7	Gauden rd SW4
149 Z 1	Gaunt st SE1
40 B 20	Gauntlett clo Nthlt
42 A 14	Gauntlett ct Wemb
41 Z 14	Gauntlett ct Wemb
154 G 12	Gauntlett rd Sutton
92 C 4	Gautrey rd SE15
150 G 6	Gavel st SE17
76 A 9	Gaverick st E14
94 H 19	Gavestone cres SE12
94 G 18	Gavestone rd SE12
79 U 11	Gavin st SE18
120 G 12	Gavina clo Mrdn
63 P 8	Gawber st E2
52 A 15	Gawsworth clo E15
44 K 14	Gay clo NW2
56 J 13	Gay gdns Dgnhm
64 H 6	Gay rd E15
26 A 5	Gaydon clo NW9
35 T 9	Gayfere rd Ilf
148 J 2	Gayfere st SW1
74 E 6	Gayford rd W12
49 X 20	Gayhurst rd E8
40 E 15	Gaylor rd Nthlt

35 R 1	Gaynes Hill rd Wdfd Grn
154 M 17	Gaynesford rd Carsh
110 F 4	Gaynesford rd SE23
35 W 17	Gaysham av Ilf
35 Y 11	Gaysham hall Ilf
46 F 12	Gayton cres NW3
23 W 19	Gayton rd Harrow
46 F 12	Gayton rd NW3
88 M 16	Gayville rd SW11
108 E 1	Gaywood clo SW2
33 O 10	Gaywood rd E17
149 X 2	Gaywood st SE1
149 W 11	Gaza st SE17
36 A 12	Geariesville gdns Ilf
44 H 14	Geary rd NW10
48 D 15	Geary st N7
30 M 4	Gedeney rd N17
31 N 3	Gedeney rd N17
143 O 20	Gedling pl SE1
134 A 16	Gee st EC1
133 Z 16	Gee st EC1
65 P 3	Geere rd E15
139 V 6	Gees ct W1
113 S 6	Gefferys homes SE9
134 M 9	Geffrye museum E2
134 M 9	Geffrye st E2
151 W 19	Geldart rd SE15
49 Y 7	Geldeston rd E5
92 D 4	Gellatly rd SE14
38 G 2	Gelsthorpe rd Rom
78 L 10	General Gordon pl SE18
93 X 1	General Wolfe rd SE10
78 M 17	Genesta rd SE18
79 N 17	Genesta rd SE18
90 G 10	Geneva dri SW9
37 Y 16	Geneva gdns Rom
116 K 8	Geneva rd Kingst
122 L 10	Geneva rd Thntn Hth
20 C 15	Genever clo E4
19 N 18	Genista rd N18
86 M 13	Genoa av SW15
124 B 1	Genoa rd SE20
8 C 13	Genotin rd Enf
87 N 14	Genova av SW15
7 Z 12	Gentlemans row Enf
65 T 10	Gentry gdns E13
90 L 5	Geoffrey clo SE5
92 K 7	Geoffrey rd SE4
146 G 3	Geological museum SW7
22 F 10	Georg V av Pinn
29 O 3	George cres N10
140 L 11	George ct WC2
142 F 15	George Inn yd SE1
126 H 19	George la Brom
34 G 8	George la E18
93 S 16	George la SE13
20 B 19	George rd E4
103 X 18	George rd Kingst
118 E 10	George rd New Mald
143 S 19	George row SE16
54 B 20	George st Bark
67 N 1	George st Bark
156 M 4	George st Croy
157 O 3	George st Croy
65 O 18	George st E16
82 E 4	George st Hounsl
84 H 12	George st Rich
39 T 19	George st Rom
70 B 11	George st S'hall
154 A 10	George st Sutton
139 T 3	George st W1
71 U 3	George st W7
22 G 11	George V clo Pinn
60 B 3	George V way Grnfd
87 S 18	George Wyver clo SW19
139 V 8	George yd W1
48 E 15	George's rd N7
76 H 20	Georgette pl SE10
35 Z 12	Georgeville gdns Ilf
122 J 2	Georgia rd Thntn Hth
126 H 19	Georgian clo Brom
10 K 20	Georgian clo Stanm
43 R 17	Georgian ct Wemb
41 S 7	Georgian way Harrow
132 B 3	Georgiana st NW1
135 O 12	Georgina gdns E2
112 G 9	Geraint rd Brom
147 V 6	Gerald ms SW1
56 A 5	Gerald rd Dgnhm
65 O 12	Gerald rd E16
147 U 6	Gerald rd SW1
149 U 2	Geraldine Mary Harmsworth pk SE11
88 C 14	Geraldine rd SW18
73 P 16	Geraldine rd W4
149 V 2	Geraldine st SE1
82 G 19	Gerard av Hounsl
23 Z 18	Gerard rd Harrow
86 D 2	Gerard rd SW13
114 A 4	Gerda rd SE9
64 M 9	Germander way E15
63 V 7	Gernon rd E3
44 K 5	Geron way NW2
140 G 8	Gerrard pl W1
133 X 8	Gerrard rd N1
140 G 8	Gerrard st W1
6 H 15	Gerrards clo N14
141 U 20	Gerridge st SE1
81 S 9	Gertrude rd Belv
146 D 15	Gertrude st SW10
43 W 9	Gervase clo Wemb
25 X 5	Gervase rd Edgw
75 N 18	Gervase st SE15
151 Y 17	Gervase st SE15
111 O 4	Ghent st SE6
10 B 7	Giant Tree hill Bushey
64 H 1	Gibbins rd E15
102 K 19	Gibbon rd Kingst
92 D 5	Gibbon rd SE15
62 A 19	Gibbon rd W3
61 Z 19	Gibbon rd W3
86 H 12	Gibbon wlk SW15
43 Z 19	Gibbons rd NW10
109 O 13	Gibbs av SE19
109 P 13	Gibbs clo SE19
145 P 9	Gibbs Green est W14
12 K 14	Gibbs grn Edg
19 P 14	Gibbs rd N18
109 O 13	Gibbs sq SE19
63 R 11	Gibson clo E1
49 U 7	Gibson gdns N16
55 T 3	Gibson rd Dgnhm
133 V 4	Gibson sq N1
76 L 14	Gibson st SE10
108 H 15	Gibson's hill SW16
144 K 9	Giddon rd W14
39 V 9	Gidea clo Rom
39 V 8	Gidea park Rom
81 U 10	Gideon clo Blvdr
89 O 7	Gideon rd SW11
39 V 10	Gides av Rom
47 W 6	Giesbach rd N19
18 D 18	Giffard rd N18
76 B 19	Giffin st SE8
59 S 14	Gifford gdns W7
132 L 2	Gifford st N1
133 N 1	Gifford st N1
65 N 3	Gift la E15
25 W 4	Gilbert gro Edg
140 J 2	Gilbert pl WC1
81 R 9	Gilbert rd Blvdr
112 E 18	Gilbert rd Brom
39 T 13	Gilbert rd Rom
149 V 6	Gilbert rd SE11
106 C 17	Gilbert rd SW19
51 Y 13	Gilbert st E15
139 V 7	Gilbert st W1
106 J 11	Gilbey rd SW17
79 X 17	Gilbourne rd SE18
9 V 16	Gilda av Enf
49 Y 5	Gilda cres N16
139 Z 2	Gilden rd W5
47 O 16	Gilden cres NW5
78 J 16	Gildersome st SE18
109 T 11	Giles coppice SE19
91 R 15	Gilkes cres SE21
91 R 16	Gilkes pl SE21
65 S 19	Gill av E16
63 Z 19	Gill st E14
57 X 18	Gillam way Rainham
10 A 7	Gillan grn Bushey
64 G 12	Gillender st E3
48 G 10	Gillespie rd N5
66 D 6	Gillett av E6
123 N 9	Gillett rd Thntn Hth
49 S 16	Gillett st N16
119 V 19	Gillian Park rd Sutton
93 P 12	Gillian st SE13
47 R 15	Gillies st NW5
147 Z 5	Gillingham ms SW1
45 S 10	Gillingham rd NW2
148 A 5	Gillingham row SW1
148 A 5	Gillingham st SW1
147 Z 5	Gillingham st SW1
65 O 3	Gilman dri E15
15 Y 5	Gilmore clo Barnt
93 W 10	Gilmore st SE13
85 Z 10	Gilpin av SW14
18 H 17	Gilpin cres N18
82 K 17	Gilpin cres Twick
50 H 12	Gilpin rd E5
57 T 19	Gilroy clo Rainhm
123 O 9	Gilsland rd Thntn Hth
88 B 4	Gilstead rd SW6
146 C 12	Gilston rd SW10
111 Z 6	Gilton rd SE6
141 X 3	Giltspur st EC1
109 S 15	Gipsy hill SE19
86 H 9	Gipsy la SW15
108 M 10	Gipsy rd SE27
109 O 11	Gipsy rd SE27
80 H 20	Gipsy rd Welling
97 W 1	Gipsy rd Welling
108 M 11	Gipsy Road gdns SE27
66 A 15	Giralda clo E16
64 C 17	Giraud st E14
144 H 4	Girdlers rd W14
47 U 7	Girdlestone wlk N19
87 T 18	Girdwood rd SW18
145 R 19	Gironde st SW6
25 R 11	Girton av NW9
40 M 19	Girton clo Nthlt
159 N 4	Girton gdns Croy
40 M 18	Girton rd Grnfd
41 N 17	Girton rd Grnfd
110 F 12	Girton rd SE26
30 C 13	Gisburn rd N8
65 P 7	Given Wilson wlk E13
53 O 11	Gladding rd E12
124 H 16	Glade gdns Croy
70 J 6	Glade la S'hall
127 O 4	Glade the Brom
124 H 15	Glade the Croy
7 T 10	Glade the Enf
152 H 12	Glade the Epsom
35 T 5	Glade the Ilf
17 O 1	Glade the N21
77 X 19	Glade the SE7
153 T 19	Glade the Sutton
159 T 6	Glade the W Wkhm
21 U 12	Glade the Wdfd Grn
124 F 17	Gladeside Croy
17 P 1	Gladeside N21
31 V 17	Glademore rd N15
81 U 10	Gladeswood rd Blvdr
92 J 18	Gladiator st SE23
49 U 11	Glading ter N16
4 G 10	Gladsmuir rd Barnt
47 V 4	Gladsmuir rd N19
53 R 19	Gladstone av E12
30 J 6	Gladstone av N22
83 R 19	Gladstone av Twick
73 X 9	Gladstone clo W4
44 L 10	Gladstone Park gdn est NW2
44 L 9	Gladstone Park gdns NW2
44 G 12	Gladstone park NW2
4 C 14	Gladstone pl Barnt
21 X 5	Gladstone rd Buck Hl
123 P 17	Gladstone rd Croy
117 R 6	Gladstone rd Kingst
70 B 7	Gladstone rd S'hall
105 X 18	Gladstone rd SW19
149 W 1	Gladstone st SE1
89 T 1	Gladstone ter SW8
23 V 10	Gladstone way Harrow
112 G 15	Gladwell rd Brom
30 C 19	Gladwell rd N8
87 O 7	Gladwyn rd SW15
45 Y 19	Gladys rd NW6
63 R 20	Glamis pl E1
75 R 1	Glamis rd E1
63 R 18	Glamis rd E1
40 M 19	Glamis way Nthlt
122 A 7	Glamorgan clo Mitch
102 E 19	Glamorgan rd Kingst
124 M 8	Glanfield rd Becknhm
129 T 4	Glangall pass NW6
97 Z 7	Glangall rd Bxly Hth
151 P 12	Glangall rd SE15
21 U 19	Glangall rd Wdfd Grn
11 U 13	Glanleam rd Stanm
52 H 17	Glanparke rd E7
126 J 7	Glanville rd Brom
90 A 14	Glanville rd SW2
100 E 2	Glasbrook av Twick
95 O 17	Glasbrook rd SE9
49 T 2	Glaserton rd N16
106 M 15	Glasford st SW17
65 U 6	Glasgow rd E13
18 L 15	Glasgow rd N18
63 S 19	Glass House fields E1
63 N 10	Glass st E2
135 Y 15	Glass st E2
141 Y 18	Glasshill st SE1
140 C 10	Glasshouse st W1
148 M 9	Glasshouse wlk SE11
149 N 9	Glasshouse wlk SE11
29 W 17	Glasslyn rd N8
126 D 5	Glassmill la Brom
119 Z 16	Glastonbury rd Mrdn
45 W 16	Glastonbury way NW6
64 C 13	Glaucus st E3
101 U 17	Glazbrook rd Tedd
109 O 3	Glazebrook clo SE21
144 L 9	Glazebury rd W14
7 W 11	Glebe av Enf
24 J 10	Glebe av Harrow
120 H 4	Glebe av Mitch
21 S 20	Glebe av Wdfd Grn
24 K 11	Glebe cres Harrow
27 N 12	Glebe cres NW4
120 L 5	Glebe ct Mitch
11 P 16	Glebe ct Stanm
118 B 16	Glebe gdns New Mald
109 T 10	Glebe Hyrst SE19
24 J 12	Glebe la Harrow
146 J 13	Glebe pl SW3
120 K 6	Glebe pth Mitch
112 F 20	Glebe rd Brom
154 M 13	Glebe rd Carsh
154 M 14	Glebe rd Carsh
56 H 19	Glebe rd Dgnhm
49 U 20	Glebe rd E8
28 E 5	Glebe rd N3
30 C 14	Glebe rd N8
44 E 18	Glebe rd NW10
11 R 16	Glebe rd Stanm
11 R 17	Glebe rd Stanm
153 S 18	Glebe rd Sutton
86 F 4	Glebe rd SW13
83 W 16	Glebe side Twick
120 K 6	Glebe sq Mitch
73 Z 13	Glebe st W4
64 C 8	Glebe ter E3
94 A 7	Glebe the SE3
93 Z 7	Glebe the SE3
118 D 19	Glebe the Worc Pk
100 G 7	Glebe way Felt
159 Y 3	Glebe way W Wkhm
21 Y 17	Glebe way Wdfd Grn
34 E 8	Glebelands av E18
54 E 1	Glebelands av Ilf
36 F 19	Glebelands av Ilf
109 T 11	Glebelands clo SE19
91 S 7	Glebelands clo SE5
99 T 10	Glebelands Drtfrd
146 A 8	Gledhow gdns SW5
144 L 11	Gledstanes rd W14
10 B 7	Gleed av Bushey
87 O 9	Glegg pl SW15
105 P 4	Glen Albyn rd SW19
21 V 20	Glen cres Wdfd Grn
155 S 18	Glen End rd Carsh
156 G 7	Glen gdns Croy
107 Y 11	Glen ms SW16
65 X 11	Glen rd E13
21 V 19	Glen ri Wdfd Grn
125 Z 3	Glen the Brom
158 G 4	Glen the Croy
7 W 14	Glen the Enf
22 C 20	Glen the Pinn
70 F 13	Glen the S'hall
42 H 12	Glen the Wemb
83 R 12	Glen wlk Islwth
154 D 7	Glena mt SM1
76 H 12	Glenaffric av E14
24 K 12	Glenalmond rd Harrow
78 C 10	Glenalvon way SE18
50 C 13	Glenarm rd E5
52 A 20	Glenavon rd E15
95 Y 8	Glenbarr clo SE9
112 A 13	Glenbow rd Brom
111 Z 14	Glenbow rd Brom
7 P 13	Glenbrook north Enf
45 X 16	Glenbrook rd NW6
7 R 13	Glenbrook south Enf
116 J 15	Glenbuck rd Surb
106 M 6	Glenburnie rd SW17
60 C 13	Glencairn dri W5
108 B 18	Glencairn rd SW16
66 B 14	Glencairne clo E16
66 B 14	Glencairne clo E16
54 F 2	Glencoe av Ilf
56 E 11	Glencoe dri Dgnhm
58 A 14	Glencoe rd
58 B 11	Glencoe rd Grnfd
12 B 15	Glendale av Edg
30 E 2	Glendale av N22
55 S 1	Glendale av Rom
95 X 8	Glendale clo SE9

105 V 12	Glendale dri SW19
42 J 5	Glendale gdns Wemb
81 Y 10	Glendale rd Erith
80 J 1	Glendale way SE28
90 C 9	Glendale st SW9
87 P 7	Glendarvon st SW15
31 Z 5	Glendish rd N17
12 M 14	Glendor gdns NW7
146 F 6	Glendower pl SW7
20 K 5	Glendower rd E8
85 Y 8	Glendower rd SW14
79 Z 14	Glendown rd SE2
62 B 20	Glendun rd W3
107 V 12	Gleneagle rd SW16
11 O 20	Gleneagles Stanm
107 Z 10	Gleneldon ms SW16
108 B 10	Gleneldon rd SW16
90 A 12	Glenelg rd SW2
95 Y 13	Glenesk rd SE9
93 W 20	Glenfarg rd SE6
107 V 1	Glenfield rd SW12
72 B 5	Glenfield rd W13
72 A 4	Glenfield ter W13
149 Y 18	Glenfinlas way SE5
77 P 13	Glenforth st SE10
76 A 8	Glengall causeway E14
76 F 8	Glengall gro E14
12 F 10	Glengall rd Edg
129 T 4	Glengall rd NW6
151 P 13	Glengall ter SE15
76 G 12	Glengarnock av E14
91 U 12	Glengarry rd SE22
35 Z 16	Glenham dri Ilf
95 Y 8	Glenhead clo SE9
27 Y 7	Glenhill clo N3
95 W 12	Glenhouse rd SE9
47 P 12	Glenhurst av NW5
72 E 15	Glenhurst rd Brentf
15 U 15	Glenhurst rd N12
108 M 18	Glenhurst ri SE19
46 J 17	Glenilla rd NW3
107 Y 19	Glenister Park rd SW16
77 P 13	Glenister rd SE10
78 K 4	Glenister st E16
95 X 11	Glenlea rd SE9
9 R 9	Glenloch rd Enf
46 J 16	Glenloch rd NW3
77 T 18	Glenluce rd SE3
95 X 12	Glenlyon rd SE9
13 T 20	Glenmere av NW7
100 F 12	Glenmill Hampt
100 F 12	Glenmill Hampt
46 J 17	Glenmore rd NW3
79 X 20	Glenmore rd SE18
96 K 2	Glenmore rd Welling
68 A 8	Glenmore way Bark
154 D 7	Glenn mt Sutton
108 F 7	Glennie rd SE27
54 B 18	Glennie rd Bark
88 C 5	Glenrosa st SW6
136 B 4	Glenroy st W12
62 M 16	Glenroy st W12
92 L 8	Glensdale rd SE4
95 X 12	Glenshiel rd SE9
108 F 7	Glentanner way SW17
74 J 16	Glentham gdns SW13
74 J 16	Glentham rd SW13
124 B 19	Glenthorne av Croy
119 X 19	Glenthorne clo Sutton
119 X 19	Glenthorne gdns Sutton
35 Y 11	Glenthorne gdns Ilf
32 H 15	Glenthorne rd E17
116 L 8	Glenthorne rd Kingst
16 B 16	Glenthorne rd N11
144 A 6	Glenthorne rd W6
74 K 11	Glenthorne rd W6
119 P 12	Glenthorpe rd Mrdn
39 P 1	Glenton clo Rom
93 Y 10	Glenton rd SE13
39 P 2	Glenton way Rom
131 P 18	Glentworth st NW1
95 X 13	Glenure rd SE9
127 O 4	Glenview rd Brom
80 K 16	Glenview SE2
8 A 4	Glenville av Enf
75 Z 20	Glenville gro SE8
87 Z 19	Glenville ms SW18
103 O 20	Glenville rd Kingst
44 A 3	Glenwood av NW9
43 Z 3	Glenwood av NW9
23 W 16	Glenwood clo Harrow
39 V 14	Glenwood dri Rom

35 V 15	Glenwood gdns Ilf
43 V 4	Glenwood gro NW9
152 G 13	Glenwood rd Epsom
83 P 8	Glenwood rd Hounsl
30 K 15	Glenwood rd N15
13 O 10	Glenwood rd N15
110 M 1	Glenwood rd SE6
111 N 1	Glenwood rd SE6
124 F 15	Glenwood way Croy
76 H 11	Glenworth av E14
64 E 8	Glergion way E3
80 L 8	Glimpsing grn Blvdr
64 E 7	Global appr E3
78 K 8	Globe la SE18
75 V 3	Globe Pond rd SE16
52 B 15	Globe rd E15
63 P 7	Globe rd E2
39 V 19	Globe rd Hornch
57 W 1	Globe rd Hornch
21 Z 18	Globe rd Wdfd Grn
142 D 20	Globe st SE1
63 P 8	Globe ter E2
139 X 7	Globe yd W1
157 P 19	Glossop rd S Croy
118 B 9	Gloster rd New Mald
96 K 11	Gloucester av Welling
131 T 2	Gloucester av NW1
114 J 5	Gloucester av Sidcp
76 G 19	Gloucester cir SE10
43 X 20	Gloucester clo NW10
131 X 4	Gloucester cres NW1
73 O 20	Gloucester ct Rich
48 K 6	Gloucester dri N4
27 Y 13	Gloucester dri NW11
131 W 7	Gloucester dri NW1
131 W 7	Gloucester Gate ms NW1
154 B 1	Gloucester gdns Sutton
6 C 15	Gloucester gdns Barnt
27 U 20	Gloucester gdns NW11
53 S 1	Gloucester gdns Ilf
25 X 5	Gloucester gro Edg
138 C 6	Gloucester Mews west W2
138 D 6	Gloucester ms W2
131 O 18	Gloucester pl NW1
139 R 2	Gloucester pl W1
139 P 2	Gloucester Place ms W1
99 Z 18	Gloucester rd Dartfd
5 O 17	Gloucester rd Barnt
5 R 18	Gloucester rd Barnt
81 O 13	Gloucester rd Blvdr
123 P 18	Gloucester rd Croy
51 N 2	Gloucester rd E10
34 J 16	Gloucester rd E11
53 T 11	Gloucester rd E12
32 F 7	Gloucester rd E17
7 Z 3	Gloucester rd Enf
100 L 17	Gloucester rd Hampt
22 K 16	Gloucester rd Harrow
82 A 11	Gloucester rd Hounsl
117 R 4	Gloucester rd Kingst
31 P 11	Gloucester rd N17
18 G 17	Gloucester rd N18
73 P 19	Gloucester rd Rich
39 S 19	Gloucester rd Rom
146 C 8	Gloucester rd SW7
101 S 13	Gloucester rd Tedd
101 N 1	Gloucester rd Twick
73 X 4	Gloucester rd W3
72 E 7	Gloucester rd W5
138 H 7	Gloucester sq W2
148 B 8	Gloucester st SW1
138 C 6	Gloucester ter W2
133 U 14	Gloucester way EC1
137 U 16	Gloucester wlk W8
22 A 18	Glover rd Pinn
89 N 8	Glycena rd SW11
5 T 14	Glyn av Barnt
152 F 20	Glyn clo Epsom
123 P 2	Glyn clo SE25
115 R 11	Glyn dri Sidcp
50 F 11	Glyn rd E5
9 P 14	Glyn rd Enf
153 O 4	Glyn rd Worc Pk
149 N 11	Glyn st SE11
146 M 3	Glynde ms SW3
97 X 8	Glynde st Bxly Hth
92 M 15	Glynde st SE4
79 R 12	Glyndon rd SE18
62 B 1	Glynfield rd NW10
110 C 5	Glynwood dri SE26
8 H 3	Goat la Enf

121 N 15	Goat rd Mitch
143 N 16	Goat st SE1
145 P 19	Goater's all SW6
38 M 1	Gobions av Rom
39 N 2	Gobions av Rom
156 B 10	Godalming av Wallgtn
64 C 16	Godalming rd E14
64 M 10	Godbold rd E15
124 G 9	Goddard rd Becknhm
58 A 3	Godfrey av Twick
83 R 18	Godfrey av Twick
78 E 12	Godfrey hill SE18
78 F 12	Godfrey rd SE18
64 G 4	Godfrey st E15
146 L 9	Godfrey st SW3
82 D 19	Godfrey way Hounsl
148 M 11	Goding st SE11
106 F 2	Godley rd SW18
141 Z 7	Godliman st EC4
91 Z 6	Godman rd SE15
74 J 4	Godolphin rd W12
58 B 3	Godrey av Grnfd
159 X 20	Godric cres Croy
156 F 6	Godson rd Croy
133 S 9	Godson st N1
154 E 7	Godstone rd Sutton
84 A 17	Godstone rd Twick
80 E 6	Godstow rd SE2
126 L 7	Godwin av Brom
52 J 12	Godwin rd E7
93 Y 3	Goffers rd SE3
155 Y 8	Goidel clo Wallgtn
129 N 19	Golborne gdns W10
136 L 1	Golborne ms W10
136 L 1	Golborne rd W10
128 M 20	Golborne rd W10
12 L 19	Gold hill Edg
12 L 20	Gold la Edg
4 C 18	Golda clo Barnt
26 A 2	Goldbeaters gro Edg
12 M 19	Goldbeaters gro Edg
13 N 20	Goldbeaters gro Edg
119 Y 16	Goldcliff clo Mrdn
66 B 15	Goldcrest clo E16
68 G 19	Goldcrest clo SE28
159 X 18	Goldcrest way Croy
84 G 13	Golden ct Rich
134 B 17	Golden la EC1
71 T 1	Golden mnor W7
59 T 20	Golden mnr W7
140 C 9	Golden sq W1
12 F 15	Golders clo Edg
45 U 1	Golders gdns NW11
45 W 2	Golders Green cres NW11
27 T 18	Golders Green rd NW11
45 V 1	Golders Green rd NW11
46 A 5	Golders Hill pk NW3
45 Z 6	Golders Hill pk NW3
27 R 19	Golders Manor dri NW11
45 Z 5	Golders Park clo NW11
27 O 15	Golders ri NW4
45 W 2	Golders way NW11
79 T 7	Goldfinch rd SE28
74 K 6	Goldhawk ms W12
136 B 19	Goldhawk rd W12
74 G 8	Goldhawk rd W12
34 M 2	Goldhaze clo Ilf
130 B 1	Goldhurst ter NW6
46 D 20	Goldhurst ter NW6
129 Y 2	Goldhurst ter NW6
127 N 13	Goldie st SE5
143 U 7	Golding st E1
132 E 7	Goldington cres NW1
132 F 8	Goldington st NW1
135 R 16	Goldman clo E2
129 T 18	Goldney rd W9
143 U 5	Goldney ter E1
148 G 20	Goldsboro' rd SW8
20 F 8	Goldsborough cres E4
89 Y 1	Goldsborough rd SW8
9 V 10	Goldsdown clo Enf
9 U 9	Goldsdown rd Enf
79 V 14	Goldsmid st SE18
79 V 14	Goldsmidt st SE18
53 R 17	Goldsmith av N12
26 B 17	Goldsmith av NW9
56 E 2	Goldsmith av Rom
61 X 20	Goldsmith av W3

40 J 5	Goldsmith clo Harrow
73 Z 1	Goldsmith clo W3
25 V 13	Goldsmith la NW9
51 P 4	Goldsmith rd E10
32 G 8	Goldsmith rd E17
15 Z 16	Goldsmith rd N11
91 X 1	Goldsmith rd SE15
73 X 1	Goldsmith rd W3
135 T 9	Goldsmith's row E2
135 U 7	Goldsmith's sq E2
75 R 12	Goldsworthy gdns SE16
122 D 8	Goldwell rd Thntn Hth
92 C 2	Goldwin clo SE14
24 C 2	Golf clo Stanm
103 Z 18	Golf Club dri Kingst
127 X 7	Golf rd Brom
60 M 17	Golf rd W5
101 S 7	Golf side Twick
54 F 10	Golfe rd Ilf
118 A 3	Golfside clo New Mald
156 A 16	Goliath clo Wallgt
77 Y 15	Gollogly ter SE7
101 Y 14	Gomer gdns Tedd
101 Y 14	Gomer pl Tedd
75 N 9	Gomm rd SE16
156 A 10	Gomshall av Wallgtn
45 V 14	Gondar gdns NW6
76 C 17	Gonson st SE8
105 S 5	Gonston clo SW19
40 L 19	Gonville cres Nrthlt
87 T 7	Gonville st SW6
51 V 10	Goodall rd E11
41 T 9	Gooden ct Harrow
105 U 18	Goodenough rd SW19
140 C 1	Goodge pl W1
140 D 1	Goodge st W1
62 C 9	Goodhall st NW10
125 Y 14	Goodhart way W Wkhm
47 Z 16	Goodlinge rd N7
107 Y 3	Goodman cres SW2
51 U 2	Goodman rd E10
143 R 6	Goodman st E1
143 O 8	Goodman's yd E1
143 S 5	Goodmans stile E1
55 N 3	Goodmayes av Ilf
55 N 6	Goodmayes la Ilf
55 O 4	Goodmayes rd Ilf
91 V 15	Goodrich rd SE22
132 J 8	Goods way NW1
62 B 1	Goodson rd NW10
64 J 17	Goodway gdns E14
115 W 6	Goodwin dri Sidcup
156 J 13	Goodwin gdns Croy
156 H 12	Goodwin rd Croy
19 S 7	Goodwin rd N9
74 H 5	Goodwin rd W12
48 F 7	Goodwin st N4
140 J 9	Goodwins ct WC2
9 P 1	Goodwood av Enf
119 Y 9	Goodwood clo Mrdn
40 G 18	Goodwood dri Nthlt
75 V 20	Goodwood rd SE14
13 P 16	Goodwyn av NW7
29 R 5	Goodwyns vale N10
150 D 16	Goodyear pl SE5
27 O 16	Goodyers gdns NW4
79 R 8	Goosander way SE28
133 U 11	Goose yd EC1
24 H 15	Gooseacre la Harrow
66 K 9	Gooseley la E6
66 L 11	Gooseley la E6
160 E 9	Gophir la EC4
134 G 6	Gopsall st N1
20 L 18	Gordon av E4
57 T 6	Gordon av Hrnch
10 K 20	Gordon av Stanm
11 O 19	Gordon av Stanm
86 A 10	Gordon av SW14
84 A 13	Gordon av Twick
83 Z 13	Gordon av Twick
97 R 2	Gordon av Welling
123 T 19	Gordon cres Croy
62 L 17	Gordon ct W12
90 J 5	Gordon gro SE5
7 Y 6	Gordon hill Enf
47 P 12	Gordon House rd NW5
137 V 17	Gordon pl W8
67 U 4	Gordon rd Bark
124 L 7	Gordon rd Becknhm
81 X 10	Gordon rd Blvdr
154 L 14	Gordon rd Carsh
34 E 19	Gordon rd E11
53 W 10	Gordon rd E12
51 U 13	Gordon rd E15
34 H 5	Gordon rd E18

21 N 4	Gordon rd E4
8 A 8	Gordon rd Enf
23 T 10	Gordon rd Harrow
82 M 9	Gordon rd Hounsl
116 M 2	Gordon rd Kingst
117 N 1	Gordon rd Kingst
117 N 19	Gordon rd Kingst
54 E 9	Gordon rd Ilf
29 X 1	Gordon rd N11
27 V 2	Gordon rd N3
19 N 8	Gordon rd N9
85 O 6	Gordon rd Rich
38 A 19	Gordon rd Rom
70 C 11	Gordon rd S'hall
92 A 7	Gordon rd SE15
91 Z 3	Gordon rd SE15
96 H 13	Gordon rd Sidcp
73 U 16	Gordon rd W4
60 D 19	Gordon rd W5
132 F 17	Gordon sq WC1
65 T 10	Gordon st E13
132 E 16	Gordon st WC1
4 J 14	Gordon way Barnt
93 N 13	Gordonbrock rd SE4
105 Z 4	Gordondale rd SW19
25 P 16	Gore ct NW9
63 R 4	Gore rd E9
118 M 3	Gore rd SW20
146 C 1	Gore st SW7
129 U 8	Gorefield pla NW6
69 P 4	Goresbrook rd Dgnhm
136 J 11	Gorham pl W11
38 J 5	Goring clo Rom
55 T 13	Goring gdns Dgnhm
57 N 19	Goring rd Dgnhm
16 M 19	Goring rd N11
17 N 19	Goring rd N11
142 L 5	Goring st EC3
59 N 7	Goring way Grnfd
31 O 15	Gorleston rd N15
144 M 6	Gorleston st W14
78 G 11	Gorman rd SE18
107 P 19	Gorringe Park av Mitch
103 V 14	Gorscombe clo Kingst
159 P 6	Gorse rd Croy
107 P 13	Gorse ri SW17
57 P 4	Gorse way Rom
61 X 11	Gorst rd NW10
88 L 17	Gorst rd SW11
135 N 11	Gorsuch pl E2
89 N 20	Gosberton rd SW12
56 E 5	Gosfield rd Dgnhm
139 Z 1	Gosfield st W1
35 T 15	Gosford gdns Ilf
140 G 5	Goslett yd WC2
58 G 8	Gosling clo Grnfd
90 F 2	Gosling way SW9
149 T 20	Gosling way SW9
30 L 3	Gospatrick rd N17
31 N 4	Gospatrick rd N17
32 L 16	Gosport rd E17
79 S 14	Gossage rd SE18
135 P 13	Gosset st E2
127 X 3	Gosshill rd Chisl
75 W 15	Gosterwood st SE8
100 J 1	Gostling rd Twick
122 F 7	Goston gdns Thntn Hth
133 X 14	Goswell pl EC1
133 Y 15	Goswell rd EC1
101 R 4	Gothic rd Twick
112 B 12	Goudhurst rd Brom
52 B 13	Gough rd E15
8 L 9	Gough rd Enf
141 U 5	Gough sq EC4
133 P 16	Gough st WC1
101 T 1	Gould rd Twick
50 A 16	Gould ter E8
143 O 4	Goulston st E1
50 A 13	Goulton rd E5
31 S 17	Gourley pl N15
31 S 17	Gourley st N15
95 W 13	Gourock rd SE9
65 N 1	Govier clo E15
87 S 2	Gowan av SW6
44 J 19	Gowan rd NW10
132 E 16	Gower ct WC1
140 F 1	Gower ms WC1
52 G 18	Gower rd E7
71 W 17	Gower rd Isl
132 C 15	Gower st WC1
132 C 16	Gower st WC1
143 S 5	Gower's wlk E1
124 L 4	Gowland pl Becknhm
91 W 8	Gowlett rd SE15
89 O 8	Gowrie rd SW11
98 C 4	Grace av Bxly Hth
113 N 8	Grace clo SE9
110 D 10	Grace pth SE26
122 L 15	Grace rd Croy
64 H 1	Grace rd E15
64 E 9	Grace st E3
143 T 9	Grace's all E1
91 P 3	Grace's ms SE5
91 R 3	Grace's rd SE5
142 H 8	Gracechurch st EC3
160 H 8	Gracechurch st EC3
107 T 12	Gracedale rd SW16
108 A 8	Gracefield gdns SW16
109 W 11	Gradient the SE26
8 C 9	Graeme rd Enf
85 T 9	Graemesdyke av SW14
100 C 1	Grafton clo Hounsl
59 Y 17	Grafton clo W13
152 B 5	Grafton clo Worc Pk
47 S 18	Grafton cres NW1
55 Z 6	Grafton gdns Dgnhm
30 K 18	Grafton gdns N4
132 B 18	Grafton ms W1
152 B 4	Grafton Park rd Worc Pk
132 F 13	Grafton pl NW1
156 G 1	Grafton rd Croy
55 Z 6	Grafton rd Dgnhm
7 P 11	Grafton rd Enf
23 O 17	Grafton rd Harrow
118 B 7	Grafton rd New Mald
47 S 17	Grafton rd NW5
61 V 19	Grafton rd W3
152 A 5	Grafton rd Worc Pk
89 V 8	Grafton sq SW4
139 Z 10	Grafton st W1
47 N 16	Grafton ter NW5
132 B 18	Grafton way W1
47 T 18	Grafton yd NW5
121 O 1	Graham av Mitch
72 B 7	Graham av W13
158 M 2	Graham clo Croy
159 N 3	Graham clo Croy
40 D 15	Graham ct Nthlt
116 J 19	Graham gdns Surb
74 J 9	Graham mans W6
98 C 10	Graham rd Bxly Hth
65 S 10	Graham rd E13
49 X 18	Graham rd E8
100 F 9	Graham rd Hampt
23 T 9	Graham rd Harrow
121 N 1	Graham rd Mitch
30 J 11	Graham rd N15
26 H 19	Graham rd NW4
105 W 19	Graham rd SW19
73 X 7	Graham rd W4
133 Z 10	Graham st N1
147 T 7	Graham ter SW1
26 D 8	Grahame Park way NW9
13 P 20	Grahame Park way NW7
40 M 16	Grainger clo Nthlt
83 W 5	Grainger rd Islwth
30 L 5	Grainger rd N22
51 Y 7	Gramer clo E11
45 S 4	Grampian gdns NW2
106 L 12	Granada st SW17
86 K 14	Granard av SW15
88 M 18	Granard rd SW12
132 E 5	Granary way NW1
149 N 7	Granby bldgs SE11
95 U 6	Granby rd SE9
135 R 15	Granby st E2
132 A 10	Granby ter NW1
141 X 1	Grand av EC1
29 P 12	Grand av N10
117 U 16	Grand av Surb
43 P 16	Grand av Wemb
78 J 13	Grand Depot rd SE18
118 M 3	Grand dri SW20
119 O 12	Grand dri SW20
87 S 12	Grand Parade ms SW15
63 V 11	Grand wlk E1
122 A 3	Grandison rd SW16
152 M 4	Grandison rd Worc Pk
88 M 12	Grandison rd SW11
89 N 13	Grandison rd SW11
88 H 2	Granfield st SW11
15 Y 4	Grange av Barnt
15 P 17	Grange av N12
14 D 4	Grange av N20
123 R 3	Grange av SE25
24 C 7	Grange av Stanm
101 U 3	Grange av Twick
34 D 1	Grange av Wdfd Grn
21 S 20	Grange av Wdfd Grn
118 F 11	Grange clo New Mald
12 J 17	Grange clo Edg
70 D 15	Grange clo Hounsl
114 M 6	Grange clo Sidcp
34 E 1	Grange clo Wdfd Grn
68 G 19	Grange cres SE28
141 P 6	Grange ct WC2
113 S 15	Grange dri Chisl
41 N 6	Grange Farm clo Harrow
16 L 6	Grange gdns N14
46 B 10	Grange gdns NW3
22 C 12	Grange gdns Pinn
123 R 3	Grange gdns SE25
48 K 18	Grange gro N1
12 J 16	Grange hill Edg
123 R 2	Grange hill SE25
109 V 4	Grange la SE21
7 X 20	Grange Park av N21
17 Y 1	Grange Park av N21
123 N 7	Grange Park rd Thntn Hth
51 P 4	Grange Park rd E10
72 K 3	Grange pk W5
151 R 3	Grange plSE16
129 T 2	Grange pl NW6
51 O 4	Grange rd E10
65 R 10	Grange rd E13
32 H 17	Grange rd E17
12 M 20	Grange rd Edg
41 P 7	Grange rd Harrow
23 Y 17	Grange rd Harrow
54 A 11	Grange rd Ilf
116 J 6	Grange rd Kingst
18 K 20	Grange rd N17
29 N 19	Grange rd N6
44 K 19	Grange rd NW10
156 M 20	Grange rd S Croy
70 B 4	Grange rd S'hall
150 L 2	Grange rd SE1
123 P 5	Grange rd SE25
154 A 16	Grange rd Sutton
153 Z 16	Grange rd Sutton
86 F 3	Grange rd SW13
73 T 13	Grange rd W4
72 G 2	Grange rd W5
134 G 6	Grange st N1
158 L 3	Grange the Croy
15 S 5	Grange the N20
150 M 1	Grange the SE1
105 P 14	Grange the SW19
61 O 1	Grange the Wemb
154 B 16	Grange vale Sutton
15 S 5	Grange View rd N20
21 Y 14	Grange way Wdfd Grn
150 L 2	Grange wlk SE1
151 N 1	Grange wlk SE1
151 N 2	Grange yd SE1
123 R 3	Grangecliffe gdns SE25
49 R 3	Grangecourt rd N16
95 V 8	Grangehill rd SE9
111 O 5	Grangemill rd SE6
111 O 5	Grangemill way SE6
39 W 19	Granger way Rom
35 R 15	Grangeway gdns Ilf
15 O 13	Grangeway N12
129 S 1	Grangeway NW6
7 X 19	Grangewood Bxly
98 A 20	Grangewood la Becknhm
66 B 3	Grangewood st E6
65 Z 3	Grangewood st E6
18 H 9	Granham gdns N9
79 Y 13	Granite st SE18
51 Z 7	Granleigh rd E11
50 A 20	Gransden av E8
74 D 6	Gransden rd W12
16 G 3	Grant clo N14
123 V 20	Grant pl Croy
123 U 20	Grant rd Croy
23 U 9	Grant rd Harrow
88 G 9	Grant rd SW11
65 S 10	Grant st E13
133 S 8	Grant st N1
71 Y 18	Grant way Islwth
133 Y 7	Grantbridge st N1
41 W 9	Grantchester clo Harrow
11 W 10	Grantham clo Edg
38 A 20	Grantham gdns Rom
139 W 15	Grantham pl W1
53 W 11	Grantham rd E12
90 A 5	Grantham rd SW9
74 A 18	Grantham rd W4
63 T 10	Grantley st E1
33 X 5	Grantock rd E17
55 N 5	Granton rd Ilf
115 T 15	Granton rd Sidcp
107 V 19	Granton rd SW16
27 N 1	Grants clo NW7
129 X 14	Grantully rd W9
82 G 14	Granville av Hounsl
19 P 11	Granville av N9
108 C 19	Granville gdns SW16
73 O 2	Granville gdns W5
93 V 8	Granville gro SE13
45 T 10	Granville ms NW2
93 U 6	Granville pk SE13
139 S 7	Granville pl W1
4 B 13	Granville rd Barnt
33 R 17	Granville rd E17
34 J 8	Granville rd E18
53 Y 5	Granville rd Ilf
28 D 1	Granville rd N12
30 J 5	Granville rd N22
17 O 18	Granville rd N22
30 D 20	Granville rd N4
45 V 7	Granville rd NW2
129 T 10	Granville rd NW6
115 O 9	Granville rd Sidcp
87 X 18	Granville rd SW18
105 Y 18	Granville rd SW19
97 U 8	Granville rd Welling
133 R 13	Granville sq WC1
133 P 13	Granville st WC1
140 J 4	Grape st WC1
80 A 18	Grasdene rd SE18
82 J 16	Grasmere av Hounsl
104 A 9	Grasmere av SW15
103 Z 10	Grasmere av SW15
119 Y 6	Grasmere av SW19
61 X 19	Grasmere av W3
42 J 4	Grasmere av Wemb
23 Z 8	Grasmere gdns Harrow
35 S 14	Grasmere gdns Ilf
112 B 19	Grasmere rd Brom
98 K 4	Grasmere rd Bxly Hth
29 S 6	Grasmere rd N10
18 J 20	Grasmere rd N17
124 A 13	Grasmere rd SE25
108 B 11	Grasmere rd SW16
65 S 6	Grasmere st E13
27 V 5	Grass pk N3
155 U 8	Grass way Wallgtn
115 N 11	Grassington rd Sidcp
110 B 3	Grassmount SE23
4 M 19	Grasvenor av Barnt
144 K 2	Gratton rd W14
45 O 10	Gratton ter NW2
98 G 13	Gravel hill Bxly Hth
98 G 15	Gravel Hill clo Bxly Hth
158 H 14	Gravel hill Croy
27 W 7	Gravel hill N3
142 M 4	Gravel la E1
101 S 2	Gravel rd Twick
114 B 8	Gravelwood clo Chisl
106 J 10	Graveney rd SW17
74 G 1	Gravesend rd W12
56 C 4	Gray av Dgnhm
57 V 16	Gray gdns Rainhm
141 V 18	Gray st SE1
141 P 1	Gray's Inn pl WC1
133 O 16	Gray's Inn rd WC1
141 R 1	Gray's Inn sq WC1
66 C 16	Grayford clo E6
117 Y 9	Grayham cres New Mald
117 X 9	Grayham rd New Mald
127 O 2	Grayland clo Brom
49 P 6	Grayling rd N16
107 X 18	Grayscroft rd SW16
89 N 6	Grayshott rd SW11
118 J 4	Grayswood gdns New Mald
28 D 1	Graywood ct N12
49 O 7	Grazebrook rd N16
98 K 12	Grazeley clo Bxly Hth
10 R 11	Grazeley ct SE19
160 E 4	Great Bell all EC2
109 V 8	Great Brownings SE21
15 O 5	Great Bushey dri N20
8 L 5	Great Cambridge rd Enf
31 N 3	Great Cambridge rd N17
18 B 11	Great Cambridge rd N9
140 A 5	Great Castle st W1
139 Z 5	Great Castle st W1
131 N 20	Great Central st NW1
44 A 15	Great Central way NW10
43 X 14	Great Central way NW10

140 E 5	Great Chapel st W1
100 H 6	Great Chertsey rd Felt
85 X 2	Great Chertsey rd W4
144 G 8	Great Church la W6
148 J 1	Great College st SW1
57 P 7	Great Cullings Rom
139 O 6	Great Cumberland ms W1
139 P 6	Great Cumberland pl W1
150 F 2	Great Dover st SE1
51 X 18	Great Eastern rd E15
51 X 20	Great Eastern rd E15
134 J 15	Great Eastern st EC2
126 L 8	Great Elms rd Brom
26 D 7	Great Field strand NW9
39 Z 18	Great Gardens rd Rom
140 H 18	Great George st SW1
142 A 13	Great Guilford st SE1
113 W 8	Great Harry dri SE9
133 O 19	Great James st WC1
140 B 6	Great Marlborough st W1
142 G 15	Great Maze pond SE1
140 H 8	Great Newport st WC2
4 H 8	Great North rd Barnt
28 E 3	Great North rd N12
74 J 14	Great North rd W6
26 L 6	Great North way NW4
27 P 9	Great North way NW4
132 M 19	Great Ormond st WC1
133 N 19	Great Ormond st WC1
133 P 12	Great Percy st WC1
148 G 2	Great Peter st SW1
148 J 2	Great Peter st SW1
140 A 4	Great Portland st W1
139 Z 2	Great Portland st W1
140 D 8	Great Pulteney st W1
140 M 5	Great Queen st WC2
140 J 2	Great Russell st WC1
140 J 14	Great Scotland yd SW1
140 G 20	Great Smith st SW1
148 H 1	Great Smith st SW1
91 R 14	Great Spilmano SE22
142 J 5	Great St Helen's EC3
160 C 8	Great St Thomas apostle EC4
142 A 19	Great Suffolk st SE1
141 Y 15	Great Suffolk st SE1
133 Y 17	Great Sutton st EC1
160 F 4	Great Swan all EC2
140 A 2	Great Titchfield st W1
131 Z 19	Great Titchfield st W1
142 J 9	Great Tower st EC3
160 C 8	Great Trinity la EC4
141 O 3	Great Turnstile WC1
72 B 17	Great West rd Brentf
82 E 3	Great West rd Hounsl
71 U 19	Great West rd Islwth
74 J 13	Great West rd W4
73 T 15	Great West rd W4
144 A 9	Great West rd W6
137 S 2	Great Western rd W11
129 R 19	Great Western rd W9
160 H 3	Great Winchester st EC2
140 E 9	Great Windmill st W1
59 V 13	Greatdown rd W7
66 G 11	Greatfield av E6
93 O 11	Greatfield clo SE4
67 T 4	Greatfields rd Bark
143 S 2	Greatorex st E1
113 V 17	Greatwood Chisl
106 H 10	Greaves pl SW17
108 K 15	Grecian cres SE19
140 G 7	Greek st W1
4 J 3	Green Acre la Barnt
141 X 4	Green Arbour ct EC4
12 M 12	Green av NW7
13 N 12	Green av NW7
72 C 8	Green av W13
75 N 3	Green bank E1
143 U 14	Green bank E1
143 Y 14	Green bank E1
15 O 13	Green bank N12
125 Z 5	Green clo Brom
154 M 3	Green clo Carsh
100 C 12	Green clo Hampt
28 C 20	Green clo NW11
25 W 17	Green clo NW9
158 A 1	Green Court av Croy
158 A 1	Green Court gdns Croy
91 R 11	Green dell SE22

72 K 14	Green Dragon la Brentf
7 T 19	Green Dragon la N21
17 X 1	Green Dragon la N21
143 R 2	Green Dragon yd E1
70 J 2	Green dri S'hall
17 X 8	Green end N21
78 G 14	Green hill SE18
141 X 1	Green Hills rents EC1
151 V 15	Green Hundred rd SE15
114 A 14	Green la Chisl
56 B 6	Green la Dgnhm
12 A 14	Green la Edg
11 Z 12	Green la Edg
100 A 12	Green la Felt
122 K 2	Green La gdns Thntn Hth
54 D 8	Green la Ilf
55 T 5	Green la Ilf
120 B 17	Green la Mrdn
119 X 14	Green la Mrdn
117 W 11	Green la New Mald
27 P 16	Green la NW4
110 E 18	Green la SE20
113 X 4	Green la SE9
95 Y 19	Green la SE9
11 O 16	Green la Stanm
108 F 19	Green la SW16
122 J 2	Green la Thntn Hth
71 T 4	Green la W7
118 H 19	Green la Worc Pk
152 B 18	Green lanes Epsom
49 N 12	Green lanes N16
17 X 4	Green lanes N21
48 L 4	Green lanes N4
30 H 16	Green lanes N8
71 Z 1	Green Man gdns W13
71 Z 1	Green Man la W13
72 A 1	Green Man pas W13
17 W 2	Green Moor link N21
139 Y 16	Green pk SW1
99 S 12	Green pl Drtfrd
32 J 9	Green Pond rd E17
6 E 18	Green rd N14
15 S 10	Green rd N20
65 X 20	Green st E13
52 K 20	Green st E7
9 P 9	Green st Enf
139 S 8	Green st W1
126 E 18	Green the Brom
98 D 3	Green the Bxly Hth
158 M 19	Green the Croy
34 H 19	Green the E11
52 A 18	Green the E15
70 F 17	Green the Hounsl
119 R 9	Green the Mrdn
119 S 9	Green the Mrdn
117 X 5	Green the N Mald
16 K 10	Green the N14
16 L 10	Green the N14
17 V 4	Green the N21
18 K 9	Green the N9
115 R 18	Green the Orp
84 G 12	Green the Rich
70 C 8	Green the S'hall
154 A 6	Green the Sutton
105 O 13	Green the SW19
101 T 2	Green the Twick
62 B 17	Green the W7
21 T 16	Green the Wdfd Grn
96 J 11	Green the Welling
41 Z 6	Green the Wemb
97 W 13	Green vale Bxly Hth
60 M 16	Green vale W5
24 F 1	Green verges Stanm
127 S 14	Green way Brom
95 N 13	Green way SE9
B2 D 9	Green Way the Hounsl
21 Y 15	Green way Wdfd Grn
99 T 11	Green wlk Drtfrd
20 H 4	Green wlk E4
27 P 14	Green wlk NW4
158 K 15	Green wlk S Croy
70 G 14	Green wlk S'hall
150 H 2	Green wlk SE1
154 K 1	Green Wrythe cres Carsh
120 H 17	Green Wrythe la Carsh
154 K 2	Green Wrythe la Carsh
140 D 8	Green's ct W1
78 L 10	Green's end SE18
16 L 11	Greenacre wlk N14
10 D 8	Greenacres Bushey
157 U 6	Greenacres Croy
11 N 20	Greenacres dri Stanm
27 U 8	Greenacres N3

95 W 16	Greenacres SE9
46 B 13	Greenaway gdns NW3
41 Y 15	Greenbank av Wemb
27 S 13	Greenbank cres NW4
78 B 19	Greenbay rd SE7
130 K 10	Greenberry st NW8
5 S 6	Greenbrook av Barnt
148 C 4	Greencoat pl SW1
148 D 3	Greencoat pl SW1
148 D 3	Greencoat row SW1
25 R 5	Greencourt av Edg
66 C 16	Greencroft clo E6
46 D 19	Greencroft gdns NW6
129 Y 1	Greencroft gdns NW6
8 E 11	Greencroft gdns Enf
82 D 2	Greencroft rd Hounsl
74 A 6	Greenend rd W4
76 M 7	Greenfell st SE10
77 N 8	Greenfell st SE10
117 T 15	Greenfield av Surb
68 H 3	Greenfield gdns Dgnhm
45 T 9	Greenfield gdns NW2
68 G 3	Greenfield rd Dgnhm
143 U 4	Greenfield rd E1
31 S 15	Greenfield rd N15
22 J 10	Greenfield way Harrow
58 H 18	Greenfields S'hall
70 E 1	Greenford av S'hall
58 E 20	Greenford av S'hall
59 T 14	Greenford av W7
58 M 8	Greenford gdns Grnfd
59 N 8	Greenford gdns Grnfd
41 T 17	Greenford grn Grnfd
59 O 10	Greenford rd Grnfd
41 T 17	Greenford rd Grnfd
71 N 1	Greenford rd S'hall
154 A 9	Greenford rd Sutton
42 A 17	Greengate Grnfd
65 V 8	Greengate st E13
28 D 14	Greenhalgh wlk N2
141 T 20	Greenham clo SE1
29 P 6	Greenham rd N10
34 C 9	Greenheys dri E18
21 X 4	Greenhill Buck Hl
58 E 6	Greenhill gdns Nthlt
53 P 14	Greenhill gro E12
5 O 18	Greenhill pk Barnt
62 A 4	Greenhill pk NW10
23 U 18	Greenhill rd Harrow
62 A 4	Greenhill rd NW10
154 D 3	Greenhill Sutton
58 E 7	Greenhill ter Grnfd
78 G 13	Greenhill ter SE18
23 U 18	Greenhill way Harrow
43 T 6	Greenhill way Wemb
43 U 6	Greenhill Wemb
141 X 1	Greenhills rents EC1
49 O 19	Greenhills Ter N1
96 F 18	Greenhithe clo Sidcp
95 Y 13	Greenholm rd SE9
108 G 12	Greenhurst rd SE27
80 F 11	Greening st SE2
75 U 14	Greenland av SE16
131 Z 4	Greenland pl NW1
75 U 10	Greenland quay SE16
4 A 19	Greenland rd Barnt
132 A 3	Greenland rd NW1
131 Z 4	Greenland rd NW1
131 Z 4	Greenland st NW1
118 E 16	Greenlaw gdns New Mald
78 H 9	Greenlaw st SE18
32 M 11	Greenleaf rd E17
33 N 11	Greenleaf rd E17
65 Y 4	Greenleaf rd E6
35 Z 10	Greenleafe dri Ilf
134 A 2	Greenman st N1
133 Z 3	Greenman st N1
105 O 8	Greenoak way SW19
107 X 20	Greenock rd SW16
73 U 9	Greenock rd W3
55 T 5	Greenside Dgnhm
122 G 16	Greenside rd Croy
74 G 7	Greenside rd W12
74 A 6	Greenside rd W4
84 H 12	Greenside Rich
34 K 1	Greenstead av Wdfd Grn
21 Z 20	Greenstead av Wdfd Grn
21 Y 19	Greenstead clo Wdfd Grn

86 H 14	Greenstead gdns SW15
21 Y 19	Greenstead gdns Wdfd Grn
34 E 18	Greenstone ms E11
95 U 11	Greenvale rd SE9
124 J 13	Greenview av Becknhm
124 H 15	Greenview av Croy
33 W 12	Greenway av E17
113 X 11	Greenway Chisl
14 L 9	Greenway clo N20
48 M 7	Greenway clo N4
25 X 9	Greenway clo NW9
55 U 5	Greenway Dgnhm
58 J 8	Greenway gdns Grnfd
23 U 6	Greenway gdns Harrow
158 K 6	Greenway gdns Croy
25 X 8	Greenway gdns NW9
24 K 16	Greenway Harrow
16 M 9	Greenway N14
17 N 7	Greenway N14
14 L 7	Greenway N20
15 N 8	Greenway N20
118 M 8	Greenway SW20
23 U 6	Greenway the Harrow
25 Y 8	Greenway the NW9
22 E 19	Greenway the Pinn
155 U 9	Greenway Wallgtn
125 O 4	Greenways Becknhm
16 C 20	Greenways clo N11
131 Z 18	Greenwell st W1
76 G 16	Greenwich Church st SE10
66 D 15	Greenwich cres E6
76 F 19	Greenwich High rd SE10
76 L 18	Greenwich pk SE10
93 S 2	Greenwich South st SE10
56 H 11	Greenwood av Dgnhm
9 U 7	Greenwood av Enf
10 E 4	Greenwood clo Bushey
119 S 9	Greenwood clo Mrdn
115 O 4	Greenwood clo Sidcp
20 H 16	Greenwood dri E4
17 V 10	Greenwood gdns N13
36 C 3	Greenwood gdns Ilf
100 L 12	Greenwood la Hampt
104 B 17	Greenwood pk Kingst
47 T 14	Greenwood pl NW5
122 K 16	Greenwood rd Croy
65 R 5	Greenwood rd E13
49 X 16	Greenwood rd E8
83 U 7	Greenwood rd Islwth
121 X 7	Greenwood rd Mitch
61 Y 4	Greenwood ter NW10
23 O 4	Greer rd Harrow
141 V 16	Greet st SE1
77 T 20	Gregor ms SE3
95 O 19	Gregory cres SE9
137 W 18	Gregory pl W8
65 X 19	Gregory rd E16
37 U 12	Gregory rd Rom
70 H 8	Gregory rd S'hall
30 A 15	Greig clo N8
149 Y 13	Greig ter SE17
85 N 11	Grena gdns Rich
85 N 11	Grena rd Rich
123 O 18	Grenaby av Croy
123 O 18	Grenaby rd Croy
77 Z 20	Grenada rd SE7
63 Z 20	Grenade st E14
78 H 4	Grenadier st E16
43 P 7	Grendon gdns Wemb
130 K 17	Grendon st NW8
57 T 4	Grenfell av Hornch
24 J 20	Grenfell gdns Harrow
107 N 17	Grenfell rd Mitch
136 H 9	Grenfell rd W11
154 E 3	Grennell clo Sutton
154 E 4	Grennell rd Sutton
17 S 18	Grenoble gdns N13
117 V 20	Grenville clo Surb
34 K 3	Grenville gdns Wdfd Grn
100 J 12	Grenville ms Hampt
146 B 6	Grenville ms SW7
12 K 16	Grenville pl NW7
146 A 4	Grenville pl SW7
159 V 20	Grenville rd Croy

48 A 4	Grenville rd N19
132 L 18	Grenville st WC1
15 Y 13	Gresham av N20
98 A 16	Gresham clo Bxly
7 Y 12	Gresham clo Enf
37 R 18	Gresham dri Rom
45 T 3	Gresham gdns NW11
124 G 3	Gresham rd Becknhm
65 W 18	Gresham rd E16
66 G 7	Gresham rd E6
12 A 20	Gresham rd Edg
100 G 15	Gresham rd Hampt
83 N 2	Gresham rd Hounsl
43 Z 16	Gresham rd NW10
123 W 10	Gresham rd SE25
90 G 8	Gresham rd SW9
160 C 4	Gresham st EC2
142 C 5	Gresham st EC2
31 N 14	Gresley clo N15
47 W 2	Gresley rd N19
140 E 3	Gresse st W1
87 V 17	Gressenhall rd SW18
115 O 7	Greswell clo Sidcp
87 O 2	Greswell st SW6
31 T 3	Greton rd N17
84 A 18	Greville clo Twick
129 W 6	Greville ms NW6
129 Y 8	Greville pl NW6
33 U 13	Greville rd E17
129 Z 8	Greville rd NW6
85 N 15	Greville rd Rich
141 T 1	Greville st EC1
28 C 18	Grey clo NW11
135 O 19	Grey Eagle st E1
148 E 3	Greycoat pl SW1
148 E 3	Greycoat st SW1
111 O 12	Greycott rd Becknhm
11 P 15	Greyfell clo Stanm
26 H 11	Greyhound hill NW4
107 Z 15	Greyhound la SW16
31 T 10	Greyhound rd N17
128 A 12	Greyhound rd NW10
62 L 8	Greyhound rd NW10
154 C 11	Greyhound rd Sutton
144 G 14	Greyhound rd W6
144 J 13	Greyhound rd W6
107 V 20	Greyhound ter SW16
99 P 15	Greyhound way Drtfrd
92 C 18	Greystead rd SE23
22 H 10	Greystoke av Pinn
6 L 14	Greystoke gdns Enf
60 L 12	Greystoke gdns W5
60 H 9	Greystoke Park ter W5
141 T 4	Greystoke pl EC4
24 D 19	Greystone gdns Harrow
36 C 6	Greystone gdns Ilf
107 T 15	Greyswood st SW16
92 G 16	Grierson rd SE23
44 K 16	Griffin clo NW10
79 T 9	Griffin Manor way SE28
31 R 8	Griffin rd N17
79 T 11	Griffin rd SE18
152 K 4	Griffiths clo Worc Pk
105 Z 17	Griffiths rd SW19
150 L 1	Grigg's pl SE1
54 B 7	Griggs app Ilf
33 V 19	Griggs rd E10
135 P 17	Grimsby st E2
22 D 2	Grimsdyke rd Pinn
87 V 6	Grimston rd SW6
157 Y 6	Grimwade av Croy
92 B 6	Grimwade cres SE15
83 X 17	Grimwood rd Twick
141 S 19	Grindal st SE1
76 A 17	Grinling pl SE8
75 Z 17	Grinling pl SE8
75 W 14	Grinstead rd SE8
129 T 16	Grittledon rd W9
43 T 19	Grittleton av Wemb
110 A 4	Grizedale ter SE23
160 E 6	Grocers Hall ct EC2
160 E 5	Grocers Hall gdns EC2
88 F 19	Groom cres SW18
139 V 20	Groom pl SW1
65 Y 15	Groombes rd E16
97 O 13	Groombridge clo Welling
63 T 1	Groombridge rd E9
107 O 9	Groomfield clo SW17
79 Y 14	Grosmont rd SE18
155 O 13	Grosvenor av Carsh
22 L 19	Grosvenor av Harrow
48 L 17	Grosvenor av N5
49 N 16	Grosvenor av N5

84 J 13	Grosvenor av Rich
86 A 8	Grosvenor av SW14
147 S 5	Grosvenor cotts SW1
139 T 18	Grosvenor Cres ms SW1
25 R 13	Grosvenor cres NW9
139 T 19	Grosvenor cres SW1
16 H 1	Grosvenor ct N14
147 X 1	Grosvenor Gardens ms north SW1
147 X 2	Grosvenor Gardens ms north SW1
147 X 3	Grosvenor Gardens ms south SW1
86 A 9	Grosvenor gdns SW14
102 H 14	Grosvenor gdns Kingst
45 N 16	Grosvenor gdns NW2
155 U 16	Grosvenor gdns Wallgtn
27 U 17	Grosvenor gdns NW1
21 U 20	Grosvenor gdns Wdfd Grn
66 A 8	Grosvenor gdns E6
29 U 11	Grosvenor gdns N10
6 K 15	Grosvenor gdns N14
147 X 2	Grosvenor gdns SW1
105 S 14	Grosvenor hill SW19
139 X 9	Grosvenor hill W1
33 P 16	Grosvenor Park rd E17
150 A 16	Grosvenor pk SE5
149 Z 17	Grosvenor pk SE5
139 W 19	Grosvenor pl SW1
159 S 1	Grosvenor rd W Wkhm
97 X 13	Grosvenor rd Bxly Hth
81 R 15	Grosvenor rd Blvdr
72 H 17	Grosvenor rd Brentf
56 C 3	Grosvenor rd Dgnhm
51 U 3	Grosvenor rd E10
34 G 17	Grosvenor rd E11
66 B 3	Grosvenor rd E6
52 H 19	Grosvenor rd E7
82 E 8	Grosvenor rd Hounsl
54 A 9	Grosvenor rd Ilf
29 S 5	Grosvenor rd N10
27 W 1	Grosvenor rd N3
19 N 5	Grosvenor rd N9
84 K 13	Grosvenor rd Rich
57 N 3	Grosvenor rd Rom
70 E 7	Grosvenor rd S'hall
123 W 8	Grosvenor rd SE25
147 Y 13	Grosvenor rd SW1
83 Y 20	Grosvenor rd Twick
73 T 14	Grosvenor rd W4
71 X 3	Grosvenor rd W7
155 S 12	Grosvenor rd Wallgtn
33 S 16	Grosvenor Rise east E17
139 V 9	Grosvenor sq W1
139 W 9	Grosvenor st W1
150 B 15	Grosvenor ter SE17
149 Z 16	Grosvenor ter SE17
76 J 12	Grosvenor Wharf rd E14
93 Z 5	Grotes pl SE3
106 B 3	Groton rd SW18
139 U 1	Grotto pas W1
101 W 4	Grotto rd Twick
29 U 8	Grove av N10
27 Y 2	Grove av N3
22 B 14	Grove av Pinn
153 Y 14	Grove av Sutton
101 W 1	Grove av Twick
59 U 17	Grove av W7
100 B 11	Grove clo Felt
116 L 9	Grove clo Kingst
92 G 20	Grove clo SE23
146 L 12	Grove cotts SW3
34 D 7	Grove cres E18
100 B 10	Grove cres Felt
116 J 7	Grove cres Kingst
25 X 13	Grove cres NW9
91 R 5	Grove cres SE5
51 Y 18	Grove Crescent rd E15
34 A 7	Grove end E18
130 F 14	Grove End rd NW8
56 K 10	Grove gdns Dgnhm
9 T 4	Grove gdns Enf
26 F 14	Grove gdns NW4
130 K 14	Grove gdns NW8
101 Z 10	Grove gdns Tedd
51 U 9	Grove Green rd E11
34 B 7	Grove hill E18
41 U 2	Grove hill Harrow

41 U 1	Grove Hill rd Harrow
91 S 7	Grove Hill rd SE5
86 E 15	Grove ho SW15
30 A 14	Grove House rd N8
116 K 8	Grove la Kingst
91 N 2	Grove la SE5
95 T 15	Grove Market pl SE9
144 B 2	Grove ms W6
74 L 8	Grove ms W6
33 P 2	Grove Park av E4
73 V 19	Grove Park bri W4
73 U 19	Grove Park gdns W4
31 S 13	Grove Park rd N15
112 M 6	Grove Park rd SE9
113 N 5	Grove Park rd SE9
73 T 19	Grove Park rd W4
73 T 18	Grove Park ter W4
101 Y 11	Grove pass Tedd
116 J 10	Grove path Surb
34 G 17	Grove pk E11
25 W 12	Grove pk NW9
91 S 6	Grove pk SE5
85 V 1	Grove pk W4
67 O 2	Grove pl Bark
46 F 11	Grove pl NW3
73 V 3	Grove pl W3
72 H 1	Grove pl W5
5 V 12	Grove rd Barnt
81 P 16	Grove rd Blvdr
72 F 14	Grove rd Brentf
98 K 11	Grove rd Bxly Hth
52 B 2	Grove rd E11
33 P 17	Grove rd E17
34 C 6	Grove rd E18
63 V 7	Grove rd E3
20 F 13	Grove rd E4
12 B 18	Grove rd Edg
82 G 10	Grove rd Hounsl
83 U 3	Grove rd Islwth
121 P 4	Grove rd Mitch
16 F 15	Grove rd N11
15 T 18	Grove rd N12
31 P 16	Grove rd N15
44 L 17	Grove rd NW2
22 D 15	Grove rd Pinn
84 M 16	Grove rd Rich
85 N 15	Grove rd Rich
55 S 1	Grove rd Rom
37 S 19	Grove rd Rom
116 G 11	Grove rd Surb
154 B 13	Grove rd Sutton
153 Y 14	Grove rd Sutton
86 D 4	Grove rd SW13
106 D 18	Grove rd SW19
122 E 10	Grove rd Thntn Hth
101 R 8	Grove rd Twick
73 W 3	Grove rd W3
72 H 1	Grove rd W5
9 R 1	Grove road west Enfield
18 H 18	Grove st N18
75 X 10	Grove st SE8
47 R 11	Grove ter NW5
101 Y 10	Grove ter Tedd
97 W 10	Grove the Bxly Hth
51 Y 18	Grove the E15
12 F 13	Grove the Edg
7 T 9	Grove the Enf
58 M 17	Grove the Grnfd
83 T 3	Grove the Islwth
17 T 13	Grove the N13
27 X 3	Grove the N3
48 D 1	Grove the N4
47 O 3	Grove the N6
45 T 1	Grove the NW11
25 Y 16	Grove the NW9
115 Z 11	Grove the Sidcp
101 Y 11	Grove the Tedd
159 T 6	Grove the W Wkhm
159 U 1	Grove the W Wkhm
72 G 2	Grove the W5
113 W 14	Grove vale Chisl
91 T 9	Grove vale SE22
64 E 19	Grove vlls E14
16 J 1	Grovebury ct N14
80 D 6	Grovebury rd SE2
47 X 5	Grovedale rd N19
108 D 18	Groveland av SW16
160 C 6	Groveland ct EC4
124 L 6	Groveland rd Becknhm
40 J 10	Grovelands clo Harrow
91 R 5	Grovelands clo SE5
16 J 4	Grovelands ct N14
17 P 4	Grovelands pk N21
17 R 12	Grovelands rd N13
31 X 18	Grovelands rd N15
115 P 19	Grovelands rd Orp

117 X 11	Grovelands way New Mald
61 R 15	Groveside clo W3
20 M 9	Groveside rd E4
21 O 10	Groveside rd E4
55 V 11	Groveway Dgnhm
90 E 3	Groveway SW9
43 U 15	Groveway Wemb
85 O 3	Grovewood rd Rich
91 U 2	Grummant rd SE15
64 D 18	Grundy st E14
28 A 1	Gruneisen rd N3
90 K 13	Gubyon av SE24
63 Y 8	Guerin sq E3
90 L 18	Guernsey gro SE24
51 W 5	Guernsey rd E11
112 G 1	Guibal rd SE12
94 G 20	Guibal rd SE12
78 B 15	Guild rd SE7
108 A 17	Guildersfield rd SW16
107 Z 18	Guildersfield rd SW16
116 M 11	Guildford av Surb
93 S 1	Guildford gro SE10
133 N 18	Guildford pl WC1
123 O 14	Guildford rd Croy
33 V 4	Guildford rd E17
66 F 18	Guildford rd E6
54 J 8	Guildford rd Ilf
90 A 1	Guildford rd SW8
132 K 19	Guildford st WC1
133 O 17	Guildford st WC1
115 L 15	Guildford vlls Surb
156 B 10	Guildford way Wallgtn
160 D 4	Guildhall bldgs EC2
142 C 4	Guildhall EC2
148 A 6	Guildhouse st SW1
15 N 12	Guildown av N12
32 K 5	Guilds way E17
63 V 1	Guinness clo E9
150 K 5	Guinness sq SE1
87 W 4	Guion rd SW6
156 A 17	Gull clo Wallgtn
57 X 19	Gull way Hornch
58 D 3	Gulliver clo Nthlt
114 G 5	Gulliver rd Sidcp
75 X 8	Gulliver st SE16
72 D 11	Gumleigh rd W5
83 X 7	Gumley gdns Islwth
142 M 1	Gun st E1
126 L 7	Gundulph rd Brom
63 X 3	Gunmakers la E3
78 K 14	Gunner la SE18
20 F 10	Gunners gro E4
106 G 3	Gunners rd SW18
73 P 9	Gunnersbury av W3
72 M 2	Gunnersbury av W5
73 P 6	Gunnersbury cres W3
73 N 7	Gunnersbury dri W5
73 P 6	Gunnersbury gdns W3
73 R 6	Gunnersbury la W3
72 K 9	Gunnersbury pk W3
79 U 10	Gunning st SE18
49 S 11	Gunstor rd N16
25 X 4	Gunter gro Edg
146 B 16	Gunter gro SW10
144 L 8	Gunterstone rd W14
145 N 8	Gunterstone rd W14
143 P 3	Gunthorpe st E1
50 A 8	Gunton rd E5
107 P 16	Gunton rd SW17
75 T 4	Gunwhale clo SE16
77 U 14	Gurdon rd SE7
59 X 11	Gurnell gro W13
52 A 14	Gurney clo E15
122 D 20	Gurney cres Croy
28 E 14	Gurney dri N2
155 N 7	Gurney rd Carsh
52 A 14	Gurney rd E15
51 Z 14	Gurney rd E15
146 J 9	Guthrie st SW3
160 B 5	Gutter la EC2
155 Y 6	Guy rd Wallgtn
142 G 17	Guy st SE1
121 P 2	Guyatt gdns Mitch
93 T 13	Guyscliffe rd SE13
87 P 9	Gwalior rd SW15
87 O 12	Gwendolen av SW15
87 O 13	Gwendolen clo SW15
65 V 3	Gwendoline av E13
144 M 9	Gwendwr rd W14
145 N 8	Gwendwr rd W14
97 O 14	Gwillim clo Sidcp
124 F 7	Gwydor rd Becknhm
126 D 5	Gwydyr rd Brom

124 E 16 Gwynne av Croy
133 P 14 Gwynne pl WC1
88 G 4 Gwynne rd SW11
148 M 10 Gye st SE11
91 P 11 Gylcote clo SE5
24 E 4 Gyles pk Stanm
54 L 10 Gyllyngdune gdns Ilf

H

78 H 16 Ha-Ha rd SE18
144 F 3 Haarlem rd W14
134 G 12 Haberdasher st N1
155 O 2 Hackbridge grn Wallgtn
155 N 2 Hackbridge Park gdns Carsh
155 P 1 Hackbridge rd Wallgtn
90 E 2 Hackford rd SW9
149 R 20 Hackford rd SW9
111 B 18 Hackington cres Becknhm
50 A 19 Hackney gro E8
135 T 9 Hackney rd E2
106 C 16 Hacombe rd SW19
41 R 17 Hadden way Grnfd
79 U 9 Hadden way SE28
111 X 9 Haddington rd Brom
76 F 17 Haddo st SE10
118 C 11 Haddon clo New Mald
8 K 20 Haddon clo Enf
96 M 18 Haddon gro Sidcp
154 A 9 Haddon rd Sutton
63 P 11 Hadleigh clo E1
18 M 2 Hadleigh rd N9
19 N 2 Hadleigh rd N9
63 P 10 Hadleigh st E2
7 U 19 Hadley clo N21
4 K 9 Hadley Common Barnt
5 N 9 Hadley Common Barnt
5 O 10 Hadley Common Barnt
70 D 14 Hadley gdns S'hall
73 Y 13 Hadley gdns W4
4 H 9 Hadley Green rd Barnt
4 G 8 Hadley Green west Barnt
4 G 10 Hadley gro Barnt
4 H 6 Hadley highstone Barnt
4 J 8 Hadley ho Barnt
6 D 3 Hadley rd Barnt
5 O 10 Hadley rd Barnt
81 O 9 Hadley rd Blvdr
7 R 4 Hadley rd Enf
121 X 9 Hadley rd Mitch
4 G 11 Hadley ridge Barnt
47 S 18 Hadley st NW1
7 T 20 Hadley way N21
109 W 17 Hadlow pl SE19
115 O 10 Hadlow rd Sidcp
80 G 19 Hadlow rd Welling
156 B 15 Hadrian clo Wall
76 M 14 Hadrian st SE10
8 H 16 Hadrians ride Enf
74 F 5 Hadyn Park rd W12
88 K 11 Hafer rd SW11
112 A 2 Hafton rd SE6
84 A 19 Haggard rd Twick
135 N 2 Haggerston rd E8
135 U 14 Hague st E2
11 R 17 Haig rd Stanm
65 Y 8 Haig Road east E13
65 X 8 Haig Road west E13
36 A 13 Haigville gdns Ilf
106 C 15 Hailes clo SW19
81 S 6 Hailey rd Blvdr
8 H 20 Haileybury av Enf
108 C 5 Hailsham av SW2
116 H 17 Hailsham clo Surb
23 S 10 Hailsham dri Harrow
107 P 16 Hailsham rd SW17
18 A 15 Hailsham ter N18
95 O 12 Haimo rd SE9
33 X 14 Hainault ct E17
38 A 17 Hainault gore Rom
37 T 11 Hainault ho Rom
33 Z 20 Hainault rd E11
38 B 18 Hainault rd Rom

38 L 10 Hainault rd Rom
54 A 7 Hainault st Ilf
114 A 2 Hainault st SE9
92 G 10 Hainsford clo SE4
108 H 8 Hainthorpe rd SE27
20 B 14 Hal la E4
56 B 11 Halbutt gdns Dgnhm
56 B 11 Halbutt st Dgnhm
134 J 6 Halcomb st N1
98 G 12 Halcot av Bxly Hth
63 O 16 Halcrow st E1
20 G 20 Haldan rd E4
33 V 1 Haldan rd E4
29 R 1 Haldane clo N10
88 A 20 Haldane pl SW18
66 D 8 Haldane rd E6
68 J 20 Haldane rd SE28
145 N 17 Haldane rd S'hall
58 M 18 Haldene rd S'hall
87 W 15 Haldon rd SW18
20 G 10 Hale clo E4
12 J 16 Hale clo Edg
12 J 19 Hale dri NW7
33 W 8 Hale End rd E17
20 J 19 Hale End rd E4
33 V 8 Hale End rd Wdfd Grn
31 X 11 Hale gdns N17
73 P 2 Hale gdns W3
12 M 16 Hale Grove gdns NW7
13 N 17 Hale Grove gdns NW7
12 E 15 Hale la Edg
12 L 16 Hale la NW7
13 O 17 Hale la NW7
66 D 12 Hale rd E6
31 X 11 Hale rd N17
64 D 19 Hale st E14
33 W 2 Hale the E4
31 X 11 Hale the N17
59 U 15 Hale wlk W7
31 Z 6 Halefield rd N17
76 A 20 Hales st SE8
120 A 19 Halesowen rd Mrdn
119 Z 18 Halesowen rd Mrdn
93 P 7 Halesworth rd SE13
26 M 18 Haley rd NW4
72 F 17 Half acre Brentf
71 S 2 Half Acre rd W7
142 A 2 Half Moon ct EC1
90 L 15 Half Moon la SE24
91 N 15 Half Moon la SE24
143 O 5 Half Moon pass E1
139 Y 14 Half Moon st W1
133 R 6 Halfmoon cres N1
33 W 16 Halford rd E10
84 J 13 Halford rd Rich
145 T 15 Halford rd SW6
96 F 20 Halfway st Sidcp
114 J 2 Halfway st Sidcp
83 Z 12 Haliburton rd Twick
49 O 17 Haliday wlk N1
50 C 14 Halidon clo E9
8 A 8 Halifax rd Enf
58 L 3 Halifax rd Grnfd
110 A 8 Halifax st SE26
80 L 10 Halifield dri Blvdr
156 L 16 Haling gro S Croy
156 K 13 Haling Park gdns S Croy
156 M 14 Haling Park rd S Croy
157 N 14 Haling Park rd S Croy
157 O 13 Haling rd S Croy
139 S 20 Halkin ms SW1
147 S 1 Halkin pl SW1
139 U 19 Halkin st SW1
110 B 11 Hall dri SE26
59 U 16 Hall dri W7
11 N 12 Hall Farm clo Stanm
83 R 18 Hall Farm dri Twick
130 E 13 Hall ga NW8
19 Z 14 Hall gdns E4
19 Y 14 Hall la E4
26 G 7 Hall la NW4
130 F 19 Hall pl W2
98 L 14 Hall Place cres Bxly
51 X 12 Hall rd E15
66 G 3 Hall rd E6
83 R 12 Hall rd Islwth
130 C 14 Hall rd NW8
37 U 18 Hall rd Rom
155 T 18 Hall rd Wallgtn
133 X 11 Hall st EC1
15 P 16 Hall st N12
94 E 8 Hall st SE3
113 N 4 Hall view SE9
113 T 13 Hallam clo Chisl
22 C 2 Hallam gdns Pinn
131 Y 20 Hallam ms W1
30 J 14 Hallam rd N5
131 Y 19 Hallam st W1

139 Z 1 Hallam st W1
49 P 17 Hallday wlk N1
93 X 10 Halley gdns SE13
63 W 14 Halley rd E12
52 K 18 Halley rd E7
53 P 16 Halley rd E7
63 V 15 Halley st E14
134 D 1 Halliford st N1
90 B 15 Halliwell rd SW2
29 O 4 Halliwick rd N10
154 A 5 Hallmead rd Sutton
153 Z 5 Hallmead rd Sutton
155 Z 7 Hallowell av Croy
121 O 5 Hallowell clo Mitch
8 G 4 Hallside rd Enf
65 O 17 Hallsville rd E16
27 V 15 Hallswelle rd NW11
95 X 1 Halons rd SE9
150 H 7 Halpin pl SE17
94 M 6 Halsbrook rd SE3
95 P 11 Halsbrook rd SE9
11 O 15 Halsbury clo Stanm
41 O 13 Halsbury Rd east Nthlt
74 H 3 Halsbury rd W12
40 L 14 Halsbury Rd west Nthlt
147 N 6 Halsey st SW3
54 K 16 Halsham cres Bark
90 K 2 Halsmere rd SE5
18 A 5 Halstead gdns N21
34 G 15 Halstead rd E11
8 E 14 Halstead rd Enf
99 P 1 Halstead rd Erith
18 A 5 Halstead rd N21
128 F 13 Halstow rd NW10
77 R 15 Halstow rd SE10
81 V 10 Halt Robin la Blvdr
81 T 10 Halt Robin rd Blvdr
133 Y 3 Halton Cross st N1
48 J 20 Halton rd N1
133 Y 2 Halton rd N1
102 D 6 Ham clo Rich
102 H 9 Ham Farm rd Rich
102 H 8 Ham Gate av Rich
102 C 2 Ham House Rich
52 E 20 Ham Park rd E7
110 A 20 Ham pl SE20
102 M 11 Ham ridings Rich
102 C 3 Ham st Rich
72 E 20 Ham the Brentf
124 J 15 Ham view Croy
140 D 9 Ham yd W1
89 V 14 Hambalt rd SW4
88 B 7 Hamble st SW6
123 U 6 Hambledon gdns SE25
87 V 19 Hambledon rd SW18
96 F 19 Hambledown rd Sidcp
126 F 19 Hambro av Brom
107 Y 13 Hambro rd SW16
123 Z 6 Hambrook rd SE25
70 B 2 Hambrough rd S'hall
56 G 9 Hamden cres Dgnhm
64 G 18 Hamelin st E14
66 J 10 Hameway E6
52 C 17 Hamfrith rd E15
36 B 14 Hamilton av Ilf
18 K 2 Hamilton av N9
38 M 8 Hamilton av Rom
39 N 8 Hamilton av Rom
153 S 1 Hamilton av Sutton
5 X 14 Hamilton clo Barnt
31 W 11 Hamilton clo N17
130 E 15 Hamilton clo NW8
75 W 6 Hamilton clo SE16
40 F 9 Hamilton cres Harrow
82 K 14 Hamilton cres Hounsl
17 U 14 Hamilton cres N13
60 L 20 Hamilton ct W5
130 D 11 Hamilton gdns NW8
48 J 13 Hamilton la N5
139 V 16 Hamilton ms N5
48 H 13 Hamilton Park west NE
48 J 13 Hamilton pk N5
139 V 16 Hamilton pl W1
123 N 5 Hamilton rd Thntn Hth
5 X 14 Hamilton rd Barnt
72 G 16 Hamilton rd Brentf
97 Z 4 Hamilton rd Bxly Hth
65 N 10 Hamilton rd E15
32 J 9 Hamilton rd E17
23 U 15 Hamilton rd Harrow
53 Z 12 Hamilton rd Ilf
28 D 10 Hamilton rd N2
18 J 3 Hamilton rd N9
44 G 14 Hamilton rd NW10

45 R 1 Hamilton rd NW11
39 Y 16 Hamilton rd Rom
70 E 2 Hamilton rd S'hall
109 O 9 Hamilton rd SE27
114 M 9 Hamilton rd Sidcp
106 B 18 Hamilton rd SW19
101 U 1 Hamilton rd Twick
74 A 7 Hamilton rd W4
60 L 19 Hamilton rd W5
130 B 12 Hamilton ter NW8
129 Z 9 Hamilton ter NW8
155 X 19 Hamilton way Wallgtn
14 K 20 Hamilton way N3
94 D 12 Hamlea clo SE12
38 D 2 Hamlet clo Rom
74 F 11 Hamlet gdns W6
38 C 2 Hamlet rd Rom
109 W 18 Hamlet rd SE19
91 R 7 Hamlet the SE5
63 Y 11 Hamlets way E3
109 R 19 Hamlyn gdns SE19
112 E 20 Hammelton rd Brom
13 U 14 Hammers la NW7
144 D 7 Hammersmith bdwy W6
144 A 11 Hammersmith br W6
74 K 15 Hammersmith br W6
144 B 10 Hammersmith Bridge rd W6
74 L 13 Hammersmith Bridge rd W6
144 D 9 Hammersmith flyover W6
74 M 13 Hammersmith flyover W6
136 A 20 Hammersmith gro W6
144 C 5 Hammersmith gro W6
74 L 7 Hammersmith gro W6
144 H 6 Hammersmith rd W6
74 E 14 Hammersmith ter W6
143 N 9 Hammett st EC3
121 R 4 Hammond av Mitch
4 F 18 Hammond clo Barnt
41 H 14 Hammond clo Grntd
9 N 10 Hammond rd Enf
70 D 9 Hammond rd S'hall
47 U 17 Hammond st NW5
68 D 20 Hammond way SE28
12 E 9 Hamonde clo Edg
124 K 4 Hampden av Becknhm
132 G 9 Hampden clo NW1
139 O 6 Hampden Gurney st W1
31 W 5 Hampden la N17
124 J 4 Hampden rd Becknhm
23 O 5 Hampden rd Harrow
117 R 5 Hampden rd Kingst
29 P 1 Hampden rd N10
31 X 4 Hampden rd N17
47 Y 8 Hampden rd N19
30 G 13 Hampden rd N8
38 H 2 Hampden rd Rom
16 E 6 Hampden way N14
18 M 17 Hampshire clo N18
30 D 1 Hampshire rd N22
47 X 16 Hampshire st NW5
90 C 1 Hampson way SW8
80 B 3 Hampstead clo SE28
27 X 19 Hampstead gdns NW11
46 J 14 Hampstead grn NW3
46 D 11 Hampstead gro NW3
46 G 6 Hampstead heath NW3
46 F 13 Hampstead High st NW3
46 H 13 Hampstead Hill gdns NW3
46 K 2 Hampstead la N6
47 N 2 Hampstead la N6
132 B 11 Hampstead rd NW1
46 E 10 Hampstead sq NW3
46 C 4 Hampstead way NW11
27 X 16 Hampstead way NW11
129 T 13 Hampton clo NW6
104 L 18 Hampton clo SW20
116 C 8 Hampton Court pk Kingst
48 H 18 Hampton ct N1
100 C 10 Hampton la Felt
122 M 14 Hampton rd Croy
51 X 5 Hampton rd E11

20 A 16	Hampton rd E4
19 X 16	Hampton rd E4
52 G 15	Hampton rd E7
54 B 13	Hampton rd Ilf
101 R 13	Hampton rd Tedd
101 R 6	Hampton rd Twick
152 H 3	Hampton rd Worc Pk
24 K 19	Hampton ri Harrow
100 G 9	Hampton Road east Felt
100 C 6	Hampton Road west Felt
149 Z 6	Hampton st SE17
114 L 5	Hamshades clo Sidcp
77 U 3	Hanameel st E16
134 B 5	Hanbury ms N1
31 Y 7	Hanbury rd N17
73 T 7	Hanbury rd W3
135 S 20	Hanbury st E1
64 F 9	Hancock rd E3
109 O 16	Hancock st SE19
141 P 2	Hand ct WC1
122 H 19	Handcroft rd Croy
11 Z 19	Handel clo Edg
132 K 16	Handel st WC1
12 C 20	Handel way Edg
25 O 1	Handel way Edg
94 C 14	Handen rd SE12
149 S 18	Handforth rd SW9
63 R 2	Handley rd E9
65 T 17	Hands wlk E16
153 P 1	Handside clo Worc Pk
20 J 19	Handsworth av E4
31 P 11	Handsworth rd N17
67 N 5	Handtrough way Bark
105 Y 1	Hanford clo SW18
104 M 14	Hanford row SW19
61 O 11	Hanger grn W5
60 K 12	Hanger Hill pk W5
60 L 14	Hanger la W5
60 M 17	Hanger Vale la W5
61 O 15	Hanger Vale la W5
61 O 16	Hanger View way W3
141 V 6	Hanging Sword all EC4
142 F 19	Hankey pl SE1
13 N 10	Hankins la NW7
48 A 5	Hanley rd N4
43 W 13	Hannah clo NW10
144 L 18	Hannell rd SW6
108 K 8	Hannen rd SE27
63 R 14	Hannibal rd E1
156 C 13	Hannibal way Croy
50 L 17	Hannington point E9
89 S 8	Hannington rd SW4
73 O 19	Hanover clo Rich
153 T 8	Hanover clo Sutton
130 M 13	Hanover ga NW1
36 B 2	Hanover gdns Ilf
149 S 16	Hanover gdns SE11
91 X 3	Hanover pk SE15
140 L 7	Hanover rd WC2
31 V 13	Hanover rd N15
128 C 3	Hanover rd NW10
62 M 2	Hanover rd NW10
106 E 17	Hanover rd SW19
139 Y 7	Hanover sq W1
156 J 6	Hanover st Croy
139 Z 7	Hanover st W1
131 N 14	Hanover ter NW1
131 N 15	Hanover Terrace ms NW1
97 X 9	Hanover way Bxly Hth
133 Z 8	Hanover yd N1
139 O 20	Hans cres SW1
147 O 2	Hans pl SW1
147 N 1	Hans rd SW3
147 P 2	Hans st SW1
136 J 18	Hansard ms W14
7 U 7	Hansart way Enf
10 J 17	Hanselin clo Stanm
25 X 4	Hanshaw dri Edgw
91 V 13	Hansler rd SE22
97 Y 12	Hansol rd Bxly Hth
89 S 19	Hanson clo SW12
70 C 5	Hanson gdns S'hall
140 A 1	Hanson st W1
132 A 20	Hanson st W1
140 F 3	Hanway pl W1
59 T 16	Hanway rd W7
140 F 4	Hanway st W1
100 J 14	Hanworth rd Hampt
82 H 14	Hanworth rd Hounsl
82 K 10	Hanworth ter Hounsl
41 P 15	Hapgood clo Har
143 T 9	Harads pl E1
46 E 20	Harben rd NW6
65 P 3	Harberson rd E15
89 R 20	Harberson rd SW12
47 V 4	Harberton rd N19
19 U 17	Harbet rd E4
138 H 2	Harbet rd W2
98 F 18	Harbex clo Bxly
76 D 12	Harbinger rd E14
87 X 1	Harbledown rd SW6
91 O 4	Harbord clo SE5
87 P 1	Harbord st SW6
96 J 18	Harborough av Sidcp
108 D 9	Harborough rd SW16
88 D 2	Harbour av SW10
90 L 7	Harbour rd SE5
86 F 18	Harbridge av SW15
154 H 17	Harbury rd Carsh
88 F 11	Harbut rd SW11
49 R 10	Harcombe rd N16
53 T 14	Harcourt av E12
12 G 11	Harcourt av Edg
97 T 18	Harcourt av Sidcp
155 T 9	Harcourt av Wallgtn
97 Z 9	Harcourt Bxly Hth
83 Z 6	Harcourt clo Islwth
155 T 8	Harcourt field Wallgtn
122 D 14	Harcourt rd Thntn Hth
65 O 6	Harcourt rd E15
29 W 4	Harcourt rd N22
92 J 9	Harcourt rd SE4
105 Y 19	Harcourt rd SW19
155 S 8	Harcourt rd Wallgtn
138 M 2	Harcourt st W1
146 A 12	Harcourt ter SW10
145 Z 11	Harcourt ter SW10
159 S 7	Hardcourts clo W Wkhm
108 G 2	Hardel ri SW2
78 D 10	Hardel st SE18
78 A 9	Hardens manorway SE7
91 Z 3	Harders rd SE15
92 A 2	Harders Road ms SE15
90 K 8	Hardess st SE24
43 W 15	Hardie clo NW10
56 K 10	Hardie rd Dgnhm
98 A 4	Harding rd Bxly Hth
18 D 18	Hardinge rd N18
128 C 6	Hardinge rd NW10
62 L 4	Hardinge rd NW10
63 R 19	Hardinge st E1
110 E 16	Hardings la SE20
116 K 2	Hardman rd Kingst
77 U 13	Hardman rd SE7
11 R 16	Hardwick clo Stanm
133 T 13	Hardwick st EC1
82 H 2	Hardwicke av Hounsl
60 B 14	Hardwicke grn W13
17 N 18	Hardwicke rd N13
102 C 9	Hardwicke rd Rich
73 X 11	Hardwicke rd W4
87 X 14	Hardwicks way SW18
142 J 17	Hardwidge st SE1
77 R 17	Hardy rd SE3
106 B 18	Hardy rd SW19
7 U 6	Hardy way Enf
94 A 4	Hare and Billet rd SE3
93 X 4	Hare and Billet rd SE3
141 S 7	Hare ct EC4
39 Y 12	Hare Hall la Rom
135 S 17	Hare marsh E2
63 N 5	Hare row E2
135 X 7	Hare row E2
78 J 9	Hare st SE18
134 L 9	Hare wlk N1
58 B 11	Harecastle clo Grnfd
48 L 17	Harecourt rd N1
90 M 11	Haredale rd SE24
92 D 18	Haredon clo SE23
29 X 15	Harefield av N8
153 R 20	Harefield av Sutton
7 U 5	Harefield clo Enf
92 K 7	Harefield ms SE4
92 L 8	Harefield rd SE4
93 N 8	Harefield rd SE4
115 W 6	Harefield rd Sidcp
108 D 18	Harefield rd SW16
56 F 19	Haresfield rd Dgnhm
58 D 1	Harewood av Nthlt
130 M 17	Harewood av NW1
131 N 20	Harewood av NW1
58 D 1	Harewood clo Nthlt
35 T 7	Harewood dri Ilf
139 Y 6	Harewood pl W1
71 V 20	Harewood rd Islwth
83 W 1	Harewood rd Islwth
157 S 14	Harewood rd S Croy
106 K 16	Harewood rd SW19
130 M 20	Harewood row NW1
70 F 11	Harewood ter S'hall
91 R 7	Harfield gdns SE5
20 E 2	Harford clo E4
20 E 2	Harford rd E4
63 U 12	Harford st E1
28 G 14	Harford wlk N2
24 K 19	Hargood clo Harrow
94 L 4	Hargood rd SE3
47 U 8	Hargrave pk N19
47 X 16	Hargrave pl N7
47 W 7	Hargrave rd N19
90 B 8	Hargwyne st SW9
30 D 13	Haringey gro N8
30 A 19	Haringey pk N8
30 A 14	Haringey rd N8
23 V 6	Harkett clo Harrow
157 W 5	Harland av Croy
114 E 6	Harland av Sidcp
94 E 20	Harland rd SE12
112 F 1	Harland rd SE12
17 O 11	Harlech rd N14
71 Z 17	Harlequin av Brentf
102 A 17	Harlequin rd Tedd
92 F 10	Harlescott rd SE15
62 D 3	Harlesden gdns NW10
62 H 2	Harlesden rd NW10
44 J 20	Harlesden rd NW10
42 G 17	Harley clo Wemb
23 R 13	Harley cres Harrow
146 C 11	Harley gdns SW10
63 Z 9	Harley gro E3
139 W 2	Harley pl W1
23 R 12	Harley rd Harrow
62 B 6	Harley rd NW10
130 H 2	Harley rd NW3
131 W 19	Harley st W1
139 X 2	Harley st W1
112 K 20	Harleyford Brom
149 O 13	Harleyford rd SE11
149 S 15	Harleyford st SE11
98 A 7	Harlington rd Bxly Hth
18 A 10	Harlow rd N13
21 O 20	Harman av Wdfd Grn
20 K 14	Harman clo E4
45 T 11	Harman clo NW2
45 T 11	Harman dri NW2
96 K 16	Harman dri Sidcup
8 G 16	Harman rd Enf
155 Z 19	Harmony clo SM6
47 R 20	Harmood st NW1
47 R 20	Harmood st NW1
149 W 12	Harmsworth st SE17
14 J 6	Harmsworth way N20
79 Z 6	Harness rd SE28
81 O 14	Harold av Belvdr
149 R 12	Harold pl SE11
51 Z 4	Harold rd E11
65 X 3	Harold rd E13
20 F 12	Harold rd E4
31 V 14	Harold rd N15
30 C 14	Harold rd N8
61 X 8	Harold rd NW10
109 R 16	Harold rd SE19
154 F 9	Harold rd Sutton
34 G 4	Harold rd Wdfd Grn
32 G 16	Haroldstone rd E17
141 V 4	Harp all EC4
43 Y 7	Harp Island clo NW10
142 K 10	Harp la EC3
59 V 12	Harp rd W7
52 K 6	Harpenden rd E12
108 H 5	Harpenden rd SE27
66 G 18	Harper rd E6
142 B 20	Harper rd SE1
150 C 1	Harper rd SE1
63 S 10	Harpley sq E1
54 B 19	Harpour rd Bark
89 O 3	Harpsden st SW11
133 N 20	Harpur st WC1
94 L 2	Harraden rd SE3
64 J 20	Harrap st E14
57 Y 19	Harrier clo Hornch
79 T 6	Harrier ms SE28
135 R 4	Harriet clo E8
157 X 2	Harriet gdns Croy
139 R 20	Harriet st SW1
10 C 3	Harriet way Bushey
139 R 19	Harriet wlk SW1
72 J 1	Harriets clo W5
30 J 14	Harringay gdns N15
30 G 12	Harringay pass N8
30 J 13	Harringay rd N15
30 J 14	Harringay rd N15
155 Z 3	Harrington clo Wallgtn
146 A 7	Harrington gdns SW7
50 B 4	Harrington hill E5
52 A 4	Harrington rd E11
124 B 8	Harrington rd SE25
123 Y 9	Harrington rd SE25
146 E 6	Harrington rd SW7
132 B 9	Harrington sq NW1
132 A 12	Harrington st NW1
18 B 12	Harrington ter N18
78 B 8	Harrington way SE18
77 O 12	Harriott clo SE10
7 V 6	Harris clo Enf
82 G 2	Harris clo Hounsl
98 A 2	Harris rd Bxly Hth
56 B 15	Harris rd Dgnhm
50 L 1	Harris st E17
150 G 19	Harris st SE5
56 F 19	Harrison rd Dgnhm
132 M 14	Harrison st WC1
156 J 5	Harrison's ri Croy
55 R 15	Harrold rd Dgnhm
18 H 1	Harrow av Enf
39 Z 3	Harrow cres Rom
57 Z 3	Harrow dri Hornch
18 G 4	Harrow dri N9
51 Z 9	Harrow grn E11
64 F 20	Harrow la E14
80 F 2	Harrow Lodge park Hornch
57 Y 7	Harrow Lodge park Hornch
80 F 7	Harrow Manor way SE2
41 U 6	Harrow pk Harrow
142 M 3	Harrow pl E1
67 V 3	Harrow rd Bark
154 J 12	Harrow rd Carsh
52 D 9	Harrow rd E11
66 D 2	Harrow rd E6
54 C 14	Harrow rd Ilf
128 D 14	Harrow rd NW10
62 J 8	Harrow rd NW10
138 B 2	Harrow rd W2
129 O 17	Harrow rd W9
43 P 17	Harrow rd Wemb
41 X 12	Harrow rd Wemb
23 R 14	Harrow view Harrow
60 C 12	Harrow view rd W5
10 D 18	Harrow Weald pk Harrow
88 F 5	Harroway rd SW11
138 M 4	Harrowby st W1
139 N 4	Harrowby st W1
42 F 14	Harrowdene clo Wemb
101 Z 17	Harrowdene gdns Tedd
42 G 10	Harrowdene rd Wemb
12 D 10	Harrowes meade Edg
41 U 10	Harrowfields gdns Harrow
50 G 19	Harrowgate rd E9
58 G 14	Hart gro S'hall
73 O 2	Hart gro W5
142 L 8	Hart st EC3
141 S 1	Hart yd EC1
82 F 5	Harte rd Hounsl
105 V 17	Hartfield cres SW19
110 B 20	Hartfield gro SE20
105 W 18	Hartfield rd SW19
64 B 7	Hartfield ter E3
24 A 10	Hartford av Harrow
23 Z 10	Hartford av Harrow
98 F 17	Hartford rd Bxly
27 H 14	Hartford wlk N2
83 X 1	Hartham clo Islwth
48 A 15	Hartham clo N7
83 X 2	Hartham rd Islwth
31 U 6	Hartham rd N17
48 A 15	Hartham rd N7
113 P 8	Harting rd SE9
41 T 12	Hartington clo Harrow
65 V 17	Hartington rd E16
32 H 19	Hartington rd E17
70 B 7	Hartington rd S'hall
148 J 20	Hartington rd SW8
89 Z 1	Hartington rd SW8
84 B 17	Hartington rd Twick
72 B 1	Hartington rd W13
73 U 20	Hartington rd W4
85 W 3	Hartington rd W4
145 R 17	Hartismere rd SW6
50 G 18	Hartlake rd E9

38 G 3	Hazell cres Rom
58 F 6	Hazelmere clo Grnfd
58 F 5	Hazelmere rd Nthlt
129 S 6	Hazelmere rd NW6
126 E 14	Hazelmere way Brom
58 F 5	Hazelmere wlk Nthlt
58 B 9	Hazeltree la Nthlt
47 X 2	Hazelville rd N19
120 B 9	Hazelwood av Mrdn
72 K 5	Hazelwood clo W5
17 T 13	Hazelwood cres N13
116 J 14	Hazelwood ct Surb
17 T 13	Hazelwood la N13
32 H 16	Hazelwood rd E17
8 J 19	Hazelwood rd Enf
88 A 4	Hazlebury rd SW6
157 R 4	Hazledean rd Croy
73 V 16	Hazledene rd W4
118 H 19	Hazlemere gdns Worc Pk
87 N 12	Hazlewell rd SW15
128 M 17	Hazlewood cres W10
129 N 17	Hazlewood cres W10
144 K 2	Hazlitt ms W14
144 K 3	Hazlitt rd W14
122 D 8	Headcorn rd Thntn Hth
112 D 12	Headcorn rd Brom
31 U 2	Headcorn rd N17
139 V 19	Headfort pl SW1
106 E 2	Headington rd SW18
89 X 17	Headlam rd SW4
63 N 12	Headlam st E1
35 Y 17	Headley appr Ilf
156 D 10	Headley av Wallgtn
159 T 16	Headley dri Croy
36 A 18	Headley dri Ilf
35 Y 17	Headley dri Ilf
92 A 6	Headley st SE15
23 P 11	Headstone dri Harrow
23 O 12	Headstone gdns Harrow
22 L 8	Headstone la Harrow
22 M 11	Headstone mnr
23 S 18	Headstone rd Harrow
152 D 20	Headway the Epsom
93 N 2	Heald st SE14
47 S 18	Healey st NW1
134 K 18	Hearn st EC2
73 P 5	Hearne rd W4
150 G 8	Hearns bldgs SE17
89 O 20	Hearnville rd SW12
80 J 17	Heath av Bxly Hth
46 C 8	Heath brow NW3
46 A 2	Heath clo NW11
39 W 10	Heath clo Rom
61 O 12	Heath clo W5
46 A 12	Heath dri NW3
45 Z 13	Heath dri NW3
39 W 9	Heath dri Rom
154 C 19	Heath dri Sutton
118 M 8	Heath dri SW20
119 N 8	Heath dri SW20
101 V 2	Heath gdns Twick
110 B 18	Heath gro SE20
46 J 13	Heath Hurst rd NW3
93 Y 6	Heath la SE3
105 O 6	Heath mead SW19
39 X 15	Heath Park rd Rom
99 T 17	Heath rd Drtfrd
23 N 20	Heath rd Harrow
82 L 11	Heath rd Hounsl
83 P 10	Heath rd Hounsl
55 Y 1	Heath rd Romford
89 R 7	Heath rd SW8
89 T 6	Heath rd SW8
122 M 5	Heath rd Thntn Hth
101 W 2	Heath rd Twick
126 D 14	Heath ri Brom
87 R 16	Heath ri SW15
46 H 11	Heath side NW3
46 D 10	Heath st NW3
28 D 12	Heath View clo N2
28 E 12	Heath view N2
79 W 15	Heath vlls SE18
98 L 2	Heath way Erith
21 Z 15	Heath way Wdfd Grn
83 V 19	Heatham pk Twick
10 G 8	Heathbourne rd Stanm
99 Y 20	Heathclose av Drtfrd
99 W 20	Heathclose rd Drtfrd
35 U 7	Heathcote ave Ilf
20 F 9	Heathcote gro E4
84 C 14	Heathcote rd Twick
133 N 15	Heathcote st WC1
46 B 3	Heathcroft NW11
61 N 12	Heathcroft W5
82 B 8	Heathdale av Hounsl
81 U 12	Heathdene dri Blvdr
155 T 16	Heathdene rd Wallgtn
81 V 12	Heathdene rd Blvdr
108 C 18	Heathdene rd SW16
39 O 7	Heather av Rom
66 L 18	Heather clo E6
100 F 20	Heather clo Hampt
39 N 5	Heather clo Rom
99 V 19	Heather dri Drtfrd
39 O 7	Heather dri Rom
27 S 19	Heather gdns NW11
39 O 6	Heather gdns Rom
153 X 14	Heather gdns Sutton
39 N 7	Heather glen Rom
61 R 2	Heather Park dri Wemb
44 D 7	Heather rd NW2
112 F 2	Heather rd SE12
39 N 6	Heather way Rom
158 F 18	Heather way S Croy
10 J 20	Heather way Stanm
12 E 16	Heather wlk Edg
127 Y 3	Heatherbank BR7
95 V 5	Heatherbank SE9
103 R 17	Heatherdale clo Kingst
120 H 10	Heatherdene clo Mitch
35 S 9	Heatherley dri Ilf
108 D 19	Heatherset gdns SW16
115 V 6	Heatherside rd Sidcp
52 K 7	Heatherwood clo E12
88 G 17	Heathfield ave SW18
114 C 16	Heathfield Chisl
66 A 14	Heathfield clo E16
73 X 13	Heathfield ct W4
20 G 10	Heathfield E4
88 F 15	Heathfield gdns SW18
27 P 20	Heathfield gdns NW11
73 V 14	Heathfield gdns W4
114 B 17	Heathfield la Chisl
83 V 17	Heathfield north Twick
44 M 19	Heathfield pk NW2
98 A 11	Heathfield rd Bxly Hth
112 D 18	Heathfield rd Brom
157 N 9	Heathfield rd Croy
88 F 16	Heathfield rd SW18
73 S 6	Heathfield rd W3
158 D 14	Heathfield rd S Croy
83 V 18	Heathfield south Twick
88 F 18	Heathfield sq SW18
79 W 16	Heathfield ter SE18
73 W 13	Heathfield ter W4
158 G 18	Heathfield vale S Croy
28 A 19	Heathgate NW11
157 R 19	Heathhurst rd S Croy
49 P 3	Heathland rd N16
99 Y 17	Heathlands ri Drtfrd
94 B 10	Heathlee rd SE3
114 C 15	Heathley end Chisl
87 W 3	Heathmans rd SW6
98 A 4	Heathside av Bxly Hth
97 Z 3	Heathside av Bxly Hth
82 E 19	Heathside Hounsl
62 H 18	Heathstan rd W12
99 S 17	Heathview av Drtfrd
99 X 20	Heathview cres Drtfrd
80 H 16	Heathview dri SE2
86 L 19	Heathview gdns SW15
122 F 8	Heathview rd Thntn Hth
48 A 2	Heathville rd N19
88 M 8	Heathwall st SW11
158 M 5	Heathway Croy
56 C 12	Heathway Dgnhm
69 R 2	Heathway Dgnhm
77 S 20	Heathway SE3
78 D 13	Heathwood gdns SE7
99 O 20	Heathwood lodge Bxly
39 Y 2	Heaton av Rom
39 U 6	Heaton Grange rd Rom
51 V 15	Heaton pl E15
107 O 17	Heaton rd Mitch
91 Y 6	Heaton rd SE15
88 G 6	Heaver clo SW11
79 R 15	Heavitree clo SE18
79 S 14	Heavitree rd SE18
106 K 7	Hebdon rd SW17
45 O 14	Hebdon rd Blvdr
91 V 15	Heber rd SE22
144 A 2	Hebron rd W6
74 L 9	Heckfield pl SW6
32 H 6	Hecham clo E17
145 T 19	Heckfield pl SW6
63 T 19	Heckford st E1
79 U 12	Hector st SE18
83 Y 9	Heddon clo Islwth
6 A 15	Heddon Court av Bark
5 Z 16	Heddon rd Barnt
140 B 10	Heddon st W1
7 W 6	Hedge hill Enf
17 V 11	Hedge la N13
35 T 13	Hedgeley Ilf
55 W 20	Hedgeman's rd Dgnhm
56 C 19	Hedgemans rd Dgnhm
55 Y 19	Hedgemans way Dgnhm
58 M 7	Hedgerly gdns Grnfd
50 H 18	Hedgers gro E9
35 V 14	Hedgewood gdns Ilf
94 B 12	Hedgley st SE12
134 A 2	Hedingham clo N1
55 P 16	Hedingham rd Dgnhm
115 R 7	Hedley clo Sidcp
49 O 14	Hedley rw N5
8 A 8	Heene rd Enf
66 C 2	Heigham rd E6
156 J 10	Heighton gdns Croy
41 Y 15	Heights av Grnfd
104 J 19	Heights clo SW20
40 F 15	Heights the Nrthlt
77 Z 15	Heights the SE7
89 Y 16	Helby rd SW4
94 C 19	Helder gro SE12
157 O 13	Helder st S Croy
83 R 9	Heldman clo Islwth
28 C 10	Helen clo N2
78 M 11	Helen st SE18
156 C 16	Helena clo Croy
60 G 14	Helena ct W5
65 R 7	Helena rd E13
33 N 17	Helena rd E17
44 J 14	Helena rd NW10
60 H 14	Helena rd NW5
5 U 2	Helens clo Barnt
45 X 4	Helenslea av NW11
90 D 15	Helix gdns SW2
90 E 16	Helix rd SW2
143 U 14	Hellings st E1
105 V 12	Helme clo SW19
134 B 15	Helmet row EC1
58 A 11	Helmsdale clo Grnfd
39 R 2	Helmsdale clo Rom
39 R 1	Helmsdale rd Rom
107 W 19	Helmsdale rd SW16
135 X 2	Helmsley pl E8
22 E 3	Helston clo Pinn
77 O 13	Helvelius clo SE10
110 L 5	Helvetia st SE6
148 H 18	Hemans st SW8
90 A 7	Hemberton rd SW9
41 P 14	Hemery clo Grnfd
25 S 1	Heming rd Edg
153 N 8	Hemingford rd Sutton
133 P 2	Hemingford rd N1
15 Y 16	Hemington av N11
86 E 3	Hemitage the SW13
62 E 20	Hemlock rd W12
100 G 20	Hemming clo Hampt
135 U 17	Hemming st E1
150 F 6	Hemp wlk SE17
21 S 8	Hempstead clo Buck Hl
33 X 9	Hempstead rd E17
63 N 2	Hemsley st E8
45 Y 20	Hemstal rd NW6
26 A 5	Hemswell dri NW9
134 J 7	Hemsworth st N1
146 L 10	Hemus pl SW3
62 D 17	Henchman st W12
26 H 10	Hendale av NW4
43 V 17	Henderson clo NW10
130 F 16	Henderson dri NW8
123 N 13	Henderson rd Croy
52 K 17	Henderson rd E7
18 M 4	Henderson rd N9
88 H 18	Henderson rd SW18
106 K 4	Hendham rd SW17
27 V 6	Hendon av N3
27 U 9	Hendon la N3
27 V 17	Hendon Park row NW11
13 S 7	Hendon pk NW7
18 K 7	Hendon rd N9
45 T 6	Hendon way NW2
26 L 18	Hendon way NW4
13 T 4	Hendon Wood la NW7
150 K 7	Hendre rd SE1
41 P 15	Hendren clo Grnfd
88 M 18	Hendrick av SW12
142 L 5	Heneage la EC3
143 P 1	Heneage st E1
98 E 15	Henfield clo Bxly
47 W 5	Henfield clo N1
119 V 1	Henfield rd SW19
105 V 20	Henfield rd SW19
120 F 9	Hengelo gdns Mitch
81 X 18	Hengist rd Erith
94 J 18	Hengist rd SE12
125 Y 9	Hengist way Brom
92 E 17	Hengrave rd SE23
146 E 13	Henley ms SW3
153 R 5	Henley av Sutton
59 O 6	Henley clo Grnfd
83 V 3	Henley clo Islwth
16 G 3	Henley ct N14
104 C 18	Henley dri Kingst
37 Y 15	Henley gdns Rom
78 H 5	Henley rd E16
54 B 13	Henley rd Ilf
18 D 13	Henley rd N18
128 D 3	Henley rd NW10
89 O 4	Henley st SW11
110 E 7	Hennel clo SE23
66 C 8	Henn" clo SE23
146 E 13	Henniker ms SW3
51 Y 15	Henniker rd E15
88 H 3	Henning st SW11
31 P 3	Henningham rd N17
139 W 5	Henrietta pl W1
51 V 15	Henrietta st E15
140 K 9	Henrietta st WC2
143 T 6	Henriques st E1
113 N 8	Henry Cooper way SE9
14 D 17	Henry Darlot dri NW7
87 O 8	Henry Jackson rd SW18
5 T 17	Henry rd Barnt
66 E 6	Henry rd E6
48 K 5	Henry rd N4
112 J 20	Henry rd Brom
21 P 16	Henrys av Wdfd Grn
36 D 2	Henrys wlk Ilf
92 M 13	Henryson rd SE4
93 N 13	Henryson rd SE4
110 A 9	Hensford gdns SE26
49 P 18	Henshall st N1
150 E 5	Henshaw st SE17
55 X 9	Henshawe rd Dgnhm
91 Y 13	Henslowe rd SE22
44 L 14	Henson av NW2
24 G 11	Henson pth Harrow
130 J 7	Henstridge pl NW8
146 L 20	Henty clo SW11
86 J 14	Henty wlk SW15
126 J 1	Henville rd Brom
95 P 8	Henwick rd SE9
75 P 9	Henwood rd SE16
84 A 4	Hepple clo Islwth
86 K 16	Hepplestone clo SW15
51 N 19	Hepscott rd E9
55 N 15	Hepworth gdns Bark
108 B 19	Hepworth rd SW16
155 Z 17	Heracles clo Wallgtn
63 O 10	Herald st E2
135 Y 15	Herald st E2
133 T 18	Herbal hill EC1
133 U 18	Herbal pl EC1
147 O 1	Herbert cres SW1
128 A 8	Herbert gdns NW10
62 J 5	Herbert gdns NW10
55 W 1	Herbert gdns Rom
73 T 17	Herbert gdns W4
127 P 11	Herbert rd Brom
98 A 5	Herbert rd Bxly Hth
97 Z 4	Herbert rd Bxly Hth
53 R 14	Herbert rd E12
32 L 20	Herbert rd E17
116 L 7	Herbert rd Kingst
54 G 6	Herbert rd Ilf
16 M 20	Herbert rd N11
31 V 15	Herbert rd N15
18 M 8	Herbert rd N9

47 S 13	Highgate rd NW5
47 O 6	Highgate West hill N6
47 O 7	Highgate West hill N6
55 S 14	Highgrove rd Dgnhm
56 K 9	Highland av Dgnhm
59 T 16	Highland av W7
155 T 9	Highland cotts Wallgtn
111 R 13	Highland croft Becknhm
26 B 1	Highland rd Brom
112 B 19	Highland rd Brom
98 E 12	Highland rd Bxly Hth
109 R 15	Highland rd SE19
61 V 20	Highlands av W3
82 K 3	Highlands clo Hounsl
53 T 2	Highlands gdns Ilf
86 L 20	Highlands heath SW15
4 M 16	Highlands rd Barnt
25 T 6	Highlands the Edg
26 B 3	Highlea clo NW9
136 C 1	Highlever rd W10
42 M 20	Highmead cres Wemb
79 X 20	Highmead SE18
77 N 18	Highmore rd SE3
91 W 3	Highshore rd SE15
12 G 14	Highview av Edg
156 C 11	Highview av Wallgtn
12 G 14	Highview gdns Edg
16 H 17	Highview gdns N11
12 M 11	Highview NW7
59 Z 16	Highview rd W13
63 S 20	Highway the E1
79 X 20	Highway the E1
143 W 10	Highway the E1
23 X 1	Highway the Stanm
154 D 20	Highway the Sutton
31 T 16	Highweek rd N15
15 R 13	Highwood av N12
35 U 14	Highwood gdns Ilf
12 M 15	Highwood gro NW7
13 S 10	Highwood hill NW7
13 R 9	Highwood ho NW7
47 Z 10	Highwood rd N19
16 L 17	Highworth rd N11
121 N 5	Hilary av Mitch
98 H 2	Hilary clo Bxly Hth
145 X 18	Hilary clo SW6
62 D 20	Hilary rd W12
153 P 6	Hilbert rd Sutton
65 N 12	Hilda rd E16
66 A 1	Hilda rd E6
112 B 14	Hildenborough gdns Brom
125 Y 3	Hildenlea pl BR2
107 R 1	Hildreth st SW12
145 U 14	Hildyard rd SW6
128 B 11	Hiley rd NW10
62 L 8	Hiley rd NW10
130 D 2	Hilgrove rd NW6
24 E 8	Hiliary gdns Stanm
127 P 1	Hill brow Brom
113 O 20	Hill brow Chisl
99 U 17	Hill brow Drtfrd
113 Y 12	Hill clo Chisl
41 T 11	Hill clo Harrow
27 Z 18	Hill clo NW11
44 J 10	Hill clo NW2
11 N 13	Hill clo Stanm
23 Y 16	Hill cres Harrow
15 N 7	Hill cres N20
117 O 10	Hill cres Surb
153 N 3	Hill cres Worc Pk
27 S 11	Hill Crest gdns N3
97 O 19	Hill crest Sidcp
40 H 15	Hill ct Grnfd
43 U 4	Hill dri NW9
136 E 1	Hill Farm rd W10
128 E 20	Hill Farm rd W10
39 P 9	Hill gro Rom
23 W 1	Hill House av Stanm
17 T 2	Hill House clo N21
108 D 13	Hill House rd SW16
108 D 13	Hill pth SW16
154 K 14	Hill rd Carsh
23 Y 16	Hill rd Harrow
107 T 19	Hill rd Mitch
29 N 6	Hill rd N10
130 D 10	Hill rd NW8
22 A 17	Hill rd Pinn
154 A 11	Hill rd Sutton
42 A 8	Hill rd Wemb
9 N 20	Hill ri Enf
59 O 2	Hill ri Grnfd
19 N 1	Hill ri N9
28 B 14	Hill ri NW11
84 H 14	Hill ri Rich

110 A 2	Hill ri SE23
84 H 14	Hill st Rich
139 V 12	Hill st W1
28 B 13	Hill top NW11
119 T 18	Hill top Sutton
35 T 18	Hill View cres Ilf
96 G 4	Hill View dri Welling
25 Y 15	Hill View gdns NW9
14 B 14	Hill View rd NW7
22 D 1	Hill View rd Pinn
83 Y 16	Hill View rd Twick
70 H 7	Hillary rd S'hall
70 H 8	Hillary rd S'hall
75 O 18	Hillbeck cl SE15
151 Z 16	Hillbeck clo SE15
59 P 3	Hillbeck way Grnfd
106 C 19	Hillborough clo SW19
135 O 3	Hillborough ct E8
107 O 9	Hillbrook rd SW17
118 E 7	Hillbrow New Mald
111 Z 16	Hillbrow rd Brom
24 C 16	Hillbury av Harrow
107 T 6	Hillbury rd SW17
108 E 18	Hillcote av SW16
15 N 18	Hillcourt av N12
91 Z 17	Hillcourt rd SE22
12 E 14	Hillcrest av Edg
27 U 14	Hillcrest av NW11
124 K 13	Hillcrest clo Becknhm
109 X 11	Hillcrest clo SE26
44 F 10	Hillcrest gdns NW2
17 U 2	Hillcrest N21
29 P 20	Hillcrest N6
112 E 11	Hillcrest rd Brom
99 S 18	Hillcrest rd Drtfrd
33 Y 7	Hillcrest rd E17
34 D 7	Hillcrest rd E18
57 V 1	Hillcrest rd Hornch
39 Y 20	Hillcrest rd Hornch
73 R 3	Hillcrest rd W3
60 L 13	Hillcrest rd W5
124 K 14	Hillcrest view Becknhm
22 E 20	Hillcroft av Pinn
60 H 16	Hillcroft cres W5
42 M 12	Hillcroft cres Wemb
43 N 12	Hillcroft cres Wemb
66 L 14	Hillcroft rd E6
154 G 13	Hillcroome rd Sutton
119 S 11	Hillcross av Mrdn
153 V 9	Hilldale rd Sutton
126 B 19	Hilldown rd Brom
108 B 17	Hilldown rd SW16
47 Y 15	Hilldrop cres N7
47 Y 15	Hilldrop la N7
112 G 15	Hilldrop rd Brom
47 Z 14	Hilldrop rd N7
95 Y 3	Hillend SE18
12 A 16	Hillerdon av Edg
86 F 4	Hillersdon av SW13
150 F 6	Hillery clo SE17
120 H 13	Hillfield av Mrdn
30 B 13	Hillfield av N8
26 B 15	Hillfield av NW9
42 M 20	Hillfield clo Harrow
23 N 13	Hillfield clo Harrow
46 J 16	Hillfield ct NW3
29 S 12	Hillfield Park ms N10
29 S 12	Hillfield pk N10
17 S 9	Hillfield pk N21
100 D 19	Hillfield rd Hampt
45 X 14	Hillfield rd NW6
38 K 5	Hillfoot av Rom
38 J 5	Hillfoot rd Rom
137 T 13	Hillgate pl W8
137 T 13	Hillgate st W8
75 O 2	Hilliards ct E1
143 Z 13	Hilliards ct E1
5 N 20	Hillier clo Barnt
156 G 11	Hillier gdns Croy
89 N 16	Hillier rd SW11
155 Z 6	Hilliers la Wallgtn
98 L 8	Hillingdon rd Bxly Hth
150 A 14	Hillingdon st SE17
149 X 16	Hillingdon st SE5
35 O 7	Hillington gdns Wdfd Grn
50 A 18	Hillman st E8
48 A 14	Hillmarton rd N7
90 H 10	Hillmead dri SW9
110 G 12	Hillmore gro SE26
78 E 13	Hillreach SE18
47 Z 1	Hillrise rd N19
140 B 6	Hills pl W1
21 V 6	Hills rd Buck Hl
91 S 13	Hillsboro rd SE22
15 Z 18	Hillside av N11

21 X 18	Hillside av Wdfd Grn
21 Z 18	Hillside av Wdfd Grn
42 L 12	Hillside av Wemb
5 S 17	Hillside Barnt
119 S 8	Hillside clo Mrdn
129 Y 9	Hillside clo NW6
21 Y 17	Hillside clo Wdfd Grn
8 B 2	Hillside cres Enf
40 M 5	Hillside cres Harrow
12 B 18	Hillside dri Edg
31 U 20	Hillside est N15
4 E 14	Hillside gdns Barnt
33 X 9	Hillside gdns E17
12 A 14	Hillside gdns Edg
42 K 1	Hillside gdns Harrow
16 H 20	Hillside gdns N11
29 R 19	Hillside gdns N6
155 V 17	Hillside gdns Wallgtn
16 K 3	Hillside gro N14
26 F 1	Hillside gro NW7
61 W 2	Hillside NW10
25 X 14	Hillside NW9
156 J 8	Hillside rd Croy
99 V 15	Hillside rd Drtfrd
31 T 19	Hillside rd N15
58 G 11	Hillside rd S'hall
117 O 10	Hillside rd Surb
153 V 16	Hillside rd Sutton
108 F 3	Hillside rd SW2
60 J 15	Hillside rd W5
105 P 16	Hillside SW19
137 R 13	Hillsleigh rd W8
50 E 8	Hillstowe st E5
26 J 6	Hilltop gdns NW4
45 Y 19	Hilltop rd NW6
10 L 11	Hilltop way Stanm
24 J 16	Hillview av Harrow
22 H 11	Hillview gdns Harrow
27 P 12	Hillview gdns NW4
113 X 11	Hillview rd Chisl
154 E 4	Hillview rd Sutton
104 J 19	Hillview SW20
47 P 7	Hillway N6
44 A 2	Hillway NW9
90 F 19	Hillworth rd SW2
93 N 9	Hilly Fields cres SE4
7 X 1	Hilly Fields pk Enf
59 U 14	Hillyard rd W7
90 E 3	Hillyard st SW9
32 G 8	Hillyfield E17
50 C 11	Hilsea st E5
15 U 18	Hilton av N12
91 S 11	Hilversum cres SE22
106 K 14	Himley rd SW17
156 C 14	Hinchcliffe clo Croy
91 W 9	Hinckley rd SE15
81 Z 18	Hind cres Erith
141 U 5	Hind ct EC4
64 B 17	Hind gro E14
139 V 4	Hinde ms W1
139 U 4	Hinde st W1
23 R 17	Hindes rd Harrow
49 S 3	Hindhead clo N16
58 B 3	Hindhead gdns Nthlt
156 A 10	Hindhead way Croy
91 X 13	Hindmans rd SE22
69 P 10	Hindmans way Dgnhm
143 U 8	Hindmarsh clo E1
50 A 14	Hindrey rd E5
110 D 3	Hindsley pl SE23
156 B 17	Hinkler clo Croy
24 G 11	Hinkler rd Harrow
80 H 7	Hinksey pth SE2
79 P 18	Hinstock rd SE18
82 A 10	Hinton av Hounsl
113 R 2	Hinton clo SE9
18 D 14	Hinton rd N18
90 K 9	Hinton rd SE24
155 V 14	Hinton rd Wallgtn
136 L 11	Hippodrome ms W11
136 L 11	Hippodrome pl W11
77 V 9	Hiroshima wlk SE7
50 K 3	Hitcham rd E17
63 W 6	Hitchin sq E3
93 V 14	Hither Green la SE13
55 Y 7	Hitherfield rd Dgnhm
108 E 5	Hitherfield rd SW16
23 O 4	Hitherwell dri Harrow
109 U 10	Hitherwood dri SE19
10 D 8	Hive clo Bushey
10 E 9	Hive rd Bushey
107 X 5	Hoadly rd SW16
15 W 8	Hobart clo N20
123 N 6	Hobart gdns Thntn Hth
84 M 18	Hobart pl Rich
147 W 2	Hobart pl SW1
55 X 12	Hobart rd Dgnhm

36 C 8	Hobart rd Ilf
152 J 5	Hobart rd Worc Pk
59 R 16	Hobbayne rd W7
86 J 14	Hobbes wlk SW15
28 E 10	Hobbs grn N2
109 N 11	Hobbs rd SE27
64 C 16	Hobday st E14
114 H 15	Hoblands end Chisl
135 R 20	Hobsons pl E1
146 D 15	Hobury st SW10
135 N 14	Hocker st E2
75 X 10	Hockett clo SE8
66 D 6	Hockley av E6
45 U 10	Hocroft av NW2
59 W 6	Hodder dri Grnfd
81 S 14	Hoddesdon rd Blvdr
45 W 3	Hodford rd NW11
68 K 20	Hodgkin clo SE28
75 R 10	Hodnet gro SE16
40 E 9	Hodson clo Nthlt
8 L 4	Hoe la Enf
9 P 3	Hoe la Enf
33 O 12	Hoe st E17
144 J 1	Hofland rd W14
38 B 2	Hog Hill rd Rom
138 E 1	Hogan ms W2
49 X 6	Hogan way E5
66 A 14	Hogarth clo E16
60 L 14	Hogarth clo W5
122 M 17	Hogarth cres Croy
120 F 1	Hogarth cres SW19
142 K 7	Hogarth ct EC3
70 H 20	Hogarth gdns Hounsl
27 W 13	Hogarth hill NW11
74 A 16	Hogarth la W4
25 O 6	Hogarth rd Edg
145 W 7	Hogarth rd SW5
18 E 8	Hoggin rd N9
96 J 16	Holbeach gdns Sidcp
93 R 18	Holbeach rd SE6
151 U 19	Holbeck row SE15
147 S 8	Holbein ms SW1
147 S 9	Holbein pl SW1
62 J 8	Holberton gdns NW10
141 S 2	Holborn bldgs EC4
141 T 2	Holborn EC1
65 V 13	Holborn rd E13
141 U 3	Holborn viaduct EC1
8 J 4	Holbrook clo Enf
47 T 5	Holbrook clo N19
114 G 19	Holbrook la Chisl
65 O 5	Holbrook rd E15
127 U 13	Holbrook way Brom
48 A 11	Holbrooke ct N7
84 H 14	Holbrooke pla Rich
94 K 3	Holburne clo SE3
94 M 3	Holburne gdns SE3
94 K 4	Holburne rd SE3
94 L 3	Holburne rd SE3
95 P 3	Holburne rd SE3
13 T 11	Holcombe dale NW7
13 T 11	Holcombe hill NW7
53 W 2	Holcombe rd Ilf
31 W 9	Holcombe rd N17
74 K 12	Holcombe st W6
80 M 10	Holcote clo Blvdr
63 R 1	Holcroft rd E9
15 N 15	Holden av N12
43 W 4	Holden av NW9
15 N 13	Holden rd N12
89 O 6	Holden st SW11
92 J 13	Holdenby rd SE4
28 C 2	Holdenhurst av N12
107 N 5	Holderness rd SW17
108 K 13	Holderness way SE27
27 P 9	Holders Hill av NW4
27 S 3	Holders Hill circus NW7
27 P 8	Holders Hill crs NW4
27 R 9	Holders Hill dri NW4
27 R 8	Holders Hill gdns NW4
27 S 4	Holders Hill rd NW7
133 P 12	Holford pl WC1
46 E 9	Holford rd NW3
133 R 11	Holford st WC1
88 F 8	Holgate av SW11
56 D 17	Holgate gdns Dgnhm
56 D 16	Holgate rd Dgnhm
153 X 19	Holland av Sutton
104 E 20	Holland av SW20
15 T 1	Holland clo Barnt
10 M 16	Holland clo Stanm
144 L 1	Holland gdns W14
149 V 19	Holland gro SW9
145 O 2	Holland ms W14

18 G 9 Hydeway N9
57 Z 2 Hyland clo Hrnch
57 Y 3 Hyland way Hrnch
33 Y 8 Hylands rd E17
79 X 10 Hylton st SE18
110 E 7 Hyndewood SE23
151 W 14 Hyndman st SE15
55 U 7 Hynton rd Dgnhm
156 K 10 Hyrstdene S Croy
75 N 12 Hyson rd SE16
80 M 20 Hythe av Bxly Hth
81 N 20 Hythe av Bxly Hth
18 L 14 Hythe clo N18
123 O 5 Hythe path Thntn Hth
62 G 11 Hythe rd NW10
123 O 5 Hythe rd Thntn Hth
12 M 2 Hyver hill NW7

I

9 S 7 Ian sq Enf
65 P 16 Ibbotson av E16
63 R 10 Ibbott st E1
155 Y 8 Iberian av Wallgtn
85 V 3 Ibis la W14
56 K 19 Ibscott clo Dgnhm
104 F 1 Ibsley gdns SW15
86 F 20 Ibsley gdns SW15
5 Y 15 Ibsley way Barnt
64 B 3 Iceland rd E3
49 Z 9 Ickburgh rd E5
113 R 10 Ickleton rd SE9
36 A 16 Icknield dri Ilf
35 Z 16 Icknield dri Ilf
32 J 12 Ickworth rd E17
31 O 14 Ida rd N15
64 F 18 Ida st E14
126 A 6 Iden clo Brom
107 O 14 Idlecombe rd SW17
118 E 18 Idmiston rd
    Worc Pk
52 B 14 Idmiston rd E15
108 L 5 Idmiston rd SE27
118 E 18 Idmiston sq
    Worc Pk
142 J 10 Idol la EC3
75 Z 19 Idonia st SE8
144 A 5 Iffley rd W6
74 L 10 Iffley rd W6
146 A 15 Ifield rd SW10
145 Y 13 Ifield rd SW10
81 S 19 Ightham rd Erith
128 H 13 Ilbert st W10
137 X 9 Ilchester gdns W2
137 P 20 Ilchester pl W14
55 T 15 Ilchester rd Dgnhm
109 O 5 Ildersley gro SE21
75 P 17 Ilderton rd SE15
75 O 13 Ilderton rd SE16
151 Y 9 Ilderton rd SE16
44 C 18 Ilex rd NW10
108 F 12 Ilex way SW16
53 X 9 Ilford hill Ilf
54 A 15 Ilford la Ilf
53 Y 10 Ilford la Ilf
55 P 1 Ilfracombe gdns Rom
112 B 7 Ilfracombe rd Brom
149 Y 8 Iliffe st SE17
149 Z 8 Iliffe St yd SE17
65 X 16 Ilkley rd E16
120 G 6 Illingworth clo Mitch
8 E 16 Illingworth rd N2
24 F 18 Ilmington rd Harrow
88 K 10 Ilminster gdns SW11
16 J 1 Imber clo N14
134 E 6 Imber st N1
22 G 19 Imperial clo Harrow
40 F 2 Imperial dri Harrow
22 H 19 Imperial dri Harrow
146 E 2 Imperial Institute rd
    SW7
66 A 7 Imperial ms E6
30 A 4 Imperial rd N22
88 C 2 Imperial rd SW6
64 F 10 Imperial st E3
149 U 3 Imperial War
    Museum SE11
114 C 2 Imperial way Chisl
156 E 15 Imperial way Croy
24 L 19 Imperial way Harrow
95 Y 19 Inca dri SE9
111 S 3 Inchmery rd SE6
159 R 8 Inchwood Croy
94 B 6 Independents rd SE3

30 D 18 Inderwick rd N8
76 C 6 Indescon ct E14
143 N 7 India st EC3
62 J 20 India way W12
77 Z 20 Indus rd SE7
65 T 13 Ingal rd E13
89 T 2 Ingate pl SW8
52 K 5 Ingatestone rd E12
34 G 2 Ingatestone rd Wdfd
    Grn
123 Y 10 Ingatestone SE25
89 R 5 Ingelow rd SW8
9 R 4 Ingersoll rd Enf
74 J 3 Ingersoll rd W12
140 D 7 Ingestre pl W1
52 F 12 Ingestre rd E7
47 T 11 Ingestre rd NW5
158 E 19 Ingham clo S Croy
45 X 13 Ingham rd NW6
158 D 19 Ingham rd S Croy
22 C 11 Ingle clo Pinn
133 S 12 Inglebert st EC1
90 E 4 Ingleborough st SW9
56 G 19 Ingleby clo Dgnhm
41 R 8 Ingleby dri Harrow
56 G 19 Ingleby rd Dgnhm
53 Z 4 Ingleby rd Ilf
48 A 9 Ingleby rd N7
113 X 13 Ingleby way Chisl
155 X 18 Ingleby way Wallgtn
79 T 13 Ingledew rd SE18
143 Y 13 Inglefield sq E1
35 T 17 Inglehurst gdns Ilf
107 N 17 Inglemere rd Mitch
110 E 6 Inglemere rd SE23
111 N 18 Ingleside clo
    Becknhm
77 R 17 Ingleside gro SE3
87 O 1 Inglethorpe st SW6
97 O 12 Ingleton av Welling
154 N 18 Ingleton rd Carsh
18 J 19 Ingleton rd N18
15 V 19 Ingleway N12
114 D 15 Inglewood Chisl
127 T 3 Inglewood Copse
    Brom
158 J 19 Inglewood Croy
98 M 9 Inglewood rd Bxly
    Hth
45 Y 16 Inglewood rd NW6
123 V 19 Inglis rd Croy
60 M 19 Inglis rd W5
61 N 20 Inglis rd W5
90 K 3 Inglis st SE5
46 D 1 Ingram av NW11
11 R 17 Ingram clo Stanm
28 K 13 Ingram rd N2
122 L 1 Ingram rd Thntn Hth
108 L 20 Ingram rd Thntn Hth
59 R 4 Ingram way Grnfd
39 O 13 Ingrave rd Rom
88 H 7 Ingrave st SW11
74 A 13 Ingress rd W4
78 C 18 Inigo Jones rd SE7
140 K 9 Inigo pl WC2
47 S 17 Inkerman rd NW5
20 F 16 Inks grn E4
62 A 2 Inman rd NW10
88 C 20 Inman rd SW6
21 T 15 Inmans row Wdfd
    Grn
131 S 13 Inner crcl NW1
105 O 1 Inner Pk rd SW19
141 T 7 Inner Temple la EC4
86 K 16 Innes gdns SW15
65 Y 7 Inniskilling rd E13
51 P 7 Inskip clo E10
55 W 5 Inskip rd Dgnhm
49 Z 16 Institute pl E8
156 B 15 Instone clo Croy
133 S 13 Insurance st WC1
79 S 15 Inverary pl SE18
37 V 14 Inverclyde gdns Rom
152 F 6 Inveresk gdns
    Worc Pk
46 C 7 Inverforth clo NW3
16 F 18 Inverforth rd N11
77 W 14 Inverine rd SE7
79 O 11 Invermore pl SE18
8 F 6 Invermore av Enf
137 W 15 Inverness gdns W8
137 Z 8 Inverness ms W2
137 Z 9 Inverness pl W2
82 F 10 Inverness rd Hounsl
18 M 15 Inverness rd N18
70 C 11 Inverness rd S'hall
119 O 20 Inverness rd Worc Pk
131 X 3 Inverness st NW1
137 Z 9 Inverness ter W2
92 E 11 Inverton rd SE15

113 W 12 Invicta clo Chisl
58 D 9 Invicta gro Nthlt
77 T 18 Invicta rd SE3
150 G 12 Inville rd SE17
82 M 8 Inwood av Hounsl
83 N 8 Inwood av Hounsl
158 J 2 Inwood clo Croy
82 M 8 Inwood rd Hounsl
88 J 4 Inworth st SW11
134 A 4 Inworth wlk N1
93 N 17 Iona clo SE6
31 T 16 Ipplepen rd N15
107 R 16 Ipswich rd SW17
141 Y 8 Ireland yd EC4
87 Y 3 Irene rd SW6
47 Y 8 Ireton rd N19
98 A 15 Iris av Bxly
97 Z 15 Iris av Bxly
124 E 19 Iris clo CR0
116 L 19 Iris clo Surb
81 O 17 Iris cres Bxly
19 Y 20 Iris way E4
8 H 5 Irkdale av Enf
99 X 10 Iron Mill la Drtfd
99 T 11 Iron Mill pl SE18
88 A 15 Iron Mill pl SW11
88 B 16 Iron Mill rd SW18
160 D 6 Ironmonger la EC2
134 C 15 Ironmonger row EC1
76 C 11 Ironmongers pl E14
38 K 2 Irons way Rom
24 A 10 Irvine av Harrow
23 Z 10 Irvine av Harrow
15 W 9 Irvine clo N20
58 A 2 Irving av Nthlt
90 B 5 Irving gr SW9
144 H 1 Irving rd W14
140 H 10 Irving st WC2
26 E 17 Irving way NW9
79 V 18 Irwin av SE18
128 A 6 Irwin gdns NW10
62 L 4 Irwin gdns NW10
90 E 2 Isabel st SW9
50 C 16 Isabella rd E9
141 V 15 Isabella st SE1
76 G 10 Isambard ms E14
39 R 2 Isbell gdns Rom
91 S 13 Isel way SE22
121 Z 3 Isham rd SW16
86 L 9 Isis clo SW15
106 C 4 Isis st SW18
79 O 17 Isla rd SE18
106 L 18 Island rd Mitch
63 X 19 Island row E14
48 E 10 Isledon rd N7
127 Y 1 Islehurst clo Chisl
133 W 5 Islington grn N1
133 V 9 Islington High st N1
48 G 20 Islington Pk st N1
12 K 20 Islip gdns Edg
40 C 20 Islip gdns Nthlt
40 C 20 Islip Manor rd Nthlt
47 V 16 Islip st NW5
52 H 20 Ismailia rd E7
65 X 10 Isom clo E13
24 B 8 Ivanhoe dri Harrow
23 Z 9 Ivanhoe dri Harrow
91 T 7 Ivanhoe rd SE5
145 R 11 Ivatt pl SW6
51 O 6 Ive Farm clo E10
61 P 5 Iveagh av NW10
63 U 2 Iveagh clo E9
61 P 6 Iveagh clo NW10
97 T 5 Ivedon rd Welling
89 U 6 Iveley rd SW4
135 U 13 Ivere dri E2
4 M 18 Ivere dri Barnt
5 N 19 Ivere dri Barnt
97 X 12 Iverhurst clo Bxly
    Hth
137 V 20 Iverna ct W8
145 V 1 Iverna gdns W8
159 S 16 Ivers way Croy
45 V 19 Iverson rd NW6
39 U 14 Ivers gdns Rom
64 L 14 Ives rd E16
146 L 6 Ives st SW3
92 C 18 Ivestor ter SE23
8 D 7 Ivinghoe clo Enf
10 B 2 Ivinghoe rd Bushey
    Watf
55 P 15 Ivinghoe rd Dgnhm
113 Z 1 Ivor gro SE9
131 O 17 Ivor pl NW1
47 U 20 Ivor st NW1
112 F 8 Ivorydown Brom
83 X 17 Ivy Bridge clo Twick
40 D 12 Ivy clo Harrow
73 U 10 Ivy cres W4
121 X 7 Ivy gdns Mitch

30 A 19 Ivy gdns N8
82 D 10 Ivy la Hounsl
116 L 15 Ivy pl Surb
65 T 17 Ivy rd E16
33 P 19 Ivy rd E17
82 L 11 Ivy rd Hounsl
16 J 3 Ivy rd N14
44 M 12 Ivy rd NW2
45 N 12 Ivy rd NW2
92 L 11 Ivy rd SE4
93 O 12 Ivy rd SE4
134 J 8 Ivy st N1
55 Y 18 Ivy wlk Dgnhm
140 M 10 Ivybridge la WC2
110 B 18 Ivychurch clo SE20
155 N 2 Ivydale rd Carsh
92 F 9 Ivydale rd SE15
108 C 8 Ivyday gro SW16
154 D 8 Ivydene clo Sutton
135 U 2 Ivydene rd E8
56 B 18 Ivyhouse rd Dgnhm
55 Y 18 Ivyhouse rd Dgnhm
108 F 8 Ivymount rd SE27
146 K 9 Ixworth pl SW3
98 A 12 Izane rd Bxly Hth

J

30 D 8 Jack Barnett way
    N22
53 W 13 Jack Cornwell st E12
21 R 14 Jacklin grn Wdfd Grn
44 A 10 Jackman ms NW10
135 V 5 Jackman st E8
67 T 4 Jackson rd Bark
5 V 20 Jackson rd Barnt
127 T 20 Jackson rd Brom
48 E 13 Jackson rd N7
78 J 16 Jackson st SE18
70 M 4 Jackson way S'hall
29 R 20 Jacksons la N6
123 P 20 Jacksons pl Croy
143 R 17 Jacob st SE1
139 U 3 Jacobs Well ms W1
58 C 3 Jacqueline clo
    Nthlt
55 T 4 Jade clo Dgnhm
66 B 18 Jade clo E16
108 K 10 Jaffray pl SE27
126 M 9 Jaffray rd Brom
88 M 20 Jaggard way SW12
79 P 16 Jago clo SE18
143 P 19 Jamaica rd SE1
75 N 7 Jamaica rd SE16
143 X 20 Jamaica rd SE16
122 H 13 Jamaica rd Thntn
    Hth
63 R 16 Jamaica st E1
56 C 5 James av Dgnhm
44 M 14 James av NW2
65 T 6 James clo E13
39 W 15 James clo Rom
30 K 2 James gdns N22
33 X 20 James la E11
31 U 3 James pl N17
99 V 17 James rd Drtfrd
67 O 1 James st Bark
8 H 16 James st Enf
83 O 8 James st Hounsl
139 V 6 James st W1
140 K 8 James st WC2
137 U 13 Jameson st W8
131 X 2 Jamestown rd NW1
143 W 5 Jane st E1
76 B 7 Janet st E14
143 U 19 Janeway st SE16
51 Z 14 Janson clo E15
44 A 8 Janson clo NW10
52 A 14 Janson rd E15
51 Z 13 Janson rd E15
31 S 11 Jansons rd N15
48 C 3 Japan cres N4
37 W 20 Japan rd Rom
150 K 13 Jardin st SE5
120 A 12 Jarratt clo SW2
31 Z 12 Jarrow rd N15
37 U 18 Jarrow rd Rom
50 K 13 Jarrow way E9
4 C 18 Jarvis clo Barnt
157 O 14 Jarvis rd S Croy
91 T 11 Jarvis rd SE22
159 P 6 Jasmine gdns Croy
40 H 7 Jasmine gdns Harrow
110 A 20 Jasmine gro SE20

139 V 4	Jason ct W1	
113 W 9	Jason wlk SE9	
9 P 4	Jasper clo Enf	
66 C 18	Jasper rd E16	
109 U 13	Jasper rd SE19	
58 A 10	Javelin way Grnfd	
138 D 19	Jay ms SW7	
90 B 16	Jebb av SW2	
64 C 7	Jebb st E3	
65 X 8	Jedburgh rd E13	
89 P 10	Jedburgh st SW8	
74 D 5	Jeddo rd W12	
36 A 16	Jefferson clo Ilf	
72 B 9	Jefferson clo W13	
64 F 9	Jefferson est E3	
9 X 14	Jeffreys rd Enf	
90 A 5	Jeffreys rd SW4	
89 Z 4	Jeffreys rd SW4	
47 T 20	Jeffreys st NW1	
9 X 12	Jeffreys way Enf	
89 Z 3	Jeffreys wlk SW4	
153 V 9	Jeffs rd Sutton	
94 L 11	Jeken rd SE9	
90 F 12	Jelf rd SW2	
10 K 18	Jellicoe gdns Stanm	
31 O 3	Jellicoe rd N17	
67 O 8	Jenkins la Bark	
65 W 12	Jenkins rd E13	
74 H 17	Jenner pl SW13	
49 W 9	Jenner rd N16	
156 F 4	Jennett rd Croy	
112 D 6	Jennifer rd Brom	
91 V 15	Jennings rd SE22	
4 A 12	Jennings way Barnt	
81 Y 3	Jenningtree way Blvdr	
109 T 18	Jenson way SE19	
97 Y 3	Jenton av Bxly Hth	
52 L 19	Jephson rd E7	
91 O 3	Jephson st SE5	
87 X 16	Jephtha rd SW18	
120 L 9	Jeppos la Mitch	
145 U 18	Jerdan pl SW6	
64 C 18	Jeremiah st E14	
19 O 13	Jeremys grn N18	
140 B 12	Jermyn st SW1	
35 Y 7	Jerningham av Ilf	
92 H 2	Jerningham rd SE14	
130 J 15	Jerome cres NW8	
135 N 19	Jerome st E1	
93 S 7	Jerrard st SE13	
24 C 9	Jersey av Stanm	
51 W 5	Jersey rd E11	
65 X 15	Jersey rd E16	
82 L 1	Jersey rd Hounsl	
70 L 20	Jersey rd Hounsl	
53 Z 13	Jersey rd Ilf	
71 P 18	Jersey rd Islwth	
107 R 16	Jersey rd SW17	
71 Y 7	Jersey rd W7	
135 X 13	Jersey st E2	
133 W 18	Jerusalem pass EC1	
108 F 14	Jerviston gdns SW16	
43 O 17	Jesmond av Wemb	
123 U 17	Jesmond rd Croy	
11 Y 15	Jesmond way Stanm	
49 Z 4	Jessam av E5	
71 V 3	Jessamine rd W7	
51 T 5	Jesse rd E10	
88 E 15	Jessica rd SW18	
90 K 11	Jessop rd SE24	
121 V 15	Jessops way Mitch	
79 O 10	Jessup clo SE18	
58 A 9	Jetstar way Nthlt	
112 J 2	Jevington way SE12	
33 N 10	Jewel rd E17	
142 M 7	Jewry st EC3	
88 B 10	Jews row SW11	
110 A 10	Jews wlk SE26	
44 L 16	Jeymer av NW2	
58 M 4	Jeymer dri Grnfd	
59 N 3	Jeymer dri Grnfd	
88 D 17	Jeypore rd SW18	
100 H 18	Jillian clo Hampt	
95 O 19	Joan cres SE9	
55 Y 6	Joan gdns Dgnhm	
55 Y 6	Joan rd Dgnhm	
141 V 15	Joan st SE1	
58 C 3	Joave clo Grnfd	
84 K 8	Jocelyn rd Rich	
141 P 1	Jockeys fields WC1	
63 Z 2	Jodrell rd E3	
141 S 18	Johanna st SE1	
140 L 11	John Adam st WC2	
16 K 6	John Bradshaw rd N14	
67 V 2	John Burns dri Bark	
49 S 15	John Campbell rd N16	
141 V 8	John Carpenter st EC4	
143 S 19	John Felton rd SE16	
143 R 10	John Fisher st E1	
148 G 8	John Islip st SW1	
97 S 8	John Newton ct Welling	
56 G 20	John Parker clo Dgnhm	
93 S 2	John Penn st SE13	
139 Z 5	John Prince's st W1	
143 Y 11	John Rennie wlk E1	
151 U 1	John Roll way SE16	
150 B 14	John Ruskin st SE5	
149 Y 17	John Ruskin st SE5	
48 K 18	John Spencer sq N1	
65 O 4	John st E15	
8 G 16	John st Enf	
82 C 4	John st Hounsl	
123 Y 9	John st SE25	
133 P 19	John st WC1	
78 J 11	John Wilson st SE18	
93 Y 9	John Woolley clo SE13	
26 L 13	Johns av NW4	
120 D 12	Johns la Mrdn	
133 O 18	Johns ms WC1	
143 Y 4	Johns pl E1	
123 P 20	Johns ter Croy	
135 T 3	Johnson clo E8	
127 N 12	Johnson rd Brom	
123 N 17	Johnson rd Croy	
63 P 19	Johnson st E1	
154 M 4	Johnsons clo Carsh	
141 U 6	Johnsons ct EC4	
148 B 12	Johnsons pl SW1	
61 S 11	Johnsons Way NW10	
21 S 18	Johnston rd Wdfd Grn	
66 H 10	Johnstone rd E6	
45 O 10	Johnstone ter NW2	
142 G 14	Joiner st SE1	
58 B 13	Jolly's la Hayes	
41 P 4	Jollys la Harrow	
149 O 8	Jonathan st SE11	
65 W 13	Jones Avenue rd E13	
65 W 13	Jones rd E13	
139 X 10	Jones st W1	
121 T 8	Jonson clo Mitch	
151 W 11	Joram way SE16	
40 E 10	Jordan clo Nthlt	
87 P 11	Jordan ct SW15	
60 D 2	Jordan rd Grnfd	
83 U 3	Jordans clo Islwth	
89 U 16	Joseph Powell clo SW12	
63 Y 13	Joseph st E3	
90 D 14	Josephine av SW2	
64 F 16	Joshua st E14	
88 M 5	Joubert st SW11	
151 P 19	Jowett st SE15	
18 H 17	Joyce av N18	
90 F 16	Joyce wlk SW2	
37 P 18	Joydon dri Rom	
20 G 18	Jubilee av E4	
38 H 17	Jubilee av Rom	
83 O 20	Jubilee av Twick	
25 Y 18	Jubilee clo NW9	
38 H 16	Jubilee clo Rom	
76 G 9	Jubilee cres E14	
18 K 4	Jubilee cres N9	
40 A 12	Jubilee dri Ruisl	
58 H 15	Jubilee gdns S'hall	
18 L 3	Jubilee pk N9	
146 M 10	Jubilee pl SW3	
60 A 2	Jubilee rd Grnfd	
153 P 15	Jubilee rd Sutton	
63 P 17	Jubilee st E1	
120 B 1	Jubilee way Mitch	
115 N 5	Jubilee way Sidcp	
132 J 14	Judd st WC1	
65 P 18	Jude st E16	
46 C 9	Judges wlk NW3	
88 K 1	Juer st SW11	
146 L 19	Juer st SW11	
68 J 5	Julia gdns Bark	
47 O 14	Julia st NW5	
61 U 20	Julian av W3	
4 M 12	Julian clo Barnt	
41 T 8	Julian hill Harrow	
76 E 12	Julian pl E14	
72 D 10	Julian rd N1	
93 T 7	Junction appr SE13	
138 K 4	Junction ms W2	
138 H 4	Junction pl W2	
65 V 6	Junction rd E13	
23 S 19	Junction rd Harrow	
31 X 9	Junction rd N17	
47 V 8	Junction rd N19	
18 K 6	Junction rd N9	
39 T 14	Junction rd Rom	
157 O 12	Junction rd S Croy	
72 F 11	Junction rd W5	
55 X 1	Junction Road west Rom	
55 Z 1	Junction Road east Rom	
53 X 11	Juniper rd Ilf	
63 P 19	Juniper st E1	
75 T 16	Juno way SE14	
48 D 18	Jupiter way N7	
64 J 1	Jupp rd E15	
64 H 2	Jupp Road west E15	
146 J 15	Justice wlk SW3	
72 H 19	Justin clo Brent	
33 N 1	Justin rd E4	
9 W 10	Jute la Enf	
65 T 12	Jutland rd E13	
93 T 19	Jutland rd SE6	
38 G 19	Jutsums la Rom	
22 L 5	Juxon clo Harrow	
149 P 5	Juxon st SE11	

K

80 K 6	Kale rd Blvdr	
88 G 6	Kambala rd SW11	
110 L 11	Kangley Bridge rd SE26	
59 R 5	Karoline gdns Grnfd	
79 X 12	Kashgar rd SE18	
78 A 18	Kashmir rd SE7	
88 M 2	Kassala rd SW11	
156 M 4	Katharine st Croy	
157 N 4	Katharine st Croy	
36 C 1	Katherine gdns Ilf	
95 N 12	Katherine gdns SE9	
66 C 3	Katherine rd E6	
52 L 16	Katherine rd E7	
83 Z 20	Katherine rd Twick	
61 W 13	Kathleen av W3	
60 K 1	Kathleen av Wemb	
42 K 20	Kathleen av Wemb	
88 L 8	Kathleen rd SW11	
90 B 6	Kay rd SW9	
64 K 1	Kay st E15	
135 T 9	Kay st E2	
97 R 2	Kay st Welling	
154 H 15	Kayemoor rd Sutton	
45 P 14	Kayes rd NW2	
141 N 6	Kean st WC2	
108 X 11	Keary ho SW15	
58 J 15	Keat's way Grnfd	
39 Y 2	Keats av Rom	
46 H 12	Keats gro NW3	
81 W 8	Keats rd Blvdr	
96 J 1	Keats rd Welling	
124 C 15	Keats way Croy	
41 O 16	Keble clo Nthlt	
118 E 20	Keble clo Worc Pk	
106 D 9	Keble st SW17	
126 F 17	Kechill gdns Brom	
112 B 11	Keedonwood rd Brom	
111 Z 11	Keedonwood rd Brom	
75 U 4	Keel clo SE16	
156 L 3	Keeley rd Croy	
141 N 5	Keeley st WC2	
94 M 13	Keeling rd SE9	
156 M 8	Keen's rd Croy	
48 J 18	Keens yd N1	
102 M 17	Keep the Kingst	
94 E 6	Keep the SE3	
151 V 1	Keeton's rd SE16	
87 R 19	Keevil dri SW19	
48 A 14	Keighley clo N7	
114 D 2	Keightley dri SE9	
88 L 11	Keildon rd SW11	
49 Z 4	Keir Hardie est E5	
68 A 1	Keir Hardie way Bark	
74 G 4	Keith gro W12	
67 T 5	Keith rd Bark	
32 L 6	Keith rd E17	
95 P 6	Kelbrook rd SE3	
114 A 8	Kelby path SE9	
44 H 5	Kelceda clo NW2	
50 M 20	Kelday rd E9	
136 E 4	Kelfield gdns W10	
141 Y 20	Kell st SE1	
65 T 11	Kelland rd E13	
94 M 5	Kellaway rd SE3	
95 N 3	Kellaway rd SE3	
93 Y 13	Kellerton rd SE13	
90 F 11	Kellett rd SW2	
122 H 16	Kelling gdns Croy	
106 L 9	Kellino st SW17	
79 X 8	Kellner rd SE28	
14 D 18	Kelly rd NW7	
47 T 18	Kelly st NW1	
37 Y 17	Kelly way Rom	
89 Y 5	Kelman clo SW4	
91 X 10	Kelmore gro SE22	
74 G 7	Kelmscot gdns W12	
32 K 6	Kelmscott clo E17	
88 K 14	Kelmscott rd SW11	
48 K 12	Kelross rd N5	
94 H 4	Kelsall clo SE3	
125 N 7	Kelsey la Becknhm	
125 R 5	Kelsey Pk av Becknhm	
125 P 3	Kelsey Pk rd Becknhm	
125 N 3	Kelsey sq Becknhm	
135 V 15	Kelsey st E2	
125 O 6	Kelsey way Becknhm	
145 Y 2	Kelso pl W8	
120 E 17	Kelso rd Carsh	
36 A 6	Kelston rd Ilf	
35 Z 7	Kelston rd Ilf	
103 O 15	Kelvedon clo Kingst	
145 P 20	Kelvedon rd SW6	
17 R 18	Kelvin av N13	
101 T 15	Kelvin av Tedd	
10 F 20	Kelvin cres Harrow	
84 C 15	Kelvin dri Twick	
58 G 17	Kelvin gdns S'hall	
110 A 7	Kelvin gro SE26	
48 K 13	Kelvin rd N5	
96 M 7	Kelvin rd Welling	
124 J 16	Kelvington clo Croy	
92 E 14	Kelvington rd SE15	
156 G 5	Kemble rd Croy	
31 W 6	Kemble rd N17	
110 G 2	Kemble rd SE23	
141 N 6	Kemble st WC2	
125 S 4	Kemerton rd Becknhm	
123 U 17	Kemerton rd Becknhm	
90 L 8	Kemerton rd SE5	
50 H 16	Kemeys st E9	
114 E 9	Kemnal manor Chisl	
114 D 13	Kemnal rd Chisl	
114 D 15	Kemnal Warren Chisl	
122 K 15	Kemp gdn Croy	
55 W 4	Kemp rd Dgnhm	
128 G 10	Kempe rd NW6	
91 S 13	Kempis way SE22	
46 G 12	Kemplay rd NW3	
145 V 11	Kempsford gdns SW5	
149 U 7	Kempsford rd SE11	
108 A 17	Kempshott rd SW16	
107 Z 17	Kempshott rd SW16	
145 W 20	Kempson rd SW6	
87 Z 1	Kempson rd SW6	
78 J 17	Kempt st SE18	
75 X 11	Kempthorne rd SE8	
40 H 16	Kempton av Northolt	
81 X 16	Kempton clo Erith	
100 B 20	Kempton pk Felt	
66 F 3	Kempton rd E6	
124 K 14	Kempton wlk Croy	
97 Z 17	Kemsing clo Bxly	
122 M 9	Kemsing clo Thntn Hth	
77 S 14	Kemsing rd SE10	
90 L 4	Kenbury st SE5	
148 K 20	Kenchester clo SW8	
81 P 6	Kencot way Blvdr	
67 U 2	Kendal av Bark	
18 B 14	Kendal av N18	
61 S 14	Kendal av W3	
21 R 9	Kendal clo Wdfd Grn	
57 V 15	Kendal croft Hornch	
18 B 14	Kendal gdns N18	
18 A 14	Kendal pde N18	
44 H 13	Kendal rd NW10	
138 M 6	Kendal st W2	
111 Z 13	Kendale rd Brom	
124 H 3	Kendall av Becknhm	
157 O 20	Kendall av S Croy	
154 D 2	Kendall gdns Sutton	
139 S 3	Kendall pl W1	
124 H 3	Kendall rd Becknhm	
83 X 5	Kendall rd Islwth	
75 R 20	Kender st SE14	
89 Y 9	Kendoa rd SW4	
34 J 17	Kendon clo E11	
120 A 4	Kendor gdns SW19	
156 J 16	Kendra Hall rd S Croy	
83 S 17	Kendrey gdns Twick	

141 Z 4	King Edward st EC1
149 T 1	King Edward wlk SE1
73 P 3	King Edward's gdns W3
102 C 15	King Edward's gro Tedd
67 S 5	King Edward's rd Bark
9 U 14	King Edwards rd Enf
63 O 2	King Edwards rd E9
135 Y 3	King Edwards rd E9
18 M 2	King Edwards rd N9
19 N 3	King Edwards rd N9
156 H 10	King gdns Croy
66 A 18	King George av E16
65 Z 17	King George av E16
38 K 11	King George clo Rom
152 B 7	King George Field Auriol pk Epsom
87 Z 20	King George pk SW18
76 H 20	King George st SE10
121 N 8	King George VI av Mitch
131 P 2	King George's ms NW1
131 P 2	King George's ter NW1
58 E 14	King Georges dri S'hall
80 M 18	King Harold's way Bxly Hth
49 S 15	King Henry st N16
159 V 18	King Henry's dri Croy
117 T 5	King Henry's rd Kingst
130 K 1	King Henry's rd NW3
131 O 1	King Henry's rd NW3
49 R 17	King Henry's wlk N1
141 Y 19	King James st SE1
134 L 16	King John ct EC2
63 T 15	King John st E1
95 P 19	King John's wk SE9
133 Z 13	King sq EC1
65 S 12	King st E13
142 C 5	King st EC2
160 D 5	King st EC2
31 U 3	King st N17
28 G 8	King st N2
84 G 13	King st Rich
70 C 9	King st S'hall
140 C 14	King st SW1
101 Y 1	King st Twick
73 U 3	King st W3
144 B 7	King st W6
74 F 12	King st W6
140 K 9	King st WC2
75 N 5	King Stairs clo SE16
142 F 7	King William st EC4
160 F 8	King William st EC4
76 H 16	King William wlk SE10
160 F 5	King's Arms yd EC2
58 L 16	King's av Grnfd
29 P 10	King's av N10
17 V 5	King's av N21
89 Z 14	King's av SW4
60 H 16	King's av W5
21 W 18	King's av Wdfd Grn
141 Y 17	King's Bench st SE1
99 O 11	King's clo Drtfd
46 H 20	King's College rd NW3
48 L 8	King's cres N4
92 A 1	King's gro SE15
151 Y 20	King's gro SE15
142 F 15	King's Head yd SE1
79 X 17	King's highway SE18
50 K 13	King's Mead way E9
95 S 15	King's orchard SE9
51 Y 1	King's rd E11
18 L 15	King's rd N17
116 D 20	King's rd Surb
147 T 4	King's rd SW1
85 Z 9	King's rd SW14
105 Y 14	King's rd SW19
146 J 12	King's rd SW3
145 Z 20	King's rd SW6
101 P 12	King's rd Tedd
60 G 15	King's rd W5
148 B 4	King's Scholars' pas SW1
132 A 6	King's ter NW1
57 V 20	Kingaby gdns Rainham
45 Y 17	Kingdon rd NW6
60 G 11	Kingfield rd W5
76 G 11	Kingfield st E14
68 H 20	Kingfisher clo SE28
102 C 9	Kingfisher dri Rich
66 E 15	Kingfisher st E6
88 C 18	Kingham clo SW18
141 Z 2	Kinghorn st EC1
150 J 11	Kinglake st SE17
150 L 9	Kinglake st SE17
140 B 8	Kingly ct W1
140 B 7	Kingly st W1
143 R 2	Kings Arms ct E1
112 B 16	Kings av Brom
21 Z 7	Kings av Buck Hl
154 K 18	Kings av Carsh
89 Z 17	Kings Av clo SW4
89 Y 13	Kings Av gdns SW4
82 L 2	Kings av Hounsl
118 C 8	Kings av New Mald
38 C 18	Kings av Rom
141 T 8	Kings Bench wlk EC4
51 R 2	Kings clo E10
27 R 13	Kings clo NW4
133 O 12	Kings Cross rd WC1
132 K 9	Kings Cross station N1
65 W 4	Kings ct E13
12 A 15	Kings dri Edg
11 Z 14	Kings dri Edg
117 P 15	Kings dri Surb
43 S 5	Kings dri Wemb
43 S 7	Kings dri Wemb
85 O 11	Kings Farm av Rich
54 D 4	Kings gdns Ilf
129 V 2	Kings gdns NW6
39 V 17	Kings gro Rom
110 F 18	Kings Hall rd SE20
160 H 10	Kings Head ct EC3
20 F 3	Kings Head hill E4
154 G 12	Kings la Sutton
86 K 12	Kings lawn clo SW15
89 Z 13	Kings ms SW4
133 P 19	Kings ms WC1
116 G 4	Kings pas Kingst
21 Z 8	Kings pl Buck Hl
142 B 20	Kings pl SE1
73 V 12	Kings pl W4
54 A 20	Kings rd Bark
4 A 13	Kings rd Barnt
20 J 5	Kings rd E4
65 Y 3	Kings rd E6
40 E 9	Kings rd Harrow
102 J 19	Kings rd Kingst
103 O 17	Kings rd Kingst
121 P 5	Kings rd Mitch
31 U 3	Kings rd N17
30 D 4	Kings rd N22
44 J 20	Kings rd NW10
84 M 12	Kings rd Rich
39 V 17	Kings rd Rom
123 Y 6	Kings rd SE25
84 C 17	Kings rd Twick
85 P 12	Kings Ride ga Rich
156 D 11	Kings way Croy
23 T 12	Kings way Harrow
21 Y 16	Kings way Wdfd Grn
102 H 19	Kings way W5
112 F 3	Kingsand rd SE12
58 A 11	Kingsash dri Grnfd
73 N 5	Kingsbridge av W3
58 E 15	Kingsbridge cres S'hall
67 T 7	Kingsbridge rd Berk
119 P 17	Kingsbridge rd Mrdn
70 D 12	Kingsbridge rd S'hall
136 D 3	Kingsbridge rd W10
49 S 17	Kingsbury rd N1
26 B 17	Kingsbury rd NW9
25 U 15	Kingsbury rd NW9
49 S 17	Kingsbury ter N1
86 F 17	Kingsclere clo SW15
105 V 3	Kingscliffe gdns SW19
123 Z 18	Kingscote rd Croy
117 Y 7	Kingscote rd New Mald
73 X 10	Kingscote rd W4
141 W 8	Kingscote st EC4
107 Z 7	Kingscourt rd SW16
45 U 17	Kingscroft rd NW2
136 H 15	Kingsdale gdns W11
79 X 17	Kingsdale rd SE18
110 F 19	Kingsdale rd SE18
156 K 20	Kingsdown av S Croy
72 C 5	Kingsdown av W13
62 B 18	Kingsdown av W3
136 J 7	Kingsdown clo W11
52 A 10	Kingsdown rd E11
48 A 7	Kingsdown rd N19
47 Z 8	Kingsdown rd N19
153 S 11	Kingsdown rd Sutton
126 E 15	Kingsdown way Brom
116 L 18	Kingsdowne rd Surb
104 D 1	Kingsfarm lodge SW15
22 L 14	Kingsfield av Harrow
23 N 15	Kingsfield av Harrow
41 S 2	Kingsfield rd Harrow
41 R 2	Kingsfield ter Harrow
156 B 17	Kingsford av Croy
46 M 15	Kingsford st NW5
27 Y 10	Kingsgate av N3
97 Y 1	Kingsgate clo Bxly Hth
129 T 2	Kingsgate pl NW6
129 U 2	Kingsgate rd NW6
45 X 20	Kingsgate rd NW6
43 U 8	Kingsgate Wemb
95 O 18	Kingsground SE9
24 B 13	Kingshill av Harrow
118 H 16	Kingshill av Worc Pk
24 B 11	Kingshill dri Harrow
63 P 1	Kingshold rd E9
95 P 9	Kingsholme gdns SE9
94 F 19	Kingshurst rd SE12
49 T 17	Kingsland High st E8
49 T 17	Kingsland pass E8
65 Y 9	Kingsland rd E13
134 L 6	Kingsland rd E2
49 T 19	Kingsland rd E8
83 N 4	Kingsley av Hounsl
58 G 20	Kingsley av S'hall
154 G 8	Kingsley av Sutton
59 Y 16	Kingsley av W13
56 G 12	Kingsley clo Dgnhm
28 C 15	Kingsley clo N2
152 E 1	Kingsley dri Worc Pk
20 B 15	Kingsley gdns E4
145 Z 2	Kingsley ms W8
47 R 2	Kingsley pl N6
122 F 19	Kingsley rd Croy
33 U 8	Kingsley rd E17
52 F 20	Kingsley rd E7
40 M 11	Kingsley rd Harrow
41 N 10	Kingsley rd Harrow
82 L 4	Kingsley rd Hounsl
83 N 6	Kingsley rd Hounsl
36 C 4	Kingsley rd Ilf
17 U 13	Kingsley rd N13
129 P 3	Kingsley rd NW6
22 E 14	Kingsley rd Pinn
106 B 12	Kingsley rd SW19
88 M 7	Kingsley st SW11
89 N 6	Kingsley st SW11
28 C 15	Kingsley way N2
113 U 7	Kingsley Wood dri SE9
123 R 1	Kingslyn cres SE19
78 G 9	Kingsman pk SE18
78 G 9	Kingsman st SE18
152 J 4	Kingsmead av Worc Pk
121 V 5	Kingsmead av Mitch
18 M 6	Kingsmead av N9
43 Y 1	Kingsmead av NW9
39 S 18	Kingsmead av Rom
4 L 14	Kingsmead Barnt
114 M 5	Kingsmead clo Sidcp
40 E 20	Kingsmead dri Nthlt
108 F 5	Kingsmead rd SW2
43 U 5	Kingsmere pk NW9
105 R 3	Kingsmere rd SW19
56 B 16	Kingsmill gdns Dgnhm
56 B 16	Kingsmill rd Dgnhm
130 G 9	Kingsmill ter NW8
103 T 16	Kingsnympton pk Kingst
34 D 9	Kingspark ct E18
110 E 10	Kingsthorpe rd SE26
153 T 5	Kingston av Sutton
116 F 3	Kingston br Kingst
118 B 12	Kingston By-pass New Mald
104 B 15	Kingston By-pass SW20
58 E 2	Kingston clo Northolt
37 Y 9	Kingston clo Rom
102 A 15	Kingston clo Tedd
124 L 1	Kingston cres Becknhm
103 P 17	Kingston gate Kingst
116 H 5	Kingston Hall rd Kingst
37 Z 9	Kingston Hill av Rom
103 S 18	Kingston hill Kingst
103 W 10	Kingston Hill place Rich
102 A 15	Kingston la Tedd
101 Z 13	Kingston la Tedd
5 U 17	Kingston rd Barnt
152 C 12	Kingston rd Epsom
152 E 17	Kingston rd Epsom
54 B 12	Kingston rd Ilf
18 L 8	Kingston rd N9
117 V 7	Kingston rd New Mald
39 U 13	Kingston rd Rom
70 D 7	Kingston rd S'hall
104 J 2	Kingston rd SW15
86 M 20	Kingston rd SW15
105 Y 19	Kingston rd SW19
119 P 2	Kingston rd SW20
102 B 15	Kingston rd Tedd
104 A 8	Kingston vale SW15
103 Y 9	Kingston vale SW15
131 S 4	Kingstown st NW1
158 D 20	Kingsway av S Croy
22 M 14	Kingsway cres Harrow
9 N 15	Kingsway Enf
140 M 4	Kingsway Hall WC2
15 R 18	Kingsway N12
118 L 10	Kingsway New Mald
153 S 15	Kingsway rd Sutton
85 U 8	Kingsway SW14
141 N 5	Kingsway WC2
42 K 12	Kingsway Wemb
47 S 9	Kingswear rd NW5
82 D 4	Kingswood av Hounsl
122 G 13	Kingswood av Thntn Hth
81 O 10	Kingswood av Blvdr
125 Y 8	Kingswood av Brom
100 K 15	Kingswood av Hampt
128 L 7	Kingswood av NW6
118 D 15	Kingswood clo New Mald
15 R 1	Kingswood clo N20
116 K 16	Kingswood clo Surb
148 L 19	Kingswood clo SW8
109 T 10	Kingswood dri SE19
27 U 6	Kingswood pk N3
93 Z 9	Kingswood pl SE13
126 A 5	Kingswood rd Brom
125 Y 6	Kingswood rd Brom
54 M 3	Kingswood rd Ilf
55 N 1	Kingswood rd Ilf
110 B 16	Kingswood rd SE20
105 W 19	Kingswood rd SW19
90 A 18	Kingswood rd SW2
89 Z 17	Kingswood rd SW2
73 V 9	Kingswood rd W4
156 A 10	Kingswood way Croy
124 H 10	Kingsworthy clo BR3
43 Y 20	Kingthorpe rd NW10
143 T 1	Kingward st E1
5 U 3	Kingwell rd Barnt
144 L 20	Kingwood rd SW6
96 B 1	Kinlet rd SE18
44 A 1	Kinloch dri NW9
43 Z 1	Kinloch dri NW9
48 D 10	Kinloch st N7
27 U 11	Kinloss gdns N3
120 D 18	Kinloss rd Carsh
112 C 16	Kinnaird av Brom
73 U 20	Kinnaird av W4
112 D 16	Kinnaird clo Brom
74 C 5	Kinnear rd W12
139 R 18	Kinnerton Place north SW1
139 R 19	Kinnerton Place south SW1
139 S 20	Kinnerton st SW1
139 S 19	Kinnerton yd SW1
144 L 14	Kinnoul rd W6
152 F 4	Kinross av Worc Pk
24 L 16	Kinross clo Harrow
142 L 19	Kinross st SE1
91 X 8	Kinsale rd SE15
151 N 4	Kintore st SE1
122 D 4	Kintyre clo SW16
78 C 14	Kinveachy gdns SE7
110 D 9	Kinver rd SE26
10 H 18	Kipling pl Stanm
97 Z 1	Kipling rd Bxly Hth
142 G 18	Kipling st SE1
18 C 9	Kipling ter N21N9
113 O 1	Kippington dri SE9
152 D 12	Kirby clo Epsom
142 J 17	Kirby gdns SE1
141 U 1	Kirby st EC1
133 U 20	Kirby st EC1
72 A 1	Kirchen rd W13
79 O 16	Kirk la SE18
32 M 18	Kirk rd E17
52 A 2	Kirkdale rd E11

110 B 9 Kirkdale SE26
66 E 16 Kirkham rd E6
79 V 18 Kirkham st SE18
35 W 7 Kirkland av Ilf
96 G 15 Kirkland clo Sidcp
55 T 16 Kirklees rd Dgnhm
122 E 10 Kirklees rd Thntn Hth
105 Z 19 Kirkley rd SW19
157 S 20 Kirkly clo S Croy
140 E 1 Kirkman pl W1
64 H 17 Kirkmichael rd E14
63 X 15 Kirks pl E3
77 S 17 Kirkside rd SE3
31 O 12 Kirkstall av N17
107 Z 1 Kirkstall gdns SW2
108 A 1 Kirkstall rd SW2
107 Z 1 Kirkstall rd SW2
119 Z 19 Kirksted rd Mrdn
112 A 17 Kirkstone way Brom
31 R 14 Kirkton rd N15
63 R 8 Kirkwall pl E2
47 O 19 Kirkwood pl NW1
92 A 3 Kirkwood rd SE15
72 A 1 Kirn rd W13
148 B 17 Kirtling st SW8
73 Y 12 Kirton clo W4
135 P 13 Kirton gdns E2
65 X 5 Kirton rd E13
25 W 2 Kirton wlk Edg
149 Z 18 Kirwyn way SE5
64 B 8 Kitcat ter E3
56 J 17 Kitchener rd Dgnhm
33 R 4 Kitchener rd E17
52 H 18 Kitchener rd E7
31 P 10 Kitchener rd N17
28 H 11 Kitchener rd N2
123 N 5 Kitchener rd Thntn Hth
123 U 1 Kitley gdns SE19
150 D 17 Kitson rd SE5
86 F 3 Kitson rd SW13
92 F 6 Kitto rd SE14
4 H 5 Kitts End rd Barnt
47 Z 7 Kiver rd N19
89 U 15 Klea av SW4
110 A 4 Knapdale clo SE23
111 P 5 Knapmill rd SE6
111 P 5 Knapmill way SE6
44 B 17 Knapp clo NW10
64 B 12 Knapp rd E3
145 X 6 Knaresborough pl SW5
61 Z 3 Knatchbull rd NW10
90 J 3 Knatchbull rd SE5
33 O 4 Knebworth av E17
49 R 11 Knebworth rd N16
80 G 11 Knee Hill cres SE2
80 G 13 Knee hill SE2
83 P 15 Kneller gdns Islwth
83 R 16 Kneller hall Twick
117 Z 17 Kneller rd New Mald
92 J 10 Kneller rd SE4
82 M 16 Kneller rd Twick
83 O 16 Kneller rd Twick
72 L 7 Knight's av W5
143 V 15 Knighten st E1
49 Z 6 Knightland rd E5
38 M 18 Knighton clo Rom
156 J 17 Knighton clo S Croy
21 V 13 Knighton clo Wdfd Grn
21 U 13 Knighton dri Wdfd Grn
21 V 9 Knighton la Buck Hl
110 G 12 Knighton Pk rd SE26
52 F 11 Knighton rd E7
38 L 18 Knighton rd Rom
141 Z 8 Knightrider st EC4
70 A 14 Knights arbour S'hall
108 J 12 Knights hill SE27
108 K 9 Knights hill sq SE27
18 K 10 Knights la N9
116 J 5 Knights pk Kingst
77 T 4 Knights rd E16
11 S 13 Knights rd Stanm
149 W 7 Knights wlk SE11
39 N 16 Knightsbridge gdns Rom
139 N 19 Knightsbridge grn SW7
138 L 18 Knightsbridge SW7
139 O 18 Knightsbridge SW7
12 G 8 Knightswood clo Edg
118 B 14 Knightwood cres New Mald
145 T 15 Knivett rd SW6
64 D 2 Knobs Hill rd E15
95 N 12 Knockholt rd SE9
99 X 19 Knole rd Drtfrd
113 W 10 Knole the SE9

16 C 3 Knoll dri N14
98 D 17 Knoll rd Bxly
115 R 12 Knoll rd Sidcp
88 C 14 Knoll rd SW18
125 R 1 Knoll the Becknhm
60 C 15 Knoll W13
117 X 20 Knollmead Surb
152 J 4 Knolls clo Worc Pk
108 G 6 Knolly's Clo SW16
108 E 6 Knolly's rd SW16
63 S 8 Knottisford st E2
33 T 18 Knotts Green rd E10
81 N 18 Knowle av Bxly Hth
90 E 7 Knowle clo SW9
101 T 2 Knowle rd Twick
93 W 13 Knowles Hill cres SE13
126 D 12 Knowlton grn Brom
70 J 3 Knowsley av S'hall
88 L 6 Knowsley rd SW11
52 D 18 Knox rd E7
139 O 1 Knox st W1
75 V 17 Knoyle st SE14
106 B 12 Kohat rd SW19
76 M 13 Kossuth st SE10
145 V 11 Kramer Mews SW5
108 D 19 Kuala gdns SW16
52 F 14 Kuhn way E7
45 Y 19 Kylemore rd NW6
23 T 19 Kymberley rd Harrow
39 T 20 Kyme rd Hornch
24 D 5 Kynance gdns Stanm
146 A 2 Kynance mans SW7
146 A 2 Kynance ms SW7
146 A 1 Kynance pl SW7
49 T 9 Kynaston av N16
122 L 11 Kynaston av Thntn Hth
23 R 1 Kynaston clo Harrow
122 M 11 Kynaston cres Thntn Hth
112 G 12 Kynaston rd Brom
8 B 7 Kynaston rd Enf
49 S 9 Kynaston rd N16
122 M 10 Kynaston rd Thntn Hth
23 R 1 Kynaston wood Harrow
19 R 15 Kynoch rd N18
89 O 14 Kyrle rd SW11
49 V 4 Kyverdale rd N16

L

57 U 9 Laburnum av Hornch
31 O 1 Laburnum av N17
18 F 9 Laburnum av N9
154 H 6 Laburnum av Sutton
19 Y 19 Laburnum clo E4
16 C 20 Laburnum clo N11
151 Z 20 Laburnum clo SE15
11 P 15 Laburnum ct Stanm
121 P 4 Laburnum est Mitch
17 Y 7 Laburnum gdns N21
82 F 11 Laburnum gro Hounsl
17 Y 7 Laburnum gro N21
117 X 4 Laburnum gro New Mald
25 W 20 Laburnum gro NW9
58 F 12 Laburnum gro S'hall
121 P 4 Laburnum rd Mitch
106 E 18 Laburnum rd SW19
134 M 6 Laburnum st E2
135 N 6 Laburnum st E2
127 Y 16 Laburnum way Brom
11 Y 13 Lacey dri Edg
134 G 20 Lackington st EC2
106 C 16 Lacock clo SW19
91 W 11 Lacon rd SE22
87 R 9 Lacy rd SW15
108 K 11 Ladas rd SE27
136 L 6 Ladbroke cres W11
137 O 9 Ladbroke gdns W11
128 H 15 Ladbroke gro W10
136 K 3 Ladbroke gro W10
137 P 13 Ladbroke gro W11
8 H 19 Ladbroke rd Enf
137 O 13 Ladbroke rd W11
137 P 10 Ladbroke Sq gdns W11
137 R 11 Ladbroke sq W11
137 R 12 Ladbroke ter W11

137 R 12 Ladbroke wlk W11
22 D 17 Ladbrook clo Pinn
123 P 8 Ladbrook rd SE25
115 X 8 Ladbrooke cres Sidcp
103 U 13 Ladderstile ride Kingst
16 G 17 Ladderswood way N11
152 C 1 Lady hay Worc Pk
70 E 1 Lady Margaret rd S'hall
58 E 17 Lady Margaret rd S'hall
47 V 13 Lady Margaret rd NW5
47 T 13 Lady Somerset rd NW5
93 P 8 Ladycroft rd SE13
24 G 6 Ladycroft wlk Stanm
158 G 20 Ladygrove S Croy
66 C 6 Ladysmith av E6
54 F 2 Ladysmith av Ilf
65 O 10 Ladysmith rd E16
8 F 12 Ladysmith rd Enf
23 T 8 Ladysmith rd Harrow
31 W 8 Ladysmith rd N17
19 N 18 Ladysmith rd N18
95 X 17 Ladysmith rd SE9
93 S 12 Ladywell rd SE13
65 P 4 Ladywell st E15
143 N 17 Lafone st SE1
75 U 3 Lagado ms SE16
123 P 15 Lahore rd Enf
120 K 2 Laings av Mitch
82 K 3 Lainlock pl Hounsl
87 X 19 Lainson st SW18
90 L 20 Lairdale clo SE21
48 B 17 Lairs clo N7
89 S 20 Laitwood rd SW12
107 T 1 Laitwood rd SW12
112 F 15 Lake av Brom
56 D 15 Lake gdns Dgnhm
102 B 6 Lake gdns Rich
155 R 7 Lake gdns Wallgtn
52 E 7 Lake House rd E11
158 L 1 Lake rd Croy
37 W 13 Lake rd Rom
105 U 13 Lake rd SW19
39 T 9 Lake rise Rom
10 B 5 Lake the Bushey Watf
11 Z 17 Lake view Edg
97 O 10 Lake View rd Welling
79 V 15 Lakedale rd SE18
30 J 9 Lakefield rd N22
122 J 12 Lakehall gdns Thntn Hth
122 J 12 Lakehall rd Thntn Hth
152 A 12 Lakehurst rd Epsom
10 C 19 Lakeland clo Harrow
6 J 17 Lakenheath N14
6 K 20 Lakenheath N14
87 U 15 Laker pl SW15
35 N 13 Lakeside av Ilf
123 W 3 Lakeside clo SE25
97 U 14 Lakeside clo Sidcp
6 A 18 Lakeside cres Barnt
48 K 6 Lakeside ct N4
6 K 13 Lakeside Enf
17 P 12 Lakeside rd N13
144 F 1 Lakeside rd W14
136 G 20 Lakeside rd W14
60 D 15 Lakeside W13
155 S 7 Lakeside Wallgtn
43 R 13 Lakeside way Wemb
108 H 12 Lakeview rd SE27
12 K 10 Laleham av NW7
93 T 18 Laleham rd SE6
87 S 3 Lalor st SW6
63 N 1 Lamb la E8
135 X 1 Lamb la E8
134 M 20 Lamb st E1
135 N 20 Lamb st E1
142 J 19 Lamb wlk SE1
113 X 9 Lambarde av SE9
56 A 4 Lamberhurst rd Dgnhm
108 F 11 Lamberhurst rd SE27
85 S 8 Lambert av Rich
65 V 17 Lambert rd E16
15 S 17 Lambert rd N12
90 C 14 Lambert rd SW2
133 R 2 Lambert st N1
15 S 17 Lambert way N12
123 P 20 Lamberts pl Croy
116 L 12 Lamberts rd Surb
148 L 4 Lambeth br SW1
149 N 5 Lambeth High st SE1

160 A 8 Lambeth hill EC4
149 O 7 Lambeth ms SE11
149 N 2 Lambeth Palace rd SE1
141 O 20 Lambeth Palace rd SE1
149 O 3 Lambeth palace SE1
148 M 3 Lambeth Pier SW1
122 G 18 Lambeth rd Croy
149 P 3 Lambeth rd SE1
143 S 6 Lambeth st E1
149 O 7 Lambeth wlk SE11
47 O 14 Lamble st NW5
55 N 18 Lambley rd Dgnhm
46 K 18 Lambolle pl NW3
46 J 18 Lambolle rd NW3
117 T 2 Lambourn clo Kingst
71 U 8 Lambourn clo W7
89 T 7 Lambourn rd SW4
105 V 9 Lambourne av SW19
67 X 1 Lambourne gdns Bark
20 B 8 Lambourne gdns E4
8 G 9 Lambourne gdns Enf
94 H 1 Lambourne pla SE3
67 W 2 Lambourne rd Bark
51 V 2 Lambourne rd E11
54 H 6 Lambourne rd Ilf
87 R 2 Lambrook ter SW6
134 D 18 Lambs bldgs EC1
18 J 8 Lambs clo N9
141 N 1 Lambs Conduit pas WC1
133 N 19 Lambs Conduit st WC1
133 X 6 Lambs ms N1
35 N 7 Lambs ms Wdfd Grn
72 M 15 Lambs pas Brentf
134 D 19 Lambs pas EC1
18 C 8 Lambs ter N9
7 Z 9 Lambs wlk Enf
112 M 8 Lambscroft av SE9
113 N 7 Lambscroft av SE9
137 S 8 Lambton pl W11
48 A 4 Lambton rd N19
118 L 2 Lambton rd SW20
104 L 20 Lambton rd SW20
112 C 9 Lamerock rd Brom
36 A 6 Lamerton rd Ilf
76 B 17 Lamerton st SE8
31 P 1 Lamford clo N17
74 J 10 Lamington st W6
149 X 4 Lamlash st SE11
121 O 3 Lammas av Mitch
121 O 4 Lammas av Mitch
109 Z 5 Lammas grn SE26
72 E 4 Lammas Pk gdns W5
72 F 4 Lammas Pk rd W5
50 H 5 Lammas rd E10
63 U 1 Lammas rd E9
102 D 11 Lammas rd Rich
89 T 19 Lammermoor rd SW12
146 E 15 Lamont Rd pas SW10
146 E 15 Lamont rd SW10
114 K 3 Lamorbey clo Sidcp
115 P 1 Lamorbey park Bxly
24 G 6 Lamorna gro Stanm
49 U 4 Lampard gro N16
144 K 15 Lampeter sq W6
94 B 12 Lampmead rd SE12
82 J 3 Lampton av Hounsl
78 G 10 Lampton clo SE18
105 O 10 Lampton Ho clo SW19
82 G 5 Lampton park Hounsl
82 J 6 Lampton Park rd Hounsl
82 J 5 Lampton rd Hounsl
25 Z 5 Lanacre av Edg
26 B 6 Lanacre av NW9
144 F 15 Lanarch rd W6
60 E 14 Lanark clo W5
130 D 17 Lanark pl W9
130 B 14 Lanark rd W9
129 Z 12 Lanark rd W9
92 F 11 Lanbury rd SE15
34 G 12 Lancashire av E18
139 Y 8 Lancashire ct W1
67 V 2 Lancaster av Bark
5 T 3 Lancaster av Barnt
112 A 9 Lancaster av Mitch
122 A 9 Lancaster av Mitch
108 K 4 Lancaster av SE27
105 R 12 Lancaster av SW19
155 Z 2 Lancaster clo Wallgtn
126 B 10 Lancaster clo Brom
102 H 12 Lancaster clo Kingst

145 S 20	Lancaster ct SW6
76 G 3	Lancaster dri E14
57 Z 16	Lancaster dri Hornch
46 H 18	Lancaster dri NW3
138 C 10	Lancaster ga W2
102 H 13	Lancaster gdns Kingst
105 S 11	Lancaster gdns SW19
72 C 4	Lancaster gdns W13
46 H 18	Lancaster gro NW3
138 D 9	Lancaster ms W2
84 J 14	Lancaster pk Rich
105 R 12	Lancaster pl SW19
83 Z 17	Lancaster pl Twick
141 N 9	Lancaster pl WC2
5 T 17	Lancaster rd Barnt
32 F 8	Lancaster rd E 17
52 A 7	Lancaster rd E11
52 F 20	Lancaster rd E7
65 U 1	Lancaster rd E7
8 C 6	Lancaster rd Enf
22 H 17	Lancaster rd Harrow
16 L 18	Lancaster rd N11
18 G 17	Lancaster rd N18
48 F 2	Lancaster rd N4
40 M 17	Lancaster rd Nthlt
44 F 14	Lancaster rd NW10
58 B 20	Lancaster rd S'hall
123 V 5	Lancaster rd SE25
105 R 12	Lancaster rd SW19
136 L 5	Lancaster rd W11
137 O 4	Lancaster rd W11
138 F 8	Lancaster ter W2
41 N 2	Lance rd Harrow
129 O 14	Lancefield st W10
49 T 8	Lancell st N16
42 G 12	Lancelot av Wemb
42 G 13	Lancelot cres Wemb
16 B 3	Lancelot gdns Barnt
139 N 19	Lancelot pl SW7
36 G 1	Lancelot rd Ilf
97 O 9	Lancelot rd Welling
42 H 15	Lancelot rd Wemb
78 B 10	Lancey clo SE7
29 N 15	Lanchester rd N6
18 H 5	Lancing gdns N9
122 D 16	Lancing rd Croy
36 E 19	Lancing rd Ilf
72 A 1	Lancing rd W13
132 F 13	Lancing st NW1
91 V 15	Landcroft rd SE22
91 V 16	Landells rd SE22
49 X 11	Landfield st E5
49 X 14	Landford clo
86 M 9	Landford rd SW15
105 X 11	Landgrove rd SW19
75 T 15	Landmann way SE14
147 O 1	Landon pl SW3
76 G 2	Landons clo E14
90 A 7	Landor rd SW9
74 F 6	Landor wlk W7
7 V 19	Landra gdns N21
87 U 4	Landridge rd SW6
30 B 18	Landrock rd N8
34 H 2	Landscape rd Wdfd Grn
53 V 15	Landseer av E12
25 R 7	Landseer clo Edg
120 E 1	Landseer clo SW19
117 Z 16	Landseer rd New Mald
8 J 18	Landseer rd Enf
48 A 8	Landseer rd N19
153 X 14	Landseer rd Sutton
14 E 17	Lane appr NW7
44 J 10	Lane clo NW2
98 F 8	Lane end Bxly Hth
10 F 4	Lane gdns Bushey
130 A 10	Lane the NW8
94 F 7	Lane the SE3
108 G 3	Lanercost clo SW2
16 M 1	Lanercost gdns N14
108 G 3	Lanercost rd SW2
56 C 2	Laneside av Dgnhm
114 A 12	Laneside Chisl
12 H 17	Laneside Edg
86 J 14	Laneway SW15
63 V 7	Lanfranc rd E3
141 T 20	Lanfranc st SE1
145 O 11	Lanfrey pl W14
63 P 11	Lang st E1
47 P 7	Langbourne av N6
95 O 6	Langbrook rd SE3
120 M 5	Langdale av Mitch
98 E 1	Langdale cres Bxly Hth
57 W 15	Langdale gdns Hornch
60 C 8	Langdale gdns Grnfd

122 F 9	Langdale rd Thntn Hth
76 F 20	Langdale rd SE10
143 V 7	Langdale st E1
66 K 5	Langdon cres E6
62 A 3	Langdon ct NW10
43 U 3	Langdon dri NW9
47 U 1	Langdon Park rd N6
85 V 7	Langdon pl SW14
66 J 4	Langdon rd E6
120 C 12	Langdon rd Mrdn
114 K 12	Langdon shaw Sidcp
49 W 14	Langford clo E8
130 D 9	Langford clo NW8
5 Z 13	Langford cres Barnt
91 R 7	Langford grn SE5
130 D 9	Langford pl NW8
115 N 7	Langford pl Sidcp
21 Z 20	Langford rd Wdfd Grn
88 B 3	Langford rd SW6
37 P 18	Langham dri Rom
42 D 7	Langham gdns Wemb
25 V 1	Langham gdns Edg
7 U 17	Langham gdns N21
102 E 9	Langham gdns Rich
60 B 20	Langham gdns W13
102 F 9	Langham House clo Rich
30 H 11	Langham pde N15
139 Z 3	Langham pl W1
12 H 20	Langham rd Edg
30 M 12	Langham rd N15
119 N 1	Langham rd SW20
102 A 14	Langham rd Tedd
139 Z 2	Langham st W1
18 G 19	Langhedge clo N18
18 H 18	Langhedge la N18
89 Y 19	Langholm clo SW12
10 A 4	Langholme Bushey
56 D 19	Langhorne rd Dgnhm
24 H 8	Langland Crescent east Stanm
24 H 8	Langland Crescent west Stanm
158 L 2	Langland gdns Croy
46 B 14	Langland gdns NW3
128 E 11	Langler rd NW10
116 H 20	Langley av Surb
153 O 2	Langley av Worc Pk
68 H 2	Langley cres Dgnhm
34 K 20	Langley cres E11
12 J 12	Langley cres Edg
125 S 9	Langley ct Becknhm
140 K 7	Langley ct WC2
34 J 19	Langley dri E11
73 T 4	Langley dri W3
126 L 9	Langley gdns Brom
127 Z 14	Langley gdns Brom
68 H 2	Langley gdns Dgnhm
118 A 3	Langley gro New Mald
117 Z 3	Langley gro New Mald
148 M 14	Langley la SW8
154 E 15	Langley Park rd Sutton
13 O 18	Langley pk NW7
124 G 9	Langley rd Becknhm
83 W 3	Langley rd Islwth
158 E 20	Langley rd S Croy
116 K 17	Langley rd Surb
119 W 1	Langley rd SW19
105 X 20	Langley rd SW19
80 F 18	Langley rd Welling
140 K 7	Langley st WC2
126 A 17	Langley way W Wckm
125 Y 18	Langley way W Wckm
10 D 4	Langmead dri Bushey
108 K 9	Langmead SE27
106 L 5	Langroyd rd SW17
86 F 10	Langside av SW15
16 L 11	Langside cres N14
160 F 3	Langthorn ct EC2
51 V 10	Langthorne rd E11
144 G 20	Langthorne st SW6
66 K 9	Langton av E6
15 S 3	Langton av N20
133 O 15	Langton clo WC1
22 M 3	Langton rd Harrow
23 N 2	Langton rd Harrow
44 M 10	Langton rd NW2
90 K 1	Langton rd SW9
149 Y 20	Langton rd SW9
91 Z 18	Langton ri SE22
92 A 18	Langton ri SE23
146 D 16	Langton st SW10
157 T 7	Langton way Croy

94 D 1	Langton way SE3
77 U 20	Langton way SE3
58 A 5	Langtry rd Nthlt
129 Y 5	Langtry rd NW8
130 A 4	Langtry wlk NW8
102 E 16	Langwood chase Tedd
129 U 16	Lanhill rd W9
93 V 15	Lanier rd SE13
28 G 6	Lankaster gdns N2
22 F 18	Lankers rd Harrow
125 T 1	Lankton clo Becknhm
114 A 1	Lannoy rd SE9
64 L 16	Lanrick rd E14
80 J 8	Lanridge rd SE2
68 A 1	Lansbury av Bark
18 C 18	Lansbury av N18
37 Z 16	Lansbury av Rom
9 T 7	Lansbury rd Enf
18 C 18	Lansbury way N18
64 H 17	Lansby gdns E14
121 O 3	Lansdell rd Mitch
52 L 19	Lansdown rd E7
115 P 7	Lansdown rd Sidcp
80 H 19	Lansdowne av Welling
105 N 18	Lansdowne clo SW20
101 V 1	Lansdowne clo Twick
137 N 10	Lansdowne cres W11
152 F 2	Lansdowne ct Worc Pk
135 V 3	Lansdowne dri E8
49 X 18	Lansdowne dri E8
90 A 1	Lansdowne gdns SW8
148 K 20	Lansdowne gdns SW8
44 B 14	Lansdowne gro NW10
108 J 6	Lansdowne hill SE27
78 A 15	Lansdowne la SE7
77 Z 15	Lansdowne la SE7
137 N 14	Lansdowne ms W11
150 G 1	Lansdowne pl SE1
109 T 17	Lansdowne pl SE19
82 K 7	Lansdowne rd Hounsl
112 G 18	Lansdowne rd Brom
157 N 2	Lansdowne rd Croy
123 O 20	Lansdowne rd Croy
52 B 7	Lansdowne rd E11
33 N 17	Lansdowne rd E17
34 E 10	Lansdowne rd E18
20 A 9	Lansdowne rd E4
54 K 2	Lansdowne rd Ilf
29 V 8	Lansdowne rd N10
31 W 5	Lansdowne rd N17
27 X 1	Lansdowne rd N3
11 S 20	Lansdowne rd Stanm
105 N 17	Lansdowne rd SW20
136 M 9	Lansdowne rd W11
137 N 12	Lansdowne rd W11
136 M 10	Lansdowne ri W11
139 Y 12	Lansdowne row W1
132 M 17	Lansdowne ter WC1
89 Z 2	Lansdowne way SW8
90 A 2	Lansdowne way SW8
137 O 12	Lansdowne wlk W11
18 L 13	Lansfield av N18
142 A 18	Lant st SE1
86 G 10	Lantern clo SW15
42 G 15	Lantern clo Wemb
76 C 7	Lanterns ct E14
92 B 5	Lanvanor rd SE15
109 Y 3	Lapsewood wlk SE26
24 D 19	Lapstone gdns Harrow
93 V 16	Lara clo SE13
107 U 19	Larbert rd SW16
74 A 3	Larch av W3
16 A 20	Larch clo N11
107 R 3	Larch clo SW12
45 N 12	Larch rd NW2
159 P 6	Larch Tree way Croy
127 W 16	Larch way Brom
85 X 10	Larches av SW14
17 Y 10	Larches the N13
114 A 5	Larchwood rd SE9
113 Z 4	Larchwood rd SE9
150 C 7	Larcom st SE17
74 B 4	Larden rd W3
63 O 4	Lark row E2
135 Z 6	Lark row E2
110 H 10	Larkbere rd SE26
10 A 5	Larken dri Bushey

24 C 10	Larkfield av Harrow
84 K 10	Larkfield rd Rich
114 K 8	Larkfield rd Sidcp
89 X 5	Larkhall la SW4
89 V 6	Larkhall ri SW4
9 N 7	Larksfield gro Enf
20 H 14	Larkshall cres E4
20 J 10	Larkshall rd E4
66 D 14	Larkspur clo E6
31 O 3	Larkspur clo N17
20 C 15	Larkswood rd E4
25 Z 14	Larkway clo NW9
86 L 13	Larpent av SW15
41 P 15	Larwood clo Grnfd
41 R 1	Lascelles av Harrow
51 X 8	Lascelles clo E11
17 R 20	Lascotts rd N22
95 S 13	Lassa rd SE9
76 L 14	Lassell st SE10
34 J 5	Latchett rd E18
62 H 8	Latchford gdns NW10
102 K 11	Latchmere clo Rich
88 L 6	Latchmere gro SW11
102 L 14	Latchmere la Kingst
88 K 5	Latchmere pas SW11
102 K 17	Latchmere rd Kingst
103 N 15	Latchmere rd Kingst
88 L 8	Latchmere rd SW11
88 L 4	Latchmere st SW11
72 G 17	Lateward rd Brentf
83 X 17	Latham clo Twick
98 F 13	Latham rd Bxly Hth
83 X 18	Latham rd Twick
156 C 1	Latham's way Croy
18 J 2	Lathkill clo Enf
66 E 16	Lathom clo E6
66 E 1	Lathom rd E6
66 G 4	Latimer av E6
152 K 8	Latimer clo Worc Pk
136 C 4	Latimer pl W10
5 N 10	Latimer rd Barnt
156 J 5	Latimer rd Croy
52 J 11	Latimer rd E7
31 S 18	Latimer rd N15
106 A 16	Latimer rd SW19
101 V 12	Latimer rd Tedd
136 D 5	Latimer rd W10
62 M 15	Latimer rd W10
63 T 15	Latimer st E1
151 R 15	Latona rd SE15
18 G 5	Latymer rd N9
18 C 9	Latymer way N9
156 L 7	Laud st Croy
149 N 10	Laud st SE11
102 G 6	Lauderdale dri Rich
130 A 15	Lauderdale rd W9
129 X 15	Lauderdale rd W9
58 A 4	Laughton rd Nthlt
112 G 10	Launcelot rd Brom
141 S 18	Launcelot st SE1
60 C 2	Launceston gdns Grnfd
146 A 2	Launceston pl W8
60 C 3	Launceston rd Grnfd
76 F 7	Launch st E14
144 K 15	Laundry rd W6
34 K 15	Laura clo E11
8 D 17	Laura clo Enf
50 B 12	Laura pl E5
29 N 12	Lauradale rd N2
101 V 1	Laurel av Twick
115 N 7	Laurel clo Sidcp
159 O 6	Laurel cres Croy
57 P 5	Laurel cres Rom
17 S 2	Laurel dri N21
20 D 2	Laurel gdns E4
82 A 11	Laurel gdns Hounsl
12 K 11	Laurel gdns NW7
71 T 2	Laurel gdns W7
110 B 18	Laurel gro SE20
110 G 11	Laurel gro SE26
86 F 5	Laurel rd SW13
104 H 20	Laurel rd SW20
101 P 13	Laurel rd Tedd
49 V 18	Laurel st E8
15 N 11	Laurel view N12
34 C 12	Laurel way E18
14 L 10	Laurel way N20
8 A 6	Laurelbank rd Enf
23 V 2	Laurels the Harrow
160 F 9	Laurence Poutney la EC4
160 F 9	Laurence Poutney hill EC4
92 J 1	Laurie gro SE14
59 T 14	Laurie rd W7
39 R 14	Laurie wlk Rom

123 U 16 Laurier rd Croy
47 S 10 Laurier rd NW5
11 P 19 Laurimel clo Stanm
63 S 1 Lauriston rd E9
105 O 15 Lauriston rd SW19
30 G 13 Lausanne rd N8
92 D 4 Lausanne rd SE15
49 O 13 Lavell st N16
120 J 1 Lavender av Mitch
43 V 3 Lavender av NW9
153 N 5 Lavender av Worc Pk
155 P 9 Lavender clo Carsh
88 M 9 Lavender gdns SW11
7 X 4 Lavender gdns Enf
49 W 20 Lavender gro E8
120 K 1 Lavender gro Mitch
7 T 5 Lavender hill Enf
88 L 9 Lavender hill SW11
89 O 8 Lavender hill SW11
155 P 10 Lavender rd Carsh
122 B 14 Lavender rd Croy
8 C 5 Lavender rd Enf
75 W 2 Lavender rd SE16
154 F 7 Lavender rd Sutton
88 G 7 Lavender rd SW11
51 Z 18 Lavender st E15
88 L 10 Lavender sweep SW11
155 X 14 Lavender vale Wallgtn
124 F 15 Lavender way Croy
88 L 10 Lavender wlk SW11
108 L 4 Lavengro rd SE27
105 X 2 Lavenham rd SW18
98 F 5 Lavernock rd Bxly Hth
49 T 9 Lavers rd N16
86 F 19 Laverstoke gdns SW15
145 Y 8 Laverton ms SW5
145 Y 7 Laverton pl SW5
113 S 5 Lavidge rd SE9
132 M 8 Lavina gro N1
156 C 7 Lavington rd Croy
72 C 3 Lavington rd W13
141 Z 14 Lavington st SE1
150 G 1 Law st SE1
156 K 8 Lawdons gdns Croy
155 Z 19 Lawford clo Wallgtn
134 J 2 Lawford rd N1
47 V 18 Lawford rd NW5
73 W 18 Lawford rd W4
132 B 2 Lawfords wharf NW1
16 E 3 Lawley rd N14
50 D 12 Lawley st E5
112 H 16 Lawn clo Brom
18 H 3 Lawn clo N9
118 A 4 Lawn clo New Mald
85 N 4 Lawn cres Rich
37 Y 11 Lawn Farm gro Rom
71 T 2 Lawn gdns W7
148 M 14 Lawn la SW8
149 N 15 Lawn la SW8
110 M 18 Lawn rd Becknhm
47 R 1 Lawn rd N6
46 L 15 Lawn rd NW3
94 B 7 Lawn ter SE3
70 H 13 Lawn the S'hall
22 A 6 Lawn vale Pinn
20 C 16 Lawns the E4
22 K 1 Lawns the Pinn
123 O 1 Lawns the SE19
94 B 7 Lawns the SE3
115 S 9 Lawns the Sidcp
153 T 17 Lawns the Sutton
38 L 2 Lawns way Rom
94 B 11 Lawnside SE3
118 A 17 Lawrence av New Mald
117 Z 15 Lawrence av New Mald
53 V 14 Lawrence av E12
32 G 4 Lawrence av E17
17 V 15 Lawrence av N13
13 P 13 Lawrence av NW7
49 U 9 Lawrence bldgs N16
15 U 10 Lawrence Campe clo N20
31 R 12 Lawrence clo N15
56 G 9 Lawrence cres Dgnhm
25 P 8 Lawrence cres Edg
13 O 15 Lawrence ct NW7
13 S 10 Lawrence gdns NW7
20 B 7 Lawrence hill E4
160 C 5 Lawrence la EC2
132 L 4 Lawrence pl N1
65 V 3 Lawrence rd E13
64 A 8 Lawrence rd E3

66 C 2 Lawrence rd E6
100 E 18 Lawrence rd Hampt
31 R 13 Lawrence rd N15
18 M 14 Lawrence rd N18
102 E 9 Lawrence rd Rich
39 Y 17 Lawrence rd Rom
123 V 9 Lawrence rd SE25
72 F 10 Lawrence rd W5
65 P 16 Lawrence st E16
13 S 12 Lawrence st NW7
146 J 15 Lawrence st SW3
60 A 4 Lawrence way Grnfd
119 X 13 Lawrence Weaver clo Mrdn
31 S 13 Lawrence yd N15
110 B 11 Lawrie Park av SE26
110 A 13 Lawrie Park cres SE26
110 B 12 Lawrie Park gdns SE26
110 B 14 Lawrie Park rd SE26
105 O 8 Lawson clo SW19
9 O 8 Lawson rd Enf
58 G 12 Lawson rd S'hall
65 Z 16 Lawsons clo E16
5 T 12 Lawton rd Barnt
51 T 4 Lawton rd E10
63 W 10 Lawton rd E3
149 Y 18 Laxley clo SE5
131 Z 16 Laxton pl NW1
8 H 5 Layard rd Enf
123 O 3 Layard rd Thntn Hth
151 X 4 Layard sq SE16
48 G 19 Laycock st N1
61 P 20 Layer gdns W3
44 K 1 Layfield clo NW4
44 J 1 Layfield cres NW4
44 K 2 Layfield rd NW4
159 Z 11 Layhams rd W Wckm
81 O 9 Laymarsh clo Blvdr
40 A 19 Laymead clo Nthlt
133 S 18 Laystall st EC1
156 H 11 Layton cres Croy
72 G 14 Layton rd Brentf
82 L 10 Layton rd Hounsl
133 U 7 Layton rd N1
112 H 6 Le May av SE12
50 E 6 Lea Bridge rd E10
33 T 18 Loo Bridgo rd E10
33 X 15 Lea Bridge rd E11
42 L 14 Lea gdns Wemb
51 O 3 Lea Hall rd E10
125 O 2 Lea rd Becknhm
8 A 6 Lea rd Enf
70 B 11 Lea rd S'hall
98 M 11 Lea vale Bxly Hth
20 B 1 Lea Valley rd E4
9 Y 19 Lea Valley rd Enf
41 T 10 Leabank clo Harrow
31 Y 17 Leabank view N15
31 W 20 Leabourne rd N16
96 K 13 Leachcroft av Sidcp
88 M 19 Leacroft av SW12
20 A 9 Leadale av E4
31 X 18 Leadale rd N15
160 H 7 Leaden Hall av EC3
142 J 6 Leadenhall mkt EC3
142 J 7 Leadenhall pl EC3
142 K 6 Leadenhall st EC3
53 X 16 Leader av E12
43 V 9 Leadings the Wemb
108 F 11 Leaf gro SE27
108 H 16 Leafield clo SW16
153 X 3 Leafield rd Sutton
119 W 5 Leafield rd SW20
112 L 8 Leafy Oak rd SE12
157 T 3 Leafy way Croy
50 D 9 Leagrave st E5
94 A 15 Leahurst rd SE13
93 X 13 Leahurst rd SE13
141 R 18 Leake st SE1
31 U 17 Lealand rd N15
112 K 12 Leamington av Brom
33 O 17 Leamington av E17
119 U 8 Leamington av Mrdn
83 O 12 Leamington clo Hounsl
112 K 11 Leamington clo Brom
53 S 15 Leamington clo E12
40 C 10 Leamington cres Harrow
54 K 7 Leamington gdns Ilf
61 X 16 Leamington pk W3
137 R 3 Leamington Road vlls W11
144 A 7 Leamore st W6
74 L 11 Leamore st W6
66 C 16 Leamouth gdns E6
64 K 18 Leamouth rd E14
58 G 6 Leander rd Nthlt
90 E 16 Leander rd SW2

122 D 8 Leander rd Thntn Hth
66 J 19 Learoyd gdns E6
113 W 7 Leas dale SE9
114 L 15 Leas grn Chisl
29 O 11 Leaside av N10
50 B 5 Leaside rd E5
51 O 3 Leasowes rd E10
81 P 7 Leather Bottle grn Blvdr
121 O 4 Leather clo Mitch
64 M 4 Leather gdns E15
133 T 19 Leather la EC1
141 T 2 Leather la EC1
63 T 10 Leatherdale st E1
49 T 3 Leatherhead clo N16
142 H 18 Leathermarket st SE1
40 L 10 Leathsail rd Harrow
88 M 11 Leathwaite rd SW11
93 R 5 Leathwell rd SE8
125 O 9 Leaveland clo Beckhm
59 S 7 Leaver gdns Grnfd
10 M 19 Leavesden rd Stanm
11 N 20 Leavesden rd Stanm
50 G 5 Leaway E10
87 X 14 Lebanon gdns SW18
84 B 20 Lebanon pk Twick
157 T 2 Lebanon rd Croy
87 X 14 Lebanon rd SW18
94 G 9 Lebrun sq SE3
34 M 7 Lechmere appr Wdfd Grn
34 M 7 Lechmere av Wdfd Grn
44 K 18 Lechmere rd NW2
106 E 2 Leckford rd SW18
80 L 17 Leckwith av Bxly Hth
146 F 10 Lecky st SW7
86 D 9 Leconfield av SW13
49 N 13 Leconfield rd N5
9 S 4 Leda av Enf
137 T 7 Ledbury ms N W11
137 S 8 Ledbury ms W W11
157 N 9 Ledbury pl Croy
157 N 9 Ledbury rd Croy
137 S 7 Ledbury rd W11
151 U 17 Ledbury st SE15
100 W 16 Ledrington rd SE19
42 M 2 Ledway dri Wemb
43 N 1 Ledway dri Wemb
37 X 19 Lee av Rom
94 A 10 Lee Church st SE13
32 E 6 Lee clo E17
50 L 14 Lee Conservancy rd E9
93 V 9 Lee High rd SE13
19 V 12 Lee Parkway N9
94 B 10 Lee pk SE3
8 K 20 Lee rd Enf
60 D 3 Lee rd Grnfd
120 B 1 Lee rd Mitch
27 R 2 Lee rd NW7
94 C 11 Lee rd SE3
134 M 3 Lee st E8
135 N 3 Lee st E8
94 A 8 Lee ter SE3
93 Z 8 Lee ter SE3
7 W 6 Lee view Enf
155 P 6 Leechcroft rd Wallgtn
4 E 14 Leecroft rd Barnt
48 D 4 Leeds pla N4
54 F 4 Leeds rd Ilf
18 J 17 Leeds st N18
133 N 12 Leeke st WC1
71 Z 2 Leeland rd W13
72 A 2 Leeland ter W13
44 C 12 Leeland way NW10
27 O 13 Leemount clo NW4
139 T 8 Lees pl W1
158 L 3 Lees the Croy
4 F 19 Leeside Barnt
27 U 18 Leeside cres NW11
19 P 20 Leeside rd N17
90 G 12 Leeson rd SE24
105 U 14 Leeward gdns SW19
22 C 2 Leeway clo Pinn
75 Y 13 Leeway SE8
63 Z 4 Lefevre wk E3
74 H 6 Leffern rd W12
74 C 5 Lefroy rd W12
48 J 11 Legard rd N5
94 M 13 Legatt rd SE9
95 N 13 Legatt rd SE9
64 G 6 Leggatt rd E15
93 T 12 Legge st SE13
62 F 5 Leghorn rd NW10
79 T 14 Leghorn rd SE18
119 Y 14 Legion ct Mrdn
59 O 4 Legion rd Grnfd

56 L 5 Legon av Rom
140 G 9 Leicester ct WC2
152 M 7 Leicester ct Worc Pk
36 J 20 Leicester gdns Ilf
140 G 9 Leicester pl WC2
5 R 14 Leicester rd Barnt
123 S 18 Leicester rd Croy
34 J 16 Leicester rd E11
28 K 11 Leicester rd N2
43 Z 20 Leicester rd NW10
140 G 10 Leicester sq WC2
140 F 9 Leicester st WC2
35 N 13 Leigh av Ilf
117 X 8 Leigh clo New Mald
159 T 16 Leigh cres Croy
41 S 5 Leigh ct Harrow
128 C 9 Leigh gdns NW10
62 M 6 Leigh gdns NW10
142 A 17 Leigh Hunt st SE1
108 C 8 Leigh Orchard clo SW16
141 T 1 Leigh pl EC1
97 O 4 Leigh pl Welling
51 V 2 Leigh rd E10
53 V 19 Leigh rd E6
83 P 10 Leigh rd Hounsl
48 J 13 Leigh rd N5
132 J 15 Leigh st WC1
108 A 7 Leigham av SW16
108 B 5 Leigham Court rd SW16
71 U 19 Leigham dri Islwth
108 E 6 Leigham vale SW16
53 W 16 Leighton av E12
22 B 10 Leighton av Pinn
25 R 7 Leighton clo Edg
47 W 14 Leighton cres NW5
128 C 7 Leighton gdns NW10
62 L 5 Leighton gdns NW10
47 W 14 Leighton gro NW5
47 V 16 Leighton pl NW5
8 H 18 Leighton rd Enf
23 O 7 Leighton rd Harrow
47 V 15 Leighton rd NW5
72 A 5 Leighton rd W13
71 Z 5 Leighton rd W13
122 H 20 Leighton st Croy
05 V 9 Leinster av SW14
138 B 7 Leinster gdns W2
138 B 10 Leinster ms W2
138 A 7 Leinster pl W2
29 T 13 Leinster rd N10
129 T 12 Leinster rd NW6
137 W 7 Leinster sq W2
138 B 10 Leinster ter W2
43 Y 4 Leith clo NW9
30 H 4 Leith rd N22
129 U 4 Leith yd NW6
108 C 9 Leithcote gdns SW16
135 S 5 Lelitia clo E8
143 R 7 Leman st E1
11 R 17 Lemark clo Stanm
76 M 15 Lemmon rd SE10
52 A 2 Lemna rd E11
96 A 15 Lemonwell ct SE9
31 Y 17 Lemsford clo N15
88 B 16 Lemuel st SW18
144 D 2 Lena gdns W6
74 M 9 Lena gdns W6
89 Y 8 Lendal ter SW4
117 P 20 Lenelby rd Surb
81 O 17 Lenham rd Bxly Hth
94 B 11 Lenham rd SE12
154 B 10 Lenham rd Sutton
123 O 4 Lenham rd Thntn Hth
110 K 19 Lennard rd Becknhm
127 U 20 Lennard rd Brom
122 K 19 Lennard rd Croy
44 M 16 Lennon rd NW2
39 T 19 Lennox clo Rom
147 N 4 Lennox Gardens ms SW1
156 K 9 Lennox gdns Croy
53 S 4 Lennox gdns Ilf
44 D 13 Lennox gdns NW10
147 N 4 Lennox gdns SW1
32 M 19 Lennox rd E17
48 E 7 Lennox rd N4
97 Y 11 Lenor clo Bxly Hth
65 X 1 Lens rd E7
80 G 7 Lensbury way SE2
146 B 5 Lenthall pl SW7
49 W 20 Lenthall rd E8
77 P 13 Lenthorpe rd SE10
112 C 7 Lentmead rd Brom
79 R 10 Lenton st SE18
151 U 10 Lenville way SE16
75 O 19 Leo st SE15
151 Z 17 Leo st SE15

108 H 13	Lindway SE27
33 V 11	Linford rd E17
89 U 2	Linford st SW8
65 T 14	Ling rd E16
81 Y 17	Ling rd Erith
93 V 11	Lingards rd SE13
114 L 3	Lingey clo Sidcp
116 K 9	Lingfield av Kingst
8 D 19	Lingfield clo Enf
96 E 10	Lingfield cres SE9
19 N 2	Lingfield gdns N9
105 P 14	Lingfield rd SW19
152 M 6	Lingfield rd Worc Pk
90 B 5	Lingham st SW9
4 C 16	Lingholm way Barnt
21 U 9	Lingrove gdns Buck HI
109 O 3	Lings coppice SE21
106 K 6	Lingwell rd SW17
71 T 18	Lingwood gdns Islwth
49 Y 1	Lingwood rd E5
31 X 20	Lingwood rd N16
131 N 18	Linhope st NW1
156 A 13	Link la Wallgtn
155 Y 13	Link la Wallgtn
69 T 7	Link rd Dgnhm
16 B 13	Link rd N11
155 O 1	Link rd Wallgtn
50 D 16	Link st E9
9 V 5	Link the Enf
40 D 16	Link the Nthlt
61 S 16	Link the W3
42 D 4	Link the Wembm
127 R 16	Link way Brom
126 E 14	Linkfield Brom
83 Y 5	Linkfield rd Islwth
26 B 3	Linklea clo NW9
119 Y 8	Links av Mrdn
39 Z 6	Links av Rom
14 M 6	Links dri N20
108 F 18	Links gdns SW16
44 C 8	Links rd NW2
107 R 17	Links rd SW17
125 V 20	Links rd W Wkhm
61 P 16	Links rd W3
21 S 16	Links rd Wdfd Grn
7 S 12	Links side Enf
32 H 13	Links the E17
10 L 20	Links View clo Stanm
27 V 3	Links view N3
159 O 4	Links View rd Croy
101 O 11	Links View rd Hampt
125 P 14	Links way Becknhm
7 S 12	Linkside clo Enf
7 R 11	Linkside gdns Enf
14 J 18	Linkside N12
118 B 4	Linkside New Mald
27 O 8	Linksway NW4
55 U 11	Linkway Dgnhm
102 B 5	Linkway Rich
118 K 7	Linkway SW20
4 M 20	Linkway the Barnt
154 E 20	Linkway the Sutton
38 J 9	Linley cres Rom
31 S 6	Linley rd N17
27 Z 19	Linnell clo NW11
27 Z 20	Linnell dri NW11
18 K 15	Linnell rd N18
91 S 3	Linnell rd SE5
68 G 20	Linnet clo SE28
89 N 18	Linnet ms SW12
20 H 13	Linnett clo E4
90 A 11	Linom rd SW4
50 C 13	Linscott rd E5
151 S 5	Linsey st SE16
151 T 3	Linsey st SE16
45 X 19	Linstead st NW6
87 S 18	Linstead way SW18
42 F 17	Linthorpe av Wemb
5 W 12	Linthorpe rd Barnt
40 T 1	Linthorpe rd N16
97 O 3	Linton clo Well
39 O 7	Linton ct Rom
66 D 16	Linton gdns E6
158 H 20	Linton glade CRO
108 L 11	Linton gro SE27
54 B 20	Linton rd Bark
67 O 1	Linton rd Bark
134 C 5	Linton st N1
87 W 5	Linver rd SW6
66 F 15	Linwood clo E6
29 Z 13	Linzee rd N8
101 V 2	Lion av Twick
84 M 6	Lion Gate gdns Rich
85 N 5	Lion gdns Rich
98 A 10	Lion rd Bxly Hth
122 L 13	Lion rd Croy
66 G 15	Lion rd E6
18 K 9	Lion rd N9
101 V 1	Lion rd Twick
72 F 18	Lion way Brentf
84 A 8	Lion Wharf rd Islwth
95 O 13	Lionel gdns SE9
128 J 9	Lionel ms W10
128 K 20	Lionel ms W10
72 M 14	Lionel rd Brentf
73 O 14	Lionel rd Brentf
95 O 13	Lionel rd SE9
112 M 8	Lions clo SE9
113 N 8	Lionsdale clo SE9
92 B 19	Liphook cres SE23
68 F 19	Lipton clo SE28
63 T 18	Lipton st E1
100 M 5	Lisbon av Twick
101 N 4	Lisbon av Twick
46 M 13	Lisburne rd NW3
91 V 1	Lisford st SE15
145 N 6	Lisgar ter W14
114 C 16	Liskeard clo Chisl
94 F 2	Liskeard gdns SE3
140 G 9	Lisle st WC2
83 X 5	Lismore clo Islwth
31 O 11	Lismore rd N17
157 R 15	Lismore rd S Croy
47 P 12	Lissenden gdns NW5
130 G 15	Lisson gro NW8
130 K 20	Lisson st NW1
18 A 16	Lister gdns N18
17 Z 16	Lister gdns N18
52 A 5	Lister rd E11
31 W 5	Liston rd N17
89 V 8	Liston rd SW4
34 L 2	Liston way Wdfd Grn
56 E 8	Listowel rd Dgnhm
149 X 20	Listowell clo SW9
149 X 20	Listowell st SW9
49 T 6	Listria pk N16
44 G 19	Litchfied gdns NW10
51 Z 18	Litchfield av E15
119 V 16	Litchfield av Mrdn
154 B 9	Litchfield rd Sutton
140 H 8	Litchfield st WC2
28 C 16	Litchfield way NW11
46 C 17	Lithos rd NW3
75 O 10	Litlington st SE16
151 Y 5	Litlington st SE16
125 P 7	Little acre Bcknhm
131 Z 14	Little Albany st NW1
140 A 6	Little Argyll st W1
114 H 5	Little birches Sidcp
146 A 11	Little Boltons the SW10
145 Z 10	Little Boltons the SW5
109 S 8	Little bournes SE21
142 A 3	Little Britain EC1
160 A 3	Little Britain EC1
141 Y 2	Little Britain EC1
18 C 4	Little Bury st N9
10 C 1	Little Bushey la Bushey
15 P 12	Little cedars N12
139 W 20	Little Chester st SW1
148 J 2	Little College st SW1
87 R 18	Little Cote clo SW19
159 Z 3	Little ct W Wkhm
107 T 3	Little dimocks SW12
142 C 16	Little Dorrit st SE1
72 F 9	Little Ealing la W5
131 Y 12	Little Edward st NW1
141 R 8	Little Essex st WC2
141 R 8	Little Essex st WC2
20 M 9	Little Friday hill E4
35 Z 14	Little Gearies Ilf
140 J 19	Little George st SW1
47 S 12	Little Green st NW5
5 X 20	Little gro Barnt
37 O 13	Little Heath lodge Rom
98 A 1	Little Heath rd Bxly IIth
81 P 20	Little Heath rd Bxly Hth
157 Z 17	Little Heath rd S Croy
37 P 14	Little Heath Rom
78 D 14	Little Heath SE7
53 U 12	Little Ilford la E12
59 V 16	Little John rd W7
140 B 7	Little Marlborough st W1
22 C 7	Little Moss la Pinn
141 V 5	Little New st EC4
140 G 9	Little Newport st WC2
22 A 7	Little Orchard clo Pinn
100 A 4	Little Park dri Felt
8 A 12	Little Park gdns Enf
21 Z 5	Little Plucketts way Buck HI
140 A 4	Little Portland st W1
10 D 2	Little Potters Bushey
101 V 15	Little Queens rd Tedd
127 P 2	Little Redlands Brom
140 J 2	Little Russell st WC1
140 H 19	Little Sanctuary SW1
148 H 2	Little Smith st SW1
143 N 6	Little Somerset st E1
140 B 15	Little St James st SW1
85 W 8	Little St Leonards SW14
26 D 7	Little strand NW9
140 A 3	Little Titchfield st W1
160 B 8	Little Trinity la EC4
141 N 3	Little turnstile WC1
38 B 1	Little Venice W2
89 X 8	Littlebury rd SW4
87 P 15	Littlecombe clo SW15
77 W 16	Littlecombe SE7
22 C 3	Littlecote pl Pinn
95 V 7	Littlecroft SE9
80 A 17	Littledale SE2
47 V 11	Littlefield clo N19
25 U 1	Littlefield rd Edg
158 A 20	Littleheath rd S Croy
113 U 7	Littlemede SE9
54 E 10	Littlemoor rd Ilf
80 A 7	Littlemoor rd SE2
106 E 20	Littlers clo SW19
111 O 16	Littlestone clo Becknhm
21 O 6	Littleton av Ev
41 W 7	Littleton cres Harrow
41 X 8	Littleton rd Harrow
106 E 5	Littleton st SW18
72 B 9	Littlewood clo W13
93 V 15	Littlewood rd SE13
135 O 2	Livermere rd E8
150 C 11	Liverpool gro SE17
122 M 7	Liverpool rd Thntn Hth
33 V 17	Liverpool rd E10
65 N 13	Liverpool rd E16
103 R 17	Liverpool rd Kingst
133 U 2	Liverpool rd N1
48 F 17	Liverpool rd N7
72 H 5	Liverpool rd W5
142 J 2	Liverpool st EC2
142 K 2	Liverpool Street sta EC2
151 T 14	Livesey pl SE15
76 F 14	Livingstone pl E14
82 M 9	Livingstone rd Hounsl
123 N 4	Livingstone rd Thntn Hth
83 N 9	Livingstone rd Hounsl
64 H 4	Livingstone rd E15
33 R 18	Livingstone rd E17
17 N 18	Livingstone rd N13
58 A 20	Livingstone rd S'hall
88 G 8	Livingstone rd SW11
66 L 18	Livingstone st E6
140 D 7	Livonia st W1
134 C 15	Lizard st EC1
77 V 19	Lizban st SE3
45 W 8	Llanelly rd NW2
78 K 18	Llanover rd SE18
42 G 10	Llanover rd Wemb
120 F 13	Llanthony rd Mrdn
45 W 7	Llanvanor rd NW2
143 T 18	Llewellyn st SE16
122 B 1	Lloyd av SW16
133 S 12	Lloyd Baker st WC1
157 U 9	Lloyd Park av Croy
157 V 8	Lloyd pk Croy
33 N 7	Lloyd pk E17
56 C 19	Lloyd rd Dgnhm
32 F 13	Lloyd rd E17
66 F 4	Lloyd rd E6
153 N 4	Lloyd rd Worc Pk
133 R 13	Lloyd sq WC1
133 S 12	Lloyd st WC1
142 L 7	Lloyds av EC3
94 A 5	Lloyds pl SE3
133 V 13	Lloyds row EC1
124 K 11	Lloyds way Becknhm
93 P 6	Loampit hills SE13
93 S 7	Loampit vale SE13
89 Z 15	Loats rd SW4
66 D 14	Lobelia clo E6
59 P 10	Locarno rd Grnfd
73 V 3	Locarno rd W3
93 Z 11	Lochaber rd SE13
144 E 13	Lochaline rd W6
58 B 12	Lochan clo Grnfd
89 R 19	Lochinvar st SW12
64 G 14	Lochnagar st E14
94 A 8	Lock chase SE3
102 E 9	Lock rd Rich
57 U 19	Locke clo Rainhm
23 U 9	Locket rd Harrow
9 X 8	Lockfield av Enf
48 C 18	Lockhart clo N7
63 Z 12	Lockhart st E3
50 F 12	Lockhurst st E5
89 T 1	Lockington rd SW8
31 Y 18	Lockmead rd N15
93 V 7	Lockmead rd SE13
81 V 17	Lockmere clo Erith
121 N 2	Locks la Mitch
63 Y 15	Locksley st E14
102 B 10	Locksmead rd Rich
110 G 10	Lockwood clo SE26
54 C 8	Lockwood rd Ilf
151 W 2	Lockwood sq SE16
32 E 9	Lockwood way E17
39 R 16	Lockwood wlk Rom
142 F 18	Lockyer st SE1
50 B 20	Loddiges rd E9
156 E 6	Lodge av Croy
68 B 4	Lodge av Dgnhm
55 P 13	Lodge av Dgnhm
24 J 14	Lodge av Harrow
39 U 12	Lodge av Rom
85 Z 8	Lodge av SW14
12 A 18	Lodge clo Edg
84 A 1	Lodge clo Islwth
18 A 17	Lodge clo N18
154 B 10	Lodge clo Sutton
155 O 1	Lodge clo Wallgtn
6 K 13	Lodge cres Enf
17 T 14	Lodge dri N13
124 M 12	Lodge gdns Becknhm
35 S 12	Lodge hill Ilf
80 E 18	Lodge hill Welling
97 V 14	Lodge la Bxly
159 P 15	Lodge la Croy
15 P 15	Lodge la N12
38 D 3	Lodge la Rom
112 K 17	Lodge rd Brom
122 K 17	Lodge rd Croy
122 L 17	Lodge rd Croy
26 M 12	Lodge rd NW4
130 H 15	Lodge rd NW8
155 R 10	Lodge rd Wallgtn
21 P 20	Lodge vlls Wdfd Grn
40 L 6	Lodgehill Park clo Harrow
26 A 15	Lodore gdns NW9
64 F 18	Lodore st E14
143 U 18	Loftie st SE16
133 S 1	Lofting rd N1
74 K 3	Loftus rd W12
9 T 7	Logan clo Enf
145 T 5	Logan ms W8
145 T 5	Logan pl W8
82 D 9	Logan rd Hounsl
19 O 9	Logan rd N9
42 J 6	Logan rd Wemb
113 R 19	Logs hill Chisl
127 S 1	Logs hill Chisl
113 R 20	Logs Hill clo Chisl
149 S 7	Lollard st SE11
141 Y 16	Loman st SE1
159 U 16	Lomas clo CRO
135 U 19	Lomas st E1
9 R 7	Lombard av Enf
54 G 5	Lombard av Ilf
160 H 8	Lombard ct EC3
141 U 7	Lombard la EC4
16 G 16	Lombard rd N11
88 F 5	Lombard rd SW11
120 B 2	Lombard rd SW19
142 G 7	Lombard rd EC3
160 G 7	Lombard st EC3
77 V 10	Lombard way SE7
137 Y 10	Lombardy pl W2
31 S 14	Lomond clo N15
43 N 20	Lomond clo Wemb
150 D 19	Lomond gro SE5
150 L 13	Loncroft rd SE5
49 R 11	Londesborough rd N16
142 F 12	London br EC4
142 H 14	London Bridge station SE1
142 F 14	London Bridge st SE1

135 W 2	London Fields East side E8
49 Y 20	London Fields West side E8
112 F 17	London la Brom
50 A 20	London la E8
138 G 5	London ms W2
137 Z 15	London museum W8
66 M 2	London rd Bark
67 O 1	London rd Bark
112 C 19	London rd Bark
99 P 13	London rd Drtfrd
65 R 7	London rd E13
8 C 14	London rd Enf
152 K 11	London rd Epsom
41 T 7	London rd Harrow
84 A 1	London rd Islwth
83 X 2	London rd Islwth
117 N 2	London rd Kingst
120 K 8	London rd Mitch
107 N 19	London rd Mitch
121 P 17	London rd Mitch
119 X 11	London rd Mrdn
38 D 19	London rd Rom
149 X 2	London rd SE1
110 B 2	London rd SE23
11 U 14	London rd Stanm
153 O 4	London rd Sutton
122 D 4	London rd SW16
83 Y 17	London rd Twick
155 S 3	London rd Wallgtn
42 M 17	London rd Wemb
142 K 8	London st EC3
138 G 6	London st W2
160 C 3	London wall EC2
142 G 3	London wall EC2
160 G 3	London wall EC2
155 P 14	Long Acre pl Carsh
140 L 6	Long acre WC2
20 M 6	Long Deacon rd E4
58 L 4	Long dri Grnfd
40 A 10	Long dri Pinn
62 B 16	Long dri W3
22 L 5	Long elmes Harrow
23 R 4	Long elmes Harrow
26 C 4	Long field NW9
80 K 20	Long la Bxly Hth
97 Z 1	Long la Bxly Hth
124 B 14	Long la Croy
141 Y 1	Long la EC1
28 D 8	Long la N2
27 Z 3	Long la N3
142 D 18	Long la SE1
20 E 19	Long leys E4
66 A 16	Long Mark rd E16
26 D 5	Long mead NW9
47 X 16	Long meadow NW5
114 G 2	Long Meadow rd Sidcp
94 A 2	Long Pond rd SE3
93 Z 3	Long Pond rd SE3
89 U 10	Long rd E2
134 M 11	Long st E2
64 J 8	Long wall E15
117 W 5	Long wlk New Mald
150 L 1	Long wlk SE1
78 L 16	Long wlk SE18
86 C 6	Long wlk SW13
133 N 18	Long yd WC1
33 W 4	Longacre rd E17
89 N 9	Longbeach rd SW11
45 V 8	Longberrys NW2
55 P 12	Longbridge rd Dgnhm
54 G 16	Longbridge rd Bark
93 T 12	Longbridge way SE13
113 V 7	Longcroft SE9
24 H 1	Longcrofte rd Edg
111 O 9	Longdown rd SE6
32 L 20	Longfellow rd E17
33 N 18	Longfellow rd E17
63 V 10	Longfellow rd E3
152 H 1	Longfellow rd Worc Pk
32 G 14	Longfield av E17
9 R 2	Longfield av Enf
57 T 1	Longfield av Hornch
26 G 3	Longfield av NW7
60 E 20	Longfield av W5
155 P 1	Longfield av Wallgtn
121 P 20	Longfield av Wallgtn
42 J 5	Longfield av Wemb
112 D 20	Longfield Brom
110 C 6	Longfield cres SE26
85 S 13	Longfield dri SW14
60 F 19	Longfield dri W5
87 X 19	Longfield st SW18
60 E 18	Longfield wlk W5
70 J 1	Longford av S'hall
58 J 20	Longford av S'hall
100 G 10	Longford clo Hampt
31 R 18	Longford clo N15
154 D 4	Longford gdns Sutton
100 J 2	Longford rd Twick
131 Z 16	Longford st NW1
37 W 12	Longhayes av Rom
124 D 12	Longheath gdns Croy
89 O 4	Longhedge st SW11
111 X 6	Longhill rd SE6
124 B 14	Longhurst rd Croy
94 A 14	Longhurst rd SE13
93 Z 14	Longhurst rd SE13
151 S 10	Longland ct SE1
15 N 9	Longland dri N20
115 N 5	Longlands la Sidcp
114 G 6	Longlands Park cres Sidcp
114 J 6	Longlands rd Sidcp
8 F 19	Longleat rd Enf
80 E 16	Longleigh la SE2
61 N 4	Longley av Wemb
122 H 18	Longley rd Croy
23 P 14	Longley rd Harrow
106 J 14	Longley rd SW17
151 S 6	Longley st SE1
45 N 10	Longley way NW2
127 Y 3	Longmead BR7
115 X 4	Longmead dri Sidcp
106 L 11	Longmead rd SW17
5 S 17	Longmere av Barnt
148 B 7	Longmore st SW1
63 U 10	Longnor rd E1
67 X 12	Longreach rd Bark
58 L 18	Longridge la S'hall
145 T 7	Longridge rd SW5
140 G 11	Longs ct WC2
20 K 11	Longshaw rd E4
75 Y 11	Longshore SE8
87 Z 17	Longstaff cres SW18
87 Z 17	Longstaff rd SW18
62 F 4	Longstone av NW10
107 S 13	Longstone rd SW17
121 W 3	Longthornton rd SW16
109 Y 10	Longton av SE26
110 A 9	Longton gro SE26
109 Z 10	Longton gro SE26
38 L 5	Longville rd SE11
149 X 5	Longville rd SE11
86 H 17	Longwood dri SW15
35 U 14	Longwood gdns Ilf
68 K 19	Longworth clo SE28
9 O 2	Loning the Enf
26 B 12	Loning the NW9
66 G 11	Lonsdale av E6
38 J 18	Lonsdale av Rom
42 L 16	Lonsdale av Wemb
66 D 11	Lonsdale clo E6
22 C 3	Lonsdale clo Pinn
35 Y 18	Lonsdale cres Ilf
6 K 14	Lonsdale dri Enf
7 O 14	Lonsdale dri Enf
122 C 8	Lonsdale gdns Thntn Hth
85 O 2	Lonsdale ms Rich
133 U 2	Lonsdale pl N1
98 B 6	Lonsdale rd Bxly Hth
34 D 20	Lonsdale rd E11
129 O 6	Lonsdale rd NW6
123 Z 8	Lonsdale rd SE25
86 D 3	Lonsdale rd SW13
74 F 18	Lonsdale rd SW13
137 R 7	Lonsdale rd W11
74 C 10	Lonsdale rd W4
133 T 2	Lonsdale sq N1
31 T 11	Loobert rd N15
36 A 9	Looe gdns Ilf
114 A 16	Loop rd Chisl
18 D 13	Lopen rd N18
9 P 17	Loraine clo Enf
48 D 12	Loraine rd N7
73 S 17	Loraine rd W4
35 V 10	Lord av Ilf
103 X 20	Lord Chancellor wlk Kingst
35 S 12	Lord gdns Ilf
129 Y 20	Lord Hills rd W2
148 J 2	Lord North st SW1
145 X 19	Lord Robert's ms SW6
78 K 15	Lord Robert's ter SE18
78 E 3	Lord st E16
78 F 9	Lord Warwick st SE18
135 P 13	Lorden wlk E2
100 C 5	Lords clo Felt
108 M 2	Lords clo SE21
130 G 13	Lords Cricket ground NW8
49 P 7	Lordship gro N16
31 O 6	Lordship la N17
30 G 6	Lordship la N22
91 V 15	Lordship la SE22
48 M 7	Lordship pk N16
49 O 6	Lordship pk N16
146 K 15	Lordship pl SW3
49 O 4	Lordship rd N16
40 B 20	Lordship rd Nthlt
49 P 8	Lordship ter N16
31 S 6	Lordsmead rd N17
133 O 11	Lorenzo st WC1
24 J 13	Loretto gdns Harrow
15 N 13	Lorian clo N12
83 V 4	Loring rd Islwth
15 V 8	Loring rd N20
144 D 2	Loris rd W6
90 E 4	Lorn rd SW9
124 F 17	Lorne av Croy
130 L 15	Lorne clo NW8
124 G 16	Lorne gdns Croy
34 K 14	Lorne gdns E11
136 J 17	Lorne gdns W11
33 N 17	Lorne rd E17
52 K 11	Lorne rd E7
23 V 8	Lorne rd Harrow
48 D 3	Lorne rd N4
84 L 13	Lorne rd Rich
23 T 2	Lorraine pk Harrow
149 Y 14	Lorrimore rd SE17
149 Z 13	Lorrimore sq SE17
151 U 10	Losberne way SE16
72 F 7	Lothair rd W5
30 J 20	Lothair Road north N4
30 H 20	Lothair Road south N4
88 H 8	Lothair st SW11
142 F 5	Lothbury EC2
160 F 5	Lothbury EC2
149 Y 20	Lothian ms SW9
90 J 1	Lothian rd SW9
149 Y 20	Lothian rd SW9
128 L 13	Lothrop st W10
146 A 19	Lots rd SW10
106 M 14	Loubet st SW17
130 D 5	Loudon rd NW8
36 A 15	Loudoun av Ilf
35 Z 14	Loudoun av Ilf
48 D 16	Lough rd N7
90 J 9	Loughborough pk SW9
90 F 4	Loughborough rd SW9
90 H 6	Loughborough rd SW9
149 R 10	Loughborough st SE11
63 S 13	Louisa st E1
52 A 17	Louise rd E15
107 O 6	Louisville rd SW17
88 G 11	Louvaine rd SW11
44 D 11	Lovat clo NW2
142 H 10	Lovat la EC3
160 H 10	Lovat la EC3
12 E 18	Lovatt clo Edg
98 C 17	Love la Bxly
160 C 4	Love la EC2
120 K 4	Love la Mitch
120 A 16	Love la Mrdn
119 Z 17	Love la Mrdn
31 U 2	Love la N17
22 A 10	Love la Pinn
78 K 11	Love la SE18
124 A 7	Love la SE25
153 T 13	Love la Sutton
153 U 12	Love la Sutton
91 N 4	Love la SE5
72 B 4	Loveday rd W13
151 T 12	Lovegrove st SE1
116 K 2	Lovekyn clo Kingst
96 M 5	Lovel av Well
97 N 4	Lovel av Welling
127 X 15	Lovelace av Brom
54 M 14	Lovelace gdns Bark
116 F 17	Lovelace gdns Surb
95 T 8	Lovelace grn SE9
15 W 2	Lovelace rd Barnt
108 L 2	Lovelace rd SE21
116 H 17	Lovelace rd Surb
75 R 16	Lovelinch st SE15
75 V 7	Lovell pl SE16
102 D 7	Lovell rd Rich
58 J 17	Lovell rd S'hall
57 V 17	Lovell wlk Rainhm
45 V 18	Loveridge rd NW6
27 X 1	Lovers wlk N3
14 H 19	Lovers wlk NW7
120 E 17	Lovett dri Carsh
43 W 15	Lovett way NW10
109 V 7	Low Cross Wood la SE21
20 B 3	Low Hall clo E4
53 Z 14	Lowbrook rd Ilf
19 N 5	Lowden rd N9
58 B 19	Lowden rd S'hall
90 K 11	Lowden rd SE24
65 T 15	Lowe av E16
63 W 17	Lowell st E14
123 W 20	Lower Addiscombe rd Croy
147 W 2	Lower Belgrave st SW1
71 T 4	Lower Boston rd W7
69 R 3	Lower Broad st Dgnhm
113 U 20	Lower Camden Chisl
127 V 1	Lower Camden Chisl
156 J 13	Lower Church st Croy
50 B 12	Lower Clapton rd E5
86 K 8	Lower Common south SW15
156 L 7	Lower Coombe st Croy
105 P 20	Lower Downs rd SW20
119 R 1	Lower Downs rd SW20
18 K 13	Lower Fore st N9
127 T 20	Lower Gravel rd Brom
120 K 7	Lower Green west Mitch
147 Y 1	Lower Grosvenor pl SW1
19 W 15	Lower Hall la E4
102 G 14	Lower Ham rd Kingst
116 H 1	Lower Ham rd Kingst
96 A 7	Lower Jackwood clo SE9
140 C 9	Lower James st W1
140 C 9	Lower John st W1
6 L 16	Lower Kenwood av N14
16 H 18	Lower Maidstone rd N11
144 B 11	Lower Mall W6
74 K 14	Lower Mall W6
69 Y 7	Lower Mardyke av Rainhm
116 M 8	Lower Marsh la Kingst
117 R 9	Lower Marsh la Kingst
141 R 19	Lower Marsh SE1
130 K 1	Lower Merton ri NW3
119 P 14	Lower Morden la Mrdn
84 J 10	Lower Mortlake rd Rich
81 T 9	Lower Park rd Blvdr
16 G 18	Lower Park rd N11
81 U 9	Lower rd Blvdr
81 Z 10	Lower rd Erith
41 P 4	Lower rd Harrow
69 Z 6	Lower rd Rainhm
75 R 8	Lower rd SE16
154 E 9	Lower rd Sutton
140 E 12	Lower Regent st W1
86 L 7	Lower Richmond rd SW15
87 O 7	Lower Richmond rd SW15
85 S 7	Lower Richmond rd SW14
147 R 8	Lower Sloane st SW1
85 U 1	Lower Staithe W4
99 P 16	Lower Station rd Drtfd
26 D 8	Lower Strand NW9
102 F 19	Lower Teddington rd Kingst
116 F 2	Lower Teddington rd Kingst
46 C 9	Lower ter NW3
142 G 10	Lower Thames st EC3
160 G 10	Lower Thames st EC3
10 B 1	Lower tub Watford
42 G 6	Loweswater clo Wemb
45 X 19	Lowfield rd NW6
61 V 17	Lowfield rd W3
32 J 19	Lowhall la E17
23 T 14	Lowick rd Harrow
38 H 17	Lowlands gdns Rom
23 S 20	Lowlands rd Harrow
48 D 13	Lowman rd N7
147 U 2	Lowndes clo SW1
140 B 7	Lowndes ct W1
147 T 2	Lowndes pl SW1
139 R 19	Lowndes sq SW1
147 S 1	Lowndes st SW1
126 F 4	Lownds av Brom
63 O 20	Lowood st E1
143 Y 9	Lowood st E1
38 F 4	Lowshoe la Rom
90 M 4	Lowth rd SE5
6 M 12	Lowther dri Enf
7 N 13	Lowther dri Enf
92 J 19	Lowther hill SE23
32 G 8	Lowther rd E17

M

135 U 10	Mansford st E2	
107 O 20	Manship rd Mitch	
46 B 9	Mansion gdns NW3	
160 F 7	Mansion House pl EC4	
142 E 6	Mansion House st EC2	
146 D 6	Manson ms SW7	
146 E 7	Manson pl SW7	
55 U 1	Mansted gdns Rom	
70 G 11	Manston av S'hall	
124 C 1	Manston clo SE20	
57 Z 19	Manston way Hornch	
45 S 14	Manstone rd NW2	
133 T 7	Mantell st N1	
79 P 13	Manthorpe rd SE18	
107 P 10	Mantilla rd SW17	
92 J 8	Mantle rd SE4	
71 X 6	Manton av W7	
80 A 11	Manton rd SE2	
79 Z 11	Manton rd SE2	
88 G 7	Mantua clo SW11	
63 P 10	Mantus clo E1	
63 P 10	Mantus rd E1	
15 P 7	Manus way N20	
107 R 5	Manville gdns SW17	
107 R 5	Manville rd SW17	
92 L 15	Manwood rd SE4	
107 T 3	Many gates SW12	
135 V 16	Mape st E2	
45 S 17	Mapesbury rd NW2	
19 Y 19	Maple av E4	
40 L 8	Maple av Harrow	
74 B 3	Maple av Harrow	
57 Y 10	Maple clo Hornch	
121 S 1	Maple clo Mitch	
31 Y 19	Maple clo N16	
89 Y 15	Maple clo SW4	
97 N 15	Maple cres Sidcp	
118 A 6	Maple ct New Mald	
114 C 14	Maple Dene Chisl	
26 A 2	Maple gdns Edg	
72 B 18	Maple gro Brentf	
43 V 1	Maple gro NW9	
58 F 13	Maple gro S'hall	
72 H 7	Maple gro W5	
63 N 14	Maple pl E1	
132 B 19	Maple pl W1	
34 A 19	Maple rd E11	
110 C 18	Maple rd SE20	
116 F 15	Maple rd Surb	
38 K 14	Maple st Rom	
132 C 19	Maple st W1	
66 C 16	Maplecroft clo E6	
157 Y 4	Mapledale av Croy	
49 W 20	Mapledene rd E8	
35 Z 11	Mapleleafe gdns Ilf	
68 D 4	Maplestead rd Dgnhm	
90 C 19	Maplestead rd SW2	
122 G 9	Maplethorpe rd Thntn Hth	
126 D 13	Mapleton clo Brom	
88 A 16	Mapleton cr SW18	
9 O 3	Mapleton cres Enf	
9 N 10	Mapleton rd Enf	
87 Z 16	Mapleton rd SW18	
7 R 18	Maplin clo N21	
65 U 17	Maplin rd E16	
33 Z 1	Mapperley dri Wdfd Grn	
80 J 7	Maran way Blvdr	
129 O 12	Marban rd W3	
73 S 3	Marble clo W3	
84 B 18	Marble Hill clo Twick	
84 A 19	Marble Hill gdns Twick	
84 E 19	Marble Hill pl Twick	
112 K 6	Marbrook ct SE12	
48 C 9	Marcellus rd N7	
83 X 18	March rd Twick	
51 Y 0	Marchant rd E11	
145 R 13	Marchbank rd SW5	
155 V 17	Marchmont rd Wallgtn	
84 M 14	Marchmont rd Rich	
85 N 14	Marchmont rd Rich	
132 K 17	Marchmont st WC1	
150 K 20	Marchwood clo SE5	
60 F 16	Marchwood cres W5	
150 M 7	Marcia rd SE1	
144 A 3	Marco rd W6	
74 L 9	Marco rd W6	
49 Z 16	Marcon pl E8	
58 K 18	Marconi way S'hall	
65 N 4	Marcus ct E15	
99 W 19	Marcus rd Drtfd	
65 O 3	Marcus st E15	
88 B 15	Marcus st SE18	
25 Z 17	Mardale dri NW9	
74 L 6	Mardale st W12	
124 E 12	Mardell rd Croy	
126 D 15	Marden av Brom	
98 L 13	Marden cres Bxly	
122 D 14	Marden cres Croy	
122 D 15	Marden rd Croy	
31 R 9	Marden rd N17	
39 S 18	Marden rd Rom	
75 O 8	Marden sq SE16	
72 A 6	Marder rd W13	
71 Z 6	Marder rd W13	
50 A 18	Mare st E8	
63 N 4	Mare st E8	
135 Y 2	Mare st E8	
114 F 6	Marechal Niel av Sidcp	
157 S 4	Maresfield Croy	
46 E 18	Maresfield gdns NW3	
67 M 1	Marg Bonfield av Bark	
20 E 1	Margaret av E4	
39 Y 16	Margaret clo Rom	
140 A 4	Margaret ct W1	
49 U 5	Margaret gdns N16	
5 V 14	Margaret rd Barnt	
97 W 15	Margaret rd Bxly	
49 U 5	Margaret rd N16	
39 Y 16	Margaret rd Rom	
140 A 4	Margaret st W1	
139 Z 4	Margaret st W1	
35 P 17	Margaret way Ilf	
146 L 13	Margaretta ter SW3	
52 L 5	Margaretting rd E12	
90 A 13	Margate rd SW2	
52 E 18	Margery Park rd E7	
55 X 8	Margery rd Dgnhm	
133 R 15	Margery st WC1	
105 P 11	Margin dri SW19	
144 H 10	Margravine gdns W6	
144 H 12	Margravine rd W6	
120 C 14	Marham gdns SW18	
106 H 3	Marham gdns SW18	
63 S 13	Maria ter E1	
117 Z 11	Maria Theresa clo New Mald	
153 T 11	Marian ct Sutton	
135 V 7	Marian pl E2	
107 V 20	Marian rd SW16	
135 V 7	Marian sq E2	
135 W 8	Marian st E2	
62 D 1	Marian way NW10	
23 P 4	Maricas av Harrow	
156 B 18	Mariette way SM6	
143 V 19	Marigold st SE16	
19 Y 20	Marigold way E4	
118 J 13	Marina av New Mald	
126 D 6	Marina clo Brom	
96 H 4	Marina dri Welling	
38 J 17	Marina gdns Rom	
102 F 17	Marina way Tedd	
78 G 11	Marine dri SE18	
151 R 1	Marine st SE16	
88 B 4	Marinefield rd SW6	
102 C 8	Mariner gdns Rich	
53 V 12	Mariner rd E12	
36 D 1	Marion clo Ilf	
21 N 15	Marion gro Wdfd Grn	
13 T 16	Marion rd NW7	
123 N 11	Marion rd Thntn Hth	
93 W 9	Marischal rd SE13	
63 Y 12	Maritime st E3	
107 O 3	Marius pass SW17	
107 O 3	Marius rd SW17	
89 N 10	Marjorie gro SW11	
20 E 1	Mark av E4	
97 Y 1	Mark clo Bxly Hth	
70 J 2	Mark clo S'hall	
142 K 8	Mark la EC3	
30 K 6	Mark rd N22	
51 Y 20	Mark st E15	
134 H 16	Mark st EC2	
140 A 5	Market ct W1	
78 K 9	Market hill SE18	
25 V 6	Market la Edg	
39 P 14	Market link Rom	
139 W 14	Market ms W1	
91 X 6	Market par SE15	
72 F 18	Market pl Brentf	
116 G 4	Market pl Kingst	
28 H 11	Market pl N2	
28 B 14	Market pl NW11	
39 R 14	Market pl Rom	
140 A 5	Market pl W1	
73 U 3	Market pl W3	
48 A 18	Market rd N7	
47 Z 19	Market rd N7	
85 P 8	Market rd Rich	
126 E 3	Market sq Brom	
64 E 18	Market sq E14	
18 L 9	Market sq N9	
66 G 6	Market st E6	
78 K 11	Market st SE18	
64 E 18	Market way E14	
42 J 16	Market way Wemb	
20 D 1	Markfield gdns E4	
31 X 14	Markfield rd N15	
147 N 9	Markham sq SW3	
146 M 9	Markham st SW3	
100 E 19	Markhole clo Hampt	
32 J 18	Markhouse av E17	
32 K 18	Markhouse rd E17	
50 M 1	Markhouse rd E17	
50 K 1	Markmanor av E17	
38 A 12	Marks hall Rom	
38 L 16	Marks rd Rom	
85 R 7	Marksbury av Rich	
109 Z 9	Markwell clo SE26	
55 R 16	Markyate rd Dgnhm	
88 B 11	Marl st SW18	
35 S 10	Marlands rd Ilf	
35 T 9	Marlands rd Ilf	
135 S 5	Marlborough av E8	
12 F 11	Marlborough av Edg	
16 G 10	Marlborough av N14	
146 L 5	Marlborough bldgs SW3	
106 H 16	Marlborough clo SW19	
15 Z 12	Marlborough clo N20	
149 Z 7	Marlborough clo SE17	
73 Z 9	Marlborough cres W4	
140 B 7	Marlborough ct W1	
35 R 10	Marlborough dri Ilf	
15 Z 11	Marlborough gdns N20	
151 S 12	Marlborough gro SE1	
130 D 6	Marlborough hill NW8	
23 U 13	Marlborough hill Harrow	
140 D 15	Marlborough ho SW1	
77 Y 18	Marlborough la SE7	
97 N 20	Marlborough Park av Sidcp	
130 B 9	Marlborough pl NW8	
72 A 20	Marlborough rd Brentf	
100 H 15	Marlborough rd Hampt	
106 H 16	Marlborough rd SW19	
126 L 9	Marlborough rd Brom	
156 M 16	Marlborough rd S Croy	
55 T 14	Marlborough rd Dgnhm	
97 W 7	Marlborough rd Bxly Hth	
153 Y 4	Marlborough rd Sutton	
52 A 13	Marlborough rd E15	
34 G 9	Marlborough rd E18	
20 C 19	Marlborough rd E4	
52 K 19	Marlborough rd E7	
48 A 6	Marlborough rd N19	
47 Y 7	Marlborough rd N19	
30 B 1	Marlborough rd N22	
17 O 20	Marlborough rd N22	
18 H 7	Marlborough rd N9	
84 L 16	Marlborough rd Rich	
38 H 13	Marlborough rd Rom	
140 D 15	Marlborough rd SW1	
73 U 13	Marlborough rd W4	
72 H 5	Marlborough rd W5	
146 K 8	Marlborough st SW3	
110 K 2	Marler rd SE23	
80 J 17	Marley clo Grnfd	
58 G 7	Marley clo Grnfd	
100 G 16	Marlingdene clo Hampt	
42 F 12	Marloes clo Wemb	
145 W 4	Marloes rd W8	
124 A 5	Marlow clo SE20	
83 V 15	Marlow cres Twick	
26 C 11	Marlow ct NW9	
153 P 4	Marlow dri Sutton	
66 F 9	Marlow rd E6	
70 E 8	Marlow rd S'hall	
124 B 4	Marlow rd SE20	
75 T 5	Marlow way SE16	
13 O 17	Marlowe clo Chisl	
36 C 5	Marlowe clo Ilf	
95 X 15	Marlowe gdns SE9	
33 U 12	Marlowe rd E17	
121 U 8	Marlowe sq Mitch	
156 B 2	Marlowe way CRO	
99 N 11	Marlowes the Drtfrd	
130 F 4	Marlowes the NW8	
131 V 18	Marylebone rd NW1	
131 N 19	Marylebone sta NW1	
79 X 10	Marmadon rd SE18	
20 A 13	Marmion av E4	
19 Y 13	Marmion av E4	
20 A 13	Marmion clo E4	
89 P 8	Marmion ms SW11	
89 P 9	Marmion rd SW11	
151 U 20	Marmont rd SE15	
91 Y 1	Marmont rd SE15	
92 C 15	Marmora rd SE22	
16 D 13	Marne av N11	
96 M 8	Marne av Welling	
128 L 12	Marne st W10	
89 O 10	Marney rd SW11	
45 S 11	Marnham av NW2	
58 K 6	Marnham cres Grnfd	
58 K 8	Marnham cres Grnfd	
92 K 14	Marnock rd SE4	
63 V 15	Maroon st E14	
48 M 20	Marquess rd N1	
49 N 18	Marquess rd N1	
61 O 1	Marquis clo Wemb	
17 R 20	Marquis rd N22	
48 E 3	Marquis rd N4	
47 Z 19	Marquis rd NW1	
86 H 9	Marrick clo SW15	
9 X 3	Marrilyne av Enf	
4 D 12	Marriot rd Barnt	
64 L 2	Marriott rd E15	
28 M 5	Marriott rd N10	
29 N 5	Marriott rd N10	
48 C 5	Marriott rd N4	
26 D 19	Marriotts clo NW9	
105 S 10	Marryat pl SW19	
105 P 12	Marryat rd SW19	
93 S 10	Marsala rd SE13	
18 M 8	Marsden rd N9	
91 V 8	Marsden rd SE15	
47 O 18	Marsden st NW5	
121 N 2	Marsh av Mitch	
13 R 11	Marsh clo NW7	
26 D 19	Marsh dri NW9	
101 U 1	Marsh Farm rd Twick	
83 V 20	Marsh Farm rd Twick	
69 R 4	Marsh Green rd Dgnhm	
50 H 15	Marsh hill E9	
51 N 5	Marsh la E10	
32 A 4	Marsh la N17	
12 M 12	Marsh la NW7	
13 O 11	Marsh la NW7	
11 S 18	Marsh la NW7	
24 G 1	Marsh la Stanm	
22 C 14	Marsh rd Pinn	
60 H 8	Marsh rd W5	
76 C 11	Marsh st E14	
76 B 4	Marsh wall E14	
41 O 1	Marshall clo Harrow	
82 E 12	Marshall clo Hounsl	
149 X 2	Marshall gdns SE1	
31 P 4	Marshall rd N17	
140 C 7	Marshall st W1	
39 P 9	Marshalls dri Rom	
78 E 10	Marshalls gro SE18	
38 M 14	Marshalls rd Rom	
154 B 8	Marshalls rd Sutton	
142 C 17	Marshalsea rd SE1	
113 Y 12	Marsham clo Chisl	
148 H 3	Marsham st SW1	
95 N 7	Marshbrook clo SE3	
76 G 8	Marshfield st E14	
64 D 3	Marshgate la E15	
51 R 20	Marshgate la E15	
149 Z 11	Marsland clo SE17	
149 Y 11	Marsland rd SE17	
56 D 8	Marston av Dgnhm	
56 D 8	Marston clo Dgnhm	
46 D 20	Marston clo NW6	
35 R 6	Marston rd Ilf	
102 B 13	Marston rd Tedd	
108 K 18	Marston way SE19	
22 A 3	Marsworth av Pinn	
140 L 8	Mart st WC2	
49 T 6	Martaban rd N16	
109 N 7	Martell rd SE21	
50 A 19	Martello st E8	
33 P 6	Marten rd E17	
98 J 10	Martens av Bxly Hth	
98 L 12	Martens av Bxly Hth	
98 J 11	Martens clo Bxly Hth	
98 J 9	Martens Grove pk Bxly Hth	
52 B 17	Martha rd E15	
63 O 18	Martha st E1	

148 M 18 Meadow pl SW8	90 E 18 Medora rd SW2	22 F 13 Melrose rd Pinn	142 E 16 Mermaid ct SE1
67 Z 2 Meadow rd Bark	93 R 16 Medusa rd SE6	86 D 3 Melrose rd SW13	70 E 9 Merrick rd S'hall
126 A 2 Meadow rd Brom	124 C 14 Medway clo Croy	87 U 17 Melrose rd SW18	150 D 1 Merrick sq SE1
56 A 18 Meadow rd Dgnhm	54 C 16 Medway clo Ilf	119 Y 2 Melrose rd SW19	7 V 19 Merridene N21
100 B 3 Meadow rd Felt	59 W 6 Medway dri Grnfd	73 U 8 Melrose rd W3	69 P 5 Merrielands cres Dgnhm
22 A 14 Meadow rd Pinn	41 Y 13 Medway gdns Wemb	136 D 20 Melrose ter W6	118 M 20 Merrilands rd Worc Pk
56 K 2 Meadow rd Rom	59 W 7 Medway pde Grnfd	74 M 7 Melrose ter W6	96 G 20 Merrilees rd Sidcp
70 F 1 Meadow rd S'hall	99 W 9 Medway rd Drtfrd	120 C 14 Melsa rd Mord	94 M 1 Merriman rd SE3
58 F 20 Meadow rd S'hall	63 W 7 Medway rd E3	151 X 11 Meltham way SE16	95 N 1 Merriman rd SE3
154 H 9 Meadow rd Sutton	148 F 3 Medway st SW1	95 P 2 Melthorpe gdns SE3	145 U 13 Merrington rd SW6
106 D 19 Meadow rd SW8	90 B 10 Medwin st SW4	57 T 1 Melton gdns Rom	11 T 15 Merrion av Stanm
149 O 15 Meadow rd SW8	94 L 8 Meerbrook rd SE3	132 D 15 Melton st NW1	92 L 13 Merritt rd SE4
150 A 3 Meadow row SE1	65 O 1 Meeson rd SE13	41 V 16 Melville av Grnfd	35 O 13 Merrivale av Ilf
114 B 15 Meadow the Chisl	50 H 13 Meeson st E5	157 V 12 Melville av S Croy	6 K 18 Merrivale N14
122 H 12 Meadow View rd Thntn Hth	75 N 2 Meeting House all E1	104 F 19 Melville av SW20	153 O 19 Merrow rd Sutton
25 Z 15 Meadow way NW9	143 X 13 Meeting House all E1	17 U 17 Melville gdns N13	150 D 12 Merrow st SE17
23 T 5 Meadow Way the Harrow	75 N 20 Meeting House la SE15	32 L 12 Melville rd E17	150 F 11 Merrow st SE17
42 H 12 Meadow way Wemb	151 W 20 Meeting House la SE15	61 Y 1 Melville rd NW10	159 V 14 Merrow way Croy
70 B 18 Meadow waye Hounsl	91 Z 1 Meeting House la SE15	38 G 3 Melville rd Rom	150 G 10 Merrow wlk SE17
56 A 17 Meadow wlk Dgnhm	50 C 16 Mehetabel rd E9	115 T 5 Melville rd Sidcp	127 S 1 Merrydown way Chisl
34 E 12 Meadow wlk E18	113 T 13 Melanda clo Chisl	86 F 2 Melville rd SW13	11 T 18 Merryfield gdns Stanm
152 D 17 Meadow wlk Epsom	97 Y 1 Melanie clo Bxly Hth	134 A 2 Melville st N1	94 D 5 Merryfield SE3
155 R 5 Meadow wlk Wallgtn	93 S 3 Melba way SE13	110 B 20 Melvin rd SE20	20 D 3 Merryhill clo E4
144 E 19 Meadowbank clo SW6	17 R 18 Melbourne av N13	47 W 13 Melyn clo N7	7 N 16 Merryhills dri Enf
131 O 2 Meadowbank NW3	22 II 8 Melbourne av Pinn	134 A 17 Memel st EC1	32 L 9 Mersey rd E17
43 X 1 Meadowbank rd NW9	71 Z 2 Melbourne av W13	64 M 8 Memorial av E15	25 R 16 Mersham dri NW9
94 D 11 Meadowcourt rd SE3	155 U 11 Melbourne clo Wallgtn	65 N 9 Memorial av E15	110 A 20 Mersham pl SE20
127 U 7 Meadowcroft Brom	109 Y 18 Melbourne ct SE20	70 E 17 Memorial clo Hounsl	123 N 4 Mersham rd Thntn Hth
17 U 9 Meadowcroft rd N13	37 Y 14 Melbourne gdns Rom	105 R 5 Mendip clo SW19	55 Z 1 Merten rd Rom
153 S 20 Meadowside rd Sutton	91 T 10 Melbourne gro SE22	88 D 9 Mendip cres SW11	74 K 17 Merthyr ter SW13
94 L 11 Meadowside SE9	90 G 3 Melbourne ms SW9	45 R 8 Mendip dri NW2	41 N 15 Merton av Nthlt
111 O 12 Meadowview clo SE6	141 O 7 Melbourne pl WC2	99 P 3 Mendip rd Bxly Hth	74 C 11 Merton av W4
152 B 19 Meadowview rd Epsom	155 T 12 Melbourne rd Wallgtn	57 W 2 Mendip rd Hornch	127 Z 11 Merton gdns Brom
98 A 17 Meadowview rd Bxly	51 P 1 Melbourne rd E10	36 G 16 Mendip rd Ilf	105 T 20 Merton Hall gdns SW20
110 M 11 Meadowview rd SE6	32 J 12 Melbourne rd E17	88 D 8 Mendip rd SW11	105 T 20 Merton Hall rd SW19
111 N 11 Meadowview rd SE6	66 G 5 Melbourne rd E6	145 N 16 Mendora rd SW6	119 U 1 Merton Hall rd SW19
97 P 17 Meadowview Sidcp	54 A 4 Melbourne rd Ilf	45 T 13 Menelik rd NW2	106 D 19 Merton High st SW19
54 H 1 Meads la Ilf	53 Z 4 Melbourne rd Ilf	109 N 18 Menlo gdns SE19	47 N 6 Merton la N6
9 V 6 Meads rd Enf	105 Z 20 Melbourne rd SW19	24 E 18 Mentmore clo Harrow	119 P 4 Merton mans SW20
30 H 9 Meads rd N22	102 F 15 Melbourne rd Tedd	50 A 20 Mentmore ter E8	67 Y 1 Merton rd Bark
12 M 19 Meads the Edg	90 F 3 Melbourne sq SW9	73 V 5 Meon rd W3	33 T 17 Merton rd E17
153 H 5 Meads the Sutton	8 H 20 Melbourne way Enf	121 U 2 Meopham rd Mitch	8 A 4 Merton rd Enf
123 V 16 Meadvale rd Croy	70 J 9 Melbury av S'hall	23 N 2 Mepham cres Harrow	41 N 4 Merton rd Harrow
60 C 11 Meadvale rd W5	113 S 15 Melbury clo Chisl	23 N 2 Mepham gdns Harrow	36 K 20 Merton rd Ilf
4 K 14 Meadway Barnt	145 R 1 Melbury ct W8	141 R 16 Mepham st SE1	123 W 11 Merton rd SE25
125 U1 Meadway Becknhm	150 J 20 Melbury dri SE5	98 F 0 Mera dri Bxly Hth	87 V 18 Merton rd SW18
21 Z 6 Meadway Buck HI	104 J 20 Melbury gdns SW20	93 X 9 Mercator rd SE13	106 A 18 Merton rd SW19
4 K 13 Meadway clo Barnt	25 N 16 Melbury rd Harrow	140 J 6 Mercer st WC2	46 J 19 Merton ri NW3
28 B 19 Meadway clo NW11	145 O 1 Melbury rd W14	63 N 12 Merceron st E1	92 F 12 Merttins rd SE15
102 C 10 Meadway clo Rich	130 M 19 Melbury ter NW1	135 X 18 Merceron st E1	90 F 12 Mervan rd SW2
27 Z 19 Meadway ga NW11	131 N 19 Melcombe pl NW1	77 P 12 Mercers clo SE10	114 C 6 Mervyn av SE9
54 J 11 Meadway Ilf	131 P 19 Melcombe st NW1	47 Y 10 Mercers rd N19	71 Z 8 Mervyn rd W13
16 L 8 Meadway N14	88 A 2 Meldon clo SW6	63 Z 10 Merchant st E3	61 X 18 Messaline av W3
17 N 8 Meadway N14	55 O 8 Meldrum rd Ilf	111 V 3 Merchiston rd SE6	94 L 12 Messent rd SE9
28 B 18 Meadway NW11	111 T 11 Melfield gdns SE6	114 C 2 Merchland rd SE9	95 W 15 Messeter pl SE9
27 Z 19 Meadway NW11	54 J 17 Melford av Bark	93 V 9 Mercia gro SE13	129 U 1 Messina av NW6
39 V 7 Meadway Rom	51 Z 7 Melford rd E11	87 S 13 Mercier rd SW15	89 P 10 Meteor st SW11
118 M 9 Meadway SW20	32 K 14 Melford rd E17	39 S 14 Mercury gdns Rom	156 A 16 Meteor way Wallgtn
119 N 8 Meadway SW20	66 G 10 Melford rd E6	72 F 15 Mercury rd Brentf	155 V 12 Meteor way Wallgtn
93 Y 6 Meadway the SE3	54 E 8 Melford rd Ilf	75 S 15 Mercury way SE14	26 A 6 Metheringham way NW9
83 P 20 Meadway Twick	91 Y 20 Melford rd SE22	93 R 12 Mercy ter SE13	149 U 11 Methley st SE11
110 A 18 Meaford way SE20	122 J 7 Melfort av Thntn Hth	87 R 18 Mere clo SW19	25 O 2 Methuen clo Edg
53 R 13 Meanley rd E12	122 K 7 Melfort rd Thntn Hth	124 F 18 Mere end Croy	29 T 9 Methuen pk N10
140 E 7 Meard st W1	48 G 16 Melgund rd N5	156 D 10 Merebank la Croy	81 V 10 Methuen rd Blvdr
65 O6 Meath rd E15	130 E 14 Melina pl NW8	45 N 14 Meredith av NW2	98 B 11 Methuen rd Bxly Hth
54 C 9 Meath rd Ilf	74 H 6 Melina rd W12	65 T 10 Meredith st E13	25 O 3 Methuen rd Edg
89 R 1 Meath st SW11	142 H 16 Melior pl SE1	133 V 14 Meredith st EC1	136 F 1 Methwold rd W10
133 N 17 Mecklenburg pl WC1	142 H 16 Melior st SE1	86 G 4 Meredyth rd SW13	128 F 20 Methwold rd W10
133 N 16 Mecklenburg sq WC1	111 Y 5 Meliot rd SE6	92 H 9 Meretone clo SE4	143 S 12 Mews st E1
133 N 15 Mecklenburg st WC1	76 M 15 Mell st SE10	120 D 14 Merevale cres Mrdn	35 O 16 Mews the Ilf
132 E 8 Medburn st NW1	155 Z 4 Meller clo Wallgtn	101 S 1 Mereway rd Twick	134 C 4 Mews the N1
133 U 10 Medcalf pl N1	79 V 17 Melling st SE18	127 V 3 Merewood clo Brom	39 P 14 Mews the Rom
9 Z 1 Medcalf rd Enf	67 X 4 Mellish ct Bark	98 J 4 Merewood rd Bxly Hth	115 O 9 Mews the Sidcp
85 U 10 Medcroft gdns SW4	106 L 13 Mellison rd SW17	126 C 12 Mereworth clo Brom	87 W 13 Mexfield rd SW15
94 F 7 Medebourne clo SE3	62 D 15 Mellitus st W12	79 O 20 Mereworth dri SE18	8 K 3 Meyer gro Enf
17 V 19 Medesenge wy N13	35 U 9 Mellows rd Ilf	113 O 19 Meriden clo Chisl	81 Y 16 Meyer rd Erith
86 H 18 Medfield st SW15	155 X 11 Mellows rd Wallgtn	36 B 4 Meriden clo Ilf	141 V 14 Meymott st SE1
63 V 7 Medhurst rd E3	113 S 10 Mells cres SE9	78 A 18 Meridian rd SE7	50 E 20 Meynell cres E9
63 V 8 Medhurst rd E3	88 D 14 Melody rd SW18	18 F 19 Meridian wlk N17	50 E 20 Meynell gdns
50 C 14 Median rd E5	137 W 16 Melon pl W8	94 L 10 Merifield rd SE9	50 F 20 Meynell rd E9
48 E 9 Medina gro N7	91 W 1 Melon rd SE15	97 O 15 Merino pl Sidcp	39 Z 1 Meynell rd Rom
48 E 9 Medina rd N7	58 L 6 Melrose av Grnfd	41 O 2 Merivale rd Harrow	44 F 17 Meyrick rd NW10
121 O 19 Medland clo Mitch	107 R 18 Melrose av Mitch	87 T 10 Merivale rd SW15	88 H 8 Meyrick rd SW11
58 A 6 Medlar clo Nthlt	30 J 4 Melrose av N22	127 T 1 Merlewood clo Chisl	13 O 17 M1 Motorway NW7
150 B 20 Medlar st SE5	44 M 19 Melrose av NW2	113 T 20 Merlewood dri Chisl	72 B 14 M4 motorway Brentf
90 M 1 Medlar st SE5	45 N 15 Melrose av NW2	43 W 3 Merley ct NW9	70 G 15 M4 motorway Hounsl
45 Y 18 Medley rd NW6	122 E 5 Melrose av SW16	157 S 7 Merlin clo Croy	110 J 8 Miall wlk SE26
115 R 8 Medomsley clo Sidcp	105 X 6 Melrose av SW19	25 N 4 Merlin cres Edgw	134 C 11 Micawber st N1
38 M 13 Medora rd Rom	82 L 19 Melrose av Twick	112 E 8 Merlin gdns Brom	71 X 3 Michael Gaynor clo W7
	58 K 6 Melrose clo Grnfd	124 M 10 Merlin gro Becknhm	52 A 4 Michael rd E11
	70 H 1 Melrose dri S'hall	125 N 10 Merlin gro Becknhm	
	25 T 9 Melrose gdns Edg	36 A 1 Merlin gro Ilf	
	117 Y 7 Melrose gdns New Mald	52 M 7 Merlin rd E12	
	144 D 1 Melrose gdns W6	96 M 9 Merlin rd Well	
		97 O 10 Merlin rd Welling	
		133 T 14 Merlin st WC1	
		40 F 9 Merlins av Harrow	

123 R 7	Michael rd SE25	50 D 19	Milborne st E9	
88 B 1	Michael rd SW6	94 A 18	Milborough cres SE12	
94 C 15	Micheldever rd SE12	141 X 19	Milcote st SE1	
101 X 6	Michelham gdns Twick	91 U 16	Mild rd SE22	

123 R 7 Michael rd SE25
88 B 1 Michael rd SW6
94 C 15 Micheldever rd SE12
101 X 6 Michelham gdns Twick
84 J 9 Michels row Rich
53 S 12 Michigan av E12
14 J 13 Michleham down N12
153 R 13 Mickleham gdns Sutton
159 X 15 Mickleham way Croy
145 U 15 Micklethwaite rd SW6
12 L 11 Middle dene NW7
130 F 3 Middle Field NW8
29 Z 17 Middle la N8
101 V 14 Middle la Tedd
94 M 15 Middle Park av SE9
95 O 18 Middle Park av SE9
113 S 1 Middle Park av SE9
41 P 5 Middle path Harrow
5 V 19 Middle rd Barnt
65 S 8 Middle rd E13
41 P 6 Middle rd Harrow
121 W 3 Middle rd SW16
128 K 17 Middle row W10
156 L 4 Middle st Croy
141 Z 1 Middle st EC1
141 S 7 Middle Temple la EC4
121 X 4 Middle way SW16
23 U 7 Middle Way the Harrow
35 Z 20 Middlefield gdns Ilf
60 A 14 Middlefielde W13
158 H 20 Middlefields Croy
18 K 19 Middleham gdns N18
18 K 19 Middleham rd N18
18 K 18 Middlesborough rd N18
74 E 12 Middlesex ct W4
141 Z 2 Middlesex pas EC1
122 A 10 Middlesex rd Mitch
142 M 3 Middlesex st E1
143 N 5 Middlesex st E1
50 D 6 Middlesex wharf E5
20 A 11 Middleton av E4
19 Z 12 Middleton av E4
59 S 5 Middleton av Grnfd
115 S 14 Middleton av Sidcp
140 A 2 Middleton bldgs W1
19 Z 12 Middleton clo E4
75 T 5 Middleton dri SE16
36 A 20 Middleton gdns Ilf
35 Z 19 Middleton gdns Ilf
47 Z 15 Middleton gro N7
134 M 1 Middleton rd E8
135 O 1 Middleton rd E8
120 B 14 Middleton rd Mrdn
120 J 17 Middleton rd Mrdn
119 Z 15 Middleton rd Mrdn
45 X 1 Middleton rd NW11
63 N 8 Middleton st E2
135 W 11 Middleton st E2
93 X 9 Middleway SE13
28 B 17 Middleway NW11
98 K 7 Midfield av Bxly Hth
115 R 20 Midfield way Orp
132 C 18 Midford pl W1
28 A 13 Midholm clo NW11
28 A 14 Midholm NW11
158 J 4 Midholm rd Croy
43 R 5 Midholm Wemb
132 L 13 Midhope st WC1
122 G 16 Midhurst av Croy
29 N 11 Midhurst av N10
57 U 13 Midhurst clo Hornch
98 D 15 Midhurst hill Bxly Hth
72 A 8 Midhurst rd W13
71 Z 6 Midhurst rd W13
76 G 14 Midland pl E14
51 U 3 Midland rd E10
132 H 12 Midland rd NW1
62 B 12 Midland ter NW10
45 O 10 Midland ter NW2
117 V 5 Midleton rd New Mald
63 X 13 Midlothian rd E3
107 V 1 Midmoor rd SW12
105 R 19 Midmoor rd SW19
44 B 12 Midstrath rd NW10
82 D 11 Midsummer av Hounsl
119 V 17 Midway Sutton
44 H 9 Midwood clo NW2
66 K 2 Miers clo E6
35 O 14 Mighell av Ilf
146 C 12 Milborne gro SW10

50 D 19 Milborne st E9
94 A 18 Milborough cres SE12
141 X 19 Milcote st SE1
91 U 16 Mild rd SE22
50 B 11 Mildenhall rd E5
49 O 16 Mildmay av N1
49 O 16 Mildmay gro N1
49 P 15 Mildmay pk N1
54 A 10 Mildmay rd Ilf
53 Z 10 Mildmay rd Ilf
49 P 15 Mildmay rd N1
38 K 15 Mildmay rd Rom
49 P 17 Mildmay st N1
40 L 16 Mildred av Nthlt
63 T 12 Mile End pl E1
63 O 13 Mile End rd E1
32 F 6 Mile End the E17
121 U 19 Mile rd Wallgtn
160 F 10 Miles la EC4
130 J 20 Miles pl NW1
116 M 9 Miles pl Surb
120 H 5 Miles rd Mitch
30 B 11 Miles rd N8
148 K 15 Miles st SW8
15 X 9 Miles way N20
13 Y 17 Milespit hill NW7
154 E 15 Milestone clo Sutton
109 U 16 Milestone rd SE19
62 G 20 Milfoil st W12
80 M 16 Milford clo SE2
25 P 3 Milford gdns Edg
42 G 14 Milford gdns Wemb
154 C 7 Milford gro Sutton
141 R 7 Milford la WC2
141 S 8 Milford la WC2
70 H 1 Milford rd S'hall
58 H 20 Milford rd S'hall
72 A 3 Milford rd W13
143 S 3 Milfred st E1
112 H 14 Milk st Brom
78 L 4 Milk st E16
160 B 5 Milk st EC2
75 P 1 Milk yd E1
34 J 1 Milkwell gdns Wdfd Grn
90 K 11 Milkwood rd SE24
155 O 3 Mill clo Carsh
4 H 7 Mill corner Barnt
82 C 20 Mill Farm cres Hounsl
100 C 1 Mill Farm cres Twick
110 A 8 Mill gdns SE26
121 O 16 Mill Green rd Mitch
13 R 16 Mill Hill cir NW7
14 D 20 Mill Hill East sta NW7
73 U 4 Mill Hill gro W3
13 T 17 Mill Hill pk NW7
86 G 6 Mill Hill rd SW13
73 S 4 Mill Hill rd W3
73 T 4 Mill Hill ter W3
121 U 11 Mill ho Mitch
155 N 8 Mill la Carsh
156 E 5 Mill la Croy
152 E 18 Mill la Epsom
45 T 16 Mill la NW6
37 Y 19 Mill la Rom
78 K 14 Mill la SE18
21 R 17 Mill la Wdfd Grn
31 Z 11 Mill Mead rd N17
113 Y 20 Mill pl Chisl
99 X 11 Mill pl Drtfrd
63 X 18 Mill pl E14
116 K 5 Mill pl Kingst
83 Y 5 Mill Plat av Islwth
84 A 6 Mill Plat Islwth
83 Z 6 Mill Plat Islwth
77 W 3 Mill rd E16
81 X 20 Mill rd Erith
53 W 9 Mill rd Ilf
106 E 19 Mill rd SW19
101 O 4 Mill rd Twick
12 B 17 Mill ridge Edg
134 L 5 Mill row N1
87 N 1 Mill Shot clo SW6
116 K 5 Mill st Kingst
143 P 18 Mill st SE1
139 Z 8 Mill st W1
126 D 4 Mill vale Brom
158 E 5 Mill View gdns Croy
143 S 8 Mill yd E1
53 X 16 Millais av E12
25 P 7 Millais gdns Edg
51 V 12 Millais rd E11
8 H 18 Millais rd E
117 Z 16 Millais rd New Mald
49 S 15 Millard clo N16
56 D 18 Millard ter Dgnhm
148 K 7 Millbank SW1
94 E 14 Millbank way SE12

100 C 9 Millbourne rd Felt
96 F 10 Millbrook av Welling
38 A 17 Millbrook gdns Rom
39 S 6 Millbrook gdns Rom
18 L 6 Millbrook rd N9
90 H 8 Millbrook rd SW9
122 E 20 Miller rd Croy
106 G 15 Miller rd SW19
132 A 7 Miller st NW1
49 U 13 Millers av E8
49 U 14 Millers ter E8
136 E 18 Millers way W12
58 L 8 Millet rd Grnfd
32 J 5 Millfield av E17
47 N 8 Millfield la N6
47 O 7 Millfield la N6
25 W 7 Millfield rd Edg
82 C 20 Millfield rd Hounsl
50 F 10 Millfields rd E5
89 N 3 Millgrove st SW11
76 D 6 Millharbour E14
37 R 18 Millhaven clo Rom
108 K 11 Millhouse pl SE27
50 M 3 Millicent rd E10
25 Y 1 Milling rd Edg
133 N 17 Millman ms WC1
133 N 18 Millman st WC1
92 J 6 Millmark gro SE14
9 Y 8 Millmarsh la Enf
64 F 16 Mills gro E14
27 O 11 Mills gro NW4
154 M 2 Millside Carsh
84 A 6 Millside clo Islwth
143 N 19 Millstream rd SE1
76 B 8 Millwall Dock rd E14
63 N 15 Millward st E1
40 E 19 Millway gdns Nthlt
13 N 14 Millway NW7
82 M 13 Millwood rd Hounsl
83 N 13 Millwood rd Hounsl
136 J 2 Millwood st W10
128 J 8 Milman rd NW6
146 G 16 Milman st SW10
22 G 1 Milne field Pinn
95 R 13 Milne gdns SE9
83 P 18 Milner dri Twick
133 V 3 Milner pl N1
55 S 7 Milner rd Dgnhm
64 M 9 Milner rd E15
116 G 7 Milner rd Kingst
120 F 11 Milner rd Mrdn
106 A 19 Milner rd SW19
123 N 5 Milner rd Thntn Hth
133 V 2 Milner sq N1
147 N 5 Milner st SW3
73 X 16 Milnthorpe rd W4
144 J 1 Milson rd W14
4 J 15 Milton av Barnt
123 P 18 Milton av Croy
66 B 1 Milton av E6
57 U 6 Milton av Hornch
47 U 1 Milton av N6
61 X 4 Milton av NW10
25 U 11 Milton av NW9
154 H 8 Milton av Sutton
28 D 17 Milton clo N2
22 A 3 Milton clo Pinn
154 G 6 Milton clo Sutton
75 X 18 Milton Court rd SE14
36 A 20 Milton cres Ilf
134 D 20 Milton ct EC2
16 J 16 Milton gro N11
49 P 13 Milton gro N16
47 U 1 Milton pk N6
48 E 15 Milton pl N7
81 R 11 Milton rd Blvdr
123 P 18 Milton rd Croy
33 O 12 Milton rd E17
100 H 19 Milton rd Hampt
23 U 13 Milton rd Harrow
107 P 18 Milton rd Mitch
30 J 12 Milton rd N15
47 V 1 Milton rd N6
13 T 15 Milton rd NW7
39 V 18 Milton rd Rom
90 H 14 Milton rd SE24
153 X 7 Milton rd Sutton
85 X 9 Milton rd SW14
106 C 15 Milton rd SW19
73 X 2 Milton rd W3
59 W 20 Milton rd W7
155 W 14 Milton rd Wallgtn
96 J 1 Milton rd Welling
65 T 5 Milton st E13
134 D 20 Milton st EC2
54 K 6 Milverton gdns Ilf
128 D 1 Milverton rd NW6
45 N 20 Milverton rd NW6
149 U 11 Milverton st SE11

113 X 9 Milverton way SE9
143 X 1 Milward st E1
87 V 2 Mimosa st SW6
150 M 9 Mina rd SE17
105 Z 20 Mina rd SW19
93 Y 19 Minard rd SE6
111 Z 3 Minard rd SE6
16 J 11 Minchenden cres N14
142 K 8 Mincing la EC3
109 Z 20 Minden rd SE20
153 U 3 Minden rd SM3
40 G 9 Minehead rd Harrow
108 C 13 Minehead rd SW16
147 U 6 Minera ms SW1
79 T 12 Mineral st SE18
114 G 9 Minerva clo Sidcp
33 R 1 Minerva rd E4
116 L 3 Minerva rd Kingst
61 X 10 Minerva rd NW10
135 W 9 Minerva st E2
62 A 5 Minet av NW10
62 A 5 Minet gdns NW10
90 J 5 Minet rd SW9
136 E 19 Minford gdns W14
64 A 20 Ming st E14
117 N 10 Minniedale rd Surb
116 M 11 Minniedale Surb
143 N 8 Minories EC3
89 W 3 Minshull st SW8
89 X 3 Minshull st SW8
63 T 2 Minson rd E9
86 D 17 Minstead gdns SW15
118 A 15 Minstead way New Mald
153 Y 4 Minster av Sutton
60 L 13 Minster ct W5
157 S 7 Minster dri Croy
112 H 17 Minster rd Brom
45 T 15 Minster rd NW2
30 A 14 Minster wlk N8
155 R 9 Mint rd Wallgtn
142 B 17 Mint st SE1
156 M 5 Mint wlk Croy
157 N 5 Mint wlk Croy
17 W 11 Mintern clo N13
134 G 8 Mintern st N1
70 H 10 Minterne av S'hall
25 O 17 Minterne rd Harrow
135 W 12 Minto pl E2
145 P 17 Mirabel rd SW6
47 W 4 Miranda rd N19
78 A 10 Mirfield st SE7
79 U 13 Miriam rd SE18
112 M 7 Mirror pth SE9
120 D 14 Missenden gdns Mrdn
32 K 15 Mission gro E17
91 X 1 Mission pl SE15
124 E 20 Mistletoe clo CR0
121 T 15 Mitcham comm Mitch
107 U 14 Mitcham la SW16
120 L 9 Mitcham pk Mitch
122 C 16 Mitcham rd Croy
66 E 9 Mitcham rd E6
36 L 20 Mitcham rd Ilf
106 L 12 Mitcham rd SW17
80 F 13 Mitchell clo SE2
17 X 15 Mitchell rd N13
134 B 15 Mitchell st EC1
43 V 18 Mitchell way NW10
43 Y 18 Mitchellbrook way NW10
49 O 19 Mitchison rd N1
31 W 9 Mitchley rd N17
48 B 7 Mitford rd N19
154 E 16 Mitre clo Sutton
160 B 5 Mitre ct EC2
64 M 5 Mitre rd E15
141 U 17 Mitre rd SE1
142 M 6 Mitre sq EC3
142 L 6 Mitre st EC3
63 Y 19 Mitre the E14
62 L 14 Mitre way NW10
27 Z 10 Moat cres N3
65 Y 8 Moat dri E13
23 O 13 Moat dri Harrow
40 F 19 Moat Farm rd Nthlt
99 X 3 Moat la Erith
90 D 7 Moat pl SW9
61 T 16 Moat pl W3
9 R 13 Moat side Enf
118 A 1 Moat the New Mald
47 N 18 Modbury gdns NW5
47 O 17 Modbury st NW5
87 P 9 Modder pl SW15
85 W 9 Model cotts SW14
72 B 4 Model cotts W13

113 R 6 Model Farm clo SE9
141 W 5 Modern ct EC4
23 X 16 Moelyn ms Harrow
120 G 7 Moffat gdns Mitch
17 N 18 Moffat rd N13
106 K 9 Moffat rd SW17
122 M 4 Moffat rd Thntn Hth
123 N 3 Moffat rd Thntn Hth
83 X 12 Mogden la Islwth
6 C 20 Mohan clo N14
76 A 7 Moiety rd E14
157 W 20 Moir clo S Croy
31 R 7 Moira clo N17
95 U 9 Moira rd N17
75 S 12 Moland mead SE16
114 B 7 Molescroft SE9
153 S 4 Molesey dri Sutton
87 Y 3 Molesford rd SW6
93 T 9 Molesworth st SE13
9 W 8 Mollison av Enf
9 X 5 Mollison av Enf
156 B 14 Mollison dri Wallgtn
155 Y 17 Mollison dri Wallgtn
24 M 9 Mollison way Edg
25 O 8 Mollison way Edg
89 U 19 Molly Huggins clo SW12
138 M 3 Molyneux st W1
92 D 4 Mona rd SE15
65 P 15 Mona st E16
81 S 9 Monarch rd Blvdr
8 B 9 Monastery gdns Enf
148 G 3 Monck st SW1
91 R 9 Monclar rd SE5
138 H 20 Moncorvo clo SW7
66 D 17 Moncrieff clo E6
91 X 4 Moncrieff st SE15
53 P 17 Monega rd E12
52 K 18 Monega rd E7
64 A 1 Monier rd E3
110 L 19 Monivea rd Becknhm
65 R 19 Monk dri E16
78 J 10 Monk st SE18
6 D 20 Monkfrith av N14
16 D 2 Monkfrith clo N14
16 D 2 Monkfrith way N14
21 V 18 Monkhams av Wdfd Grn
21 V 17 Monkhams dri Wdfd Grn
21 T 15 Monkhams la Wdfd Grn
21 X 11 Monkhams la Buck Hl
119 T 8 Monkleigh rd Mrdn
15 S 1 Monks av Barnt
5 S 20 Monks av Barnt
7 X 9 Monks clo Enf
80 H 10 Monks clo SE2
61 P 16 Monks dri W3
125 P 16 Monks Orchard rd Becknhm
43 T 19 Monks Park gdns Wemb
43 U 16 Monks Park Wemb
7 X 8 Monks rd Enf
125 O 13 Monks way Becknhm
154 B 4 Monksdene gdns Sutton
29 P 4 Monkswell ct N10
35 W 11 Monkswood gdns Ilf
96 L 4 Monkton rd Welling
149 U 5 Monkton st SE11
27 V 13 Monkville av NW11
160 B 2 Monkwell sq EC2
34 H 11 Monmouth av E18
102 F 19 Monmouth av Kingst
97 N 9 Monmouth clo Welling
122 B 8 Monmouth clo Mitch
137 W 6 Monmouth pl W2
56 B 15 Monmouth rd Dgnhm
66 F 10 Monmouth rd E6
18 M 8 Monmouth rd N9
19 P 9 Monmouth rd N9
137 W 7 Monmouth rd W2
140 J 8 Monmouth st WC2
47 V 10 Monnery rd N19
151 T 6 Monnow rd SE1
32 M 4 Monoux gro E17
23 S 1 Monro gdns Harrow
8 M 7 Monroe cres Enf
85 T 13 Monroe dri SW14
127 R 14 Mons way Brom
48 J 9 Monsell rd N4
62 H 6 Monson rd NW10
75 S 20 Monson rd SE14
10 G 2 Montacute rd Bushey
159 T 20 Montacute rd Croy

120 E 15 Montacute rd Mrdn
92 L 18 Montacute rd SE6
19 N 15 Montagu cres N18
155 V 9 Montagu gdns Wallgtn
19 N 14 Montagu gdns N18
139 N 14 Montagu mans W1
139 P 2 Montagu Mews north W1
139 P 5 Montagu Mews south W1
139 P 4 Montagu Mews west W1
140 H 1 Montagu pl W1
139 P 2 Montagu pl W1
31 W 12 Montagu rd N15
19 O 12 Montagu rd N18
139 R 2 Montagu row W1
139 P 3 Montagu sq W1
139 P 4 Montagu st W1
92 M 10 Montague av SE4
93 N 10 Montague av SE4
71 V 3 Montague av W7
142 E 13 Montague clo SE1
61 P 19 Montague gdns W3
64 F 20 Montague pl E14
132 H 20 Montague pl WC1
122 J 19 Montague rd Croy
52 B 8 Montague rd E11
49 W 15 Montague rd E8
82 K 7 Montague rd Hounsl
30 C 16 Montague rd N8
26 G 19 Montague rd NW4
84 K 15 Montague rd Rich
70 B 10 Montague rd S'hall
105 Z 18 Montague rd SW19
60 B 17 Montague rd W13
71 V 4 Montague rd W7
75 P 20 Montague sq SE14
140 J 1 Montague st WC1
70 A 9 Montague waye S'hall
21 O 14 Montalt rd Wdfd Grn
21 O 16 Montalt rd Wdfd Grn
107 O 8 Montana rd SW17
105 N 20 Montana rd SW20
113 Z 7 Montbelle rd SE9
126 F 15 Montcalm clo Brom
78 A 18 Montcalm rd SE7
54 C 18 Monteagle av Bark
89 S 5 Montefiore st SW8
63 Y 3 Monteith rd E3
118 A 9 Montem rd New Mald
117 Z 8 Montem rd New Mald
92 K 19 Montem rd SE23
48 C 5 Montem st N4
29 W 17 Montenotte rd N8
149 S 12 Montford pl SE11
87 R 20 Montford pl SW19
122 B 9 Montgomery clo Mitch
96 J 15 Montgomery clo Sidcp
12 A 20 Montgomery rd Edg
73 V 10 Montgomery rd W4
88 M 16 Montholme rd SW11
143 R 2 Monthope st E1
86 L 12 Montolieu gdns SW15
97 W 19 Montpelier av Bxly
60 E 15 Montpelier av W5
66 B 8 Montpelier gdns E6
55 T 1 Montpelier gdns Rom
47 V 14 Montpelier gdns NW5
138 M 20 Montpelier ms SW7
138 L 20 Montpelier pl SW7
28 C 6 Montpelier rd N3
92 A 1 Montpelier rd SE15
151 X 20 Montpelier rd SE15
154 E 8 Montpelier rd Sutton
60 G 15 Montpelier rd W5
45 S 1 Montpelier ri NW11
42 F 5 Montpelier ri Wemb
84 D 19 Montpelier row Twick
94 C 4 Montpelier row SE3
138 L 20 Montpelier sq SW7
138 M 20 Montpelier st SW7
94 B 5 Montpelier vale SE3
45 S 1 Montpelier way NW11
138 L 20 Montpelier wlk SW7
110 C 16 Montrave rd SE20
141 O 8 Montreal pl WC2
54 A 2 Montreal rd Ilf
90 A 20 Montrell rd SW2
25 W 7 Montrose av Edg
128 M 7 Montrose av NW6

97 O 18 Montrose av Sidcp
82 L 20 Montrose av Twick
96 G 8 Montrose av Welling
21 S 13 Montrose clo Wdfd Grn
96 J 7 Montrose clo Welling
28 C 1 Montrose cres N12
15 O 20 Montrose cres N12
42 J 17 Montrose cres Wemb
138 H 20 Montrose ct SW7
154 B 4 Montrose gdns Sutton
120 M 5 Montrose gdns Mitch
139 U 19 Montrose pl SW1
23 V 8 Montrose rd Harrow
110 E 2 Montrose wy SE23
33 X 2 Montserrat av Wdfd Grn
33 X 2 Montserrat av Wdfd Grn
87 S 10 Montserrat rd SW15
142 H 10 Monument st EC3
160 H 10 Monument st EC3
31 V 11 Monument way N17
75 P 1 Monza st E1
75 R 7 Moodkee st SE16
63 T 10 Moody st E1
4 H 12 Moon la Barnt
133 V 4 Moon st N1
94 F 11 Moons ct SE12
25 O 17 Moor ct NW9
142 D 1 Moor la EC2
160 D 2 Moor la EC2
134 E 20 Moor la EC2
142 F 2 Moor pl EC2
160 F 2 Moor pl EC2
140 G 7 Moor st W1
107 Z 6 Moorcroft rd SW16
22 A 16 Moorcroft way Pinn
78 L 20 Moordown SE18
95 Y 2 Moordown SE18
121 S 4 Moore clo Mitch
85 W 8 Moore clo SW14
156 A 18 Moore clo Wallgtn
145 V 20 Moore Park rd SW6
108 K 14 Moore rd SE19
147 O 5 Moore st SW3
52 G 13 Moore wlk E7
31 U 9 Moorefield rd N17
94 H 8 Moorehead way SE3
112 D 19 Mooreland rd Brom
65 O4 Moorey clo E15
60 H 11 Moorfield av W5
9 O 7 Moorfield rd Enf
142 E 2 Moorfields EC2
160 E 2 Moorfields EC2
160 E 4 Moorgate EC2
142 F 2 Moorgate EC2
24 H 10 Moorhouse rd Harrow
137 T 5 Moorhouse rd W2
100 E 13 Moorland clo Hampt
38 H 3 Moorland clo Rom
24 K 14 Moorland rd Harrow
90 H 10 Moorland rd SW9
13 X 20 Moorlands av NW7
152 B 11 Moormead dri Epsom
83 Z 16 Moormead rd Twick
112 A 7 Moorside rd Brom
44 M 11 Mora rd NW2
45 N 11 Mora rd NW2
134 C 13 Mora st EC1
30 C 4 Morant pl N22
64 B 19 Morant st E14
90 E 1 Morat st SW9
149 P 20 Morat st SW9
146 G 16 Moravian pl SW10
63 P 8 Moravian st E2
39 O 3 Moray clo Rom
48 D 6 Moray ms N4
48 E 5 Moray rd N4
39 O 3 Moray way Rom
61 Z 4 Mordant rd NW10
68 M 1 Mordaunt gdns Dgnhm
90 C 8 Mordaunt st SW9
93 U 3 Morden clo SE13
119 Z 9 Morden ct Mrdn
41 X 15 Morden gdns Grnfd
120 G 9 Morden gdns Mrdn
120 C 7 Morden hall Mrdn
120 D 6 Morden Hall pk Mrdn
120 B 7 Morden Hall rd Mrdn
93 U 4 Morden hill SE13
93 U 3 Morden la SE13
119 U 13 Morden pk Mrdn
36 K 20 Morden rd Ilf
120 A 3 Morden rd Mitch
38 A 20 Morden rd Rom

37 Z 20 Morden rd Rom
94 E 4 Morden rd SE3
94 F 5 Morden rd SE3
106 A 20 Morden rd SW19
94 E 5 Morden Road ms SE3
93 S 3 Morden st SE13
119 X 18 Morden way Sutton
76 M 9 Morden Wharf rd SE10
65 P 17 More clo E16
144 J 7 More clo W14
57 Z 16 Morecambe clo Hornch
11 V 14 Morecambe gdns Stanm
150 C 8 Morecambe st SE17
18 A 13 Morecambe ter N18
103 T 17 Morecoombe clo Kingst
18 J 15 Moree way N18
99 Z 14 Moreland av Drtfrd
46 B 4 Moreland clo NW11
133 Y 12 Moreland st EC1
20 E 10 Moreland way E4
5 R 11 Morell clo Barnt
88 L 18 Morella rd SW12
110 M 10 Moremead rd SE6
111 O 10 Moremead rd SE6
93 R 18 Morena st SE6
117 T 17 Moresby av Surb
50 A 4 Moresby rd E5
49 Z 5 Moresby rd E5
83 S 1 Moreton av Islwth
50 B 5 Moreton clo E5
31 O 18 Moreton clo N15
13 Z 20 Moreton clo NW7
148 C 9 Moreton pl SW1
31 P 18 Moreton rd N15
157 P 12 Moreton rd S Croy
152 H 3 Moreton rd Worc Pk
148 D 10 Moreton st SW1
148 C 9 Moreton ter SW1
33 Y 13 Morgan av E17
69 R 1 Morgan clo Dgnhm
112 E 19 Morgan rd Brom
48 F 16 Morgan rd N7
137 N 1 Morgan rd W10
65 P 14 Morgan st E16
63 W 9 Morgan st E3
142 J 14 Morgans la SE1
146 J 19 Morgans wlk SW11
88 A 12 Morie st SW18
50 L 4 Morieux rd E10
107 P 10 Moring rd SW17
109 R 6 Morkyns wlk SE21
123 S 19 Morland av Croy
61 Y 1 Morland gdns NW10
70 L 3 Morland gdns S'hall
133 U 1 Morland ms N1
123 U 18 Morland rd Croy
69 T 2 Morland rd Dgnhm
32 G 17 Morland rd E17
53 Y 6 Morland rd Ilf
110 F 16 Morland rd SE20
154 D 12 Morland rd Sutton
33 W 2 Morley av E4
18 K 14 Morley av N18
30 J 6 Morley av N22
24 F 9 Morley Cres east Stanm
12 G 9 Morley cres Edg
24 E 9 Morley cres Stanm
24 E 10 Morley Cres west Stanm
8 B 4 Morley hill Enf
67 S 4 Morley rd Bark
51 U 5 Morley rd E10
65 P 6 Morley rd E15
37 Y 17 Morley rd Rom
93 U 11 Morley rd SE13
119 V 20 Morley rd Sutton
84 F 16 Morley rd Twick
141 U 19 Morley st SE1
90 M 3 Morna st SE5
50 B 17 Morning la E9
152 L 3 Morningside rd Worc Pk
126 M 7 Mornington av Brom
35 V 20 Mornington av Ilf
145 O 8 Mornington av W14
21 S 13 Mornington clo Wdfd Grn
132 A 8 Mornington cres NW1
64 A 9 Mornington gro E3
90 K 1 Mornington ms SE5
132 A 9 Mornington pl NW1
131 Z 9 Mornington pl NW1
21 S 13 Mornington rd Wdfd Grn

52 B 2	Mornington rd E11
20 J 2	Mornington rd E4
58 K 12	Mornington rd Grnfd
75 Z 20	Mornington rd SE8
131 Y 8	Mornington st NW1
131 Y 7	Mornington ter NW1
102 E 9	Mornington wlk Rich
142 J 19	Morocco st SE1
63 S 4	Morpeth gro E9
63 S 4	Morpeth rd E9
63 S 9	Morpeth st E2
148 B 3	Morpeth ter SW1
54 K 9	Morrab gdns Ilf
53 T 15	Morris av E12
87 X 17	Morris gdns SW18
48 F 6	Morris pl N4
56 C 7	Morris rd Dgnhm
64 D 15	Morris rd E14
51 Y 12	Morris rd E15
83 V 7	Morris rd Islwth
39 Z 1	Morris rd Rom
63 N 18	Morris st E1
143 Y 7	Morris st E1
90 A 19	Morrish rd SW2
31 S 10	Morrison av N17
68 K 6	Morrison rd Bark
89 O 6	Morrison st SW11
65 R 10	Morse clo E13
129 W 14	Morshead rd W9
113 T 10	Morston gdns SE9
89 X 16	Morten clo SW4
31 O 4	Morteyne rd N17
64 L 4	Mortham st E15
45 W 8	Mortimer clo NW2
107 X 3	Mortimer clo SW16
129 Y 6	Mortimer cres NW6
132 D 18	Mortimer mkt WC1
129 X 6	Mortimer pl NW6
66 F 9	Mortimer rd E6
81 Z 17	Mortimer rd Erith
120 L 2	Mortimer rd Mitch
134 K 2	Mortimer rd N1
49 S 20	Mortimer rd N1
128 D 12	Mortimer rd NW10
60 C 17	Mortimer rd W13
136 H 11	Mortimer sq W11
140 B 3	Mortimer st W1
139 Z 3	Mortimer st W1
47 R 12	Mortimer ter NW5
156 B 5	Mortlake clo Croy
85 Y 6	Mortlake High st SW14
65 W 16	Mortlake rd E16
54 D 13	Mortlake rd Ilf
73 O 19	Mortlake rd Rich
85 S 3	Mortlake rd Rich
91 Z 2	Mortlock clo SE15
16 J 13	Morton cres N14
155 V 10	Morton gdns Wallgtn
145 X 7	Morton ms SW5
149 S 2	Morton pl SE1
65 O 2	Morton rd E15
120 F 12	Morton rd Mrdn
134 D 2	Morton rd N1
16 H 12	Morton way N14
90 F 14	Morval rd SW2
81 O 11	Morvale clo Blvdr
106 L 7	Morven rd SW17
64 A 6	Morville st E3
140 F 2	Morwell st WC1
137 X 8	Moscow pl W2
137 W 9	Moscow rd W2
30 H 6	Moselle av N22
30 B 11	Moselle clo N8
31 V 2	Moselle pl N17
31 V 2	Moselle st N17
154 H 10	Moss clo Carsh
143 U 1	Moss clo E1
22 D 8	Moss clo Pinn
158 E 17	Moss gdn S Croy
15 O 19	Moss Hall cres N12
15 N 19	Moss Hall gro N12
22 C 8	Moss la Pinn
39 V 18	Moss la Rom
56 F 20	Moss rd Dgnhm
15 N 19	Mossborough clo N12
88 K 9	Mossbury rd SW11
81 T 12	Mossdown clo Blvdr
35 Z 8	Mossford ct Ilf
36 A 9	Mossford grn Ilf
36 B 5	Mossford la Ilf
63 X 12	Mossford st E3
151 Z 6	Mossington rd SE16
127 O 12	Mosslea rd Brom
110 C 16	Mosslea rd SE20
146 L 6	Mossop st SW3
119 V 7	Mossville gdns Mrdn
42 M 14	Mostyn av Wemb
43 N 14	Mostyn av Wemb
128 F 11	Mostyn gdns NW10
63 Z 7	Mostyn gro E3
26 A 3	Mostyn rd Edg
25 Z 2	Mostyn rd Edg
119 W 1	Mostyn rd SW19
90 F 3	Mostyn rd SW9
127 R 15	Mosul way Brom
139 S 20	Motcomb st SW1
13 R 7	Mote end NW7
118 G 13	Motspur pk New Mald
113 O 2	Mottingham gdns SE9
112 K 2	Mottingham hall SE9
94 K 19	Mottingham la SE9
112 L 1	Mottingham la SE9
113 N 2	Mottingham la SE9
19 S 1	Mottingham rd N9
113 S 6	Mottingham rd SE9
80 A 10	Mottisfont rd SE2
79 Z 9	Mottisfont rd SE2
63 R 2	Moulins rd E9
82 D 4	Moulton av Hounsl
113 V 8	Mound the SE9
31 X 19	Moundfield rd N16
91 X 19	Mount Adon pk SE22
86 E 19	Mount Angelus rd SW15
84 K 13	Mount Ararat rd Rich
110 A 6	Mount Ash rd SE26
109 Z 7	Mount Ash rd SE26
20 C 12	Mount av E4
58 G 18	Mount av S'hall
60 H 13	Mount av W5
6 B 15	Mount clo Barnt
113 P 20	Mount clo Chisl
155 P 19	Mount clo Wallgtn
159 Z 2	Mount ct W Wkhm
115 X 15	Mount Culver av Sidcp
97 Y 13	Mount dri Bxly Hth
22 E 15	Mount dri Harrow
43 V 7	Mount dri Wemb
108 C 6	Mount Earl gdns SW16
20 D 6	Mount Echo av E4
20 E 4	Mount Echo dri E4
107 Y 7	Mount Ephraim la SW16
107 Y 6	Mount Ephraim rd SW16
109 Z 6	Mount gdns SE26
12 K 12	Mount gro Edg
48 K 9	Mount Grove rd N5
49 L 7	Mount ho Barnt
133 Z 14	Mount mills EC1
3 T 16	Mount Morres rd E1
108 C 6	Mount Nod rd SW16
41 S 7	Mount Park av Harrow
156 J 20	Mount Park av S Croy
60 G 18	Mount Park cres W5
41 R 9	Mount Park rd Harrow
60 G 15	Mount Park rd W5
155 P 18	Mount pk Wallgtn
60 K 2	Mount pleasant Wemb
61 N 2	Mount pleasant Wemb
6 A 14	Mount pleasant Barnt
5 Y 14	Mount pleasant Barnt
48 C 2	Mount Pleasant cres N4
50 B 6	Mount Pleasant hill E5
50 A 4	Mount Pleasant la E5
128 C 2	Mount Pleasant rd NW10
60 E 13	Mount Pleasant rd W5
32 H 7	Mount Pleasant rd E17
31 R 7	Mount Pleasant rd N17
93 T 15	Mount Pleasant rd SE13
117 X 5	Mount Pleasant rd New Mald
48 C 1	Mount Pleasant vlls N4
133 R 17	Mount pleasant WC1
133 R 18	Mount pleasant WC1
98 K 14	Mount Pleasant wlk Bxly
5 W 16	Mount rd Barnt
97 X 13	Mount rd Bxly Hth
56 C 3	Mount rd Dgnhm
99 U 15	Mount rd Drtfrd
100 B 6	Mount rd Felt
53 Z 16	Mount rd Ilf
120 G 2	Mount rd Mitch
117 X 6	Mount rd New Mald
44 L 9	Mount rd NW2
26 G 20	Mount rd NW4
109 P 16	Mount rd SE19
105 Z 4	Mount rd SW19
139 W 10	Mount row W1
139 W 10	Mount st W1
24 F 20	Mount Stewart av Harrow
143 V 2	Mount ter E1
15 R 8	Mount the N20
118 E 7	Mount the New Mald
46 D 10	Mount the NW3
43 U 7	Mount the Wemb
152 K 9	Mount the Worc Pk
7 R 3	Mount view Enf
12 L 11	Mount view NW7
20 J 3	Mount View rd E4
48 B 1	Mount View rd N4
30 E 19	Mount View rd N4
25 Y 14	Mount View rd NW9
108 J 7	Mount vlls SE27
155 P 20	Mount way Wallgtn
109 W 8	Mountacre clo SE26
109 S 13	Mountbatten clo SE19
79 U 17	Mountbatten clo SE18
88 C 20	Mountbatten ms SW18
23 Y 6	Mountbel rd Stanm
116 J 16	Mountcombe clo Surb
66 H 8	Mountfield rd E6
27 X 9	Mountfield rd N3
60 H 18	Mountfield rd W5
143 S 4	Mountford st E1
133 R 1	Mountfort ter N1
126 C 18	Mounthurst rd Brom
80 D 5	Mountjoy clo SE2
93 W 4	Mounts Pond rd SE3
93 W 15	Mountsfield ct SE13
23 X 4	Mountside Stanm
30 H 13	Mountview ct N15
67 T 4	Movers la Bark
47 Y 5	Mowatt clo N19
5 P 16	Mowbray rd Barnt
12 D 13	Mowbray rd Edg
45 T 19	Mowbray rd NW6
102 D 7	Mowbray rd Rich
109 V 19	Mowbray rd SE19
38 K 6	Mowbrays clo Rom
38 K 7	Mowbrays rd Rom
63 O 5	Mowlem st E2
135 Y 7	Mowlem st E2
149 S 20	Mowll st SW9
65 P 7	Moxon clo E13
4 H 13	Moxon st Barnt
139 T 2	Moxon st W1
135 T 7	Moye clo E2
51 U 2	Moyers rd E10
144 M 15	Moylan rd W6
61 R 7	Moyne pl NW10
107 U 14	Moyser rd SW16
129 O 14	Mozart st W10
120 E 14	Muchelney rd Mrdn
77 S 8	Mudlarks way SE7
56 G 12	Muggeridge rd Dgnhm
49 Y 11	Muir rd E5
78 F 3	Muir st E16
85 X 10	Muirdown av SW14
62 C 18	Muirfield W3
111 V 2	Muirkirk rd SE6
5 U 14	Mulberry clo Barnt
20 C 8	Mulberry clo E4
58 B 5	Mulberry clo Nthlt
46 F 14	Mulberry clo NW3
26 M 12	Mulberry clo NW4
107 U 10	Mulberry clo SW16
72 C 19	Mulberry cres Brentf
54 K 19	Mulberry ct Bark
157 V 1	Mulberry la Croy
155 U 13	Mulberry ms Wallgtn
74 E 14	Mulberry pl W6
143 S 3	Mulberry st E1
81 Y 5	Mulberry way Blvdr
34 H 8	Mulberry way E18
36 C 13	Mulberry way Ilf
146 G 12	Mulberry wlk SW3
157 O 7	Mulgrave rd Croy
41 X 8	Mulgrave rd Harrow
44 E 13	Mulgrave rd NW10
154 B 14	Mulgrave rd Sutton
153 V 16	Mulgrave rd Sutton
145 O 14	Mulgrave rd W14
60 H 10	Mulgrave rd W5
121 T 3	Mulholland clo Mitch
89 Y 17	Muller rd SW4
85 Y 7	Mullins pth SW14
22 J 3	Mullion clo Harrow
130 J 18	Mulready st NW8
74 A 5	Multi way W3
88 G 20	Multon rd SW18
142 G 18	Mulvaney way SE1
160 C 5	Mumford ct EC2
90 J 14	Mumford rd SE24
89 N 12	Muncaster rd SW11
145 P 11	Mund st W14
92 B 15	Mundania rd SE22
65 S 19	Munday rd E16
144 K 6	Munden st W14
50 C 6	Mundford rd E5
54 E 4	Mundon gdns Ilf
10 A 8	Mungo Park clo Bushy
57 W 17	Mungo Park rd Rainhm
83 P 14	Munnings gdns Islwth
128 M 20	Munro ms W10
82 C 12	Munster av Hounsl
17 X 13	Munster gdns N13
144 K 18	Munster rd SW6
87 U 3	Munster rd SW6
102 C 16	Munster rd Tedd
131 Z 15	Munster sq NW1
150 D 5	Munton rd SE17
115 X 1	Murchison av Bxly
97 Y 20	Murchison av Bxly
51 U 5	Murchison rd E10
65 R 16	Murdock clo E16
63 W 10	Murdock cottages E3
105 R 4	Murfett clo SW19
133 P 7	Muriel st N1
93 Y 11	Murillo rd SE13
141 S 19	Murphy st SE1
126 J 3	Murray av Brom
82 K 14	Murray av Hounsl
134 E 10	Murray gro N1
47 X 19	Murray ms NW1
102 C 4	Murray rd Rich
105 P 15	Murray rd SW19
72 D 12	Murray rd W5
65 U 19	Murray sq E16
47 W 19	Murray st NW1
144 L 14	Musard rd W6
63 P 17	Musbury st E1
154 J 3	Muschamp rd Carsh
91 V 8	Muschamp rd SE15
142 L 9	Muscovy st EC3
140 J 2	Museum st WC1
5 R 6	Musgrave clo Barnt
145 V 20	Musgrave cres SW6
87 Z 1	Musgrave cres SW6
83 V 1	Musgrave rd Islwth
92 G 3	Musgrove rd SE14
88 G 6	Musjid clo SW11
49 Z 6	Muston rd E5
29 R 6	Muswell av N10
29 S 8	Muswell av N10
29 R 11	Muswell Hill bdwy N10
29 U 11	Muswell hill N10
29 T 12	Muswell Hill pl N10
29 R 16	Muswell Hill rd N10
29 S 9	Muswell ms N10
29 T 9	Muswell rd N10
129 V 3	Mutrix rd NW6
117 V 4	Muybridge rd New Mald
90 J 1	Myatt rd SW9
77 S 18	Mycenae rd SE3
17 X 2	Myddelton gdns N21
133 T 12	Myddelton pas EC1
15 V 8	Myddelton pk N20
30 B 11	Myddelton rd N8
133 T 11	Myddelton sq EC1
133 U 14	Myddelton st EC1
8 F 4	Myddleton av Enf
8 G 5	Myddleton clo Enf
30 A 1	Myddleton ms N22
30 A 1	Myddleton rd N22
30 B 12	Myddleton rd N8
110 A 9	Mylis clo SE26
133 T 11	Mylne st EC1
80 A 11	Myra st SE2
143 U 4	Myrdle st E1
93 V 8	Myron pl SE13
16 A 5	Myrtle clo Barnt
99 R 1	Myrtle clo Erith
71 T 2	Myrtle gdns W7
8 C 4	Myrtle gro Enf
117 W 4	Myrtle gro New Mald
159 P 5	Myrtle rd Croy
32 J 19	Myrtle rd E17
66 E 4	Myrtle rd E6
100 M 16	Myrtle rd Hampt
82 M 6	Myrtle rd Hounsl
53 Z 7	Myrtle rd Ilf
17 Z 11	Myrtle rd N13

108 B 8	Newcombe gdns SW16
61 N 2	Newcombe pk Wemb
13 O 16	Newcombe pk NW7
137 U 13	Newcombe st W8
52 B 9	Newcomen rd E11
88 F 7	Newcomen rd SW11
142 E 16	Newcomen st SE1
130 K 10	Newcourt st NW8
18 L 9	Newdale clo N9
63 Y 19	Newell st E14
120 L 19	Newent clo Carsh
150 J 16	Newent clo SE15
100 G 20	Newfield clo Hampt
100 H 19	Newfield clo Hampt
44 H 9	Newfield ri NW2
24 M 4	Newgale gdns Edg
100 C 6	Newgate clo Felt
122 M 19	Newgate Croy
20 M 12	Newgate st E4
21 N 11	Newgate st E4
141 X 4	Newgate st EC1
67 S 7	Newham way Bark
65 Y 14	Newham way E16
66 F 13	Newham way E6
142 L 20	Newhams row SE1
95 N 9	Newhaven gdns SE9
123 P 11	Newhaven rd SE25
37 W 10	Newhouse av Rom
118 B 18	Newhouse clo New Mald
98 G 15	Newick clo Bxly
50 B 10	Newick rd E5
113 O 18	Newing grn Chisl
48 C 8	Newington Barrow way N7
149 Y 6	Newington butts SE11
149 Z 2	Newington causeway SE1
149 Y 8	Newington cres SE17
49 O 16	Newington Green rd N1
49 O 14	Newington grn N16
43 P 7	Newland ct Wemb
8 M 6	Newland dri Enf
71 Y 6	Newland gdns W13
30 A 10	Newland rd N8
78 E 3	Newland st E16
11 X 10	Newlands clo Edg
70 B 13	Newlands clo S'hall
42 E 17	Newlands clo Wemb
110 D 13	Newlands pk SE26
4 B 16	Newlands pl Barnt
21 R 9	Newlands rd Wdfd Grn
122 B 3	Newlands rd SW16
155 X 17	Newlands the Wallgtn
158 K 19	Newlands wood Croy
66 H 17	Newling clo E6
40 C 2	Newlyn gdns Harrow
4 G 15	Newlyn rd Barnt
31 U 6	Newlyn rd N17
44 L 4	Newlyn rd NW2
96 K 5	Newlyn rd Welling
140 D 3	Newman pas W1
126 G 2	Newman rd Brom
122 C 18	Newman rd Croy
65 U 10	Newman rd E13
32 G 14	Newman rd E17
140 C 2	Newman st W1
160 H 6	Newmans ct EC4
141 P 3	Newmans row WC2
5 S 7	Newmans way Barnt
40 K 16	Newmarket av Nthlt
95 O 18	Newmarket grn SE9
120 D 15	Newminster rd Mrdn
122 L 3	Newnham clo Thntn Hth
40 M 16	Newnham clo Nthlt
41 N 17	Newnham gdns Nthlt
30 E 4	Newnham rd N22
149 R 1	Newnham ter SE1
141 R 20	Newnham ter SE1
24 L 14	Newnham way Harrow
127 V 6	Newnhams clo Brom
49 O 1	Newnton clo N4
65 W 12	Newport av E13
140 G 8	Newport ct WC2
140 G 8	Newport pl WC2
51 V 6	Newport rd E10
32 J 14	Newport rd E17
86 H 1	Newport rd SW13
149 O 6	Newport st SE11
40 C 7	Newquay cres Harrow
111 S 4	Newquay rd SE6

83 Z 12	Newry rd Twick
31 O 15	Newsam av N15
94 B 18	Newstead rd SE12
105 R 8	Newstead way SW19
120 D 17	Newstead wlk Carsh
29 R 3	Newton av N10
73 V 6	Newton av W3
74 A 10	Newton gro W4
40 H 7	Newton pk Harrow
51 Y 14	Newton rd E15
23 T 6	Newton rd Harrow
83 V 4	Newton rd Islwth
31 W 14	Newton rd N15
44 M 11	Newton rd NW2
105 U 18	Newton rd SW19
137 W 5	Newton rd W2
96 M 8	Newton rd Welling
60 M 1	Newton rd Wemb
89 S 2	Newton st SW11
140 M 4	Newton st WC2
17 Z 16	Newton way N18
25 T 4	Newton wlk Edg
87 Z 14	Newtons yd SW18
72 C 10	Niagra av W5
23 T 15	Nibthwaite rd Harrow
16 J 4	Nichol clo N14
112 G 17	Nichol la Brom
58 L 5	Nicholas clo Grnfd
72 F 4	Nicholas gdns W5
160 G 8	Nicholas la EC4
156 B 8	Nicholas rd Croy
56 B 8	Nicholas rd Dgnhm
63 R 12	Nicholas st E1
82 G 11	Nicholes rd Hounsl
135 S 7	Nicholl st E2
60 J 14	Nichols grn W5
123 V 20	Nicholson rd Croy
141 X 14	Nicholson st SE1
84 C 15	Nicol clo Twick
23 R 7	Nicola clo Harrow
156 L 14	Nicola clo S Croy
26 K 26	Nicoll pl NW4
62 B 4	Nicoll rd NW10
10 A 7	Nicolson dri Bushey
88 H 18	Nicosia rd SW18
110 G 8	Niederwald rd SE26
58 B 4	Nigel clo Nthlt
53 Y 12	Nigel ms Ilf
74 J 12	Nigel Playfair av W6
52 M 15	Nigel rd E7
91 X 7	Nigel rd SE15
77 Z 19	Nigeria rd SE7
20 L 15	Nightingale av E4
155 N 3	Nightingale clo Carsh
20 L 13	Nightingale clo E4
73 V 18	Nightingale clo W4
93 X 13	Nightingale gro SE13
126 L 4	Nightingale la Brom
127 N 5	Nightingale la Brom
34 G 15	Nightingale la E11
46 J 3	Nightingale la N6
29 Z 13	Nightingale la N8
84 K 18	Nightingale la Rich
88 L 19	Nightingale la SW12
89 O 17	Nightingale la SW12
78 K 15	Nightingale pl SE18
155 N 4	Nightingale rd Carsh
49 Y 9	Nightingale rd E5
100 H 15	Nightingale rd Hampt
30 C 3	Nightingale rd N22
19 S 6	Nightingale rd N9
62 E 7	Nightingale rd NW10
71 V 2	Nightingale rd W7
89 O 18	Nightingale sq SW12
78 K 16	Nightingale vale SE18
66 E 14	Nightingale way E6
89 R 15	Nightingale wlk SW4
65 X 7	Nile rd E13
134 D 12	Nile st N1
151 O 12	Nile ter SE15
91 S 12	Nimegen way SE22
10 D 4	Nimmo dri Bushey
107 T 12	Nimrod rd SW16
53 R 15	Nine Acres clo E12
148 H 15	Nine Elms la SW8
78 M 18	Nithdale rd SE18
79 N 18	Nithdale rd SE18
4 B 19	Niton clo Barnt
85 P 8	Niton rd Rich
144 F 18	Niton st SW6
19 R 15	Noble st E1
160 A 4	Noble st EC2
30 F 8	Noel Park rd N22
66 C 12	Noel rd E6
133 X 8	Noel rd N1
61 P 17	Noel rd W3
55 T 11	Noel sq Dgnhm

140 C 6	Noel st W1
49 Y 11	Nolan way E5
25 N 6	Nolton pla Edg
152 L 15	Nonsuch pk Epsom Sutton
153 N 13	Nonsuch pk Epsom Sutton
153 O 19	Nonsuch wlk Sutton
153 P 20	Nonsuch wlk Sutton
27 P 13	Nora gdns NW4
41 T 3	Nora ter Harrow
117 R 3	Norbiton av Kingst
117 U 5	Norbiton Comm rd Kingst
63 X 17	Norbiton rd E14
62 D 19	Norbroke st W12
136 J 2	Norburn st W10
83 P 11	Norbury av Hounsl
108 C 20	Norbury av SW16
122 E 1	Norbury av SW16
108 H 19	Norbury clo SW16
122 C 4	Norbury Court rd SW16
121 Z 4	Norbury Court rd SW16
122 C 1	Norbury cres SW16
121 Z 5	Norbury cross SW16
37 V 16	Norbury gdns Rom
13 O 10	Norbury gro NW7
108 J 17	Norbury hill SW16
20 A 15	Norbury rd E4
122 M 4	Norbury rd Thntn Hth
123 N 4	Norbury rd Thntn Hth
122 A 5	Norbury ri SW16
121 Z 5	Norbury ri SW16
24 D 17	Norcombe gdns Harrow
49 X 8	Norcott rd N16
91 W 17	Norcroft gdns SE22
101 T 1	Norcutt rd Twick
17 X 20	Norfolk av N13
31 V 18	Norfolk av N15
6 B 14	Norfolk clo Barnt
17 X 19	Norfolk clo N13
28 H 10	Norfolk clo N2
84 B 15	Norfolk clo Twick
96 H 18	Norfolk cres Sidcp
138 L 5	Norfolk cres W2
98 B 1	Norfolk gdns Bxly Hth
107 Y 6	Norfolk House rd SW16
138 H 5	Norfolk pl W2
96 M 4	Norfolk pl Welling
67 U 2	Norfolk rd Bark
4 M 12	Norfolk rd Barnt
56 H 15	Norfolk rd Dgnhm
32 G 7	Norfolk rd E17
66 H 3	Norfolk rd E6
9 O 18	Norfolk rd Enf
22 L 16	Norfolk rd Harrow
54 H 1	Norfolk rd Ilf
44 B 20	Norfolk rd NW10
130 J 5	Norfolk rd NW8
38 L 18	Norfolk rd Rom
106 J 16	Norfolk rd SW19
122 M 6	Norfolk rd Thntn Hth
149 O 4	Norfolk row SE11
138 G 5	Norfolk sq W2
138 G 6	Norfolk Square ms W2
52 F 14	Norfolk st E7
144 K 12	Norfolk ter W6
89 P 20	Norgrove st SW12
123 U 5	Norhyrst av SE25
136 L 14	Norland pl W11
136 H 15	Norland rd W11
136 L 14	Norland sq W11
127 Z 1	Norlands cres BR7
104 H 2	Norley vale SW15
51 V 4	Norlington rd E10
100 C 4	Norman av Felt
30 K 4	Norman av N22
58 C 19	Norman av S'hall
84 C 18	Norman av Twick
38 J 6	Norman clo Rom
63 X 7	Norman gro E3
100 E 4	Norman ho Felt
126 J 14	Norman pk Brom
81 T 7	Norman rd Blvdr
51 Y 7	Norman rd E11
66 H 11	Norman rd E6
57 X 1	Norman rd Hornch
54 A 16	Norman rd Ilf
53 Z 16	Norman rd Ilf
31 V 15	Norman rd N15
76 E 17	Norman rd SE10
153 X 11	Norman rd Sutton
106 D 17	Norman rd SW19
122 J 11	Norman rd Thntn Hth
134 B 15	Norman st EC1

16 M 9	Norman way N14
61 T 16	Norman way W3
87 U 13	Normanby clo SW15
44 E 13	Normanby rd NW10
144 M 13	Normand ms W14
145 N 15	Normand pk W14
145 N 13	Normand rd W14
4 H 14	Normandy av Barnt
90 F 2	Normandy rd SW9
65 U 18	Normandy ter E16
99 P 2	Normandy way Erith
97 W 3	Normanhurst av Bxly Hth
83 Z 13	Normanhurst dri Twick
108 D 3	Normanhurst rd SW2
43 X 18	Normans clo NW10
43 X 18	Normans mead NW10
102 E 18	Normansfield av Tedd
20 F 13	Normanshire av E4
20 C 14	Normanshire dri E4
105 X 5	Normanton av SW19
20 M 10	Normanton pk E4
21 N 9	Normanton pk E4
157 R 13	Normanton rd S Croy
110 G 5	Normanton st SE23
108 F 11	Normington clo SW16
28 F 17	Norrice lea N2
140 E 11	Norris st SW1
99 U 6	Norris way Drtfd
87 P 11	Norroy rd SW15
5 Z 15	Norrys clo Barnt
5 Y 15	Norrys rd Barnt
58 L 4	Norseman way Grnfd
104 F 4	Norstead pl SW15
32 G 18	North Access rd E17
26 B 6	North acre NW9
61 Y 8	North Acton rd NW10
139 T 8	North Audley st W1
155 N 16	North av Carsh
22 L 18	North av Harrow
132 M 9	North av N1
18 L 13	North av N18
85 O 3	North av Rich
58 F 20	North av S'hall
60 B 15	North av W13
130 J 14	North Bank NW8
51 X 10	North Birbeck rd E11
44 D 6	North Circular rd NW2
18 F 15	North Circular rd N18
60 L 8	North Circular rd Wemb
45 N 1	North Circular rd NW2
53 R 17	North Circular rd E12
61 R 3	North Circular rd NW10
53 S 5	North Circular rd Ilf
17 V 16	North Circular rd N13
43 W 18	North Circular rd NW10
19 V 17	North Circular rd E4
66 G 10	North Circular rd E6
28 C 8	North Circular rd N2
27 X 11	North Circular rd N3
97 W 10	North clo Bxly Hth
69 S 4	North clo Dgnhm
119 S 8	North clo Mrdn
60 L 20	North Common rd W5
32 L 6	North Countess rd E17
115 Y 15	North Cray rd Sidcp
27 V 9	North cres N3
132 E 20	North cres WC1
36 A 14	North Cross rd Ilf
91 V 12	North Cross rd SE22
132 C 20	North ct W1
82 J 3	North dene Hounsl
12 L 10	North dene NW7
159 S 20	North Downs cres Croy
83 O 6	North dri Hounsl
107 V 9	North dri SW16
46 D 6	North End av NW3
21 Y 3	North end Buck Hl
145 N 7	North End cres W14
156 L 3	North end Croy
46 C 5	North end NW3
45 Z 4	North End rd NW11
46 B 4	North End rd NW3

144 L 5   North End rd SW6
145 R 13   North End rd W14
43 R 10   North End rd Wemb
46 C 7   North End way NW3
74 E 13   North Eyot gdns W6
106 G 17   North gdns SW19
98 B 20   North Glade the Bxly
132 B 14   North Gower st NW1
31 O 16   North gro N15
47 O 2   North gro N6
29 N 17   North Hill av N6
29 O 19   North hill N6
70 A 13   North Hyde la S'hall
101 V 14   North la Tedd
87 P 14   North Lodge clo
    SW15
133 P 18   North ms WC1
87 V 12   North pas SW18
95 U 17   North pk SE9
106 L 17   North pl Mitch
136 B 3   North Pole rd W10
62 L 15   North Pole rd W10
81 U 6   North rd Blvdr
72 L 16   North rd Brentf
112 H 20   North rd Brom
99 U 17   North rd Drtfrd
25 T 3   North rd Edg
54 G 7   North rd Ilf
47 P 1   North rd N6
48 B 16   North rd N7
47 Z 17   North rd N7
18 M 4   North rd N9
85 O 8   North rd Rich
37 X 16   North rd Rom
58 F 20   North rd S'hall
70 G 1   North rd S'hall
79 W 9   North rd SE18
116 G 14   North rd Surb
106 D 15   North rd SW19
125 S 20   North rd W Wkhm
72 G 9   North rd W5
139 T 7   North row W1
93 Y 4   North several SE3
153 W 5   North Spur rd Sutton
27 Z 17   North sq NW11
54 A 20   North st Bark
67 N 1   North st Bark
126 E 2   North st Brom
98 E 9   North st Bxly Hth
154 M 8   North st Carsh
155 N 9   North st Carsh
65 U 6   North st E13
83 Y 6   North st Islwth
27 N 15   North st NW4
39 O 13   North st Rom
89 U 6   North st SW4
143 P 6   North Tenter st E1
146 J 4   North ter SW3
35 N 7   North View dri
    Wdfd Grn
29 Y 11   North View rd N8
104 L 20   North view SW19
60 D 11   North view W5
47 Y 18   North vlls NW1
19 S 8   North way N9
25 S 10   North way NW9
138 F 3   North Wharf rd W2
159 U 13   North wlk Croy
78 A 4   North Woolwich rd
    E16
77 S 3   North Woolwich rd
    E16
86 A 7   North Worple way
    SW14
85 Z 7   North Worple way
    SW14
98 J 6   Northall rd Bxly Hth
49 N 16   Northampton gro N1
49 N 16   Northampton pk N1
157 X 2   Northampton rd Croy
133 T 16   Northampton rd EC1
9 X 15   Northampton rd Enf
133 T 16   Northampton row
    EC1
133 X 13   Northampton sq EC1
48 L 20   Northampton st N1
107 Z 16   Northanger rd SW16
33 T 7   Northbank rd E17
122 C 4   Northborough rd
    SW16
121 Y 5   Northborough rd
    SW16
126 F 16   Northbourne Brom
89 Y 12   Northbourne rd SW4
4 F 20   Northbrook rd Barnt
123 N 12   Northbrook rd Croy
53 V 7   Northbrook rd Ilf
30 B 1   Northbrook rd N22
93 Y 12   Northbrook rd SE13
133 X 17   Northburgh st EC1

43 O 18   Northchurch rd
    Wemb
49 N 20   Northchurch rd N1
134 J 1   Northchurch ter N1
152 B 6   Northcliffe clo
    Worc Pk
14 H 5   Northcliffe dr N20
58 C 20   Northcote av S'hall
70 D 1   Northcote av S'hall
117 S 16   Northcote av Surb
83 Y 12   Northcote av Twick
60 J 20   Northcote av W5
117 X 7   Northcote rd
    New Mald
123 P 14   Northcote rd Croy
32 J 14   Northcote rd E17
62 B 1   Northcote rd NW10
114 H 10   Northcote rd Sidcp
88 K 12   Northcote rd SW11
84 A 12   Northcote rd Twick
83 Z 12   Northcote rd Twick
30 A 4   Northcott av N22
152 A 17   Northcroft rd Epsom
72 B 7   Northcroft rd W13
31 U 19   Northdene gdns N15
36 G 15   Northdown gdns Ilf
97 P 5   Northdown rd
    Welling
57 Y 2   Northdown rd
    Hornch
132 M 10   Northdown st N1
99 S 2   Northend rd Erith
18 F 9   Northern av N9
65 W 5   Northern rd E13
119 T 10   Northernhay wlk
    Mrdn
63 W 20   Northey st E14
72 B 3   Northfield av W13
153 S 9   Northfield cres
    Sutton
56 B 12   Northfield gdns
    Dgnhm
5 W 12   Northfield rd Barnt
56 B 12   Northfield rd Dgnhm
53 V 20   Northfield rd E6
9 P 19   Northfield rd Enf
49 T 1   Northfield rd N16
72 A 5   Northfield rd W13
61 U 14   Northfields rd W3
87 X 11   Northfields SW18
14 K 12   Northiam N12
14 M 12   Northiam N12
63 O 4   Northiam st E8
135 Y 6   Northiam st E9
133 P 19   Northington st WC1
90 L 6   Northlands st SE5
12 K 14   Northolm Edg
25 P 4   Northolme gdns
    Edg
48 K 11   Northolme rd N5
41 W 15   Northolt gdns Grnfd
40 K 12   Northolt rd Harrow
41 O 7   Northolt rd Harrow
112 C 7   Northover Brom
134 H 6   Northport st N1
108 G 4   Northstead rd SW2
18 H 10   Northumberland
    gdns N9
121 Y 11   Northumberland
    gdns Mitch
142 M 7   Northumberland all
    EC3
96 G 9   Northumberland av
    Welling
140 K 13   Northumberland av
    WC2
52 L 4   Northumberland av
    E12
9 N 5   Northumberland av
    Enf
83 V 1   Northumberland av
    Islwth
71 X 20   Northumberland av
    Islwth
98 K 1   Northumberland clo
    Erith
31 Z 2   Northumberland gro
    N17
81 X 19   Northumberland pk
    Erith
31 Y 1   Northumberland pk
    N17
84 G 16   Northumberland pl
    Rich
137 U 5   Northumberland pl
    W2
22 H 16   Northumberland rd
    Harrow
51 N 1   Northumberland rd
    E17

15 P 1   Northumberland rd
    Barnt
66 E 16   Northumberland rd E6
140 J 12   Northumberland st
    WC2
99 N 2   Northumberland way
    Erith
64 B 17   Northumbria st E14
44 C 13   Northview cres
    NW10
12 L 12   Northway cir NW7
12 M 13   Northway cres NW7
119 T 8   Northway Mrdn
28 A 17   Northway NW11
28 B 15   Northway NW11
16 G 19   Northway NW11
123 U 15   Northway rd Croy
90 L 8   Northway rd SE5
155 V 8   Northway Wallgtn
24 A 20   Northwick av Harrow
23 Z 19   Northwick av Harrow
28 D 18   Northwick cir Harrow
130 F 17   Northwick clo NW8
42 B 2   Northwick pk Harrow
23 X 18   Northwick Park rd
    Harrow
60 H 4   Northwick rd Wemb
130 E 17   Northwick ter NW8
41 W 1   Northwick wlk
    Harrow
49 Y 7   Northwold rd E5
49 U 7   Northwold rd N16
57 X 12   Northwood av
    Hornch
15 T 16   Northwood gdns
    N12
41 W 15   Northwood gdns
    Grnfd
35 W 12   Northwood gdns Ilf
81 N 7   Northwood pl Blvdr
122 L 3   Northwood rd
    Thntn Hth
123 N 1   Northwood rd
    Thntn Hth
155 O 14   Northwood rd Carsh
47 T 1   Northwood rd N6
110 K 2   Northwood rd SE23
117 T 16   Norton av Surb
20 B 15   Norton clo E4
8 M 9   Norton clo Enf
134 L 19   Norton folgate E1
122 A 3   Norton gdns SW16
57 N 18   Norton rd Dgnhm
50 M 3   Norton rd E10
42 G 18   Norton rd Wemb
75 W 8   Norway ga SE16
63 X 18   Norway pl E14
76 E 16   Norway st SE10
122 M 7   Norwich rd
    Thntn Hth
69 S 7   Norwich rd Dgnhm
52 E 16   Norwich rd E7
58 L 3   Norwich rd Grnfd
141 T 3   Norwich st EC4
25 W 2   Norwich wlk Edg
57 P 3   Norwood av Rom
60 M 5   Norwood av Wemb
70 F 12   Norwood clo S'hall
22 G 18   Norwood dri Harrow
70 D 10   Norwood gdns S'hall
70 H 12   Norwood Grn rd
    S'hall
108 K 8   Norwood High st
    SE27
108 M 12   Norwood Park rd
    SE27
109 N 12   Norwood Park rd
    SE27
70 G 12   Norwood rd S'hall
108 J 7   Norwood rd SE27
150 E 18   Notley st SE5
123 Z 10   Notson rd SE25
137 T 12   Notting Hill ga W11
65 Y 16   Nottingham av E16
140 K 6   Nottingham ct WC2
131 T 19   Nottingham pl W1
156 L 10   Nottingham rd
    S Croy
156 L 11   Nottingham rd
    S Croy
33 U 18   Nottingham rd E10
83 V 4   Nottingham rd Islwth
106 L 2   Nottingham rd SW17
131 T 20   Nottingham st W1
119 S 18   Nova ms Sutton
122 K 18   Nova rd Croy
114 B 2   Nova rd SE9
87 X 2   Novello st SW6
74 G 17   Nowell rd SW13
22 E 12   Nower hill Pinn

106 M 6   Noyna rd SW17
93 P 8   Nuding clo SE13
48 A 4   Nugent rd N19
123 T 6   Nugent rd SE25
130 C 11   Nugent ter NW8
22 C 4   Nugents pk Pinn
160 E 3   Nun ct EC2
68 K 1   Nuneaton rd Dgnhm
91 Y 8   Nunhead cres SE15
92 A 7   Nunhead grn SE15
92 B 8   Nunhead gro SE15
92 A 8   Nunhead la SE15
113 R 7   Nunnington clo SE9
7 Z 8   Nunns rd Enf
4 A 19   Nupton dri Barnt
15 W 20   Nursery app N12
98 C 7   Nursery av Bxly Hth
158 E 3   Nursery av Croy
28 C 7   Nursery av N3
158 E 4   Nursery clo Croy
9 T 5   Nursery clo Enf
100 E 11   Nursery clo Hampt
37 W 19   Nursery clo Rom
87 O 11   Nursery clo SW15
21 U 16   Nursery clo Wdfd Grn
9 T 6   Nursery gdns Enf
52 G 17   Nursery la E7
136 B 2   Nursery la W10
62 M 14   Nursery la W10
120 J 7   Nursery rd Mitch
120 A 1   Nursery rd Mrdn
16 H 3   Nursery rd N14
28 G 5   Nursery rd N2
154 D 9   Nursery rd Sutton
105 R 19   Nursery rd SW19
90 D 9   Nursery rd SW9
123 O 9   Nursery rd Thntn Hth
150 D 8   Nursery row SE17
31 U 3   Nursery st N17
89 S 7   Nursery st SW8
26 L 10   Nursery wlk NW4
39 N 20   Nursery wlk Rom
81 T 20   Nurstead rd Erith
128 K 12   Nutbourne st W10
91 W 8   Nutbrook st SE15
69 P 3   Nutbrowne rd
    Dgnhm
151 V 18   Nutcroft rd SE16
18 J 19   Nutfield clo N18
54 L 7   Nutfield gdns Ilf
51 U 12   Nutfield rd E15
44 F 9   Nutfield rd NW2
91 V 11   Nutfield rd SE22
122 H 9   Nutfield rd Thntn Hth
139 N 4   Nutford pl W1
79 T 6   Nuthatch gdns SE28
103 D 3   Nuthurst av SW2
46 E 17   Nutley ter NW3
11 U 8   Nutt gro Edg
151 P 18   Nutt st SE15
134 L 7   Nuttall st N1
34 K 16   Nutter la E11
81 R 14   Nuxley rd Blvdr
79 T 18   Nyanza st SE18
85 P 4   Nylands av Rich
118 J 5   Nymans gdns SW20
75 V 18   Nynehead st SE14
110 K 5   Nyon gro SE6
47 Z 4   Nyton clo N19

O

63 P 14   O'Leary sq E1
142 C 15   O'meara st SE1
63 Y 3   O'Shea gro E3
159 P 1   Oak av Croy
7 P 3   Oak av Enf
100 C 14   Oak av Hampt
70 A 20   Oak av Hounsl
29 S 2   Oak av N10
31 P 1   Oak av N17
29 Z 14   Oak av N8
159 V 13   Oak bank Croy
99 S 11   Oak clo Drtfrd
16 D 3   Oak clo N14
154 D 4   Oak clo Sutton
62 C 17   Oak common W3
112 A 2   Oak Cottage clo SE6
65 N 15   Oak cres E16
39 Y 19   Oak Dene clo Rom
60 A 14   Oak dene W13
159 O 1   Oak gdns Croy
25 U 7   Oak gdns Edg
45 R 12   Oak gro NW2

159 V 1 Oak gro W Wkhm
124 C 2 Oak Grove rd SE20
34 H 19 Oak Hall rd E11
33 X 2 Oak Hill clo Wdfd Grn
33 Y 1 Oak Hill cres Wdfd Grn
34 A 3 Oak Hill gdns Wdfd Grn
46 C 12 Oak Hill Park ms NW3
116 K 16 Oak hill Surb
46 B 11 Oak hill way NW3
34 A 2 Oak hill Wdfd Grn
33 X 1 Oak hill Wdfd Grn
33 Z 1 Oak hill Wdfd Grn
63 X 19 Oak la E14
16 L 19 Oak la N11
28 F 7 Oak la N2
28 F 7 Oak la N2
83 U 9 Oak la Twick
83 Z 19 Oak la Twick
21 R 13 Oak la Wdfd Grn
11 S 15 Oak Lodge clo Stanm
125 S 18 Oak Lodge dri W Wkhm
103 O 3 Oak lodge Rich
87 P 20 Oak Park gdns SW19
81 X 20 Oak rd Erith
99 X 3 Oak rd Erith
117 X 3 Oak rd New Mald
121 U 3 Oak row Mitch
38 J 14 Oak st Rom
72 H 1 Oak st W5
24 C 3 Oak Tree clo Stanm
60 E 18 Oak Tree clo W13
25 X 16 Oak Tree dell NW9
15 O 6 Oak Tree dri N20
112 J 11 Oak Tree rd NW8
130 J 14 Oak Tree rd NW8
47 O 13 Oak village NW5
124 G 13 Oak way Croy
16 D 2 Oak way N14
74 A 2 Oak way W3
90 L 10 Oakbank gro SE24
112 H 9 Oakbrook clo SE12
88 A 5 Oakbury rd SW6
104 A 19 Oakcombe clo New Mald
93 W 5 Oakcroft rd SE13
24 K 15 Oakdale av Harrow
125 T 2 Oakdale Becknhm
20 G 15 Oakdale ct E4
16 G 4 Oakdale N14
51 W 7 Oakdale rd E11
34 J 8 Oakdale rd E18
52 J 20 Oakdale rd E7
30 M 18 Oakdale rd N4
31 N 18 Oakdale rd N4
92 D 7 Oakdale rd SE15
108 B 12 Oakdale rd SW16
149 U 6 Oakden st SE11
113 V 11 Oakdene av Chisl
81 X 17 Oakdene av Erith
22 E 1 Oakdene clo Pinn
117 V 19 Oakdene dri Surb
27 W 1 Oakdene pk N3
116 K 17 Oakenshaw clo Surb
66 H 18 Oakes clo E6
47 P 6 Oakeshott av N6
30 F 20 Oakfied rd N4
24 B 10 Oakfield av Harrow
118 D 12 Oakfield clo New Mald
27 P 20 Oakfield ct NW11
20 C 16 Oakfield E4
125 P 13 Oakfield gdns Becknhm
120 K 20 Oakfield gdns Carsh
59 P 10 Oakfield gdns Grnfd
18 C 14 Oakfield gdns N18
109 T 12 Oakfield gdns SE19
122 L 20 Oakfield rd Croy
32 J 7 Oakfield rd E17
66 C 4 Oakfield rd E6
54 A 9 Oakfield rd Ilf
17 N 9 Oakfield rd N14
28 A 5 Oakfield rd N3
48 G 1 Oakfield rd N4
110 B 17 Oakfield SE20
105 R 6 Oakfield rd SW19
146 A 13 Oakfield rd SW10
27 T 17 Oakfields rd NW11
47 U 12 Oakfield rd NW5
34 J 18 Oakhall ct E11
126 D 10 Oakham dri Brom
27 P 3 Oakhampton rd NW7
46 A 12 Oakhill av NW3
22 A 7 Oakhill av Pinn
116 K 16 Oakhill cres Surb

116 L 17 Oakhill dri Surb
16 B 1 Oakhill gro Surb
116 J 15 Oakhill gro Surb
15 Z 2 Oakhill pk Barnt
87 X 12 Oakhill pl SW15
116 J 15 Oakhill pth Surb
125 T 4 Oakhill rd Bcknhm
116 K 16 Oakhill rd Surb
154 B 6 Oakhill rd Sutton
87 X 12 Oakhill rd SW15
122 B 2 Oakhill rd SW19
98 E 12 Oakhouse rd Bxly Hth
15 V 2 Oakhurst av Barnt
80 L 20 Oakhurst av Bxly Hth
33 Z 12 Oakhurst clo E17
21 P 5 Oakhurst clo E4
80 M 20 Oakhurst gdns Bxly Hth
33 Z 13 Oakhurst gdns E17
21 P 5 Oakhurst gdns E4
91 X 10 Oakhurst gro SE22
40 G 2 Oakington av Harrow
42 M 9 Oakington av Wemb
43 O 9 Oakington av Wemb
43 P 15 Oakington Manor dri Wemb
129 U 17 Oakington rd W9
30 A 20 Oakington way N8
152 A 13 Oakland way Epsom
122 F 8 Oaklands av Thntn Hth
159 T 5 Oaklands av W Wkhm
98 C 13 Oaklands clo Bxly Hth
9 N 20 Oaklands av Enf
71 W 16 Oaklands av Islwth
39 S 12 Oaklands av Rom
96 K 18 Oaklands av Sidcp
42 F 16 Oaklands ct Wemb
74 H 3 Oaklands gro W12
17 P 8 Oaklands N21
54 C 7 Oaklands Park av Ilf
112 B 17 Oaklands rd Brom
98 B 12 Oaklands rd Bxly Hth
14 G 2 Oaklands rd N20
45 O 13 Oaklands rd NW2
85 X 8 Oaklands rd SW14
71 W 5 Oaklands rd W7
82 M 19 Oaklands Twick
155 W 16 Oaklands way SM6
116 H 6 Oaklea pas Kingst
35 Y 10 Oakleafe gdns Ilf
25 T 5 Oakleigh av Edg
15 V 7 Oakleigh av N20
16 A 11 Oakleigh clo N20
15 X 10 Oakleigh cres N20
25 V 8 Oakleigh ct Edg
12 A 15 Oakleigh gdns Edg
15 S 5 Oakleigh gdns N20
127 X 2 Oakleigh Park av Chisl
15 U 5 Oakleigh Park north N20
15 V 4 Oakleigh Park south N20
15 V 2 Oakleigh pk Barnt
16 A 11 Oakleigh Road north N20
15 U 7 Oakleigh Road north N20
16 C 13 Oakleigh Road south N11
121 S 1 Oakleigh way Mitch
54 L 20 Oakley av Bark
156 B 8 Oakley av Croy
61 P 19 Oakley av W5
66 E 17 Oakley clo E6
83 R 2 Oakley clo Islwth
59 S 19 Oakley clo W7
133 X 10 Oakley cres N1
114 E 3 Oakley dri Sidcp
30 C 15 Oakley gdns N8
146 L 13 Oakley gdns SW3
127 O 18 Oakley ho Brom
97 S 19 Oakley pk Sidcp
151 N 11 Oakley pl SE1
127 P 20 Oakley rd Brom
23 S 17 Oakley rd Harrow
49 O 20 Oakley rd N1
124 A 11 Oakley rd SE25
123 Z 12 Oakley rd SE25
132 C 8 Oakley sq NW1
146 K 14 Oakley st SW3
144 J 14 Oakley wk W6
126 F 15 Oakmead av Brom
12 K 13 Oakmead gdns Edg
121 X 14 Oakmead rd Mitch
107 R 2 Oakmead rd SW12
80 A 16 Oakmere rd SE2

111 X 11 Oakridge rd Brom
100 A 4 Oaks av Felt
38 L 8 Oaks av Rom
109 R 11 Oaks av SE19
152 L 8 Oaks av Worc Pk
20 M 8 Oaks gro E4
158 D 4 Oaks la Croy
36 G 14 Oaks la Ilf
158 C 8 Oaks rd Croy
157 Z 10 Oaks rd Croy
15 P 14 Oaks the N12
79 O 15 Oaks the SE18
154 M 17 Oaks way Carsh
155 N 17 Oaks way Carsh
109 Z 8 Oaksford av SE26
111 Y 9 Oakshade rd Brom
88 B 19 Oakshaw rd SW18
17 S 15 Oakthorpe rd N13
17 U 10 Oaktree av N13
124 K 19 Oakview gro Croy
111 R 12 Oakview rd SE6
125 W 4 Oakway Brom
97 Z 16 Oakway clo Bxly
118 M 9 Oakway SW20
119 N 9 Oakway SW20
95 Y 15 Oakways SE9
125 U 3 Oakwood av Becknhm
126 H 7 Oakwood av Brom
120 G 3 Oakwood av Mitch
70 H 1 Oakwood av S'hall
58 H 20 Oakwood av S'hall
113 V 16 Oakwood clo Chisl
6 J 20 Oakwood clo N14
42 A 18 Oakwood cres Grnfd
41 Z 17 Oakwood cres Grnfd
7 O 18 Oakwood cres N21
145 O 1 Oakwood ct W14
98 L 9 Oakwood dri Bxly Hth
12 G 18 Oakwood dri Edg
109 P 15 Oakwood dri SE19
54 K 7 Oakwood gdns Ilf
137 O 20 Oakwood la W14
16 M 1 Oakwood Park rd N14
17 N 1 Oakwood Park rd N14
122 F 15 Oakwood pl Croy
122 F 15 Oakwood rd Croy
28 A 15 Oakwood rd NW11
27 Z 14 Oakwood rd NW11
104 H 20 Oakwood rd SW20
16 L 1 Oakwood view N14
155 T 19 Oakwood Wallgtn
136 E 1 Oakworth rd W10
160 B 3 Oat la EC2
125 X 5 Oates clo BR2
32 H 9 Oatland ri E17
9 P 7 Oatlands rd Enf
65 Z 10 Oban rd E13
123 O 8 Oban rd SE25
64 K 16 Oban st E13
88 G 10 Oberstein rd SW11
90 K 14 Oborne clo SE24
137 U 17 Observatory gdns W8
85 V 11 Observatory rd SW14
95 Z 1 Occupation la SE18
72 G 11 Occupation la W5
150 A 9 Occupation rd SE17
72 A 10 Occupation rd W13
72 B 4 Occupation rd W13
63 U 14 Ocean st E1
49 O 19 Ockendon rd N1
115 O 18 Ockham dri Orp
122 C 17 Ockley rd Croy
107 Z 8 Ockley rd SW16
120 H 11 Octavia clo Mrdn
83 V 6 Octavia rd Islwth
76 A 19 Octavia st SE8
88 J 3 Octavia st SW11
80 E 1 Octavia way SE28
52 E 14 Odessa rd E7
62 H 7 Odessa rd NW10
75 X 7 Odessa st SE16
88 M 5 Odger st SW11
50 K 13 Offa's mead E9
113 U 9 Offenham rd SE9
89 V 8 Offerton rd SW4
14 H 16 Offham slope N12
149 S 18 Offley rd SW9
48 D 20 Offord rd N1
78 F 12 Ogilby st SE18
91 V 8 Oglander rd SE15
140 A 1 Ogle st W1
56 D 9 Oglethorpe rd Dgnhm
65 P 13 Ohio rd E13
44 C 20 Oldfield clo NW10

107 O 11 Okeburn rd SW17
15 T 15 Okehampton clo N12
80 H 20 Okehampton cres Welling
97 S 1 Okehampton cres Welling
128 E 6 Okehampton rd NW10
136 G 11 Olaf st W11
141 X 5 Old bailey EC4
153 S 16 Old Barn clo Sutton
98 L 9 Old Barn way Bxly Hth
139 T 18 Old Barrack yd SW1
65 N 4 Old Barrowfield E15
135 T 12 Old Bethnal Green rd E2
141 R 4 Old bldgs WC2
140 A 12 Old Bond st W1
46 F 13 Old Brewery ms NW3
58 H 4 Old Bridge clo Nthlt
116 F 2 Old Bridge st Hamp
142 H 3 Old Broad st EC2
160 H 3 Old Broad st EC2
111 X 12 Old Bromley rd Brom
146 B 9 Old Brompton rd SW5
140 A 10 Old Burlington st W1
143 O 4 Old Castle st E1
139 X 5 Old Cavendish st W1
160 A 7 Old Change ct EC4
43 X 7 Old Church la NW9
24 E 1 Old Church la Stanm
11 P 19 Old Church la Stanm
11 T 20 Old Church la Stanm
63 T 17 Old Church rd E1
20 B 11 Old Church rd E4
146 J 15 Old Church st SW3
140 E 8 Old Compton st W1
70 G 17 Old Cote dri Hounsl
137 X 17 Old Court pl W8
84 K 8 Old Deer Park gdns Rich
84 F 7 Old Deer pk Rich
89 S 20 Old Devonshire rd SW12
73 P 17 Old Dock clo Rich
77 U 19 Old Dover rd SE3
16 H 2 Old Farm av N14
114 E 2 Old Farm av Sidcup
82 E 9 Old Farm clo Hounsl
100 G 15 Old Farm rd Hampt
28 G 4 Old Farm rd N2
114 L 3 Old Farm Rd west Sidcp
114 M 3 Old Farm Road east Sidcp
4 G 7 Old Fold clo Barnt
4 G 7 Old Fold la Barnt
4 A 12 Old Fold view Barnt
135 Z 11 Old Ford rd E2
63 U 5 Old Ford rd E3
10 M 13 Old Forge clo Stanm
8 G 4 Old Forge rd Enf
10 M 14 Old Forge Stanm
115 R 11 Old Forge way Sidcp
132 L 20 Old Gloucester st WC1
140 M 1 Old Gloucester st WC1
22 B 5 Old Hall clo Pinn
22 B 5 Old Hall dri Pinn
113 Y 20 Old hill Chisl
105 S 12 Old House clo SW19
151 R 1 Old Jamaica rd SE16
91 Z 8 Old James st SE15
142 D 6 Old Jewry EC2
160 D 6 Old Jewry EC2
150 K 7 Old Kent rd SE1
75 O 18 Old Kent rd SE15
151 X 16 Old Kent rd SE15
25 T 16 Old Kenton la NW9
10 M 16 Old Lodge way Stanm
83 O 15 Old Manor dri Islwth
98 M 7 Old Manor way Bxly Hth
145 W 8 Old Manor yd SW5
138 L 2 Old Marylebone rd NW1
34 K 9 Old Mill ct E18
79 S 16 Old Mill rd SE18
141 T 7 Old Mitre ct EC4
143 R 2 Old Montague st E1
135 U 20 Old Montague st E1
23 S 17 Old ms Harrow
134 M 15 Old Nichol st E2
135 N 15 Old Nichol st E2
141 N 1 Old North st WC1

62 C 11	Old Oak Comm la NW10
62 C 18	Old Oak Comm la W3
62 C 9	Old Oak la NW10
62 D 20	Old Oak rd W3
74 E 3	Old Oak rd W3
46 L 12	Old Orchard the NW3
84 E 12	Old Palace la Rich
156 K 4	Old Palace rd Croy
84 F 12	Old Palace yd Rich
149 O 5	Old Paradise st SE11
7 Z 12	Old Park av Enf
89 P 16	Old Park av SW12
7 Y 15	Old Park gro Enf
139 W 16	Old Park la W1
70 F 20	Old Park ms Hounsl
7 W 12	Old Park rd Enf
17 R 12	Old Park rd N13
80 A 14	Old Park rd SE2
7 X 18	Old Park ridings N21
7 V 14	Old Park Road south Enf
7 U 11	Old Park view Enf
114 G 17	Old Perry st Chisl
148 F 1	Old Pye st SW1
139 R 7	Old Quebec st W1
140 G 19	Old Queen st SW1
98 M 12	Old rd Drtfrd
9 P 6	Old rd Enf
93 Z 11	Old rd SE13
12 C 18	Old Rectory gdns Edg
10 C 14	Old Redding Harrow
152 C 19	Old Schools la Epsom
141 W 5	Old Seacoal la EC4
148 L 18	Old South Lambeth rd SW8
141 R 4	Old sq WC2
65 W 7	Old st E13
134 J 14	Old st EC1
127 W 1	Old Station hill Chisl
154 L 9	Old Swan yd Carsh
156 K 5	Old Town Croy
89 U 9	Old Town SW4
76 K 15	Old Woolwich rd SE10
88 B 12	Old York rd SW18
12 M 19	Oldberry rd Edg
42 D 9	Oldborough rd Wemb
131 T 19	Oldbury pl W1
8 L 9	Oldbury rd Enf
57 P 1	Oldchurch pk Rom
39 O 20	Oldchurch rd Rom
39 P 20	Oldchurch ri Rom
127 V 9	Oldfield clo Brom
41 T 17	Oldfield clo Grnfd
10 L 15	Oldfield clo Stanm
59 P 4	Oldfield Farm gdns Grnfd
75 T 11	Oldfield gro SE16
59 P 5	Oldfield la Grnfd
41 R 19	Oldfield Lane north Grnfd
47 V 2	Oldfield ms N6
127 U 8	Oldfield rd Brom
98 A 5	Oldfield rd Bxly Hth
97 Z 5	Oldfield rd Bxly Hth
49 S 9	Oldfield rd N16
88 A 11	Oldfield rd SW18
105 S 14	Oldfield rd SW19
74 D 5	Oldfield rd W12
41 O 17	Oldfields cir Grnfd
153 X 3	Oldfields rd Sutton
73 V 4	Oldhams ter W3
49 X 3	Oldhill st N16
89 R 18	Oldridge rd SW12
111 W 10	Oldstead rd Brom
63 S 15	Oley pl E1
63 W 7	Olga st E3
76 H 9	Oliffe st E14
31 U 19	Olinda rd N16
128 K 11	Oliphant st W10
65 Z 9	Olive rd E13
44 L 12	Olive rd NW2
45 N 12	Olive rd NW2
106 D 18	Olive rd SW19
72 G 9	Olive rd W5
39 N 15	Olive st Rom
123 U 7	Oliver av SE25
51 P 7	Oliver clo E10
66 E 16	Oliver gdns E6
123 V 8	Oliver gro SE25
51 P 7	Oliver rd E10
33 V 14	Oliver rd E17
117 W 3	Oliver rd New Mald
154 E 9	Oliver rd Sutton
73 R 16	Olivers clo W4
134 F 17	Olivers yd EC2
87 P 9	Olivette st SW15
63 Z 2	Ollerton grn E3
16 K 17	Ollerton rd N11
74 F 3	Ollgar clo W12
151 R 13	Olmar st SE1
150 A 14	Olney rd SE17
149 Z 14	Olney rd SE17
97 X 14	Olron cres Bxly Hth
79 P 18	Olven rd SE18
120 G 14	Olveston wlk Carsh
97 O 3	Olyffe av Welling
111 T 20	Olyffe dri Becknhm
144 M 3	Olympia rd W14
144 L 4	Olympia W14
137 Z 9	Olympia yd W2
58 M 4	Olympic way Grnfd
43 P 10	Olympic way Wemb
44 K 13	Oman av NW2
132 M 10	Omega pl N1
92 G 3	Ommaney rd SE14
91 V 9	Ondine rd SE15
92 D 17	One Tree clo SE23
75 V 8	Onega ga SE16
37 T 14	Ongar clo Rom
145 T 13	Ongar rd SW6
33 O 20	Onra rd E7
84 K 14	Onslow av Rich
20 H 9	Onslow av Rich
127 Z 1	Onslow cres BR7
115 V 5	Onslow dri Sidcp
34 J 10	Onslow gdns E18
29 S 15	Onslow gdns N10
7 U 17	Onslow gdns N21
146 E 8	Onslow gdns SW7
155 U 16	Onslow gdns Wllgtn
146 F 7	Onslow Mews east SW7
146 E 8	Onslow Mews west SW7
122 F 19	Onslow rd Croy
118 F 8	Onslow rd New Mald
84 K 14	Onslow rd Rich
146 G 6	Onslow sq SW7
133 U 19	Onslow st EC1
149 Y 2	Ontario st SE1
66 B 18	Opal clo E16
53 Z 8	Opal ms Ilf
149 V 9	Upal st SE11
80 C 12	Openshaw rd SE2
106 E 2	Openview SW18
91 W 3	Ophir ter SE15
131 O 2	Oppidans ms NW3
131 O 1	Oppidans rd NW3
143 U 14	Orange ct E1
25 V 1	Orange Hill rd Edg
75 P 9	Orange pl SE16
140 F 11	Orange st WC2
140 G 6	Orange yd W1
95 U 14	Orangery la SE9
150 E 8	Orb st SE17
144 M 19	Orbain rd SW6
88 H 3	Orbel st SW11
118 C 5	Orchard av New Mald
80 M 16	Orchard av Blvdr
81 N 16	Orchard av Blvdr
158 H 1	Orchard av Croy
124 J 18	Orchard av Croy
124 J 20	Orchard av Croy
99 Y 20	Orchard av Drtfrd
70 C 20	Orchard av Hounsl
121 O 19	Orchard av Mitch
16 H 1	Orchard av N14
15 U 8	Orchard av N20
27 X 10	Orchard av N20
70 D 2	Orchard av S'hall
10 C 5	Orchard clo Bxly Hth
97 Y 2	Orchard clo Bxly Hth
11 Y 18	Orchard clo Edg
41 N 17	Orchard clo Nthlt
44 F 10	Orchard clo NW2
92 C 17	Orchard clo SE23
116 B 19	Orchard clo Surb
118 L 8	Orchard clo SW20
60 K 2	Orchard clo Wemb
12 H 17	Orchard cres Edg
8 G 6	Orchard cres Enf
152 E 1	Orchard ct Worc Pk
11 Z 15	Orchard dri Edg
93 Y 4	Orchard dri SE3
93 S 4	Orchard est SE13
42 C 18	Orchard ga Grnfd
26 A 12	Orchard ga NW9
153 X 10	Orchard gdns Sutton
124 J 17	Orchard gro Croy
25 R 5	Orchard gro Edg
25 N 15	Orchard gro Harrow
155 N 10	Orchard hill Carsh
99 O 12	Orchard hill Drtfrd
93 S 3	Orchard hill SE13
104 K 20	Orchard la SW20
21 X 13	Orchard la Wdfd Grn
109 X 20	Orchard lodge SE20
134 G 2	Orchard ms N1
64 M 19	Orchard pl E14
31 U 3	Orchard pl N17
4 G 14	Orchard rd Barnt
81 R 12	Orchard rd Blvdr
72 E 16	Orchard rd Brentf
112 M 20	Orchard rd Brom
69 T 3	Orchard rd Dgnhm
9 R 18	Orchard rd Enf
100 F 17	Orchard rd Hampt
82 F 12	Orchard rd Hounsl
116 J 5	Orchard rd Kingst
121 O 19	Orchard rd Mitch
29 T 20	Orchard rd N6
85 P 9	Orchard rd Rich
38 G 6	Orchard rd Rom
93 Y 4	Orchard rd SE3
114 J 9	Orchard rd Sidcp
93 Y 10	Orchard rd Sutton
84 A 14	Orchard rd Twick
83 Z 14	Orchard rd Twick
97 R 6	Orchard rd Welling
124 K 19	Orchard ri Croy
103 V 20	Orchard ri Kingst
85 S 11	Orchard ri Rich
96 J 13	Orchard Rise east Sidcp
96 G 13	Orchard Rise west Sidcp
32 H 12	Orchard st E17
139 T 6	Orchard st W1
8 A 19	Orchard the Enf
83 O 5	Orchard the Hounsl
152 D 16	Orchard the KT17
27 X 16	Orchard the NW11
93 X 4	Orchard the SE3
73 Z 10	Orchard the W4
124 J 16	Orchard way Croy
8 D 11	Orchard way Enf
154 G 8	Orchard way Sutton
9 O 9	Orchardleigh av Enf
8 B 19	Orchardmede Enf
130 F 18	Orchardson st NW8
66 D 14	Orchid clo E6
10 G 3	Orchid rd N14
62 G 20	Orchid st W12
133 N 19	Orde Hall st WC1
63 Z 7	Ordell rd E3
76 M 5	Ordnance cres SE10
130 G 6	Ordnance hill NW8
130 H 8	Ordnance ms NW8
65 O 14	Ordnance rd E16
78 J 18	Ordnance rd SE18
53 S 11	Oregon av E12
101 V 5	Orford gdns Twick
34 G 10	Orford rd E17
33 P 16	Orford rd E17
20 G 9	Organ la E4
121 X 7	Oriel clo Mitch
35 T 11	Oriel gdns Ilf
46 E 13	Oriel pl NW3
50 G 17	Oriel rd E9
40 K 19	Oriel way Nthlt
149 W 4	Orient st SE11
50 F 9	Orient way E5
78 A 3	Oriental rd E16
80 D 1	Oriole way SE28
68 D 20	Oriole way SE28
72 C 9	Orion pk W13
79 U 13	Orissa rd SE18
89 N 3	Orkney rd SW11
89 U 9	Orkney rd SW4
109 P 17	Orleans rd SE19
84 C 19	Orleans rd Twick
48 G 18	Orleston ms N7
48 G 18	Orleston rd N7
41 S 11	Orley Farm rd Harrow
76 L 14	Orlop st SE10
109 Y 11	Ormanton rd SE26
137 Y 10	Orme Court ms W2
137 Y 9	Orme ct W2
137 X 10	Orme la W2
117 T 3	Orme rd Kingst
137 X 10	Orme sq W2
102 J 7	Ormeley lodge Rich
89 S 20	Ormeley rd SW12
121 P 2	Ormerod gdns Mitch
59 N 7	Ormesby gdns Grnfd
24 M 17	Ormesby way Harrow
74 H 3	Ormiston gro W12
77 S 14	Ormiston rd SE10
100 K 20	Ormond av Hampt
132 M 20	Ormond clo WC1
100 K 20	Ormond cres Hampt
100 L 19	Ormond cres Hampt
100 L 18	Ormond dri Hampt
132 M 18	Ormond ms WC1
48 A 4	Ormond rd N19
84 H 14	Ormond rd Rich
140 C 12	Ormond yd SW1
147 O 11	Ormonde ga SW3
85 U 9	Ormonde rd SW14
21 Y 5	Ormonde rise Buck Hl
131 O 6	Ormonde ter NW8
N 8	Ormsby st E2
46 H 15	Ornan rd NW3
49 S 11	Orpen wlk N16
91 N 3	Orpheus st SE5
18 D 12	Orpington gdns N18
17 V 6	Orpington rd N21
100 D 14	Orpwood clo Hampt
138 A 4	Orsett ms W2
137 Z 4	Orsett ms W2
149 P 9	Orsett st SE11
138 A 4	Orsett ter W2
137 Z 4	Orsett ter W2
34 K 3	Orsett ter Wdfd Grn
134 L 5	Orsman rd N1
143 T 14	Orton st E1
88 G 4	Orville rd SW11
65 X 5	Orwell rd E13
49 W 5	Osbaldeston rd N16
148 E 7	Osbert st SW1
94 E 13	Osberton rd SE12
135 S 5	Osborn clo E8
92 J 20	Osborn la SE23
143 P 3	Osborn st E1
94 C 11	Osborn ter SE3
124 J 9	Osborne clo Becknhm
39 Z 19	Osborne clo Hornch
154 F 12	Osborne clo Sutton
60 K 14	Osborne ct W5
27 O 2	Osborne gdns NW7
122 L 3	Osborne gdns Thntn Hth
32 L 14	Osborne gro E17
81 O 15	Osborne rd Blvdr
21 V 6	Osborne rd Buck Hl
56 C 14	Osborne rd Dgnhm
51 S 8	Osborne rd E10
52 G 15	Osborne rd E7
50 M 17	Osborne rd E9
9 V 9	Osborne rd Enf
39 Y 18	Osborne rd Hornch
82 E 9	Osborne rd Hounsl
102 K 17	Osborne rd Kingst
17 U 11	Osborne rd N13
48 E 4	Osborne rd N4
44 K 17	Osborne rd NW2
58 M 17	Osborne rd S'hall
122 L 3	Osborne rd Thntn Hth
73 S 7	Osborne rd W3
56 B 13	Osborne sq Dgnhm
93 N 3	Oscar st SE8
47 W 17	Oseney cres NW5
16 E 4	Osidge la N14
63 R 12	Osier st E1
51 P 8	Osier way E10
120 K 11	Osier way Mitch
87 Y 11	Osiers rd SW18
111 S 12	Oslac rd SE6
31 P 18	Osman clo N15
18 K 12	Osman rd N9
41 O 7	Osmond clo Harrow
155 V 10	Osmond gdns Wllgtn
62 E 16	Osmund st W12
131 Z 16	Osnaburgh st NW1
131 Z 17	Osnaburgh ter NW1
120 G 14	Osney wlk Carsh
66 C 15	Osprey clo E6
96 F 17	Ospringe ct SE9
47 U 13	Ospringe rd NW5
134 J 9	Osric pth N1
48 C 1	Ossian rd N4
139 T 1	Ossington bldgs W1
137 W 11	Ossington st W2
151 R 12	Ossory rd SE1
132 F 11	Ossulston st NW1
28 D 11	Ossulton way N2
90 D 18	Ostade rd SW2
145 Z 3	Osten ms SW7
71 P 19	Osterley av Islwth
83 U 1	Osterley cres Islwth
122 L 2	Osterley gdns Thntn Hth
70 K 13	Osterley la S'hall
71 O 15	Osterley Park ho Islwth
70 D 7	Osterley Park rd S'hall
71 U 6	Osterley Park View rd W7
70 M 10	Osterley pk S'hall

85 Z 11 Park av SW14
159 U 3 Park av W Wkhm
21 V 16 Park av Wdfd Grn
60 L 7 Park av Wemb
152 F 15 Park Av west Epsom
32 A 2 Park Avenue rd N17
39 T 6 Park blvd Rom
42 M 12 Park chase Wemb
43 N 11 Park chase Wemb
155 N 13 Park clo Carsh
23 T 3 Park clo Harrow
83 N 13 Park clo Hounsl
61 N 7 Park clo NW10
44 H 10 Park clo NW2
8 B 16 Park cres Enf
81 Y 17 Park cres Erith
23 T 4 Park cres Harrow
39 V 20 Park cres Hornch
131 Y 18 Park Cres Mews east W1
131 W 19 Park Cres Mews west W1
28 C 3 Park cres N3
83 R 20 Park cres Twick
131 X 18 Park cres W1
25 W 4 Park croft Edg
116 D 1 Park ct Kingst
117 Z 9 Park ct New Mald
42 L 14 Park ct Wemb
56 L 10 Park dri Dgnhm
10 D 20 Park dri Harrow
22 F 20 Park dri Harrow
17 Y 1 Park dri N21
7 Y 20 Park dri N21
45 Z 5 Park dri NW11
39 P 12 Park dri SE7
78 D 15 Park dri SE7
85 Z 11 Park dri SW14
73 P 8 Park dri W3
78 D 15 Park Drive clo SE7
112 C 20 Park end Brom
46 K 12 Park end NW3
39 R 13 Park End rd Rom
28 D 11 Park Farm clo N2
127 O 1 Park Farm rd Brom
102 L 17 Park Farm rd Kingst
28 G 10 Park ga N2
17 O 3 Park ga N21
60 F 14 Park ga W5
103 T 14 Park Gate clo Kingst
81 Y 11 Park gdns Erith
103 O 14 Park gdns Kingst
25 U 11 Park gdns NW9
126 H 1 Park gro Brom
98 J 11 Park gro Bxly Hth
65 S 3 Park gro E15
12 A 16 Park gro Edg
29 Y 2 Park gro N11
51 Z 7 Park Grove rd E11
28 K 12 Park Hall rd N2
109 N 6 Park Hall rd SE21
127 T 9 Park hill Brom
154 L 13 Park hill Carsh
154 K 12 Park Hill clo Carsh
125 Y 3 Park Hill rd Brom
157 R 8 Park Hill rd Croy
114 G 6 Park Hill rd Sidcp
155 S 16 Park Hill rd Wallgtn
157 T 4 Park Hill ri Croy
84 M 16 Park hill Rich
110 B 3 Park hill SE23
89 Y 12 Park hill SW4
60 H 15 Park hill Twick
84 D 14 Park House gdns Twick
155 P 9 Park la Carsh
64 H 2 Park la E15
40 J 9 Park la Harrow
39 U 19 Park la Hornch
57 V 2 Park la Hornch
57 Y 17 Park la Hornch
32 A 3 Park la N17
31 W 3 Park la N17
18 H 12 Park la N9
84 G 11 Park la Rich
37 V 19 Park la Rom
153 R 14 Park la Sutton
101 W 15 Park la Tedd
42 L 14 Park la Wemb
31 X 3 Park Lane clo N17
42 L 13 Park lawns Wemb
40 K 10 Park mead Harrow
97 T 15 Park mead Sidcp
62 E 5 Park pde NW10
100 M 15 Park pl Hampt
140 B 14 Park pl SW1
73 R 9 Park pl W3
72 H 3 Park pl W5
42 M 13 Park pl Wemb
43 N 13 Park pl Wemb
130 D 20 Park Place vlls W2

4 H 13 Park rd Barnt
5 X 15 Park rd Barnt
110 M 17 Park rd Becknhm
111 O 19 Park rd Becknhm
126 G 2 Park rd Brom
114 A 14 Park rd Chisl
51 O 4 Park rd E10
52 J 5 Park rd E12
65 R 3 Park rd E15
32 L 16 Park rd E17
65 Y 3 Park rd E6
103 N 12 Park Rd east Kingst
73 U 5 Park Rd east W3
100 L 11 Park rd Hampt
82 L 13 Park rd Hounsl
83 N 13 Park rd Hounsl
54 D 9 Park rd Ilf
84 A 4 Park rd Islwth
116 D 1 Park rd Kingst
103 O 15 Park rd Kingst
29 Z 2 Park rd N11
16 K 4 Park rd N14
30 J 14 Park rd N15
18 J 13 Park rd N18
28 H 10 Park rd N2
28 H 11 Park rd N2
29 X 15 Park rd N8
117 Z 10 Park rd New Mald
73 U 6 Park Rd north W3
131 O 17 Park rd NW1
62 A 3 Park rd NW10
26 K 20 Park rd NW4
130 L 13 Park rd NW8
43 Y 1 Park rd NW9
84 M 15 Park rd Rich
123 T 9 Park rd SE25
117 N 13 Park rd Surb
153 S 13 Park rd Sutton
106 H 15 Park rd SW19
90 B 18 Park rd SW2
101 W 15 Park rd Tedd
84 E 14 Park rd Twick
73 Y 16 Park rd W4
59 X 19 Park rd W7
155 R 3 Park rd Wallgtn
155 T 10 Park rd Wallgtn
42 K 18 Park rd Wemb
103 N 12 Park Rd west Kingst
23 T 5 Park ri Harrow
92 J 20 Park ri SE23
30 E 10 Park ridings N8
110 J 1 Park Rise rd SE23
76 J 15 Park row SE10
61 S 8 Park royal NW10
61 W 11 Park Royal rd NW10
131 X 17 Park Square east NW1
131 W 17 Park Square ms NW1
131 W 17 Park Square west NW1
156 M 4 Park st Croy
157 N 4 Park st Croy
142 B 12 Park st SE1
101 U 14 Park st Tedd
139 S 7 Park st W1
139 T 11 Park st W1
9 V 4 Park ter Enf
152 F 1 Park ter Worc Pk
155 N 12 Park the Carsh
29 P 20 Park the N6
46 A 4 Park the NW11
109 T 18 Park the SE19
110 B 3 Park the SE23
114 M 11 Park the Sidcp
72 G 4 Park the W5
16 E 14 Park View cres N11
67 U 7 Park View gdns Bark
35 T 13 Park View gdns Ilf
30 G 4 Park View gdns N22
27 O 17 Park View gdns NW4
17 P 2 Park view N21
118 E 7 Park view New Mald
22 F 3 Park view Pinn
31 X 10 Park View rd N17
28 B 4 Park View rd N3
44 E 12 Park View rd NW10
70 G 1 Park View rd S'hall
60 K 15 Park View rd W5
97 U 8 Park View rd Welling
61 W 14 Park view W3
43 U 14 Park view Wemb
131 Y 9 Park Village east NW1
131 X 8 Park Village west NW1
76 L 17 Park vista SE10
37 W 19 Park vlls Rom
77 T 19 Park vlls SE3
25 T 6 Park way Edg
7 S 10 Park way Enf
15 Y 14 Park way N20
27 T 16 Park way NW11

21 Z 16 Park way Wdfd Grn
138 L 5 Park West pl W2
29 P 20 Park wlk N6
146 D 13 Park wlk SW10
16 A 12 Park wood N20
98 B 20 Park Wood rd Bxly
94 B 18 Parkcroft rd SE12
79 U 14 Parkdale rd SE18
74 E 20 Parke rd SW13
86 F 1 Parke rd SW13
156 M 8 Parker rd Croy
78 C 3 Parker st E16
140 M 4 Parker st WC2
143 R 19 Parkers row SE1
22 M 7 Parkfield av Harrow
23 N 8 Parkfield av Harrow
58 B 6 Parkfield av Nthlt
86 A 10 Parkfield av SW14
12 E 20 Parkfield clo Edg
58 C 5 Parkfield clo Nthlt
22 M 8 Parkfield cres Harrow
40 B 8 Parkfield cres Ruis
58 A 7 Parkfield dri Nthlt
22 L 10 Parkfield gdns Harrow
41 N 9 Parkfield rd Harrow
58 B 5 Parkfield rd Nthlt
44 H 20 Parkfield rd NW10
92 K 1 Parkfield rd SE14
133 U 8 Parkfield st N1
127 V 13 Parkfield way Brom
44 A 3 Parkfields av NW9
43 Z 3 Parkfields av NW9
118 J 1 Parkfields av SW20
124 L 20 Parkfields Croy
103 N 13 Parkfields rd Kingst
86 M 11 Parkfields SW15
5 P 5 Parkgate av Barnt
5 P 7 Parkgate cres Barnt
85 X 14 Parkgate gdns SW14
102 M 8 Parkgate ho Rich
146 K 20 Parkgate rd SW11
155 S 11 Parkgate rd Wallgtn
94 D 9 Parkgate SE3
106 M 6 Parkhall rd SE27
88 H 2 Parkham st SW11
98 B 19 Parkhill rd Bxly
98 D 19 Parkhill rd Bxly
20 H 4 Parkhill rd E4
46 M 17 Parkhill rd NW3
46 M 16 Parkhill wlk NW3
49 V 18 Parkholme rd E8
150 G 17 Parkhouse st SE5
98 D 19 Parkhurst gdns Bxly
98 E 18 Parkhurst rd Bxly
53 W 14 Parkhurst rd E12
16 C 15 Parkhurst rd N11
32 J 14 Parkhurst rd N17
31 W 7 Parkhurst rd N17
30 D 1 Parkhurst rd N22
17 R 20 Parkhurst rd N22
48 A 12 Parkhurst rd N7
154 F 7 Parkhurst rd Sutton
39 S 9 Parkland av Rom
105 P 1 Parkland gdns SW19
34 G 2 Parkland rd Wdfd Grn
30 D 7 Parkland rd N22
29 X 20 Parkland wlk N6
27 S 11 Parklands rd N3
107 T 12 Parklands rd SW16
116 M 13 Parklands Surb
152 B 4 Parklands way Worc Pk
26 B 4 Parklea clo NW9
120 A 2 Parkleigh rd SW19
102 G 10 Parkleys Rich
13 R 18 Parkmead gdns NW7
86 J 16 Parkmead SW15
21 S 15 Parkmore clo Wdfd Grn
8 A 2 Parknook gdns Enf
84 H 10 Parkshot Rich
127 R 9 Parkside av Brom
99 S 6 Parkside av Bxly Hth
20 M 6 Parkside av Rom
105 O 11 Parkside av SW19
21 V 7 Parkside Buck Hl
117 V 15 Parkside cres Surb
99 O 5 Parkside cross Bxly Hth
12 B 12 Parkside dri Edg
16 A 4 Parkside gdns Barnt
105 O 10 Parkside gdns SW19
101 O 13 Parkside Hampt
6 G 2 Parkside ho Barnt
28 A 3 Parkside N3
44 H 11 Parkside NW2
26 E 1 Parkside NW7

13 T 19 Parkside NW7
81 W 10 Parkside rd Blvdr
82 J 12 Parkside rd Housnl
115 R 6 Parkside Sidcp
89 N 2 Parkside st SW11
153 S 14 Parkside Sutton
105 N 9 Parkside SW19
18 A 13 Parkside ter N13
22 M 13 Parkside way Harrow
23 N 12 Parkside way Harrow
86 H 13 Parkstead rd SW15
18 F 18 Parkstone av N18
33 U 10 Parkstone rd E17
91 Y 5 Parkstone rd SE15
22 K 19 Parkthorne clo Harrow
22 J 19 Parkthorne dri Harrow
89 X 19 Parkthorne rd SW12
123 Y 19 Parkview rd Croy
113 Y 3 Parkview rd SE9
145 O 19 Parkville rd SW6
111 O 9 Parkway Becknhm
80 L 7 Parkway Belvdr
159 T 20 Parkway Croy
54 K 10 Parkway Ilf
16 M 7 Parkway N14
131 X 5 Parkway NW1
39 T 7 Parkway Rom
119 O 9 Parkway SW20
83 W 1 Parkwood rd Islwth
105 W 13 Parkwood rd SW19
46 L 11 Parliament hill NW3
140 J 19 Parliament sq SW1
140 J 18 Parliament st SW1
88 L 10 Parma cres SW11
135 Y 8 Parmiter pl E2
63 O 6 Parmiter st E2
135 Y 9 Parmiter st E2
12 G 12 Parnell clo Edg
63 Y 2 Parnell rd E3
63 X 17 Parnham st E14
47 W 4 Parolles rd N19
81 R 9 Paroma rd Blvdr
66 A 4 Parr rd E6
24 H 4 Parr rd Stanm
134 D 7 Parr st N1
157 O 19 Parrs clo S Croy
66 G 19 Parry av E6
152 H 15 Parry clo Epsom
79 N 10 Parry pl SE18
123 R 7 Parry rd SE25
148 K 14 Parry st SW8
45 Y 14 Parsifal rd NW6
56 B 16 Parsloes av Dgnhm
55 X 14 Parsloes av Dgnhm
55 X 17 Parsloes pk Dgnhm
26 M 12 Parson st NW4
27 O 9 Parson st NW4
8 A 10 Parsonage gdns Enf
8 A 9 Parsonage la Enf
81 T 17 Parsonage Manor way Blvdr
76 G 12 Parsonage st E14
12 B 10 Parsons cres Edg
87 W 2 Parsons Green la SW6
87 X 3 Parsons grn SW6
12 C 10 Parsons gro Edg
78 H 9 Parsons hill SE18
122 J 20 Parsons mead Croy
156 K 1 Parsons mead Croy
65 X 7 Parsons rd E13
87 Y 2 Parthenia rd SW6
14 C 16 Partingdale la NW7
47 Y 3 Partington clo N19
66 A 16 Partridge clo E16
113 V 6 Partridge grn SE9
100 G 15 Partridge rd Hampt
114 G 8 Partridge rd Sidcp
66 E 14 Partridge sq E6
30 B 4 Partridge way N22
89 X 1 Parvin st SW8
148 H 18 Pascal st SW8
93 X 13 Pascoe rd SE13
149 Z 11 Pasley rd SE17
32 J 10 Pasquier rd E17
95 U 15 Passey pl SE9
64 E 14 Passfield dri E14
16 K 20 Passmore gdns N11
147 T 8 Passmore st SW1
141 Y 5 Pasternoster sq EC4
18 A 17 Pasteur gdns N18
17 X 17 Pasteur gdns N18
94 J 19 Paston cres SE12
149 Y 4 Pastor st SE11
42 B 10 Pasture clo Wemb
56 A 14 Pasture rd Dgnhm
112 B 1 Pasture rd SE6
42 A 8 Pasture rd Wemb
14 H 5 Pastures the N20

154 C 18	Patcham ct Sutton
89 S 1	Patcham ter SW8
145 T 2	Pater st W8
160 A 5	Paternoster row EC4
106 A 20	Path the SW19
107 Y 15	Pathfield rd SW16
88 J 6	Patience rd SW11
89 X 15	Patio clo SW4
89 V 1	Patmore st SW8
90 H 1	Patmos rd SW9
149 W 20	Patmos rd SW9
64 B 8	Paton clo E3
134 A 14	Paton st EC1
80 C 20	Patricia ct SE2
88 H 4	Patrick pass SW11
65 Z 9	Patrick rd E13
63 O 7	Patriot sq E2
135 Y 10	Patriot sq E2
93 R 17	Patrol pl SE6
47 V 18	Patshull pl NW5
47 U 18	Patshull rd NW5
84 H 14	Patten all Rich
88 J 19	Patten rd SW18
110 M 2	Pattenden rd SE6
112 B 16	Patterdale clo Brom
75 P 18	Patterdale rd SE15
109 U 17	Patterson ct SE19
109 U 16	Patterson rd SE19
45 X 10	Pattison rd NW2
64 L 2	Paul clo E15
157 U 4	Paul gdns Croy
64 L 2	Paul st E15
134 H 18	Paul st EC2
90 K 4	Paulet rd SE5
24 G 12	Paulhan rd Harrow
17 T 2	Paulin dri N21
100 M 1	Pauline cres Twick
83 N 20	Paulins rd N19
146 H 14	Paultons sq SW3
146 H 15	Paultons st SW3
47 V 5	Pauntley st N19
146 J 19	Paveley dri SW11
130 L 15	Paveley st NW8
89 V 10	Pavement the SW4
56 G 18	Pavet clo Dgnhm
53 U 1	Pavilion Ilf
139 P 20	Pavilion rd SW1
147 P 4	Pavilion rd SW1
147 P 3	Pavilion st SW1
25 U 2	Pavilion way Edg
110 C 19	Pawleyne clo SE20
65 U 2	Pawsey clo E13
122 L 13	Pawsons rd Croy
42 A 7	Paxford rd Wemb
85 N 4	Paxton clo Rich
109 P 10	Paxton pl SE27
112 F 18	Paxton rd Brom
31 W 2	Paxton rd N17
74 A 17	Paxton rd W4
64 D 7	Payne rd E3
76 A 18	Payne st SE8
75 Z 18	Payne st SE8
144 K 14	Paynes wlk W6
85 Y 9	Paynesfield av SW14
10 G 3	Paynesfield rd Bushey
147 X 16	Peabody av SW1
147 Y 12	Peabody clo SW1
31 R 5	Peabody est N17
90 K 19	Peabody est SE24
148 F 11	Peabody est SW6
128 C 19	Peabody est W10
90 K 20	Peabody Hill est SE24
43 T 8	Peace gro Wemb
135 T 17	Peace st E1
78 K 16	Peace st SE18
153 R 17	Peaches clo Sutton
77 P 16	Peachum rd SE3
149 Y 8	Peacock st SE17
149 Z 8	Peacock yd SE17
110 C 10	Peak Hill av SE26
110 D 10	Peak Hill gdns SE26
110 C 10	Peak Hill south SE26
110 C 8	Peak the SE26
35 O 14	Peaketon av Ilf
59 Y 10	Peal gdns W13
122 C 14	Peall rd Croy
25 Y 16	Pear clo NW9
141 T 17	Pear pl SE1
99 N 2	Pear Tree clo Erith
133 U 17	Pear Tree ct EC1
55 P 13	Pear Tree gdns Dgnhm
134 A 15	Pear Tree st E1
133 Z 15	Pear Tree st EC1
110 C 2	Pearcefield av SE23
51 W 7	Pearcroft rd E11
89 T 6	Peardon st SW8
24 H 6	Peareswood gdns Stanm
110 G 6	Pearfield rd SE23
66 J 17	Pearl clo E6
33 N 10	Pearl rd E17
75 O 1	Pearl st E1
75 O 2	Pearl st E1
141 T 19	Pearman st SE1
83 O 7	Pears rd Hounsl
88 B 3	Pearscroft ct SW6
88 A 3	Pearscroft rd SW6
134 M 8	Pearson st E2
135 N 8	Pearson st E2
120 K 4	Peartree clo Mitch
38 G 7	Peartree gdns Rom
8 E 12	Peartree rd Enf
63 R 8	Peary pl E2
41 Y 6	Pebworth rd Harrow
109 X 6	Peckarmans wood SE26
48 K 13	Peckett sq N5
90 F 6	Peckford pl SW9
150 K 18	Peckham gro SE15
91 V 2	Peckham High st SE15
151 R 19	Peckham Hill st SE15
91 X 1	Peckham Hill st SE15
151 U 14	Peckham Park rd SE15
91 S 2	Peckham rd SE5
92 B 11	Peckham Rye east SE15
92 A 12	Peckham Rye pk SE22
91 Y 9	Peckham rye SE15
47 V 16	Peckwater st NW5
48 B 17	Pedlers wlk N7
55 T 4	Pedley rd Dgnhm
135 R 18	Pedley st E1
50 G 11	Pedro st E5
151 Z 7	Pedworth rd SE16
105 P 12	Peek cres SW19
35 R 8	Peel dri Ilf
63 O 7	Peel gro E2
135 Z 10	Peel gro E2
35 P 8	Peel pl Ilf
129 S 10	Peel Precinct ct NW6
34 B 5	Peel rd E18
23 U 10	Peel rd Harrow
42 F 9	Peel rd Wemb
137 U 14	Peel st W8
134 E 14	Peerless st EC1
19 P 12	Pegamoid rd N18
149 S 13	Pegasus pl SE11
156 F 15	Pegasus rd Croy
112 G 3	Pegley gdns SE12
79 U 18	Pegwell st SE18
64 B 18	Pekin st E14
85 N 12	Peldon ct Rich
84 M 12	Peldon pas Rich
84 M 12	Peldon pas Rich
67 W 4	Pelham av Bark
91 S 6	Pelham clo SE5
146 J 7	Pelham cres SW7
146 J 6	Pelham pl SW7
124 D 3	Pelham rd Becknhm
98 F 8	Pelham rd Bxly Hth
34 G 10	Pelham rd E18
54 F 8	Pelham rd Ilf
31 U 13	Pelham rd N15
30 F 8	Pelham rd N22
106 A 17	Pelham rd SW19
105 Y 18	Pelham rd SW19
146 J 6	Pelham st SW7
150 B 13	Pelier st SE17
111 Y 5	Pelinore rd SE6
144 M 16	Pellant rd SW6
30 E 5	Pellatt gro N22
91 V 14	Pellatt rd SE22
49 S 14	Pellerin rd N16
64 A 17	Pelling st E14
17 S 11	Pellipar clo N13
78 F 13	Pellipar gdns SE18
65 T 4	Pelly rd E13
65 T 6	Pelly rd E13
135 N 12	Pelter st E2
76 M 13	Pelton rd SE10
32 G 11	Pember rd NW10
128 F 13	Pember rd NW10
39 Z 10	Pemberton av Rom
37 Y 16	Pemberton gdns Rom
47 V 8	Pemberton gdns N19
47 X 8	Pemberton gdns N19
30 H 17	Pemberton rd N4
141 U 5	Pemberton row EC4
100 D 1	Pembridge av Twick
137 S 9	Pembridge cres W11
137 U 11	Pembridge gdns W2
137 S 9	Pembridge ms W11
137 U 8	Pembridge pl W2
137 T 10	Pembridge rd W11
137 U 9	Pembridge sq W2
137 T 8	Pembridge vlls W11
9 N 7	Pembroke av Enf
24 A 9	Pembroke av Harrow
23 Z 9	Pembroke av Harrow
117 T 11	Pembroke av Surb
121 O 4	Pembroke clo Mitch
139 U 18	Pembroke clo SW1
145 S 4	Pembroke Gardens clo W8
56 G 10	Pembroke gdns Dgnhm
145 S 5	Pembroke gdns W8
102 L 3	Pembroke lodge Rich
145 T 3	Pembroke ms W8
25 P 3	Pembroke pl Edg
83 S 4	Pembroke pl Islwth
145 T 2	Pembroke pl W8
126 M 4	Pembroke rd Brom
127 N 4	Pembroke rd Brom
33 R 15	Pembroke rd E17
81 Y 12	Pembroke rd Erith
58 L 10	Pembroke rd Grnfd
54 K 2	Pembroke rd Ilf
29 P 3	Pembroke rd N10
18 A 12	Pembroke rd N13
17 Z 12	Pembroke rd N13
31 V 15	Pembroke rd N15
30 A 12	Pembroke rd N8
123 R 9	Pembroke rd SE25
145 R 6	Pembroke rd W14
42 H 10	Pembroke rd Wemb
145 T 4	Pembroke sq W8
132 M 3	Pembroke st N1
145 R 3	Pembroke studios W8
84 F 11	Pembroke vlls Rich
145 T 4	Pembroke vlls W8
145 T 4	Pembroke wlk W8
118 G 18	Pembury av Worc Pk
126 D 17	Pembury clo Brom
115 Y 5	Pembury clo Sidcp
50 A 13	Pembury est E5
80 M 18	Pembury rd Bxly Hth
81 N 17	Pembury rd Bxly Hth
49 Z 14	Pembury rd E5
31 U 6	Pembury rd N17
123 Y 9	Pembury rd SE25
122 G 17	Pemdevon rd Croy
63 R 11	Pemell clo E1
134 F 4	Penally pl N1
75 O 2	Penang st E1
143 Y 12	Penang st E1
75 O 16	Penarth st SE15
111 V 3	Penberth rd SE6
70 D 12	Penbury rd S'hall
151 V 15	Pencraig way SE15
50 H 12	Penda rd E5
81 W 18	Penda rd Erith
50 K 12	Penda's mead E9
104 L 20	Pendarves rd SW20
31 O 10	Pendennis rd N17
108 A 8	Pendennis rd SW16
76 C 18	Pender st SE8
82 H 12	Penderel rd Hounsl
111 V 4	Penderry ri SE6
47 Z 12	Penderyn way N7
107 T 13	Pendle rd SW16
33 P 17	Pendlestone rd E17
112 D 7	Pendragon rd Brom
92 G 6	Pendrell rd SE4
79 T 17	Pendrell st SE18
111 R 1	Penerley rd SE6
111 T 2	Penerley rd SE6
115 W 2	Penfold la Bxly
115 W 4	Penfold la Bxly
130 H 19	Penfold pl NW8
19 S 5	Penfold rd N9
95 N 8	Penford gdns SE9
90 J 4	Penford st SE5
97 W 14	Pengarth rd Bxly
110 D 17	Penge la SE20
65 X 3	Penge rd E13
123 X 6	Penge rd SE25
77 Z 10	Penhall rd SE7
97 U 18	Penhill rd Bxly
36 A 2	Penhurst rd Ilf
59 S 8	Penifather la Grnfd
108 A 17	Penistone rd SW16
41 P 9	Penketh dri Harrow
80 B 8	Penmon rd SE2
58 M 7	Penn clo Grnfd
24 C 14	Penn clo Harrow
127 Z 2	Penn gdns BR7
38 E 1	Penn gdns Rom
48 A 14	Penn rd N7
134 G 5	Penn st N1
145 X 4	Pennant ms W8
32 L 7	Pennant ter E17
136 C 16	Pennard rd W12
74 M 5	Pennard rd W12
105 S 5	Penner clo SW19
63 O 4	Pennethorne clo E9
151 V 20	Pennethorne rd SE15
45 S 5	Pennine dri NW2
99 P 3	Pennine way Bxly Hth
143 V 11	Pennington st E1
61 T 8	Penny rd NW10
158 G 19	Pennycroft S Croy
64 A 20	Pennyfields E14
66 K 18	Pennyroyal av E6
50 A 17	Penpoll rd E8
97 R 9	Penpool la Welling
32 M 6	Penrhyn av E17
33 O 4	Penrhyn av E17
33 P 4	Penrhyn cres E17
85 W 10	Penrhyn cres SW14
33 N 5	Penrhyn gro E17
116 H 8	Penrhyn rd Kingst
107 U 14	Penrith st SW16
87 T 14	Penrith clo SW15
57 X 16	Penrith cres Hornch
31 O 15	Penrith rd N15
117 Z 9	Penrith rd New Mald
122 M 2	Penrith rd Thntn Hth
150 A 11	Penrose gro SE17
150 A 10	Penrose st SE17
150 A 12	Penrose st SE17
150 L 8	Penry st SE1
132 E 8	Penryn st NW1
89 V 4	Pensbury pl SW8
89 V 4	Pensbury st SW8
85 R 4	Pensford av Rich
35 Z 15	Penshore clo
97 O 15	Penshurst av Sidcp
12 F 16	Penshurst gdns Edg
126 C 12	Penshurst grn Brom
98 B 1	Penshurst rd Bxly Hth
122 H 11	Penshurst rd Thntn Hth
63 T 2	Penshurst rd E9
31 U 2	Penshurst rd N17
153 Y 18	Penshurst way Sutton
33 W 5	Pentire rd E17
45 S 8	Pentland clo NW11
88 B 15	Pentland gdns SW18
88 C 16	Pentland st SW18
121 R 6	Pentlands clo Mitch
86 M 6	Pentlow st SW15
20 H 5	Pentney rd E4
107 U 1	Pentney rd SW12
105 R 19	Pentney rd SW19
133 S 9	Penton gro N1
150 A 10	Penton pl SE17
149 X 8	Penton pl SE17
133 P 11	Penton ri WC1
133 S 9	Penton st N1
133 R 10	Pentonville rd N1
8 K 4	Pentrich av Enf
150 M 20	Pentridge st SE15
18 B 16	Pentyre av N18
71 N 20	Penwerris av Islwth
106 A 3	Penwith rd SW18
105 Z 3	Penwith rd SW18
107 T 15	Penwortham rd SW16
25 R 3	Penylan pl Edg
145 V 9	Penywern rd SW5
136 L 12	Penzance pl W11
136 L 13	Penzance st W11
62 F 19	Peony gdns W12
128 H 9	Peploe rd NW6
142 A 16	Pepper st SE1
4 B 17	Peppys cres Barnt
92 F 2	Pepys rd SE14
104 L 19	Pepys rd SW20
118 M 1	Pepys rd SW20
142 L 9	Pepys st EC3
46 H 15	Perceval av NW3
49 V 13	Perch st E8
31 V 1	Percival ct N17
37 U 18	Percival gdns Rom
8 H 14	Percival rd Enf
85 V 12	Percival rd SW14
133 W 15	Percival st EC1
80 G 10	Percival st SE2
133 P 12	Percy cir WC1
9 T 17	Percy gdns Enf
117 Z 19	Percy gdns Worc Pk
140 E 3	Percy ms W1
98 A 6	Percy rd Bxly Hth
97 Z 6	Percy rd Bxly Hth
33 Z 20	Percy rd E11
65 N 14	Percy rd E16

100 G 17 Percy rd Hampt
36 M 20 Percy rd Ilf
37 N 20 Percy rd Ilf
83 Z 9 Percy rd Islwth
121 O 17 Percy rd Mitch
15 R 16 Percy rd N12
17 Z 3 Percy rd N21
38 J 9 Percy rd Rom
124 E 1 Percy rd SE20
123 V 11 Percy rd SE25
100 K 3 Percy rd Twick
82 M 20 Percy rd Twick
74 G 6 Percy rd W12
140 E 2 Percy st W1
100 M 1 Percy way Twick
133 P 13 Percy yd WC1
104 M 17 Peregrine way SW19
57 X 19 Peregrine wlk Hornch
144 M 12 Perham rd W14
145 N 12 Perham rd W14
66 E 15 Peridot st E6
109 N 1 Perifield SE7
60 E 5 Perimeade rd Grnfd
95 N 11 Periton rd SE9
60 A 11 Perivale gdns W13
59 Y 8 Perivale la Grnfd
59 T 10 Perivale pk Grnfd
42 A 14 Perkins clo Wemb
36 E 16 Perkins rd Ilf
148 F 2 Perkins rents SW1
93 Y 6 Perks clo SE3
96 F 17 Perpins rd SE9
108 H 2 Perran rd SW2
72 J 15 Perran wlk Brentf
47 S 18 Perren st NW5
74 J 9 Perrers rd W6
42 A 12 Perrin rd Wemb
46 E 13 Perrins la NW3
46 D 13 Perrins wlk NW3
61 Y 17 Perry av W3
69 Z 6 Perry clo Rainhm
31 R 18 Perry ct N15
18 C 10 Perry gdns N9
110 L 5 Perry hill SE6
118 C 19 Perry how Worc Pk
7 W 7 Perry mead Enf
110 J 8 Perry ri SE23
114 K 15 Perry st Chisl
114 H 16 Perry Street gdns Chisl
114 H 17 Perry Street shaw Chisl
110 D 3 Perry vale SE23
26 E 20 Perryfield way NW9
102 B 5 Perryfield way Rich
36 D 17 Perrymans Farm rd Ilf
87 Z 4 Perrymead st SW6
73 Y 1 Perryn rd W3
61 Z 19 Perryn rd W3
140 E 4 Perrys pl W1
111 Z 5 Persant rd SE6
149 U 20 Perseverance pl SW9
35 Z 15 Pershore clo Ilf
120 G 14 Pershore gro Carsh
29 R 1 Pert clo N10
43 Z 2 Perth av NW9
118 F 3 Perth clo SW20
67 T 5 Perth rd Bark
125 U 3 Perth rd Becknhm
50 K 4 Perth rd E10
65 V 8 Perth rd E13
36 A 20 Perth rd Ilf
54 B 1 Perth rd Ilf
35 X 18 Perth rd Ilf
30 H 5 Perth rd N22
48 F 4 Perth rd N4
63 R 16 Perth st E1
54 C 2 Perth ter Ilf
40 E 5 Perwell av Harrow
44 J 20 Peter av NW10
62 J1 Peter av NW10
140 E 7 Peter st W1
77 N 10 Peterboat clo SE10
87 X 4 Peterborough ms SW6
120 H 13 Peterborough rd Carsh
41 U 3 Peterborough rd Harrow
87 X 4 Peterborough rd SW6
33 W 18 Peterborough rd E10
88 A 2 Peterborough vlls SW6
88 D 10 Petergate SW11
11 U 18 Peters clo Stanm
141 Z 7 Peters hill EC4
133 X 20 Peters la EC1

109 Z 9 Peters pth SE26
17 Y 17 Petersfield clo N18
73 W 5 Petersfield rd W3
86 J 20 Petersfield ri SW15
102 H 3 Petersham clo Rich
153 W 12 Petersham clo Sutton
146 B 1 Petersham la SW7
102 G 1 Petersham lodge Rich
146 B 2 Petersham ms SW7
102 L 2 Petersham pk Rich
146 B 2 Petersham pl SW7
102 H 3 Petersham rd Rich
84 J 16 Petersham rd Rich
80 D 7 Peterstone rd SE2
105 T 3 Peterstow clo SW19
49 N 13 Petherton rd N5
144 E 16 Petley rd W6
131 Y 17 Peto pl NW1
65 O 19 Peto st E16
45 T 17 Petrie clo NW2
78 D 10 Pett st SE18
142 M 4 Petticoat la E1
39 R 6 Pettits blvd Rom
39 P 7 Pettits clo Rom
39 P 7 Pettits la Rom
39 N 4 Pettits Lane north Rom
56 D 16 Pettits pl Dgnhm
56 D 15 Pettits rd Dgnhm
39 N 16 Pettley gdns Rom
79 R 9 Pettman cres SE28
42 E 14 Petts Grove av Wemb
40 K 16 Petts hill Nthlt
140 D 20 Petty France SW1
40 E 20 Petworth clo Nthlt
154 B 5 Petworth clo Sutton
118 J 5 Petworth gdn New Mald
98 D 14 Petworth rd Bxly Hth
15 X 17 Petworth rd N12
88 K 2 Petworth st SW11
57 U 13 Petworth way Hornch
146 J 15 Petyt pl SW3
146 M 7 Petyward SW3
8 C 8 Pevensey av Enf
16 K 17 Pevensey av N11
52 D 12 Pevensey rd E7
100 B 2 Pevensey rd Felt
106 G 10 Pevensey rd SW17
101 R 12 Peveril dri Tedd
19 Z 17 Pewsy clo E4
76 G 19 Peyton pl SE10
150 E 13 Phelp st SE17
146 L 14 Phene st SW3
145 T 9 Philbeach gdns SW5
143 T 7 Philchurch pl E1
57 N 4 Philip av Rom
57 N 4 Philip clo Rom
158 K 2 Philip gdns Croy
31 U 11 Philip la N15
91 Y 7 Philip rd SE15
65 R 12 Philip rd SE9
95 U 16 Philipot pth SE9
95 N 12 Philippa gdns SE9
128 B 4 Phillimore gdns NW10
62 L 3 Phillimore gdns NW10
137 S 19 Phillimore gdns W8
137 T 19 Phillimore pl W8
137 T 20 Phillimore wlk W8
134 L 6 Phillipp st N1
99 Y 15 Phillips gdns Drtfrd
126 F 4 Phillips way Brom
142 H 9 Philpot la EC3
160 H 9 Philpot la EC3
143 X 4 Philpot st E1
105 O 2 Philsdon clo SW19
95 R 7 Phineas Pett rd SE9
134 J 17 Phipp st EC2
120 E 1 Phipps Bridge rd SW19
120 E 4 Phipps Bridge rd SW19
8 A 2 Phipps Hatch la Enf
7 Z 2 Phipps Hatch la Enf
147 X 4 Phipps ms SW1
120 F 1 Phipps ter SW19
93 O 13 Phoebeth rd SE4
133 R 16 Phoenix pl WC1
132 E 11 Phoenix rd NW1
132 G 10 Phoenix rd NW1
110 C 16 Phoenix rd SE20
140 H 6 Phoenix st WC2
118 K 10 Phyllis av New Mald
81 U 7 Picardy Manorway Blvdr
81 S 13 Picardy rd Blvdr

81 S 9 Picardy st Blvdr
140 B 12 Piccadilly arc SW1
140 E 10 Piccadilly cir W1
140 C 11 Piccadilly pl W1
140 B 12 Piccadilly W1
139 Y 14 Piccadilly W1
133 Z 12 Pickard st EC1
66 K 7 Pickering av E6
137 Y 5 Pickering ms W2
133 Z 3 Pickering st N1
10 D 5 Pickets clo Bushey
89 R 18 Pickets st SW12
24 F 5 Pickett croft Stanm
19 U 8 Picketts Lock la N9
97 Y 5 Pickford clo Bxly Hth
97 Z 2 Pickford la Bxly Hth
97 Y 9 Pickford rd Bxly Hth
126 B 17 Pickhurst grn Brom
126 A 13 Pickhurst la W Wkhm
125 Z 12 Pickhurst la W Wkhm
126 B 17 Pickhurst mead Brom
126 B 13 Pickhurst pk Brom
126 A 18 Pickhurst ri W Wkhm
125 Y 19 Pickhurst ri W Wkhm
142 L 14 Pickle Herring st SE1
148 L 20 Pickwick clo SW8
18 E 15 Pickwick ms N18
41 T 1 Pickwick pl Harrow
91 R 18 Pickwick rd SE21
142 B 18 Pickwick st SE1
114 C 15 Pickwick way Chisl
139 U 6 Picton pl W1
150 F 19 Picton st SE5
79 T 14 Piedmont rd SE18
78 J 4 Pier pde E16
78 J 4 Pier rd E16
76 H 10 Pier st E14
88 B 10 Pier ter SW18
79 R 7 Pier way SE18
91 Z 13 Piermont grn SE22
91 Z 13 Piermont rd SE22
61 T 19 Pierrepoint rd W3
133 W 7 Pierrepont row N1
100 G 11 Pigeon la Hampt
64 A 17 Piggot st E14
112 G 13 Pike clo Brom
58 B 12 Pikestone clo Grnfd
108 L 8 Pilgrim hill SE27
141 W 6 Pilgrim st EC4
43 T 4 Pilgrim's way Wemb
142 F 19 Pilgrimage st SE1
41 N 16 Pilgrims clo Nthlt
46 G 13 Pilgrims la NW3
5 X 17 Pilgrims ri Barnt
47 X 3 Pilgrims way N6
157 V 12 Pilgrims way S Croy
91 Z 5 Pilkington rd SE15
115 S 17 Pilmans clo Sidcp
150 C 9 Pilton pl SE17
148 E 13 Pimlico gdns SW1
147 U 8 Pimlico rd SW1
5 V 14 Pimms Brook dri Barnt
20 K 8 Pimp Hall pk E4
95 O 11 Pin pl SE9
143 T 8 Pinchin st E1
98 E 11 Pincott rd Bxly Hth
106 B 20 Pincott rd SW19
134 K 20 Pindar st EC2
129 Z 17 Pindock ms W9
125 R 19 Pine av W Wkhm
16 H 3 Pine clo N14
11 N 12 Pine clo Stanm
158 F 9 Pine coombe Croy
117 R 14 Pine gdns Surb
14 K 5 Pine gro N20
48 B 7 Pine gro N4
105 U 13 Pine gro SW19
16 A 8 Pine rd N11
45 N 12 Pine rd NW2
155 O 19 Pine ridge Carsh
133 T 16 Pine st EC1
117 H 13 Pine wlk Surb
64 A 19 Pinefield clo E14
127 R 3 Pines rd Brom
21 R 10 Pines the Wdfd Grn
114 H 2 Pinewood av Sidcp
158 H 6 Pinewood clo Croy
60 E 17 Pinewood gro W13
126 F 8 Pinewood rd Brom
80 H 16 Pinewood rd SE2
108 A 9 Pinfold rd SW16
16 F 19 Pinkham way N11
68 C 2 Pinley gdns Dgnhm
98 H 11 Pinnacle hill Bxly Hth
95 O 12 Pinnell rd SE9

22 G 13 Pinner ct Pinn
22 B 15 Pinner gro Pinn
22 L 9 Pinner Park av Harrow
23 N 8 Pinner Park av Harrow
23 O 9 Pinner Park gdns Harrow
22 F 6 Pinner pk Pinn
22 J 14 Pinner rd Harrow
23 O 19 Pinner rd Harrow
23 N 17 Pinner view Harrow
66 D 15 Pintail rd E6
34 J 1 Pintail rd Wdfd Grn
94 G 10 Pinto way SE3
48 C 17 Piper clo N7
117 O 5 Piper rd Kingst
11 W 11 Pipers Green la Edg
25 W 17 Pipers grn NW9
120 H 14 Pipewell rd Carsh
124 K 19 Pippin clo Croy
124 C 4 Piquet rd SE20
159 V 14 Pirbright cres Croy
87 X 20 Pirbright rd SW18
77 V 3 Pirie st E16
38 E 12 Pitcairn clo Rom
106 M 17 Pitcairn rd Mitch
80 S 6 Pitcairn st SW8
64 L 2 Pitchford st E15
134 H 14 Pitfield st N1
9 P 5 Pitfield way Enf
43 V 18 Pitfield way NW10
43 W 17 Pitfield way NW10
94 F 17 Pitfold clo SE12
94 E 17 Pitfold rd SE12
156 J 2 Pitlake Croy
150 A 18 Pitman st SE5
63 T 18 Pitsea pl E1
63 T 18 Pitsea st E1
60 D 12 Pitshanger la W5
60 B 9 Pitshanger pk Grnfd
106 A 10 Pitt cres SW19
105 Z 10 Pitt cres SW19
41 N 7 Pitt rd Harrow
122 M 12 Pitt rd Thntn Hth
137 V 17 Pitt st W8
142 K 14 Pitts ct SE1
139 V 14 Pitts Head ms W1
126 E 18 Pittsmead av Brom
123 X 5 Pittville gdns SE25
63 Y 17 Pixley st E14
158 H 20 Pixton way Croy
142 F 18 Plaintain pl SE1
112 G 18 Plaistow gro Brom
65 O 4 Plaistow gro E15
112 G 18 Plaistow la Brom
126 M 2 Plaistow la Brom
65 U 5 Plaistow Park rd E13
65 R 6 Plaistow rd E15
109 Z 8 Plane st SE26
55 W 2 Plantagenet gdns Rom
55 X 2 Plantagenet pl Rom
5 P 14 Plantagenet rd Barnt
99 V 1 Plantation rd Erith
94 F 5 Plantation the SE3
66 A 1 Plashet gro E6
53 O 20 Plashet gro E6
65 X 2 Plashet gro E6
65 U 2 Plashet rd E13
93 S 19 Plassy rd SE6
134 G 17 Platina st EC2
90 A 11 Plato rd SW2
132 F 9 Platt st NW1
87 R 8 Platt the SW15
45 Y 11 Platts la NW3
9 R 7 Platts rd Enf
110 G 20 Plawsfield rd Becknhm
126 L 2 Plaxtol clo Brom
77 T 14 Plaxtol pl SE10
81 T 18 Plaxtol rd Erith
144 E 12 Playfair st W6
38 J 4 Playfield av Rom
91 T 13 Playfield cres SE22
25 W 6 Playfield rd Edg
48 E 6 Playford rd N4
48 F 8 Playford rd N4
111 O 8 Playgreen way SE6
124 G 4 Playground clo Becknhm
141 X 8 Playhouse yd EC4
86 J 12 Pleasance rd SW15
86 J 11 Pleasance the SW15
158 L 5 Pleasant gro Croy
133 Z 2 Pleasant pl N1
131 Z 5 Pleasant row NW1
60 F 5 Pleasant way Wemb
20 B 8 Pleasaunce E4
132 B 6 Plender pl NW1

132 B 6	Plender st NW1
47 W 13	Pleshey rd N7
156 A 18	Plesman way SM6
31 S 18	Plevna clo N15
31 S 17	Plevna cres N15
18 L 10	Plevna rd N9
76 F 7	Plevna st E14
66 K 19	Plevna st E6
109 V 17	Pleydell av SE19
74 E 10	Pleydell av W6
141 U 6	Pleydell ct EC4
141 U 6	Pleydell ct EC4
48 G 8	Plimsoll rd N4
160 G 8	Plough ct EC3
91 W 17	Plough la SE22
106 B 11	Plough la SW19
156 A 12	Plough la Wallgtn
156 B 20	Plough la Wallgtn
155 Z 8	Plough la Wallgtn
155 Z 10	Plough Lane clo Wallgtn
141 T 4	Plough pl EC4
88 G 10	Plough rd SW11
88 G 10	Plough ter SW11
75 W 10	Plough way SE16
134 K 18	Plough yd EC2
132 E 3	Ploughmans clo NW1
83 R 13	Ploughmans end Islwth
55 U 3	Plowman rd Dgnhm
70 B 9	Pluckington pl S'hall
72 H 12	Plum garth Brentf
79 O 18	Plum la SE18
93 T 2	Plumb st SE10
133 U 15	Plumbers pl EC1
143 T 3	Plumbers row E1
120 L 2	Plummer la Mitch
89 X 18	Plummer rd SW4
40 G 17	Plumpton clo Nthlt
154 J 5	Plumpton way Carsh
78 L 15	Plumstead Common rd SE18
79 P 16	Plumstead Common rd SE18
79 W 12	Plumstead High st SE18
79 O 10	Plumstead rd SE18
155 X 16	Plumtree clo Dgnhm
141 V 3	Plumtree ct EC4
112 J 20	Plymouth rd Brom
65 S 16	Plymouth rd E16
76 J 10	Plymouth wharf E14
129 N 2	Plympton av NW6
80 L 10	Plympton clo Blvdr
130 K 18	Plympton pl NW8
129 O 1	Plympton rd NW6
130 K 18	Plympton st NW8
80 F 20	Plymstock rd Welling
26 A 7	Pocklington clo NW9
141 X 17	Pocock st SE1
88 C 11	Podmore rd SW18
49 N 14	Poets rd N5
23 U 14	Poets way Harrow
93 U 2	Point clo SE10
93 V 2	Point hill SE10
87 X 11	Point pleasant SW18
28 D 6	Pointalls clo N3
140 C 5	Poland st W1
20 F 3	Pole Hill rd E4
94 L 6	Polebrook rd SE3
110 L 4	Polecroft la SE6
118 J 4	Polesden gdns New Mald
68 K 1	Polesworth rd Dgnhm
55 X 20	Polesworth rd Dgnhm
65 S 19	Pollard clo E16
48 D 14	Pollard clo N7
120 G 12	Pollard rd Mrdn
15 W 9	Pollard rd N20
135 U 13	Pollard row E2
135 U 13	Pollard st E2
122 B 6	Pollards cres SW16
122 C 5	Pollards Hill east SW16
122 C 5	Pollards Hill north SW16
122 C 7	Pollards Hill south SW16
122 B 6	Pollards Hill west SW16
122 A 5	Pollards Wood rd SW16
139 Z 7	Pollen st W1
130 G 16	Pollitt dri NW8
92 L 19	Polsted rd SE6
79 R 10	Polthorne gro SE18
108 A 13	Polworth rd SW16
132 D 11	Polygon rd NW1

89 U 9	Polygon the SW4
78 K 11	Polytechnic st SE18
143 O 4	Pomell way E1
75 P 26	Pomeroy sq SE14
92 C 2	Pomeroy st SE14
90 K 7	Pomfret rd SE5
94 D 5	Pond clo SE3
91 P 15	Pond mead SE21
146 J 8	Pond pl SW3
64 L 6	Pond rd E15
94 D 5	Pond rd SE3
47 P 3	Pond sq N6
46 H 14	Pond st NW3
102 D 16	Pond way Tedd
48 C 20	Ponder st N7
126 A 20	Pondfield rd Brom
56 G 14	Pondfield rd Dgnhm
153 R 12	Pondhill gdns Sutton
143 V 7	Ponler st E1
62 J 8	Ponsard rd NW10
50 D 16	Ponsford st E9
148 H 9	Ponsonby pl SW1
86 J 19	Ponsonby rd SW15
148 H 9	Ponsonby ter SW1
147 R 2	Pont st SW1
147 N 2	Pont Street ms SW3
112 D 12	Pontefract rd Brom
148 F 16	Ponton rd SW8
141 V 17	Pontypool pl SE1
41 P 2	Pool rd Harrow
82 B 4	Poole Court rd Hounsl
50 E 19	Poole rd E9
134 E 6	Poole st N1
68 M 5	Pooles la Dgnhm
146 B 20	Pooles la SW10
48 E 8	Pooles pk N4
75 T 5	Poolmans st SE16
26 B 13	Poolsford rd NW9
63 P 19	Poonah st E1
127 N 12	Pope rd Brom
142 M 19	Pope st SE1
160 F 7	Pope's Head all EC3
101 U 3	Popes av Twick
27 Y 3	Popes dri N3
158 L 4	Popes gro Croy
101 V 4	Popes gro Twick
72 G 9	Popes la W5
90 F 9	Popes rd SW9
100 D 8	Popham clo Felt
134 A 3	Popham rd N1
134 A 4	Popham st N1
133 Y 4	Popham st N1
120 M 1	Poplar av Mitch
70 K 8	Poplar av S'hall
64 E 19	Poplar Bath st E14
105 Y 11	Poplar ct SW19
117 Z 4	Poplar gdns New Mald
16 A 20	Poplar gro N11
117 Z 6	Poplar gro New Mald
136 D 20	Poplar gro W6
43 X 9	Poplar gro Wemb
64 D 20	Poplar High st E14
81 V 10	Poplar mt Blvdr
80 G 2	Poplar pl SE2
137 Y 9	Poplar pl W2
119 Y 6	Poplar rd S SW19
90 K 9	Poplar rd SE24
119 U 20	Poplar rd Sutton
38 K 13	Poplar st Rom
36 C 13	Poplar way Ilf
156 L 1	Poplar wlk Croy
90 L 10	Poplar wlk SE24
44 M 19	Poplars av NW2
33 R 18	Poplars rd E17
141 V 5	Poppins ct EC4
34 A 20	Poppleton rd E11
15 Y 11	Porch way N20
91 N 10	Porchester clo SE5
137 Z 4	Porchester ms W2
138 L 6	Porchester pl W2
117 T 4	Porchester rd Kingst
137 Y 5	Porchester rd W2
137 Y 4	Porchester sq W2
138 K 4	Porchester st W2
138 B 10	Porchester ter W2
137 Z 3	Porchester Terrace north W2
113 S 4	Porcupine clo SE9
90 D 11	Porden rd SW2
41 N 3	Porlock av Harrow
18 F 3	Porlock rd Enf
142 F 18	Porlock st SE1
113 V 20	Porrington clo Chisl
108 G 6	Portal clo SE27
8 B 11	Portcullis Lodge rd Enf
63 S 10	Portelet rd E1
144 J 2	Porten rd W14
66 H 18	Porter rd E6

131 R 20	Porter st W1
55 V 14	Porters av Dgnhm
138 E 1	Porteus rd W2
129 P 15	Portgate clo W9
110 J 10	Porthcawe rd SE26
97 N 9	Porthkerry av Welling
63 Y 13	Portia way E3
87 U 14	Portinscale rd SW15
118 E 16	Portland av New Mald
49 U 2	Portland av N16
97 O 17	Portland av Sidcp
58 L 13	Portland cres Grnfd
113 P 4	Portland cres SE9
24 G 8	Portland cres Stanm
24 J 8	Portland cres Stanm
30 K 19	Portland gdns N4
37 X 15	Portland gdns Rom
90 B 1	Portland gro SW8
140 C 7	Portland ms W1
139 Y 1	Portland pl W1
131 Y 19	Portland pl W1
112 L 11	Portland rd Brom
116 K 7	Portland rd Kingst
120 J 3	Portland rd Mitch
31 T 13	Portland rd N15
70 D 7	Portland rd S'hall
123 X 9	Portland rd SE25
113 R 4	Portland rd SE9
136 M 12	Portland rd W11
48 K 4	Portland ri N4
48 K 4	Portland Rise est N4
143 W 13	Portland sq E1
150 E 11	Portland st SE17
84 G 11	Portland ter Rich
85 Y 9	Portman av SW14
139 S 4	Portman clo W1
97 X 8	Portman ct Bxly Hth
35 N 8	Portman dri Wdfd Grn
25 X 9	Portman gdns NW9
139 S 6	Portman ms S W1
63 R 9	Portman pl E2
117 N 4	Portman rd Kingst
139 S 6	Portman sq W1
139 R 6	Portman st W1
80 H 4	Portmeadow wlk SE2
129 O 11	Portnall rd W9
39 N 7	Portnoi clo Rom
137 T 10	Portobello ms W11
136 M 2	Portobello rd W10
128 K 19	Portobello rd W11
137 T 10	Portobello rd W11
133 S 20	Portpool la EC1
30 C 3	Portree clo N22
64 K 16	Portree st E14
27 V 19	Portsdown av NW11
138 M 6	Portsea ms W2
138 M 6	Portsea st W2
89 V 4	Portslade rd SW8
116 F 12	Portsmouth rd Surb & Kingst
86 L 19	Portsmouth rd SW15
141 O 5	Portsmouth st WC2
143 O 8	Portsoken st E1
86 D 17	Portswood pl SW15
100 M 4	Portugal gdns Twick
141 P 5	Portugal st WC2
65 O 2	Portway E15
152 G 20	Portway Epsom
31 S 4	Pospect pl N17
52 G 16	Post Office appr E7
148 F 16	Post Office way SW8
7 U 10	Postern grn Enf
150 G 2	Potier st SE1
63 N 10	Pott st E2
135 X 14	Pott st E2
121 T 4	Potter clo Mitch
87 P 19	Potterne clo SW19
142 L 15	Potters fields SE1
117 W 9	Potters gro New Mald
4 M 14	Potters la Barnt
107 W 14	Potters la SW16
5 O 13	Potters rd Barnt
136 L 12	Pottery la W11
72 K 16	Pottery rd Brentf
143 V 18	Pottery st SE16
101 X 2	Poulett gdns Twick
66 G 5	Poulett rd E6
120 J 13	Poulter pk Carsh
154 H 5	Poulton av Sutton
142 D 6	Poultry EC2
160 D 6	Poultry EC2
116 D 19	Pound clo Surb
44 F 18	Pound la NW10
78 A 12	Pound Park rd SE7
95 V 15	Pound pl SE9
154 L 11	Pound st Carsh

89 O 7	Pountney rd SW11
82 E 20	Powder Mill la Twick
100 G 1	Powder Mill la Twick
11 Z 18	Powell clo Edg
155 Z 16	Powell clo Wallgtn
56 D 12	Powell gdns Dgnhm
21 Z 3	Powell rd Buck Hl
50 A 11	Powell rd E5
74 B 17	Powells wlk W4
73 B 12	Power rd W4
84 G 18	Powers ct Twick
50 D 11	Powerscroft rd E5
115 T 17	Powerscroft rd Sidcp
45 U 2	Powis gdns NW11
137 P 5	Powis gdns W11
136 R 5	Powis ms W11
132 L 19	Powis pl WC1
64 D 9	Powis rd E3
137 R 6	Powis sq W11
64 L 9	Powis st E15
78 J 9	Powis st SE18
137 R 5	Powis ter W11
47 R 19	Powlett pl NW1
82 L 10	Pownall gdns Hounsl
135 R 5	Pownall rd E8
82 L 10	Pownall rd Hounsl
112 G 12	Powster rd Brom
80 K 18	Powys clo Bxly Hth
16 M 14	Powys la N13
17 N 14	Powys la N13
16 M 13	Powys la N14
89 V 18	Poynders gdns SW4
89 W 18	Poynders rd SW4
47 U 9	Poynings rd N19
14 K 17	Poynings way N12
114 F 20	Poyntell cres Chisl
8 J 18	Poynter rd Enf
31 Z 6	Poynton rd N17
88 L 6	Poyntz rd SW11
63 N 7	Poyser st E2
135 Y 11	Poyser st E2
138 G 5	Praed ms W2
138 F 6	Praed st W2
65 X 8	Pragel st E13
112 G 3	Pragnell rd SE12
90 A 14	Prague clo SW2
48 G 8	Prah rd N4
89 R 4	Prairie st SW8
132 A 5	Pratt ms NW1
132 C 3	Pratt st NW1
149 O 4	Pratt wlk SE11
45 P 3	Prayle gro NW2
74 D 11	Prebend gdns W4
134 B 5	Prebend st N1
87 R 10	Premier pl SW15
94 A 7	Prendergast rd SE3
107 Z 9	Prentis rd SW16
78 A 12	Prentiss ct SE7
118 B 10	Presburg rd New Mald
25 N 5	Prescelly pl Edg
143 O 8	Prescot st E1
127 Y 15	Prescott av Brom
108 A 17	Prescott clo SW16
89 X 9	Prescott pl SW4
134 A 13	President st EC1
143 W 12	Presidents dri E1
43 Z 9	Press rd NW10
64 H 20	Prestage st E14
64 J 20	Prestage st E14
52 L 20	Prestbury rd E7
113 T 9	Prestbury sq SE9
88 J 9	Prested rd SW11
20 J 20	Preston av E4
150 J 6	Preston clo SE1
101 S 5	Preston clo Twick
97 W 3	Preston dri Bxly Hth
34 K 16	Preston dri E11
152 C 13	Preston dri Epsom
9 X 1	Preston gdns Enf
35 S 19	Preston gdns Ilf
44 C 18	Preston gdns NW10
42 K 1	Preston hill Harrow
24 M 18	Preston hill Harrow
44 H 18	Preston pl NW2
84 L 13	Preston pl Rich
34 A 20	Preston rd E11
64 G 20	Preston rd E15
20 J 20	Preston rd E4
42 K 2	Preston rd Harrow
108 J 15	Preston rd SE19
104 E 18	Preston rd SW20
42 J 3	Preston waye Harrow
76 G 3	Prestons rd E14
70 B 14	Prestwick clo S'hall
24 B 13	Prestwood av Harrow
24 C 13	Prestwood clo Harrow
122 L 16	Prestwood gdns Croy
32 G 12	Pretoria av E17

108 M 16 Pytchley cres SE19
91 T 8 Pytchley rd SE22

Q

39 R 15 Quadrant arc Rom
47 N 16 Quadrant gro NW5
122 J 8 Quadrant rd Thntn Hth
84 H 11 Quadrant rd Rich
80 K 20 Quadrant the Bxly Hth
84 J 11 Quadrant the Rich
154 C 13 Quadrant the Sutton
105 S 20 Quadrant the SW20
94 E 10 Quaggy wlk SE3
43 Y 10 Quainton st NW10
71 X 19 Quaker la Islwth
83 Z 1 Quaker la Islwth
70 H 7 Quaker rd S'hall
135 N 18 Quaker st E1
26 C 5 Quakers course NW9
8 A 20 Quakers wlk Enf
141 S 4 Quality ct WC2
45 O 7 Quantock gdns NW2
99 R 3 Quantock rd Bxly Hth
120 G 14 Quarr rd Carsh
87 Y 4 Quarrendon st SW6
153 U 13 Quarry Park rd Sutton
88 E 15 Quarry rd SW18
153 U 13 Quarry ri Sutton
94 E 10 Quarry wlk SE3
51 P 12 Quarter Mile la E10
139 P 6 Quebec ms W1
54 A 1 Quebec rd Ilf
36 B 19 Quebec rd Ilf
75 U 7 Quebec way SE16
110 D 17 Queen Adelaide rd SE20
97 X 8 Queen Ann ga Bxly Hth
126 D 7 Queen Anne av Brom
120 K 6 Queen Anne gdns Mitch
139 Y 3 Queen Anne ms W1
50 F 19 Queen Anne rd E9
139 X 3 Queen Anne st W1
31 T 15 Queen Annes av N15
101 R 7 Queen Annes clo Twick
140 F 19 Queen Annes ga SW1
74 A 8 Queen Annes gdns W4
8 E 20 Queen Annes gdns Enf
72 J 6 Queen Annes gdns W5
74 A 9 Queen Annes gro W4
72 K 5 Queen Annes gro W5
18 C 2 Queen Annes gro Enf
8 F 19 Queen Annes pl Enf
74 L 14 Queen Caroline st W6
144 C 10 Queen Caroline st W6
119 Y 9 Queen Elizabeth gdns Mrdn
141 P 13 Queen Elizabeth hall SE1
32 H 10 Queen Elizabeth rd E 17
116 L 3 Queen Elizabeth rd Kingst
142 M 16 Queen Elizabeth st SE1
143 O 17 Queen Elizabeth st SE1
49 N 6 Queen Elizabeths clo N16
16 M 6 Queen Elizabeths dri N14
17 N 4 Queen Elizabeths dri N14
159 W 20 Queen Elizabeths dri Croy
49 N 4 Queen Elizabeths wlk N16
155 Y 8 Queen Elizabeths wlk Wallgtn
49 R 16 Queen Margarets gro N1
119 O 12 Queen Mary av Mrdn

108 K 14 Queen Mary rd SE19
154 L 17 Queen Marys av Carsh
131 S 15 Queen Marys gdns NW1
132 K 19 Queen sq WC1
132 K 19 Queen Square pl WC1
98 A 9 Queen st Bxly Hth
156 L 7 Queen st Croy
160 C 7 Queen st EC4
142 C 9 Queen st EC4
139 X 13 Queen st Mayfair W1
39 O 17 Queen st Rom
142 C 10 Queen Street pl EC4
160 C 10 Queen Street pl EC4
42 G 20 Queen Victoria av Wemb
160 A 8 Queen Victoria st EC4
142 B 8 Queen Victoria st EC4
141 Y 8 Queen Victoria st EC4
144 M 13 Queen's Club gdns W14
145 N 13 Queen's Club gdns W14
144 L 12 Queen's Club the W14
35 X 12 Queenborough gdns Ilf
158 A 20 Queenhill rd S Croy
160 B 9 Queenhithe EC4
153 R 16 Queens av Sutton
58 M 16 Queens av Grnfd
59 N 16 Queens av Grnfd
29 R 10 Queens av N10
15 U 9 Queens av N20
17 X 6 Queens av N21
28 D 4 Queens av N3
24 D 9 Queens av Stanm
21 W 16 Queens av Wdfd Grn
147 X 20 Queens cir SW11
12 C 17 Queens clo Edg
155 S 10 Queens clo Wallgtn
84 G 4 Queens cott Rich
47 O 18 Queens cres NW5
85 N 13 Queens cres Rich
110 B 3 Queens ct SE23
51 O 1 Queens dri E10
48 J 6 Queens dri N4
117 R 15 Queens dri Surb
61 O 17 Queens dri W3
60 M 18 Queens dri W5
146 G 10 Queens Elm pde SW3
146 G 11 Queens Elm sq SW3
138 D 20 Queens ga SW7
146 D 3 Queens ga SW7
139 Z 19 Queens Gallery SW1
146 B 3 Queens Gate gdns SW7
146 B 1 Queens Gate ms SW7
138 C 20 Queens Gate ms SW7
146 D 3 Queens Gate pl SW7
146 D 4 Queens Gate Place Ms SW7
146 C 1 Queens Gate ter SW7
69 Z 7 Queens gdns Rainhm
82 B 2 Queens gdns Hounsl
27 N 16 Queens gdns NW4
138 B 8 Queens gdns W2
60 E 13 Queens gdns W5
130 F 7 Queens gro NW8
20 K 5 Queens Grove rd E4
133 Y 5 Queens Head st N1
142 E 15 Queens Head yd SE1
76 L 17 Queens ho SE10
29 S 10 Queens la N10
126 B 4 Queens Mead rd Brom
137 Y 8 Queens ms W2
15 Z 18 Queens Parade clo N11
128 K 7 Queens pk NW6
119 Z 8 Queens pl Mrdn
54 A 20 Queens rd Bark
4 C 13 Queens rd Barnt
124 J 3 Queens rd Becknhm
126 F 3 Queens rd Brom
21 W 7 Queens rd Buck Hl
114 A 15 Queens rd Chisl
122 K 14 Queens rd Croy
51 Y 2 Queens rd E11
65 V 5 Queens rd E13
32 L 19 Queens rd E17
33 N 17 Queens rd E17
8 E 13 Queens rd Enf
100 K 10 Queens rd Hampt

82 J 7 Queens rd Hounsl
103 R 19 Queens rd Kingst
119 Z 8 Queens rd Mrdn
16 M 20 Queens rd N11
28 D 5 Queens rd N3
18 M 9 Queens rd N9
118 E 10 Queens rd New Mald
26 M 17 Queens rd NW4
27 N 16 Queens rd NW4
84 L 17 Queens rd Rich
85 N 12 Queens rd Rich
85 N 14 Queens rd Rich
70 A 7 Queens rd S'hall
92 C 2 Queens rd SE14
147 V 18 Queens rd SW11
85 Z 8 Queens rd SW14
106 B 13 Queens rd SW19
120 E 4 Queens rd SW19
105 Z 14 Queens rd SW19
101 W 16 Queens rd Tedd
83 X 20 Queens rd Twick
101 Y 1 Queens rd Twick
60 J 16 Queens rd W5
155 S 10 Queens rd Wallgtn
97 P 3 Queens rd Welling
84 M 15 Queens ri Rich
86 G 9 Queens ride SW13
65 U 5 Queens Road west E13
150 D 13 Queens row SE17
83 Z 8 Queens sq Islwth
18 E 20 Queens st N17
65 W 4 Queens ter E13
83 Z 9 Queens ter Islwth
130 F 7 Queens ter NW8
27 N 15 Queens way NW4
20 J 4 Queens wlk E4
23 S 12 Queens wlk Harrow
43 W 6 Queens wlk NW9
60 D 14 Queens wlk W5
146 E 5 Queensberry Mews west SW7
146 E 5 Queensberry pl SW7
146 F 5 Queensberry way SW7
138 A 8 Queensborough pas W2
138 A 10 Queensborough ter W2
83 T 14 Queensbridge pk Islwth
135 P 3 Queensbridge rd E8
49 V 18 Queensbridge rd E8
24 M 12 Queensbury pk Harrow
60 M 6 Queensbury rd Wemb
61 O 5 Queensbury rd Wemb
43 X 2 Queensbury rd NW9
134 C 2 Queensbury st N1
25 N 10 Queensbury Station pde Edg
42 K 12 Queenscourt Wemb
95 P 15 Queenscroft rd SE9
136 H 13 Queensdale cres W11
136 J 14 Queensdale pl W11
136 H 15 Queensdale rd W11
136 K 14 Queensdale wlk W11
49 Z 12 Queensdown rd E5
129 T 2 Queensgate pl NW6
106 A 20 Queensland av SW19
17 Z 18 Queensland av N18
48 G 13 Queensland pl N7
48 F 13 Queensland rd N7
153 N 20 Queensmead Sutton
105 O 5 Queensmere clo SW19
105 O 5 Queensmere rd SW19
144 G 19 Queensmill rd SW6
110 E 10 Queensthorpe rd SE26
89 R 6 Queenstown rd SW8
147 W 17 Queenstown rd SW8
89 X 19 Queensville rd SW12
156 C 13 Queensway Croy
156 E 12 Queensway Croy
9 P 16 Queensway Enf
137 Y 6 Queensway W2
15 W 12 Queenswell av N20
82 E 4 Queenswood av Hounsl
122 G 12 Queenswood av Thntn Hth
100 K 15 Queenswood av Hampt

155 X 9 Queenswood av Wallgtn
33 U 6 Queenswood av E17
52 G 5 Queenswood gdns E11
27 T 6 Queenswood pk N3
110 G 8 Queenswood rd SE23
96 K 15 Queenswood rd Sidcp
29 T 17 Queenswood rd N10
48 C 14 Quemerford rd N7
94 A 8 Quentin rd SE13
112 E 15 Quernmore clo Brom
112 E 15 Quernmore rd Brom
30 F 19 Quernmore rd N4
88 C 5 Querrin st SW6
129 U 4 Quex ms NW6
129 V 3 Quex rd NW6
133 X 5 Quick pl N1
74 A 14 Quick rd W4
133 X 9 Quick st N1
106 C 17 Quicks rd SW19
46 K 20 Quickswood NW3
130 M 1 Quickswood NW3
87 P 10 Quill la SW15
142 B 17 Quilp st SE1
135 R 12 Quilter st E2
4 A 18 Quinta dri Barnt
119 U 1 Quinton av SW20
125 V 6 Quinton clo Becknhm
155 R 8 Quinton clo Wallgtn
106 C 5 Quinton st SW18
64 J 20 Quixley st E14
91 T 9 Quorn rd SE22

R

137 V 12 Rabbit row W8
53 R 11 Rabbits rd E12
40 B 16 Rabounmead dri Nthlt
117 Z 8 Raby rd New Mald
63 V 17 Raby st E14
145 S 15 Racton rd SW6
72 E 10 Radbourne av W5
33 W 9 Radbourne cres E17
107 W 1 Radbourne rd SW12
89 W 19 Radbourne rd SW12
8 A 5 Radcliffe av Enf
62 F 5 Radcliffe av NW10
154 J 18 Radcliffe gdns Carsh
157 V 3 Radcliffe rd Croy
23 Y 8 Radcliffe rd Harrow
17 W 4 Radcliffe rd N21
87 P 15 Radcliffe sq SW15
149 U 11 Radcot st SE11
137 N 2 Raddington rd W10
96 F 18 Radfield way Sidcp
93 V 15 Radford rd SE13
67 X 9 Radford way Bark
87 V 1 Radipole rd SW6
65 R 18 Radland rd E16
110 B 5 Radlett av SE26
52 D 17 Radlett clo E7
130 K 5 Radlett pl NW8
54 L 13 Radley av Ilf
24 L 14 Radley gdns Harrow
34 E 8 Radley la E18
145 V 4 Radley ms W8
31 T 7 Radley rd N17
50 C 6 Radley sq E5
56 G 18 Radleys mead Dgnhm
51 N 4 Radlix rd E10
23 S 15 Radnor av Harrow
97 R 13 Radnor av Welling
114 H 16 Radnor clo Chisl
122 A 10 Radnor clo Mitch
35 T 17 Radnor cres Ilf
8 E 5 Radnor gdns Enf
101 V 3 Radnor gdns Twick
138 H 6 Radnor ms W2
138 J 6 Radnor pl W2
23 T 16 Radnor rd Harrow
128 L 5 Radnor rd NW6
151 S 17 Radnor rd SE15
101 W 2 Radnor rd Twick
134 C 14 Radnor st EC1
148 K 17 Radnor ter SW8
145 O 4 Radnor ter W14
61 S 10 Radnor way NW10
124 K 16 Radnor wlk Croy

146 M 11	Radnor wlk SW3
147 N 13	Radnor wlk SW3
151 T 13	Radsley st SE1
24 A 11	Radstock av Harrow
23 Z 11	Radstock av Harrow
146 K 19	Radstock st SW11
99 Z 14	Raeburn av Drtfrd
117 S 19	Raeburn av Surb
102 F 19	Raeburn clo Kingst
28 C 19	Raeburn clo NW11
25 O 6	Raeburn rd Edg
96 J 16	Raeburn rd Sidcp
90 B 11	Raeburn st SW2
126 G 4	Rafford way Brom
113 X 20	Raggleswood Chisl
156 K 10	Raglan ct S Croy
81 O 12	Raglan rd Blvdr
126 M 9	Raglan rd Brom
33 V 15	Raglan rd E17
18 F 2	Raglan rd Enf
47 T 17	Raglan st NW5
40 K 13	Raglan ter Harrow
41 N 18	Raglan way Northolt
73 U 4	Ragley clo W3
38 F 5	Raider clo Rom
47 U 14	Railey ms NW5
84 A 10	Railshead rd Twick
90 G 12	Railton rd SE24
23 V 13	Railway appr Harrow
30 G 19	Railway appr N8
142 F 14	Railway appr SE1
83 Y 20	Railway appr Twick
155 S 12	Railway appr Wallgtn
75 P 5	Railway av SE16
136 L 5	Railway ms W10
101 X 15	Railway pas Tedd
81 T 8	Railway pl Blvdr
142 L 8	Railway pl EC3
105 V 16	Railway pl SW19
101 V 11	Railway rd Tedd
86 B 7	Railway side SW13
132 L 9	Railway st N1
55 T 2	Railway st Rom
33 V 5	Railway ter E17
93 R 13	Railway ter SE13
43 V 16	Rainborough clo NW10
150 J 17	Rainbow st SE5
75 N 2	Raine st E l
143 Y 12	Raine st E1
96 F 15	Rainham clo SE9
88 K 15	Rainham clo SW11
128 D 13	Rainham rd NW10
57 T 18	Rainham rd Rainhm
56 H 9	Rainham Road north Dgnhm
56 K 19	Rainham Road south Dgnhm
64 C 9	Rainhill way E3
75 V 12	Rainsborough av SE8
11 P 15	Rainsford clo Stanm
61 S 7	Rainsford rd NW10
138 J 4	Rainsford st W2
57 U 4	Rainsford way Hornch
77 U 13	Rainton rd SE7
144 E 16	Rainville rd W6
16 K 12	Raith av N14
76 H 2	Raleana rd E14
101 U 16	Raleigh av Tedd
155 X 8	Raleigh av Wallgtn
26 L 15	Raleigh clo NW4
155 T 15	Raleigh ct Wallgtn
15 X 10	Raleigh dri N20
117 V 20	Raleigh dri Surb
120 L 4	Raleigh gdns Mitch
8 B 15	Raleigh rd Enf
30 G 13	Raleigh rd N8
85 N 8	Raleigh rd Rich
70 B 12	Raleigh rd S'hall
110 E 18	Raleigh rd SE20
133 Z 6	Raleigh st N1
16 L 4	Raleigh way N14
150 C 2	Ralph st SE1
147 O 11	Ralston st SW3
50 C 17	Ram pl E9
41 T 7	Rama ct Harrow
77 U 12	Ramac way SE7
107 U 10	Rambler clo SW16
90 A 15	Ramillies clo SW2
140 B 5	Ramillies pl W1
13 O 9	Ramillies rd NW7
97 P 16	Ramillies rd Sidcp
73 Y 9	Ramillies rd W4
140 B 6	Ramillies st W1
148 F 9	Rampayne st SW1
20 A 10	Rampton clo E4
37 Z 12	Rams gro Rom
41 O 15	Ramsay clo Grnfd
52 C 11	Ramsay rd E7

73 V 7	Ramsay rd W3
18 C 4	Ramscroft clo N9
107 R 13	Ramsdale rd SW17
38 F 3	Ramsden dri Rom
81 Z 20	Ramsden rd Erith
15 Z 16	Ramsden rd N11
89 P 20	Ramsden rd SW12
26 D 19	Ramsey rd NW9
122 E 13	Ramsey rd Thntn Hth
135 T 16	Ramsey st E2
16 H 4	Ramsey way N14
49 V 17	Ramsgate st E8
36 K 14	Ramsgill appr Ilf
36 K 14	Ramsgill dri Ilf
58 A 12	Ramulis dri Hay
95 P 9	Rancliffe gdns SE9
66 E 7	Rancliffe rd E6
44 C 8	Randall av NW2
81 Y 17	Randall clo Erith
88 J 2	Randall clo SW11
76 F 18	Randall pl SE10
39 T 18	Randall rd Rom
149 N 8	Randall rd SE11
149 N 8	Randall row SE11
64 L 13	Randall st E16
132 L 3	Randell's rd N1
102 E 9	Randle rd Rich
111 R 7	Randlesdown rd SE6
65 Z 17	Randolph appr E16
130 C 17	Randolph av W9
129 Z 12	Randolph av W9
98 J 7	Randolph clo Bxly Hth
103 W 13	Randolph clo Kingst
130 B 17	Randolph cres W9
129 X 10	Randolph gdns NW6
130 C 18	Randolph ms W9
33 S 15	Randolph rd E17
70 D 5	Randolph rd S'hall
130 C 18	Randolph rd W9
132 B 1	Randolph st NW1
22 K 7	Randon clo Harrow
86 G 5	Ranelagh av SW13
87 U 7	Ranelagh av SW6
12 B 13	Ranelagh clo Edg
12 B 13	Ranelagh dri Edg
84 C 12	Ranelagh dri Twick
34 K 15	Ranelagh gdns E11
53 U 3	Ranelagh gdns Ilf
87 U 8	Ranelagh gdns SW6
73 U 18	Ranelagh gdns W4
147 V 9	Ranelagh gro SW1
118 A 10	Ranelagh pl New Mald
51 Z 11	Ranelagh rd E11
65 O 6	Ranelagh rd E15
66 J 4	Ranelagh rd E6
31 T 10	Ranelagh rd N17
30 C 6	Ranelagh rd N22
62 D 7	Ranelagh rd NW10
70 A 1	Ranelagh rd S'hall
148 C 11	Ranelagh rd SW1
72 G 5	Ranelagh rd W5
42 H 17	Ranelagh rd Wemb
153 Z 2	Ranfurly rd Sutton
112 C 13	Rangefield rd Brom
111 Z 11	Rangefield rd Brom
31 V 16	Rangemoor rd N15
21 R 2	Rangers rd E4
93 W 1	Rangers sq SE10
142 M 7	Rangoon st EC3
26 B 10	Rankin clo NW9
81 P 19	Ranleigh gdns Bxly Hth
89 T 20	Ranmere st SW12
23 R 14	Ranmoor clo Harrow
23 S 13	Ranmoor gdns Harrow
157 V 7	Ranmore av Croy
153 O 20	Ranmore rd Sutton
144 D 13	Rannoch rd W6
144 E 16	Rannoch rd W6
44 A 1	Rannock av NW9
77 Y 12	Ransom rd SE7
130 K 20	Ranston st NW1
45 V 11	Ranulf rd NW2
63 X 4	Ranwell clo E3
99 S 4	Ranworth clo Erith
19 O 10	Ranworth rd N9
39 S 9	Raphael av Rom
39 T 8	Raphael pk Rom
139 N 19	Raphael st SW7
15 S 9	Rasper rd N20
107 X 3	Rastell av SW2
134 C 14	Ratcliff gro EC1
52 K 16	Ratcliff rd E7
63 T 18	Ratcliffe Cross st E1
63 U 18	Ratcliffe la E1
63 T 19	Ratcliffe orchard E1
63 N 20	Ratcliffe st E1

140 E 3	Rathbone pl W1
65 O 16	Rathbone st E16
140 D 2	Rathbone st W1
30 D 15	Rathcoole av N8
30 D 15	Rathcoole gdns N8
110 M 2	Rathfern rd SE6
72 C 4	Rathgar av W13
27 V 6	Rathgar clo N3
90 J 7	Rathgar rd SW9
89 X 16	Rathmell dri SW4
77 V 13	Rathmore rd SE7
90 F 12	Rattray rd SW2
91 X 3	Raul rd SE15
47 U 13	Raveley st NW5
34 K 6	Raven rd E18
63 N 14	Raven row E1
143 X 1	Raven row E1
89 R 2	Ravenet st SW11
106 M 8	Ravenfield rd SW17
65 Y 6	Ravenhill rd E13
87 P 12	Ravenna rd SW15
58 L 8	Ravenor Park rd Grnfd
59 N 9	Ravenor Park rd Grnfd
58 M 9	Ravenor pk Grnfd
126 C 5	Ravens clo Brom
8 D 9	Ravens clo Enf
94 E 12	Ravens way SE12
111 X 19	Ravensbourne av Brom
125 Y 1	Ravensbourne av Brom
60 A 15	Ravensbourne gdns W13
36 A 5	Ravensbourne gdns Ilf
35 X 4	Ravensbourne gdns Ilf
92 M 18	Ravensbourne Park cres SE6
93 N 18	Ravensbourne pk SE6
84 D 14	Ravensbourne rd Twick
126 E 6	Ravensbourne rd Brom
92 K 20	Ravensbourne rd SE6
99 V 7	Ravensbourne rd Drtfrd
120 D 11	Ravensbury av Mordn
121 N 4	Ravensbury clo Mitch
120 F 9	Ravensbury gro Mitch
120 F 9	Ravensbury la Mitch
120 F 8	Ravensbury pth Mitch
106 A 3	Ravensbury rd SW18
105 Z 3	Ravensbury rd SW18
111 Z 10	Ravenscar rd Brom
74 G 11	Ravenscourt av W6
74 F 10	Ravenscourt gdns W6
74 G 11	Ravenscourt pk W6
74 H 11	Ravenscourt pl W6
74 H 12	Ravenscourt rd W6
74 F 9	Ravenscourt sq W6
16 G 14	Ravenscraig rd N11
42 L 3	Ravenscroft av Wemb
45 V 1	Ravenscroft av NW11
27 W 20	Ravenscroft av NW11
65 S 14	Ravenscroft clo E16
4 D 12	Ravenscroft Park rd Barnt
4 D 13	Ravenscroft pk Barnt
124 F 1	Ravenscroft rd Becknhm
65 T 14	Ravenscroft rd E16
73 W 11	Ravenscroft rd W4
135 P 10	Ravenscroft st E2
15 S 14	Ravensdale av N12
109 P 19	Ravensdale gdns SE19
82 B 7	Ravensdale rd Hounsl
31 V 20	Ravensdale rd N16
149 U 11	Ravensdon st SE11
55 X 12	Ravensfield clo Dgnhm
152 B 10	Ravensfield gdns Epsom
45 W 17	Ravenshaw st NW6
127 Y 2	Ravenshill Chisl
26 L 12	Ravenshurst av NW4
88 M 19	Ravenslea rd SW12

111 X 18	Ravensmead rd Brom
74 D 12	Ravensmeade way W4
30 E 11	Ravenstone rd N8
26 E 19	Ravenstone rd NW9
107 R 2	Ravenstone st SW12
125 T 20	Ravenswood av W Wkhm
115 Z 1	Ravenswood Bxly
156 J 6	Ravenswood clo Croy
40 D 7	Ravenswood cres Harrow
125 T 19	Ravenswood cres W Wkhm
103 U 16	Ravenswood ct Kingst
83 T 1	Ravenswood gdns Islwth
89 S 19	Ravenswood rd SW12
156 J 6	Ravenswood rd Croy
33 T 14	Ravenswood rd E17
62 K 8	Ravensworth rd NW10
113 T 8	Ravensworth rd SE9
149 P 5	Ravent rd SE11
134 J 16	Ravey st EC2
79 U 17	Ravine gro SE18
147 N 6	Rawlings st SW3
27 S 9	Rawlins clo N3
158 K 16	Rawlins clo S Croy
31 V 11	Rawlinson ter N17
120 G 10	Rawnsley av Mrdn
89 R 3	Rawson st SW11
65 S 6	Rawstone wlk E13
133 W 12	Rawstorne pl EC1
133 W 12	Rawstorne st EC1
68 A 6	Ray gdns Bark
11 P 16	Ray gdns Stanm
21 Z 18	Ray Lodge rd Wdfd Grn
133 U 18	Ray st EC1
4 M 18	Raydean rd Barnt
47 S 7	Raydon st N19
55 Z 14	Raydons gdns Dgnhm
56 A 14	Raydons rd Dgnhm
55 Y 15	Raydons rd Dgnhm
127 P 14	Rayfield clo Brom
94 C 19	Rayford av SE12
95 Z 2	Rayleas clo SE18
18 A 10	Rayleigh clo N13
117 O 3	Rayleigh ct Kingst
34 L 1	Rayleigh rd Wdfd Grn
21 X 20	Rayleigh rd Wdfd Grn
18 A 10	Rayleigh rd N13
17 Z 10	Rayleigh rd N13
105 U 20	Rayleigh rd SW19
157 S 14	Rayleigh ri S Croy
122 G 11	Raymead av Thntn Hth
27 N 11	Raymead NW4
79 T 19	Raymere gdns SE18
34 B 9	Raymond av E18
71 Z 8	Raymond av W13
110 C 11	Raymond clo SE26
124 H 10	Raymond rd Becknhm
65 X 2	Raymond rd E13
54 D 2	Raymond rd Ilf
105 T 15	Raymond rd SW19
75 O 11	Raymouth rd SE16
151 Y 6	Raymouth rd SE16
34 C 12	Rayne ct E18
40 F 4	Rayners la Harrow
22 F 20	Rayners la Pinn
87 R 13	Rayners rd SW15
52 L 1	Raynes av E11
18 K 18	Raynham av N18
18 K 16	Raynham rd N18
74 J 10	Raynham rd W6
18 K 17	Raynham ter N18
70 D 3	Raynor clo S'hall
134 C 3	Raynor pl N1
42 G 14	Raynors clo Wemb
40 B 3	Raynton clo Harrow
19 P 15	Rays av N18
19 P 15	Rays rd N18
89 T 1	Raywood st SW8
132 C 2	Reachview clo NW1
50 A 18	Reading la E8
49 Z 19	Reading la E8
40 L 14	Reading rd Nthlt
154 D 12	Reading rd Sutton
14 D 16	Reading way NW7
132 E 3	Reapers clo NW1
83 R 13	Reapers way Islwth
75 N 3	Reardon pth E1

98 F 15 Rochester dri Bxly Hth
157 T 5 Rochester gdns Croy
53 T 2 Rochester gdns Ilf
47 V 19 Rochester ms NW1
47 U 19 Rochester pl NW1
155 N 8 Rochester rd Carsh
47 U 19 Rochester rd NW1
148 C 5 Rochester row SW1
47 W 20 Rochester sq NW1
148 E 4 Rochester st SW1
47 U 19 Rochester ter NW1
99 O 19 Rochester way Bxly
96 C 9 Rochester Way east SE9
94 H 2 Rochester way SE3
94 K 6 Rochester way SE3
95 V 8 Rochester way SE3
37 T 14 Rochford av Rom
66 A 6 Rochford clo E6
57 Y 19 Rochford clo Hornch
121 Z 15 Rochford way Croy
85 Z 8 Rock av SW14
56 G 15 Rock gdns Dgnhm
109 U 10 Rock hill SE26
48 G 7 Rock st N4
110 E 2 Rockbourne rd SE23
92 A 17 Rockell's pl SE22
60 A 7 Rockford av Grnfd
45 O 13 Rockhall rd NW2
108 F 10 Rockhampton clo SE27
108 F 9 Rockhampton rd SE27
157 R 14 Rockhampton rd S Croy
39 Z 20 Rockingham av Hornch
86 D 11 Rockingham clo SW15
150 B 2 Rockingham st SE1
24 C 8 Rocklands dri Stanm
136 F 18 Rockley rd W14
79 Y 13 Rockmount rd SE18
86 G 8 Rocks la SW13
59 S 2 Rockware av Grnfd
109 T 11 Rockwell gdns SE19
56 G 15 Rockwell rd Dgnhm
136 C 17 Rockwood pl W12
133 Y 9 Rocliffe st N1
94 C 7 Rocque la SE3
45 W 4 Rodborough rd NW11
123 R 15 Roden gdns SE25
48 C 11 Roden st N7
53 X 9 Roden way Ilf
89 Y 14 Rodenhurst rd SW4
46 M 13 Roderick rd NW3
66 M 1 Roding av Bark
34 M 13 Roding la South Ilf
35 N 12 Roding la South Ilf
35 N 14 Roding la South Ilf
35 O 8 Roding Lane north Wdfd Grn
50 G 13 Roding rd E5
66 L 14 Roding rd E6
21 Y 19 Rodings the Wdfd Grn
139 R 2 Rodmarton st W1
14 H 15 Rodmell slope N12
77 O 14 Rodmere st SE10
90 A 20 Rodmill la SW2
118 A 10 Rodney clo New Mald
32 J 7 Rodney pl E17
150 C 5 Rodney pl SE17
106 C 20 Rodney pl SW19
34 G 13 Rodney rd E11
120 H 5 Rodney rd Mitch
118 A 10 Rodney rd New Mald
150 D 6 Rodney rd SE17
150 F 7 Rodney rd SE17
82 G 17 Rodney rd Twick
133 P 8 Rodney st N1
78 L 8 Rodney st SE18
38 F 6 Rodney way Rom
112 H 19 Rodway rd Brom
86 G 18 Rodway rd SW15
12 B 19 Rodwell pl Edg
91 V 14 Rodwell rd SE22
25 V 12 Roe end NW9
25 T 12 Roe la NW9
156 B 14 Roe way Wallgtn
78 J 4 Roebourne way E16
18 H 20 Roebuck clo N17
21 Y 4 Roebuck la Buck Hl
9 O 4 Roedean av Enf
9 O 4 Roedean clo Enf
86 A 14 Roedean cres SW15

86 G 11 Roehampton clo SW15
47 N 13 Rona rd SW3
114 C 16 Roehampton dri Chisl
86 B 15 Roehampton ga SW15
86 H 18 Roehampton High st SW15
86 F 11 Roehampton la SW15
104 K 1 Roehampton la SW15
104 C 6 Roehampton vale SW15
76 F 6 Roffey st E14
133 O 18 Roger st WC1
56 F 15 Rogers gdns Dgnhm
56 F 17 Rogers rd Dgnhm
65 R 18 Rogers rd E16
106 H 9 Rogers rd SW17
110 E 1 Rojack rd SE23
34 F 4 Rokeby gdns Wdfd Grn
92 L 3 Rokeby rd SE4
64 L 3 Rokeby st E15
96 F 4 Rokesby clo Welling
42 F 16 Rokesby pl Wemb
30 A 15 Rokesly av N8
146 C 9 Roland gdns SW7
63 S 13 Roland ms E1
33 W 14 Roland rd E17
150 F 12 Roland way SE17
146 C 9 Roland way SW7
37 X 12 Roles gro Rom
5 X 16 Rolfe rd Barnt
35 W 16 Roll gdns Ilf
68 F 19 Rollesby way SE28
127 Z 15 Rolleston av Brom
127 Z 16 Rolleston clo Orp
157 O 17 Rolleston rd S Croy
75 R 16 Rollins st SE15
82 H 13 Rollit cres Hounsl
48 E 14 Rollit st N7
141 S 5 Rolls bldgs EC4
20 C 18 Rolls Park av E4
20 D 17 Rolls Park rd E4
141 S 4 Rolls pas EC4
151 R 9 Rolls rd SE1
90 L 13 Rollscourt av SE24
75 X 16 Rolt st SE8
113 O 18 Rolvenden gdns Chisl
57 S 2 Rom cres Rom
32 J 10 Roma rd E17
86 H 20 Roma Read clo SW15
73 T 6 Roman clo W3
63 U 7 Roman rd E3
66 E 12 Roman rd E6
54 A 17 Roman rd Ilf
53 Z 17 Roman rd Ilf
29 R 2 Roman rd N10
74 C 10 Roman rd W4
109 P 14 Roman ri SE19
156 J 2 Roman way Croy
99 R 14 Roman way Drtfrd
8 H 16 Roman way Enf
48 C 18 Roman way N7
126 A 10 Romanhurst av Brom
125 Z 9 Romanhurst av Brom
125 Y 9 Romanhurst gdns Brom
32 G 4 Romany gdns E17
119 X 18 Romany gdns Sutton
107 O 7 Romberg rd SW17
93 T 13 Romborough gdns SE13
94 K 11 Romero sq SE9
108 D 7 Romeyn rd SW16
53 U 11 Romford rd E12
51 Z 19 Romford rd E15
52 K 16 Romford rd E7
37 Z 1 Romford rd Rom
143 U 3 Romford st E1
48 H 8 Romilly rd N4
140 G 7 Romilly st W1
109 N 8 Rommany rd SE27
40 J 1 Romney clo Harrow
31 Z 4 Romney clo N17
46 B 4 Romney clo NW11
113 O 18 Romney dri Chisl
22 H 20 Romney dri Harrow
40 J 1 Romney dri Harrow
98 C 1 Romney gdns Bxly Hth
117 Y 15 Romney rd New Mald
76 J 17 Romney rd SE10
148 H 3 Romney st SW1
108 H 1 Romola rd SE24
68 J 2 Romsey gdns Dgnhm
68 J 3 Romsey rd Dgnhm

71 Y 1 Romsey rd W13
47 N 13 Rona rd NW3
65 N 10 Ronald av E15
124 M 10 Ronald clo Becknhm
63 R 18 Ronald st E1
112 F 20 Ronalds rd Brom
48 G 15 Ronalds rd N5
96 J 15 Ronaldstone rd Sidcp
45 S 14 Rondu rd NW2
94 D 20 Ronver rd SE12
142 J 9 Rood la EC3
57 X 20 Rook clo Hornch
57 Y 20 Rook clo Hornch
17 W 8 Rookby ct N21
77 O 13 Rookel way SE10
26 D 15 Rookery clo NW9
69 V 1 Rookery cres Dgnhm
126 L 14 Rookery la Brom
127 N 14 Rookery la Brom
89 U 11 Rookery rd SW4
26 C 16 Rookery way NW9
29 U 12 Rookfield av N10
29 U 12 Rookfield clo N10
106 L 13 Rookstone rd SW17
118 F 9 Rookwood av New Mald
155 X 8 Rookwood av Wallgtn
21 O 7 Rookwood gdns E4
31 W 20 Rookwood rd N16
57 O 19 Roosevelt way Dgnhm
75 W 9 Rope st SE16
78 L 8 Rope Yard rails SE18
75 V 7 Ropemaker rd SE16
142 F 1 Ropemaker st EC2
160 F 1 Ropemaker st EC2
63 X 20 Ropemakers fields E14
142 L 18 Roper la SE1
95 V 14 Roper st SE9
121 P 2 Roper way Mitch
20 G 17 Ropers av E4
146 J 16 Ropers gdns SW3
63 Y 12 Ropery st E3
135 R 10 Ropley st E2
48 K 12 Rosa Alba ms N5
144 L 19 Rosaline rd SW6
109 Z 8 Rosamond st SE26
82 B 5 Rosary clo Hounsl
146 C 8 Rosary gdns SW7
145 O 19 Rosaville rd SW6
134 C 18 Roscoe st EC1
25 T 3 Roscoff clo Edg
140 C 13 Rose & Crown yd SW1
142 B 12 Rose all SE1
34 J 7 Rose av E18
120 M 1 Rose av Mitch
106 M 20 Rose av Mitch
120 D 11 Rose av Mrdn
32 L 11 Rose Bank gro E17
109 Z 17 Rose Bank st SE20
144 E 19 Rose Bank SW6
25 O 13 Rose Bates dri NW9
119 N 20 Rose end Worc Pk
58 H 11 Rose gdns S'hall
72 H 8 Rose gdns W5
25 X 12 Rose glen NW9
57 P 4 Rose glen Rom
154 B 2 Rose hill Sutton
120 B 20 Rose hill Sutton
37 Z 12 Rose la Rom
10 A 6 Rose lawn Bushey
140 J 8 Rose st WC2
117 T 10 Rose wlk Surb
159 W 2 Rose wlk W Wkhm
60 A 13 Roseacre clo W13
97 S 9 Roseacre rd Welling
41 V 13 Rosebank av Wemb
63 X 7 Rosebank gdns E3
33 P 19 Rosebank rd E17
71 U 6 Rosebank rd W7
33 O 14 Rosebank vlls E17
61 X 16 Rosebank way W3
30 J 18 Roseberry gdns N4
49 U 19 Roseberry pl E8
49 U 19 Roseberry pl E8
151 W 7 Roseberry st SE16
118 C 5 Rosebery av New Mald
122 M 3 Rosebery av Thntn Hth
53 R 18 Rosebery av E12
133 T 14 Rosebery av EC1
40 C 11 Rosebery av Harrow
31 Z 7 Rosebery av N17
96 H 18 Rosebery av Sidcp
119 O 15 Rosebery clo Mrdn
30 A 16 Rosebery gdns N8

59 Z 17 Rosebery gdns W13
29 U 6 Rosebery ms N10
83 O 13 Rosebery rd Hounsl
117 S 4 Rosebery rd Kingst
29 U 7 Rosebery rd N10
18 K 10 Rosebery rd N9
153 V 14 Rosebery rd Sutton
90 A 16 Rosebery rd SW2
89 Z 16 Rosebery rd SW2
117 R 4 Rosebery sq Kingst
83 R 19 Rosebine av Twick
88 B 6 Rosebury rd SW6
122 C 15 Rosecourt rd Croy
45 Z 10 Rosecroft av NW3
83 R 20 Rosecroft gdns Twick
44 G 10 Rosecroft gdns NW2
58 H 12 Rosecroft rd S'hall
80 C 8 Rosedale clo SE2
11 O 20 Rosedale clo Stanm
71 V 6 Rosedale clo W7
68 C 1 Rosedale gdns Dgnhm
68 C 1 Rosedale rd Dgnhm
52 L 16 Rosedale rd E7
152 G 10 Rosedale rd Epsom
84 J 9 Rosedale rd Rich
38 L 10 Rosedale rd Rom
122 B 17 Rosedene av Croy
58 H 8 Rosedene av Grnfd
119 Y 12 Rosedene av Mrdn
108 D 7 Rosedene av SW16
35 X 12 Rosedene gdns Ilf
128 H 3 Rosedene NW6
51 R 7 Rosedene ter E10
144 F 14 Rosedew rd W6
64 A 19 Rosefield gdns E14
11 Y 18 Rosegarden clo Edg
137 U 7 Rosehart ms W11
37 W 10 Rosehatch av Rom
82 E 12 Roseheath rd Hounsl
120 C 19 Rosehill av Sutton
41 W 15 Rosehill gdns Grnfd
154 C 1 Rosehill gdns Sutton
154 C 1 Rosehill Park west Sutton
154 A 1 Rosehill pk Sutton
88 C 15 Rosehill rd SW18
31 O 2 Roseland clo N17
48 J 13 Roseleigh av N5
84 F 17 Roselieu clo Twick
8 D 5 Rosemary av Enf
82 A 6 Rosemary av Hounsl
28 B 8 Rosemary av N3
18 M 6 Rosemary av N9
19 N 7 Rosemary av N9
39 T 10 Rosemary av Rom
35 O 16 Rosemary dri Ilf
56 B 4 Rosemary gdns Dgnhm
85 W 7 Rosemary la SW14
151 O 18 Rosemary rd SE15
106 B 8 Rosemary rd SW17
96 L 2 Rosemary rd Welling
134 F 3 Rosemary st N1
121 V 4 Rosemead av Mitch
42 L 16 Rosemead av Wemb
15 R 19 Rosemont av N12
117 V 6 Rosemont rd New Mald
46 C 17 Rosemont rd NW3
84 L 16 Rosemont rd Rich
61 S 20 Rosemont rd W3
73 T 1 Rosemont rd W3
60 J 4 Rosemont rd Wemb
147 N 6 Rosemoor st SW3
127 U 8 Rosemount dri Brom
59 Z 16 Rosemount rd W13
12 F 11 Rosen's wlk Edg
88 K 2 Rosenau cres SW11
88 K 1 Rosenau rd SW11
90 K 19 Rosendale rd SE21
108 M 1 Rosendale rd SE21
17 V 5 Roseneath av N21
89 O 15 Roseneath rd SW11
8 C 14 Roseneath wlk Enf
93 S 17 Rosenthal rd SE6
92 E 13 Rosenthorpe rd SE15
76 G 6 Roserton st E14
124 E 14 Rosery the Croy
34 C 1 Roses the Wdfd Grn
148 K 18 Rosetta st SW8
112 L 9 Roseveare rd SE12
82 G 13 Roseville av Hounsl
118 M 1 Rosevine rd SW20
94 E 14 Roseway SE12
91 P 17 Roseway SE21
41 Y 17 Rosewood av Grnfd
57 X 15 Rosewood av Hornch
115 S 6 Rosewood clo Sidcp

Grid	Street
155 U 13	Rosewood gdns Wallgtn
154 E 2	Rosewood gro Sutton
64 H 1	Rosher clo E15
50 E 16	Rosina st E9
87 O 7	Roskell rd SW15
73 T 8	Roslin rd W3
112 F 14	Roslin way Brom
120 F 3	Roslyn clo Mitch
39 S 7	Roslyn gdns Rom
31 P 15	Roslyn rd N15
136 M 9	Rosmead rd W11
133 V 15	Rosoman pl EC1
133 T 16	Rosoman st EC1
56 A 5	Ross av Dgnhm
14 E 17	Ross av NW7
23 N 1	Ross clo Harrow
155 T 12	Ross pde Wallgtn
99 V 17	Ross rd Drtfrd
123 S 4	Ross rd SE25
100 L 2	Ross rd Twick
155 V 12	Ross rd Wallgtn
95 R 7	Ross way SE9
39 W 19	Rossall clo Hornch
60 M 9	Rossall cres NW10
9 O 20	Rossdale dri Enf
10 O 9	Rossdale dri N9
43 U 4	Rossdale dri N9
87 N 9	Rossdale rd SW15
154 K 9	Rossdale Sutton
94 G 1	Rosse ms SE3
132 D 2	Rossendale way NW1
82 H 12	Rossindel rd Hounsl
49 Y 6	Rossington st E5
107 T 1	Rossiter rd SW12
98 F 13	Rossland clo Bxly Hth
15 W 1	Rosslyn av Barnt
56 D 2	Rosslyn av Dgnhm
21 O 8	Rosslyn av E4
86 C 8	Rosslyn av SW13
23 W 14	Rosslyn cres Harrow
42 J 11	Rosslyn cres Wemb
23 W 14	Rosslyn Crescent south Harrow
46 H 14	Rosslyn hill NW3
46 G 14	Rosslyn Park ms NW3
54 F 20	Rosslyn rd Bark
67 S 1	Rosslyn rd Bark
33 U 14	Rosslyn rd E17
84 D 16	Rosslyn rd Twick
130 L 17	Rossmore rd NW1
131 N 16	Rossmore rd NW1
155 T 13	Rosswood gdns SM6
106 G 10	Rostella rd SW17
31 V 19	Rostrevor av N15
70 C 14	Rostrevor gdns S'hall
105 X 13	Rostrevor rd SW19
87 U 2	Rostrevor rd SW6
141 X 20	Rotary st SE1
71 Z 20	Rothbury gdns Islwth
50 M 20	Rothbury rd E9
31 Y 3	Rothbury wlk N17
155 P 10	Rotherfield rd Carsh
9 T 1	Rotherfield rd Enf
134 B 1	Rotherfield st N1
107 Y 16	Rotherhithe av SW16
75 R 11	Rotherhithe New rd SE16
151 V 11	Rotherhithe New rd SE16
75 S 10	Rotherhithe Old rd SE16
75 T 2	Rotherhithe st SE16
143 X 18	Rotherhithe st SE16
75 S 1	Rotherhithe tunnel E1
156 E 12	Rothermere rd Croy
61 O 13	Rotherwick hill W5
45 X 2	Rotherwick rd NW11
87 O 7	Rotherwood rd SW15
133 X 4	Rothery st N1
41 O 18	Rothesay av Grnfd
85 S 9	Rothesay av Rich
119 T 2	Rothesay av SW20
123 P 9	Rothesay rd SE25
52 L 19	Rothsay rd E7
150 H 2	Rothsay st SE1
73 V 9	Rothschild rd W4
108 K 10	Rothschild st SE27
68 G 2	Rothwell gdns Dgnhm
68 G 3	Rothwell rd Dgnhm
131 R 3	Rothwell st NW1
76 H 8	Rotterdam dri E14
78 E 14	Rotunda clo SE18
151 S 5	Rouel rd SE16
119 X 15	Rougemont av Mrdn
124 G 17	Round gro Croy
110 B 6	Round hill SE26
127 Y 3	Round wood BR7
110 E 5	Roundhay clo SE23
7 R 3	Roundhedge way Enf
7 P 15	Roundhill dri Enf
112 D 6	Roundtable rd Brom
42 A 15	Roundtree rd Wemb
30 M 4	Roundway N17
31 O 3	Roundway N17
35 T 6	Roundway rd Ilf
62 F 2	Roundwood pk NW10
44 C 19	Roundwood rd NW10
64 B 11	Rounton rd E3
108 D 1	Roupell rd SW2
90 E 20	Roupell rd SW2
141 U 15	Roupell st SE1
132 B 1	Rousden st NW1
109 S 9	Rouse gdns SE21
88 J 19	Routh rd SW18
151 R 3	Rovel rd SE16
144 K 19	Rowallan rd SW6
19 Z 19	Rowan av E4
118 A 4	Rowan clo New Mald
121 Y 1	Rowan clo SW16
72 L 6	Rowan clo W5
41 Z 10	Rowan clo Wemb
121 V 1	Rowan cres SW16
26 F 11	Rowan dri N9
157 V 4	Rowan gdn Croy
72 B 20	Rowan rd Brentf
98 A 8	Rowan rd Bxly Hth
97 Z 8	Rowan rd Bxly Hth
121 V 2	Rowan rd SW16
144 F 6	Rowan rd W6
144 F 6	Rowan ter W6
37 U 11	Rowan way Rom
28 E 17	Rowan wlk N2
17 X 11	Rowans The N13
18 B 4	Rowantree clo N21
7 W 9	Rowantree rd Enf
18 B 4	Rowantree rd N21
15 N 5	Rowben clo N20
151 O 10	Rowcross pl SE1
151 O 9	Rowcross st SE1
58 H 2	Rowdell rd Nthlt
110 K 20	Rowden rd Becknhm
20 C 20	Rowden rd E4
89 N 4	Rowditch la SW11
44 K 20	Rowdon av NW10
159 Z 20	Rowdown cres Croy
69 O 1	Rowdowns rd Dgnhm
67 Z 7	Rowe gdns Bark
40 G 9	Rowe wlk Harrow
88 J 5	Rowena cres SW11
107 O 2	Rowfant rd SW17
50 A 12	Rowhill rd E5
129 Y 20	Rowington clo W2
24 E 11	Rowland av Harrow
65 O 12	Rowland ct E16
18 A 20	Rowland Hill av N17
46 J 14	Rowland Hill st NW3
106 A 20	Rowland way SW19
22 J 1	Rowlands av Pinn
29 O 19	Rowlands clo N6
26 F 2	Rowlands clo NW7
56 B 8	Rowlands rd Dgnhm
97 P 19	Rowley av Sidcp
61 N 1	Rowley clo Wemb
43 N 20	Rowley clo Wemb
48 K 1	Rowley gdns N4
30 L 16	Rowley rd N15
130 A 4	Rowley way NW8
129 Z 4	Rowley way NW8
117 O 5	Rowlls rd Kingst
55 S 18	Rowney gdns Dgnhm
55 R 18	Rowney rd Dgnhm
101 S 1	Rowntree rd Twick
64 G 2	Rowse clo E15
26 L 9	Rowsley av NW4
47 Z 16	Rowstock gdns N7
79 P 18	Rowton rd SE18
41 S 1	Roxborough av Harrow
71 W 19	Roxborough av Islwth
40 A 19	Roxborough Nthlt
23 S 20	Roxborough pk Harrow
41 T 2	Roxborough pk Harrow
40 A 19	Roxbourne clo Nthlt
40 A 4	Roxbourne pk Harrow
108 H 11	Roxburgh rd SE27
145 V 13	Roxby pl SW6
40 L 7	Roxeth Green av Harrow
40 L 12	Roxeth gro Harrow
41 R 6	Roxeth hill Harrow
93 S 16	Roxley rd SE13
159 N 12	Roxton gdns Croy
68 B 7	Roxwell rd Bark
74 G 5	Roxwell rd W12
34 M 1	Roxwell way Wdfd Grn
37 S 20	Roxy av Rom
36 J 14	Roy gdns Ilf
100 K 14	Roy gro Hampt
140 B 11	Royal Academy W1
138 E 20	Royal Albert hall SW7
81 U 12	Royal Alfred home Blvdr
140 A 11	Royal arc W1
147 O 9	Royal av SW3
152 B 3	Royal av Worc Pk
84 K 5	Royal Botanic Gardens Rich
108 H 7	Royal cir SE27
152 A 3	Royal clo Worc Pk
132 C 3	Royal College st NW1
47 U 20	Royal College st NW1
136 H 15	Royal Cres ms W11
40 A 11	Royal cres Ruis
136 J 15	Royal cres W11
43 O 13	Royal ct Wemb
160 F 6	Royal Exchange bldgs EC2
141 O 14	Royal Festival Hall SE1
76 F 20	Royal hill SE10
76 G 19	Royal hill SE10
147 P 12	Royal Hospital rd SW3
78 F 14	Royal Military repository SE18
143 P 9	Royal Mint E1
143 P 9	Royal Mint st E1
76 H 16	Royal Naval College SE10
92 A 16	Royal Oak pl SE22
98 C 12	Royal Oak rd Bxly Hth
49 Y 18	Royal Oak rd E8
140 F 13	Royal Opera arc SW1
114 C 19	Royal pde Chisl
94 B 5	Royal pde SE3
60 K 10	Royal pde W5
76 G 20	Royal pl SE10
65 Z 18	Royal rd E16
149 W 14	Royal rd SE17
115 W 6	Royal rd Sidcp
101 R 11	Royal rd Tedd
141 P 20	Royal st SE1
63 T 6	Royal Victor pl E3
155 S 4	Royal wlk Wallgtn
67 X 7	Roycraft av Bark
67 X 6	Roycraft clo Bark
67 Y 6	Roycraft gdns Bark
34 H 5	Roycroft clo E18
108 F 2	Roycroft clo SW2
79 U 14	Roydene rd SE18
39 Y 17	Royle clo Rom
59 Y 12	Royle cres W13
20 C 17	Royston av E4
154 G 5	Royston av Sutton
155 Y 8	Royston av Wallgtn
35 N 19	Royston gdns Ilf
154 F 5	Royston pk Sutton
99 S 16	Royston rd Drtfrd
84 L 14	Royston rd Rich
124 F 1	Royston rd SE20
110 F 20	Royston rd SE20
63 R 8	Royston st E2
117 S 11	Roystons the Surb
89 U 6	Rozel rd SW4
110 M 5	Rubens st SE6
9 Y 1	Ruberoid rd Enf
33 O 10	Ruby rd E17
151 W 15	Ruby st SE15
151 W 13	Ruby triangle SE15
51 S 10	Ruckholt clo E10
51 P 12	Ruckholt rd E10
62 E 6	Rucklidge av NW10
46 F 12	Rudall cres NW3
79 N 11	Rudd st SE18
75 W 19	Ruddigore rd SE14
98 H 8	Rudland rd Bxly Hth
89 U 17	Rudloe rd SW12
65 R 7	Rudolph rd E13
12 H 18	Rudyard gro NW7
157 Z 15	Ruffetts clo S Croy
158 A 16	Ruffetts the S Croy
23 Z 19	Rufford clo Harrow
132 K 3	Rufford st N1
40 A 10	Rufus clo Ruis
134 J 14	Rufus st EC1
41 S 17	Rugby av Grnfd
18 G 5	Rugby av N9
42 C 14	Rugby av Wemb
23 S 14	Rugby clo Harrow
55 S 19	Rugby gdns Dgnhm
153 P 20	Rugby la Sutton
55 P 19	Rugby rd Dgnhm
25 S 12	Rugby rd NW9
83 U 15	Rugby rd Twick
73 Z 6	Rugby rd W4
133 N 19	Rugby st WC1
58 K 11	Ruislip clo Grnfd
59 P 11	Ruislip rd East Grnfd
58 L 11	Ruislip rd Grnfd
58 B 8	Ruislip rd Nthlt
106 M 9	Ruislip st SW17
75 O 2	Rum clo E1
143 Z 10	Rum clo E1
145 Y 19	Rumbold rd SW6
100 E 15	Rumsey clo Hampt
90 D 7	Rumsley rd SW9
43 Y 5	Runbury cir NW9
136 J 9	Runcorn pl W11
26 J 17	Rundell cres NW4
41 T 10	Runnelfield Harrow
141 W 14	Running Horse yd SE1
82 L 17	Runnymede clo Twick
107 Z 20	Runnymede cres SW16
82 K 17	Runnymede gdns Twick
59 T 6	Runnymede gdns Grnfd
82 L 16	Runnymede rd Twick
106 P 20	Runnymede SW19
75 P 6	Rupack st SE16
42 K 16	Rupert av Wemb
140 F 9	Rupert ct W1
90 J 6	Rupert gdns SW9
47 Y 8	Rupert rd N19
129 R 10	Rupert rd NW6
74 B 9	Rupert rd W4
140 E 8	Rupert st W1
107 T 17	Rural way SW16
65 P 17	Ruscoe rd E16
152 F 1	Rush ct Worc Pk
56 L 3	Rush Green gdns Rom
56 K 4	Rush Green rd Rom
78 H 12	Rush Grove st SE18
89 P 8	Rush Hill rd SW11
88 M 17	Rusham rd SW12
89 N 17	Rusham rd SW12
32 M 6	Rushbrook cres E17
114 A 5	Rushbrook rd SE9
33 P 1	Rushcroft dri E4
33 R 1	Rushcroft rd E4
90 F 11	Rushcroft rd SW2
109 P 18	Rushden clo SE19
35 X 10	Rushden gdns Ilf
14 A 18	Rushden gdns NW7
15 X 3	Rushdene av Barnt
80 G 9	Rushdene SE2
120 G 19	Rushen wlk Carsh
116 A 19	Rushett clo Surb
116 A 18	Rushett rd Surb
117 X 10	Rushey clo New Mald
93 S 18	Rushey grn SE6
7 P 15	Rushey hill Enf
93 O 14	Rushey mead SE13
93 O 14	Rushey mead SE13
92 M 16	Rushford rd SE4
26 D 13	Rushgrove av NW9
157 U 8	Rushmead clo Croy
12 G 7	Rushmead clo Edg
102 B 8	Rushmead Rich
127 R 7	Rushmore clo Brom
50 E 12	Rushmore cres E5
50 C 12	Rushmore rd E5
56 E 9	Rusholme av Dgnhm
109 T 12	Rusholme gro SE19
87 R 17	Rusholme rd SW15
24 A 19	Rushout av Harrow
134 F 8	Rushton st N1
26 G 11	Rushworth av NW4
26 G 12	Rushworth gdns NW4
141 Y 18	Rushworth st SE1
53 T 17	Ruskin av E12
73 R 20	Ruskin av Rich
96 M 6	Ruskin av Welling

97 N 6	Ruskin av Welling
28 A 18	Ruskin clo NW11
97 N 6	Ruskin dri Welling
152 L 2	Ruskin dri Worc Pk
24 M 15	Ruskin gdns Harrow
25 N 13	Ruskin gdns Harrow
39 Y 4	Ruskin gdns Rom
60 F 11	Ruskin gdns W5
97 N 6	Ruskin gro Welling
81 R 11	Ruskin rd Blvdr
155 O 11	Ruskin rd Carsh
156 K 2	Ruskin rd Croy
83 V 8	Ruskin rd Islwth
31 U 4	Ruskin rd N17
58 A 20	Ruskin rd S'hall
120 F 1	Ruskin way SW19
127 T 13	Ruskin wlk Brom
18 J 8	Ruskin wlk N9
90 L 14	Ruskin wlk SE24
23 T 14	Rusland Park rd Harrow
44 M 10	Rusper clo NW2
11 S 14	Rusper clo Stanm
55 U 18	Rusper rd Dgnhm
30 L 9	Rusper rd N22
30 H 8	Russell av N22
125 S 5	Russell clo Becknhm
98 D 10	Russell clo Bxly Hth
99 W 9	Russell clo Drtfrd
61 V 1	Russell clo NW10
77 W 19	Russell clo SE7
140 B 15	Russell ct SW1
136 K 20	Russell Gardens ms W14
15 X 8	Russell gdns N20
27 T 19	Russell gdns NW11
102 C 4	Russell gdns Rich
144 L 1	Russell gdns W14
13 N 14	Russell gro NW7
16 A 6	Russell la N20
15 X 8	Russell la N20
23 V 3	Russell mead Harrow
148 F 9	Russell pl SW1
21 X 6	Russell rd Buck Hl
21 Y 5	Russell rd Buck Hl
33 R 20	Russell rd E10
65 U 17	Russell rd E16
32 K 11	Russell rd E17
19 X 14	Russell rd E4
8 G 3	Russell rd Enf
120 K 6	Russell rd Mitch
17 O 18	Russell rd N13
31 R 16	Russell rd N15
15 X 7	Russell rd N20
41 N 13	Russell rd Nthlt
26 E 19	Russell rd NW9
105 X 17	Russell rd SW19
83 V 17	Russell rd Twick
144 M 2	Russell rd W14
132 J 19	Russell sq WC1
140 M 8	Russell st WC2
153 Z 11	Russell way SM1
108 C 12	Russells footpath SW16
48 C 14	Russet cres N7
20 J 13	Russets clo E4
160 C 5	Russia ct EC2
75 W 4	Russia Dock rd SE16
63 O 6	Russia la E2
135 Z 8	Russia la E2
160 C 5	Russia row EC2
75 U 6	Russia wlk SE16
150 D 17	Rust sq SE5
73 Y 8	Rusthall av W4
124 C 13	Rusthall clo Croy
107 T 17	Rustic av SW16
42 F 11	Rustic pl Wemb
119 V 16	Rustington wlk Mrdn
117 S 17	Ruston av Surb
136 K 5	Ruston ms W11
63 Z 3	Ruston st E3
108 A 12	Rutford rd SW16
24 M 11	Ruth clo Harrow
154 F 13	Rutherford clo Sutton
148 F 4	Rutherford st SW1
10 D 5	Rutherford way Bushey
43 R 11	Rutherford way Wemb
79 Z 15	Rutherglen rd SE2
152 G 14	Rutherwyke clo Epsom
26 A 18	Ruthin clo NW9
77 T 16	Ruthin rd SE3
63 T 3	Ruthven st E9
97 N 18	Rutland av Sidcp
115 W 3	Rutland clo Bxly
85 U 7	Rutland clo SW14

106 H 16	Rutland clo SW19
119 W 15	Rutland dri Mrdn
81 U 14	Rutland ga Blvdr
126 D 9	Rutland ga Brom
138 K 19	Rutland ga SW7
138 L 19	Rutland Gardens ms SW7
138 K 20	Rutland Gate ms SW7
157 T 9	Rutland gdns Croy
55 S 14	Rutland gdns Dgnhm
30 J 18	Rutland gdns N4
138 L 19	Rutland gdns SW7
59 Y 15	Rutland gdns W13
144 A 10	Rutland gro W6
74 K 14	Rutland gro W6
146 K 1	Rutland Mews south SW7
146 K 1	Rutland Mews west SW7
45 N 18	Rutland pk NW2
110 M 5	Rutland pk SE6
34 J 14	Rutland rd E11
33 O 18	Rutland rd E17
53 N 20	Rutland rd E7
63 S 3	Rutland rd E9
9 N 18	Rutland rd Enf
23 N 18	Rutland rd Harrow
54 A 11	Rutland rd Ilf
53 Z 11	Rutland rd Ilf
58 G 14	Rutland rd S'hall
106 J 16	Rutland rd SW19
101 P 4	Rutland rd Twick
146 K 1	Rutland st SW7
110 M 4	Rutland wlk SE6
105 Y 20	Rutlish rd SW19
120 E 9	Rutter gdns Mitch
92 E 4	Rutts ter SE14
10 D 5	Rutts the Bushey
87 P 7	Ruvigny gdns SW15
115 X 15	Ruxley clo Sidcp
115 X 16	Ruxley corner Sidcp
94 J 10	Ryan clo SE9
91 W 18	Rycott pth SE22
94 C 4	Ryculff sq SE3
27 R 5	Rydal clo NW4
60 C 7	Rydal cres Grnfd
98 H 3	Rydal dri Bxly Hth
82 K 16	Rydal gdns Hounsl
26 B 15	Rydal gdns NW9
104 A 12	Rydal gdns SW15
42 E 3	Rydal gdns Wemb
107 X 11	Rydal rd SW16
9 R 19	Rydal way Enf
84 F 15	Ryde pl Twick
112 H 13	Ryder clo Brom
140 B 13	Ryder ct SW1
66 K 17	Ryder gdns E6
57 U 18	Ryder gdns Rainhm
140 C 13	Ryder st SW1
140 C 12	Ryder yd SW1
130 A 8	Ryders ter NW8
107 T 3	Rydevale rd SW12
134 C 4	Rydon st N1
95 P 7	Rydons clo SE9
48 B 20	Rydston clo N7
98 G 15	Rye Hill pk SE15
92 B 11	Rye rd SE15
91 X 4	Rye la SE15
92 E 12	Rye rd SE15
16 J 2	Rye the N14
12 A 19	Rye way Edg
87 P 14	Rye wlk SW15
109 S 1	Ryecotes mead SE21
35 Z 7	Ryecroft av Ilf
100 L 2	Ryecroft av Twick
82 L 20	Ryecroft av Twick
93 V 13	Ryecroft rd SE13
108 G 15	Ryecroft rd SW16
87 Z 3	Ryecroft st SW6
31 V 10	Ryecroft way N17
91 Z 16	Ryedale SE22
108 M 15	Ryefield rd SE19
105 X 6	Ryfold rd SW19
16 F 13	Ryhope rd N11
47 S 17	Ryland rd NW5
44 G 9	Rylandes rd NW2
94 J 16	Rylands cres SE12
74 D 7	Rylett cres W12
74 F 8	Rylett rd W12
18 A 11	Rylston rd N13
145 O 16	Rylston rd SW6
123 T 17	Rymer rd Croy
88 B 12	Rymer rd SW18
90 J 15	Rymer st SE24
78 J 4	Rymill st E16
139 O 20	Rysbrack st SW3

S

65 O 18	Sabbarton st E16
88 M 7	Sabine rd SW11
89 N 7	Sabine rd SW8
48 J 20	Sable st N1
50 A 6	Sach rd E5
126 E 19	Sackville av Brom
41 P 10	Sackville clo Harrow
53 T 3	Sackville gdns Ilf
153 X 17	Sackville rd Sutton
140 B 11	Sackville st W1
14 K 16	Saddlescombe way N12
120 L 3	Sadler clo Mitch
30 G 9	Sadlings the N22
112 H 4	Sadstone rd SE12
27 V 17	Saffron clo NW11
133 U 19	Saffron hill EC1
141 V 1	Saffron hill EC1
38 L 7	Saffron rd Rom
133 U 19	Saffron st EC1
66 A 18	Saigasso clo E16
149 P 4	Sail st SE11
107 P 4	Sainfoin rd SW17
109 R 12	Sainsbury rd SE19
97 O 3	St Abb's St Welling
103 N 16	St Agathas clo Kingst
63 P 4	St Agnes clo E9
149 V 15	St Agnes pl SE11
72 C 6	St Aidan's rd W13
91 Z 14	St Aidans rd SE22
66 J 9	St Alban's av E6
101 Z 12	St Alban's gdns Tedd
120 K 18	St Alban's gro Carsh
146 A 1	St Alban's gro W8
145 Z 1	St Alban's gro W8
133 V 5	St Alban's pl N1
54 K 2	St Alban's rd Ilf
62 A 3	St Alban's rd NW10
47 P 9	St Alban's rd NW5
144 K 12	St Alban's ter W6
73 Y 10	St Albans av W4
34 E 3	St Albans cres Wdfd Grn
30 F 6	St Albans cres N22
45 Y 4	St Albans la NW11
138 H 1	St Albans ms W2
34 D 3	St Albans rd Wdfd Grn
4 C 4	St Albans rd Barnt
102 K 16	St Albans rd Kingst
153 U 9	St Albans rd Sutton
140 F 12	St Albans rd SW1
76 G 17	St Alfege pas SE10
78 B 15	St Alfege rd SE7
142 C 2	St Alphage gdn EC2
160 C 2	St Alphage gdn EC2
25 W 7	St Alphage wlk Edgw
19 O 3	St Alphage rd N9
89 W 11	St Alphonsus rd SW4
111 O 9	St Amund's clo SE6
141 V 3	St Andrew st EC4
41 Y 12	St Andrew's av Wemb
24 E 7	St Andrew's clo Stanm
44 J 10	St Andrew's clo NW2
41 Y 11	St Andrew's clo Wemb
15 P 13	St Andrew's clo N12
49 O 4	St Andrew's gro N16
49 R 3	St Andrew's ms N16
131 X 16	St Andrew's pl NW1
44 J 19	St Andrew's rd NW10
27 W 19	St Andrew's rd NW11
154 K 4	St Andrew's rd Carsh
156 L 8	St Andrew's rd Croy
65 V 10	St Andrew's rd E13
32 G 9	St Andrew's rd E17
8 C 12	St Andrew's rd Enf
53 U 1	St Andrew's rd Ilf
19 P 4	St Andrew's rd N9
43 X 5	St Andrew's rd NW9
116 G 14	St Andrew's rd Surb
62 B 18	St Andrew's rd W3
116 F 14	St Andrew's sq Surb
106 C 3	St Andrews ct SW18
24 E 5	St Andrews dri Stanm
141 Y 7	St Andrews hill EC4
33 Z 19	St Andrews rd E11
63 N 4	St Andrews rd E2
39 O 18	St Andrews rd Rom

115 X 7	St Andrews rd Sidcp
144 M 12	St Andrews rd W14
71 S 5	St Andrews rd W7
136 J 6	St Andrews sq W11
31 P 18	St Ann's clo N15
88 C 15	St Ann's cres SW18
47 O 18	St Ann's gdns NW5
88 C 17	St Ann's hill SW18
88 C 17	St Ann's Park rd SW18
23 U 18	St Ann's rd Harrow
30 J 16	St Ann's rd N15
18 G 7	St Ann's rd N9
86 D 3	St Ann's rd SW13
136 H 13	St Ann's rd W11
67 R 4	St Ann's st Bark
148 G 1	St Ann's st SW1
130 G 8	St Ann's ter NW8
156 K 14	St Ann's way Croy
63 Z 18	St Anne st E14
42 H 15	St Anne's rd Wemb
63 Z 18	St Anne's row E14
47 P 8	St Annes clo N6
140 E 6	St Annes ct W1
60 L 8	St Annes gdns Wemb
63 Y 19	St Annes pas E14
51 V 5	St Annes rd E11
148 G 2	St Anns la SW1
86 C 7	St Anns pas SW13
30 B 13	St Anns rd N8
136 J 14	St Anns vlls W11
139 V 7	St Anselm's pl W1
34 K 1	St Anthony's av Wdfd Grn
143 S 13	St Anthony's clo E1
106 J 4	St Anthony's clo SW17
52 G 20	St Anthony's rd E7
65 U 1	St Anthony's rd E7
157 T 5	St Arvan's clo Croy
92 F 7	St Asaph rd SE4
82 G 14	St Aubyn's av Hounsl
105 U 12	St Aubyn's av SW19
109 T 16	St Aubyn's rd SE19
98 F 4	St Audrey av Bxly Hth
42 K 9	St Augustine's av Wemb
156 L 15	St Augustine's av S Croy
127 R 12	St Augustine's av Brom
60 L 7	St Augustine's av W5
81 P 9	Saint Augustine's rd Blvdr
47 Y 19	St Augustine's rd NW1
24 M 8	St Austell clo Edg
93 V 4	St Austell rd SE13
67 S 2	St Awdry's rd Bark
67 P 1	St Awdrys wlk Bark
125 T 3	St Barnabas clo Becknhm
154 F 10	St Barnabas rd Sutton
34 J 2	St Barnabas rd Wdfd Grn
21 X 20	St Barnabas rd Wdfd Grn
33 N 18	St Barnabas rd E17
107 P 18	St Barnabas rd Mitch
147 V 10	St Barnabas st SW1
90 A 1	St Barnabas vlls SW8
66 F 5	St Bartholomews rd E6
133 Z 19	St Barts Medical School EC1
107 P 13	St Benedicts clo SW17
106 J 4	St Benet clo SW17
120 C 18	St Benet's gro Carsh
66 B 4	St Bernard's rd E6
109 O 9	St Bernards clo SE27
157 S 7	St Bernards Croy
126 G 3	St Blaise av Brom
143 N 5	St Botolph St EC3
24 M 5	St Bride's av Edg
141 W 7	St Bride's pas EC4
141 V 5	St Bride's st EC4
106 J 4	St Catherines clo SW17
92 F 6	St Catherines dri SE14
20 B 9	St Catherines rd E4
132 M 11	St Chad's pl WC1
37 X 20	St Chad's rd Rom
132 L 12	St Chad's rd WC1
55 Y 1	St Chads gdns Rom
37 W 18	St Chads pk Rom
136 K 2	St Charles pl W10

60 J 11 Sandall rd W5
63 V 12 Sandalwood clo E1
119 Z 4 Sandbourne av SW19
92 H 4 Sandbourne rd SE4
12 M 18 Sandbrook clo NW7
49 R 10 Sandbrook rd N16
95 R 8 Sandby grn SE9
81 Z 12 Sandcliff rd Erith
141 T 16 Sandell st SE1
26 M 1 Sanders la NW7
27 O 1 Sanders la NW7
47 Z 5 Sanders way N19
47 R 14 Sanderson clo NW5
59 Z 4 Sanderson cres Grnfd
45 S 8 Sanderstead av NW2
89 V 18 Sanderstead clo SW12
157 O 18 Sanderstead rd S Croy
50 J 3 Sanderstead rd E10
42 A 15 Sanderton rd Wemb
122 K 6 Sandfield gdns Thntn Hth
122 K 6 Sandfield rd Thntn Hth
30 L 3 Sandford av N22
66 F 11 Sandford clo E6
49 R 3 Sandford ct N16
126 F 8 Sandford rd Brom
97 Z 9 Sandford rd Bxly Hth
66 F 9 Sandford rd E6
146 A 20 Sandford rd SW6
150 F 9 Sandford row SE17
75 U 17 Sandford wlk SE14
80 F 18 Sandgate rd Welling
151 V 13 Sandgate st SE15
155 Y 7 Sandhills Wallgtn
22 L 19 Sandhurst av Harrow
117 S 17 Sandhurst av Surb
25 O 10 Sandhurst clo NW9
157 T 18 Sandhurst clo S Croy
54 L 13 Sandhurst dri Ilf
97 V 14 Sandhurst rd Bxly
9 R 20 Sandhurst rd Enf
19 S 1 Sandhurst rd N9
25 P 11 Sandhurst rd NW9
111 X 1 Sandhurst rd SE6
114 M 7 Sandhurst rd Sidcp
157 T 18 Sandhurst way S Croy
153 U 3 Sandiford rd Sutton
157 X 3 Sandilands Croy
88 A 3 Sandilands rd SW6
91 W 6 Sandison st SE15
141 O 2 Sandland st WC1
113 V 7 Sandling ri SE9
30 G 9 Sandlings the N22
90 A 10 Sandmere rd SW4
89 Z 9 Sandmere rd SW4
56 J 18 Sandown av Dgnhm
155 N 19 Sandown dri Carsh
124 A 11 Sandown rd SE25
123 Z 11 Sandown rd SE25
40 C 17 Sandown way Nthlt
111 Y 13 Sandpit rd Brom
158 F 7 Sandpits rd Croy
102 H 3 Sandpits rd Rich
82 K 14 Sandra clo Hounsl
23 U 12 Sandridge clo Harrow
119 T 2 Sandringham av SW20
8 E 8 Sandringham clo Enf
36 C 10 Sandringham clo Ilf
40 H 8 Sandringham cres Harrow
96 H 4 Sandringham dri Welling
30 B 19 Sandringham gdns N8
36 C 10 Sandringham gdns Ilf
15 T 19 Sandringham gdns N12
112 F 13 Sandringham rd Brom
40 H 20 Sandringham rd Nthlt
152 H 5 Sandringham rd Worc Pk
44 J 17 Sandringham rd NW2
45 S 2 Sandringham rd NW11
54 L 16 Sandringham rd Bark
122 M 12 Sandringham rd Croy
33 X 19 Sandringham rd E10
52 K 16 Sandringham rd E7
49 X 15 Sandringham rd E8
30 L 9 Sandringham rd N22

158 F 8 Sandrock pl Croy
93 P 7 Sandrock rd SE13
78 C 10 Sands st SE18
47 T 7 Sandstone pl N19
77 V 16 Sandtoft rd SE7
45 Y 17 Sandwell cres NW6
132 J 14 Sandwich st WC1
78 L 15 Sandy Hill rd SE18
78 L 13 Sandy Hill rd SE18
155 V 19 Sandy Hill rd Wallgtn
121 P 1 Sandy la Mitch
155 Z 11 Sandy la North Wallgtn
115 X 18 Sandy la Orp
102 E 5 Sandy la Rich
155 X 13 Sandy la South Wallgtn
153 T 18 Sandy la Sutton
102 A 19 Sandy la Tedd
101 Y 17 Sandy la Tedd
46 B 6 Sandy rd NW3
113 V 15 Sandy ridge Chisl
158 K 5 Sandy way Croy
84 C 17 Sandycombe rd Twick
85 O 8 Sandycombe rd Rich
79 Z 16 Sandycroft SE2
53 Y 13 Sandyhill rd Ilf
11 T 17 Sandymount av Stanm
142 L 1 Sandys row E1
49 U 8 Sanford la SE14
75 U 16 Sanford st SE14
49 V 8 Sanford ter N16
123 T 8 Sangley rd SE25
93 R 20 Sangley rd SE6
111 U 1 Sangley rd SE6
88 G 11 Sangora rd SW11
133 V 16 Sans wlk EC1
52 B 7 Sansom rd E11
52 B 8 Sansom rd E11
150 F 20 Sansom st SE5
91 P 1 Sansom st SE5
66 A 17 Santana clo E16
90 B 10 Santley st SW4
87 X 13 Santos rd SW18
10 E 17 Santway the Stanm
66 H 17 Sapphire clo E6
75 W 12 Sapphire rd SE8
123 O 13 Saracen clo Croy
64 B 18 Saracen st E14
142 M 7 Saracen's Head yd EC3
134 K 12 Sarah st N1
50 C 11 Saratoga rd E5
141 O 5 Sardinia st WC2
23 O 7 Sarita clo Harrow
105 R 5 Sarjant clo SW19
70 H 20 Sark clo Hounsl
65 V 16 Sark wlk E16
8 A 13 Sarnesfield rd Enf
45 V 14 Sarre rd NW2
82 F 4 Sarsen av Hounsl
106 M 2 Sarsfeld rd SW12
107 N 2 Sarsfeld rd SW12
60 C 5 Sarsfield rd Grnfd
26 D 4 Satchell mead NW9
135 R 14 Satchwell rd E2
135 R 14 Satchwell st E2
92 E 11 Sator rd SE15
52 A 9 Sauls Green E11
100 L 13 Saunders clo Hampt
76 J 12 Saunders Ness rd E14
79 X 13 Saunders rd SE18
68 D 20 Saunders way SE28
42 B 15 Saunderton gdns Wemb
57 V 7 Saunton rd Hornch
66 H 18 Savage gdns E6
142 M 9 Savage gdns EC3
18 K 1 Savernake rd N9
47 N 12 Savernake rd NW3
118 B 12 Savile clo New Mald
157 V 3 Savile gdns Croy
140 A 10 Savile row W1
118 H 5 Savill gdns New Mald
21 R 18 Savill row Wdfd Grn
78 D 3 Saville rd E16
38 B 20 Saville rd Rom
101 V 2 Saville rd Twick
73 X 8 Saville rd W4
9 S 10 Saville row Enf
140 A 10 Saville row W1
105 H 17 Savona clo SW19
148 A 19 Savona st SW8
140 M 9 Savoy bldgs WC2
12 B 16 Savoy clo Edg
141 N 10 Savoy hill WC2
140 M 11 Savoy pl WC2

141 N 11 Savoy pl WC2
141 N 10 Savoy row WC2
141 N 10 Savoy st WC2
141 N 10 Savoy steps WC2
140 M 10 Savoy way WC2
105 R 4 Sawkin clo SW19
74 F 2 Sawley rd W12
120 H 17 Sawtry clo Carsh
142 A 17 Sawyer st SE1
141 Z 16 Sawyer st SE1
56 J 18 Sawyers clo Dgnhm
59 Y 18 Sawyers lawn W13
90 A 17 Saxby rd SW2
67 V 5 Saxham rd Berk
20 L 11 Saxlingham rd E4
115 T 14 Saxon and Mallard wlk Sidcp
100 G 6 Saxon av Felt
61 T 15 Saxon dri W3
58 C 20 Saxon gdns S'hall
100 E 4 Saxon ho Felt
112 D 18 Saxon rd Brom
63 X 7 Saxon rd E3
66 F 12 Saxon rd E6
54 A 17 Saxon rd Ilf
53 Z 17 Saxon rd Ilf
30 J 4 Saxon rd N22
70 C 1 Saxon rd S'hall
123 O 12 Saxon rd SE25
43 U 9 Saxon rd Wemb
6 J 19 Saxon way N14
120 F 6 Saxonbury clo Mitch
116 E 20 Saxonbury gdns Surb
93 X 9 Saxton clo SE13
150 A 4 Sayer st SE17
84 M 18 Sayers wlk Rich
75 Z 15 Sayes Court st SE8
114 L 16 Scadbury pk Chisl
140 D 1 Scala st W1
31 W 10 Scales rd N17
136 G 5 Scamps ms W10
143 W 14 Scandrett st E1
51 W 4 Scarborough rd E11
48 G 3 Scarborough rd N4
19 P 2 Scarborough rd N9
143 P 7 Scarborough st E1
156 L 5 Scarborough rd Croy
42 H 18 Scarle rd Wemb
111 Y 6 Scarlet rd SE6
95 O 7 Scarsbrook rd SE3
145 X 1 Scarsdale pl W8
40 M 11 Scarsdale rd Harrow
145 U 3 Scarsdale vlls W8
86 F 7 Scarth rd SW13
75 V 13 Scawen rd SE8
135 P 9 Scawfell st E2
14 K 14 Scaynes link N12
63 P 9 Sceptre rd E2
20 J 6 Scholar's rd E4
107 U 2 Scholar's rd SW12
47 Y 6 Scholefield rd N19
63 S 19 School House la E1
116 D 1 School la Kingst
22 B 12 School la Pinn
97 S 7 School la Welling
70 F 1 School pass S'hall
63 N 12 School pl E1
100 M 14 School Rd av Hampt
114 C 19 School rd Chisl
69 T 3 School rd Dgnhm
53 T 13 School rd E12
100 M 14 School rd Hampt
83 N 8 School rd Hounsl
116 E 1 School rd Kingst
31 P 19 School rd N15
61 Z 12 School rd NW10
15 U 19 School way N12
63 W 7 Schoolbell ms E3
102 C 19 Schoolhouse la Tedd
76 G 13 Schooner st E14
87 V 13 Schubert rd SW15
146 G 2 Science museum SW7
135 O 17 Sclater st E1
49 V 10 Scoble pl N16
108 G 1 Scoles cres SW2
141 X 15 Scoresby st SE1
59 Y 6 Scorton av Grnfd
22 A 2 Scot gro Pinn
60 A 13 Scotch comm W13
59 Z 13 Scotch comm W13
34 J 1 Scoter clo Wdfd Grn
9 T 17 Scotland Green rd Enf
9 U 15 Scotland Green Road north Enf
31 V 7 Scotland grn N17
140 K 14 Scotland pl SW1
21 Y 6 Scotland rd Buck Hl

153 T 15 Scotsdale clo Sutton
94 J 15 Scotsdale rd SE12
133 V 16 Scotswood st EC1
31 Y 1 Scotswood wlk N17
122 B 1 Scott clo SW16
99 T 2 Scott cres Erith
40 J 5 Scott cres Harrow
130 E 14 Scott Ellis gdns NW8
143 T 20 Scott Lidgett cres SE16
51 T 5 Scott's rd E10
136 A 18 Scott's rd W12
74 K 6 Scott's rd W12
55 W 3 Scottes la Dgnhm
125 Y 3 Scotts av Brom
100 K 17 Scotts dri Hampt
125 W 7 Scotts la Brom
112 E 19 Scotts rd Brom
65 R 17 Scoulding rd E16
64 H 20 Scouler st E14
64 J 20 Scouler st E14
89 U 8 Scout la SW4
12 M 13 Scout way NW7
53 Z 10 Scrafton rd Ilf
68 J 5 Scrattons ter Bark
135 P 3 Scriven st E8
93 R 17 Scrooby st SE6
62 H 10 Scrubs la NW10
89 X 19 Scrutton clo SW12
134 J 17 Scrutton st EC2
25 U 12 Scudamore la NW9
92 B 14 Scutari rd SE22
91 Y 7 Scylla rd SE15
159 Z 3 Seabrook dri W Wkhm
56 E 2 Seabrook gdns Rom
55 V 9 Seabrook rd Dgnhm
141 X 5 Seacoal la EC4
80 H 5 Seacourt rd SE2
16 K 15 Seafield rd N11
33 R 11 Seaford rd E17
8 F 14 Seaford rd Enf
31 P 14 Seaford rd N15
72 A 3 Seaford rd W13
132 M 14 Seaford rd WC1
118 K 9 Seaforth av New Mald
39 R 1 Seaforth clo Rom
40 L 16 Seaforth cres N6
152 D 9 Seaforth gdns Epsom
17 S 4 Seaforth gdns N21
21 Y 17 Seaforth gdns Wdfd Grn
63 Y 14 Seager pl E3
145 U 13 Seagrave rd SW6
34 F 20 Seagry rd E11
49 V 13 Seal st E8
48 D 4 Searle pl N4
146 L 20 Searles clo SW11
150 F 4 Searles rd SE1
150 E 18 Sears st SE5
54 J 14 Seaton av Ilf
65 T 13 Seaton clo E13
86 K 20 Seaton clo SW15
83 P 16 Seaton clo Twick
99 W 19 Seaton rd Drtfrd
120 J 4 Seaton rd Mitch
83 O 16 Seaton rd Twick
80 F 20 Seaton rd Welling
60 J 5 Seaton rd Wemb
18 L 17 Seaton rd N18
133 X 14 Sebastian st EC1
18 K 12 Sebastopol rd N9
133 X 1 Sebbon st N1
52 L 13 Sebert rd E7
135 U 9 Sebright pas E2
4 D 10 Sebright rd Barnt
22 M 6 Secker cres Harrow
141 S 15 Secker st SE1
69 V 5 Second av Dgnhm
53 S 14 Second av E12
65 T 9 Second av E13
33 P 15 Second av E17
8 G 17 Second av Enf
19 P 13 Second av N18
27 O 12 Second av NW4
37 T 15 Second av Rom
86 A 6 Second av SW14
129 N 15 Second av W10
74 D 3 Second av W3
42 G 6 Second av Wemb
101 S 3 Second Cross rd Twick
43 T 13 Second way Wemb
150 H 9 Sedan way SE17
9 S 16 Sedcote rd Enf
147 S 6 Sedding st SW1
120 G 12 Seddon rd Mrdn
133 O 14 Seddon st WC1
95 O 6 Sedgebrook rd SE3

24 E 16	Sedgecombe av Harrow	

24 E 16 Sedgecombe av Harrow
74 E 2 Sedgeford rd W12
111 R 12 Sedgehill rd SE6
28 D 10 Sedgemere av N2
80 G 9 Sedgemere rd SE2
56 E 11 Sedgemoor dri Dgnhm
150 J 20 Sedgemoor pl SE5
112 B 2 Sedgeway SE6
126 C 16 Sedgewood clo Brom
51 T 7 Sedgwick rd E10
50 F 16 Sedgwick st E9
87 W 15 Sedleigh rd SW18
145 S 14 Sedlescombe rd SW6
139 X 7 Sedley pl W1
109 T 9 Seeley dri SE21
44 F 2 Seelig av NW9
107 N 14 Seely rd SW17
142 L 9 Seething la EC3
116 E 15 Seething Wells la Surb
23 R 5 Sefton av Harrow
12 K 18 Sefton av NW7
157 Y 1 Sefton rd Croy
123 Y 20 Sefton rd Croy
86 M 6 Sefton st SW15
92 H 20 Segal clo SE23
133 W 16 Sekforde st EC1
44 D 15 Selbie av NW10
115 Y 1 Selborne av Bxly
53 W 11 Selborne av E12
59 Y 5 Selborne gdns Grnfd
26 G 13 Selborne gdns NW4
118 A 3 Selborne rd New Mald
157 T 7 Selborne rd Croy
32 M 15 Selborne rd E17
33 O 14 Selborne rd E17
53 W 8 Selborne rd Ilf
16 M 10 Selborne rd N14
17 O 10 Selborne rd N14
30 C 5 Selborne rd N22
115 R 10 Selborne rd Sidcp
113 W 14 Selby clo Chisl
66 D 16 Selby clo E6
58 H 12 Selby gdns S'hall
120 K 16 Selby grn Carsh
120 J 16 Selby rd Carsh
52 A 10 Selby rd E11
51 Z 10 Selby rd E11
65 V 14 Selby rd E13
18 D 20 Selby rd N17
31 R 1 Selby rd N17
123 Y 3 Selby rd SE20
60 C 12 Selby rd W5
135 U 18 Selby st E1
92 D 5 Selden rd SE15
123 R 14 Selhurst New rd SE25
123 R 15 Selhurst pl SE25
18 C 11 Selhurst rd N9
123 S 11 Selhurst rd SE25
56 A 2 Selinas la Dgnhm
99 S 2 Selkirk dri Erith
106 K 10 Selkirk rd SW17
100 M 3 Selkirk rd Twick
101 N 2 Selkirk rd Twick
27 X 3 Sellers Hall clo N3
106 K 13 Sellincourt rd SW17
110 M 19 Sellindge clo Becknhm
149 O 7 Sellon ms SE11
62 E 4 Sellons av NW10
4 C 17 Sellwood dr Barnt
132 C 5 Selous st NW1
157 O 13 Selsdon av S Croy
38 J 4 Selsdon clo Rom
116 K 12 Selsdon clo Surb
158 G 19 Selsdon Park rd S Croy
34 E 20 Selsdon rd E11
65 Y 6 Selsdon rd E13
65 Y 4 Selsdon rd E6
44 F 8 Selsdon rd NW2
157 O 12 Selsdon rd S Croy
108 H 8 Selsdon rd SE27
49 T 15 Selsea pl N16
97 V 2 Selsey cres Welling
49 T 15 Selsey pl N16
64 A 15 Selsey st E14
12 K 14 Selvage la NW7
146 E 9 Selwood pl SW7
124 A 20 Selwood rd Croy
157 Z 1 Selwood rd Croy
119 V 19 Selwood rd Sutton
146 F 10 Selwood ter SW7
34 E 17 Selworthy clo E11
110 K 7 Selworthy rd SE6

20 H 19 Selwyn av E4
36 J 18 Selwyn av Ilf
84 L 8 Selwyn av Rich
82 B 9 Selwyn clo Hounsl
97 O 9 Selwyn cres Welling
25 R 3 Selwyn ct Edg
65 U 4 Selwyn rd E13
63 X 7 Selwyn rd E3
117 Y 11 Selwyn rd New Mald
43 Z 20 Selwyn rd NW10
147 W 7 Semley pl SW1
122 C 2 Semley rd SW16
92 D 6 Senate st SE5
90 A 10 Seneca rd SW4
122 L 9 Seneca rd Thntn Hth
121 P 20 Senga rd Wallgtn
153 N 6 Senhouse rd Sutton
129 Y 20 Senior st W2
112 H 2 Senlac rd SE12
18 F 2 Sennen rd Enf
113 R 7 Sennen wlk SE9
63 S 17 Senrab st E1
27 N 14 Sentinel sq NW4
11 P 19 September way Stanm
10 B 6 Sequoia clo Bushey
51 V 2 Serbin clo E10
141 P 5 Serle st WC2
141 Z 7 Sermon la EC4
113 N 19 Serviden dri Chisl
151 N 5 Setchell rd SE1
150 M 5 Setchell way SE1
75 R 6 Seth st SE16
68 G 1 Seton gdns Dgnhm
65 R 7 Settle rd E13
143 U 4 Settles st E1
87 Z 6 Settrington rd SW6
36 L 19 Seven Kings pk Ilf
54 J 6 Seven Kings rd Ilf
31 P 18 Seven Sisters rd N15
48 J 5 Seven Sisters rd N4
48 D 9 Seven Sisters rd N7
63 N 20 Seven Star all E1
98 H 11 Sevenoaks clo Bxly Hth
92 K 15 Sevenoaks rd SE4
115 S 19 Sevenoaks way Sidcup
53 U 12 Seventh av E12
39 Z 9 Severn av Rom
8 L 2 Severn dri Enf
44 C 15 Severn way NW10
88 J 10 Severus rd SW11
139 P 18 Seville st SW1
26 H 19 Sevington rd NW4
129 W 18 Sevington st W9
124 F 3 Seward rd Becknhm
71 Y 5 Seward rd W7
134 A 14 Seward st EC1
133 Z 15 Seward st EC1
63 R 5 Sewardstone rd E2
20 C 1 Sewardstone rd E4
50 E 11 Sewdley st E5
80 B 6 Sewell rd SE2
65 T 9 Sewell st E13
76 J 10 Sextant av E14
39 O 10 Seymer rd Rom
152 K 20 Seymour av Epsom
119 P 17 Seymour av Mrdn
31 W 7 Seymour av N17
21 P 8 Seymour ct E4
44 H 7 Seymour ct NW2
127 U 20 Seymour dri BR2
53 T 4 Seymour gdns Ilf
117 N 12 Seymour gdns Surb
84 A 19 Seymour gdns Twick
139 N 3 Seymour hall W1
139 T 5 Seymour ms W1
123 Z 9 Seymour pl SE25
139 N 4 Seymour pl W1
155 O 11 Seymour rd Carsh
50 L 4 Seymour rd E10
20 D 4 Seymour rd E4
66 A 5 Seymour rd E6
101 N 11 Seymour rd Hampt
116 F 1 Seymour rd Kingst
102 F 20 Seymour rd Kingst
121 O 18 Seymour rd Mitch
28 B 2 Seymour rd N3
30 H 16 Seymour rd N8
19 N 9 Seymour rd N9
87 W 17 Seymour rd SW18
105 P 5 Seymour rd SW19
73 W 9 Seymour rd W4
139 R 6 Seymour rd W1
123 Z 1 Seymour ter SE20
123 Z 1 Seymour vlls SE20
146 C 13 Seymour wlk SW10
76 H 11 Seyssel st E14
73 Z 1 Shaa rd W3

101 U 10 Shacklegate la Tedd
58 F 20 Shackleton rd S'hall
49 V 13 Shacklewell grn E8
49 V 13 Shacklewell la E8
49 U 12 Shacklewell rd N16
49 U 13 Shacklewell row E8
135 P 15 Shacklewell st E2
143 P 18 Shad Thames SE1
152 D 3 Shadbolt clo Worc Pk
58 E 7 Shadwell dri Nthlt
63 O 19 Shadwell pl E1
143 Z 7 Shadwell pl E1
10 A 2 Shadybush clo
101 Z 17 Shaef way Tedd
56 J 17 Shafter rd Dgnhm
24 H 19 Shaftesbury av Harrow
42 J 1 Shaftesbury av Harrow
40 M 3 Shaftesbury av Harrow
41 O 6 Shaftesbury av Harrow
5 P 13 Shaftesbury av Barnt
9 S 9 Shaftesbury av Enf
70 H 9 Shaftesbury av S'hall
140 E 10 Shaftesbury av W1
145 U 4 Shaftesbury ms W8
124 M 4 Shaftesbury rd Becknhm
120 H 16 Shaftesbury rd Carsh
51 O 5 Shaftesbury rd E10
33 R 17 Shaftesbury rd E17
20 K 5 Shaftesbury rd E4
52 M 20 Shaftesbury rd E7
65 X 1 Shaftesbury rd E7
18 F 19 Shaftesbury rd N19
48 A 3 Shaftesbury rd N19
84 J 9 Shaftesbury rd Rich
39 U 17 Shaftesbury rd Rom
134 D 9 Shaftesbury st N1
101 S 7 Shaftesbury way Twick
67 O 5 Shaftesburys the Bark
147 O 3 Shafto ms SW1
63 T 3 Shafton rd E9
61 X 3 Shakespeare av NW10
16 H 16 Shakespeare av N11
25 O 20 Shakespeare clo Harrow
53 T 19 Shakespeare cres E12
61 Y 3 Shakespeare cres NW10
25 O 20 Shakespeare ct Harrow
25 N 20 Shakespeare dri Harrow
28 M 13 Shakespeare gdns N2
90 J 10 Shakespeare rd SE24
97 Y 2 Shakespeare rd Bxly Hth
32 G 8 Shakespeare rd E17
13 T 14 Shakespeare rd NW7
39 U 18 Shakespeare rd Rom
73 W 1 Shakespeare rd W3
59 W 19 Shakespeare rd W7
49 R 12 Shakespeare wlk N16
146 D 15 Shalcomb st SW10
119 S 11 Shaldon dri Mrdn
24 M 7 Shaldon rd Edg
136 F 8 Shalfleet dri W10
61 U 19 Shalimar gdns W3
61 U 19 Shalimar rd W3
113 Y 9 Shallons rd SE9
116 L 15 Shalston vlls Surb
85 T 7 Shalstone rd SW14
122 C 13 Shamrock rd Croy
89 W 7 Shamrock st SW4
16 E 5 Shamrock way N14
142 K 16 Shand st SE1
89 V 15 Shandon rd SW4
63 T 13 Shandy st E1
31 X 13 Shanklin rd N15
29 Y 17 Shanklin rd N8
70 A 14 Shannon clo S'hall
90 D 10 Shannon gro SW9
130 L 8 Shannon pl NW8
120 L 19 Shap cres Carsh
135 N 8 Shap st E2
151 U 14 Shard's sq SE15
90 K 13 Shardcroft av SE24
92 K 3 Shardeloes rd SE14
114 M 10 Sharman ct Sidcp
64 C 15 Sharman st E14

97 T 8 Sharnbrooke clo Welling
116 E 19 Sharon clo Surb
63 P 3 Sharon gdns E9
9 V 8 Sharon rd Enf
73 Y 13 Sharon rd W4
131 R 2 Sharpleshall st NW1
75 P 16 Sharratt st SE15
149 W 11 Sharsted st SE17
140 F 10 Shaver's pl SW1
68 L 6 Shaw av Bark
10 D 8 Shaw clo Bushey
80 E 3 Shaw clo SE28
68 L 6 Shaw gdns Bark
112 B 8 Shaw rd Brom
9 S 6 Shaw rd Enf
32 J 5 Shaw sq E17
155 Z 15 Shaw way Wallgtn
94 M 13 Shawbrooke rd SE9
95 N 11 Shawbrooke rd SE9
91 V 12 Shawbury rd SE22
127 O 2 Shawfield pk Brom
146 M 11 Shawfield st SW3
86 H 19 Shawford ct SW15
159 V 20 Shaxton cres Croy
48 A 17 Shearling way N7
94 B 9 Shearman rd SE3
99 V 7 Shearwood cres Drtfrd
26 B 13 Sheaveshill av NW9
135 P 18 Sheba st E1
85 R 12 Sheen Common dri Rich
85 R 10 Sheen Court rd Rich
85 V 10 Sheen Gate gdns SW14
133 R 4 Sheen gro N1
85 W 7 Sheen la SW14
84 L 11 Sheen pk Rich
84 K 12 Sheen rd Rich
85 P 12 Sheen rd Rich
156 C 10 Sheen way Wallgtn
85 V 13 Sheen wood SW14
84 M 9 Sheendale rd Rich
110 A 11 Sheenewood SE26
135 W 5 Sheep la E8
88 M 5 Sheepcote la SW11
89 N 5 Sheepcote la SW11
23 W 18 Sheepcote rd Harrow
37 X 13 Sheepcotes rd Rom
118 A 18 Sheephouse way New Mald
117 Z 18 Sheephouse way New Mald
66 A 14 Sheerwater rd E16
63 Z 8 Sheffield sq E3
141 O 6 Sheffield st WC2
137 U 15 Sheffield ter W8
38 G 1 Sheila clo Rom
38 G 1 Sheila rd Rom
22 D 11 Shelbourne clo Pinn
31 Z 6 Shelbourne rd N17
48 D 12 Shelburne rd N7
115 N 9 Shelbury clo Sidcp
92 B 14 Shelbury rd SE22
35 Y 7 Sheldon av Ilf
46 K 1 Sheldon av N6
28 M 17 Sheldon av N6
98 B 3 Sheldon rd Bxly Hth
55 Y 20 Sheldon rd Dgnhm
18 F 14 Sheldon rd N18
45 P 13 Sheldon rd NW2
156 L 6 Sheldon st Croy
137 S 17 Sheldrake pl W8
120 F 2 Sheldrick clo Mitch
127 R 14 Sheldwick ter BR2
49 O 10 Shelford pl N16
4 A 20 Shelford rd Barnt
109 T 19 Shelford ri SE19
88 L 12 Shelgate rd SW11
127 S 15 Shell clo Brom
93 P 7 Shell rd SE13
53 P 18 Shelley av E12
59 P 8 Shelley av Grnfd
57 U 6 Shelley av Hornch
12 B 15 Shelley clo Edg
59 P 9 Shelley clo Grnfd
58 F 18 Shelley cres S'hall
96 J 2 Shelley dri SE18
42 D 8 Shelley gdns Wemb
50 A 14 Shellness rd E5
88 M 6 Shellwood rd SW11
64 A 14 Shelmerdine clo E3
105 Y 19 Shelton rd SW19
140 J 7 Shelton st WC2
34 G 2 Shenfield rd Wdfd Grn
34 G 2 Shenfield rd Wdfd Grn
134 K 10 Shenfield st N1

82 B 2 Shenley rd Hounsl
91 S 2 Shenley rd SE5
98 L 11 Shenstone clo Bxly Hth
36 L 15 Shenstone gdns Ifl
36 L 15 Shenstone gdns Ilf
139 X 13 Shepherd mkt W1
139 X 14 Shepherd st W1
29 T 19 Shepherd's clo N6
99 Y 19 Shepherd's la Drtfrd
46 F 14 Shepherd's wlk NW3
134 D 12 Shepherdess pl N1
134 B 8 Shepherdess wlk N1
136 G 18 Shepherds Bush shopping centre W12
136 E 17 Shepherds Bush comm W12
136 F 17 Shepherds Bush grn W12
136 C 16 Shepherds Bush mkt W12
74 M 5 Shepherds Bush mkt W12
136 G 16 Shepherds Bush pl W12
144 D 5 Shepherds Bush rd W6
100 E 10 Shepherds Bush rd W6
37 V 15 Shepherds clo Rom
114 E 18 Shepherds grn Chisl
29 S 19 Shepherds hill N6
50 E 16 Shepherds la E9
139 T 8 Shepherds pl W1
40 C 19 Shepherds pth Nthlt
158 E 17 Shepherds way S Croy
155 O 4 Shepley clo Carsh
9 N 4 Sheppard clo Enf
116 J 10 Sheppard clo Surb
65 P 12 Sheppard st E16
134 C 3 Shepperton rd N1
55 U 20 Sheppey gdns Dgnhm
55 P 20 Sheppey rd Dgnhm
66 K 19 Shepstone st E6
95 S 12 Sherard rd SE9
140 D 6 Sheraton st W1
70 G 10 Sherborne av S'hall
120 H 17 Sherborne cres Carsh
60 B 15 Sherborne gdns W13
25 P 10 Sherborne gdns NW9
160 F 8 Sherborne la EC4
153 X 1 Sherborne rd Sutton
134 E 3 Sherborne st N1
31 T 18 Sherboro rd N15
17 W 3 Sherbrook gdns N21
98 D 9 Sherbrooke clo Bxly Hth
66 H 16 Sherbrooke gdns E6
144 L 19 Sherbrooke rd SW6
35 Y 16 Shere rd Ilf
20 L 17 Sheredan rd E4
86 C 16 Sherfield gdns SW15
24 F 19 Sheridan gdns Harrow
81 R 10 Sheridan rd Blvdr
97 Z 7 Sheridan rd Bxly Hth
53 T 16 Sheridan rd E12
52 D 10 Sheridan rd E7
102 D 8 Sheridan rd Rich
119 W 1 Sheridan rd SW19
63 O 18 Sheridan st E1
143 Z 6 Sheridan st E1
143 Z 7 Sheridan st E1
154 L 12 Sheridan wlk Carsh
27 X 18 Sheridan wlk NW11
127 Z 2 Sheriden cres BR7
53 U 12 Sheringham av E12
6 K 18 Sheringham av N14
100 F 2 Sheringham av Twick
54 L 16 Sheringham dri Bark
48 E 17 Sheringham rd N7
124 B 5 Sheringham rd SE20
22 H 1 Sherington av Pinn
77 V 17 Sherington rd SE7
101 X 1 Sherland rd Twick
83 X 20 Sherland rd Twick
147 X 9 Sherland st SW1
126 G 1 Sherman rd Brom
64 F 8 Sherman st E3
33 T 13 Shernhall st E17
53 O 16 Sherrard rd E12
52 K 17 Sherrard rd E7
4 M 19 Sherrards way Barnt

44 J 15 Sherrick Green rd NW10
45 Y 19 Sherriff rd NW6
31 X 7 Sherringham av N17
38 L 19 Sherringham av Rom
26 H 12 Sherrock gdns NW4
92 F 3 Sherwin rd SE14
34 H 11 Sherwood av E18
41 U 16 Sherwood av Grnfd
108 A 20 Sherwood av SW16
107 Y 19 Sherwood av SW16
97 T 17 Sherwood clo Bxly
86 K 8 Sherwood clo SW15
72 A 3 Sherwood clo W13
54 E 20 Sherwood gdns Bark
97 S 16 Sherwood Park av Sidcp
121 V 8 Sherwood Park rd Mitch
153 Y 12 Sherwood Park rd Sutton
123 Z 18 Sherwood rd Croy
100 M 11 Sherwood rd Hampt
40 M 8 Sherwood rd Harrow
41 N 8 Sherwood rd Harrow
36 D 14 Sherwood rd Ilf
26 M 10 Sherwood rd NW4
27 N 9 Sherwood rd NW4
100 M 10 Sherwood rd NW4
96 G 6 Sherwood rd Welling
15 S 10 Sherwood st N20
140 D 9 Sherwood st W1
15 T 10 Sherwood ter N20
159 T 2 Sherwood way W Wkhm
63 Y 6 Shetland rd E3
72 A 16 Shield dri Brentf
71 Z 17 Shield dri Brentf
80 E 11 Shieldhall st SE2
138 M 1 Shillibeer pl W1
133 X 2 Shillingford st N1
17 X 16 Shillitoe rd N13
136 B 5 Shinfield st W12
62 M 17 Shinfield st W12
110 F 6 Shinford pth SE23
81 R 18 Shinglewell rd Erith
78 M 8 Ship & Half Moon pas SE18
142 H 17 Ship & Mermaid row SE1
85 W 6 Ship la SW14
93 N 2 Ship st SE8
160 H 7 Ship Tavern pas EC3
107 S 1 Shipka rd SW12
65 X 18 Shipman rd E16
110 G 4 Shipman rd SE23
55 V 9 Shipton clo Dgnhm
135 R 11 Shipton st E2
75 W 6 Shipwright rd SE16
142 H 14 Shipwright yd SE1
92 D 20 Shirburn clo SE23
64 C 19 Shirbutt st E14
95 O 6 Shirebrook rd SE3
27 P 18 Shirehall clo NW4
27 P 18 Shirehall gdns NW4
27 P 17 Shirehall la NW4
27 O 19 Shirehall pk NW4
102 J 10 Shires the Rich
129 R 15 Shirland ms W9
129 P 14 Shirland rd W9
97 V 20 Shirley av Bxly
158 C 1 Shirley av Croy
154 H 8 Shirley av Sutton
153 U 20 Shirley av Sutton
158 F 5 Shirley Church rd Croy
159 N 9 Shirley Church rd CR0
33 S 14 Shirley clo E17
82 M 14 Shirley clo Hounsl
124 G 10 Shirley cres Becknhm
82 L 14 Shirley dri Hounsl
54 G 17 Shirley gdns Bark
71 X 2 Shirley gdns W7
19 S 3 Shirley gro N9
89 P 7 Shirley gro SW11
158 C 2 Shirley Hills rd Croy
77 Y 18 Shirley House dri SE7
158 E 1 Shirley Oaks rd CR0
124 B 19 Shirley Park rd Croy
158 C 2 Shirley rd Croy
52 A 20 Shirley rd E15
7 Y 12 Shirley rd Enf
114 H 7 Shirley rd Sidcp
73 Z 7 Shirley rd W4
155 U 19 Shirley rd Wallgtn
65 P 17 Shirley st E16
133 P 4 Shirley st N1
158 L 4 Shirley way Croy

159 N 3 Shirley way Croy
46 M 12 Shirlock rd NW3
47 N 13 Shirlock rd NW3
31 O 5 Shobden rd N17
141 V 6 Shoe la EC4
53 U 20 Shoebury rd E6
45 T 17 Shoot Up hill NW2
24 E 12 Shooters av Harrow
95 S 2 Shooters Hill rd SE18
94 A 2 Shooters Hill rd SE3
77 Y 20 Shooters Hill rd SE3
96 C 4 Shooters hill SE18
7 V 5 Shooters rd Enf
100 C 14 Shore clo Hampt
100 F 4 Shore gro Felt
63 P 1 Shore pl E9
63 P 1 Shore rd E9
120 E 1 Shore st SW19
134 M 15 Shoreditch High st EC2
115 W 2 Shoreham clo Bxly
124 C 13 Shoreham clo Croy
88 A 13 Shoreham clo SW18
126 D 15 Shoreham way Brom
150 M 10 Shorncliffe rd SE1
93 U 20 Shorndean st SE6
97 R 15 Shorne clo Sidcp
147 W 16 Shornefield clo SE9
80 E 12 Shornells way SE2
145 R 18 Shorrold's rd SW6
14 J 12 Short ga N12
82 H 3 Short hedges Hounsl
51 Y 6 Short rd E11
64 J 2 Short rd E15
74 A 16 Short rd W4
67 P 3 Short st Bark
141 V 16 Short st SE1
64 G 8 Short wall E15
15 X 19 Short way N12
95 P 8 Short way SE9
83 N 19 Short way Twick
152 E 16 Shortcroft rd Epsom
56 B 17 Shortcrofts rd Dgnhm
143 O 9 Shorter st E1
18 C 12 Shortlands clo N18
126 A 2 Shortlands gdns Brom
125 X 5 Shortlands gro Brom
125 Y 5 Shortlands rd Brom
51 R 1 Shortlands rd E10
102 M 19 Shortlands rd Kingst
103 O 18 Shortlands rd Kingst
144 G 8 Shortlands W6
25 U 13 Shorts croft NW9
140 J 6 Shorts gdns WC2
154 K 10 Shorts rd Carsh
155 S 14 Shotfield Wallgtn
87 X 1 Shottendane rd SW6
113 R 6 Shottery clo SE9
86 A 10 Shottfield av SW14
139 N 3 Shouldham st W1
95 T 8 Shrapnel rd SE9
24 K 14 Shrewsbury av Harrow
85 X 11 Shrewsbury av SW14
61 Z 3 Shrewsbury cres NW10
95 Z 3 Shrewsbury la SE18
137 T 3 Shrewsbury ms W2
79 R 20 Shrewsbury pk SE18
124 J 6 Shrewsbury rd Becknhm
120 K 18 Shrewsbury rd Carsh
53 N 16 Shrewsbury rd E7
53 N 20 Shrewsbury rd E7
16 J 18 Shrewsbury rd N11
137 T 5 Shrewsbury rd W2
106 M 16 Shrewton rd SW17
112 B 8 Shroffold rd Brom
111 Z 9 Shroffold rd Brom
122 A 9 Shropshire clo Mitch
132 D 19 Shropshire pl W1
30 C 1 Shropshire rd N22
130 L 19 Shroton st NW1
34 F 7 Shrubberies the E18
17 W 3 Shrubbery gdns N21
18 J 12 Shrubbery rd N9
70 F 1 Shrubbery rd S'hall
108 A 10 Shrubbery rd SW16
152 L 6 Shrubland gro Worc Pk
33 P 20 Shrubland rd E10
33 N 16 Shrubland rd E17
135 R 2 Shrubland rd E8
159 O 7 Shrublands av Croy
15 U 7 Shrublands clo N20
5 U 20 Shurland av Barnt

15 V 1 Shurland av Barnt
151 P 18 Shurland gdns SE15
96 K 19 Shuttle clo Sidcp
99 V 8 Shuttle rd Drtfrd
135 R 18 Shuttle st E1
98 B 18 Shuttlemead Bxly
88 H 4 Shuttleworth rd SW11
89 X 6 Sibella rd SW4
97 Y 13 Sibley clo Bxly Hth
53 R 20 Sibley gro E12
120 L 3 Sibthorp rd Mitch
94 J 18 Sibthorpe rd SE12
120 J 17 Sibton rd Carsh
140 L 2 Sicilian av WC1
48 M 20 Sickert ct N1
69 W 10 Sickle corner Dgnhm
87 S 1 Sidbury st SW6
114 J 12 Sidcup By-pass rd Sidcp
115 U 17 Sidcup By-pass rd Sidcp
114 M 9 Sidcup High st Sidcp
115 T 14 Sidcup Hill gdns Sidcp
115 R 12 Sidcup hill Sidcp
94 J 14 Sidcup rd SE12
114 C 6 Sidcup rd SE9
119 O 1 Sidcup rd SE9
131 P 18 Siddons la NW1
156 G 4 Siddons rd Croy
31 X 5 Siddons rd N17
110 G 5 Siddons rd SE23
32 K 16 Side rd E17
114 E 1 Sidewood rd SE9
149 R 2 Sidford pl SE1
51 T 8 Sidings the E11
83 T 4 Sidmouth av Islwth
51 T 8 Sidmouth rd E10
128 B 1 Sidmouth rd NW10
62 M 1 Sidmouth rd NW10
45 N 19 Sidmouth rd NW2
91 V 1 Sidmouth rd SE15
80 F 20 Sidmouth rd Welling
132 M 15 Sidmouth st WC1
17 R 18 Sidney av N13
129 W 1 Sidney Boyd ct NW6
72 F 16 Sidney gdns Brentf
133 W 11 Sidney gro EC1
124 H 2 Sidney rd Becknhm
52 E 10 Sidney rd E7
23 O 11 Sidney rd Harrow
123 W 1 Sidney rd SE25
90 D 5 Sidney rd SW9
83 Z 16 Sidney rd Twick
63 O 16 Sidney sq E1
143 Z 3 Sidney sq E1
63 O 17 Sidney st E1
143 Z 1 Sidney st E1
135 Z 20 Sidney st E1
63 P 15 Sidney Street est E1
63 N 1 Sidworth st E8
135 X 2 Sidworth st E8
77 T 17 Siebert rd SE3
78 B 9 Siemens rd SE18
49 Y 15 Sigdon rd E8
136 H 7 Silchester rd W10
98 F 3 Silecroft rd Bxly Hth
141 Y 19 Silex st SE1
94 E 14 Silk clo SE12
93 T 5 Silk Mills pth SE13
142 D 1 Silk st EC2
160 D 1 Silk st EC2
26 C 15 Silkfield rd NW9
25 X 6 Silkstream rd Edg
30 D 9 Silsoe rd N8
20 A 19 Silver Birch av E4
19 Y 19 Silver Birch av E4
16 B 20 Silver Birch clo N11
23 P 2 Silver clo Harrow
73 T 12 Silver cres W4
159 X 2 Silver la W Wkhm
140 C 8 Silver pl W1
136 E 12 Silver rd W12
81 V 16 Silver Spring clo Erith
8 C 12 Silver st Enf
18 C 15 Silver st N18
38 F 11 Silver way Rom
75 X 3 Silver wlk SE16
5 W 15 Silvercliffe gdns Barnt
36 J 17 Silverdale av Ilf
40 E 16 Silverdale clo Nthlt
153 U 8 Silverdale clo Sutton
71 U 2 Silverdale clo W7
57 X 16 Silverdale dri Hornch
7 O 15 Silverdale Enf
98 G 6 Silverdale rd Bxly Hth
156 J 4 Silverdale rd Croy

20 K 19	Silverdale rd E4
110 D 9	Silverdale SE26
83 Y 6	Silverhall st Islwth
42 J 2	Silverholme Harrow
78 G 3	Silverland st E16
122 C 9	Silverleigh rd Thntn Hth
93 P 17	Silvermere rd SE6
40 L 18	Silverst clo Grnfd
11 S 19	Silverston clo Stanm
11 S 19	Silverston way Stanm
20 C 7	Silverthorne gdns E4
89 T 5	Silverthorne rd SW8
144 F 16	Silverton rd W6
78 B 3	Silvertown By-pass E16
65 O 18	Silvertown way E16
77 S 3	Silvertown way E16
59 R 8	Silvertree la Grnfd
91 V 14	Silvester rd SE22
142 D 18	Silvester st SE1
75 R 12	Silwood st SE16
94 B 10	Sim's wlk SE3
75 V 18	Simla clo SE14
15 X 7	Simmons clo N20
20 K 9	Simmons la E4
78 L 13	Simmons rd SE18
15 W 7	Simmons way N20
154 J 3	Simms clo Carsh
94 H 18	Simnel rd SE12
137 S 9	Simon clo W11
51 O 6	Simonds rd E10
127 P 1	Simone clo Brom
51 X 16	Simons wlk E15
82 E 17	Simpson rd Hounsl
57 U 19	Simpson rd Rainhm
102 C 9	Simpson rd Rich
88 H 5	Simpson st SW11
126 F 7	Simpson's rd Brom
64 E 20	Simpsons rd E14
87 Y 14	Simrose ct SW18
39 T 14	Sims clo Rom
136 H 19	Sinclair gdns W14
27 R 18	Sinclair gro NW11
19 X 17	Sinclair rd E4
19 X 18	Sinclair rd E4
136 J 19	Sinclair rd W14
144 K 1	Sinclair rd W14
60 A 5	Sindall rd Grnfd
71 Z 1	Singapore rd W13
134 G 15	Singer st EC2
122 K 16	Singleton clo Croy
106 L 16	Singleton clo SW17
56 C 16	Singleton rd Dgnhm
14 L 15	Singleton scarp N12
32 F 4	Sinnott rd E17
84 A 20	Sion rd Twick
74 C 2	Sir Alexander clo W3
74 D 2	Sir Alexander rd W3
30 K 8	Sirdar rd N22
136 J 11	Sirdar rd W11
160 D 7	Sise la EC4
67 X 3	Sisley rd Bark
87 V 15	Sispara gdns SW18
123 Y 17	Sissinghurst rd Croy
89 N 8	Sisters av SW11
107 T 1	Sistova rd SW12
18 B 1	Sittingbourne av Enf
8 C 20	Sittingbourne av Enf
10 H 17	Sitwell gro Stanm
56 H 20	Siviter way Dgnhm
126 J 7	Siward rd Brom
31 O 5	Siward rd N17
106 C 7	Siward rd SW17
53 U 14	Sixth av E12
128 J 15	Sixth av W10
100 M 6	Sixth Cross rd Twick
101 O 8	Sixth Cross rd Twick
45 S 14	Skardu rd NW2
87 T 19	Skeena hill SW18
66 F 3	Skeffington rd E6
106 B 4	Skelbrook st SW18
87 V 11	Skelgill rd SW15
65 O 1	Skelly rd E15
52 G 19	Skelton rd E7
51 S 1	Skeltons la E10
144 D 15	Skelwith rd W6
75 S 13	Sketchley gdns SE16
8 H 12	Sketty rd Enf
64 L 3	Skiers st E15
90 G 20	Skiffington clo SW2
142 A 12	Skin Market pl SE1
147 T 7	Skinner pl SW1
133 V 15	Skinner st EC1
160 C 8	Skinners la EC4
82 J 1	Skinners la Hounsl
66 H 10	Skipsey av E6
149 Y 2	Skipton st SE1
63 R 3	Skipworth rd E9
33 W 3	Sky Peals rd Wdfd Grn
99 U 1	Slade gdns Erith
99 V 1	Slade Green rd Erith
79 U 16	Slade the SE18
150 C 19	Slade wlk SE5
95 O 7	Sladebrook rd SE3
79 V 14	Sladedale rd SE18
7 T 11	Slades clo Enf
114 B 9	Slades dri Chisl
7 S 10	Slades gdns Enf
7 U 11	Slades hill Enf
7 T 11	Slades ri Enf
93 P 12	Slagrove pl SE13
146 C 16	Slaidburn st SW10
93 U 11	Slaithwaite rd SE13
48 E 14	Slaney pl N7
148 B 18	Sleaford st SW8
140 J 8	Slingsby pl WC2
151 X 1	Slippers pl SE16
146 K 6	Sloane av SW3
147 R 9	Sloane Court east SW3
147 R 9	Sloane Court west SW3
147 S 7	Sloane gdns SW1
147 R 7	Sloane sq SW1
139 P 19	Sloane st SW1
147 R 4	Sloane st SW1
147 R 5	Sloane ter SW1
124 K 14	Sloane wlk Croy
80 F 1	Slocum clo SE28
25 V 19	Slough la NW9
143 W 5	Sly st E1
143 W 6	Sly st E1
83 W 4	Smallberry av Islwth
138 E 7	Smallbrook ms W2
49 U 8	Smalley clo N16
106 F 10	Smallwood rd SW17
88 C 12	Smardale rd SW18
81 R 12	Smarden clo Blvdr
113 T 8	Smarden gro SE9
39 Z 4	Smart clo Rom
63 T 8	Smart st E2
140 L 4	Smarts pl WC2
87 X 19	Smeaton rd SW18
143 V 13	Smeaton st E1
89 Y 4	Smedley st SW8 & SW4
64 A 1	Smeed rd E3
72 K 17	Smith hill Brentf
148 J 3	Smith sq SW1
116 M 15	Smith st Surb
147 N 10	Smith st SW3
147 N 11	Smith ter SW3
141 X 3	Smithfield st EC1
51 T 14	Smithies ct E15
80 C 11	Smithies rd SE2
31 O 4	Smithson rd N17
105 S 3	Smithwood clo SW19
63 P 15	Smithy st E1
122 M 15	Smock wlk Croy
88 A 10	Smugglers way SW18
150 L 9	Smyrk's rd SE17
129 U 2	Smyrna rd NW6
64 E 20	Smythe st E14
6 G 11	Snakes la Barnt
21 S 17	Snakes la Wdfd Grn
21 T 18	Snakes la Wdfd Grn
11 V 14	Snaresbrook dri Stanm
34 E 12	Snaresbrook hall E18
34 C 14	Snaresbrook rd E11
33 Z 14	Snaresbrook rd E11
136 C 3	Snarsgate st W10
62 M 16	Snarsgate st W10
27 U 20	Sneath av NW11
18 H 18	Snells pk N18
44 M 13	Sneyd rd NW2
141 W 3	Snow hill EC1
88 B 5	Snowbury rd SW6
26 A 18	Snowden dri NW9
134 J 19	Snowden st EC2
142 G 17	Snowsfields SE1
53 N 15	Snowshill rd E12
53 P 14	Snowshill rd E12
91 U 8	Soames st SE15
118 A 1	Soames wlk New Mald
141 O 4	Soane Museum WC2
126 G 15	Socket la Brom
140 F 6	Soho sq W1
140 E 5	Soho st W1
45 X 15	Solent rd NW6
133 S 12	Soley ms WC1
86 L 14	Solna av SW15
18 A 3	Solna rd N21
92 A 10	Solomon's pass SE15
90 A 10	Solon New rd SW4
90 A 11	Solon rd SW2
82 C 7	Solway clo Hounsl
30 H 4	Solway rd N22
91 X 10	Solway rd SE22
5 U 19	Somaford gro Barnt
45 U 14	Somali rd NW2
54 D 20	Somerby rd Bark
5 X 11	Somercoates clo Barnt
101 U 12	Somerest rd Tedd
48 J 7	Somerfield rd N4
49 U 13	Somerford gro N16
31 Y 2	Somerford gro N17
135 X 17	Somerford st E1
75 W 6	Somerford way SE16
97 O 18	Somerhill av Sidcp
97 R 4	Somerhill rd Welling
90 G 10	Somerleyton rd SW9
132 F 9	Somers clo NW1
138 J 6	Somers cres W2
90 C 17	Somers pl SW2
32 L 14	Somers rd E17
90 C 17	Somers rd SW2
35 T 15	Somersby gdns Ilf
118 J 3	Somerset av SW20
96 L 11	Somerset av Welling
118 B 13	Somerset clo New Mald
34 G 4	Somerset clo E18
122 D 6	Somerset gdns SW16
47 R 1	Somerset gdns N6
93 P 5	Somerset gdns SE13
101 T 12	Somerset gdns Tedd
141 O 9	Somerset Ho WC2
5 O 16	Somerset rd Barnt
5 R 16	Somerset rd Barnt
72 F 17	Somerset rd Brentf
99 Z 17	Somerset rd Drtfrd
33 O 17	Somerset rd E17
22 M 17	Somerset rd Harrow
117 N 4	Somerset rd Kingst
31 V 11	Somerset rd N17
18 G 16	Somerset rd N18
26 L 13	Somerset rd NW4
58 H 15	Somerset rd S'hall
105 O 8	Somerset rd SW19
72 C 3	Somerset rd W13
73 X 7	Somerset rd W4
137 N 19	Somerset sq W14
70 A 18	Somerset waye Hounsl
97 Z 5	Somersham rd Bxly Hth
85 S 8	Somerton av Rich
45 S 9	Somerton rd NW2
92 A 10	Somerton rd SE15
112 H 5	Somertrees av SE12
40 J 14	Somervell rd Harrow
37 U 15	Somerville rd Rom
110 F 17	Somerville rd SE20
48 D 8	Sonderburg rd N7
150 F 13	Sondes st SE17
23 V 20	Sonia ct Harrow
70 G 20	Sonia gdns Hounsl
15 P 14	Sonia gdns N12
44 D 12	Sonia gdns NW10
123 X 15	Sonning rd SE25
48 C 18	Sophia clo N7
51 P 2	Sophia rd E10
65 V 16	Sophia rd E16
64 C 16	Sophia st E14
80 B 3	Sorrel clo SE18
39 S 10	Sorrel wlk Rom
66 D 14	Sorrell gdns E6
154 A 6	Sorrento rd Sutton
153 Z 6	Sorrento rd Sutton
48 K 11	Sotheby rd N5
135 T 4	Sotheran clo E8
145 Z 20	Sotheron rd SW6
88 M 3	Soudan rd SW11
144 H 4	Souldern rd W14
32 H 19	South Access rd E17
26 C 8	South acre NW9
136 A 10	South Africa rd W12
74 J 1	South Africa rd W12
62 L 20	South Africa rd W12
139 V 12	South Audley st W1
155 N 17	South av Carsh
20 E 1	South av E4
85 O 4	South av Rich
58 D 20	South av S'hall
58 D 20	South Avenue gdns S'hall
116 K 14	South bank Surb
58 H 15	South Bank ter Surb
51 X 10	South Birkbeck rd E11
74 F 14	South Black Lion la W6
146 A 10	South Bolton gdns SW5
17 R 16	South Church ct N13
4 H 12	South clo Barnt
97 W 11	South clo Bxly Hth
69 S 5	South clo Dgnhm
119 X 14	South clo Mrdn
29 R 17	South clo N6
40 E 2	South clo Pinn
100 H 6	South clo Twick
32 K 10	South Countess rd E17
140 F 1	South cres WC1
36 A 15	South Cross rd Ilf
109 O 6	South Croxted rd SE21
12 L 12	South dene NW7
153 S 20	South dri Sutton
72 G 9	South Ealing rd W5
18 G 11	South Eastern av N9
147 V 6	South Eaton pl SW1
125 R 16	South Eden Park rd Becknhm
145 S 3	South Edwardes sq W8
46 J 13	South End clo NW3
156 M 8	South end Croy
46 K 14	South End grn NW3
57 Z 14	South End rd Hornch
46 J 12	South End rd NW3
145 Y 1	South End row W8
145 X 1	South end W8
52 K 19	South Esk rd E7
106 G 18	South gdns SW19
32 K 16	South gro E17
31 P 16	South gro N15
47 P 4	South gro N6
41 O 10	South Hill av Harrow
113 S 16	South hill Chisl
41 T 12	South Hill gro Harrow
46 K 11	South Hill Park gdns NW3
46 K 12	South Hill pk NW3
126 A 9	South Hill rd Brom
125 Z 8	South Hill rd Brom
113 T 17	South Hill rd Chisl
149 S 19	South Island pl SW9
116 G 6	South la Kingst
118 B 17	South la New Mald
117 Z 15	South la New Mald
149 O 19	South Lambeth est SW8
148 L 13	South Lambeth pl SE1
148 L 17	South Lambeth rd SW8
117 X 9	South Lane west New Mald
122 A 8	South Lodge av Mitch
121 Z 8	South Lodge av Mitch
6 K 13	South Lodge cres Enf
6 J 14	South Lodge dri N14
7 N 17	South Lodge dri N14
26 D 5	South mead NW9
139 W 7	South Molton la W1
139 W 7	South Molton pas W1
65 T 16	South Molton rd E16
139 W 7	South Molton st W1
123 T 4	South Norwood hill SE25
108 D 9	South Oak rd SW16
76 K 19	South observatory SE10
54 F 9	South Park cres Ilf
94 A 20	South Park cres SE6
112 B 1	South Park cres SE6
54 G 9	South Park dri Ilf
117 V 10	South Park gro New Mald
157 P 10	South Park Hill rd S Croy
54 F 9	South Park rd Ilf
106 A 16	South Park rd SW19
105 X 16	South Park rd SW19
54 F 11	South Park ter Ilf
146 G 10	South pde SW3
73 Y 10	South pde W4
160 F 1	South pl EC2
142 G 1	South pl EC2
116 L 16	South pl Surb
142 F 2	South Place ms EC2
160 G 1	South Place ms EC2
25 U 4	South rd Edg
100 A 14	South rd Felt
100 D 16	South rd Hampt
18 L 5	South rd N9
37 X 18	South rd Rom

70 E 4	South rd S'hall
110 E 4	South rd SE23
106 D 16	South rd Twick
101 R 8	South rd Twick
72 G 10	South rd W5
154 K 19	South ri Carsh
94 C 4	South row SE3
75 X 8	South Sea st SE16
74 D 9	South side W6
27 Z 18	South sq NW11
141 R 1	South sq WC1
126 F 2	South st Brom
9 S 18	South st Enf
69 Y 7	South st Rainhm
39 P 15	South st Rom
139 T 12	South st W1
143 P 7	South Tenter st E1
116 K 13	South ter Surb
146 J 5	South ter SW7
41 U 12	South vale Harrow
109 R 16	South vale SE19
126 J 3	South view Brom
98 B 17	South View clo Bxly
35 Y 18	South View cres Ilf
34 J 11	South View dri E18
99 O 13	South View Drtfrd
29 Z 11	South View rd N8
47 Y 18	South vlls NW1
158 K 5	South way Croy
22 H 14	South way Harrow
14 M 7	South way N20
19 R 8	South way N9
43 P 14	South way Wemb
84 A 16	South Western rd Twick
83 Z 15	South Western rd Twick
138 G 4	South Wharf rd W2
159 Z 5	South wlk W Wkhm
86 A 8	South Worple av SW14
86 A 8	South Worple way SW14
85 Y 8	South Worple way SW14
142 E 19	Southall pl SE1
89 S 2	Southalm st SW11
128 M 19	Southam st W10
141 R 3	Southampton bldgs WC2
121 Z 11	Southampton gdns Mitch
140 L 2	Southampton pl WC1
46 M 14	Southampton rd NW5
132 K 19	Southampton row WC1
140 L 9	Southampton st WC2
150 G 18	Southampton way SE5
150 K 19	Southampton way SE5
91 T 1	Southampton way SE5
114 A 8	Southbank Chisl
116 A 17	Southbank Surb
116 G 19	Southborough clo Surb
127 S 12	Southborough la Brom
116 J 20	Southborough rd Surb
127 S 12	Southborough rd Brom
63 S 2	Southborough rd E9
25 W 8	Southbourne av NW9
126 F 18	Southbourne Brom
22 B 20	Southbourne clo Pinn
27 S 13	Southbourne cres NW4
94 H 12	Southbourne gdns SE12
54 B 16	Southbourne gdns Ilf
156 K 7	Southbridge pl Croy
156 M 8	Southbridge rd Croy
70 D 6	Southbridge way S'hall
94 C 15	Southbrook rd SE12
122 A 1	Southbrook rd SW16
136 A 19	Southbrook st W12
8 K 15	Southbury av Enf
8 G 13	Southbury rd Enf
66 G 7	Southchurch rd E6
144 L 6	Southcombe st W14
117 S 18	Southcote av Surb
32 F 15	Southcote rd E17
47 V 12	Southcote rd N19
124 B 13	Southcote rd SE25
96 H 7	Southcroft av Welling
159 U 3	Southcroft av W Wkhm
107 N 14	Southcroft rd SW17
105 U 3	Southdean gdns SW19
16 F 12	Southdene ct N11
71 X 9	Southdown av W7
40 L 5	Southdown cres Harrow
36 G 15	Southdown cres Ilf
105 O 19	Southdown dri SW20
57 X 2	Southdown rd Hornch
155 O 19	Southdown rd Carsh
105 R 20	Southdown rd SW20
95 Y 15	Southend clo SE9
95 Y 15	Southend cres SE9
110 K 9	Southend la SE6 & SE26
111 O 10	Southend la SE6 & SE26
35 N 8	Southend rd Wdfd Grn
111 P 17	Southend rd Becknhm
33 X 5	Southend rd E17
34 F 6	Southend rd E18
53 U 19	Southend rd E6
77 T 16	Southern appr SE10
123 V 6	Southern av SE25
63 Y 10	Southern gro E3
65 W 6	Southern rd E13
28 L 13	Southern rd N2
128 K 18	Southern row W10
133 N 9	Southern st N1
38 F 19	Southern way Rom
144 B 5	Southerton rd W6
74 L 10	Southerton rd W6
31 S 15	Southey rd N15
105 Z 14	Southey rd SW19
90 E 1	Southey rd SW9
110 D 18	Southey st SE20
4 B 20	Southfield Barnt
71 W 5	Southfield cotts W7
101 V 8	Southfield gdns Twick
22 J 14	Southfield pk Harrow
9 P 19	Southfield rd Enf
74 A 7	Southfield rd W4
73 X 6	Southfield rd W4
26 H 9	Southfields NW4
87 X 16	Southfields rd SW18
134 G 1	Southgate gro N1
134 G 2	Southgate rd N1
49 P 18	Southgate rd N1
79 Z 18	Southgate rd SE18
83 P 13	Southland way Hounsl
127 R 7	Southlands gro Brom
126 M 10	Southlands rd Brom
127 P 8	Southlands rd Brom
153 X 6	Southly clo Sutton
152 C 16	Southmead Epsom
87 S 20	Southmead rd SW19
42 L 15	Southmeadows Wemb
113 V 8	Southold ri SE9
112 F 14	Southover Brom
14 K 11	Southover N12
14 L 14	Southover N12
79 S 11	Southport rd SE18
116 J 9	Southsea rd Kingst
105 O 14	Southside comm SW19
96 F 18	Southspring Sidcp
94 A 6	Southvale rd SE3
44 D 14	Southview av NW10
155 V 17	Southview gdns Wallgtn
111 X 9	Southview rd Brom
89 Y 2	Southville N12
142 C 11	Southwark br SE1
142 B 16	Southwark Bridge rd SE1
142 A 14	Southwark gro SE1
151 T 5	Southwark Park rd SE16
151 X 2	Southwark Park rd SE16
143 X 20	Southwark Park rd SE16
127 U 7	Southwark pl Brom
142 C 14	Southwark st SE1
63 Y 17	Southwater clo E14
126 E 18	Southway Brom
74 L 6	Southway clo W12
14 L 9	Southway N20
28 B 17	Southway NW11
119 N 10	Southway SW20
155 V 9	Southway Wallgtn
40 J 17	Southwell av Nthlt
146 B 4	Southwell gdns SW7
51 Z 7	Southwell Grove rd E11
122 F 15	Southwell rd Croy
24 H 18	Southwell rd Harrow
90 L 7	Southwell rd SE5
51 X 3	Southwest rd E11
138 J 5	Southwick ms W2
138 J 7	Southwick pl W2
138 J 5	Southwick st W2
55 N 15	Southwold dri Bark
98 G 17	Southwold rd Bxly
50 A 7	Southwold rd E5
103 W 20	Southwood av Kingst
29 R 20	Southwood av N6
153 P 1	Southwood clo Worc Pk
127 V 9	Southwood clo Brom
117 W 17	Southwood dri Surb
35 Z 14	Southwood gdns Ilf
47 P 2	Southwood la N6
29 P 20	Southwood la N6
47 R 1	Southwood Lawn rd N6
47 R 1	Southwood pk N6
80 D 3	Southwood rd SE28
114 A 3	Southwood rd SE9
113 Y 4	Southwood rd SE9
60 D 15	Sovereign clo W5
95 T 14	Sowerby clo SE9
57 U 17	Sowrey av Rainhm
123 R 2	Spa clo SE25
109 O 19	Spa hill SE19
151 O 2	Spa rd SE16
151 S 2	Spa rd SE16
133 T 15	Spafield st EC1
107 S 13	Spalding rd SW17
64 B 12	Spanby rd E3
46 E 3	Spaniards clo NW11
46 F 4	Spaniards end NW3
46 E 6	Spaniards rd NW3
139 U 3	Spanish pl W1
88 E 12	Spanish rd SW18
23 T 13	Sparkbridge rd Harrow
152 H 9	Sparrow Farm rd Epsom
56 G 8	Sparrow grn Dgnhm
96 B 20	Sparrows la SE9
114 C 1	Sparrows la SE9
10 A 4	Sparrows way Bushey
67 V 4	Sparsholt rd Bark
48 B 3	Sparsholt rd N19
93 T 3	Sparta st SE10
145 V 7	Spear ms SW5
78 K 17	Spearman st SE18
36 K 14	Spearpoint gdns Ilf
48 A 4	Spears rd N19
70 B 20	Speart la Hounsl
46 B 10	Spedan clo NW3
76 A 20	Speedwell st SE8
132 K 14	Speedy pl WC1
113 U 8	Speke hill SE9
123 N 3	Speke rd Thntn Hth
126 D 13	Speldhurst clo Brom
63 S 2	Speldhurst rd E9
73 Z 7	Speldhurst rd W4
143 R 1	Spelman st E1
135 R 20	Spelman st E1
17 R 19	Spencer av N13
21 Y 17	Spencer clo Wdfd Grn
123 P 17	Spencer clo Croy
61 N 7	Spencer clo NW10
28 D 19	Spencer dri N2
95 T 13	Spencer gdns SE9
105 T 17	Spencer Hill rd SW19
105 S 17	Spencer hill SW19
144 K 14	Spencer ms W6
88 F 13	Spencer pk SW18
112 B 18	Spencer rd Brom
33 U 6	Spencer rd E17
66 B 3	Spencer rd E6
23 U 8	Spencer rd Harrow
54 L 4	Spencer rd Ilf
83 O 3	Spencer rd Islwth
121 N 18	Spencer rd Mitch
121 P 6	Spencer rd Mitch
16 D 14	Spencer rd N11
31 X 5	Spencer rd N17
30 C 16	Spencer rd N8
157 S 11	Spencer rd S Croy
88 G 12	Spencer rd SW18
118 K 1	Spencer rd SW20
101 T 5	Spencer rd Twick
73 V 2	Spencer rd W3
73 V 20	Spencer rd W4
42 C 6	Spencer rd Wemb
47 T 11	Spencer ri NW5
133 X 13	Spencer st EC1
87 O 10	Spencer wlk SW15
49 R 13	Spenser gro N16
90 G 14	Spenser rd SE24
148 C 1	Spenser st SW1
49 P 9	Spensley wlk N16
79 X 13	Speranza st SE18
31 T 9	Sperling rd N17
63 V 20	Spert st E14
6 G 20	Spey side N14
64 F 15	Spey st E14
39 P 2	Spey way Rom
62 G 6	Spezia rd NW10
157 N 9	Spice's yd CRO
90 J 5	Spicer clo SE5
118 E 13	Spiers clo New Mald
31 N 5	Spigurnell rd N17
58 C 18	Spikes Br rd S'hall
26 A 7	Spilsby clo NW9
79 V 14	Spindel st SE18
157 R 8	Spindlewood gdns Croy
76 D 11	Spindrift av E14
79 Y 14	Spinel clo SE18
40 D 4	Spinnells rd Harrow
118 A 11	Spinney clo New Mald
56 A 14	Spinney gdns Dgnhm
127 S 3	Spinney oak Brom
5 O 10	Spinney the Barnt
17 S 2	Spinney the N21
115 Y 12	Spinney the Sidcp
11 X 14	Spinney the Stanm
152 M 9	Spinney the Sutton
107 V 6	Spinney the SW16
41 X 10	Spinney the Wemb
127 T 3	Spinneys the Brom
143 U 12	Spirit Quay E1
134 L 20	Spital sq E1
135 R 19	Spital st E1
134 M 20	Spitalfields mkt E1
31 W 13	Spondon rd N15
155 Y 10	Spooner wlk Wallgtn
93 U 20	Sportsbank st SE6
30 L 3	Spottons gro N17
159 O 11	Spout hill Croy
34 F 18	Spratt Hall rd E11
83 R 14	Spray la Islwth
78 M 10	Spray st SE18
79 N 10	Spray st SE18
147 N 8	Sprimont pl SW3
17 P 1	Spring bank N21
60 G 19	Spring Bridge rd W5
153 S 12	Spring Close la Sutton
7 S 3	Spring Court rd Enf
34 J 1	Spring gdns Wdfd Grn
57 Y 13	Spring gdns Hrnch
48 L 16	Spring gdns N5
38 J 17	Spring gdns Rom
140 H 13	Spring gdns SW1
155 U 11	Spring gdns Wallgtn
148 M 11	Spring Gdns wlk SE11
73 O 15	Spring gro W4
82 M 2	Spring Grove cres Hounsl
82 L 3	Spring Grove rd Hounsl
83 N 3	Spring Grove rd Hounsl
84 M 12	Spring Grove rd Rich
85 N 13	Spring Grove rd Rich
49 X 2	Spring hill E5
50 A 2	Spring la E5
124 A 15	Spring la SE25
123 Z 14	Spring la SE25
11 N 13	Spring lake Stanm
139 R 1	Spring ms W1
158 G 4	Spring Park av Croy
158 F 3	Spring Park rd Croy
159 T 7	Spring pk Croy
47 R 16	Spring pl NW5
152 D 20	Spring st Epsom
138 F 7	Spring st W2
98 H 10	Spring vale Bxly Hth
144 G 2	Spring Vale ter W14
25 P 1	Spring Villa rd Edg
75 N 20	Springall st SE15
151 X 19	Springall st SE15
93 Z 17	Springbank rd SE13

111 U 20	Springbourne ct Becknhm
28 L 12	Springcroft av N2
49 N 12	Springdale rd N16
100 K 14	Springfield av Hampt
29 V 11	Springfield av N10
119 U 5	Springfield av SW20
10 C 4	Springfield Bushey
10 L 11	Springfield clo Stanm
14 M 16	Springfield clo N12
36 B 17	Springfield dri Ilf
50 A 3	Springfield E5
49 Y 4	Springfield E5
34 L 2	Springfield gdns Wdfd Grn
159 T 2	Springfield gdns W Wkhm
127 U 9	Springfield gdns Brom
25 Z 16	Springfield gdns NW9
50 A 4	Springfield gdns E5
77 Y 17	Springfield gro SE7
129 W 6	Springfield la NW6
26 A 15	Springfield mt NW9
49 Z 2	Springfield pk E5
98 G 10	Springfield rd Bxly Hth
122 L 1	Springfield rd Thntn Hth
108 L 20	Springfield rd Thntn Hth
97 P 7	Springfield rd Welling
155 S 11	Springfield rd Wallgtn
127 U 9	Springfield rd Brom
65 N 8	Springfield rd E15
32 K 19	Springfield rd E17
20 L 4	Springfield rd E6
53 U 19	Springfield rd E6
116 K 7	Springfield rd Kingst
16 G 17	Springfield rd N11
31 X 12	Springfield rd N15
130 A 6	Springfield rd NW8
110 B 14	Springfield rd SE26
105 W 13	Springfield rd SW19
101 Y 13	Springfield rd Tedd
82 H 20	Springfield rd Twick
71 T 2	Springfield ri SE26
109 Z 8	Springfield wlk NW6
129 W 5	Springhill clo SE5
91 P 8	Springhurst clo CR0
158 L 8	Springpark dri Becknhm
48 M 3	Springpark dri N4
56 Z 15	Springpond rd Dgnhm
93 W 16	Springrice rd SE13
72 H 13	Springvale av Brentf
95 W 2	Springwater clo SE18
62 E 4	Springwell av NW10
108 D 10	Springwell clo SW16
70 A 20	Springwell rd Hounsl
108 E 11	Springwell rd SW16
12 F 7	Springwood cres Edg
39 V 16	Springwood way Rom
52 F 16	Sprowston ms E7
52 F 16	Sprowston rd E7
33 T 9	Spruce Hills rd E17
158 F 8	Sprucedale gdn Croy
155 Z 20	Sprucedale gdns Wallgtn
92 H 6	Sprules rd SE4
67 O 8	Spur rd Bark
67 O 9	Spur rd Bark
11 Y 12	Spur rd Edg
71 Z 20	Spur rd Islwth
31 O 13	Spur rd N15
140 B 19	Spur rd SW1
109 O 19	Spurgeon av SE19
109 O 19	Spurgeon rd SE19
150 E 1	Spurgeon st SE1
56 C 17	Spurling rd Dgnhm
91 V 10	Spurling rd SE22
49 Z 16	Spurstowe rd E8
49 Y 16	Spurstowe ter E8
155 N 10	Square the Carsh
53 W 1	Square the Ilf
21 R 17	Square the Wdfd Grn
106 E 7	Square SW17
28 E 4	Squire's la N3
46 F 10	Squires mt NW3
113 S 18	Squires Wood cres Chisl
15 P 13	Squirrels clo N12
152 E 2	Squirrels grn Worc Pk
39 Y 11	Squirrels Heath av Rom
22 E 11	Squirrels the Pinn
135 T 13	Squirries st E2
132 E 15	Sta fore ct NW1
58 G 5	Stable clo Nthlt
28 G 4	Stable wk N2
140 B 16	Stable Yard rd SW1
140 B 16	Stable yd SW1
21 Y 2	Stables the Buck Hl
149 S 10	Stables way SE11
19 P 14	Stacey av N18
33 W 17	Stacey clo E10
140 H 6	Stacey st WC2
139 P 20	Stackhouse st SW3
78 F 18	Stadium rd SE18
146 D 19	Stadium st SW10
99 R 14	Stadium way Drtfrd
43 P 13	Stadium way Wemb
50 G 3	Staffa rd E10
6 G 16	Stafford clo N14
129 T 13	Stafford clo NW6
153 T 13	Stafford clo Sutton
156 D 10	Stafford gdns Croy
84 L 18	Stafford pl Rich
140 A 20	Stafford pl SW1
117 V 6	Stafford rd New Mald
156 E 10	Stafford rd Croy & Wallgtn
63 Y 7	Stafford rd E3
52 M 19	Stafford rd E7
23 N 3	Stafford rd Harrow
129 T 11	Stafford rd NW6
114 H 9	Stafford rd Sidcp
156 B 12	Stafford rd Wallgtn
155 U 14	Stafford rd Wallgtn
140 A 12	Stafford st W1
137 T 19	Stafford ter W8
91 Y 1	Staffordshire st SE15
25 U 7	Stag clo Edg
21 V 7	Stag la Buck Hl
25 V 10	Stag la NW9
104 E 5	Stag la SW15
148 A 1	Stag pl SW1
71 V 18	Stags way Islwth
121 S 5	Stainbank rd Mitch
31 V 12	Stainby rd N15
142 G 15	Stainer st SE1
153 P 3	Staines av Sutton
82 E 10	Staines rd Hounsl
54 D 14	Staines rd Ilf
100 H 7	Staines rd Twick
101 O 4	Staines rd Twick
115 U 15	Staines wlk Sidcp
33 P 13	Stainforth rd E17
54 F 1	Stainforth rd Ilf
36 F 20	Stainforth rd Ilf
160 B 4	Staining la EC2
114 E 20	Stainmore clo Chisl
63 R 7	Stainsbury st E2
64 A 16	Stainsby pl E14
64 A 17	Stainsby rd E14
9 R 5	Stainton rd Enf
93 W 18	Stainton rd SE6
130 L 20	Stalbridge st NW1
75 N 9	Stalham st SE16
151 Y 3	Stalham st SE16
109 S 19	Stambourne way SE19
159 V 4	Stambourne way W Wkhm
148 M 18	Stamford bldgs SW8
145 Y 18	Stamford Bridge stadium SW6
74 E 10	Stamford Brook av W6
74 E 9	Stamford Brook gdns W6
74 E 9	Stamford Brook rd W6
23 T 1	Stamford clo Harrow
31 X 14	Stamford clo N15
70 H 1	Stamford clo S'hall
126 D 10	Stamford dri Brom
49 W 3	Stamford Green east N16
49 W 4	Stamford Green west N16
49 U 4	Stamford hill N16
68 C 2	Stamford rd Dgnhm
55 U 20	Stamford rd Dgnhm
66 C 3	Stamford rd E6
31 W 14	Stamford rd N15
141 T 13	Stamford st SE1
135 O 11	Stamp pl E2
49 S 1	Stanard clo N16
100 E 14	Stanborough clo Hampt
83 R 7	Stanborough rd Hounsl
87 N 8	Stanbridge rd SW15
80 C 6	Stanbrook rd SE2
92 B 4	Stanbury rd SE15
26 A 15	Stancroft NW9
81 R 14	Standard rd Blvdr
97 Z 10	Standard rd Bxly Hth
9 W 1	Standard rd Enf
82 C 7	Standard rd Hounsl
61 X 10	Standard rd Hounsl
87 X 20	Standen rd SW18
74 G 12	Standish rd W6
106 B 19	Stane clo SW19
107 Z 11	Stane pas SW16
56 F 7	Stanfield gdns Dgnhm
56 F 15	Stanfield rd Dgnhm
63 W 7	Stanfield rd E3
100 E 15	Stanford clo Hampt
38 G 18	Stanford clo Rom
150 J 7	Stanford pl SE17
16 A 16	Stanford rd N11
122 B 2	Stanford rd SW16
121 Z 2	Stanford rd SW16
145 Y 2	Stanford rd W8
148 E 6	Stanford st SW1
121 X 3	Stanford way SW16
123 X 10	Stanger rd SE25
99 X 11	Stanham pl Drtfrd
126 E 20	Stanhope av Brom
23 P 5	Stanhope av Harrow
27 W 10	Stanhope av N3
139 U 13	Stanhope ga W1
56 A 8	Stanhope gdns Dgnhm
53 T 3	Stanhope gdns Ilf
30 K 18	Stanhope gdns N4
29 U 19	Stanhope gdns N6
13 R 17	Stanhope gdns NW7
146 D 6	Stanhope gdns SW7
124 L 10	Stanhope gro Becknhm
146 D 5	Stanhope Mews east SW7
146 C 6	Stanhope Mews south SW7
146 C 5	Stanhope Mews west SW7
59 N 10	Stanhope Park rd Grnfd
139 N 7	Stanhope pl W2
4 B 19	Stanhope rd Barnt
98 A 4	Stanhope rd Bxly Hth
97 Z 4	Stanhope rd Bxly Hth
155 O 17	Stanhope rd Carsh
157 R 7	Stanhope rd Croy
56 A 8	Stanhope rd Dgnhm
33 R 16	Stanhope rd E17
59 N 13	Stanhope rd Grnfd
15 S 16	Stanhope rd N12
47 V 1	Stanhope rd N6
29 V 20	Stanhope rd N6
114 M 8	Stanhope rd Sidcp
139 W 15	Stanhope row W1
132 A 12	Stanhope st NW1
138 G 8	Stanhope ter W2
145 R 11	Stanier clo W14
74 L 3	Stanlake ms W12
136 A 14	Stanlake rd W12
74 K 2	Stanlake rd W12
136 A 15	Stanlake vlls W12
74 L 3	Stanlake vlls W12
67 X 8	Stanley av Bark
125 U 5	Stanley av Becknhm
56 C 3	Stanley av Dgnhm
58 M 3	Stanley av Grnfd
59 N 3	Stanley av Grnfd
118 F 11	Stanley av New Mald
39 W 14	Stanley av Rom
60 K 1	Stanley av Wemb
39 X 12	Stanley clo Rom
149 N 16	Stanley clo SW8
60 K 1	Stanley clo Wemb
137 O 9	Stanley cres W11
101 T 11	Stanley Gardens rd Tedd
45 N 16	Stanley gdns NW2
107 N 16	Stanley gdns SW17
137 P 9	Stanley gdns W11
74 A 5	Stanley gdns W3
155 U 15	Stanley gdns Wallgtn
122 F 15	Stanley gro Croy
89 R 5	Stanley gro SW8
60 M 2	Stanley Park dri Wemb
155 S 14	Stanley Park rd Wallgtn
154 M 16	Stanley Park rd Carsh
132 J 9	Stanley pas NW1
126 K 8	Stanley rd Brom
155 O 18	Stanley rd Carsh
122 G 15	Stanley rd Croy
33 R 19	Stanley rd E10
53 R 16	Stanley rd E12
64 H 4	Stanley rd E15
34 C 5	Stanley rd E18
20 K 4	Stanley rd E4
8 F 13	Stanley rd Enf
40 M 7	Stanley rd Harrow
41 N 8	Stanley rd Harrow
82 M 9	Stanley rd Hounsl
83 N 9	Stanley rd Hounsl
54 D 8	Stanley rd Ilf
119 Y 8	Stanley rd Mrdn
29 R 2	Stanley rd N10
16 L 17	Stanley rd N11
30 K 13	Stanley rd N15
28 G 12	Stanley rd N2
18 F 7	Stanley rd N9
58 A 20	Stanley rd S'hall
115 O 8	Stanley rd Sidcp
154 A 16	Stanley rd Sutton
153 Z 16	Stanley rd Sutton
85 T 10	Stanley rd SW14
105 Y 16	Stanley rd SW19
101 U 13	Stanley rd Tedd
73 U 8	Stanley rd W3
43 N 17	Stanley rd Wemb
155 N 19	Stanley sq Carsh
66 L 19	Stanley st E6
75 Y 19	Stanley st SE8
48 A 8	Stanley ter N4
83 R 3	Stanleycroft clo Islwth
88 K 4	Stanmer st SW11
154 D 6	Stanmore gdns Sutton
85 N 8	Stanmore gdns Rich
10 L 11	Stanmore hill Stanm
11 O 14	Stanmore hill Stanm
131 Y 4	Stanmore pl NW1
81 Y 10	Stanmore rd Blvdr
52 C 4	Stanmore rd E11
30 K 12	Stanmore rd N15
84 M 7	Stanmore rd Rich
133 N 3	Stanmore st N1
125 P 2	Stanmore ter Becknhm
66 K 17	Stannard cres E6
49 W 17	Stannard rd E8
149 U 12	Stannary pl SE11
149 U 13	Stannary st SE11
90 D 7	Stansfield rd SW9
56 E 9	Stansgate rd Dgnhm
126 C 13	Stanstead clo Brom
153 Z 13	Stanstead manor Sutton
34 H 15	Stanstead rd E11
110 J 1	Stanstead rd SE23
57 Z 19	Stansted clo Hornch
115 V 2	Stansted cres Bxly
150 K 20	Stanswood gdns SE5
108 A 11	Stanthorpe rd SW16
107 Z 11	Stanthorpe rd SW16
101 T 14	Stanton av Tedd
153 O 1	Stanton clo Worc Pk
122 L 18	Stanton rd Croy
86 D 4	Stanton rd SW13
119 O 1	Stanton rd SW20
91 W 1	Stanton st SE15
110 K 9	Stanton way SE26
12 G 17	Stanway gdns Edg
73 P 1	Stanway gdns W3
134 K 9	Stanway st N1
145 O 7	Stanwick rd W14
42 A 9	Stapenhill rd Wemb
22 A 1	Staple Field clo Pinn
41 S 3	Staple Inn bldgs WC1
141 S 3	Staple Inn WC1
142 G 19	Staple st SE1
108 A 1	Staplefield clo SW2
36 H 17	Stapleford av Ilf
117 P 5	Stapleford clo Kingst
87 R 20	Stapleford clo SW19
42 G 20	Stapleford rd Wemb
68 D 8	Stapleford way Bark
154 J 17	Staplehurst rd Carsh
93 Y 14	Staplehurst rd SE13
57 W 19	Stapleton cres Rainhm
156 F 10	Stapleton gdns Croy
48 D 3	Stapleton Hall rd N4
30 E 20	Stapleton Hall rd N4
107 N 7	Stapleton rd SW17
81 R 14	Stapley rd Blvdr
4 F 12	Stapylton rd Barnt

Ref	Entry
84 L 20	Star & Garter hill Rich
63 N20	Star & Garter rd E1
142 K 8	Star all EC3
99 O 12	Star hill Drtfrd
64 M 12	Star la E16
65 N 13	Star la E16
83 P 5	Star rd Islwth
145 O 12	Star rd W14
65 P 13	Star st E16
138 J 4	Star st W2
141 S 5	Star yd WC2
76 C 8	Starboard way E14
36 E 7	Starch House la Ilf
132 C 14	Starcross st NW1
74 G 6	Starfield rd W12
151 X 10	Starkleigh way SE16
21 U 6	Starling clo Buck HI
79 S 6	Starling ms SE18
101 W 1	Staten gdns Twick
83 W 20	Staten gdns Twick
49 N 11	Statham gro N16
18 D 15	Statham gro N18
98 F 20	Station appr Bxly
98 J 5	Station appr Bxly Hth
113 R 16	Station appr Chisl
127 W 2	Station appr Chisl
99 S 14	Station appr Drtfrd
152 F 11	Station appr Epsom
100 H 20	Station appr Hampt
23 U 20	Station appr Harrow
117 R 2	Station appr Kingst
16 D 16	Station appr N11
22 B 12	Station appr Pinn
73 V 20	Station Appr rd W4
85 O 1	Station appr Rich
95 S 12	Station appr SE9
113 T 1	Station appr SE9
153 T 16	Station appr Sutton
107 Y 12	Station appr SW16
87 U 6	Station appr SW6
97 O 5	Station appr Welling
42 C 17	Station appr Wemb
118 C 6	Station av New Mald
152 C 19	Station av Epsom
85 O 3	Station av Rich
90 K 7	Station av SW9
100 K 20	Station clo Hampt
27 Z 6	Station clo N3
31 N 14	Station cres N15
77 S 15	Station cres SE3
42 B 17	Station cres Wemb
73 W 20	Station gdns W4
42 J 17	Station gro Wemb
57 X 13	Station pde Hornch
44 M 17	Station pde NW2
45 N 17	Station pde NW2
25 N 10	Station pde NW9
85 O 2	Station pde Rich
48 G 7	Station pl N4
81 T 9	Station rd Blvdr
126 A 3	Station rd Brom
98 A 6	Station rd Bxly Hth
97 Z 6	Station rd Bxly Hth
155 N 7	Station rd Carsh
122 L 20	Station rd Croy
157 P 3	Station rd Croy
99 T 15	Station rd Drtfrd
51 V 10	Station rd E10
53 O 13	Station rd E12
51 W 18	Station rd E15
32 J 17	Station rd E17
20 K 3	Station rd E4
52 F 13	Station rd E7
12 D 18	Station rd Edg
100 H 20	Station rd Hampt
22 K 15	Station rd Harrow
23 V 19	Station rd Harrow
82 K 12	Station rd Hounsl
117 P 1	Station rd Kingst
36 F 11	Station rd Ilf
53 Z 8	Station rd Ilf
16 E 17	Station rd N11
31 Y 11	Station rd N17
47 V 10	Station rd N19
17 W 5	Station rd N21
30 A 1	Station rd N22
30 D 7	Station rd N22
28 A 7	Station rd N3
27 Y 5	Station rd N3
118 J 12	Station rd New Mald
26 G 18	Station rd NW4
13 P 18	Station rd NW7
55 W 1	Station rd Rom
110 C 15	Station rd SE20
123 V 9	Station rd SE25
115 N 8	Station rd Sidcp
86 D 9	Station rd SW13
86 F 7	Station rd SW13
106 F 20	Station rd SW19
101 X 14	Station rd Tedd
83 W 20	Station rd Twick
159 U 1	Station rd W Wkhm
125 U 20	Station rd W Wkhm
60 M 18	Station rd W5
61 N 17	Station rd W5
71 T 2	Station rd W7
108 J 3	Station ri SE27
81 U 8	Station Road north Blvdr
51 W 20	Station st E15
78 L 4	Station st E16
128 E 9	Station ter NW10
90 M 2	Station ter SE5
92 Y 2	Station view Grnfd
153 S 15	Station way Sutton
83 X 19	Station yd Twick
141 Y 6	Stationers Hall ct EC4
102 L 17	Staunton rd Kingst
75 Y 17	Staunton st SE8
75 V 3	Stave yard rd SE16
48 B 14	Staveley clo N7
92 A 1	Staveley clo SE15
85 Z 1	Staveley gdns W4
73 W 18	Staveley rd W4
44 M 19	Staverton rd NW2
120 C 18	Stavordale rd Carsh
48 G 13	Stavordale rd N5
63 S 12	Stayners rd E1
153 X 4	Stayton rd Sutton
150 D 7	Stead st SE17
135 N 4	Stean st E8
108 A 6	Steatham ct SW16
68 B 6	Stebbing way Bark
76 H 10	Stebondale st E14
140 J 3	Stedham pl WC1
149 Z 7	Stedman st SE17
28 M 6	Steeds rd N10
46 M 18	Steel's rd NW3
51 Z 12	Steele rd E11
83 Y 11	Steele rd Islwth
31 T 9	Steele rd N17
61 W 7	Steele rd NW10
73 X 8	Steele rd SW9
46 M 18	Steeles ms NW3
63 R 18	Steels la E1
91 S 12	Steen way SE22
107 Y 8	Steep hill SW16
105 T 11	Steeple clo SW19
87 T 6	Steeple clo SW6
17 Y 17	Steeplestone clo N18
106 C 5	Steerforth st SW18
120 K 1	Steers mead Mitch
106 L 20	Steers mead Mitch
75 W 6	Steers way SE16
107 N 14	Stella rd SW17
49 W 11	Stellman clo E5
124 A 4	Stembridge rd SE20
135 U 4	Stephan clo E8
57 V 17	Stephen av Rainhm
140 E 3	Stephen ms W1
98 K 9	Stephen rd Bxly Hth
140 E 3	Stephen st W1
88 B 6	Stephendale rd SW6
65 O 4	Stephens rd E15
59 W 16	Stephenson rd W7
62 C 8	Stephenson st NW10
64 M 15	Stephenson st E16
132 C 15	Stephensons way NW1
63 T 19	Stepney causeway E1
63 S 13	Stepney grn E1
63 U 16	Stepney High st E1
63 R 15	Stepney way E1
143 W 2	Stepney way E1
12 A 13	Sterling av Edg
11 Z 13	Sterling av Edg
8 A 5	Sterling rd Enf
138 L 20	Sterling st SW7
18 C 15	Sterling way N18
144 E 2	Sterndale rd W14
136 F 16	Sterne st W12
91 Y 6	Sternhall la SE15
108 A 4	Sternhold av SW2
107 Y 3	Sternhold av SW2
56 D 14	Sterry cres Dgnhm
152 A 8	Sterry dri Epsom
56 E 17	Sterry gdns Dgnhm
67 X 4	Sterry rd Bark
56 D 12	Sterry rd Dgnhm
142 E 19	Sterry st SE1
92 J 20	Steucers la SE23
97 U 5	Stevedale rd Welling
53 V 18	Stevenage rd E6
144 E 20	Stevenage rd SW6
87 O 3	Stevenage rd SW6
50 D 17	Stevens av E9
100 D 14	Stevens clo Hampt
10 B 6	Stevens grn Bushey
55 R 9	Stevens rd Dgnhm
142 L 20	Stevens st SE1
74 E 1	Steventon rd W12
142 L 1	Steward st E1
134 M 20	Steward st E1
39 R 16	Steward wlk Rom
100 C 15	Steward clo Hampt
25 W 19	Stewart clo NW9
51 V 13	Stewart rd E15
76 H 6	Stewart st E14
146 J 9	Stewart's gro SW3
147 Z 20	Stewart's la SW8
148 A 20	Stewart's rd SW8
89 W 3	Stewart's rd SW8
17 X 17	Stewartsby clo N18
73 T 2	Steyne rd W3
113 T 10	Steyning gro SE9
14 K 17	Steynings way N12
115 X 3	Steynton av Bxly
81 S 10	Stickland rd Blvdr
58 K 10	Stickleton clo Grnfd
73 P 14	Stile Hall gdns W4
42 B 11	Stilecroft gdns Wemb
127 U 13	Stiles clo Brom
74 G 18	Stillingfleet rd SW13
148 C 4	Stillington st SW1
92 K 17	Stillness rd SE23
61 X 1	Stilton cres NW10
58 B 11	Stipulakis dri Grnfd
65 V 7	Stirling rd E13
32 G 9	Stirling rd E17
23 V 9	Stirling rd Harrow
31 X 5	Stirling rd N17
30 H 4	Stirling rd N22
90 A 6	Stirling rd SW9
82 H 20	Stirling rd Twick
73 T 8	Stirling rd W3
32 G 9	Stirling Road pth E17
122 A 18	Stirling way Croy
117 T 14	Stirling wlk Surb
40 E 10	Stiven cres Harrow
48 C 14	Stock Orchard cres N7
48 C 15	Stock Orchard st N7
65 T 8	Stock st E13
124 B 14	Stockbury rd Croy
56 B 6	Stockdale rd Dgnhm
59 X 9	Stockdove way Grnfd
87 Z 3	Stockenchurch st SW6
108 D 6	Stockfield rd SW16
87 N 6	Stockhurst clo SW15
9 X 10	Stockingswater la Enf
38 M 19	Stockland rd Rom
107 X 20	Stockport rd SW16
33 V 11	Stocksfield rd E17
30 L 3	Stockton gdns N17
12 M 10	Stockton gdns NW7
13 N 10	Stockton gdns NW7
30 L 3	Stockton rd N17
18 L 18	Stockton rd N18
90 D 8	Stockwell av SW9
90 C 3	Stockwell gdns SW9
90 C 6	Stockwell grn SW9
90 C 5	Stockwell la SW9
90 C 6	Stockwell ms SW9
90 D 4	Stockwell Park cres SW9
90 D 4	Stockwell Park rd SW9
90 E 7	Stockwell Park wlk SW9
90 C 5	Stockwell rd SW9
76 H 18	Stockwell st SE10
90 B 2	Stockwell ter SW9
124 B 1	Stodart rd SE20
110 B 20	Stodart rd SE20
87 S 20	Stoford clo SW19
49 U 9	Stoke Newington High st N16
49 V 8	Stoke Newington comm N16
49 O 9	Stoke Newington Church st N16
49 T 13	Stoke Newington rd N16
62 D 9	Stoke pl NW10
103 V 18	Stoke rd Kingst
124 G 15	Stokes rd Croy
66 C 11	Stokes rd E6
62 E 17	Stokesley st W12
55 R 14	Stonard rd Dgnhm
17 U 9	Stonard rd N13
92 H 16	Stondon pk SE23
141 R 3	Stone bldgs WC2
56 C 8	Stone clo Dgnhm
11 Y 14	Stone gro Edg
17 S 2	Stone Hall rd N21
142 K 3	Stone House ct EC3
125 P 8	Stone Park av Becknhm
152 G 2	Stone pl Worc Pk
126 D 10	Stone rd Brom
156 E 12	Stone st Croy
61 Y 1	Stonebridge pk NW10
31 T 16	Stonebridge rd N15
43 T 18	Stonebridge way Wemb
119 S 20	Stonecot clo Sutton
81 X 20	Stonecroft rd Erith
122 A 16	Stonecroft way Croy
141 V 4	Stonecutter st EC4
98 E 8	Stonefield clo Bxly Hth
40 A 14	Stonefield clo Ruislip
133 T 4	Stonefield st N1
40 B 14	Stonefield way Ruislip
78 B 19	Stonefield way SE7
11 Y 16	Stonegrove gdns Edg
35 R 19	Stonehall av Ilf
16 J 18	Stoneham rd N11
85 Y 13	Stonehill clo SW14
85 X 13	Stonehill rd SW14
75 X 18	Stonehill rd W4
109 T 6	Stonehills ct SE21
9 R 16	Stonehorse rd Enf
152 G 7	Stoneleigh av Worc Pk
9 N 5	Stoneleigh av Enf
152 E 10	Stoneleigh cres Epsom
124 G 13	Stoneleigh Park av Croy
152 F 10	Stoneleigh Park rd Epsom
136 H 10	Stoneleigh pl W11
120 H 16	Stoneleigh rd Carsh
35 S 11	Stoneleigh rd Ilf
31 V 9	Stoneleigh rd N17
136 H 10	Stoneleigh st W11
88 M 15	Stonells rd SW11
48 D 5	Stonenest st N4
142 A 19	Stones End st SE1
95 Y 4	Stoney all SE18
142 M 4	Stoney la E1
109 T 17	Stoney la SE19
142 D 13	Stoney st SE1
94 C 18	Stoneycroft clo SE12
32 H 13	Stoneydown av E17
32 G 13	Stoneydown E17
12 J 14	Stoneyfields gdns Edg
12 J 13	Stoneyfields la Edg
89 W 9	Stonhouse st SW4
145 P 7	Stonor rd W14
65 T 3	Stopford rd E13
149 Z 11	Stopford rd SE17
78 H 5	Store rd E16
51 Y 16	Store st E15
140 H 19	Store st WC1
76 J 11	Storers quay E14
32 L 14	Storey rd E17
29 N 18	Storey rd N6
78 K 4	Storey st E16
140 H 19	Storeys ga SW1
91 R 7	Stories rd SE5
52 D 19	Stork rd E7
151 U 3	Stork's rd SE16
26 A 2	Storksmead rd Edg
46 L 1	Stormont rd N6
28 L 20	Stormont rd N6
89 O 10	Stormont rd W11
123 U 19	Storrington rd Croy
133 N 3	Story st N1
63 P 12	Stothard st E1
153 R 10	Stoughton av Sutton
104 G 1	Stoughton clo SW15
70 H 9	Stour av S'hall
56 F 7	Stour rd Dgnhm
99 V 8	Stour rd Drtfrd
64 A 2	Stour rd E3
139 N 5	Stourcliffe st W1
87 R 19	Stourhead clo SW19
118 H 5	Stourhead gdns New Mald
100 D 9	Stourton av Felt
32 J 3	Stow ct E17
76 C 16	Stowage the SE8
18 H 6	Stowe gdns N9
31 S 11	Stowe pl N15
74 J 6	Stowe rd W12

23 P 5 Stoxmead Harrow
52 F 13 Stracey rd E7
61 Z 3 Stracey rd NW10
104 M 16 Strachan pl SW19
35 S 9 Stradbroke gro Ilf
48 L 13 Stradbroke rd N5
90 L 16 Stradella rd SE24
35 X 7 Strafford av Ilf
4 E 11 Strafford rd Barnt
82 F 8 Strafford rd Hounsl
84 A 19 Strafford rd Twick
83 Z 18 Strafford rd Twick
73 U 6 Strafford rd W3
76 B 5 Strafford st E14
63 W 8 Strahan rd E3
70 A 6 Straight the S'hall
76 G 18 Straightsmouth SE10
66 G 19 Strait rd E6
92 A 11 Straker's rd SE15
91 Z 11 Straker's rd SE22
18 D 15 Strand pl N18
140 L 10 Strand WC2
141 P 8 Strand WC2
73 R 17 Strand-on-the-Green W4
79 V 13 Strandfield clo SE18
145 O 2 Strangways ter W14
132 M 3 Stranraer way N1
67 Z 2 Stratford clo Bark
56 J 20 Stratford clo Dgnhm
117 Y 8 Stratford ct New Mald
87 R 10 Stratford gro SW15
139 V 6 Stratford pl W1
122 G 8 Stratford rd Thntn Hth
65 S 5 Stratford rd E13
70 A 11 Stratford rd S'hall
145 V 4 Stratford rd W8
145 V 3 Stratford studios W8
47 W 20 Stratford vlls NW1
88 H 11 Strath ter SW11
87 U 16 Strathan clo SW18
94 H 15 Strathaven rd SE12
88 H 12 Strathblaine rd SW11
108 C 18 Strathbrook rd SW16
42 F 7 Strathcona rd Wemb
108 D 12 Strathdale SW16
106 F 8 Strathdon dri SW17
100 L 1 Strathearn av Twick
82 M 20 Strathearn av Twick
138 J 8 Strathearn pl W2
153 Y 10 Strathearn rd Sutton
105 Y 11 Strathearn rd SW19
94 E 1 Stratheden rd SE3
77 S 20 Stratheden rd SE3
54 F 18 Strathfield gdns Bark
90 A 12 Strathleven rd SW2
57 U 5 Strathmore gdns Hornch
25 S 7 Strathmore gdns Edg
28 A 6 Strathmore gdns N3
137 V 13 Strathmore gdns W8
123 N 17 Strathmore rd Croy
105 Y 6 Strathmore rd SW19
101 S 9 Strathmore rd Tedd
151 T 7 Strathnairn st SE1
46 H 19 Strathray gdns NW3
106 A 2 Strathville rd SW18
105 Z 2 Strathville rd SW18
122 E 6 Strathyre av SW16
8 C 2 Stratton av Enf
155 X 20 Stratton av Wallgtn
97 Z 7 Stratton clo Bxly Hth
11 Z 20 Stratton clo Edg
82 F 4 Stratton clo Hounsl
119 W 3 Stratton clo SW19
54 J 16 Stratton dri Bark
58 F 17 Stratton gdns S'hall
97 Z 8 Stratton rd Bxly Hth
119 X 3 Stratton rd SW19
139 Z 13 Stratton st W1
76 F 8 Strattondale st E14
73 Y 7 Strauss rd W4
101 V 8 Strawberry Hill clo Twick
101 V 6 Strawberry Hill rd Twick
101 V 6 Strawberry hill Twick
155 N 5 Strawberry la Carsh
101 X 6 Strawberry vale Twick
28 F 5 Strawberry vale N2
44 G 5 Streakes Field rd NW2
81 R 16 Stream way Blvdr
80 B 17 Streamdale SE2
126 F 8 Streamside clo Brom

66 F 4 Streatfield av E6
24 F 10 Streatfield rd Harrow
108 B 5 Streatham clo SW16
108 B 15 Streatham Common south SW16
108 C 14 Streatham Common north SW16
108 A 17 Streatham High rd SW16
107 Z 12 Streatham High rd SW16
108 B 2 Streatham hill SW2
90 A 20 Streatham pl SW2
107 P 19 Streatham rd Mitch
140 J 3 Streatham st WC1
107 W 18 Streatham vale SW16
107 O 5 Streathbourne rd SW17
46 E 12 Streatley pl NW3
129 P 1 Streatley rd NW6
94 G 7 Streetfield ms SE3
64 H 6 Streimer rd E15
62 A 19 Strelley way W3
123 S 17 Stretton rd Croy
102 C 5 Stretton rd Rich
88 F 19 Strickland row SW18
93 O 3 Strickland st SE8
65 P 7 Stride rd E13
29 P 1 Strode clo N10
52 F 12 Strode rd E7
31 S 9 Strode rd N17
44 H 19 Strode rd NW10
144 K 17 Strode rd SW6
53 O 17 Strone rd E12
52 K 19 Strone rd E7
95 T 13 Strongbow cres SE9
95 U 13 Strongbow rd SE9
40 H 3 Strongbridge clo Harrow
74 D 5 Stronsa rd W12
56 M 4 Strood av Rom
104 F 6 Stroud cres SW15
40 B 19 Stroud field Nthlt
40 K 13 Stroud ga Harrow
124 B 16 Stroud Green gdns Croy
48 D 3 Stroud Green rd N4
124 B 15 Stroud Green way Croy
124 B 16 Stroud Green way Croy
123 Y 15 Stroud rd SE25
105 X 6 Stroud rd SW19
118 C 18 Stroudes clo Worc Pk
64 D 9 Stroudley wlk E3
135 N 12 Strouts pl E2
148 E 3 Strutton ground SW1
142 M 2 Strype st E1
126 E 19 Stuart av Brom
40 D 10 Stuart av Harrow
44 G 2 Stuart av NW9
73 N 4 Stuart av W5
158 L 6 Stuart cres Croy
30 E 5 Stuart cres N22
97 T 7 Stuart Evans clo Welling
101 U 12 Stuart gro Tedd
106 L 20 Stuart pl Mitch
67 X 2 Stuart rd Bark
15 X 3 Stuart rd Barnt
23 W 10 Stuart rd Harrow
129 U 14 Stuart rd NW6
102 C 5 Stuart rd Rich
92 D 11 Stuart rd SE15
105 X 5 Stuart rd SW19
122 M 8 Stuart rd Thntn Hth
73 V 1 Stuart rd W3
97 R 1 Stuart rd Welling
120 F 1 Stubbs way SW19
70 M 20 Stucley rd Hounsl
131 Y 1 Studd st N1
133 W 4 Studd st N1
87 Y 5 Studdridge st SW6
45 Z 13 Studholme ct NW3
75 N 19 Studholme st SE15
151 X 18 Studholme st SE15
139 R 18 Studio pl SW1
114 L 7 Studland clo Sidcup
102 K 15 Studland rd Kingst
110 E 14 Studland rd SE26
59 S 16 Studland rd W7
74 J 11 Studland st W6
20 J 20 Studley av E4
33 W 1 Studley av E4
50 H 15 Studley clo E5
115 S 12 Studley ct Sidcp

35 O 18 Studley dri Ilf
71 U 6 Studley Grange dri W7
68 K 2 Studley rd Dgnhm
52 H 18 Studley rd E7
90 A 3 Studley rd SW4
90 A 4 Studley rd SW4
65 V 1 Stukeley rd E7
140 L 4 Stukeley st WC2
111 O 16 Stumps Hill la Becknhm
92 A 6 Sturdy rd SE15
33 T 8 Sturge av E17
141 Z 17 Sturge st SE1
149 Z 11 Sturgeon rd SE17
114 E 16 Sturges field Chisl
44 H 1 Sturgess av NW4
26 K 20 Sturgess av NW4
48 C 14 Sturmer way N7
31 O 14 Sturrock clo N15
64 D 18 Sturry st E14
134 B 10 Sturt st N1
143 U 7 Stutfield st E1
90 J 7 Styles gdns SW9
125 U 10 Styles way Becknhm
90 C 12 Sudbourne rd SW2
102 H 7 Sudbrook gdns Rich
102 J 2 Sudbrook la Rich
102 J 6 Sudbrook pk Rich
89 O 17 Sudbrooke rd SW12
42 F 10 Sudbury av Wemb
41 X 9 Sudbury Court dri Harrow
41 X 10 Sudbury Court rd Harrow
112 E 13 Sudbury cres Brom
42 B 15 Sudbury cres Wemb
41 X 11 Sudbury croft Wemb
157 T 7 Sudbury gdns Croy
42 A 16 Sudbury Heights av Grnfd
41 Y 15 Sudbury Heights av Grnfd
41 X 10 Sudbury Hill clo Wemb
41 U 10 Sudbury hill Harrow
54 K 15 Sudbury rd Bark
133 X 9 Sudeley st N1
87 Y 12 Sudlow rd SW18
142 A 18 Sudrey st SE1
59 W 6 Suez av Grnfd
9 W 13 Suez rd Enf
9 W 15 Suez rd Enf
20 E 13 Suffield rd E4
31 T 15 Suffield rd N15
124 B 5 Suffield rd SE20
51 O 2 Suffolk ct E10
36 H 18 Suffolk ct Ilf
160 E 9 Suffolk la EC4
32 J 13 Suffolk pk E17
140 F 12 Suffolk pl SW1
67 U 2 Suffolk rd Bark
56 J 15 Suffolk rd Dgnhm
65 R 10 Suffolk rd E13
9 N 18 Suffolk rd Enf
22 F 17 Suffolk rd Harrow
36 H 18 Suffolk rd Ilf
31 O 17 Suffolk rd N15
44 B 20 Suffolk rd NW10
123 V 7 Suffolk rd SE25
115 T 15 Suffolk rd Sidcup
74 F 20 Suffolk rd SW13
152 E 3 Suffolk rd Worc Pk
52 E 14 Suffolk st E7
140 F 12 Suffolk st SW1
64 F 6 Sugar House la E15
63 O 8 Sugar Loaf wlk E2
116 A 20 Sugden rd Surb
89 O 10 Sugden rd SW11
150 E 16 Sugden st SE5
67 Y 6 Sugden way Bark
144 C 1 Sulgrave rd W6
136 D 19 Sulgrave rd W6
74 M 8 Sulgrave rd W6
90 A 19 Sulina rd SW2
66 A 14 Sullivan av E16
88 H 7 Sullivan clo SW11
87 Y 6 Sullivan ct SW6
149 V 5 Sullivan rd SE11
87 Y 8 Sullivan rd SW6
11 S 1 Sullivan way Borhm Wd
34 G 14 Sultan rd E11
124 G 3 Sultan st Becknhm
150 A 18 Sultan st SE5
45 X 17 Sumatra rd NW6
127 X 3 Summer hill Chisl
113 Z 20 Summer hill Chisl
63 R 17 Summercourt rd E1
128 M 8 Summerfield av NW6

129 N 8 Summerfield av NW6
18 D 1 Summerfield gro Enf
60 B 12 Summerfield rd W5
94 D 20 Summerfield st SE12
31 P 13 Summerhill rd N15
82 B 1 Summerhouse av Hounsl
49 T 7 Summerhouse rd N16
29 S 11 Summerland gdns N10
73 V 1 Summerlands av W3
28 L 12 Summerlee av N2
28 L 13 Summerlee gdns N2
106 B 4 Summerley st SW18
153 Y 17 Summers clo Sutton
43 T 4 Summers clo Wemb
28 F 1 Summers la N12
15 X 19 Summers la N12
15 X 19 Summers row N12
133 T 18 Summers st EC1
29 R 17 Summersby rd N6
106 D 8 Summerstown SW17
68 K 18 Summerton way SE28
153 U 14 Summerville gdns Sutton
83 W 14 Summerwood rd Islwth
25 Y 15 Summit av NW9
25 P 2 Summit clo Edgw
16 G 8 Summit clo N14
45 S 17 Summit clo NW2
25 Y 14 Summit clo NW9
35 O 6 Summit dri Wdfd Grn
33 T 13 Summit rd E17
58 H 1 Summit rd Nthlt
16 F 8 Summit way N14
109 T 19 Summit way SE19
91 V 1 Sumner av SE15
122 G 19 Sumner gdns Croy
146 G 7 Sumner pl SW7
146 G 6 Sumner Place ms SW7
122 H 19 Sumner rd Croy
41 N 1 Sumner rd Harrow
122 G 20 Sumner rd S Croy
151 O 15 Sumner rd SE15
91 V 1 Sumner rd SE15
142 A 13 Sumner st SE1
141 Z 13 Sumner st SE1
46 E 18 Sumpter clo NW3
84 H 10 Sun all Rich
160 H 6 Sun ct EC2
77 V 20 Sun la SE3
145 O 12 Sun rd W14
134 H 20 Sun st EC2
142 J 1 Sun St pas EC2
134 J 20 Sun St pas EC2
61 X 12 Sunbeam rd NW10
89 P 15 Sunburgh rd SW12
12 L 15 Sunbury av NW7
85 Z 11 Sunbury av SW14
12 L 15 Sunbury gdns NW7
88 G 2 Sunbury la SW11
153 R 5 Sunbury rd Sutton
78 G 9 Sunbury st SE18
99 U 4 Suncourt Erith
110 B 7 Suncroft pl SE26
158 F 20 Sundale av S Croy
91 Y 19 Sunderland ct SE22
110 F 2 Sunderland rd SE23
72 G 8 Sunderland rd W5
137 W 5 Sunderland ter W2
53 N 5 Sunderland way E12
74 F 1 Sundew av W12
62 G 19 Sundew av W12
123 U 5 Sundial av SE25
77 X 14 Sundorne rd SE7
96 F 6 Sundridge av Welling
127 N 1 Sundridge av Brom
113 O 19 Sundridge av Chisl
113 N 17 Sundridge Park mans Chisl
113 O 15 Sundridge pk Chisl
123 W 19 Sundridge rd Croy
77 V 19 Sunfields pl SE3
156 A 18 Sunkist way SM6
97 Z 11 Sunland av Bxly Hth
60 K 3 Sunleigh rd Wemb
59 Y 4 Sunley gdns Grnfd
67 R 2 Sunningdale av Bark
100 B 4 Sunningdale av Felt
62 B 19 Sunningdale av W3
10 M 20 Sunningdale clo Stanm
25 U 17 Sunningdale gdns NW9
16 L 15 Sunningdale N14

T

57 Y 13	Tadworth pde Hornch
44 G 7	Tadworth rd NW2
76 D 10	Taeping st E14
120 K 5	Taffy's how Mitch
64 F 8	Taft st E3
143 P 2	Tailworth st E1
123 R 16	Tait rd Croy
38 L 7	Takeley clo Rom
47 R 18	Talacre rd NW5
28 F 11	Talbot av N2
31 U 13	Talbot clo N15
26 G 16	Talbot cres NW4
54 M 7	Talbot gdns Ilf
94 A 3	Talbot pl SE3
93 Z 3	Talbot pl SE3
126 G 7	Talbot rd Brom
155 O 10	Talbot rd Carsh
56 B 19	Talbot rd Dgnhm
66 H 5	Talbot rd E6
52 E 12	Talbot rd E7
23 X 9	Talbot rd Harrow
83 Z 10	Talbot rd Islwth
31 V 13	Talbot rd N15
29 W 6	Talbot rd N22
29 O 19	Talbot rd N6
70 C 10	Talbot rd S'hall
123 O 9	Talbot rd Thntn Hth
101 U 1	Talbot rd Twick
83 U 20	Talbot rd Twick
137 P 6	Talbot rd W11
71 Y 2	Talbot rd W13
137 U 4	Talbot rd W2
42 G 17	Talbot rd Wemb
138 G 6	Talbot sq W2
142 F 15	Talbot yd SE1
91 U 2	Talfourd pl SE15
91 T 2	Talfourd rd SE15
144 J 9	Talgarth rd W14
109 W 9	Talisman sq SE26
42 L 9	Talisman way Wemb
126 C 10	Tall Elms clo Brom
23 U 3	Tallack clo Harrow
50 M 4	Tallack rd E10
77 W 16	Tallis gro SE7
141 U 8	Tallis st EC4
15 R 17	Tallyho corner N12
83 T 17	Talma gdns Twick
90 G 12	Talma rd SW2
92 C 20	Talmage clo SE23
11 T 18	Talman gro Stanm
64 E 10	Talwin st E3
21 W 19	Tamar sq Wdfd Grn
78 B 10	Tamar st SE7
31 W 10	Tamar way N17
62 E 20	Tamarisk sq W12
152 A 1	Tamesis gdns KT4
129 S 16	Tamplin ms W9
21 N 18	Tamworth av Wdfd Grn
121 R 4	Tamworth la Mitch
121 T 8	Tamworth Lodge est Mitch
121 S 7	Tamworth pk Mitch
145 T 14	Tamworth st SW6
121 T 8	Tamworth vlls Mitch
30 J 20	Tancred rd N4
44 C 11	Tanfield av NW2
156 L 8	Tanfield rd Croy
85 R 9	Tangier rd Rich
10 F 10	Tanglewood clo Stanm
158 D 5	Tanglewood clo Croy
86 E 17	Tangley gro SW15
100 E 13	Tangley Park rd Hampt
57 Z 19	Tangmere cres Hornch
26 B 7	Tangmere way NW9
132 L 13	Tankerton st WC1
107 Y 17	Tankerville rd SW16
44 K 7	Tankridge rd NW2
54 B 18	Tanner st Bark
142 K 18	Tanner st SE1
143 O 18	Tanner st SE1
18 E 15	Tanners End la N18
92 M 3	Tanners hill SE8
93 N 1	Tanners hill SE8
36 C 10	Tanners la Ilf
124 E 10	Tannery clo Becknhm
56 G 8	Tannery clo Dgnhm
48 G 10	Tannington ter N4
110 E 12	Tannsfeld rd SE26
47 Z 15	Tansley clo N7
141 T 18	Tanswell st SE1
66 K 18	Tansy clo E6
65 P 16	Tant av E16
89 N 20	Tantallon rd SW12
37 X 11	Tantony gro Rom
156 K 3	Tanworth pl Croy
156 K 3	Tanworth rd Croy
46 L 11	Tanza rd NW3
154 A 16	Tapestry clo Sutton
134 B 10	Taplow st N1
135 X 17	Tapp st E1
92 B 7	Tappesfield rd SE15
4 G 13	Tapster st Barnt
91 T 12	Tarbert rd SE22
18 L 20	Tariff rd N17
110 A 3	Tarleton gdns SE23
115 R 8	Tarling clo Sidcp
65 R 19	Tarling rd E16
28 E 6	Tarling rd N2
63 O 18	Tarling st E1
143 Y 6	Tarling st E1
7 O 16	Tarn bank Enf
95 U 20	Tarnwood pk SE9
107 X 8	Tarrington clo SW16
149 Y 10	Tarver rd SE17
76 E 18	Tarves way SE10
16 E 16	Tash pl N11
46 M 16	Tasker rd NW3
90 A 8	Tasman rd SW9
66 A 18	Tasman wk E16
17 Z 19	Tasmania ter N18
144 K 14	Tasso rd W6
43 X 19	Tatam rd NW10
148 J 7	Tate gallery SW1
78 E 3	Tate rd E16
153 X 12	Tate rd Sutton
92 H 16	Tatnell rd SE23
95 R 12	Tattersall clo SE9
150 G 7	Tatum st SE17
82 M 4	Taunton av Hounsl
83 N 3	Taunton av Hounsl
118 J 3	Taunton av SW20
99 N 6	Taunton clo Bxly Hth
119 W 20	Taunton clo Sutton
7 T 11	Taunton dri Enf
131 O 18	Taunton ms NW1
131 N 17	Taunton pl NW1
58 K 2	Taunton rd Grnfd
94 C 13	Taunton rd SE12
24 K 8	Taunton way Stanm
24 K 9	Taunton way Stanm
48 K 13	Taverner sq N5
136 K 15	Taverners clo W11
32 G 11	Tavistock av E17
60 A 6	Tavistock av Grnfd
59 Z 7	Tavistock av Grnfd
49 Y 15	Tavistock clo N16
122 A 9	Tavistock cres Mitch
121 Z 9	Tavistock cres Mitch
137 O 2	Tavistock cres W10
54 H 13	Tavistock gdns Ilf
123 N 18	Tavistock gro Croy
137 N 5	Tavistock ms W11
34 F 11	Tavistock pl E18
16 E 1	Tavistock pl N14
132 H 16	Tavistock pl WC1
126 D 8	Tavistock rd Brom
120 G 20	Tavistock rd Carsh
123 N 19	Tavistock rd Croy
52 B 19	Tavistock rd E15
34 E 11	Tavistock rd E18
52 B 11	Tavistock rd E7
25 O 5	Tavistock rd Edg
31 N 19	Tavistock rd N4
62 D 5	Tavistock rd NW10
137 O 3	Tavistock rd W11
97 T 2	Tavistock rd Welling
132 G 16	Tavistock sq WC1
140 M 9	Tavistock st WC2
141 N 7	Tavistock st WC2
47 Z 9	Tavistock ter N19
120 G 20	Tavistock wlk Carsh
132 F 16	Taviton st WC1
75 T 10	Tawny way SE16
39 S 4	Tay way Rom
83 U 16	Tayben av Twick
89 P 10	Taybridge rd SW11
64 F 17	Tayburn clo E14
85 S 4	Taylor av Rich
101 N 12	Taylor clo Hampt
31 X 1	Taylor clo N17
38 E 1	Taylor clo Rom
106 K 18	Taylor rd Mitch
155 R 11	Taylor rd Wallgtn
78 M 11	Taylor st SE18
44 A 20	Taylor's la NW10
62 B 16	Taylors grn W3
4 G 6	Taylors la Barnt
109 Y 10	Taylors la SE26
110 B 3	Taymount ri SE23
132 M 2	Tayport clo N1
58 E 9	Taywood rd Nthlt
75 V 4	Teak clo SE16
66 A 16	Teal clo E16
135 U 8	Teale st E2
124 D 20	Teasel clo CR0
64 M 8	Teasel way E15
31 T 3	Tebworth rd N17
158 E 18	Tedder rd S Croy
101 X 17	Teddington lodge Tedd
101 W 10	Teddington Park rd Tedd
101 W 11	Teddington pk Tedd
147 N 11	Tedworth gdns SW3
147 N 11	Tedworth sq SW3
62 A 17	Tee the W3
59 V 6	Tees av Grnfd
83 Z 2	Teesdale av Islwth
83 Z 2	Teesdale gdns Islwth
34 B 20	Teesdale rd E11
135 V 10	Teesdale yd E2
123 X 17	Teevan clo Croy
123 X 18	Teevan rd Croy
25 N 8	Teignmouth clo SE9
89 X 11	Teignmouth clo SW4
59 Y 7	Teignmouth gdns Grnfd
97 T 3	Teignmouth rd Welling
45 O 16	Teignmouth rd NW2
45 Z 9	Telegraph hill NW3
55 N 2	Telegraph ms Ilf
86 K 17	Telegraph rd SW15
160 F 4	Telegraph st EC2
94 J 9	Telemann sq SE9
145 R 14	Telephone pl W14
107 W 1	Telferscot rd SW12
108 A 2	Telford av SW2
107 Y 2	Telford av SW2
16 H 18	Telford rd N11
58 K 18	Telford rd S'hall
114 D 5	Telford rd SE9
128 K 20	Telford rd W10
62 A 15	Telford way W3
66 H 7	Telham rd E6
91 U 11	Tell gro SE22
95 P 1	Tellson av SE18
89 P 18	Temperley rd SW12
57 W 18	Tempest way Rainhm
45 U 17	Templar ho NW2
100 G 17	Templar pl Hampt
90 J 3	Templar st SE5
27 W 19	Templars av NW11
27 X 8	Templars cres N3
10 B 19	Templars dri Harrow
158 L 4	Temple av Dgnhm
56 D 3	Temple av Dgnhm
141 U 8	Temple av EC4
15 T 3	Temple av N20
27 V 8	Temple clo N3
79 P 7	Temple clo SE18
27 Y 16	Temple Fortune hill NW11
27 Y 18	Temple Fortune la NW11
55 V 9	Temple gdns Dgnhm
17 W 9	Temple gdns N21
27 V 18	Temple gdns NW11
7 W 10	Temple gro Enf
27 X 17	Temple gro NW11
141 U 7	Temple la EC4
11 N 20	Temple Mead clo Stanm
62 A 18	Temple Mead clo W3
51 R 13	Temple Mill la E15
51 P 13	Temple Mill rd E15
141 P 9	Temple pl WC2
157 O 9	Temple rd Croy
66 C 3	Temple rd E6
82 L 9	Temple rd Hounsl
30 C 13	Temple rd N8
44 M 11	Temple rd NW2
45 N 10	Temple rd NW2
85 N 6	Temple rd Rich
73 V 9	Temple rd W4
72 F 9	Temple rd W5
85 T 11	Temple Sheen rd SW14
85 U 12	Temple sheen SW14
135 V 9	Temple st E2
154 G 6	Temple way Sutton
63 O 3	Templecombe rd E9
135 Z 3	Templecombe rd E9
119 R 11	Templecombe way Mrdn
44 M 1	Templehof av NW4
59 W 14	Templeman rd W7
20 C 12	Templeton av E4
123 P 1	Templeton clo SE19
145 U 6	Templeton pl SW5
31 O 18	Templeton rd N15
46 B 10	Templewood av NW3
46 B 10	Templewood gdns NW3
60 B 14	Templewood W13
22 M 8	Temsford clo Harrow
89 Z 20	Tenbury ct SW2
24 B 8	Tenby av Harrow
31 V 13	Tenby clo N15
37 Y 19	Tenby clo Rom
40 G 18	Tenby gdns Nthlt
32 G 15	Tenby rd E17
25 N 6	Tenby rd Edgw
9 P 13	Tenby rd Enf
37 Y 19	Tenby rd Rom
97 Y 1	Tenby rd Welling
143 W 13	Tench st E1
151 V 8	Tenda rd SE16
37 S 15	Tendring way Rom
107 X 2	Tenham av SW2
140 B 8	Tenison ct W1
141 R 14	Tenison way SE1
138 A 8	Tenniel clo W2
142 E 17	Tennis st SE1
123 T 10	Tennison rd SE25
8 F 7	Tenniswood rd Enf
118 K 12	Tennyson av New Mald
52 F 1	Tennyson av E11
53 P 20	Tennyson av E12
25 V 11	Tennyson av NW9
101 X 2	Tennyson av Twick
96 J 2	Tennyson clo SE18
51 S 5	Tennyson rd E10
51 Z 19	Tennyson rd E15
32 L 18	Tennyson rd E17
82 M 3	Tennyson rd Hounsl
129 P 5	Tennyson rd NW6
13 T 15	Tennyson rd NW7
110 F 17	Tennyson rd SE20
106 C 14	Tennyson rd SW19
59 V 20	Tennyson rd W7
89 S 5	Tennyson st SW8
57 U 6	Tennyson way Hornch
70 G 8	Tensing rd S'hall
135 V 17	Tent st E1
70 H 12	Tentelow la S'hall
143 N 2	Tenter ground E1
27 O 10	Tenterden clo NW4
27 P 11	Tenterden dri NW4
27 O 11	Tenterden gdns NW4
27 O 11	Tenterden gro NW4
123 Y 16	Tenterden rd Croy
56 B 5	Tenterden rd Dgnhm
31 T 2	Tenterden rd N17
139 Y 6	Tenterden st W1
91 R 13	Terborch way SE22
52 B 9	Terling clo E11
56 D 5	Terling rd Dgnhm
147 Z 4	Terminus pl SW1
86 C 4	Terrace gdns SW13
84 K 17	Terrace la Rich
65 U 4	Terrace rd E13
50 D 20	Terrace rd E9
21 S 18	Terrace the Wdfd Grn
129 S 3	Terrace the NW6
56 A 16	Terrace wlk Dgnhm
55 Z 16	Terrace wlk Dgnhm
147 P 16	Terrace wlk SW11
107 S 5	Terrapin rd SW17
133 W 2	Terretts pl N1
30 A 6	Terrick rd N22
62 K 18	Terrick st W12
22 D 10	Terrilands Pinn
30 L 14	Terront rd N15
75 V 11	Terry la SE8
59 T 20	Testwood ct W7
133 V 6	Tetbury pl N1
29 O 8	Tetherdown N10
151 U 10	Tetterby way SE16
126 E 4	Tetty way Brom
90 A 1	Teversham la SW8
97 R 1	Teviot rd Welling
64 F 13	Teviot st E14
22 C 17	Tewkesbury av Pinn
92 A 20	Tewkesbury av SE23
31 O 19	Tewkesbury clo N15
25 U 10	Tewkesbury gdns SE9
120 F 19	Tewkesbury rd Carsh
31 O 20	Tewkesbury rd N15
71 Y 1	Tewkesbury rd W13
16 H 18	Tewkesbury ter N11
79 V 13	Tewson rd SE18
8 B 20	Teynham av Enf
30 M 5	Teynton ter N17
31 X 8	Thackeray av N17
40 H 4	Thackeray clo Harrow

105 P 18 Thackeray clo SW19
55 O 2 Thackeray dri Rom
66 B 6 Thackeray rd E6
89 S 5 Thackeray rd SW8
137 Y 20 Thackeray st W8
109 Z 11 Thakeham clo SE26
28 E 8 Thakrah clo N2
76 K 16 Thalia clo SE10
75 T 5 Thame rd SE16
69 W 8 Thames av Dgnhm
59 V 6 Thames av Grnfd
88 E 1 Thames av SW10
85 W 5 Thames bank SW14
38 L 8 Thames Hill av Rom
75 Z 1 Thames pl E1
84 B 11 Thames promenade Twick
68 A 8 Thames rd Bark
67 W 9 Thames rd Bark
99 W 8 Thames rd Drtfrd
78 A 4 Thames rd E16
73 R 17 Thames rd W4
102 F 17 Thames side Kingst
116 G 2 Thames side Kingst
76 E 16 Thames st SE10
85 V 2 Thames Village W4
68 G 17 Thamesbank pl SE28
102 B 10 Thamesgate clo Rich
80 B 10 Thamesmere dri SE28
82 H 6 Thamesville clo Hounsl
48 D 9 Thane vlls N7
157 T 6 Thanescroft gdns Croy
156 M 3 Thanet pl Croy
157 N 7 Thanet pl Croy
98 E 19 Thanet rd Bxly
132 J 14 Thanet st WC1
155 X 11 Tharp rd Wallgtn
15 R 3 Thatcham gdns N20
83 R 13 Thatchers way Islwth
37 Y 12 Thatches gro Rom
141 U 3 Thavies in El
105 O 18 Thaxted clo SW20
114 B 5 Thaxted rd SE9
145 R 13 Thaxton rd SW6
139 U 4 Thayer st W1
124 J 1 Thayers Farm rd Becknhm
88 M 8 Theatre st SW11
133 V 4 Theberton st N1
141 T 14 Theed st SE1
95 P 2 Thelma gdns SE3
101 X 14 Thelma gro Tedd
22 L 5 Theobald cres Harrow
156 J 2 Theobald rd Croy
150 E 3 Theobald st SE1
133 O 20 Theobald's rd WC1
15 P 14 Theobalds av N12
93 V 15 Theodore rd SE13
122 A 15 Therapia la Croy
121 X 17 Therapia la Croy
92 C 15 Therapia rd SE22
74 G 12 Theresa rd W6
74 G 12 Theresa st W6
76 E 11 Thermopylae ga E14
110 F 17 Thesiger rd SE20
148 A 19 Thessally rd SW8
89 X 3 Thessally rd SW8
17 W 20 Thetford clo N13
68 K 2 Thetford gdns Dgnhm
118 A 12 Thetford rd New Mald
117 Z 13 Thetford rd New Mald
68 K 2 Thetford rd Dgnhm
21 X 19 Theydon gro Wdfd Grn
50 C 5 Theydon rd E5
50 L 1 Theydon st E17
154 E 8 Thicket cres Sutton
55 U 17 Thicket gro Dgnhm
109 X 17 Thicket gro SE20
110 A 16 Thicket rd SE20
109 Y 18 Thicket rd SE20
154 E 7 Thicket rd Sutton
69 V 5 Third av Dgnhm
53 S 13 Third av E12
65 T 9 Third av E13
33 P 15 Third av E17
8 G 17 Third av Enf
37 T 17 Third av Rom
128 M 15 Third av W10
74 C 3 Third av W3
42 G 6 Third av Wemb
101 S 4 Third Cross rd Twick
43 U 13 Third way Wemb
25 X 4 Thirleby rd SE18

148 C 3 Thirleby rd SW1
60 C 8 Thirlmere av Grnfd
42 E 4 Thirlmere gdns Wemb
98 K 3 Thirlmere rd Bxly Hth
29 T 5 Thirlmere rd N10
107 X 10 Thirlmere rd SW16
112 B 16 Thirlmere ri Brom
40 J 17 Thirsk clo Nthlt
107 P 17 Thirsk rd Mitch
123 P 8 Thirsk rd SE25
89 N 8 Thirsk rd SW11
146 C 9 Thistle gro SW5
80 F 7 Thistlebrook SE2
24 G 6 Thistlecroft gdns Stanm
40 C 10 Thistledown av Harrow
127 Y 3 Thistlemead BR7
50 B 10 Thistlewaite rd E5
48 D 7 Thistlewood clo N7
71 P 18 Thistleworth clo Islwth
41 W 11 Thomas à Beckett clo W11
88 G 9 Thomas Baines rd SW11
140 X 1 Thomas Doyle st SE1
93 P 19 Thomas la SE6
143 S 12 Thomas More st SE1
28 C 9 Thomas More way N3
64 A 15 Thomas rd E14
63 Z 16 Thomas rd E14
78 K 10 Thomas st SE18
85 S 6 Thompson av Rich
56 C 10 Thompson rd Dgnhm
91 V 16 Thompson rd SE22
150 A 17 Thompsons av SE15
156 F 1 Thomson cres Croy
122 F 19 Thomson cres Croy
23 U 9 Thomson rd Harrow
151 S 7 Thorburn sq SE1
134 B 11 Thoresby st N1
116 A 17 Thorkhill rd Surb
10 A 6 Thorn av Bushey
12 D 20 Thorn bank Edg
127 X 14 Thorn clo Brom
58 E 8 Thorn clo Nthlt
18 L 18 Thornaby gdns N18
71 P 20 Thornbury av Islwth
71 R 19 Thornbury rd Islwth
83 R 4 Thornbury rd SW2
90 A 17 Thornbury rd SW2
89 Z 16 Thornbury rd SW2
47 U 4 Thornbury sq N19
50 C 10 Thornby rd E5
70 F 12 Thorncliffe rd S'hall
89 Z 17 Thorncliffe rd SW2
91 T 12 Thorncombe rd SE22
39 Y 18 Thorncroft Hornch
153 Z 10 Thorncroft rd Sutton
148 J 19 Thorncroft st SW8
106 C 5 Thorndean st SW18
16 A 7 Thorndene av N11
146 B 18 Thorndike clo SW10
148 D 8 Thorndike st SW1
152 C 9 Thorndon gdns Epsom
51 Y 11 Thorne clo E11
65 R 17 Thorne clo E16
81 W 16 Thorne clo Erith
117 V 8 Thorne clo New Mald
86 B 6 Thorne pas SW13
117 V 8 Thorne rd New Mald
148 L 20 Thorne rd SW8
65 R 17 Thorne st E16
86 B 6 Thorne st SW13
156 H 12 Thorneloe gdns Croy
125 T 6 Thornes clo Becknhm
127 W 7 Thornet Wood rd Brom
73 T 12 Thorney Hedge rd W4
148 J 6 Thorney st SW1
27 S 3 Thornfield av NW7
136 A 17 Thornfield rd W12
74 K 5 Thornfield rd W12
93 U 14 Thornford rd SE13
129 V 17 Thorngate rd W9
65 W 3 Thorngrove rd E13
51 V 16 Thornham gro E15
132 H 19 Thornhaugh st WC1
79 V 19 Thornhill av SE18
133 O 7 Thornhill bri N1
133 N 7 Thornhill Bridge wharf N1
133 O 3 Thornhill cres N1
54 H 20 Thornhill gdns Bark
51 S 7 Thornhill gdns E10

116 A 19 Thornhill gdns Surb
133 R 2 Thornhill gro N1
122 M 17 Thornhill rd Croy
51 R 7 Thornhill rd E10
48 F 20 Thornhill rd N1
133 S 2 Thornhill rd N1
133 O 2 Thornhill sq N1
108 H 9 Thornlaw rd SE27
31 Z 1 Thornley clo N17
146 H 19 Thornley cres SW11
40 L 7 Thornley dri Harrow
76 L 13 Thornley pl SE10
111 U 3 Thornsbeach rd SE6
123 Z 4 Thornsett pl SE20
124 A 5 Thornsett rd SE20
123 Z 4 Thornsett rd SE20
106 B 3 Thornsett rd SW18
122 C 15 Thornton av Croy
107 Y 1 Thornton av SW2
74 B 11 Thornton av W4
125 O 3 Thornton dene Becknhm
107 X 1 Thornton gdns SW12
105 R 18 Thornton hill SW19
122 E 13 Thornton rd Thntn Hth
4 E 13 Thornton rd Barnt
81 T 9 Thornton rd Blvdr
112 F 12 Thornton rd Brom
120 J 18 Thornton rd Carsh
51 X 6 Thornton rd E11
53 Y 13 Thornton rd Ilf
89 W 19 Thornton rd SW12
85 X 9 Thornton rd SW14
105 P 17 Thornton rd SW19
122 F 11 Thornton row Thntn Hth
90 E 5 Thornton st SW9
28 B 17 Thornton way NW11
56 M 5 Thorntons Farm av Rom
78 B 14 Thorntree rd SE7
93 N 3 Thornville st SE8
34 J 7 Thornwood clo E18
94 A 13 Thornwood rd SE13
93 Z 13 Thornwood rd SE13
52 A 16 Thorogood gdns E15
54 C 4 Thorold rd Ilf
53 Z 7 Thorold rd Ilf
30 B 2 Thorold rd N22
148 G 20 Thorparch rd SW8
89 Y 1 Thorparch rd SW8
32 L 6 Thorpe cres E17
33 V 6 Thorpe Hall rd E17
136 M 4 Thorpe ms W10
54 D 20 Thorpe rd Bark
33 T 7 Thorpe rd E17
66 F 4 Thorpe rd E6
52 C 11 Thorpe rd E7
102 K 18 Thorpe rd Kingst
31 T 19 Thorpe rd N15
74 G 3 Thorpebank rd W12
35 Y 12 Thorpedale gdns Ilf
48 B 5 Thorpedale rd N4
110 B 5 Thorpewood av SE26
109 R 11 Thorsden way SE19
45 R 10 Thorverton rd NW2
63 V 7 Thoydon rd E3
107 U 13 Thrale rd SW16
142 C 14 Thrale st SE1
143 O 2 Thrawl st E1
142 G 6 Threadneedle st EC2
160 G 6 Threadneedle st EC2
63 Y 19 Three Colt st E14
63 N 11 Three Colts la E2
135 Y 16 Three Colts la E2
98 H 6 Three corners Bxly Hth
121 N 6 Three Kings rd Mitch
139 W 8 Three Kings' yd W1
64 F 9 Three Mill la E3
143 N 17 Three Oak la SE1
142 E 16 Three Tuns ct SE1
136 J 9 Threshers pl W11
110 D 8 Thriftwood SE23
65 W 18 Throckmorten rd E16
160 G 4 Throgmorton av EC2
142 G 5 Throgmorton st EC2
80 E 8 Throwley clo SE2
154 B 12 Throwley rd Sutton
154 C 11 Throwley rd Sutton
154 B 8 Throwley way Sutton
121 T 3 Thrupp clo Mitch
149 Z 9 Thrush st SE17
111 R 12 Thurbarn rd SE6
151 S 1 Thurland rd SE16
108 G 9 Thurlby rd SE27

42 H 19 Thurlby rd Wemb
89 P 16 Thurleigh av SW12
88 L 17 Thurleigh rd SW12
89 O 16 Thurleigh rd SW12
119 R 11 Thurleston av Mrdn
54 K 14 Thurlestone av Ilf
15 Y 19 Thurlestone av N12
108 H 9 Thurlestone rd SE27
146 J 4 Thurloe clo SW7
39 S 19 Thurloe gdns Rom
146 H 4 Thurloe pl SW7
146 G 4 Thurloe Place ms SW7
146 H 5 Thurloe sq SW7
146 G 5 Thurloe st SW7
42 H 16 Thurlow gdns Wemb
108 K 2 Thurlow hill SE21
108 K 3 Thurlow Park rd SE21
46 G 14 Thurlow rd NW3
71 Y 6 Thurlow rd W7
150 H 10 Thurlow st SE17
47 N 17 Thurlow ter NW5
115 Y 14 Thursland rd Sidcup
159 W 16 Thursley cres Croy
105 P 5 Thursley gdns SW19
113 S 8 Thursley rd SE9
106 G 9 Thurso st SW17
58 F 18 Thurston rd S'hall
93 S 6 Thurston rd SE13
104 J 17 Thurston rd SW20
135 O 7 Thurtle rd E2
81 W 16 Thwaite clo Erith
15 O 19 Thyra gro N12
64 D 11 Tibbatt's rd E3
134 A 2 Tibberton sq N1
105 O 2 Tibbets clo SW19
87 O 17 Tibbets ride SW15
132 L 6 Tiber gdns N1
110 J 5 Ticehurst rd SE23
138 K 6 Tichbourne row W2
88 G 20 Tichwell rd SW18
80 E 5 Tickford clo SE2
65 R 20 Tidal Basin rd E16
157 T 5 Tidenham gdns Croy
86 L 15 Tidesley rd SW15
158 M 5 Tideswell rd Croy
87 N 12 Tideswell rd SW15
102 B 10 Tideway clo Rich
64 B 13 Tidey st E3
96 K 4 Tidford rd Welling
108 A 1 Tierney rd SW2
90 A 20 Tierney rd SW2
75 R 8 Tiger bay SE16
126 H 8 Tiger la Brom
49 Y 11 Tiger way E5
94 M 8 Tilbrook rd SE3
51 T 2 Tilbury rd E10
66 G 7 Tilbury rd E6
17 Y 16 Tile Kiln la N13
47 U 3 Tile Kiln la N6
153 R 11 Tilehurst rd Sutton
106 G 2 Tilehurst rd SW18
47 Z 20 Tileyard rd N1
159 U 18 Tilford av Croy
105 P 2 Tilford gdns SW19
50 A 13 Tilia rd E5
76 B 8 Tiller rd E14
43 V 19 Tillett clo NW10
135 T 12 Tillett way E2
45 N 1 Tilling rd NW2
27 W 11 Tillingbourne gdns N3
27 W 12 Tillingbourne way N3
14 M 13 Tillingham way N12
143 X 7 Tillman st E1
133 N 2 Tilloch st N1
22 K 3 Tillotson rd Harrow
53 W 1 Tillotson rd Ilf
18 F 7 Tillotson rd N9
63 S 15 Tillotson st E1
134 C 16 Tilney ct EC1
21 U 8 Tilney dri Buck Hl
49 O 18 Tilney gdns N1
56 B 19 Tilney rd Dgnhm
139 U 13 Tilney st W1
89 Z 18 Tilson gdns SW2
31 X 5 Tilson rd N17
144 M 15 Tilton st SW6
61 X 20 Tiltwood The W3
95 T 17 Tiltyard appr SE9
127 W 2 Timber clo Chisl
75 U 4 Timber pond rd SE16
134 A 17 Timber st EC1
152 A 8 Timbercroft Epsom
79 U 18 Timbercroft la SE18
27 R 7 Timberdene NW4
63 N 18 Timberland rd E1
143 Y 6 Timberland rd E1
89 Y 7 Timbermill way SW4
155 Y 20 Timberslip dri SM6
31 Y 19 Timberwharf rd N16

128 J 19	Treverton st W10
86 J 18	Treville st SW15
110 G 3	Treviso rd SE23
76 B 15	Trevithick st SE8
22 C 18	Trevone gdns Pinn
5 U 18	Trevor clo Barnt
126 D 18	Trevor clo Brom
23 W 1	Trevor clo Harrow
83 W 12	Trevor clo Islwth
25 Y 4	Trevor gdns Edg
138 M 20	Trevor pl SW7
25 Y 4	Trevor rd Edg
105 T 19	Trevor rd SW19
34 G 1	Trevor rd Wdfd Grn
138 M 20	Trevor sq SW7
139 N 19	Trevor sq SW7
138 M 19	Trevor st SW7
33 W 4	Trevose rd E17
118 M 1	Trewince rd SW20
106 B 4	Trewint st SW18
110 F 12	Trewsbury rd SE26
58 A 13	Triandra way Hayes
66 A 14	Triangle ct E16
65 Z 15	Triangle ct E16
89 X 10	Triangle pl SW4
135 W 3	Triangle rd E8
117 U 4	Triangle the New Mald
63 N 2	Triangle the E8
149 P 16	Trigon rd SW8
110 G 3	Trilby rd SE23
48 B 3	Trinder gdns N19
4 A 17	Trinder rd Barnt
48 B 3	Trinder rd N19
58 E 16	Tring av S'hall
73 N 3	Tring av W5
43 P 18	Tring av Wemb
36 D 17	Tring clo Ilf
69 Z 1	Trinidad gdns Dgnhm
63 Z 20	Trinidad st E14
8 J 20	Trinity av Enf
28 F 11	Trinity av N2
74 K 17	Trinity Church rd SW13
142 C 20	Trinity Church sq SE1
52 A 6	Trinity clo E11
82 B 9	Trinity clo Hounsl
46 F 13	Trinity clo NW3
157 T 19	Trinity clo S Croy
93 W 11	Trinity clo SE13
106 M 5	Trinity cres SW17
107 N 5	Trinity cres SW17
134 J 3	Trinity ct N1
65 P 13	Trinity gdns E16
90 C 10	Trinity gdns SW9
93 T 2	Trinity gro SE10
98 B 10	Trinity pl Bxly Hth
36 A 9	Trinity rd Ilf
28 F 9	Trinity rd N2
30 A 2	Trinity rd N22
85 N 9	Trinity rd Rich
70 A 2	Trinity rd S'hall
106 L 3	Trinity rd SW17
107 N 6	Trinity rd SW17
88 G 17	Trinity rd SW18
105 Z 16	Trinity rd SW19
90 H 20	Trinity ri SW2
142 M 9	Trinity sq EC3
65 R 16	Trinity st E16
7 Y 8	Trinity st Enf
142 C 20	Trinity st SE1
62 C 20	Trinity way W3
142 C 20	Trio pl SE1
94 A 8	Tristan sq SE3
33 X 9	Tristram clo E17
112 D 9	Tristram rd Brom
132 A 16	Triton sq NW1
156 A 7	Tritton av Croydon
109 O 7	Tritton rd SE21
66 G 16	Triumph rd E6
156 D 4	Trojan way Croy
81 R 17	Trosley rd Blvdr
91 T 12	Trossachs rd SE22
151 T 6	Trothy rd SE1
29 N 2	Trott rd N10
88 H 3	Trott st SW11
77 W 13	Troughton rd SE7
92 G 2	Troutbeck rd SE14
89 U 16	Trouville rd SW4
50 M 18	Trowbridge rd E9
102 E 15	Trowlock av Tedd
102 F 15	Trowlock wy Tedd
109 P 15	Troy rd SE19
91 X 7	Troy town SE15
66 G 18	Truesdale rd E6
31 X 1	Trulock ct N17
31 X 2	Trulock rd N17
75 N 7	Truman st SE16
49 T 14	Trumans rd N16
122 K 10	Trumble gdns Thntn Hth
160 C 5	Trump st EC2
71 V 7	Trumpers way W7
52 B 11	Trumpington rd E7
142 A 17	Trundle st SE1
10 E 5	Trundlers way Bushey
75 U 14	Trundley's rd SE8
53 R 2	Truro gdns Ilf
32 L 14	Truro rd E17
30 A 3	Truro rd N22
47 O 19	Truro st NW5
108 H 12	Truslove rd SE27
144 B 2	Trussley rd W6
74 L 8	Trussley rd W6
57 V 2	Truston's gdns Hornch
35 P 15	Tryfan clo Ilf
147 N 9	Tryon st SW3
79 R 17	Tuam rd SE18
62 E 7	Tubbs rd NW10
57 W 18	Tuck rd Rainhm
86 E 18	Tuckton wlk SW15
100 L 20	Tudinghall la Felt
100 H 17	Tudor av Hampt
39 W 11	Tudor av Rom
152 L 9	Tudor av Worc Pk
127 U 1	Tudor clo Chisl
113 U 20	Tudor clo Chisl
99 Y 16	Tudor clo Drtfrd
46 J 16	Tudor clo NW3
13 V 20	Tudor clo NW7
43 W 6	Tudor clo NW9
153 P 12	Tudor clo Sutton
155 W 17	Tudor clo Wallgtn
21 V 16	Tudor clo Wdfd Grn
43 R 16	Tudor Court north Wemb
43 R 17	Tudor Court south Wemb
7 X 4	Tudor cres Enf
32 K 20	Tudor ct E17
102 H 11	Tudor dri Kingst
103 N 14	Tudor dri Kingst
119 T 17	Tudor dri Mrdn
39 V 12	Tudor dri Rom
43 W 7	Tudor gdns NW9
39 W 12	Tudor gdns Rom
86 C 8	Tudor gdns SW13
101 W 1	Tudor gdns Twick
159 T 6	Tudor gdns W Wkhm
61 R 15	Tudor gdns W3
63 O 1	Tudor gro E9
135 Z 2	Tudor gro E9
106 K 19	Tudor pl Mitch
140 F 3	Tudor pl W1
67 X 3	Tudor rd Bark
4 M 11	Tudor rd Barnt
5 N 11	Tudor rd Barnt
125 S 6	Tudor rd Becknhm
20 E 19	Tudor rd E4
65 Z 4	Tudor rd E6
63 O 2	Tudor rd E9
135 Y 3	Tudor rd E9
100 H 18	Tudor rd Hampt
23 P 8	Tudor rd Harrow
83 P 10	Tudor rd Hounsl
103 P 18	Tudor rd Kingst
19 O 4	Tudor rd N9
58 B 20	Tudor rd S'hall
109 U 18	Tudor rd SE19
124 B 13	Tudor rd SE25
141 U 8	Tudor st EC4
16 K 5	Tudor way N14
73 O 6	Tudor way W3
11 P 17	Tudor Well clo Stanm
97 Z 15	Tudor wlk Bxly
94 K 9	Tudway rd SE3
47 V 11	Tufnell Park rd N19
48 A 11	Tufnell Park rd N7
20 A 14	Tufton rd E4
148 H 2	Tufton st SW1
123 O 14	Tugela rd Croy
110 M 4	Tugela st SE6
135 S 9	Tuilerie st E2
124 E 20	Tulip clo CR0
125 U 6	Tulse clo Becknhm
90 F 18	Tulse hill SW2
108 G 1	Tulse hill SW2
108 M 4	Tulsmere rd SE27
18 D 12	Tuncombe rd N18
136 A 14	Tunis rd W12
74 L 3	Tunis rd W12
62 B 2	Tunley rd NW10
107 N 3	Tunley rd SW17
65 X 10	Tunmarsh la E13
63 T 19	Tunnel appr E14
76 L 6	Tunnel appr SE10
76 L 6	Tunnel av SE10
77 O 11	Tunnel av SE10
75 P 6	Tunnel entrance SE16
29 V 2	Tunnel gdns N11
157 T 1	Tunstall rd Croy
90 D 10	Tunstall rd SW9
81 N 9	Tunstock way Blvdr
25 V 19	Tunworth clo NW9
86 C 17	Tunworth cres SW15
88 E 11	Turenne clo SW18
19 P 4	Turin rd N9
135 S 14	Turin st E2
109 R 19	Turkey oak clo SE19
133 W 19	Turks Head yd EC1
147 R 9	Turks row SW3
48 C 5	Turle rd N4
121 Z 2	Turle rd SW16
48 C 5	Turlewray clo N4
65 N 4	Turley clo E15
141 W 4	Turnagain la EC4
55 Y 5	Turnage rd Dgnhm
89 S 8	Turnchapel ms SW4
106 L 20	Turner av Mitch
31 R 14	Turner av N15
101 O 6	Turner av Twick
28 A 19	Turner clo NW11
28 A 19	Turner dri NW11
33 T 11	Turner rd E17
24 L 8	Turner rd Edg
117 Y 16	Turner rd New Mald
143 W 4	Turner st E1
65 P 17	Turner st E16
124 K 1	Turners Meadow way BR3
63 Y 15	Turners rd E3
156 F 3	Turners way CR0
46 D 2	Turners wood NW11
35 O 13	Turneville rd E2
145 O 13	Turneville rd W14
90 M 19	Turney rd SE21
91 O 18	Turney rd SE21
145 O 13	Turney rd W14
74 A 11	Turnham Green ter W4
92 H 12	Turnham rd SE4
133 V 19	Turnmill st EC1
75 Y 18	Turnpike clo SE8
30 E 12	Turnpike la N8
154 D 11	Turnpike la SM1
157 S 4	Turnpike link Croy
147 X 10	Turpentine la SW1
38 E 1	Turpin av Rom
47 X 5	Turpin way N19
155 T 16	Turpin way Wallgtn
127 P 16	Turpington clo Brom
127 P 16	Turpington la Brom
150 C 8	Turquand st SE17
89 U 6	Turret gro SW4
42 J 15	Turton rd Wemb
79 T 14	Tuscan rd SE18
76 M 15	Tuskar st SE10
21 U 8	Tuttlebee la Buck Hl
39 O 3	Tweed way Rom
51 S 14	Tweedale st E15
120 F 19	Tweedale rd Carsh
65 V 7	Tweedmouth rd E13
126 F 2	Tweedy rd Brom
141 R 8	Tweezer's all WC2
64 F 11	Twelve Trees ct E14
21 U 15	Twentyman clo Wdfd Grn
84 D 13	Twickenham br Twick
156 B 5	Twickenham clo Croy
23 T 2	Twickenham gdns Harrow
41 X 15	Twickenham gdns Grnfd
83 X 12	Twickenham rd Islwth
51 V 6	Twickenham rd E11
84 E 12	Twickenham rd Rich
101 Y 9	Twickenham rd Tedd
88 A 18	Twilley st SW18
14 M 13	Twineham grn N12
101 O 6	Twining av Twick
14 E 19	Twinn rd NW7
47 S 11	Twisden rd NW5
61 W 1	Twybridge way NW10
43 W 20	Twybridge way NW10
60 M 9	Twyford Abbey rd NW10
28 L 11	Twyford av N2
29 N 10	Twyford av N2
73 P 1	Twyford av W3
61 P 19	Twyford av W3
73 R 2	Twyford cres W3
141 N 4	Twyford pl WC2
120 F 19	Twyford rd Carsh
40 J 2	Twyford rd Harrow
54 B 14	Twyford rd Ilf
133 N 4	Twyford st N1
65 O 13	Tyas rd E16
119 X 5	Tybenham rd SW19
9 O 10	Tyberry rd Enf
139 O 8	Tyburn way W1
142 J 18	Tyers ga SE1
149 O 8	Tyers st SE11
149 O 10	Tyers ter SE11
81 O 14	Tyeshurst clo SE2
122 C 3	Tylecroft rd SW16
121 Z 3	Tylecroft rd SW16
54 B 14	Tylehurst gdns Ilf
135 N 8	Tyler clo E2
111 R 20	Tyler rd Becknhm
77 N 14	Tyler st SE10
24 L 19	Tylers ga Harrow
109 U 12	Tylney av SE19
127 N 3	Tylney rd Brom
52 K 11	Tylney rd E7
48 J 20	Tyndale ter N1
51 T 7	Tyndall rd E10
96 L 8	Tyndall rd Welling
54 A 7	Tyne rd Ilf
89 O 6	Tyneham rd SW11
8 L 3	Tynemouth dri Enf
107 O 17	Tynemouth rd Mitch
31 W 13	Tynemouth rd N15
88 C 4	Tynemouth st SW6
63 S 6	Type st E2
87 Z 1	Tyrawley rd SW6
41 T 12	Tyrell clo Harrow
154 M 8	Tyrell ct Carsh
91 X 11	Tyrell rd SE22
114 J 11	Tyron way Sidcp
66 H 7	Tyrone rd E6
26 D 20	Tyrrel way NW9
97 P 13	Tyrrell av Welling
93 O 6	Tyrwhitt rd SE4
133 T 15	Tysoe st EC1
92 D 19	Tyson rd SE23
49 U 17	Tyssen pas E8
49 V 17	Tyssen st E8
47 X 10	Tytherton rd N19

U

64 E 14	Uamvar st E14
107 P 19	Uckfield gro Mitch
9 U 1	Uckfield rd Enf
148 D 6	Udall st SW1
101 Z 13	Udney Park rd Tedd
62 H 3	Uffington rd NW10
108 G 9	Uffington rd SE27
22 L 2	Ufford clo Harrow
22 L 2	Ufford rd Harrow
141 W 17	Ufford st SE1
49 P 20	Ufton gro N1
134 H 2	Ufton rd N1
49 R 20	Ufton rd N1
107 V 10	Ullathorne rd SW16
17 P 11	Ulleswater rd N13
103 Y 10	Ullswater clo SW15
104 A 10	Ullswater cres SW15
103 Y 9	Ullswater cres SW15
108 J 5	Ullswater rd SE27
74 G 20	Ullswater rd SW13
57 W 14	Ullswater way Hornch
17 X 13	Ulster gdns N13
48 C 12	Ulster ms N7
131 W 18	Ulster pl NW1
77 N 16	Ulundi rd SE3
87 P 12	Ulva rd SW15
91 W 13	Ulverscroft rd SE22
33 X 7	Ulverston rd E17
108 J 5	Ulverstone rd SE27
45 W 14	Ulysses rd NW6
143 V 5	Umberton st E1
86 G 17	Umbria st SW15
30 H 19	Umfreville rd N4
93 P 6	Undercliff rd SE13
4 K 16	Underhill Barnt
131 Z 5	Underhill pas NW1
91 Z 19	Underhill rd SE22
131 Z 5	Underhill st NW1
16 F 9	Underne av N14
77 V 20	Underpass SE3
142 J 6	Undershaft EC3
112 B 8	Undershaw rd Brom

V

90 M 5 Venetian rd SE5
89 W 9 Venn st SW4
110 D 14 Venner st SE26
99 P 4 Venners clo Bxly Hth
24 C 6 Ventnor av Stanm
15 N 9 Ventnor dri N20
54 G 17 Ventnor gdns Bark
75 T 19 Ventnor rd SE14
154 B 17 Ventnor rd Sutton
97 Y 18 Venture clo Bxly
78 F 8 Venus rd SE18
7 U 18 Vera av N21
87 T 2 Vera rd SW6
74 F 14 Verbena gdns W6
112 A 2 Verdant la SE6
158 F 2 Verdayne av Croy
80 A 18 Verdun rd SE18
74 F 19 Verdun rd SW13
139 X 6 Vere st W1
145 N 12 Vereker rd W14
136 J 7 Verity clo W11
109 P 16 Vermont rd SE19
154 A 4 Vermont rd Sutton
88 B 16 Vermont rd SW18
55 Y 13 Verney gdns Dgnhm
55 Y 12 Verney rd Dgnhm
75 O 14 Verney rd SE16
151 V 12 Verney rd SE16
43 Y 10 Verney st NW10
151 V 11 Verney way SE16
79 O 16 Vernham rd SE18
53 T 13 Vernon av E12
119 O 3 Vernon av SW20
34 G 1 Vernon av Wdfd Grn
6 B 18 Vernon cres Barnt
24 A 4 Vernon ct Stanm
24 A 4 Vernon dri Stanm
23 Z 4 Vernon dri Stanm
144 L 6 Vernon ms W14
140 L 2 Vernon pl WC1
52 A 5 Vernon rd E11
51 Z 4 Vernon rd E11
51 Z 19 Vernon rd E15
32 L 14 Vernon rd E17
63 Z 6 Vernon rd E3
54 K 5 Vernon rd Ilf
30 G 11 Vernon rd N8
154 E 10 Vernon rd Sutton
85 Y 8 Vernon rd SW14
41 P 16 Vernon ri Grnfd
133 P 12 Vernon ri WC1
133 O 11 Vernon sq WC1
144 L 6 Vernon st W14
97 Y 5 Veroan rd Bxly Hth
52 F 20 Verona rd E7
107 S 5 Veronica rd SW17
36 A 15 Veronique gdns Ilf
89 R 19 Verran rd SW12
109 X 19 Versailles rd SE20
32 K 20 Verulam av E17
58 J 11 Verulam rd Grnfd
133 S 20 Verulam st EC1
22 M 8 Verwood rd Harrow
74 F 4 Vespan rd W12
92 J 5 Vesta rd SE4
110 G 4 Vestris rd SE23
91 R 2 Vestry ms SE5
33 R 14 Vestry rd E17
91 S 2 Vestry rd SE5
134 F 12 Vestry st N1
110 K 5 Vevey st SE6
56 D 9 Veysey gdns Dgnhm
141 V 2 Viaduct bldgs EC1
135 W 14 Viaduct pl E2
135 W 14 Viaduct st E2
34 G 8 Viaduct the E18
93 S 8 Vian st SE13
90 D 20 Vibart gdns SW2
132 L 4 Vibart wlk N1
135 Z 5 Vicar's clo E9
109 S 15 Vicar's Oak rd SE19
47 O 14 Vicar's rd NW5
77 T 20 Vicarage av SE3
81 X 16 Vicarage clo Erith
58 F 1 Vicarage clo Ruis
88 G 3 Vicarage cres SW11
67 R 2 Vicarage dri Bark
85 X 12 Vicarage dri SW14
70 C 20 Vicarage Farm rd Hounsl
82 C 3 Vicarage Farm rd Hounsl
137 W 16 Vicarage ga W8
120 J 7 Vicarage gdns Mitch
137 W 15 Vicarage gdns W8
91 P 1 Vicarage gro SE5
52 B 19 Vicarage la E15
65 O 2 Vicarage la E15
66 K 8 Vicarage la E6
152 G 19 Vicarage la Epsom

54 D 5 Vicarage la Ilf
79 P 14 Vicarage pk SE18
47 Z 1 Vicarage pth N8
35 S 2 Vicarage rd Wdfd Grn
156 G 4 Vicarage rd Croy
56 F 20 Vicarage rd Dgnhm
51 O 1 Vicarage rd E10
52 B 20 Vicarage rd E15
57 X 4 Vicarage rd Hornch
116 G 2 Vicarage rd Kingst
31 X 3 Vicarage rd N17
26 G 20 Vicarage rd NW4
153 Z 7 Vicarage rd Sutton
85 Y 12 Vicarage rd SW14
101 X 12 Vicarage rd Tedd
82 M 16 Vicarage rd Twick
101 T 4 Vicarage rd Twick
40 G 1 Vicarage way Harrow
43 Z 10 Vicarage way NW10
88 G 2 Vicarage wlk SW11
60 K 6 Vicars Br clo Wemb
65 S 3 Vicars clo E15
63 O 4 Vicars clo E9
8 F 10 Vicars clo Enf
93 P 9 Vicars hill SE13
17 U 3 Vicars Moor la N21
55 R 10 Vicars wlk Dgnhm
90 A 1 Viceroy rd SW8
148 J 7 Vickers Building SW1
42 L 20 Victor gro Wemb
23 O 11 Victor rd Harrow
62 K 7 Victor rd NW10
110 F 17 Victor rd SE20
101 T 11 Victor rd Tedd
18 C 10 Victor vlls N9
146 H 3 Victoria and Albert Museum SW7
5 U 15 Victoria av Barnt
66 A 3 Victoria av E6
142 K 2 Victoria av EC2
82 G 12 Victoria av Hounsl
27 W 5 Victoria av N3
116 F 16 Victoria av Surb
155 P 5 Victoria av Wallgtn
5 V 15 Victoria clo Barnt
85 O 3 Victoria cotts Rich
31 R 16 Victoria cres N15
109 R 14 Victoria cres SE19
105 W 17 Victoria cres SW19
43 P 17 Victoria ct Wemb
65 N 17 Victoria Dock rd E16
65 T 19 Victoria Dock rd E16
105 R 3 Victoria dri SW19
105 S 4 Victoria dri SW19
140 L 16 Victoria emb EC4 WC2 SW1
141 S 9 Victoria emb EC4 WC2 SW1
82 A 1 Victoria gdns Hounsl
137 S 12 Victoria gdns SW11
15 T 15 Victoria gro N12
146 A 1 Victoria gro W8
137 V 10 Victoria Grove ms W2
4 H 14 Victoria la Barnt
129 S 4 Victoria ms NW6
63 W 2 Victoria park E9
63 P 3 Victoria Park rd E9
135 Y 5 Victoria Park rd E9
63 O 8 Victoria Park sq E2
135 Z 11 Victoria Park sq E2
84 H 13 Victoria pl Rich
54 A 18 Victoria rd Bark
53 Z 18 Victoria rd Bark
5 U 16 Victoria rd Barnt
127 P 12 Victoria rd Brom
98 D 12 Victoria rd Bxly Hth
113 X 12 Victoria rd Chisl
56 J 14 Victoria rd Dgnhm
51 Y 12 Victoria rd E11
65 S 7 Victoria rd E13
33 T 7 Victoria rd E17
34 H 8 Victoria rd E18
20 M 5 Victoria rd E4
21 N 4 Victoria rd E4
36 A 15 Victoria rd Ilf
117 N 3 Victoria rd Kingst
106 K 19 Victoria rd Mitch
31 W 14 Victoria rd N15
29 W 5 Victoria rd N22
48 E 3 Victoria rd N4
18 J 9 Victoria rd N9
62 A 11 Victoria rd NW10
27 N 13 Victoria rd NW4
129 O 8 Victoria rd NW6
129 T 4 Victoria rd NW6
13 R 15 Victoria rd NW7
39 S 18 Victoria rd Rom
40 B 13 Victoria rd Ruis

70 D 9 Victoria rd S'hall
114 M 8 Victoria rd Sidcp
116 G 15 Victoria rd Surb
154 F 12 Victoria rd Sutton
85 X 7 Victoria rd SW14
101 X 15 Victoria rd Tedd
84 A 18 Victoria rd Twick
61 Y 13 Victoria rd W3
60 C 14 Victoria rd W5
138 A 19 Victoria rd W8
89 S 10 Victoria ri SW4
147 Y 1 Victoria sq SW1
81 P 14 Victoria st Blvdr
51 Y 20 Victoria st E15
148 D 2 Victoria st SW1
140 G 20 Victoria sta SW1
147 Y 5 Victoria sta SW1
41 S 4 Victoria ter Harrow
48 F 4 Victoria ter N4
148 K 1 Victoria Tower gdns SW1
85 N 9 Victoria vlls Rich
77 V 13 Victoria way SE7
49 T 10 Victorian gro N16
49 T 11 Victorian rd N16
100 D 15 Victors dri Hampt
120 D 11 Victory av Mrdn
150 D 5 Victory pl SE17
109 T 16 Victory pl SE19
106 C 18 Victory rd SW19
150 G 17 Victory sq SE5
38 F 7 Victory way Rom
75 W 6 Victory way SE16
93 O 2 Victory wlk SE8
23 P 12 View clo Harrow
28 M 20 View rd N6
29 N 19 View rd N6
81 N 13 View the SE2
42 J 2 Viewfield clo Harrow
97 T 20 Viewfield rd Sidcp
87 V 16 Viewfield rd SW18
79 W 14 Viewland rd SE18
7 U 19 Viga rd N21
109 X 9 Vigilant clo SE26
56 F 1 Vignoles rd E2
140 B 10 Vigo st W1
58 C 19 Viking rd S'hall
90 F 7 Villa rd SW9
150 F 10 Villa st SE17
150 G 12 Villa st SE17
80 A 18 Villacourt rd SE18
20 H 16 Village clo E4
99 U 11 Village Green rd Drtfrd
8 D 19 Village rd Enf
27 S 7 Village rd N3
153 X 15 Village row Sutton
78 A 16 Village the SE7
77 Z 16 Village the SE7
125 N 3 Village way Becknhm
40 F 1 Village way E Harrow
44 A 12 Village way NW10
43 Z 12 Village way NW10
40 D 1 Village way Pinn
91 O 15 Village way SE21
79 P 12 Villas rd SE18
116 L 11 Villiers av Surb
100 F 2 Villiers av Twick
51 O 6 Villiers clo E10
117 N 9 Villiers clo Surb
15 S 4 Villiers ct N20
116 L 11 Villiers pth Surb
124 F 4 Villiers rd Becknhm
83 S 4 Villiers rd Islwth
116 M 6 Villiers rd Kingst
44 G 17 Villiers rd NW2
70 F 4 Villiers rd S'hall
140 K 12 Villiers st WC2
82 H 18 Vincam clo Twick
134 G 14 Vince st EC1
4 M 11 Vincent clo Barnt
126 J 10 Vincent clo Brom
75 V 6 Vincent clo SE16
114 G 2 Vincent clo Sidcp
44 E 10 Vincent gdns NW2
123 S 18 Vincent rd Croy
68 L 2 Vincent rd Dgnhm
20 K 20 Vincent rd E4
83 P 3 Vincent rd Islwth
117 P 5 Vincent rd Kingst
30 L 13 Vincent rd N15
30 F 7 Vincent rd N22
79 N 11 Vincent rd SE18
73 U 8 Vincent rd W3
61 N 1 Vincent rd Wemb
100 M 14 Vincent row Hampt
148 E 5 Vincent sq SW1
65 P 16 Vincent st E16
148 F 6 Vincent st SW1

133 X 9 Vincent ter N1
40 B 18 Vincents pth Nthlt
117 N 13 Vine clo Surb
154 C 5 Vine clo Sutton
143 U 2 Vine ct E1
143 U 2 Vine ct E1
24 K 17 Vine ct Harrow
54 B 15 Vine gdns Ilf
133 S 18 Vine hill EC1
142 L 15 Vine la SE1
82 J 10 Vine pl Hounsl
86 D 9 Vine rd SW13
143 N 7 Vine st EC3
38 L 14 Vine st Rom
140 C 11 Vine st W1
142 B 18 Vine yd SE1
33 T 13 Vinegar all E17
143 W 13 Vinegar st E1
13 X 16 Vineries bank NW7
56 C 16 Vineries clo Dgnhm
8 E 11 Vineries the Enf
6 H 18 Vineries the N14
130 K 14 Vinery vlls NW8
28 A 5 Vines av N3
158 L 18 Viney bank Croy
93 S 8 Viney rd SE13
27 S 2 Vineyard av NW7
105 X 9 Vineyard Hill rd SW19
84 J 13 Vineyard pas Rich
85 X 7 Vineyard pth SW14
84 K 14 Vineyard the Rich
133 T 16 Vineyard wlk EC1
90 F 10 Vining st SW9
160 C 9 Vinters pl EC4
80 C 12 Viola av SE2
62 E 20 Viola sq W12
8 B 3 Violet av Enf
156 J 12 Violet gdns Croy
130 B 10 Violet hill NW8
156 J 9 Violet la Croy
33 P 19 Violet rd E17
34 H 7 Violet rd E18
64 C 12 Violet rd E3
139 N 1 Virgil pl W1
149 R 1 Virgil st SE1
36 D 8 Virginia gdns Ilf
134 M 14 Virginia rd E2
108 J 20 Virginia rd Thtn Hth
143 T 10 Virginia st E1
90 D 16 Virginia wlk SW2
134 B 19 Viscount st EC1
9 T 9 Vista av Enf
35 O 16 Vista dri Ilf
95 P 19 Vista the SE9
24 J 19 Vista way Harrow
26 J 17 Vivian av NW4
43 S 17 Vivian av Wemb
43 O 15 Vivian gdns Wemb
63 V 6 Vivian rd E3
91 Z 7 Vivian sq SE15
28 G 15 Vivian way N2
84 F 17 Vivienne clo Twick
96 F 1 Voce rd SE18
79 T 20 Voce rd SE18
118 D 14 Voewood clo New Mald
89 X 8 Voltaire rd SW4
34 E 18 Voluntary pl E11
47 V 7 Vorley rd N19
108 B 16 Voss ct SW16
135 U 14 Voss st E2
156 C 15 Vulcan clo Croy
7 U 9 Vulcan ga Enf
92 K 5 Vulcan rd SE4
92 L 4 Vulcan ter SE4
48 D 17 Vulcan way N7
98 H 8 Vyne the Bxly Hth
61 Z 20 Vyner rd W3
63 N 4 Vyner st E2
135 Y 7 Vyner st E2

W

150 D 7 Wadding st SE17
51 X 16 Waddington rd E15
51 X 17 Waddington st E15
98 F 11 Waddington ter Bxly Hth
108 M 19 Waddington way SE19
109 N 20 Waddington way SE19
156 G 4 Waddon clo Croy

90 M 15 Warmington rd SE24
65 T 11 Warmington st E13
123 W 4 Warminster gdns SE25
123 W 5 Warminster rd SE25
123 X 3 Warminster sq SE25
121 T 2 Warminster way Mitch
24 H 11 Warneford rd Harrow
135 Y 4 Warneford st E9
153 S 2 Warner av Sutton
52 A 16 Warner clo E15
135 T 10 Warner pl E2
112 C 18 Warner rd Brom
32 H 13 Warner rd E17
29 X 13 Warner rd N8
90 M 2 Warner rd SE5
133 R 17 Warner st EC1
133 S 18 Warner yd EC1
21 S 16 Warners clo Wdfd Grn
154 M 16 Warnham Court rd Carsh
15 V 17 Warnham rd N12
74 A 4 Warple way W3
111 Z 17 Warren av Brom
51 V 8 Warren av E11
85 T 9 Warren av Rich
158 E 17 Warren av S Croy
98 E 12 Warren clo Bxly Hth
19 S 4 Warren clo N9
42 H 6 Warren clo Wemb
18 H 3 Warren cres N9
111 N 19 Warren ct Becknhm
103 X 17 Warren cutting Kingst
58 L 11 Warren dri Grnfd
57 X 10 Warren dri Hornch
117 S 20 Warren dri N Surb
117 U 20 Warren dri S Surb
52 K 1 Warren dri The E11
51 X 16 Warren gdns E15
103 W 15 Warren ho Kingst
78 L 8 Warren la SE18
78 M 9 Warren la SE18
10 K 9 Warren la Stanm
131 Z 18 Warren ms W1
154 H 12 Warren Park rd Sutton
103 X 16 Warren pk Kingst
21 P 3 Warren Pond rd E4
10 B 5 Warren rd Bushey
98 D 12 Warren rd Bxly Hth
123 T 19 Warren rd Croy
51 V 9 Warren rd E10
34 K 19 Warren rd E11
52 L 1 Warren rd E11
20 G 8 Warren rd E4
36 D 15 Warren rd Ilf
103 V 15 Warren rd Kingst
44 E 8 Warren rd NW2
115 T 8 Warren rd Sidcp
106 J 16 Warren rd SW19
83 O 17 Warren rd Twick
103 Y 20 Warren ri Kingst
132 B 17 Warren st W1
37 X 14 Warren ter Rom
154 H 20 Warren the Carsh
53 R 12 Warren the E12
70 D 20 Warren the Hounsl
14 E 18 Warren way NW7
77 Y 16 Warren wlk SE7
47 V 11 Warrender rd N19
12 F 6 Warrens Shawe la Edg
89 N 2 Warriner gdns SW11
130 A 17 Warrington cres W9
130 A 19 Warrington gdns W9
23 T 16 Warrington rd Harrow
55 X 7 Warrington rd Dgnhm
156 H 6 Warrington rd Croy
55 X 7 Warrington sq Dgnhm
149 Z 18 Warrior rd SE5
53 V 12 Warrior sq E12
78 C 8 Warspite rd SE18
64 G 3 Warton rd E15
12 G 11 Warwick av Edg
40 D 13 Warwick av Harrow
130 A 19 Warwick av W9
129 Y 17 Warwick av W9
5 V 16 Warwick clo Barnt
10 F 3 Warwick clo Bushey
100 M 18 Warwick clo Hampt
138 B 1 Warwick cres W2
141 R 2 Warwick ct WC1
72 K 3 Warwick dene W5
86 J 9 Warwick dri SW15
54 A 5 Warwick gdns Ilf

30 L 17 Warwick gdns N4
145 P 3 Warwick gdns W14
50 A 5 Warwick gro E5
49 Z 5 Warwick gro E5
116 L 16 Warwick gro Surb
140 F 13 Warwick House st SW1
141 Y 5 Warwick la EC4
129 Z 18 Warwick ms W9
72 G 4 Warwick pl W5
130 A 20 Warwick pl W9
147 Z 8 Warwick Place north SW1
122 E 7 Warwick rd Thntn Hth
117 U 5 Warwick rd New Mald
5 N 15 Warwick rd Barnt
34 J 15 Warwick rd E11
53 R 16 Warwick rd E12
52 D 18 Warwick rd E15
32 K 6 Warwick rd E17
20 A 16 Warwick rd E4
9 Z 1 Warwick rd Enf
16 L 17 Warwick rd N11
18 F 15 Warwick rd N18
70 E 8 Warwick rd S'hall
124 B 6 Warwick rd SE20
115 R 13 Warwick rd Sidcp
154 C 10 Warwick rd Sutton
145 T 8 Warwick rd SW5
102 D 20 Warwick rd Tedd
101 U 1 Warwick rd Twick
145 P 5 Warwick rd W14
72 G 4 Warwick rd W5
97 T 7 Warwick rd Welling
148 A 1 Warwick row SW1
147 Z 2 Warwick row SW1
141 Y 5 Warwick sq EC4
148 A 8 Warwick sq SW1
148 A 8 Warwick Square ms SW1
140 C 9 Warwick st W1
79 T 16 Warwick ter SE18
148 B 6 Warwick way SW1
147 X 9 Warwick way SW1
75 Z 18 Warwickshire pth SE8
53 S 11 Washington av E12
74 G 10 Washington rd SW13
152 J 1 Washington rd Worc Pk
34 C 7 Washington rd E18
65 Y 2 Washington rd E6
117 O 4 Washington rd Kingst
64 E 9 Washington st E3
110 G 1 Wastdale rd SE23
93 W 3 Wat Tyler rd SE10
73 P 17 Watcombe cotts Rich
124 A 10 Watcombe rd SE25
123 Z 11 Watcombe rd SE25
11 O 19 Water gdns Stanm
52 A 18 Water la E15
54 J 10 Water la Ilf
116 G 2 Water la Kingst
84 G 13 Water la Rich
101 Z 1 Water la Twick
18 D 17 Water mill la N18
100 G 5 Water Mill way Felt
61 N 4 Water rd Wemb
141 R 8 Water st WC2
157 P 8 Water Tower hill Croy
156 L 5 Water Works yd Croy
111 T 8 Waterbank rd SE6
26 B 8 Waterbeach rd NW9
55 T 18 Waterbeach rd Dgnhm
27 N 16 Waterbrook la NW4
80 A 17 Waterdale rd SE2
51 P 18 Waterden rd E15
155 Y 14 Waterer ri Wallgtn
16 G 10 Waterfall clo N14
16 F 14 Waterfall rd N11
106 H 15 Waterfall rd SW19
106 J 14 Waterfall ter SW17
80 C 2 Waterfield clo SE18
88 A 1 Waterford rd SW6
141 W 8 Watergate EC4
76 A 15 Watergate st SE8
140 L 12 Watergate wlk WC2
20 L 13 Waterhall av E4
66 A 14 Waterhouse clo E16
46 G 14 Waterhouse clo NW3
144 H 8 Waterhouse clo W6
141 O 11 Waterloo br WC2
50 D 14 Waterloo clo E9
63 P 5 Waterloo gdns E2
39 O 18 Waterloo gdns Rom

129 R 1 Waterloo pas NW6
84 J 12 Waterloo pl Rich
140 F 13 Waterloo pl SW1
51 N 2 Waterloo rd E10
65 Y 2 Waterloo rd E6
52 D 14 Waterloo rd E7
36 B 7 Waterloo rd Ilf
44 G 5 Waterloo rd NW2
39 O 17 Waterloo rd Rom
141 U 18 Waterloo rd SE1
154 F 10 Waterloo rd Sutton
141 R 16 Waterloo sta SE1
133 W 2 Waterloo ter N1
47 U 4 Waterlow rd N19
87 R 9 Waterman st SW15
143 W 12 Waterman way E1
102 H 18 Watermans clo Kingst
120 M 15 Watermead la Carsh
111 T 9 Watermead rd SE6
102 C 8 Watermill clo Rich
56 E 16 Waters gdns Dgnhm
117 S 5 Waters rd Kingst
112 B 6 Waters rd SE6
111 Y 7 Waters rd SE6
117 S 5 Waters sq Kingst
24 H 2 Watersfield way Edg
124 M 1 Waterside Becknhm
58 F 7 Waterside clo Nthlt
143 T 19 Waterside clo SE16
99 S 12 Waterside Drtfrd
131 U 3 Waterside pl NW1
70 G 7 Waterside rd S'hall
134 L 12 Waterson st N1
50 E 8 Waterworks la E5
90 B 15 Waterworks rd SW2
115 S 17 Watery la Sidcp
119 V 2 Watery la SW20
120 L 14 Wates way Mitch
30 M 5 Wateville rd N17
10 M 1 Watford By-pass Borhm Wd
11 P 3 Watford By-pass Borhm Wd
88 K 1 Watford clo SW11
65 T 15 Watford rd E16
41 Y 2 Watford rd Harrow
42 A 12 Watford rd Wemb
26 E 4 Watford way NW7
13 O 14 Watford way NW7
43 S 11 Watkin rd Wemb
48 C 17 Watkinson rd N7
26 A 1 Watling av Edg
25 U 6 Watling av SE9
160 B 7 Watling ct EC4
11 R 5 Watling Farm clo Borhm Wd
98 H 11 Watling st Bxly Hth
99 X 15 Watling st Drtfrd
142 B 7 Watling st EC4
160 B 7 Watling st EC4
110 H 12 Watlington gro SE26
143 Y 6 Watney mkt E1
143 R 18 Watney pas SE1
85 V 6 Watney rd SW14
63 N 18 Watney st E1
143 Y 8 Watney st E1
121 W 12 Watneys rd Mitch
53 W 20 Watson av E6
153 S 2 Watson av Sutton
49 P 14 Watson clo N16
106 K 16 Watson clo SW19
65 U 5 Watson st E13
49 P 14 Watson st N16
75 Z 20 Watson's st SE8
30 D 6 Watsons rd N22
44 F 6 Watsons yd NW2
30 K 11 Watt way N17
101 Y 12 Watt's la Tedd
50 C 9 Wattisfield rd E5
64 C 13 Watts gro E3
114 A 20 Watts la Chisl
113 Z 20 Watts la Chisl
75 N 3 Watts st E1
143 X 13 Watts st E1
17 V 15 Wauthier clo N13
129 W 2 Wavel ms NW6
96 J 15 Wavell dri Sidcp
73 Y 14 Wavendon av W4
92 A 10 Waveney av SE15
33 W 10 Waverley av E17
19 X 15 Waverley av E4
117 U 14 Waverley av Surb
154 B 4 Waverley av Sutton
82 E 20 Waverley av Twick
100 G 1 Waverley av Wemb
43 N 16 Waverley av Wemb
127 N 12 Waverley clo Brom
34 K 6 Waverley clo E18
79 R 15 Waverley cres SE18

67 U 7 Waverley gdns Bark
66 E 16 Waverley gdns E6
36 D 8 Waverley gdns Ilf
61 N 7 Waverley gdns NW10
27 R 10 Waverley gro N3
130 F 8 Waverley pl NW8
33 V 10 Waverley rd E17
34 K 6 Waverley rd E18
7 X 12 Waverley rd Enf
152 J 11 Waverley rd Epsom
40 C 4 Waverley rd Harrow
31 V 8 Waverley rd N17
31 Y 2 Waverley rd N17
29 Z 20 Waverley rd N8
58 H 19 Waverley rd S'hall
79 R 14 Waverley rd SE18
124 A 8 Waverley rd SE25
154 K 14 Waverley way Carsh
88 C 19 Waverton rd SW18
139 V 12 Waverton st W1
34 F 7 Wavertree rd E18
108 B 2 Wavertree rd SW2
58 G 17 Waxlow cres S'hall
61 X 6 Waxlow rd NW10
22 A 8 Waxwell clo Pinn
22 A 9 Waxwell la Pinn
141 P 20 Waxwell ter SE1
58 A 10 Wayfarer rd Nthlt
88 K 6 Wayford st SW11
49 X 15 Wayland av E8
108 J 6 Waylett pl SE27
42 F 11 Waylett pl Wemb
136 F 7 Wayneflete sq W10
156 J 7 Wayneflete av Croy
106 D 4 Wayneflete st SW18
10 C 1 Wayside av Bushey
6 J 19 Wayside clo N14
39 S 10 Wayside clo Rom
84 D 15 Wayside ct Twick
56 D 14 Wayside gdns Dgnhm
113 U 10 Wayside gdns SE9
113 T 10 Wayside gro SE9
45 T 4 Wayside NW11
85 W 12 Wayside SW14
23 S 5 Weald la Harrow
23 V 3 Weald ri Harrow
49 V 6 Weald sq E5
113 U 15 Weald the Chisl
38 G 19 Weald way Rom
153 V 3 Wealdstone rd Sutton
20 K 10 Weale rd E4
135 W 13 Wear pl E2
8 C 6 Weardale gdns Enf
93 X 11 Weardale rd SE13
63 Z 14 Weatherley clo E3
135 S 18 Weaver st E1
108 K 10 Weaver wlk SE27
83 U 9 Weavers clo Islwth
142 L 15 Weavers la SE1
132 E 2 Weavers way NW1
49 Y 2 Webb est E5
77 P 17 Webb rd SE3
150 J 3 Webb st SE1
141 V 19 Webber row SE1
141 X 18 Webber st SE1
88 L 12 Webbs rd SW11
88 M 14 Webbs rd SW11
72 G 3 Webster gdns W5
53 V 11 Webster rd E11
151 U 2 Webster rd SE16
67 T 4 Wedderburn rd Bark
46 G 15 Wedderburn rd NW3
108 L 16 Wedgewood way SE19
128 M 17 Wedlake st W10
35 W 4 Wedmore av Ilf
47 X 8 Wedmore gdns N19
47 Y 8 Wedmore ms N19
59 R 10 Wedmore rd Grnfd
47 Y 9 Wedmore st N19
45 X 13 Weech rd NW6
47 O 15 Weedington rd NW5
143 T 5 Wehill rd E1
94 F 12 Weigall rd SE12
139 V 7 Weighhouse st W1
124 A 3 Weighton ms SE20
23 R 4 Weighton rd Harrow
123 Y 2 Weighton rd SE20
154 G 11 Weihurst gdns Sutton
87 R 9 Weimar st SW15
18 B 19 Weir Hall av N18
18 A 15 Weir Hall gdns N18
31 P 1 Weir Hall rd N17
18 C 17 Weir Hall rd N18
98 G 19 Weir rd Bxly
89 V 19 Weir rd SW12
106 B 9 Weir rd SW19

132 G 13 Weir's pas NW1
15 Z 7 Weirdale av N20
15 Z 8 Weirdale av N20
87 P 8 Weiss rd SW15
112 G 10 Welbeck av Brom
115 N 2 Welbeck av Sidcp
118 C 11 Welbeck clo
   New Mald
152 F 17 Welbeck clo Epsom
15 T 15 Welbeck clo N12
5 V 19 Welbeck rd Barnt
120 H 20 Welbeck rd Carsh
66 A 8 Welbeck rd E6
40 K 3 Welbeck rd Harrow
154 G 2 Welbeck rd Sutton
139 W 5 Welbeck st W1
139 W 4 Welbeck way W1
90 K 3 Welby st SE5
16 F 17 Weld pl N11
105 T 10 Welford pl SW19
107 R 13 Welham rd SW17
154 H 1 Welhouse rd Carsh
4 A 16 Well appr Barnt
40 B 10 Well clo Ruis
34 K 19 Well Cottage clo E11
160 C 6 Well ct EC4
95 T 13 Well Hall rd SE9
85 V 12 Well la SW14
46 F 10 Well pass NW3
4 A 17 Well rd Barnt
46 G 10 Well rd NW3
51 Y 17 Well st E15
50 D 20 Well st E9
63 P 1 Well st E9
135 Z 1 Well st E9
46 G 10 Well wlk NW3
24 C 18 Wellacre rd Harrow
97 P 13 Wellan clo Welling
59 W 7 Welland gdns Grnfd
76 G 17 Welland st SE10
127 U 3 Wellands clo Brom
143 T 8 Wellclose sq E1
143 T 10 Wellclose st E1
23 T 17 Welldon cres Harrow
142 A 17 Weller st SE1
132 J 10 Wellers ct NW1
74 H 8 Wellesley av W6
157 N 3 Wellesley Court rd
   Croy
101 S 5 Wellesley cres Twick
157 O 3 Wellesley gro Croy
156 M 2 Wellesley rd Croy
122 M 20 Wellesley rd Croy
157 N 3 Wellesley rd Croy
34 F 16 Wellesley rd E11
33 O 18 Wellesley rd E17
23 T 17 Wellesley rd Harrow
54 B 4 Wellesley rd Ilf
53 Y 6 Wellesley rd Ilf
30 F 7 Wellesley rd N22
47 O 14 Wellesley rd NW5
154 D 13 Wellesley rd Sutton
101 S 6 Wellesley rd Twick
73 P 14 Wellesley rd W4
63 R 16 Wellesley st E1
134 C 12 Wellesley ter N1
29 S 9 Wellfield av N10
108 B 10 Wellfield rd SW16
108 D 11 Wellfield wlk SW16
90 K 8 Wellfit rd SE24
42 A 18 Wellgarth gdns Grnfd
46 A 4 Wellgarth rd NW11
4 B 14 Wellhouse la Barnt
125 N 9 Wellhouse rd
   Becknhm
97 R 8 Welling High st
   Welling
96 D 7 Welling way SE9
152 M 6 Wellington av
   Worc Pk
20 C 9 Wellington av E4
82 G 13 Wellington av Hounsl
31 W 18 Wellington av N15
19 N 10 Wellington av N9
22 E 4 Wellington av Pinn
97 N 15 Wellington av Sidcp
147 V 11 Wellington bldgs SW1
69 X 1 Wellington clo
   Dgnhm
92 E 3 Wellington clo SE14
137 S 6 Wellington clo W11
117 W 7 Wellington cres
   New Mald
69 Y 1 Wellington dri
   Dgnhm
101 P 9 Wellington gdns
   Hampt
77 X 14 Wellington gdns SE7
77 X 15 Wellington ms SE7
130 H 12 Wellington pl NW8

23 T 9 Wellington rd
   Harrow
81 P 12 Wellington rd Blvdr
126 L 9 Wellington rd Brom
97 V 14 Wellington rd Bxly
122 J 17 Wellington rd Croy
50 H 3 Wellington rd E10
34 G 14 Wellington rd E11
32 J 12 Wellington rd E17
66 G 5 Wellington rd E6
52 D 14 Wellington rd E7
8 E 18 Wellington rd Enf
18 E 4 Wellington rd Enf
101 P 10 Wellington rd Hampt
128 G 14 Wellington rd NW10
130 G 10 Wellington rd NW8
22 D 4 Wellington rd Pinn
105 Z 5 Wellington rd SW19
72 D 9 Wellington rd W5
82 E 10 Wellington Road north
   Hounsl
82 G 14 Wellington Road south
   Hounsl
135 R 12 Wellington row E2
147 N 10 Wellington sq SW3
67 O 2 Wellington st Bark
64 L 14 Wellington st E16
78 K 11 Wellington st SE18
140 M 8 Wellington st WC2
141 N 8 Wellington st WC2
41 R 4 Wellington ter
   Harrow
143 W 12 Wellington ter E1
137 W 11 Wellington ter W2
64 A 10 Wellington way E3
93 Z 18 Wellmeadow rd
   SE13
111 Z 3 Wellmeadow rd SE6
71 Y 10 Wellmeadow rd W7
120 G 20 Wellow wlk Carsh
43 X 5 Wells dri NW9
56 G 16 Wells gdns Dgnhm
53 R 1 Wells gdns Ilf
57 U 18 Wells gdns Rainhm
62 B 13 Wells House rd
   NW10
140 B 3 Wells ms W1
110 A 8 Wells Park rd SE26
109 X 8 Wells Park rd SE26
127 U 3 Wells rd Brom
136 C 19 Wells rd W12
74 M 7 Wells rd W12
131 O 6 Wells ri NW8
133 O 14 Wells sq WC1
140 B 3 Wells st W1
48 F 6 Wells ter N4
16 L 4 Wells The N14
150 H 16 Wells way SE5
48 E 15 Wells yd N7
4 A 15 Wellside clo Barnt
85 V 12 Wellside gdns SW14
127 W 5 Wellsmoor gdns
   Brom
43 U 9 Wellsprings cres
   Wemb
19 R 4 Wellstead av N9
66 J 7 Wellstead rd E6
55 N 2 Wellwood rd Ilf
151 S 8 Welsford st SE1
65 R 10 Welsh clo E13
135 U 4 Welshpool st E8
74 G 13 Weltje rd W6
79 U 20 Welton rd SE18
63 P 8 Welwyn st E2
42 L 10 Wembley Hill rd
   Wemb
43 N 13 Wembley Hill rd
   Wemb
42 M 11 Wembley Park dri
   Wemb
43 O 10 Wembley Park dri
   Wemb
100 G 19 Wembley rd Hampt
43 U 17 Wembley way Wemb
24 E 3 Wemborough rd
   Stanm
47 U 1 Wembury rd N6
94 C 5 Wemyss rd SE3
41 S 8 Wendela ct Harrow
74 C 7 Wendell rd W12
154 F 1 Wendling rd Sutton
63 Z 3 Wendon st E3
118 E 14 Wendover dri
   New Mald
126 H 7 Wendover rd Brom
62 D 6 Wendover rd NW10
95 O 7 Wendover rd SE9
150 H 10 Wendover SE17
97 O 11 Wendover way
   Welling

150 J 12 Wendover wlk SE17
8 G 19 Wendy clo Enf
60 K 4 Wendy way Wemb
12 G 20 Wenlock rd Edg
134 B 10 Wenlock rd N1
134 D 10 Wenlock st N1
63 T 6 Wennington rd E3
34 D 1 Wensley av
   Wdfd Grn
18 M 19 Wensley rd N18
35 S 5 Wensleydale av Ilf
100 K 18 Wensleydale gdns
   Hampt
100 J 19 Wensleydale pass
   Hampt
100 J 17 Wensleydale rd
   Hampt
111 Y 4 Wentland clo SE6
111 Y 5 Wentland rd SE6
14 M 20 Wentworth av N3
27 Z 1 Wentworth av N3
119 W 17 Wentworth clo Mrdn
151 T 20 Wentworth cres SE15
99 V 17 Wentworth dri Drtfrd
17 V 12 Wentworth gdns
   N13
42 M 3 Wentworth hill
   Wemb
43 N 3 Wentworth hill
   Wemb
63 X 11 Wentworth ms E3
27 Z 2 Wentworth pk N3
4 D 11 Wentworth rd Brentf
122 F 18 Wentworth rd Croy
53 N 14 Wentworth rd E12
27 V 19 Wentworth rd NW11
143 P 3 Wentworth st E1
22 A 13 Wentworth way Pinn
98 F 4 Wenvoe av Bxly Hth
79 P 15 Wernbrook st SE18
123 X 10 Werndee rd SE25
35 V 10 Werneth Hall rd Ilf
132 D 10 Werrington st NW1
87 R 11 Werter rd SW15
82 D 4 Wesley av Hounsl
61 X 8 Wesley av NW10
41 N 6 Wesley clo Harrow
48 D 8 Wesley clo N7
149 X 8 Wesley clo SE17
51 U 2 Wesley rd E10
61 X 3 Wesley rd NW10
139 V 1 Wesley st W1
47 R 12 Wesleyan pl NW5
119 Z 5 Wessex av SW19
36 H 18 Wessex clo Ilf
117 S 2 Wessex clo Kingst
99 S 3 Wessex dri Erith
22 B 2 Wessex dri Pinn
45 S 3 Wessex gdns NW11
59 R 7 Wessex la Grnfd
63 P 10 Wessex st E2
45 S 2 Wessex way NW11
63 R 17 West Arbour st E1
33 R 15 West av E17
14 L 19 West av N3
27 O 15 West av NW4
22 D 19 West av Pinn
58 D 19 West av S'hall
56 B 12 West av Wallgtn
33 P 14 West Avenue rd E17
66 M 3 West bank Bark
7 Y 10 West bank Enf
49 S 2 West bank N16
118 L 9 West Barnes la
   New Mald
30 G 9 West Beech rd N22
140 K 4 West Central st WC1
22 J 4 West chantry Harrow
6 B 14 West clo Barnt
59 N 6 West clo Grnfd
100 C 15 West clo Hampt
18 H 10 West clo N9
42 M 4 West clo Wemb
43 N 4 West clo Wemb
45 Y 15 West cotts NW6
145 T 6 West Cromwell rd
   SW5
72 A 17 West Cross way Brentf
71 Z 18 West Cross way Brentf
42 D 8 West ct Wemb
10 C 19 West dri Harrow
153 P 19 West dri Suttton
107 U 9 West dri SW16
10 C 20 West Drive gdns
   Harrow
147 S 4 West Eaton pl SW1
147 S 4 West Eaton Place ms
   SW1
62 A 1 West Ella rd NW10
33 V 16 West End av E10

22 A 13 West End av Pinn
4 C 14 West End la Barnt
129 V 4 West End la NW6
45 Z 15 West End la NW6
45 Z 20 West End la NW6
22 A 15 West End la Pinn
70 B 2 West End rd S'hall
76 D 12 West Ferry rd E14
143 Z 10 West gdns E1
106 J 15 West gdns SW17
30 K 13 West Green rd N15
31 P 14 West Green rd N15
21 Z 17 West gro Wdfd Grn
147 S 1 West Halkin st SW1
85 S 3 West Hall rd Rich
113 O 1 West Hallowes SE9
64 M 2 West Ham la E15
65 R 1 West Ham pk E15
45 Z 19 West Hampstead ms
   NW6
141 T 5 West Harding st EC4
45 Y 5 West Heath av
   NW11
99 U 16 West Heath clo
   Drtfrd
45 Y 9 West Heath clo NW3
45 Y 4 West Heath dri
   NW11
45 Y 8 West Heath gdns
   NW3
99 U 16 West Heath rd Drtfrd
46 B 9 West Heath rd NW3
45 Y 7 West Heath rd NW3
80 H 17 West Heath rd SE2
44 H 3 West Hendon bdwy
   NW9 NW2
47 O 8 West Hill ct N6
41 S 6 West hill Harrow
47 P 3 West hill N6
47 N 6 West Hill pk N6
87 W 16 West Hill rd SW18
157 S 19 West hill S Croy
87 S 17 West Hill SW15
15 N 6 West Hill way N20
42 M 4 West hill Wemb
43 O 4 West hill Wemb
98 L 1 West Holme Erith
64 A 20 West India Dock rd
   E14
143 W 19 West la SE16
73 P 3 West Lodge av W3
137 V 12 West mall W8
152 B 14 West Mead Epsom
147 Z 8 West ms SW1
111 W 20 West oak Becknhm
85 R 2 West Park av Rich
37 X 16 West Park clo Rom
85 P 3 West Park rd Rich
113 R 2 West pk SE9
104 L 12 West pl SW19
141 W 2 West Poultry av EC1
62 F 17 West Quarters W12
16 B 5 West rd Barnt
65 R 3 West rd E15
103 W 20 West rd Kingst
18 M 20 West rd N17
31 Z 1 West rd N17
56 M 3 West rd Rom
37 X 17 West rd Rom
89 Z 12 West rd SW4
60 J 14 West rd W5
58 M 6 West Ridge gdns
   Grnfd
128 J 17 West row W10
84 L 10 West Sheen vale Rich
104 M 13 West Side comm
   SW19
105 N 15 West Side comm
   SW19
141 X 2 West Smithfield EC1
149 W 3 West sq SE11
126 E 2 West st Brom
98 A 9 West st Bxly Hth
154 L 8 West st Carsh
156 M 7 West st Croy
51 Z 8 West st E11
33 R 16 West st E17
63 N 7 West st E2
156 M 7 West st Harrow
154 A 11 West st Sutton
140 H 7 West st WC2
154 M 8 West Street la Carsh
85 T 12 West Temple sheen
   SW14
143 O 7 West Tenter st E1
18 D 3 West View cres N9
26 M 15 West view NW4
147 Z 8 West Warwick pl
   SW1
12 G 19 West way Edg

145 R 20 Wheatsheaf ter SW6	51 X 17 Whitear wlk E15	40 M 2 Whitmore rd Harrow	121 X 6 Wide way Mitch
56 K 9 Wheel Farm dri Dgnhm	69 S 3 Whitebarn la Dgnhm	41 N 2 Whitmore rd Harrow	35 R 12 Widecombe gdns Ilf
132 K 4 Wheeler gdns N1	127 W 16 Whitebeam av Brom	87 O 14 Whitnell way SW15	113 S 7 Widecombe rd SE9
67 S 7 Wheelers cross Bark	143 R 3 Whitechapel High st E1	35 N 12 Whitney av Ilf	28 F 15 Widecombe way N2
153 X 5 Wheelers st Sutton	143 R 4 Whitechapel pas E1	51 P 1 Whitney rd E10	142 L 2 Widegate st E1
48 C 20 Wheelwright st N7	143 U 2 Whitechapel rd E1	115 Y 16 Whitney wlk Sidcp	129 V 15 Widley rd W9
155 Y 5 Whelan way Wallgtn	135 X 20 Whitechapel rd E1	53 O 12 Whitta rd E12	127 O 4 Widmore Lodge rd Brom
135 N 18 Wheler st E1	58 L 18 Whitecote rd S'hall	65 Z 2 Whittaker rd E6	126 K 2 Widmore rd Brom
74 A 7 Whernside clo W4	125 W 8 Whitecroft clo Becknhm	153 V 5 Whittaker rd Sutton	127 O 3 Widmore rd Brom
80 H 1 Whernside clo SE28		147 S 7 Whittaker st SW1	79 S 7 Wigeon pth SE28
15 S 8 Whetstone clo N20	125 V 9 Whitecroft way Becknhm	110 C 8 Whittall gdns SE26	43 R 19 Wiggington av Wemb
141 O 3 Whetstone pk WC2	134 H 20 Whitecross pl EC2	87 V 2 Whittingstall rd SW6	102 C 4 Wiggins and Pointers cotts Rich
94 L 4 Whetstone rd SE3	134 C 17 Whitecross st EC1	142 J 7 Whittington av EC3	26 D 3 Wiggins mead NW9
48 A 7 Whewell rd N19	134 C 17 Whitecross st EC2	30 A 1 Whittington rd N22	30 G 17 Wightman rd N4
132 K 13 Whidborne st WC1	45 N 2 Whitefield av NW2	17 O 20 Whittington rd N22	100 A 2 Wigley rd Felt
68 G 19 Whimbrel clo SE2	87 T 17 Whitefield clo SW18	22 C 16 Whittington way Pinn	139 X 4 Wigmore pl W1
107 X 11 Whinfell clo SW16	112 A 7 Whitefoot la Brom		154 H 1 Wigmore rd Carsh
95 R 8 Whinyates rd SE9	112 B 7 Whitefoot ter Brom	58 K 17 Whittle clo S'hall	139 W 4 Wigmore st W1
33 W 15 Whipps cross E17	23 S 8 Whitefriars av Harrow	155 N 17 Whittlebury clo Carsh	154 G 2 Wigmore wlk Carsh
34 B 18 Whipps Cross rd E11		22 M 4 Whittlesea pth Harrow	34 K 18 Wigram rd E11
33 X 16 Whipps Cross rd E11	23 S 7 Whitefriars dri Harrow	23 N 3 Whittlesea rd Harrow	33 V 9 Wigram sq E17
133 V 14 Whiskin st EC1	141 U 6 Whitefriars st EC4	23 N 4 Whittlesea rd Harrow	65 W 11 Wigston rd E13
25 N 7 Whistler gdns Edg	140 K 14 Whitehall ct SW1	141 T 15 Whittlesey st SE1	24 J 5 Wigton gdns Stanm
48 H 14 Whistler st N5	20 L 6 Whitehall gdns E4	41 V 15 Whitton Avenue east Grnfd	149 T 11 Wigton pl SE11
146 H 20 Whistlers av SW11	140 K 15 Whitehall gdns SW1		32 L 5 Wigton rd E17
134 M 7 Whiston rd E2	73 R 3 Whitehall gdns W3	41 P 16 Whitton Avenue west Nthlt	48 H 6 Wilberforce rd N4
135 S 6 Whiston rd E2	73 T 16 Whitehall gdns W4		26 F 18 Wilberforce rd NW9
31 W 4 Whitbread clo N17	21 U 8 Whitehall la Buck Hl	42 B 19 Whitton clo Grnfd	105 O 15 Wilberforce way SW19
92 K 11 Whitbread rd SE4	99 Y 3 Whitehall la Erith	82 M 14 Whitton dene Hounsl	
93 S 11 Whitburn rd SE13	73 T 16 Whitehall Park rd W4	83 T 13 Whitton dene Islwth	147 R 5 Wilbraham pl SW1
61 S 8 Whitby av NW10	47 V 3 Whitehall pk N19	41 Z 17 Whitton dri Grnfd	18 B 17 Wilbury way N18
25 R 10 Whitby gdns NW9	140 K 13 Whitehall pl SW1	83 O 14 Whitton Manor rd Islwth	137 P 12 Wilby ms W11
154 F 1 Whitby gdns Sutton	155 R 9 Whitehall pl Wallgtn		148 K 19 Wilcox clo SW8
40 M 10 Whitby rd Harrow	122 F 13 Whitehall rd Thntn Hth	82 L 13 Whitton rd Hounsl	153 Z 9 Wilcox rd Sutton
41 N 10 Whitby rd Harrow		83 T 16 Whitton rd Twick	148 J 18 Wilcox rd SW8
78 F 11 Whitby rd SE18	21 P 7 Whitehall rd Wdfd Grn	82 H 16 Whitton waye Hounsl	101 R 9 Wilcox rd Tedd
135 N 16 Whitby st E1		65 S 10 Whitwell rd E13	140 M 5 Wild ct WC2
75 V 17 Whitcher clo SE14	127 O 10 Whitehall rd Brom	78 K 18 Whitworth rd SE18	92 D 3 Wild Goose dri SE14
47 V 19 Whitcher pl NW1	23 S 20 Whitehall rd Harrow	123 U 8 Whitworth rd SE25	27 Z 20 Wild hatch NW11
24 M 2 Whitchurch av Edg	71 Y 7 Whitehall rd W7	77 N 13 Whitworth rd SE10	140 M 6 Wild st WC2
11 Z 19 Whitchurch clo Edg	31 U 2 Whitehall st N17	91 Y 8 Whorlton rd SE15	150 H 1 Wild's rents SE1
11 Z 20 Whitchurch gdns Edg	140 J 15 Whitehall SW1	30 G 10 Whymark av N22	11 U 20 Wildcroft gdns Edg
	126 F 3 Whitehart slip Brom	52 H 18 Whyteville rd E7	86 M 20 Wildcroft rd SW15
12 B 20 Whitchurch la Edg	126 E 9 Whitehaven clo BR2	64 A 3 Wick la E3	87 N 17 Wildcroft rd SW15
24 K 2 Whitchurch la Edg	130 J 19 Whitehaven st NW8	50 E 18 Wick rd E9	135 T 4 Wilde clo E8
136 G 9 Whitchurch rd W11	88 B 19 Whitehead clo SW18	89 P 5 Wick rd SW11	113 Z 18 Wilderness rd Chisl
140 G 11 Whitcomb st WC2	146 M 8 Whitehead's gro SW3	102 C 19 Wick rd Tedd	100 K 10 Wilderness the Hampt
26 C 7 White acre NW9		143 V 7 Wicker st E1	
76 D 10 White Adder way E14	99 W 14 Whitehill rd Drtfrd	109 U 11 Wickers Oake SE19	49 T 2 Wilderton rd N16
103 P 5 White Ash lodge Rich	123 P 8 Whitehorse la SE25	89 P 7 Wickersley rd SW11	93 R 18 Wildfell rd SE6
	122 M 17 Whitehorse rd Croy	159 O 11 Wicket the Croy	142 H 20 Wilds rents SE1
133 T 19 White Bear yd EC1	123 N 13 Whitehorse rd Croy	63 O 11 Wickford st E1	94 D 18 Wildwood clo SE12
143 S 4 White Church la E1	16 L 9 Whitehouse ct N14	135 Z 17 Wickford st E1	46 C 5 Wildwood gro NW3
136 B 10 White City clo W12	16 E 10 Whitehouse way N14	32 E 12 Wickford way E17	28 C 19 Wildwood rd NW11
62 L 20 White City clo W12		158 H 1 Wickham av Croy	46 C 2 Wildwood rd NW11
136 A 9 White City rd W12	60 D 17 Whiteledges W13	152 M 10 Wickham av Sutton	46 E 3 Wildwood rd NW11
62 K 19 White City rd W12	65 P 7 Whiteleg rd E13	153 O 11 Wickham av Sutton	8 A 12 Wilford cl Enf
136 B 9 White City Stadium W10	65 P 7 Whitelegg rd E13	126 A 16 Wickham chase W Wkhm	148 B 1 Wilfred st SW1
	109 P 12 Whiteley rd SE19		61 V 13 Wilfrid gdns W3
133 T 7 White Conduit st N1	100 H 7 Whiteley's way Felt	125 X 18 Wickham chase W Wkhm	17 V 18 Wilk pl N13
23 V 2 White Gate gdns Harrow	145 P 8 Whiteleys cotts		109 U 11 Wilkers oak SE19
	125 V 3 Whiteoak dri Becknhm	118 C 13 Wickham clo New Mald	143 O 1 Wilkes st E1
56 D 17 White gdns Dgnhm			135 O 19 Wilkes st E1
142 J 3 White Hart ct EC2	59 R 8 Whiteoaks la Grnfd	9 O 11 Wickham clo Enf	135 O 20 Wilkes st E1
31 S 1 White Hart la N17	93 O 8 Whitepost la SE13	159 V 2 Wickham Court rd W Wkhm	135 P 18 Wilkes st E1
30 J 2 White Hart la N22	36 G 17 Whites av Ilf		91 X 20 Wilkie way SE22
44 D 18 White Hart la NW10	142 L 17 Whites grounds SE1	159 V 2 Wickham cres W Wkhm	47 R 11 Wilkin st NW5
38 E 4 White Hart la Rom	72 E 13 Whitestile rd Brentf		65 Y 16 Wilkinson rd E16
86 B 6 White Hart la SW13	46 E 9 Whitestone la NW3	159 Y 9 Wickham ct W Wkhm	149 N 20 Wilkinson st SW8
79 V 11 White Hart rd SE18	158 A 1 Whitethorn gdns Croy		73 X 6 Wilkinson way W4
149 V 9 White Hart st SE11	8 A 16 Whitethorn gdns Enf	92 L 8 Wickham gdns SE4	134 K 9 Wilks pl N1
142 F 15 White Hart yd SE1	64 B 13 Whitethorn st E3	80 B 18 Wickham la SE2	95 N 10 Will Crooks gdns SE9
113 V 10 White Horse hill Chisl	132 B 18 Whitfield pl W1	79 Z 14 Wickham la SE2	
	81 N 18 Whitfield rd Bxly Hth	92 M 6 Wickham ms SE4	94 M 10 Will Crooks gdns SE9
63 T 13 White Horse la E1	65 Z 2 Whitfield rd E6	125 S 5 Wickham rd Becknhm	
63 U 17 White Horse rd E1	93 X 3 Whitfield rd SE3		31 P 8 Willan rd N17
66 G 8 White Horse rd E6	132 B 18 Whitfield st W1	158 F 3 Wickham rd Croy	65 O 19 Willan wall E16
139 Y 14 White Horse st W1	140 D 1 Whitfield st W1	159 N 1 Wickham rd Croy	89 S 7 Willard st SW8
160 D 3 White Horse yd EC2	120 L 6 Whitford gdns Mitch	33 U 1 Wickham rd E4	73 R 3 Willcott rd W3
11 S 14 White House dri Stanm	156 L 11 Whitgift av S Croy	23 R 8 Wickham rd Harrow	5 P 20 Willenhall av Barnt
7 Z 5 White House la Enf	156 M 2 Whitgift sq Croy	92 M 6 Wickham rd SE4	78 L 15 Willenhall rd SE18
142 M 4 White Kennett st E1	156 L 5 Whitgift st Croy	93 N 4 Wickham rd SE4	114 K 2 Willersley av Sidcp
160 H 6 White Lion ct EC2	149 N 6 Whitgift st SE11	149 O 9 Wickham st SE11	96 L 19 Willersley av Sidcp
141 Z 9 White Lion hill EC4	67 N 1 Whiting av Bark	96 M 3 Wickham st Welling	114 K 1 Willersley clo Sidcp
133 S 9 White Lion st N1	4 A 18 Whitings rd Barnt	97 O 1 Wickham st Welling	47 S 17 Willes rd NW5
139 X 8 White Lion yd W1	154 G 1 Whitland rd Carsh	125 T 8 Wickham way Becknhm	128 M 1 Willesden la NW6 & NW2
154 E 15 White Lodge clo Sutton	31 T 7 Whitley rd N17		
	87 T 20 Whitlock dri SW19	27 T 9 Wickliffe av N3	129 R 2 Willesden la NW6 & NW2
28 H 19 White Lodge clo N2	63 V 10 Whitman rd E3	43 R 6 Wickliffe gdns Wemb	
103 Y 1 White lodge Rich	16 E 17 Whitmore clo N11		45 O 19 Willesden la NW6
108 K 17 White lodge SE19	128 C 8 Whitmore gdns NW10	132 M 12 Wicklow st WC1	151 X 11 Willet way SE16
10 K 17 White orchards Stanm		133 N 12 Wickow st WC1	122 F 11 Willett pl Thntn Hth
	62 M 6 Whitmore gdns NW10	113 N 8 Wicks clo SE9	122 F 11 Willett rd Thntn Hth
14 G 3 White orchards N20		90 K 6 Wickwood st SE5	113 X 5 William Barefoot dri SE9
51 N 19 White Post la	124 L 6 Whitmore rd Becknhm	48 C 13 Widdenham rd N7	
75 P 19 White Post st SE15		40 B 7 Widdicombe av Harrow	109 Y 20 William Booth rd SE20
52 A 20 White rd E15			
143 N 2 White's row E1		64 L 1 Widdin st E15	
89 Y 10 White's sq SW4			

75 O 1	Wine clo E1	
75 O 2	Wine clo E1	
143 Z 11	Wine clo E1	
141 V 5	Wine Office ct EC4	
93 U 1	Winforton st SE10	
88 C 20	Winfrith rd SW18	
121 Z 13	Wingate cres Croy	
53 Z 15	Wingate rd Ilf	
115 T 14	Wingate rd Sidcp	
74 H 8	Wingate rd W6	
51 Y 13	Wingfield rd E15	
33 R 15	Wingfield rd E17	
103 O 14	Wingfield rd Kingst	
91 W 7	Wingfield st SE15	
90 A 16	Wingford rd SW2	
90 L 8	Wingmore rd SE24	
144 E 15	Wingrave rd W6	
112 A 5	Winifred gro SE6	
89 N 10	Winifred gro SW11	
56 A 5	Winifred rd Dgnhm	
99 Y 14	Winifred rd Drtfrd	
100 G 9	Winifred rd Hampt	
105 Y 20	Winifred rd SW19	
78 G 3	Winifred st E16	
18 G 3	Winifred ter N9	
65 U 8	Winkfield rd E13	
30 G 5	Winkfield rd N22	
25 N 15	Winkley clo Harrow	
111 Y 10	Winlaton rd Brom	
56 A 10	Winmill rd Dgnhm	
79 W 15	Winn Common rd SE18	
94 F 20	Winn rd SE12	
112 J 1	Winn rd SE12	
140 E 8	Winnett st W1	
40 B 18	Winnings wlk Nthlt	
28 F 18	Winnington clo N2	
9 O 1	Winnington rd Enf	
46 F 2	Winnington rd N2	
28 G 17	Winnington rd N2	
32 K 10	Winns av E17	
33 N 9	Winns av E17	
31 S 14	Winns ms N15	
33 N 9	Winns ter E17	
33 W 9	Winsbeach E17	
60 F 12	Winscombe cres W5	
47 T 8	Winscombe st N19	
10 M 15	Winscombe way Stanm	
110 L 6	Winsford rd SE6	
18 A 16	Winsford ter N18	
89 O 13	Winsham gro SW11	
138 G 5	Winslade ms W2	
90 B 13	Winslade rd SW2	
93 R 19	Winslade way SE6	
138 F 4	Winsland st W2	
140 B 4	Winsley st W1	
20 M 9	Winslow gro E4	
144 E 12	Winslow rd W6	
100 A 7	Winslow way Felt	
66 J 15	Winsor ter E6	
88 G 8	Winstanley rd SW11	
56 K 14	Winstead gdns Dgnhm	
44 A 1	Winston av NW9	
10 H 20	Winston clo Harrow	
38 H 13	Winston clo Rom	
22 J 3	Winston ct Harrow	
49 O 12	Winston rd N16	
54 B 8	Winston way Ilf	
53 Z 9	Winston way Ilf	
73 X 10	Winston wlk W4	
66 E 4	Winter av E6	
122 F 8	Winterbourne rd Thntn Hth	
55 T 7	Winterbourne rd Dgnhm	
92 L 20	Winterbourne rd SE6	
90 L 16	Winterbrook rd SE24	
105 S 4	Winterfold clo SW19	
116 B 16	Winters rd Surb	
13 U 16	Winterstoke gdns NW7	
110 L 1	Winterstoke rd SE6	
146 D 13	Winterton pl SW10	
90 B 13	Winterwell rd SW2	
87 T 11	Winthorpe rd SW15	
135 W 20	Winthrop st E1	
29 V 2	Winton av N11	
19 S 3	Winton clo N9	
25 N 1	Winton gdns Edg	
65 X 19	Winton rd E16	
108 G 13	Winton way SW16	
123 P 11	Wisbeach rd Croy	
157 V 20	Wisborough rd S Croy	
56 H 5	Wisdons clo Rom	
13 U 18	Wise la NW7	
13 X 19	Wise la NW7	
64 J 3	Wise rd E15	
51 N 6	Wiseman rd E10	
106 K 1	Wiseton rd SW17	
95 N 3	Wishart rd SE3	
115 P 18	Wisley rd Orp	
89 N 14	Wisley rd SW11	
93 W 11	Wisteria rd SE13	
135 Y 15	Witan st E2	
56 F 15	Witham rd Dgnhm	
39 Y 15	Witham rd Dgnhm	
83 R 3	Witham rd Islwth	
124 C 5	Witham rd SE20	
71 Z 1	Witham rd W13	
157 S 10	Witherby clo Croy	
151 X 10	Witherfield way SE16	
48 G 15	Witherington rd N5	
26 D 4	Withers mead NW9	
113 V 5	Witherston way SE9	
20 K 12	Withy Mead E4	
87 O 20	Withycombe rd SW19	
159 U 15	Witley cres Croy	
70 E 11	Witley gdns S'hall	
47 W 7	Witley rd N19	
110 F 6	Witney path SE23	
20 K 10	Wittenham way E4	
112 B 12	Wittersham rd Brom	
91 Z 6	Wivenhoe clo SE15	
68 C 6	Wivenhoe rd Bark	
110 D 14	Wiverton rd SE26	
68 J 3	Wix rd Dgnhm	
89 R 10	Wix's la SW4	
57 W 12	Woburn av Hornch	
106 D 16	Woburn clo SW19	
132 H 17	Woburn pl WC1	
154 J 1	Woburn rd Carsh	
122 M 20	Woburn rd Croy	
123 N 20	Woburn rd Croy	
132 G 18	Woburn sq WC1	
132 G 15	Woburn wlk WC1	
102 D 19	Woffington clo Kingst	
86 D 10	Woking clo SW15	
86 D 11	Woking clo SW15	
126 K 7	Woldham rd Brom	
70 F 10	Wolf br S'hall	
126 F 14	Wolfe clo Brom	
78 A 14	Wolfe cres SE7	
53 U 12	Wolferton rd E12	
52 B 18	Wolffe gdns E15	
108 J 9	Wolfington rd SE27	
93 Y 12	Wolfram clo SE13	
88 H 7	Wolftencroft clo SW11	
12 D 12	Wolmer clo Edg	
12 C 11	Wolmer gdns Edg	
105 X 4	Wolseley av SW19	
73 T 15	Wolseley gdns W4	
52 H 20	Wolseley rd E7	
23 T 9	Wolseley rd Harrow	
121 O 17	Wolseley rd Mitch	
30 C 6	Wolseley rd N22	
29 X 17	Wolseley rd N8	
57 N 2	Wolseley rd Rom	
73 W 10	Wolseley rd W4	
143 R 18	Wolseley st SE1	
32 L 11	Wolsey av E17	
66 K 9	Wolsey av E6	
83 N 11	Wolsey clo Hounsl	
117 T 1	Wolsey clo Kingst	
103 T 20	Wolsey clo Kingst	
152 F 7	Wolsey clo Worc Pk	
159 U 19	Wolsey cres Croy	
119 T 16	Wolsey cres Mrdn	
102 J 14	Wolsey dri Kingst	
25 Z 1	Wolsey gro Edg	
47 U 16	Wolsey ms NW5	
9 N 9	Wolsey rd Enf	
100 L 14	Wolsey rd Hampt	
49 P 15	Wolsey rd N1	
63 O 15	Wolsey st E1	
143 Z 1	Wolsey st E1	
14 J 16	Wolsley clo Drtfrd	
14 J 16	Wolstonbury N12	
80 H 6	Wolvercote rd SE2	
117 R 1	Wolverton av Kingst	
103 R 20	Wolverton av Kingst	
73 N 1	Wolverton gdns W5	
144 E 6	Wolverton gdns W6	
24 C 1	Wolverton rd Stanm	
11 P 20	Wolverton rd Stanm	
6 J 17	Wolverton way N14	
30 G 2	Wolves la N22	
17 U 20	Wolves la N22	
30 B 19	Womersley rd N8	
153 O 19	Wonersh way Sutton	
104 B 20	Wonford clo New Mald	
107 N 3	Wontner rd SW17	
135 S 16	Wood clo E2	
41 P 2	Wood clo Harrow	
43 Y 2	Wood clo NW9	
113 R 14	Wood dri Chisl	
40 L 12	Wood End av Harrow	
41 N 13	Wood End av Harrow	
41 O 14	Wood End clo Nthlt	
41 O 14	Wood End gdns Nthlt	
40 L 16	Wood End la Nthlt	
41 R 12	Wood End rd Harrow	
41 O 15	Wood End way Nthlt	
56 C 9	Wood la Dgnhm	
56 G 5	Wood la Dgnhm	
55 W 12	Wood la Dgnhm	
57 V 16	Wood la Hornch	
71 U 18	Wood la Islwth	
83 W 2	Wood la Islwth	
29 R 18	Wood la N6	
44 A 2	Wood la NW9	
43 Y 2	Wood la NW9	
10 M 12	Wood la Stanm	
11 S 7	Wood la Stanm	
136 C 10	Wood la W12	
62 L 17	Wood la W12	
74 M 2	Wood la W12	
21 O 15	Wood la Wdfd Grn	
113 P 18	Wood Lodge gdns Brom	
159 W 5	Wood Lodge la W Wkhm	
4 C 13	Wood st Barnt	
51 Y 10	Wood st E11	
65 V 19	Wood st E16	
33 V 12	Wood st E17	
33 W 14	Wood st E17	
160 B 5	Wood st EC2	
142 C 2	Wood st EC2	
116 H 2	Wood st Kingst	
121 N 17	Wood st Mitch	
74 A 14	Wood st W4	
92 A 18	Wood Vale est SE23	
29 U 16	Wood vale N10	
92 B 17	Wood vale SE23	
109 Z 1	Wood vale SE23	
91 Z 20	Wood vale SE23	
76 F 16	Wood wharf SE10	
150 K 2	Wood's pl SE1	
64 E 19	Woodall clo E14	
9 U 19	Woodall rd Enf	
112 C 7	Woodbank rd Brom	
110 G 14	Woodbastwick rd SE26	
22 M 13	Woodberry av Harrow	
23 N 13	Woodberry av Harrow	
17 U 8	Woodberry av N21	
29 R 9	Woodberry cres N10	
48 L 3	Woodberry down N4	
15 P 20	Woodberry gdns N12	
15 R 19	Woodberry gro N12	
48 L 2	Woodberry gro N4	
49 N 2	Woodberry gro N4	
20 G 3	Woodberry way E4	
15 P 20	Woodberry way N12	
116 H 7	Woodbine av Kingst	
101 P 5	Woodbine clo Twick	
8 C 3	Woodbine gro Enf	
110 A 19	Woodbine gro SE20	
152 L 5	Woodbine la Worc Pk	
34 G 18	Woodbine pl E11	
96 G 20	Woodbine rd Sidcp	
50 C 17	Woodbine ter E9	
86 K 10	Woodborough rd SW15	
107 Z 7	Woodbourne av SW16	
155 T 17	Woodbourne gdns Wallgtn	
44 H 9	Woodbridge clo NW2	
48 D 7	Woodbridge clo N7	
35 S 2	Woodbridge ct Wdfd Grn	
54 K 16	Woodbridge rd Bark	
55 N 16	Woodbridge rd Bark	
133 V 16	Woodbridge st EC1	
80 A 17	Woodbrook rd SE2	
27 R 17	Woodburn clo NW4	
157 V 3	Woodbury clo Croy	
34 H 14	Woodbury clo E11	
60 B 12	Woodbury Park rd W13	
33 R 13	Woodbury rd E17	
106 K 12	Woodbury st SW17	
129 X 20	Woodchester sq W2	
114 G 8	Woodchurch clo Sidcp	
113 O 18	Woodchurch dri Chisl	
129 W 1	Woodchurch rd NW6	
127 X 2	Woodclyffe dri Chisl	
42 F 2	Woodcock Dell av Harrow	
24 E 16	Woodcock hill Harrow	
42 F 1	Woodcock hill Harrow	
24 G 17	Woodcock pk Harrow	
110 D 1	Woodcombe cres SE23	
122 J 9	Woodcote av Thntn Hth	
155 R 19	Woodcote av Wallgtn	
57 W 11	Woodcote av Hornch	
13 Z 18	Woodcote av NW7	
9 R 20	Woodcote clo Enf	
103 N 13	Woodcote clo Kingst	
155 U 20	Woodcote grn Wallgtn	
155 T 13	Woodcote ms Wallgtn	
156 A 20	Woodcote pk Wallgtn	
108 K 12	Woodcote pl SE27	
52 E 1	Woodcote rd E11	
155 T 15	Woodcote rd Wallgtn	
13 O 20	Woodcroft av NW7	
23 X 3	Woodcroft av Stanm	
41 Z 18	Woodcroft cres Grnfd	
17 S 6	Woodcroft N21	
122 H 13	Woodcroft rd Thntn Hth	
113 U 6	Woodcroft SE9	
21 O 5	Woodedge clo E4	
7 N 15	Woodend gdns Enf	
33 U 7	Woodend rd E17	
108 L 14	Woodend SE19	
154 C 3	Woodend Sutton	
155 R 19	Woodend the Wallgtn	
52 D 13	Wooder gdns E7	
4 J 16	Woodfall av Barnt	
99 S 10	Woodfall dri Drtfrd	
48 E 6	Woodfall rd N4	
147 O 10	Woodfall st SW3	
91 P 11	Woodfarrs SE5	
155 N 15	Woodfield av Carsh	
107 X 5	Woodfield av SW16	
60 E 12	Woodfield av W5	
42 D 10	Woodfield av Wemb	
108 L 17	Woodfield clo SE19	
60 F 12	Woodfield cres W5	
16 A 4	Woodfield dri Barnt	
39 X 13	Woodfield dri Rom	
118 D 11	Woodfield gdns New Mald	
107 Y 6	Woodfield gro SW16	
107 X 6	Woodfield la SW16	
44 B 4	Woodfield pk NW9	
129 S 19	Woodfield pl W9	
60 E 13	Woodfield rd W5	
129 R 20	Woodfield rd W9	
10 D 2	Woodfield ri Bushey	
16 J 20	Woodfield way N11	
29 W 1	Woodfield way N11	
35 S 13	Woodford av Ilf	
35 R 12	Woodford Bridge rd Ilf	
34 B 3	Woodford New rd Wdfd Grn	
33 Z 11	Woodford New rd E17	
42 H 4	Woodford pl Wemb	
34 D 13	Woodford rd E18	
34 E 9	Woodford rd E18	
52 G 11	Woodford rd E7	
74 M 7	Woodger rd W12	
136 C 19	Woodger rd W6	
66 D 16	Woodget clo E6	
24 F 15	Woodgrange av Harrow	
8 K 19	Woodgrange av Enf	
15 T 19	Woodgrange av N12	
73 O 2	Woodgrange av W5	
24 F 16	Woodgrange clo Harrow	
8 L 19	Woodgrange gdns Enf	
52 G 14	Woodgrange rd E7	
22 A 6	Woodhall av Pinn	
109 U 6	Woodhall av SE21	
22 A 4	Woodhall dri Pinn	
109 U 7	Woodhall dri SE21	
22 A 5	Woodhall ga Pinn	
34 B 14	Woodham ct E18	
111 U 6	Woodham rd SE6	

66 C 16	Woodhatch clo E6
36 A 12	Woodhaven gdns Ilf
113 Y 16	Woodhayes Chisl
104 M 17	Woodhayes rd SW19
105 N 15	Woodhayes rd SW19
43 Z 17	Woodheyes rd NW10
24 G 19	Woodhill cres Harrow
78 E 12	Woodhill SE18
59 X 5	Woodhouse av Grnfd
59 W 4	Woodhouse clo Grnfd
53 P 19	Woodhouse gro E12
52 A 9	Woodhouse rd E11
15 T 18	Woodhouse rd N12
80 A 12	Woodhurst rd SE2
73 V 1	Woodhurst rd W3
95 V 16	Woodington clo SE9
63 W 13	Woodison st E3
127 T 2	Woodknoll dri Brom
41 Z 17	Woodland appr Grnfd
21 V 10	Woodland clo Wdfd Grn
152 B 15	Woodland clo Epsom
29 V 1	Woodland clo Islwth
109 T 14	Woodland clo SE19
76 L 15	Woodland cres SE10
83 T 7	Woodland gdns Islwth
29 S 14	Woodland gdns N10
109 T 14	Woodland hill SE19
122 G 10	Woodland rd Thntn Hth
20 H 5	Woodland rd E4
16 E 16	Woodland rd N11
109 T 14	Woodland rd SE19
41 Z 18	Woodland ri Grnfd
29 S 14	Woodland ri N10
78 C 12	Woodland ter SE7
159 U 4	Woodland way W Wkhm
21 V 10	Woodland way Wdfd Grn
124 H 20	Woodland way Croy
107 P 18	Woodland way Mitch
119 V 9	Woodland way N21
17 T 6	Woodland way NW7
13 P 18	Woodland way NW7
80 H 12	Woodland way SE2
76 M 14	Woodland wlk SE10
28 C 4	Woodland's av N3
33 V 10	Woodland's rd E17
152 E 2	Woodlands av Worc Pk
96 H 20	Woodlands av Sidcp
117 X 2	Woodlands av New Mald
52 G 4	Woodlands av E11
37 Y 20	Woodlands av Rom
114 H 1	Woodlands av Sidcp
73 T 3	Woodlands av W3
27 S 16	Woodlands clo NW11
127 U 4	Woodlands clo Brom
10 H 19	Woodlands dri Stanm
83 U 5	Woodlands gro Islwth
22 F 14	Woodlands Harrow
15 R 19	Woodlands N12
27 S 17	Woodlands NW11
30 L 14	Woodlands Park rd N15
76 M 15	Woodlands Park rd SE10
98 A 7	Woodlands rd Bxly Hth
23 W 15	Woodlands rd Harrow
97 Z 7	Woodlands rd Bxly Hth
127 S 4	Woodlands rd Brom
51 Z 6	Woodlands rd E11
8 A 5	Woodlands rd Enf
54 A 10	Woodlands rd Ilf
83 S 7	Woodlands rd Islwth
19 P 6	Woodlands rd N9
39 T 11	Woodlands rd Rom
70 A 2	Woodlands rd S'hall
116 G 18	Woodlands rd Surb
86 D 8	Woodlands rd SW13
93 X 17	Woodlands rd SE13
119 N 9	Woodlands SW20
155 R 19	Woodlands the Wallgtn
83 U 6	Woodlands the Islwth
16 E 6	Woodlands the N14
93 X 18	Woodlands the SE13
108 M 18	Woodlands the SE19
87 U 12	Woodlands way SW15
87 V 14	Woodlawn clo SW15
100 J 3	Woodlawn cres Twick
100 A 4	Woodlawn dri Felt
144 F 19	Woodlawn rd SW6
87 O 1	Woodlawn rd SW6
87 P 2	Woodlawn rd SW6
126 A 12	Woodlea dri Brom
49 R 9	Woodlea rd N16
15 X 18	Woodleigh av N12
108 A 7	Woodleigh gdns SW16
78 K 4	Woodman st E16
136 A 2	Woodmans ms W10
62 K 15	Woodmans ms W10
155 U 20	Woodmansterne la Wallgtn
154 K 18	Woodmansterne rd Carsh
107 X 20	Woodmansterne rd SW16
1 A 1 18	Woodmansterne rd SW16
124 G 17	Woodmere clo Croy
124 E 18	Woodmere gdns Croy
95 T 20	Woodmere SE9
125 W 11	Woodmere way Becknhm
107 T 11	Woodnook rd SW16
8 M 20	Woodpecker clo Enf
158 J 19	Woodpecker mt Croy
75 V 17	Woodpecker rd SE14
68 G 20	Woodpecker rd SE2
90 K 13	Woodquest av SE24
5 T 5	Woodride Barnt
22 E 4	Woodridings av Pinn
22 C 2	Woodridings clo Pinn
51 Y 1	Woodriffe rd E11
60 B 2	Woodrow clo Grnfd
78 F 12	Woodrow SE18
37 V 13	Woodrush way Rom
139 S 9	Woods ms W1
92 A 3	Woods rd SE15
135 R 20	Woodseer st E1
136 M 17	Woodsford sq W14
56 H 10	Woodshire rd Dgnhm
114 B 14	Woodside av Chisl
23 P 13	Woodside av N10
15 O 14	Woodside av N12
28 M 15	Woodside av N6
123 Y 14	Woodside av SE25
60 K 3	Woodside av Wemb
21 X 8	Woodside Buck Hl
99 O 9	Woodside clo Bxly Hth
11 N 16	Woodside clo Stanm
117 U 18	Woodside clo Surb
60 L 3	Woodside clo Wemb
123 Y 18	Woodside Court rd Croy
114 H 7	Woodside cres Sidcp
60 L 4	Woodside end Wemb
20 E 18	Woodside gdns E4
31 T 8	Woodside gdns N17
15 O 13	Woodside Grange rd N12
123 Y 14	Woodside grn SE25
123 Y 14	Woodside grn W13
15 P 12	Woodside gro N12
97 X 15	Woodside la Bxly
15 P 11	Woodside la N12
27 Y 14	Woodside NW11
33 X 14	Woodside Park av E17
15 P 14	Woodside Park rd N12
123 Y 13	Woodside pk SE25
60 L 4	Woodside pl Wemb
118 A 4	Woodside rd New Mald
99 N 10	Woodside rd Bxly Hth
21 S 12	Woodside rd Wdfd Grn
117 Z 3	Woodside rd New Mald
127 R 11	Woodside rd Brom
65 X 12	Woodside rd E13
102 J 18	Woodside rd Kingst
30 E 2	Woodside rd N22
123 Z 15	Woodside rd SE25
114 H 7	Woodside rd Sidcp
154 C 6	Woodside rd Sutton
105 U 14	Woodside SW19
123 Z 14	Woodside view SE25
124 B 14	Woodside way Croy
121 T 1	Woodside way Mitch
47 S 10	Woodsome rd NW5
105 T 3	Woodspring rd SW19
11 Y 20	Woodstead gro Edg
83 Y 12	Woodstock av Islwth
45 T 1	Woodstock av NW11
58 F 9	Woodstock av S'hall
119 V 17	Woodstock av Sutton
71 Z 7	Woodstock av W13
24 L 9	Woodstock clo Stanm
98 B 20	Woodstock clo Bxly
8 M 19	Woodstock cres Enf
94 D 17	Woodstock ct SE12
54 M 6	Woodstock gdns Ilf
136 H 18	Woodstock gro W12
139 V 1	Woodstock ms W1
10 G 2	Woodstock rd Bushey
155 P 12	Woodstock rd Carsh
155 O 7	Woodstock rd Croy
33 W 7	Woodstock rd E17
50 K 20	Woodstock rd E7
48 G 5	Woodstock rd N4
45 W 3	Woodstock rd NW11
74 A 9	Woodstock rd W4
60 M 1	Woodstock rd Wemb
119 U 18	Woodstock ri Sutton
65 N 17	Woodstock st E16
139 X 7	Woodstock st W1
64 D 19	Woodstock ter E14
121 T 2	Woodstock way Mitch
152 H 11	Woodstone av Epsom
109 V 9	Woodsyre SE26
86 K 11	Woodthorpe rd SW15
123 U 5	Woodvale av SE25
20 G 13	Woodview av E4
94 E 13	Woodville clo SE12
101 X 10	Woodville clo Tedd
45 P 1	Woodville gdns NW11
54 C 3	Woodville gdns Ilf
60 L 17	Woodville gdns W5
122 M 8	Woodville rd Thntn Hth
123 N 7	Woodville rd Thntn Hth
5 N 14	Woodville rd Barnt
52 C 3	Woodville rd E11
32 J 14	Woodville rd E17
34 H 8	Woodville rd E18
119 X 8	Woodville rd Mrdn
49 P 15	Woodville rd N16
45 R 1	Woodville rd NW11
129 R 8	Woodville rd NW6
102 C 6	Woodville rd Rich
60 H 18	Woodville rd W5
94 J 1	Woodville SE3
26 G 17	Woodward av NW4
55 S 20	Woodward gdns Dgnhm
68 C 1	Woodward rd Dgnhm
55 U 20	Woodward rd Dgnhm
91 T 16	Woodwarde rd SE22
83 O 16	Woodwards Foot path Twick
23 Z 17	Woodway cres Harrow
88 D 13	Woodwell st SW18
91 S 19	Woodyard la SE21
94 D 16	Woodyates rd SE12
104 K 16	Wool rd SW20
94 J 4	Woolacombe rd SE3
30 H 19	Woolaston rd N4
150 F 10	Wooler st SE17
80 D 3	Woolf clo SE28
44 F 2	Woolmead av NW9
18 L 18	Woolmer gdns N18
18 L 17	Woolmer rd N18
64 G 19	Woolmore st E14
88 A 7	Woolneigh st SW6
87 Z 7	Woolneigh st SW6
87 Z 7	Woolneigh st SW6
151 R 4	Woolstaplers way SE16
110 J 4	Woolstone rd SE23
78 G 19	Woolwich Church st SE18
78 G 18	Woolwich comm SE18
78 H 8	Woolwich High st E16
78 L 4	Woolwich manorway SE18
78 K 13	Woolwich New rd SE18
98 D 10	Woolwich rd Bxly Hth
98 E 6	Woolwich rd Bxly Hth
77 O 13	Woolwich rd SE10
80 K 15	Woolwich rd SE2
81 P 13	Woolwich rd SE2
78 B 10	Woolwich rd SE7
77 Y 12	Woolwich rd SE7
64 J 17	Wooster gdns E14
27 Y 6	Wootton gro N3
141 U 15	Wootton st SE1
124 B 3	Worbeck rd SE20
8 K 3	Worcester av N17
31 W 1	Worcester av N17
158 M 3	Worcester clo Croy
159 N 3	Worcester clo Croy
121 R 5	Worcester clo Mitch
21 X 14	Worcester cres Wdfd Grn
13 O 10	Worcester cres NW7
152 C 5	Worcester gdns Worc Pk
41 O 18	Worcester gdns Grnfd
35 R 20	Worcester gdns Ilf
160 C 9	Worcester pl EC4
53 T 11	Worcester rd E12
32 F 6	Worcester rd E17
154 A 15	Worcester rd Sutton
153 Z 15	Worcester rd Sutton
105 V 13	Worcester rd SW19
59 P 7	Wordsworth av Grnfd
53 P 19	Wordsworth av E12
34 C 9	Wordsworth av E18
153 N 9	Wordsworth dri Sutton
30 H 13	Wordsworth pde N8
100 E 10	Wordsworth rd Hampt
155 W 15	Wordsworth rd Wallgtn
49 S 13	Wordsworth rd N16
96 H 2	Wordsworth rd SE18
110 E 18	Wordsworth rd SE20
27 X 14	Wordsworth wlk NW11
146 M 19	Worfield st SW11
149 N 9	Worgan st SE11
52 A 19	Worland rd E15
7 S 13	World's End la Enf
144 C 10	Worlidge st W6
74 L 13	Worlidge st W6
91 V 10	Worlingham rd SE22
74 G 3	Wormholt rd W12
142 H 3	Wormwood st EC2
128 K 18	Wornington rd W10
128 M 19	Wornington rd W10
137 N 1	Wornington rd W10
130 H 5	Woronzow rd NW8
83 Y 13	Worple av Islwth
105 S 18	Worple av SW19
40 E 3	Worple clo Harrow
83 Z 8	Worple rd Islwth
105 T 18	Worple rd SW19
118 M 2	Worple rd SW20
119 O 1	Worple rd SW20
105 U 16	Worple Road ms SW19
85 Y 7	Worple st SW14
40 E 4	Worple way Harrow
84 L 12	Worple way Rich
134 G 19	Worship st EC2
106 F 11	Worslade rd SW17
110 M 11	Worsley Bridge rd SE26
111 N 13	Worsley Bridge rd SE26
52 A 11	Worsley rd E11
51 Z 11	Worsley rd E11
89 V 12	Worsopp dri SW4
64 M 4	Worthing clo E15
70 D 17	Worthing rd Hounsl
116 M 20	Worthington rd Surb
122 E 16	Wortley rd Croy
66 A 1	Wortley rd E6
83 P 4	Worton gdns Islwth
83 R 9	Worton rd Islwth
83 P 5	Worton way Islwth
44 M 11	Wotton rd NW2
75 Z 17	Wotton rd SE8
65 O 17	Wouldham rd E16
52 A 10	Wragby rd E11
18 K 7	Wrampling pl N9

NICHOLSON

THE BEST IN LONDON

£3.95

NEW £3.50

£2.95

£3.95

LONDON Arts and CULTURAL GUIDE
THEATRE Dance MUSEUMS Music Festivals HISTORIC HOUSES Ga

LOOKING Good IN LONDON
The HAIR, BEAUTY, FASHION AND FITNESS GUIDE

THE GUIDE TO LONDON BY BUS & TUBE

The London Guide
The most comprehensive guide to London

NEW EDITION

LONDON RESTAURANT GUIDE
Over 700 places to eat More than 30 national cuisines

NEW EDITION £3.50

LONDON PUB GUIDE
• More than 800 pubs and bars
• Real Ale Specials
• Food and Entertainment

£3.50

LONDON DOCKLANDS MAP

NEW LAR 5 IN

£2.75

LONDON DOCKLANDS STREET ATLAS & GUIDE
NEW LARGE-SCALE COLOUR STREET MAPS

£5.95

Nicholson publishes a large range of guide books covering various aspects of London life. Whatever your interest you can rely on Nicholson to give you accurate up-to-date information in a compact and portable form.

LONDON INFORMATION

BREAKDOWN SERVICES

AA Breakdown Service
(0800) 887766 – freephone, for breakdown only. For information: 01-954 9599.
RAC Breakdown Service
(0923) 33555 (north of the Thames). 01-681 3611 (south of the Thames and Kent, Surrey, Sussex). *24hrs.*
Cavendish Motors   *45 U 20*
Cavendish Rd NW6. 01-459 0046. *Not 24hrs.*

24-HOUR GARAGES

Chiswick Flyover Service Station   *73 R 13*
1 Great West Rd W4. 01-994 1119.
Fina   *65 R 13*
95–99 Barking Rd, Barking E16. 01-476 6953.
Heron Service Station   *49 N 19*
316 Essex Rd N1. 01-226 5991.
Heron Station   *65 O 18*
51 Brunel St E16. 01-474 5746.
St Nicholas Filling Station   *148 D 7*
148 Vauxhall Bridge Rd SW1. 01-828 1371.
Sealand Garage   *146 L 7*
Sloane Ave SW3. 01-589 1226.

Star Service Station   *150 M 3*
Grange Rd SE1. 01-237 4171.
Star Service Station   *45 X 14*
63 Fortune Green Rd NW6. 01-453 2211.
Texaco Station   *149 T 6*
212 Kennington Rd SE11. 01-735 2191.

WHEELCLAMPED

How to get released
Take the label attached to your vehicle along with the fixed penalty notice to one of the police car pounds listed below. You will have to pay a fine before the clamp is removed. All major credit cards (A.Ax.Dc.V.) accepted. In an emergency contact the Metropolitan Police at the Bermondsey Communications Centre, 20 Maltby Street SE1. 01-252 2222.
Hyde Park Car Pound   *139 R 12*
NCP Park Lane Car Park, Marble Arch W1. *Open 24hrs Mon–Sun.*
Camden Town Car Pound   *131 W 4*
Oval Rd NW1. *Open 09.00–23.00 Mon–Sat, 09.00–17.00 Sun.*
Warwick Road Car Pound   *145 T 8*
245 Warwick Rd W14. *Open 08.00–24.00 Mon–Sat.*

THEATRES

Adelphi *836 7611*
Albery *867 1115*
Aldwych *836 6404*
Ambassadors *836 1171*
Apollo *437 2663*
Apollo Victoria *828 8665*
Arts *836 3334*
Astoria *434 0403*
Bloomsbury *387 9629*
Coliseum *836 3161*
Comedy *930 2578*
Criterion *867 1117*
Dominion *580 9562*
Donmar Warehouse
867 1111
Drury Lane, Theatre Royal
836 8108
Duchess (Players) *836 8243*
Duke of York's *836 5122*
Fortune *836 2238*
Garrick *379 6107*
Globe *437 3667*
Haymarket *930 9832*
Her Majesty's *839 2244*
ICA *930 3647*
Jeannetta Cochrane
242 7040
Lyric *437 3686*
Mayfair *629 3036*
Mermaid *236 5568*
National *928 2252*
New London *405 0072*
Old Vic *928 7616*
Palace *434 0909*
Palladium *437 7373*
Phoenix *836 2294*
Piccadilly *437 4506*
Playhouse *839 4401*
Prince Edward *734 8951*
Prince of Wales *839 5987*
Queen's *734 1166*
Royal Court *730 1745*
Royal Festival Hall
928 8800
Royal Opera House
240 1066
St Martin's *836 1443*
Savoy *836 8888*
Shaftesbury *379 5399*
Strand *836 2660*
Vaudeville *836 9987*
Victoria Palace *834 1317*
Westminster *834 0283*
Whitehall *867 1119*
Wigmore Hall *935 2141*
Wyndham's *867 1116*
Young Vic *928 6363*

CINEMAS

Cannon Haymarket
839 1527
Cannon Oxford St *636 0310*
Cannon Panton St *930 0631*
Cannon Piccadilly *437 3561*
Cannon Première *439 4470*
Cannon Shaftesbury Ave
836 8861
Cannon Tott Ct Rd
636 6148
Curzon Mayfair *499 3737*
Curzon Phoenix *240 9661*
Curzon West End *439 4805*
Empire 1, 2 & 3 *437 1234*
ICA *930 3647*
Lumière *836 0691*
Metro *437 0757*
Minema *235 4225*
Moulin *437 1653*
National Film Theatre
928 3232
Odeon Haymarket *839 7697*
Odeon Leicester Sq *930 6111*
Odeon Marble Arch
723 2011
Odeon West End *930 5252*
Plaza 1, 2, 3 & 4 *437 1234*
Prince Charles *437 8181*
Renoir *837 8402*
Warner West End *439 0791*

SHOPS

Aquascutum *734 6090*
Army & Navy *834 1234*
Asprey *493 6767*
Austin Reed *734 6789*
BHS (Oxford St) *629 2011*
C & A *629 7272*
Cartier *493 6962*
Christies *839 9060*
Conran Shop *589 7401*
Covent Garden Market
836 9137
Debenhams *580 3000*
Design Centre *839 8000*
Dickins & Jones *734 7070*
Fenwick *629 9161*
Fortnum & Mason *734 8040*
Foyles *437 5660*
General Trading Company
730 0411
Habitat (King's Rd)
351 1211
Habitat (Tott Ct Rd)
631 3880
Hamleys *734 3161*
Harrods *730 1234*
Harvey Nichols *235 5000*
Hatchard's *437 3924*
Heal's *636 1666*
HMV *631 3423*
House of Fraser (Ken High
St) *937 5432*
House of Fraser (Oxford St)
629 8800
Jaeger *734 8211*
John Lewis *629 7711*
Laura Ashley (Regent St)
437 9760
Laura Ashley (Sloane St)
235 9728
Liberty *734 1234*
Lillywhites *930 3181*
London Pavilion *437 1838*
Maples *387 7000*
Marks & Spencer (Marble
Arch) *935 7954*
Marks & Spencer (Oxford
St) *437 7722*
Marks & Spencer (Ken High
St) *938 3711*
Mothercare *629 6621*
Next (Ken High St)
937 0498
Next (Regent St) *434 2515*
Peter Jones *730 3434*
Plaza on Oxford St
436 4425
Reject Shop *352 2750*
Selfridges *629 1234*
Simpson *734 2002*
Sotheby's *493 8080*
Top Shop *636 7700*
Tower Records *439 2500*
Trocadero *439 1791*
Victoria Place Shopping
Centre *931 8811*
Virgin Megastore *631 1234*

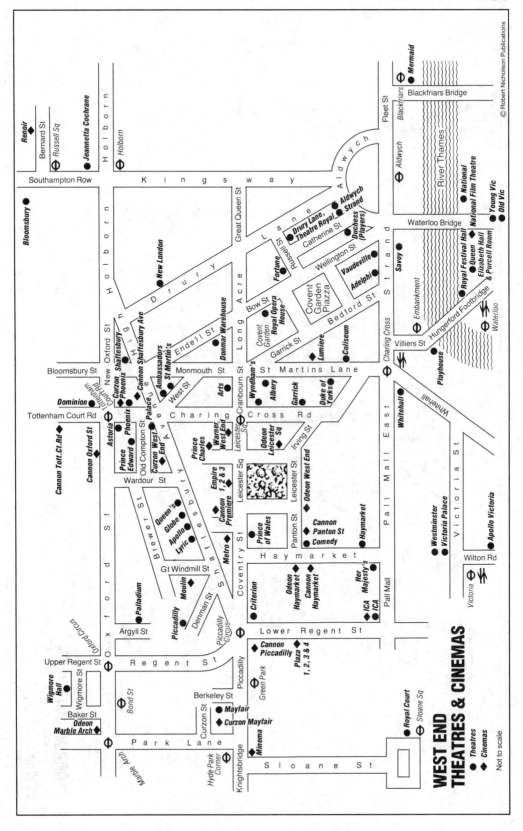

© Robert Nicholson Publications

WEST END
THEATRES & CINEMAS

● Theatres
◆ Cinemas
Not to scale

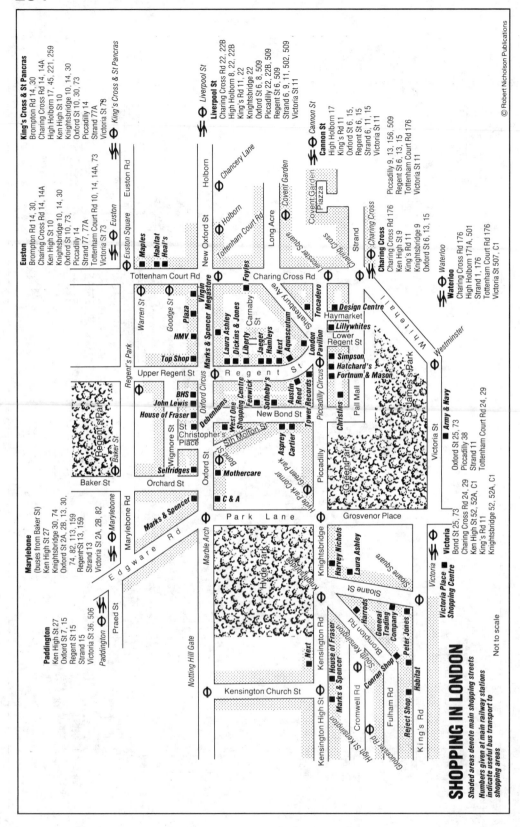

LONDON INFORMATION

LONDON TRANSPORT

London Transport   **140 E 20**
Travel Information Centre
St James's Park Underground Station
SW1. 01-222 1234. For enquiries on
London Transport buses, London
Underground and Docklands Light
Railway routes, fares and times of
running. Other travel information
centres at these Underground
stations:
Euston   **132 D 13**
Heathrow Airport
King's Cross   **132 K 10**
Oxford Circus   **139 Z 5**
Piccadilly Circus   **140 E 10**
Victoria   **147 Z 3**
Underground
London Underground tube trains run
*05.30–00.15 Mon–Sat, 07.30–23.30
Sun.* Weekly, monthly, quarterly or
annual Travelcards provide
considerable savings. Travelcards can
be used on both the Underground and
buses.
Buses
London Transport buses run *06.00–
24.00 Mon–Sat, 07.30–23.00 Sun.* They
tend to be slower, especially in the
rush hours, but more pleasant and
you see so much more. They cover the
whole of Greater London. Many routes
now have night bus services, with a
greatly extended service to the
suburbs as well. Consult *Buses for
Night Owls* for night buses, available
from London Transport and British
Rail travel information centres.

BRITISH RAIL

Booking centres for rail travel in
Britain, rail and sea journeys to the
Continent and Ireland, motorail and
rail package holidays and tours.
Several languages spoken.

British Travel Centre   **140 E 12**
4–12 Lower Regent St SW1.
01-730 3400.
And at:
14 Kingsgate Pde, Victoria   **148 D 2**
St SW1.
87 King William St EC4.   **142 F 8**
407 Oxford St W1.   **139 T 6**
170b Strand WC2.   **140 M 10**
Heathrow Airport.
British Rail trains generally run *06.00–
24.00 Mon–Sat, 07.00–22.30 Sun.*
Blackfriars   **141 X 9**
Queen Victoria St EC4. 01-928 5100.
Serves south and south east London
suburbs. *Closed Sat & Sun.*
Broad Street   **142 H 2**
Liverpool St EC2. 01-387 7070. North
London line to Richmond and peak
hour trains to Watford.
Cannon Street   **142 D 10**
Cannon St EC4. 01-928 5100. Serves
south east London suburbs, Kent, East
Sussex. *Closed Sat & Sun.*
Charing Cross   **140 K 12**
Strand WC2. 01-928 5100. Serves
south east London suburbs, Kent.
Trains from here go over Hungerford
Bridge.
Euston   **132 D 13**
Euston Rd NW1. 01-387 7070. Fast
trains to Birmingham, Manchester,
Liverpool, Glasgow, Inverness,
Northampton, Holyhead, Crewe.
Suburban line to Watford.
Fenchurch Street   **142 M 8**
Railway Pl, Fenchurch St EC3. 01-928
5100. Trains to Tilbury and Southend.
Holborn Viaduct   **141 U 3**
Holborn Viaduct EC1. 01-928 5100.
Serves south and south east London
suburbs. *Closed Sat & Sun.*
King's Cross   **131 K 10**
Euston Rd N1. 01-278 2477. Fast trains
to Leeds, York, Newcastle, Edinburgh,
Aberdeen.
Liverpool Street   **142 K 2**
Liverpool St EC2. 01-283 7171. Serves
east and north east London suburbs.

Fast trains to Cambridge, Colchester, Norwich, Harwich Docks.

London Bridge   **142 H 14**
Borough High St SE1. 01-928 5100. Serves south and south east London suburbs, Kent, Sussex, East Surrey.

Marylebone   **131 N 19**
Boston Pl NW1. 01-387 7070. Suburban lines to Amersham, High Wycombe, Banbury, Aylesbury.

Moorgate   **142 E 1**
Moorgate EC2. 01-278 2477. Suburban services to Welwyn Garden City, Hertford.

Paddington   **138 E 5**
Praed St W2. 01-262 6767. Fast trains to Bath, Bristol, Cardiff, Hereford, Swansea, Reading, Swindon, Devon, Cornwall.

St Pancras   **132 J 11**
Euston Rd NW1. Information 01-387 7070. Fast trains to Nottingham, Leicester, Sheffield, Derby. Suburban services to Luton, Bedford, St Albans.

Victoria   **147 Y 5**
Terminus Pl SW1. 01-928 5100. Serves south and south east London suburbs, Kent, Sussex, East Surrey. Fast trains to Brighton. 'Gatwick Express' *every 15 mins from 05.30–22.00, every 30 mins from 22.00–24.00, every hour from 24.00–05.30.*

Waterloo   **141 S 17**
York Rd SE1. Information 01-928 5100. Serves south west London suburbs, west Surrey, Hampshire, Dorset. Fast trains to Portsmouth, Southampton, Bournemouth. There is also a separate station, Waterloo East, where all trains from Charing Cross stop.

THAMESLINE RIVERBUS

Information 01-987 0311. Waterjet propelled catamaran service between Chelsea Harbour Pier and Greenland Pier with seven stops in between, including Charing Cross Pier, South Bank Festival Pier, Swan Lane Pier for the City, and London Bridge Pier for Hay's Galleria. Boats run *Mon–Fri* at 15-minute intervals between *07.00–10.00* and *16.00–19.00*; and at 30- minute intervals between *10.00–16.00* and *19.00–22.00*. On *Sat & Sun* boats run every 30 minutes between *10.00–18.00.*

COACHES

Green Line Coaches
Enquiries: 01-668 7261. These are express buses run by the London Country Bus company. Most run from central London to outlying areas, departing from Eccleston Bridge, Victoria or Regent Street. There is a special service, route 747, from Gatwick to Heathrow and Luton airports. Services generally run every hour. Green Line can be used for travel within central London but the bus stops are quite far apart and the fares are high for short journeys.

Victoria Coach Station   **147 Z 3**
164 Buckingham Palace Rd SW1. 01-730 0202. The main provincial coach companies operate from here, travelling all over Britain and the Continent. Booking necessary.

AIRPORTS

London City Airport   **78 E 2**
Gate 20, King George V Dock, Connaught Rd E16. 01-474 5555.

London Gatwick Airport
Horley, Surrey. (0293) 28822 or 01-668 4211.

London Heathrow Airport
Hounslow, Middx. 01-759 4321.

London Stansted Airport
Stansted, Essex. (0279) 502380.

Luton Airport
Luton, Beds. (0582) 405100.

Southend Airport
Southend-on-Sea, Essex. (0702) 340201.

AIRPORT BUS SERVICES

London Regional Transport
A1 Victoria – Marble Arch – Heathrow
A2 Euston – Earl's Court – Heathrow

Flightline
747 London – Gatwick, Heathrow
757 Victoria – Luton
767 Victoria – Heathrow
777 Victoria – Gatwick

EXCHANGE FACILITIES

Chequepoint Bureaux de Change
222 Earl's Court Rd SW5.   **145 W 7**
01-370 3238. *Open 7 days, 24hrs.*
47 Old Brompton Rd SW7.   **146 G 6**
01-584 7214. *Open 7 days 08.30–23.00.*
548 Oxford St W1   **139 R 7**
(Marble Arch). 01-723 2646. *Open 7 days, 24hrs.*
58 Queensway W2. 01-229   **137 Z 9**
4268. *Open 7 days, 24hrs.*
78 Strand WC2. 01-836 5292. **140 K 11**
Open 7 days 08.30–24.00.
Eurochange Bureaux
Knightsbridge Underground   **139 P 18**
Station SW3. 01-589 1891.
Open 7 days 08.00–19.00.
Paddington Underground   **138 F 6**
Station, 179 Praed St W2.
01-258 0442. *Open 7 days 08.00–21.00.*
Tottenham Court Rd   **140 G 4**
Underground Station W1. 01-734 0279.
Open 7 days 08.00–22.00.
Thomas Cook
104 Kensington High St W8.   **137 V 20**
01-937 3673. *Open 09.00–17.30 Mon–Fri, 09.30–17.00 Sat.*
Marks & Spencer   **139 S 7**
(Marble Arch), 458 Oxford St W1.
01-935 7954. *Open 09.00–20.00 Mon–Fri, 09.00–18.00 Sat.*
Selfridges, 400 Oxford St   **139 U 6**
W1. 01-629 1234. *Open 09.30–18.00 Mon–Sat (to 20.00 Thur).*
Victoria Station SW1.   **147 Z 3**
01-828 4422. *Open 7 days 07.45–22.00.*

LOST OR STOLEN CREDIT CARDS

During office hours the loss or theft of a credit card can be reported to any branch of the credit card company.

Outside office hours contact the *24hr* number listed and confirm by letter within seven days.
Access/Mastercard/Eurocard
Joint Credit Card Company, Access House, 200 Priory Cres, Southend-on-Sea, Essex. (0702) 352211.
American Express
Lost and Stolen Dept, American Express Company, PO Box 68, Edward St, Brighton, East Sussex. (0273) 69355 or 01-222 9633 *(until 18.00).*
Barclaycard/Visa
Barclaycard Centre, Dept G, Northampton. (0604) 230230.
Diners Club
Diners Club House, Kingsmead, Farnborough, Hants. (0252) 513500.

LOST PROPERTY

British Rail
Contact the final destination of the train on which you were travelling. They will be able to tell you if your lost property has been recovered and where it has been taken to.
London Transport   **131 R 19**
Lost Property Office, 200 Baker St W1 (next to Baker Street Underground Station). Call in person, send someone with written authority or apply by letter. No telephone enquiries. *Open 09.30–17.30 Mon–Fri.*
Taxis   **133 S 9**
Apply to 15 Penton St N1 or nearest police station.
Lost anywhere else
Apply to the nearest police station.

LATE CHEMISTS

Bliss Chemist   **139 P 7**
5 Marble Arch W1. 01-723 6116. *Open 09.00–24.00 Mon–Sun.*
Also at 50–56 Willesden   **129 R 2**
Lane NW6. 01-624 8000. *Open 09.00–02.00 Mon–Sun.*
Boots   **140 D 10**
Piccadilly Circus W1. 01-734 6126. *Open 08.00–20.00 Mon–Sat.*

Underwoods   *140 F 9*
62 Shaftesbury Ave W1. 01-434 3647.
Open 09.00–23.00 Mon–Sat, 11.00–
22.00 Sun.
Warman Freed   *45 W 3*
45 Golders Green Rd NW11. 01-455
4351. *Open 08.00–24.00 daily*
throughout year.

LATE POST

Post Office   *140 J 11*
St Martin's Pl, Trafalgar Sq WC2.
01-930 9580. *Open 08.00 (08.30 Fri)–*
20.00 Mon–Sat. Closed Sun.

24-HOUR CASUALTY

In an emergency dial 999 and ask for
an ambulance, or make your own way
to one of the casualty departments
listed below. If at all practicable,
contact your doctor as casualty
hospitals are for serious emergencies
only.
Barnet General Hospital   *4 B 14*
Wellhouse Lane, Barnet, Herts. 01-440
5111.
Chase Farm Hospital   *7 T 4*
The Ridgeway, Enfield, Middx. 01-366
6600.
Ealing General Hospital   *71 P 4*
Uxbridge Rd, Southall, Middx. 01-574
2444.
Greenwich District Hospital   *77 O 14*
Vanbrugh Hill SE10. 01-858 8141.
Guy's Hospital   *142 F 16*
St Thomas St SE1. 01-407 7600.
Hammersmith Hospital   *62 H 17*
150 Du Cane Rd W12. 01-743 2030.
Hillingdon Hospital
Pield Heath Rd, Hillingdon, Middx.
(0895) 38282.
Kingston Hospital   *103 R 20*
Galsworthy Rd, Kingston-upon-
Thames, Surrey. 01-546 7711.
Mayday Hospital   *122 H 13*
Mayday Road, Thornton Heath,
Surrey. 01-684 6999.
New Charing Cross Hospital *144 F 12*
Fulham Palace Rd W6. 01-748 2040.

Newham General Hospital   *65 Y 11*
Glen Road E13. 01-476 1400.
Northwick Park Hospital   *41 Y 1*
Watford Rd, Harrow, Middx. 01-864
5311.
Queen Mary's Hospital   *86 G 16*
Roehampton Lane SW15. 01-789 6611.
Queen Mary's Hospital   *115 N 14*
Frognal Ave, Sidcup, Kent. 01-302
2678.
Royal Free Hospital   *46 H 14*
Pond St NW3. 01-794 0500.
St Bartholomew's Hospital *141 X 2*
West Smithfield EC1. 01-601 8888.
St George's Hospital   *106 G 12*
Blackshaw Rd SW17. 01 072 1200.
St Mary's Hospital   *138 F 6*
Praed St W2. 01-725 6666.
St Stephen's Hospital   *146 C 15*
369 Fulham Rd SW10. 01-352 8161.
St Thomas's Hospital   *141 N 20*
Lambeth Palace Rd SE1. 01-928 9292.
University College Hospital *132 D 17*
Gower St WC1. 01-387 9300.
Westminster Hospital   *148 J 4*
Dean Ryle St, Horseferry Rd SW1.
01-828 9811.
Whipps Cross Hospital   *33 X 17*
Whipps Cross Rd E11. 01-539 5522.

Medical Express   *139 X 5*
Chapel Place, Oxford St W1. 01-499
1991. Emergency medical centre, no
appointment needed for minor
accident treatment. Not part of the
National Health Service – you will be
charged.

TAXIS

If you can't hail a black cab in the
street, or find one at a taxi rank
contact one of the following *24hr* taxi
services:
Computercab: 01-286 0286.
Datacab: 01-727 7200.
Dial A Cab: 01-253 5000.
Radio Taxicabs: 01-272 0272.
Lady Cabs   *49 N 11*
150 Green Lanes N16. 01-254 3501.
Late night cabs for women, driven by
women. *Open to 24.30 Mon–Thur, to*
01.00 Fri, to 02.00 Sat, to 24.00 Sun.